# Building Scalable Cisco Networks

**Catherine Paquet**
**Diane Teare**

Cisco Press
201 W 103rd Street
Indianapolis, IN 46290 USA

# Building Scalable Cisco Networks

Catherine Paquet
Diane Teare

Copyright© 2001 Cisco Systems, Inc.

Cisco Press logo is a trademark of Cisco Systems, Inc.

Published by:
Cisco Press
201 West 103rd Street
Indianapolis, IN 46290 USA

Printed in the United States of America    2 3 4 5 6 7 8 9 0   04 03 02 01

First Printing November 2000

Library of Congress Cataloging-in-Publication Number: 99-67941

ISBN: 1-57870-228-3

## Warning and Disclaimer

This book is designed to provide information about building scalable Cisco networks. Every effort has been made to make this book as complete and as accurate as possible, but no warranty or fitness is implied.

The information is provided on an "as is" basis. The authors, Cisco Press, and Cisco Systems, Inc., shall have neither liability nor responsibility to any person or entity with respect to any loss or damages arising from the information contained in this book or from the use of the discs or programs that may accompany it.

The opinions expressed in this book belong to the authors and are not necessarily those of Cisco Systems, Inc.

## Trademark Acknowledgments

All terms mentioned in this book that are known to be trademarks or service marks have been appropriately capitalized. Cisco Press or Cisco Systems, Inc., cannot attest to the accuracy of this information. Use of a term in this book should not be regarded as affecting the validity of any trademark or service mark.

## Feedback Information

At Cisco Press, our goal is to create in-depth technical books of the highest quality and value. Each book is crafted with care and precision, undergoing rigorous development that involves the unique expertise of members from the professional technical community.

Readers' feedback is a natural continuation of this process. If you have any comments regarding how we could improve the quality of this book or otherwise alter it to better suit your needs, you can contact us through e-mail at ciscopress@mcp.com. Please make sure to include the book title and ISBN in your message.

We greatly appreciate your assistance.

| | |
|---|---|
| Publisher | John Wait |
| Editor-in-Chief | John Kane |
| Executive Editor | Brett Bartow |
| Cisco Systems Program Manager | Bob Anstey |
| Managing Editor | Patrick Kanouse |
| Development Editor | Andrew Cupp |
| Senior Editor | Jennifer Chisholm |
| Copy Editor | Krista Hansing |
| Course Developers | Catherine Paquet |
| | Diane Teare |
| | Kip Peterson |
| | Patrick Lao |
| Technical Editors | Hassan Jabi |
| | Patrick Lao |
| Team Coordinator | Amy Lewis |
| Cover Designer | Louisa Klucznik |
| Production Team | Argosy |
| Indexer | Tim Wright |

CISCO SYSTEMS

CISCO PRESS

**Corporate Headquarters**
Cisco Systems, Inc.
170 West Tasman Drive
San Jose, CA 95134-1706
USA
http://www.cisco.com
Tel: 408 526-4000
 800 553-NETS (6387)
Fax: 408 526-4100

**European Headquarters**
Cisco Systems Europe s.a.r.l.
Parc Evolic, Batiment L1/L2
16 Avenue du Quebec
Villebon, BP 706
91961 Courtaboeuf Cedex
France
http://www-europe.cisco.com
Tel: 33 1 69 18 61 00
Fax: 33 1 69 28 83 26

**American Headquarters**
Cisco Systems, Inc.
170 West Tasman Drive
San Jose, CA 95134-1706
USA
http://www.cisco.com
Tel: 408 526-7660
Fax: 408 527-0883

**Asia Headquarters**
Nihon Cisco Systems K.K.
Fuji Building, 9th Floor
3-2-3 Marunouchi
Chiyoda-ku, Tokyo 100
Japan
http://www.cisco.com
Tel: 81 3 5219 6250
Fax: 81 3 5219 6001

Cisco Systems has more than 200 offices in the following countries. Addresses, phone numbers, and fax numbers are listed on the Cisco Connection Online Web site at http://www.cisco.com/offices.

Argentina • Australia • Austria • Belgium • Brazil • Canada • Chile • China • Colombia • Costa Rica • Croatia • Czech Republic • Denmark • Dubai, UAE Finland • France • Germany • Greece • Hong Kong • Hungary • India • Indonesia • Ireland • Israel • Italy • Japan • Korea • Luxembourg • Malaysia • Mexico • The Netherlands • New Zealand • Norway • Peru • Philippines • Poland • Portugal • Puerto Rico • Romania • Russia • Saudi Arabia • Singapore • Slovakia • Slovenia • South Africa • Spain • Sweden • Switzerland • Taiwan • Thailand • Turkey • Ukraine • United Kingdom • United States • Venezuela

# About the Authors

**Catherine Paquet** and **Diane Teare** are senior network architects with Global Knowledge Network (Canada) Inc., Cisco's largest worldwide training partner. There, they provide consulting and training services to customers in North America and Europe. Catherine and Diane are both Cisco Certified Systems Instructors (CCSIs) and Cisco Certified Network Professionals (CCNPs), and both have authored and edited networking books and articles. Catherine and Diane also were members of the team at Cisco Systems that developed the Building Scalable Cisco Networks (BSCN) instructor-led course.

Catherine has in-depth knowledge of routing technologies and access services, mainly in the area of Frame Relay, ISDN, and asynchronous connections. Catherine's internetworking career started as a LAN manager; she was promoted to MAN manager and eventually became the nationwide WAN manager for a federal department. She currently is the course director/master instructor for the Building Cisco Remote Access Networks (BCRAN) and Managing Cisco Networks Security (MCNS) courses at Global Knowledge Network (Canada) Inc. She has a master's degree in business administration, with a major in management information systems. Catherine edited *Building Cisco Remote Access Networks* from Cisco Press (ISBN 1-57870-091-4).

Diane has more than 15 years of experience in design, implementation, and troubleshooting of network hardware and software. She also has been involved in teaching, course design, and project management. Diane is the course director/master instructor for the BSCN and Designing Cisco Networks (DCN) courses at Global Knowledge Network (Canada) Inc. She is also a Cisco Certified Design Associate (CCDA). Diane has a bachelor's degree in applied science in electrical engineering and a master's degree in applied science in management science. She edited *Designing Cisco Networks* from Cisco Press (ISBN 1-57870-105-8).

## About the Technical Reviewers

**Hassan Jabi** has 11 years of experience in the computing industry. He is a Cisco Certified Network Associate (CCNA) and a Cisco Certified Systems Instructor. He currently holds a senior internetwork architect position with Global Knowledge Network (Canada) Inc.

**Patrick Lao** has been a Cisco Systems Education Specialist since 1998. He has Cisco Certified Internetwork Expert (CCIE) (#4952), CCSI, CCNP, and CCNA certifications. As part of the BSCN development team, Patrick developed all the labs for the BSCN instructor-led course. He has a bachelor of science degree in electrical engineering technology from Cal Poly Pomona and a master of science degree in telecommunications management from Golden Gate University.

# Dedications

From Diane:

This book is dedicated to my loving husband, Allan Mertin, who has given me wonderful encouragement and support during the editing of this book and always; to our soon-to-be-born son—we can't wait to meet you; and to my parents, Syd and Beryl, who have continually encouraged my brothers and me, and our families, in everything we've done.

*"And I think to myself, what a wonderful world"*—as sung by Louis Armstrong

From Catherine:

To my parents and sister, Maurice, Florence, and Hélène Paquet, for your continuous support, thank you. To my children, Laurence and Simon, thank you for your countless smiles, laughs, and hugs, which remind me of what is important in life. And, finally, to Pierre Rivard, my soul mate and husband, through whom I have discovered the true joys of life: to learn and to love, thank you *et amours éternels*.

God bless you all.

To Laurence and Simon:

*"Reserve your right to think, for even to think wrongly is better than not to think at all"*—Theon of Alexandria, 370 A.D.

# Acknowledgments

We would like to thank many people for helping us put this book together:

**The Cisco Press team:** Brett Bartow, the executive editor, was the catalyst for this project, coordinating the team and ensuring that sufficient resources were available for the completion of the book. Amy Lewis was instrumental in organizing the logistics and administration. Drew Cupp, the development editor, has been invaluable in producing a high-quality manuscript. His great suggestions and keen eye caught some technical errors and really improved the presentation of the book. We would also like to thank Jen Chisholm, the senior project editor, and Krista Hansing, the copy editor, for their excellent work in shepherding this book through the editorial process.

**The Cisco Systems team:** Many thanks to the other members of the development team of the original BSCN course, including Roger Beatty, Patrick Lao, Kip Peterson, Keith Serrao, Kevin Calkins, Won Lee, and Imran Quershi.

**The technical reviewers:** We would like to thank the technical reviewers of this book, Patrick Lao and Hassan Jabi, for their thorough, detailed review and very valuable input.

**Global Knowledge Network (Canada) team:** Many thanks go to Richard Gordon, vice president and managing director, Dan O'Brien, director of operations, and Kent Clapham, logistics manager, for their enthusiastic support and for providing us with the tools needed to complete this book. Special thanks also to Eric Dragowski, network architect, and to Mark Martinovic, training centre technician, for providing us with equipment when we needed to run some tests.

**Our families:** Of course, this book would not have been possible without the constant understanding and patience of our families. They have lived through the long days and nights it took to complete this project, and have always been there to motivate and inspire us. We thank you all.

**Each other:** Last, but not least, this book is a product of work by two friends and colleagues, which made it even more of a pleasure to complete.

# Contents at a Glance

# Table of Contents

**Chapter 5**   Configuring EIGRP   246

# Foreword

In April 1998, Cisco Systems, Inc., announced a new professional development initiative called the Cisco Career Certifications. These certifications address the growing worldwide demand for more (and better) trained computer networking experts. Building upon our highly successful Cisco Certified Internetwork Expert (CCIE) program—the industry's most respected networking certification vehicle—Cisco Career Certifications enable you to be certified at various technical proficiency levels.

*Building Scalable Cisco Networks* presents in book format all the topics covered in the challenging instructor-led and e-learning certification preparation courses of the same name. The BSCN courses replace the Advanced Cisco Router Configuration 11.3 course. As such, BSCN addresses those tasks that network engineers need to perform when managing access and controlling overhead traffic in growing, routed networks after basic connectivity has been established. This is one of four recommended training courses for CCNP or CCDP certification. Whether you are studying to become CCNP- or CCDP-certified or simply are seeking to gain a better understanding of the products, services, and policies that enable you to control traffic over LANs and WANs and to connect corporate networks to an Internet service provider, you will benefit from the information presented in this book.

Cisco and Cisco Press present this material in text-based format to provide another learning vehicle for our customers and the broader user community in general. Although a publication does not duplicate the instructor-led or e-learning environments, we acknowledge that not everyone responds in the same way to the same delivery mechanism. It is our intent that presenting this material via a Cisco Press publication will enhance the transfer of knowledge to a broad audience of networking professionals.

Along with *Interconnecting Cisco Network Devices*, *Designing Cisco Networks*, *Building Cisco Remote Access Networks*, *Building Cisco Multilayer Switched Networks*, *Cisco Internetwork Troubleshooting*, and *Cisco Internetwork Design*, this course supplement covers all of the most current recommended training courses developed by Cisco Systems for the CCNA, CCDA, CCNP, and CCDP routing and switching certification tracks.

Cisco Press will present existing and future courses through these coursebooks to help achieve Cisco Worldwide Training's principal objectives: to educate the Cisco community of networking professionals and to enable that community to build and maintain reliable, scalable networks. The Cisco Career Certifications and classes that support these certifications are directed at meeting these objectives through a disciplined approach to progressive learning. The books Cisco Press creates in partnership with Cisco Systems will meet the same standards for content quality demanded of our courses and certifications. It is our intent that you will find this and subsequent Cisco Press certification and training publications of value as you build your networking knowledge base.

Thomas M. Kelly
Vice President, Worldwide Training
Cisco Systems, Inc.
June 2000

# Introduction

Internetworks are growing at a fast pace to support more protocols and users, and are becoming more complex. As the premier designer and provider of internetworking devices, Cisco Systems is committed to supporting these growing networks.

Based on the new Cisco instructor-led course of the same name, *Building Scalable Cisco Networks* teaches you how to design, configure, maintain, and scale a routed network. This book focuses on using Cisco routers connected in LANs and WANs typically found at medium-to-large network sites. Upon completion of this book, you will be able to select and implement the appropriate Cisco IOS services required to build a scalable, routed network.

In *Building Scalable Cisco Networks*, you will study a broad range of technical details on topics related to routing, including routing principles, IP addressing issues such as variable-length subnet masks (VLSMs), route summarization, and protocol redistribution. The routing protocols Open Shortest Path First (OSPF), Enhanced Interior Gateway Routing Protocol (EIGRP), and Border Gateway Protocol (BGP) are investigated in detail. Configuration examples and sample verification outputs demonstrate troubleshooting techniques, and a case study is used throughout the book to review key concepts and to discuss critical issues surrounding network operation. Chapter-ending Configuration Exercises and Review Questions illustrate and help solidify the concepts presented in the book. This will start you down the path for attaining your Cisco Certified Network Professional (CCNP) or Cisco Certified Design Professional (CCDP) certification, as this book provides in-depth information to help you prepare for the BSCN exam, also known as the Routing Exam.

The commands and configuration examples presented in this book are based on Cisco IOS Release 12.0.

## Objectives of This Book

When you complete the readings and exercises in this book, you will be able to select and configure the appropriate services when given a network specification that calls for simplifying IP address management at branch offices by centralizing addresses. You will also be able to implement the appropriate technologies when given a network specification calling for a scalable, routed network that includes link-state protocols and redistribution. When given a network specification calling for either a single or a multihomed interconnection into a BGP network, you will be able to configure the edge routers to properly interconnect into the BGP cloud. You will also be able to implement case studies that reflect a scalable internetwork when given various network specifications calling for multiple routed and routing protocols.

The book is divided into four parts: "Scalable Internetworks," "Scalable Routing Protocols," "Controlling Scalable Internetworks," and "Appendixes." An overview of each part follows.

## Part I: Scalable Internetworks

This part serves as a review of routing principles and an introduction to the challenges of implementing a scalable routed network.

Chapter 1, "Routing Principles," covers the principles of routing. Classful and classless routing are reviewed, as are the differences between distance vector and link-state routing protocol behavior. Convergence issues surrounding the most commonly used interior routing protocols for the Internet Protocol (IP) are also presented.

Chapter 2, "Extending IP Addresses," discusses various aspects of IP addressing, including VLSMs, route summarization, and classless interdomain routing (CIDR).

## Part II: Scalable Routing Protocols

This part provides in-depth coverage of the scalable routing protocols OSPF, EIGRP, and BGP.

Chapter 3, "Configuring OSPF in a Single Area," introduces the OSPF routing protocol. Topics include OSPF terminology and operation in a broadcast multiaccess topology, a point-to-point topology, and an NBMA topology.

Chapter 4, "Interconnecting Multiple OSPF Areas," covers the use, operation, configuration, and verification of OSPF in multiple areas.

Chapter 5, "Configuring EIGRP," introduces EIGRP. Topics include EIGRP features, modes of operations, and support of VLSM and route summarization.

Chapter 6, "Configuring Basic Border Gateway Protocol," introduces BGP, including BGP terminology and the fundamentals of BGP operation.

Chapter 7, "Implementing BGP in Scalable Networks," starts with a discussion of problems that may occur when scaling internal BGP (IBGP). Various solutions, including route reflectors and policy control using prefix lists, are explained. Connecting an autonomous system (AS) with more than one BGP connection is known as multihoming, and different ways to accomplish this are explored.

## Part III: Controlling Scalable Internetworks

This part discusses different ways to control routing update information, and provides a review of the rest of the book.

Chapter 8, "Optimizing Routing Update Operation," discusses different ways to control routing update information. Route redistribution to interconnect networks that use multiple routing protocols is explained. Controlling information between the protocols can be accomplished by using filters, changing the administrative distance, and configuring metrics. The configuration of each of these techniques is discussed. Policy-based routing using route maps is also explained and configured.

Chapter 9, "Implementing Scalability Features in Your Internetwork," is a review of the contents in the rest of the book. This chapter culminates with a large Configuration Exercise that allows you to configure many of the features discussed.

## Part IV: Appendixes

This part contains appendixes to supplement the BSCN material.

Appendix A, "Job Aids and Supplements," contains job aids and supplements for the following topics: extending IP addressing, addressing review, IP access lists, OSPF, EIGRP, BGP, and route optimization.

Appendix B, "Router Password Recovery Procedure," contains the procedure for password recovery on Cisco routers.

Appendix C, "Summary of ICND Router Commands," contains a listing of some of the Cisco router IOS commands that you may find in the Cisco Press *Interconnecting Cisco Network Devices* (ICND) coursebook, organized in various categories.

Appendix D, "Summary of BSCN Router Commands," contains a listing of some of the Cisco router IOS commands that you may find in this Cisco Press *Building Scalable Cisco Networks* coursebook, organized in various categories.

Appendix E, "Open Systems Interconnection (OSI) Reference Model," is a brief overview of the Open Systems Interconnection seven-layer model.

Appendix F, "Common Requests For Comments," lists some common Requests For Comments (RFCs).

Appendix G, "Answers to the Review Questions," contains the answers to the review questions that appear at the end of each chapter in the book.

Appendix H, "Configuration Exercise Equipment Requirements and Backbone Configurations," contains information on the equipment requirements for the Configuration Exercises in this book, along with the configuration commands for the backbone routers.

Appendix I, "Glossary," provides definitions for networking terms and acronyms used throughout the book.

# Case Studies, Configuration Exercises, and Review Questions

Throughout the book, a case study of JKL Corporation, as shown in Figure 1, is used to discuss various aspects of scalable routing. The case study sections are used to review key concepts, to discuss critical issues surrounding network operation, and to provide a focus for the configuration exercises.

**Figure 1**    *The JKL Corporation Used in Case Study Sections Throughout the Book*

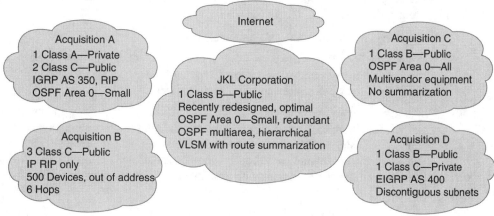

Internet

Acquisition A
1 Class A—Private
2 Class C—Public
IGRP AS 350, RIP
OSPF Area 0—Small

Acquisition C
1 Class B—Public
OSPF Area 0—All
Multivendor equipment
No summarization

JKL Corporation
1 Class B—Public
Recently redesigned, optimal
OSPF Area 0—Small, redundant
OSPF multiarea, hierarchical
VLSM with route summarization

Acquisition B
3 Class C—Public
IP RIP only
500 Devices, out of address
6 Hops

Acquisition D
1 Class B—Public
1 Class C—Private
EIGRP AS 400
Discontiguous subnets

JKL's problem: How to integrate Acquisitions A–D?

In the case study, JKL is an enterprise that will be making four acquisitions—A, B, C, and D. JKL's ultimate goal is to integrate the acquisitioned networks with its own network. Suggestions for topics to analyze are given in each chapter with a case study, and suggested solutions and answers are provided after the case study material.

Configuration Exercises at the end of most chapters provide you with the opportunity to practice configuring routers with the commands presented. If you have access to real hardware, you can try these exercises on your routers; refer to Appendix H, "Configuration Exercise Equipment Requirements and Backbone Configurations," for a list of recommended equipment and configuration commands for the backbone routers. However, even if you don't have access to any routers, you can go through the exercises and keep a log of your own "running configurations" on separate sheets of paper. Commands used and answers to the Configuration Exercises are provided after the exercise sections.

At the end of each chapter, you will have an opportunity to test your knowledge by answering Review Questions on the subjects covered in the chapter. You can compare your answers to the correct answers provided in Appendix G, "Answers to the Review Questions," to find out how you did and what material you might need to study further.

# Who Should Read This Book

This book is intended for network architects, network designers, systems engineers, network managers, and network administrators who are responsible for implementing and troubleshooting growing routed networks.

If you are planning to take the BSCN exam (the Routing Exam) toward your CCNP or CCDP certification, this book provides you with in-depth study material.

To fully benefit from this book, you should be CCNA certified or already possess the following knowledge:

- Working knowledge of the OSI reference model

- Understanding of internetworking fundamentals, including commonly used networking terms, numbering schemes, topologies, distance vector routing protocol operation, and when to use static and default routes

- Ability to operate and configure a Cisco router, including displaying and interpreting a router's routing table, configuring static and default routes, enabling a WAN serial connection using HDLC, configuring Frame Relay permanent virtual circuits (PVCs) on interfaces and subinterfaces, configuring IP standard and extended access lists, and verifying router configurations with available tools such as **show** and **debug** commands

- Working knowledge of the TCP/IP stack, configuring IP addresses, and configuring RIP and IGRP

If you lack this knowledge and these skills, you can gain them by completing Cisco's interactive, self-paced *Internetworking Multimedia CD-ROM* or by reading *Internetworking Technologies Handbook,* Second Edition (Cisco Press*),* plus one of the combinations of Cisco's instructor-led training courses or Cisco Press books, as outlined here:

- *Introduction to Cisco Router Configuration* (ICRC) contains router configuration basics, and *Cisco LAN Switch Configuration* (CLSC) contains LAN switch configuration basics. (Note that these courses/books are being phased out by Cisco and are being replaced by *Interconnecting Cisco Network Devices* (ICND) and *Building Cisco Multilayer Switched Networks* (BCMSN) respectively.)

- *Cisco Router and LAN Switches* (CRLS) contains router and LAN switch configuration basics. (Note that CRLS has been phased out by Cisco and is now replaced by ICND.)

- *Interconnecting Cisco Network Devices* (ICND) contains router and LAN switch configuration basics. See Appendix C, "Summary of ICND Router Commands," for a listing of some of the Cisco router IOS commands that you may find in ICND, organized in various categories.

# Conventions Used in This Book

This book contains several helpful elements such as figures, configuration examples, notes, and sidebars to help you learn about scalable routed networks. This section covers the standard conventions that you will encounter in this book.

## Graphic Symbols

The icons displayed in Figure 2 are used in the figures presented throughout this book.

**Figure 2**    *Icons Used in This Book*

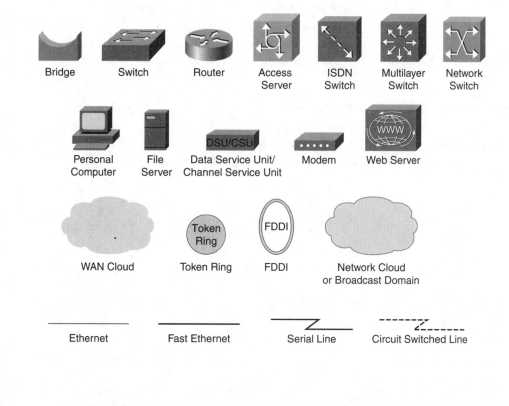

| | |
| NOTE | The example topologies in this book are for demonstration purposes only and do not necessarily represent optimal network design. |

## Command Syntax Conventions

The conventions used to present command syntax in this book are the same conventions used in the *Cisco IOS Command Reference*, as follows:

- **Boldface** indicates commands and keywords that are entered literally as shown. In examples (not syntax), boldface indicates user input (for example, a **show** command).

- *Italics* indicates arguments for which you supply values.

- Square brackets [ ] indicate optional elements.

- Braces { } contain a choice of required keywords.

- Vertical bars (|) separate alternative, mutually exclusive elements.

- Braces and vertical bars within square brackets—for example, [x {y | z}]—indicate a required choice within an optional element. You do not need to enter what is in the brackets, but if you do, you have some required choices in the braces.

## Author's Notes, Sidebars, and Cautions

The author's notes, sidebars, and cautions found in this book are included to provide you with extra information on a subject. You will probably find these asides to be very beneficial in real-world implementation.

# PART I

# Scalable Internetworks

This chapter covers the following topics:

- Routing Fundamentals
- Routing Protocols
- Routing Table Analysis
- Introduction to the Case Study
- Summary
- Configuration Exercise: Discovering the Network
- Answers to Configuration Exercise: Discovering the Network
- Review Questions

The material in this chapter is a review of topics that you are probably already familiar with. You may also wish to refer to Appendix A, "Job Aids and Supplements," for further review material, especially regarding IP addressing and subnetting.

# CHAPTER 1

# Routing Principles

This chapter covers the principles of routing. Classful and classless routing are reviewed, as are the differences between distance vector and link-state routing protocol behavior. Convergence issues surrounding the most commonly used interior routing protocols for the Internet Protocol (IP) are also presented.

After reading this chapter, you will be able to list the key information routers need to route data, describe classful and classless routing protocols, compare distance vector and link-state protocol operation, and describe the use of the fields in a routing table. Finally, given a preconfigured network, you should be able to discover the topology, analyze the routing table, and test connectivity using accepted troubleshooting techniques.

## Routing Fundamentals

This section reviews routing in general, the requirements for routing, and how routing decisions are made, including the use of administrative distance and metrics.

### Routing Defined

Routing is a relay process in which items are forwarded from one location to another. In computer networks, user-generated traffic—such as electronic mail or graphic and text documents—is forwarded from a logical source to a logical destination. Each device in the network has a logical address so that it can be reached individually; in some cases, devices can also be reached as part of a larger group of devices.

For a router to act as an effective relay device, it must have knowledge of the logical topology of the network and be capable of communicating with its neighboring devices. A router can be configured to recognize several different logical addressing schemes and to regularly exchange topology information with other devices in the network.

The mechanism of learning and maintaining awareness of the network topology is considered to be the *routing* function. The actual movement of transient traffic through the router, from an inbound interface to an outbound interface, is a separate function and is considered to be the *switching* function. A routing device must perform both the routing and the switching functions to be an effective relay device.

**NOTE**      Appendix E, "Open System Interconnection (OSI) Reference Model," contains a review of
the Open System Interconnection (OSI) reference model. Under this reference model, a
router is an OSI Layer 3 device that has an understanding of the logical topology of the
network. The routing and switching functions described here refer to the forwarding of a
Layer 3 protocol data unit (PDU), also referred to as a packet (or datagram). A packet
contains a logical source and a logical destination address that the routing device interprets
during the packet forwarding process.

## Routing Requirements

A router must know three items in order to route:

- The router must determine whether it has the protocol suite active.
- The router must know the destination network.
- The router must know which outbound interface is the best path to the destination.

For a routing device to make a routing decision, it must first understand the logical
destination address. For this to happen, the protocol suite that uses that logical addressing
scheme must be enabled and currently active on the router. Some examples of common
protocol suites are Transmission Control Protocol/Internet Protocol (TCP/IP), Internetwork
Packet Exchange (IPX), and Digital Equipment Corporation's DECnet.

After the router can understand the addressing scheme, the second decision is to determine
whether the destination logical network is a valid destination within the current routing
table. If the destination logical network does not exist in the routing table, routing devices
might be programmed to discard the packet and to generate an error message (for example,
an IP Internet Control Message Protocol [ICMP] message) to notify the sender of the event.
Some network managers have successfully reduced the size of their network's routing
tables by including only a few destination networks and then specifying a default route
entry. If specified, a default route will be followed if the destination logical network is not
included as part of the device's routing table.

The final decision that the routing device must make if the destination network is in the
routing table is to determine through which outbound interface the packet will be
forwarded. The routing table will contain only the best path (or paths) to any given
destination logical network. The best path to a destination network will be associated with
a particular outbound interface by the routing protocol process. Routing protocols use a
*metric* to determine the best path to a destination. A smaller metric indicates a preferred
path; if two or more paths have an equal lowest metric, then all those paths will be equally
shared. Sharing packet traffic across multiple paths is referred to as *load balancing* to the
destination. When the outbound interface is known, the router must also have an
encapsulation method (in other words, a Layer 2 frame type) to use when forwarding the
packet to the next-hop logical device in the relay path.

## Routing Information

The information required to perform the routing operation is included in the router's routing table and is generated by one or more routing protocol processes. The routing table is composed of multiple entries, each of which indicates the following:

- The mechanism by which the route was learned. Learning methods can be either dynamic or manual.

- The logical destination, either a major network or a subnetwork (also called a subnet) of a major network. In isolated cases, host addresses may be contained in the routing table.

- The administrative distance, which is a measure of the *trustworthiness* of the learning mechanism. Administrative distance is discussed further in the next section, "Administrative Distance."

- The metric, which is a measure of the aggregate path "cost," as defined by the routing protocol. Routing metrics are discussed further in the section "Routing Metric," later in this chapter.

- The address of the next-hop relay device (router) in the path to the destination.

- How current the information about the route is. This field indicates the amount of time the information has been in the routing table since the last update. Depending on the routing protocol in use, route entry information may be refreshed periodically to ensure that it is current.

- The interface associated with reaching the destination network. This is the port through which the packet will leave the router and be forwarded to the next-hop relay device.

Example 1-1 shows a sample line in an IP routing table on a router. Table 1-1 shows how the information in the shaded sample line in Example 1-1 is interpreted.

**Example 1-1**  *A Routing Table Shows the Metric and the Next-Hop Router for Each Network*

```
RouterA#show ip route
Codes: C - connected, S - static, I - IGRP, R - RIP, M - mobile, B - BGP
       D - EIGRP, EX - EIGRP external, O - OSPF, IA - OSPF inter area
       N1 - OSPF NSSA external type 1, N2 - OSPF NSSA external type 2
       E1 - OSPF external type 1, E2 - OSPF external type 2, E - EGP
       i - IS-IS, L1 - IS-IS level-1, L2 - IS-IS level-2, * - candidate default
       U - per-user static route, o - ODR
       T - traffic engineered route

Gateway of last resort is not set

172.16.0.0/16 is subnetted, 2 subnets
I    172.16.8.0    [100/118654]  via 172.16.7.9,  00:00:23,  Serial0
<output omitted>
```

**Table 1-1** *Interpretation of Routing Table Components in Example 1-1*

| Routing Table Entry Component | Description |
|---|---|
| I | How the route was learned—in this case, by the Interior Gateway Routing Protocol (IGRP). |
|  | The other codes possible for this component are shown in the "Codes" legend in Example 1-1. |
| 172.16.8.0 | Destination logical network/subnet. |
| [100 | Administrative distance (trustworthiness factor) of IGRP. |
| /118654] | Metric value (reachability); by default for IGRP, this is a combination of the bandwidth and delay. |
| via 172.16.7.9 | Next-hop logical address (the next router). |
| 00:00:23 | Age of entry (in hours: minutes: seconds) since the last update. |
| Serial0 | Interface through which the route was learned and through which packets for the destination will leave. |

## Administrative Distance

The routing process is responsible for selecting the best path to any destination network. Because more than one learning mechanism can exist on a router at any given time, a method to choose between routes is needed when the same route is learned from multiple sources. For IP within a Cisco router, the concept of an *administrative distance* is used as a selection method for IP routing protocols.

Administrative distance is used as a measure of the *trustworthiness* of the source of the IP routing information. It is important only when a router learns about a destination route from more than one source.

Lower values of administrative distance are preferred over higher values. In general, default administrative distances have been assigned with a preference for manual entries over dynamically learned entries, and routing protocols with more sophisticated metrics over routing protocols with simple metrics. A comparison chart of the default administrative distances is presented in Table 1-2.

**Table 1-2** *Default Administrative Distances of Sources of Routes*

| Route Source | Default Administrative Distance |
|---|---|
| Connected interface | 0 |
| Static route out an interface | 0 |
| Static route to a next hop | 1 |
| EIGRP summary route | 5 |

**Table 1-2**    *Default Administrative Distances of Sources of Routes (Continued)*

| Route Source | Default Administrative Distance |
|---|---|
| External BGP | 20 |
| Internal EIGRP | 90 |
| IGRP | 100 |
| OSPF | 110 |
| IS-IS | 115 |
| RIP (v1 and v2) | 120 |
| EGP | 140 |
| External EIGRP | 170 |
| Internal BGP | 200 |
| Unknown | 255 |

**EIGRP Summary Routes**

Enhanced Interior Gateway Routing Protocol (EIGRP) summary routes with an administrative distance of 5 exist, but they are not visible in the routing table except on the router that configured the summary address. These routes can be viewed using the **show ip route** *network* command for the specific summarized network. EIGRP is discussed in detail in Chapter 5, "Configuring EIGRP."

# Routing Metric

In a routed network, the routing process relies on the routing protocol to maintain a loop-free topology and to locate the best path to every destination network.

The definition of what is the best path to any destination is one feature that distinguishes different routing protocols. Each routing protocol uses a different measurement for what is best. Routers advertise the path to a network in terms of a *metric* value. Some common examples of metrics are hop count (how many routers to pass through), cost (based on bandwidth), and a composite value (using several parameters in the calculation). If the destination network is not local to a router, then the path is represented by the sum of the metric values defined for all the links that must be traversed from the router to reach that network.

When the routing process knows the metric values associated with the different paths (assuming that multiple paths exist), then the routing decision can be made. The routing process will select the path that has the smallest metric value. In Cisco routers, if multiple lowest equal metric paths exist in an IP environment, then load sharing (also known as load balancing) will be in effect across the multiple paths. For IP, Cisco supports by default four equal metric paths to a common destination network. A maximum of six equal metric paths can be configured in the Cisco Internetwork Operating System (IOS) by using the **maximum-paths** router configuration command.

The next two sections review the Routing Information Protocol (RIP) and IGRP routing metrics.

## RIP Routing Metrics

RIP is a commonly used routing protocol in small- to medium-sized TCP/IP networks. RIP uses hop count as a metric, equal to the number of neighboring routers that must be passed through to reach the destination. In the topology shown in Figure 1-1, traditional RIP implementations would cause Router A to arbitrarily choose one path to reach network 192.168.10.0, and only the selected path would be displayed in the routing table.

**Figure 1-1** *An Example Network Using the RIP Routing Protocol*

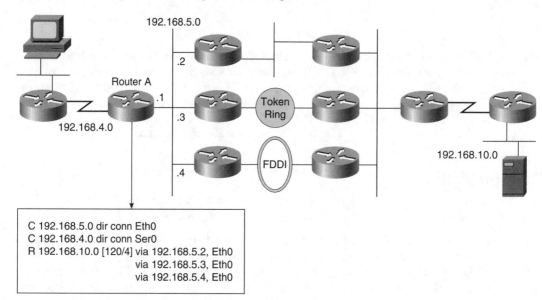

```
C 192.168.5.0 dir conn Eth0
C 192.168.4.0 dir conn Ser0
R 192.168.10.0 [120/4] via 192.168.5.2, Eth0
                       via 192.168.5.3, Eth0
                       via 192.168.5.4, Eth0
```

However, in Cisco routers, the RIP implementation is such that multiple equal hop paths can be shared because load balancing is on by default. In Figure 1-1, notice that Router A can reach network 192.168.10.0 using three different paths that have an equal hop count. As a result of the equal metric, all three paths will be displayed in the routing table as the lowest metric path. Remember that even though the three paths in Figure 1-1 are of different bandwidths, RIP does not consider bandwidth in its best path decision.

| NOTE | The example topologies in this book are for demonstration purposes only and do not necessarily represent optimal network design. |
| --- | --- |

## IGRP Routing Metrics

Cisco's IGRP is a commonly used routing protocol in medium- to large-sized TCP/IP networks. IGRP uses a composite metric, based upon bandwidth, delay, reliability, load, and maximum transmission unit (MTU). In the IGRP standard algorithm computation, only the bandwidth and delay values are enabled by default. (Refer to the "IGRP Metric Calculation" sidebar later in this section for a description of the IGRP metric calculation.)

The IGRP composite metric can distinguish subtle differences in link characteristics, and therefore will select the highest-bandwidth (fastest) path to the destination network. In Figure 1-2, Router A selects only one path to network 192.168.10.0; this is the Fiber Distributed Data Interface (FDDI) path because the 100 megabits per second (Mbps) bandwidth is higher than the other available paths. If equal-metric (at least, equal within 1 percent) paths exist, load balancing will be in effect.

**Figure 1-2**    *An Example Network Using the IGRP Routing Protocol*

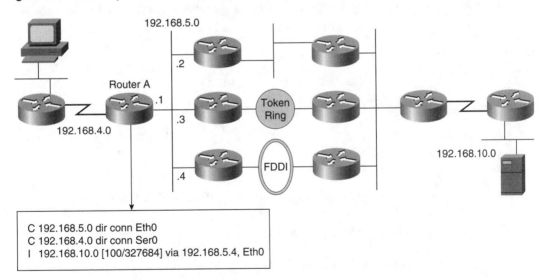

```
C 192.168.5.0 dir conn Eth0
C 192.168.4.0 dir conn Ser0
I   192.168.10.0 [100/327684] via 192.168.5.4, Eth0
```

IGRP is also capable of load balancing across unequal-cost paths, within a specified variance. This capability is also part of the EIGRP protocol and is discussed further in Chapter 5.

## IGRP Metric Calculation

IGRP calculates the metric by adding weighted values of different characteristics of the link to a destination network. The formula used is as follows:

Metric = (K1 × bandwidth) + (K2 × bandwidth) ÷ (256 − load) + (K3 × delay)

If K5 does not equal 0, then an additional operation is done:

Metric = Metric × (K5 ÷ [reliability + K4])

The K values in these formulas are constants that can be defined using the **metric weights** router configuration command. The default constant values are K1 = K3 = 1 and K2 = K4 = K5 = 0, so by default the formula is:

Metric = bandwidth + delay

To determine the bandwidth that is used in this calculation, find the smallest of all the bandwidths from the outgoing interfaces along the path to the destination, in kilobits per second (kbps), and divide 10,000,000 by that number. Note that bandwidth given in the Cisco IOS **show interfaces** command is in kilobits per second.

To determine the delay that is used in this calculation, add all the delays from the outgoing interfaces along the path to the destination, in microseconds, and divide this number by 10. Note that the delay given in the Cisco IOS **show interfaces** command is in microseconds.

Figure 1-3 presents a sample network to illustrate the IGRP metric calculation.

**Figure 1-3**    *Network for IGRP Metric Calculation Example*

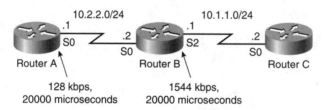

In Figure 1-3, Router B advertises network 10.1.1.0 to Router A. The metric that Router B advertises for 10.1.1.0 is calculated as follows:

Bandwidth = 10,000,000 ÷ 1544 = 6476
Delay = 20,000 ÷ 10 = 2000
Metric = Bandwidth + Delay = 8476

Router A will calculate the metric that it puts in its routing table for 10.1.1.0 as follows:

Bandwidth = 10,000,000 ÷ 128 = 78,125 (using the minimum bandwidth in the path— in this case, 128 kbps)
Delay = (20,000 + 20,000) ÷ 10 = 4000
Metric = Bandwidth + Delay = 82,125

(This information was adapted from www.cisco.com/warp/public/103/3.html.)

# Neighbor Relationships

The concept of routing is based upon a relay system. Traffic is relayed from one routing device to the next until the destination is reached. The next-hop logical address required for delivery is shown in the routing table (as the *via* address). This information is discovered when a neighboring router advertises the route. This section discusses how routers communicate with their neighboring routers.

Immediately after a router starts up, it attempts to establish a routing relationship with neighboring routing devices. The purpose of this initial communication is to identify the neighboring devices and to begin communicating and learning the network topology. The method of establishing neighbor relationships and the initial learning of the topology vary among different routing protocols. Often broadcast frames are used to send to the neighboring devices, especially until the Layer 2 addresses of the adjacent devices (for example, the addresses of the network interface cards [NICs]) are learned.

The routing process within the routing protocol establishes a peer relationship with the neighboring routers at the software (upper) layers of the OSI reference model. Different routing protocols exist at different upper layers of the OSI reference model (Layers 4 through 7). The routing protocol exchanges either periodic hello messages or periodic routing updates to maintain the ongoing communication between the neighbors.

When the network topology is understood and the routing table contains the best path to known destination networks, traffic forwarding to those destinations can begin. As discussed earlier, the function of forwarding transient packets by the router is referred to as switching.

Figure 1-4 summarizes the switching operation performed by the router.

The switching function is all about moving data through the router. The switching function relies on Layer 2 (ARP or equivalent information) and Layer 3 (routing information) lookup tables. If these tables have the necessary information, then traffic forwarding can be accomplished in an efficient manner. Incomplete tables will cause delays or will result in an incapability to forward traffic to the next-hop device.

The switching function needs the end result of the routing function, which is a routing table entry that points to the destination logical network. The switching function has four basic steps, as indicated in Figure 1-4:

1 A packet transiting the router will be accepted into the router if the frame header (of the frame in which the packet resides) contains the Layer 2 address of one of the router's interfaces, or the broadcast address, or multicast address that the router is configured to accept. If properly addressed, when the framing is checked, the frame content (the packet) will be buffered pending further processing. The buffering occurs in main memory or some other specialized memory location.

**Figure 1-4**    *A Router Performs Basic Switching Functions*

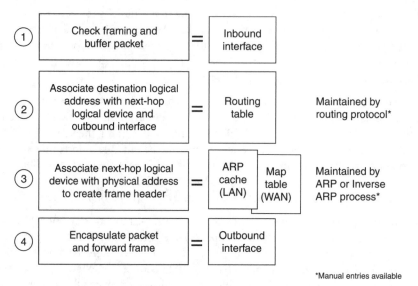

*Manual entries available

2   The router checks the destination logical network portion of the packet header against the network and subnetwork entries in the routing table. If there is a match, the destination network is associated with a next-hop logical device and an outbound interface.

3   After the next-hop logical device address is known, a lookup is performed to locate a physical address (the Layer 2 address) of the next-hop device. The lookup is performed in an Address Resolution Protocol (ARP) table for local-area network (LAN) interfaces, or a map table for wide-area network (WAN) interfaces. The contents of these tables can be created either dynamically or manually.

4   After the physical address of the next-hop device is known, the appropriate frame header is created in the router memory. (For IP packets, the router will also modify the IP header by decrementing the Time To Live [TTL] field and updating the IP header checksum.) After the frame header is created, the frame is moved to the outbound interface for transmission onto the media. As the frame is placed on the media, the outbound interface adds the cyclic redundancy check (CRC) character and ending delimiters to the frame. These characters will be validated at the arriving interface on the next-hop relay device.

### Time To Live Field in IP Packets

The TTL field of the IP header is defined to be a timer limiting the lifetime of an IP packet. It is an 8-bit field, and the units are seconds. Each router that handles a packet must decrement the TTL by at least 1, even if the elapsed time was much less than a second. Because this is very often the case, the TTL is effectively a hop count limit on how far a packet can propagate through a network.

When a router forwards a packet, it must reduce the TTL by at least 1. If it holds a packet for more than 1 second, it may decrement the TTL by 1 for each second.

If the TTL is reduced to zero (or less), the packet must be discarded, and if the destination is not a multicast address, the router must send an ICMP Time Exceeded message, Code 0 (TTL Exceeded in Transit) message to the source. Note that a router must not discard an IP unicast or broadcast packet with a nonzero TTL merely because it can predict that another router on the path to the packet's final destination will decrement the TTL to zero. However, a router may do so for IP multicasts.

Thus, you can see that the IP TTL is used as both a hop count limit and a time limit. Its hop count function is critical to ensuring that routing problems won't cause packets to loop infinitely in the network. The time limit function is used by transport protocols such as TCP to ensure reliable data transfer. Many current implementations treat TTL as a pure hop count, and in parts of the Internet community, there is a strong sentiment that the time limit function should instead be performed by the transport protocols that need it.

The RFC 1812 specification allows the time limit function to be optional. Most router vendors argued that implementation of the time limit function is difficult enough that it is currently not generally done.

(This information was adapted from RFC 1812, available at www.cis.ohio-state.edu/htbin/rfc/rfc1812.html.)

# Routing Protocols

There are many ways to categorize routing protocols. The following sections discuss two such categories—classful versus classless, and distance vector versus link-state. Each of these terms is defined, and examples are provided. Note that some routing protocols have characteristics that cross over category boundaries.

## Classful Routing Overview

Routing protocols that do not send subnet mask information along with each network address are known as *classful* routing protocols; RIP version 1 (RIPv1) and IGRP are classful routing protocols.

When using a classful routing protocol, all subnets of the same major (Class A, B, or C) network number must use the same subnet mask. Upon receiving a routing update packet, a router running a classful routing protocol does one of the following to determine the network portion of the route:

- If the routing update information is about the same major network number as configured on the receiving interface, the router applies the subnet mask that is configured on the receiving interface.

- If the routing update information is about a different major network as configured on the receiving interface, the router will apply the default (by address class) subnet mask.

**NOTE**    You may see the term *routing mask* used instead of *subnet mask*. A routing mask refers to the mask that defines the network portion of an IP address. A routing mask encompasses both natural (default) masks and subnet masks. The terms *routing mask* and *subnet mask* are interchangeable in this book.

## Classful Routes

Classful routing protocols, such as RIPv1 and IGRP, exchange routes to subnetworks within the same major (Class A, B, or C) network. This is possible because all the subnetworks in the major network should have the same subnet mask; the network administrators must enforce the use of consistent masks.

When routes are exchanged with foreign networks (in other words, with different major networks), receiving routers will not know the subnet mask in use because subnet masks are not included in the routing updates. As a result, the subnetwork information from each major network must be summarized to a classful boundary, using the default classful mask, before inclusion in the routing update. Thus, only routers configured to participate in the major network to which the subnets belong exchange subnet routes; routers that participate in different major networks exchange classful summary routes. The creation of a classful summary route at major network boundaries is handled automatically by classful routing protocols. Summarization at other bit positions within the major network address is *not* allowed by classful routing protocols.

This automatic summarization is illustrated in Figure 1-5. As shown in Figure 1-5, devices within the same major network share subnetwork routes, while only classful summary routes are exchanged between foreign networks. The classful summary routes are automatically created at Class A, B, and C network boundaries by routers running a classful routing protocol.

**Figure 1-5**  *An Example Network Showing the Routing Tables of Routers Running a Classful Routing Protocol*

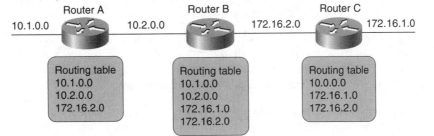

Another example is shown in Figure 1-6. In Figure 1-6, the routers are running RIPv1. Router B is attached to network 172.16.1.0/24 on its left interface. Therefore, if Router B learns about any network on this interface that is also a subnet of the 172.16.0.0 network, it will apply the subnet mask configured on its receiving interface (/24) to that learned network. Router B summarizes the routing information about the 172.16.0.0 network when sending it to Router C because it is sent over an interface in a different major network (the 192.168.5.16/28 network). Notice how Router C, which is attached to Router B via the 192.168.5.16/28 network, handles routing information about network 172.16.0.0. Rather than using the subnet mask that Router B knows about (/24), Router C applies the default (classful) subnet mask for a Class B address (/16) when it receives information about 172.16.0.0.

**Figure 1-6**  *An Example Network Showing That Routers Running RIPv1 Do Not Pass Subnet Mask Information to Their Neighbors*

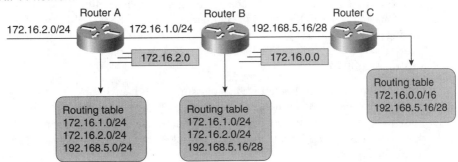

## Classful Subnetting Requirements

When performing subnetting in conjunction with a classful routing protocol, care must be taken to assign the same subnet mask to all router interfaces on all routers in the same major network within the classful routing domain. This consistency is a requirement for subnetwork routes to be advertised correctly.

This requirement has a potential downside from the standpoint of efficient address allocation. For example, as shown in Figure 1-7, while a 27-bit mask allocates the proper number of host addresses (30 addresses) for each Ethernet segment, not all of the 30 addresses can be utilized on the point-to-point serial link.

**Figure 1-7**    *Routers Running a Classful Routing Protocol Must Use the Same Mask on All Interfaces*

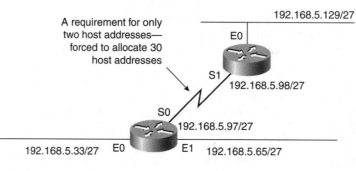

The next section describes classless routing, which overcomes some of the classful protocol restrictions.

# Classless Routing Overview

*Classless* routing protocols can be considered as second-generation protocols because they are designed to deal with some of the limitations of the earlier classful protocols. Classless routing protocols include Open Shortest Path First (OSPF), EIGRP, RIP version 2 (RIPv2), Intermediate System-to-Intermediate System (IS-IS), and the Border Gateway Protocol version 4 (BGP-4).

One of the most serious limitations in a classful network environment is that the subnet mask is not exchanged during the routing update process. This approach requires the same mask to be used on all subnetworks of a major network. The classless approach advertises the subnet mask for each route, so a more precise (sophisticated) lookup can be performed in the routing table.

Classless routing protocols also address another limitation of classful routing protocols: the automatic summarization to a classful network with a default classful subnet mask at major network boundaries. In the classless environment, the summarization process is manually controlled and can usually be invoked at any bit position within the network. (As you will see in Chapter 4, "Interconnecting Multiple OSPF Areas," hierarchical designs using OSPF allow summarization at any bit position but restrict configuring summarization to specific routers in the network.) Because subnet routes are propagated throughout the routing domain, summarization is often required to keep the routing tables at a manageable size.

In the OSPF network in Figure 1-8, Router B passes the subnet and subnet mask information to Router C; Router C puts the subnet details into its routing table. Router C does not have to use any default masks for the received routing information.

**Figure 1-8**  *An Example Network Showing That Routers Running OSPF Pass Subnet Mask Information to Their Neighbors*

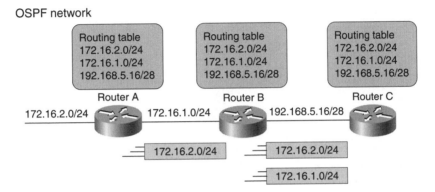

## Classless Subnetting Requirement

Recall that another limitation of classful routing protocols is the requirement for a consistent mask to be applied to all router interfaces within the major network. This strict classful approach results in inefficient utilization of host addresses.

Classless routing protocols understand that different routes within a major network can have different masks. The use of different masks within a major network is referred to as variable-length subnet masking (VLSM). Classless routing protocols support VLSM, and that, in turn, leads to more efficient allocation of subnet masks to meet different host requirements on different subnetworks, resulting in better utilization of host addresses. In Figure 1-9, the serial link has been configured with a subnet mask that properly supports the link requirement for only two host addresses (a mask of 255.255.255.252, which corresponds to a prefix length of 30). The Ethernet links can use a mask appropriate for the number of hosts attached—in this case, 255.255.255.224 (which corresponds to a prefix length of 27).

**Figure 1-9** *Routers Running a Classless Routing Protocol May Use Different IP Address Masks*

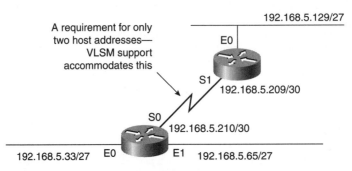

The next two sections describe another way to categorize routing protocols—distance vector versus link-state. The following sections also discuss differences between distance vector and link-state protocols and how they relate to the classful and classless categories.

## Distance Vector Operation

The periodic, routine routing updates generated by most distance vector routing protocols go only to directly connected routing devices. The addressing most commonly used by devices sending updates is a logical broadcast, although in some cases, unicast updates can be specified.

In a pure distance vector environment, the routing update includes a complete routing table, as shown in Figure 1-10. By receiving a neighbor's full table, a router can verify all the known routes and then make changes to the local table based upon the received updated information; this process is easy to understand. A router's understanding of the network is based upon the neighbor's perspective of the network topology; thus, the distance vector approach to routing is sometimes referred to as "routing by rumor."

**Figure 1-10** *Pure Distance Vector Routing Protocols Send Their Entire Routing Table*

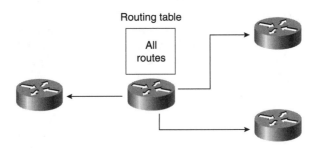

The Cisco IOS supports several distance vector routing protocols, including RIPv1, RIPv2, and IGRP. Cisco routers also support EIGRP, an advanced distance vector protocol, which is discussed in detail in Chapter 5.

Traditionally, distance vector protocols were also classful protocols. RIPv2 and EIGRP are examples of more advanced distance vector protocols that exhibit classless behavior. EIGRP also exhibits some link-state characteristics, as discussed in the next section.

Routing protocols are commonly associated with the network layer of a protocol suite. However, routing protocols use the network layer delivery mechanism to exchange routing information, but the routing protocol process itself does not exist at the network layer. Figure 1-11 shows the location of the IP distance vector routing protocols within the OSI reference model.

**Figure 1-11** *Distance Vector Routing Traffic Is Carried Within IP Packets*

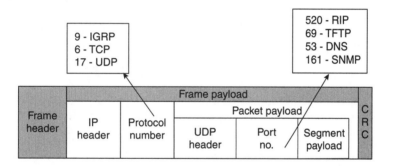

As shown in Figure 1-11, IGRP resides at the transport layer, as protocol 9. Some other recognizable protocol numbers are 6 and 17, for TCP and the User Datagram Protocol (UDP), respectively. RIP resides at the application layer and has a UDP port number of 520. Some other well-known UDP port numbers are port 53 for Domain Name Server (DNS), port 69 for Trivial File Transfer Protocol (TFTP), and port 161 for Simple Network Management Protocol (SNMP).

Table 1-3 compares the characteristics of the different distance vector routing protocols supported on Cisco routers. Most distance vector routing protocols use the Bellman-Ford algorithm for route calculation. EIGRP is an advanced distance vector protocol and uses the Diffusing Update Algorithm (DUAL).

**Table 1-3** *Comparison of Cisco's IP Distance Vector Routing Protocols*

| Characteristic | RIPv1 | RIPv2 | IGRP | EIGRP |
|---|---|---|---|---|
| Count to infinity | X | X | X | |
| Split horizon | X | X | X | X |
| Holddown timer | X | X | X | |
| Triggered updates with route poisoning | X | X | X | X |
| Load balancing—equal paths | X | X | X | X |
| Load balancing—unequal paths | | | X | X |
| VLSM support | | X | | X |
| Routing algorithm | Bellman-Ford | Bellman-Ford | Bellman-Ford | DUAL |
| Metric | Hops | Hops | Composite | Composite |
| Hop count limit | 15 | 15 | 100 | 100 |
| Scalability | Small | Small | Medium | Large |

**NOTE**
Some routing protocol features, such as split horizon, holddown time, and hop-count limit, are configurable for some routing protocols.

The hop-count limit for IGRP and EIGRP defaults to 100 but is configurable up to a maximum of 255 hops.

# Link-State Operation

Link-state routing protocols generate routing updates only when there is a change in the topology. When a link changes state, the device that detects the change creates a link-state advertisement (LSA) concerning that link (route); the LSA is then propagated to all neighboring devices using a special multicast address. Each routing device takes a copy of the LSA, forwards the LSA to all neighboring devices (this process is called *flooding*), and then updates its topological database (a table containing all the link-state information for the network). This flooding of the LSA is required to ensure that all routing devices learn about the change so that they can update their databases and create an updated routing table that reflects the new topology.

Most link-state routing protocols require a hierarchical design. The hierarchical approach, such as creating multiple logical areas for OSPF, reduces the need to flood an LSA to all devices in the routing domain because the use of areas restricts the flooding to the logical boundary of the area rather than to all devices in the OSPF domain. In other words, a change in one area should cause routing table recalculation only in that area, not in the entire domain.

Table 1-4 compares some of the characteristics exhibited by link-state routing protocols. Note that EIGRP is technically an advanced distance vector protocol, but it demonstrates some link-state features. Also, IS-IS is shown for comparison purposes only and is not covered further in this book.

**Table 1-4**   *Comparison of Cisco's IP Link-State Routing Protocols*

| Characteristic | OSPF | IS-IS | EIGRP |
| --- | --- | --- | --- |
| Hierarchical topology—required | X | X | |
| Retains knowledge of all possible routes | X | X | X |
| Route summarization—manual | X | X | X |
| Route summarization—automatic | | | X |
| Event-triggered announcements | X | X | X |
| Load balancing—equal paths | X | X | X |
| Load balancing—unequal paths | | | X |
| VLSM support | X | X | X |
| Routing algorithm | Dijkstra | IS-IS | DUAL |
| Metric | Cost | Cost | Composite |
| Hop-count limit | Unlimited | 1024 | 100 |
| Scalability | Large | Very large | Large |

**NOTE**   OSPF uses the Dijkstra algorithm, also called the shortest path first (SPF) algorithm. EIGRP uses the DUAL algorithm in its route calculations. OSPF is covered in detail in Chapter 3, "Configuring OSPF in a Single Area," and Chapter 4. EIGRP is covered in detail in Chapter 5.

IS-IS is the routing algorithm used by the International Organization for Standardization (ISO) protocol suite, which includes Connectionless Network Service (CLNS). The IS-IS protocol is not covered further in this book; introductory and configuration information is available at the following URLs:

- www.cisco.com/cpress/cc/td/cpress/fund/ith2nd/it2441.htm

- www.cisco.com/univercd/cc/td/doc/product/software/ios100/rpcg/ 66010.htm#xtocid2841339

# Convergence

This section describes how different routing protocols converge after a change in network topology. In a routed network, the routing process in each router must maintain a loop-free, single path to each possible destination logical network. When all the routing tables are synchronized and each contains a usable route to each destination network, the network is *converged*. Convergence is the activity associated with making the routing tables synchronized after a topology change occurs, such as new routes being added or existing routes changing state. Convergence efforts are different within different routing protocols, and the default timers used within the same routing protocol can vary by vendor implementation.

Convergence time is the time it takes for all routers in a network to agree on the current topology. Convergence time can be affected by the size of the network, the routing protocol in use, and numerous configurable timers.

One critical piece of information when measuring convergence time is how the link change was detected. Using the OSI reference model as a guideline, there are at least two different detection methods:

- When the physical or data link layer (for example, a NIC on a LAN) fails to receive some number (typically three) of consecutive keepalive messages, the link is considered to be down.

- When the routing protocol fails to receive some number (typically three) of consecutive hello messages or routing updates (or similar messages), the link is considered to be down.

After the detection method is understood, factors associated with routing protocol operation come into play. Most routing protocols have timers that prevent topological loops from forming during periods of link transition. For example, when a distance vector route is suspect, it is placed in holddown, and no new routing information about that route will be accepted until the holddown timer expires (unless the new routing information has a metric that is better than the original metric). This approach gives the network topology an opportunity to stabilize before new route calculations are performed. Unfortunately, a network cannot converge more rapidly than the duration of the holddown timer. In another example, a router running OSPF has a built-in delay, an amount of time it will wait before recalculating the routing table after it learns of a change. This delay exists so that multiple changes can be recalculated at the same time. This feature helps reduce the CPU overhead of performing multiple SPF recalculations within a short period of time, which can be caused by a *flapping* route (a route that is going down and up quickly).

In addition to timer values, other factors such as the size of the network, the efficiency of the routing algorithm, and how the failure information is radiated all affect convergence time. The following sections show how an example network would converge when running different routing protocols.

Figure 1-12 shows the network used in all the following convergence examples.

**Figure 1-12** *Network Used to Show How Different Routing Protocols Converge After a Link Failure*

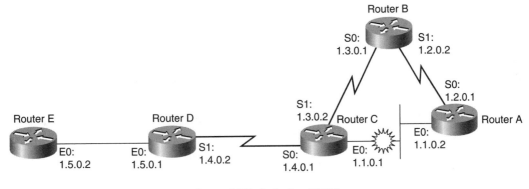

All S1 are DCE; clockrate = 64000

## RIP Convergence

The sequence of events for RIP convergence when Router C in Figure 1-12 detects the failure of network 1.1.0.0 is as follows:

1  Router C detects the link failure on the Ethernet between Routers A and C. Router C sends a *flash* update (an update that is sent when a change occurs rather than at the normal periodic interval), including a *poisoned* route (a route with an unreachable metric—in RIP's case, a hop count of 16), to Routers B and D. Router D creates a new flash update and sends it to Router E. Router C purges the entry for the directly connected down link in its routing table and also removes all routes associated with that link from its routing table.

2  Router C sends a query to its neighbors, using the broadcast address (255.255.255.255) for RIPv1 or a multicast address (224.0.0.9) for RIPv2, looking for an alternate path to network 1.1.0.0.

**3**  Router D responds with a poisoned route to network 1.1.0.0 (this is the *poison reverse* feature operating), and Router B responds with a route to network 1.1.0.0 with a weaker metric. Router C immediately installs the route from Router B in the routing table. Note that Router C does not go into holddown because the entry was already purged from its routing table.

---

**NOTE**     Because of the split horizon rule, Router D normally will not send routing updates about network 1.1.0.0 to Router C. However, poison reverse updates override the split horizon rule.

---

**4**  Router D goes into holddown for the failed route. When Router C makes its periodic advertisement that the route is available with a weaker metric, Router D ignores the route because it is in holddown. (During holddown, routes with the same metric or a worse metric than a router originally had for a network are ignored.) Router D continues to send a poisoned route to Router C in Router D's updates.

**5**  As Routers D and E come out of holddown, the new route announced by Router C causes their routing table entries to be updated.

---

**NOTE**     The default update time for RIP is 30 seconds, and the default holddown time for RIP is 180 seconds.

---

From Router E's perspective, the convergence time is the total of detection time, plus the holddown time, plus one update time (Router D to Router E), plus one partial or full update time. The actual time to converge at Router E could exceed 210 seconds (3 1/2 minutes).

---

### RIP Convergence Testing Details

During testing of RIP convergence, some other interesting characteristics were observed, including these:

— Routers add the metric (the hop count) for the link to the metric in their table before sending out the update. For example, Router D sends updates about network 1.3.0.0 to Router E with a hop count of 2, not 1. The metric that Router D sends to Router E has itself included as a hop already.

— Flash updates are full routing tables, not just what has changed.

— Replies to queries are also full routing tables.

— The **debug ip rip**, **debug ip routing**, and **show ip route** command outputs shown in Example 1-2 were obtained from Router D in Figure 1-12. Note that comment lines (starting with a ! character) have been added to the output in Example 1-2, and that some of the debug output has been omitted. The shaded lines in Example 1-2 highlight some of the more important events and information for understanding how RIP converges.

**Example 1-2**  *Example Debug Output on Router D in Figure 1-12 When Running RIP*

```
D#
06:07:30: RIP: sending v1 update to 255.255.255.255 via Ethernet0 (1.5.0.1)
06:07:30:       subnet 1.1.0.0, metric 2
06:07:30:       subnet 1.3.0.0, metric 2
06:07:30:       subnet 1.2.0.0, metric 3
06:07:30:       subnet 1.4.0.0, metric 1
06:07:30: RIP: sending v1 update to 255.255.255.255 via Serial1 (1.4.0.2)
06:07:30:       subnet 1.5.0.0, metric 1
!link has gone down
06:07:36: RIP: received v1 update from 1.4.0.1 on Serial1
06:07:36:       1.1.0.0 in 16 hops (inaccessible)
06:07:36: RT: metric change to 1.1.0.0 via 1.4.0.1, rip metric [120/1] new metric
[120/-1]
06:07:36: RT: delete route to 1.1.0.0 via 1.4.0.1, rip metric [120/4294967295]
06:07:36: RT: no routes to 1.1.0.0, entering holddown
06:07:36:       1.3.0.0 in 1 hops
06:07:36:       1.2.0.0 in 2 hops

!this is a flash update
06:07:36: RIP: sending v1 update to 255.255.255.255 via Ethernet0 (1.5.0.1)
06:07:36:       subnet 1.1.0.0, metric 16
06:07:36:       subnet 1.3.0.0, metric 2
06:07:36:       subnet 1.2.0.0, metric 3
06:07:36:       subnet 1.4.0.0, metric 1
06:07:36: RIP: sending v1 update to 255.255.255.255 via Serial1 (1.4.0.2)
06:07:36:       subnet 1.1.0.0, metric 16
06:07:36:       subnet 1.5.0.0, metric 1
06:07:36: RIP: received v1 update from 1.5.0.2 on Ethernet0
06:07:36:       1.1.0.0 in 16 hops (inaccessible)
06:07:36: RIP: received v1 request from 1.4.0.1 on Serial1

!this is the reply for the v1 request
06:07:36: RIP: sending v1 update to 1.4.0.1 via Serial1 (1.4.0.2)
06:07:36:       subnet 1.1.0.0, metric 16
06:07:36:       subnet 1.5.0.0, metric 1

06:07:36: RIP: received v2 request from 1.4.0.1 on Serial1
!Router D doesn't reply to the v2 request because it is running v1

06:07:37: RIP: received v1 update from 1.4.0.1 on Serial1
06:07:37:       1.1.0.0 in 3 hops
06:07:37:       1.3.0.0 in 1 hops
```

*continues*

**Example 1-2** *Example Debug Output on Router D in Figure 1-12 When Running RIP (Continued)*

```
06:07:37:       1.2.0.0 in 2 hops
06:07:42: RIP: received v1 update from 1.4.0.1 on Serial1
06:07:42:       1.1.0.0 in 3 hops
06:07:42:       1.3.0.0 in 1 hops
06:07:42:       1.2.0.0 in 2 hops
06:07:52: RIP: received v1 update from 1.5.0.2 on Ethernet0
06:07:52:       1.1.0.0 in 16 hops (inaccessible)
06:07:56: RIP: sending v1 update to 255.255.255.255 via Ethernet0 (1.5.0.1)
06:07:56:       subnet 1.1.0.0, metric 16
06:07:56:       subnet 1.3.0.0, metric 2
06:07:56:       subnet 1.2.0.0, metric 3
06:07:56:       subnet 1.4.0.0, metric 1
06:07:56: RIP: sending v1 update to 255.255.255.255 via Serial1 (1.4.0.2)
06:07:56:       subnet 1.1.0.0, metric 16
06:07:56:       subnet 1.5.0.0, metric 1

D#show ip route
!output omitted
     1.0.0.0/16 is subnetted, 5 subnets
R       1.1.0.0/16 is possibly down,
          routing via 1.4.0.1, Serial1
R       1.3.0.0 [120/1] via 1.4.0.1, 00:00:21, Serial1
R       1.2.0.0 [120/2] via 1.4.0.1, 00:00:21, Serial1
C       1.5.0.0 is directly connected, Ethernet0
C       1.4.0.0 is directly connected, Serial1
!Router D 1.1.0.0 is in holddown and ignores routes for 1.1.0.0 from Router C

!after a while, Router D route to 1.1.0.0 exits holddown
06:10:59: RT: 1.1.0.0 came out of holddown
!This took 10:59 - 7:36 = 3 min and 17 seconds = 197 seconds.
!This is the holddown timer (180 seconds) plus a bit
06:10:59: RT: add 1.1.0.0/16 via 1.4.0.1, rip metric [120/3]
06:10:59:       1.3.0.0 in 1 hops
06:10:59:       1.2.0.0 in 2 hops

!this is a flash update (only 20 seconds after last update)
06:10:59: RIP: sending v1 update to 255.255.255.255 via Ethernet0 (1.5.0.1)
06:10:59:       subnet 1.1.0.0, metric 4
06:10:59:       subnet 1.3.0.0, metric 2
06:10:59:       subnet 1.2.0.0, metric 3
06:10:59:       subnet 1.4.0.0, metric 1
06:10:59: RIP: sending v1 update to 255.255.255.255 via Serial1 (1.4.0.2)
06:10:59:       subnet 1.5.0.0, metric 1
!resumes sending 10 seconds later, which is 30 seconds after last "non-flash" update
06:11:09: RIP: sending v1 update to 255.255.255.255 via Ethernet0 (1.5.0.1)
06:11:09:       subnet 1.1.0.0, metric 4
06:11:09:       subnet 1.3.0.0, metric 2
06:11:09:       subnet 1.2.0.0, metric 3
06:11:09:       subnet 1.4.0.0, metric 1
06:11:09: RIP: sending v1 update to 255.255.255.255 via Serial1 (1.4.0.2)
06:11:09:       subnet 1.5.0.0, metric 1
```

## IGRP Convergence

The sequence of events for IGRP convergence when Router C in Figure 1-12 detects the failure of network 1.1.0.0 is as follows:

1   Router C detects the link failure on the Ethernet between Routers A and C. Router C sends a flash update with a poisoned route to Routers B and D. For IGRP, a poisoned route has an unreachable metric of 4,294,967,295. Router D creates a new flash update and sends it to Router E. Router C purges the entry for the directly connected down link from its routing table and also removes all routes associated with that link from its routing table.

2   Router C sends a query to its neighbors using the broadcast address (255.255.255.255), looking for an alternate path to network 1.1.0.0. (Note that Router C tries to send this query out all its interfaces, including the one that is down.) Router D responds with a poisoned route (this is the *poison reverse* feature operating), and Router C sends (out all interfaces) a flash update without the failed link entry.

| | |
|---|---|
| **NOTE** | Because of the split horizon rule, Router D normally will not send routing updates about network 1.1.0.0 to Router C. Poison reverse updates, however, override the split horizon rule. |

3   Router B responds with a route to network 1.1.0.0 with a weaker metric. The route from Router B is immediately installed in Router C's routing table. Router C does not go into holddown because the entry was already purged. Router C sends a flash update with the new route information out all interfaces.

4   Router D is in holddown for the failed route. When Router C makes its flash advertisement that the route is available with a weaker metric, Router D ignores the route because it is in holddown. (During holddown, routes with the same metric or a worse metric than a router originally had for a network are ignored.) Router D continues to send a poisoned route to Router C in Router D's updates.

5   As Routers D and E come out of holddown, the new route announced by Router C causes their routing table entries to be updated.

| | |
|---|---|
| **NOTE** | The default update time for IGRP is 90 seconds, and the default holddown time for IGRP is 280 seconds. |

From Router E's perspective, convergence time is the total of detection time, plus holddown time, plus one update time (Router D to Router E), plus one partial or full update time. The actual time to converge at Router E could exceed 400 seconds (almost 7 minutes).

### IGRP Convergence Testing Details

During testing of IGRP convergence, the **debug ip routing** and **debug ip igrp transactions** command outputs shown in Example 1-3 was obtained from routers C and D in Figure 1-12. Note that comment lines (starting with a ! character) have been added to the output in Example 1-3 and that some of the debug output has been omitted. The shaded lines in Example 1-3 highlight some of the more important events and information for understanding how IGRP converges.

**Example 1-3** *Example Debug Output on Routers C and D in Figure 1-12 When Running IGRP*

```
C#
!this is output from Router C
20:43:09: %LINEPROTO-5-UPDOWN: Line protocol on Interface Ethernet0, changed state
to down
20:43:09: IGRP: edition is now 3
!this is a flash update
20:43:09: IGRP: sending update to 255.255.255.255 via Serial0 (1.4.0.1)
!metric = 4294967295 = unreachable
20:43:09:        subnet 1.1.0.0, metric=4294967295
20:43:09:        subnet 1.3.0.0, metric=8476
20:43:09:        subnet 1.2.0.0, metric=4294967295
20:43:10: IGRP: sending update to 255.255.255.255 via Serial1 (1.3.0.2)
20:43:10:        subnet 1.1.0.0, metric=4294967295
20:43:10:        subnet 1.2.0.0, metric=4294967295
20:43:10:        subnet 1.5.0.0, metric=8576
20:43:10:        subnet 1.4.0.0, metric=8476
20:43:10: RT: interface Ethernet0 removed from routing table
20:43:10: RT: del 1.1.0.0/16 via 0.0.0.0, connected metric [0/0]
20:43:10: RT: delete subnet route to 1.1.0.0/16
20:43:10: RT: delete route to 1.2.0.0 via 1.1.0.2, Ethernet0
20:43:10: RT: no routes to 1.2.0.0

!interesting that a request was sent on Ethernet 0, even though it is down!
20:43:10: IGRP: broadcasting request on Ethernet0
20:43:10: IGRP: broadcasting request on Serial0
20:43:10: IGRP: broadcasting request on Serial1
20:43:10: IGRP: received update from 1.4.0.2 on Serial0
20:43:10:        subnet 1.1.0.0, metric 4294967295 (inaccessible)
20:43:10:        subnet 1.2.0.0, metric 4294967295 (inaccessible)
20:43:10:        subnet 1.5.0.0, metric 8576 (neighbor 1100)
20:43:10: IGRP: edition is now 4

!another flash update, note that 1.1.0.0 not in update anymore
```

**Example 1-3**    *Example Debug Output on Routers C and D in Figure 1-12 When Running IGRP (Continued)*

```
20:43:10: IGRP: sending update to 255.255.255.255 via Serial0 (1.4.0.1)
20:43:10:       subnet 1.3.0.0, metric=8476
20:43:10:       subnet 1.2.0.0, metric=4294967295
20:43:10: IGRP: sending update to 255.255.255.255 via Serial1 (1.3.0.2)
20:43:10:       subnet 1.2.0.0, metric=4294967295
20:43:10:       subnet 1.5.0.0, metric=8576
20:43:10:       subnet 1.4.0.0, metric=8476
20:43:10: IGRP: received update from 1.3.0.1 on Serial1
20:43:10:       subnet 1.1.0.0, metric 10576 (neighbor 8576)
20:43:10: RT: add 1.1.0.0/16 via 1.3.0.1, igrp metric [100/10576]
20:43:10:       subnet 1.2.0.0, metric 10476 (neighbor 8476)
20:43:10: RT: add 1.2.0.0/16 via 1.3.0.1, igrp metric [100/10476]
20:43:10: IGRP: received update from 1.4.0.2 on Serial0
20:43:10:       subnet 1.1.0.0, metric 4294967295 (inaccessible)
20:43:10:       subnet 1.2.0.0, metric 4294967295 (inaccessible)
20:43:10:       subnet 1.5.0.0, metric 8576 (neighbor 1100)
20:43:10: IGRP: edition is now 5

!another flash update with latest information
20:43:10: IGRP: sending update to 255.255.255.255 via Serial0 (1.4.0.1)
20:43:10:       subnet 1.1.0.0, metric=10576
20:43:10:       subnet 1.3.0.0, metric=8476
20:43:10:       subnet 1.2.0.0, metric=10476
20:43:11: IGRP: sending update to 255.255.255.255 via Serial1 (1.3.0.2)
20:43:11:       subnet 1.5.0.0, metric=8576
20:43:11:       subnet 1.4.0.0, metric=8476
20:43:11: IGRP: received update from 1.3.0.1 on Serial1
20:43:11:       subnet 1.1.0.0, metric 10576 (neighbor 8576)
20:43:11:       subnet 1.2.0.0, metric 10476 (neighbor 8476)


D#
!this is output from Router D
00:04:13: IGRP: received update from 1.4.0.1 on Serial1
00:04:13:       subnet 1.1.0.0, metric 4294967295 (inaccessible)
00:04:13: RT: delete route to 1.1.0.0 via 1.4.0.1, igrp metric [100/8576]
00:04:13: RT: no routes to 1.1.0.0, entering holddown
00:04:13:       subnet 1.3.0.0, metric 10476 (neighbor 8476)
00:04:13:       subnet 1.2.0.0, metric 4294967295 (inaccessible)
00:04:13: RT: delete route to 1.2.0.0 via 1.4.0.1, igrp metric [100/10576]
00:04:13: RT: no routes to 1.2.0.0, entering holddown
00:04:13: IGRP: edition is now 2
!sending flash update
00:04:13: IGRP: sending update to 255.255.255.255 via Ethernet0 (1.5.0.1)
00:04:13:       subnet 1.1.0.0, metric=4294967295
00:04:13:       subnet 1.3.0.0, metric=10476
00:04:13:       subnet 1.2.0.0, metric=4294967295
00:04:13:       subnet 1.4.0.0, metric=8476
00:04:13: IGRP: sending update to 255.255.255.255 via Serial1 (1.4.0.2)
00:04:13:       subnet 1.1.0.0, metric=4294967295
00:04:13:       subnet 1.2.0.0, metric=4294967295
00:04:13:       subnet 1.5.0.0, metric=1100
```

*continues*

**Example 1-3**   *Example Debug Output on Routers C and D in Figure 1-12 When Running IGRP (Continued)*

```
00:04:13: IGRP: received request from 1.4.0.1 on Serial1
00:04:13: IGRP: sending update to 1.4.0.1 via Serial1 (1.4.0.2)
00:04:13:        subnet 1.1.0.0, metric=4294967295
00:04:13:        subnet 1.2.0.0, metric=4294967295
00:04:13:        subnet 1.5.0.0, metric=1100

!some time later Router D comes out of holddown
00:09:25: IGRP: received update from 1.5.0.2 on Ethernet0
00:09:25:        subnet 1.1.0.0, metric 4294967295 (inaccessible)
00:09:25: RT: 1.1.0.0 came out of holddown
00:09:25:        subnet 1.2.0.0, metric 4294967295 (inaccessible)
00:09:25: RT: 1.2.0.0 came out of holddown

00:10:01: IGRP: received update from 1.4.0.1 on Serial1
00:10:01:        subnet 1.1.0.0, metric 12576 (neighbor 10576)
00:10:01: RT: add 1.1.0.0/16 via 1.4.0.1, igrp metric [100/12576]
00:10:01:        subnet 1.3.0.0, metric 10476 (neighbor 8476)
00:10:01:        subnet 1.2.0.0, metric 12476 (neighbor 10476)
00:10:01: RT: add 1.2.0.0/16 via 1.4.0.1, igrp metric [100/12476]
00:10:01: IGRP: edition is now 3
```

## EIGRP Convergence

EIGRP is discussed in detail in Chapter 5. The convergence steps for EIGRP are presented here for comparison with other protocols. The following are some of the terms used in this section that will help you understand how EIGRP converges:

- **Topology table**—EIGRP keeps a copy of its neighbors' routing tables in its topology table.

- **Successor**—This is the best route to a destination, selected from the topology table and put in the routing table.

- **Feasible successor**—This is another route to a destination—not the best route, but one that could be used if the best route becomes unavailable. It is kept in the topology table.

- **Advertised distance**—This is the EIGRP metric advertised by a neighbor for a destination.

- **Feasible distance**—This is the EIGRP metric to a destination network.

A router running EIGRP uses reliable multicast messages when it sends queries and updates to other routers.

The sequence of events for EIGRP convergence when Router C in Figure 1-12 detects the failure of network 1.1.0.0 is as follows:

1  Router C detects the link failure on the Ethernet between Routers A and C, checks the topology table for a feasible successor, doesn't find a qualifying alternate route, and enters the active state (indicating that it must actively look for a new route).

2  Router C sends a query out all interfaces looking for alternate routes to the failed link (the EIGRP multicast address 224.0.0.10 is used for the queries). The neighboring routers acknowledge the query.

3  The reply from Router D indicates no other route to the network 1.1.0.0.

4  Router B's reply contains a route to the failed link, although it has a higher feasible distance.

5  Router C accepts the new path and metric information, places it in the topology table, and creates an entry in its routing table.

6  Router C sends an update about the new route out all interfaces. All neighbors acknowledge the update and send updates of their own (which are acknowledged) back to the sender. These bidirectional updates are necessary to ensure that the routing tables are synchronized and to validate the neighbor's awareness of the new topology.

From Router E's perspective, convergence time is the total of detection time, plus query and reply times, plus update times. The actual time to converge at Router E is very rapid, approximately 2 seconds.

---

### EIGRP Convergence Testing Details

During testing of EIGRP convergence, the **debug ip routing, debug ip eigrp neighbors, debug ip eigrp summary, debug ip eigrp, debug ip eigrp notification**, and **show ip route** command outputs shown in Example 1-4 was obtained from Router C in Figure 1-12. Note that comment lines (starting with a ! character) have been added to the output in Example 1-4 and that some of the debug output has been omitted. The shaded lines in Example 1-4 highlight some of the more important events and information for understanding how EIGRP converges.

---

**NOTE**    For the EIGRP metric, 4294967295 = hex FFFFFFFF. This is the maximum metric; in other words, it indicates that the route is unreachable.

From the documentation on the **debug ip eigrp** command, the **SM** and **M** values in the output of this command have the following meanings:

— **SM**—Shows the metric as reported by the neighbor.

> — **M**—Shows the computed metric, which includes SM and the cost between the router and its neighbor. The first number is the composite metric. The next two numbers are the inverse bandwidth and the delay, respectively.

For example, in the following output:

```
M 2707456 - 1657856 1049600 SM 2195456 - 1657856 537600
```

The composite metric is 2707456, the inverse bandwidth is 1657856, and the delay is 1049600. The metric reported by the neighbor is 2195456; this includes the inverse bandwidth of 1657856 and the delay of 537600.

**Example 1-4**  *Example Debug Output on Router C in Figure 1-12 When Running EIGRP*

```
C#
02:27:51: %LINEPROTO-5-UPDOWN: Line protocol on Interface Ethernet0, changed state
to down
02:27:51: IP-EIGRP: Callback: route_adjust Ethernet0
02:27:51: IP-EIGRP: conn_summary_depend: Ethernet0 1.1.0.0/16 0
02:27:51: RT: delete route to 1.2.0.0 via 1.1.0.2, eigrp metric [90/2195456]
02:27:51: RT: no routes to 1.2.0.0
02:27:51: RT: add 1.2.0.0/16 via 1.3.0.1, eigrp metric [90/2681856]

!send a query on serial 0 and serial 1 about 1.1.0.0
02:27:52: IP-EIGRP: Int 1.1.0.0/16 metric 4294967295 - 0 4294967295
02:27:52: EIGRP: Sending QUERY on Serial0 nbr 1.4.0.2
02:27:52: IP-EIGRP: Int 1.1.0.0/16 metric 4294967295 - 0 4294967295
02:27:52: EIGRP: Sending QUERY on Serial1 nbr 1.3.0.1

!tell serial 0 and serial 1 about 1.2.0.0 metric change
02:27:52: IP-EIGRP: Int 1.2.0.0/16 metric 2681856 - 1657856 1024000
02:27:52: EIGRP: Sending UPDATE on Serial0 nbr 1.4.0.2
02:27:52: IP-EIGRP: Int 1.2.0.0/16 metric 2681856 - 1657856 1024000
02:27:52: EIGRP: Sending UPDATE on Serial1 nbr 1.3.0.1

!reply received from serial 1 (Router B) from query about 1.1.0.0
02:27:52: EIGRP: Received REPLY on Serial1 nbr 1.3.0.1
02:27:52: IP-EIGRP: Processing incoming REPLY packet
!Router B has another way to 1.1.0.0
02:27:52: IP-EIGRP: Int 1.1.0.0/16 M 2707456 - 1657856 1049600 SM 2195456 - 1657856
537600

!reply received from serial 0 (Router D) from query about 1.1.0.0
02:27:52: EIGRP: Received REPLY on Serial0 nbr 1.4.0.2
02:27:52: IP-EIGRP: Processing incoming REPLY packet
!Router D does not have another way to 1.1.0.0; it has unreachable metric
02:27:52: IP-EIGRP: Int 1.1.0.0/16 M 4294967295 - 0 4294967295 SM 4294967295 - 0
4294967295

!add route to 1.1.0.0 from Router B
02:27:52: RT: add 1.1.0.0/16 via 1.3.0.1, eigrp metric [90/2707456]
```

**Example 1-4**  *Example Debug Output on Router C in Figure 1-12 When Running EIGRP (Continued)*

```
!tell serial 0 (Router D) about new metric to 1.1.0.0
02:27:52: IP-EIGRP: Int 1.1.0.0/16 metric 2707456 - 1657856 1049600
02:27:52: EIGRP: Sending UPDATE on Serial0 nbr 1.4.0.2
!tell serial 1 (Router B) about new metric to 1.1.0.0
02:27:52: IP-EIGRP: Int 1.1.0.0/16 metric 2707456 - 1657856 1049600
02:27:52: EIGRP: Sending UPDATE on Serial1 nbr 1.3.0.1

C#show ip route
!output omitted
1.0.0.0/16 is subnetted, 5 subnets
D       1.1.0.0 [90/2707456] via 1.3.0.1, 00:00:39, Serial1
C       1.3.0.0 is directly connected, Serial1
D       1.2.0.0 [90/2681856] via 1.3.0.1, 00:00:40, Serial1
D       1.5.0.0 [90/2195456] via 1.4.0.2, 00:02:40, Serial0
C       1.4.0.0 is directly connected, Serial0
```

## OSPF Convergence

OSPF is discussed in detail in Chapters 3 and 4. The convergence steps for OSPF are presented here for comparison with other protocols. The following are some of the terms used in this section:

- **Designated router (DR)**—A router elected on each LAN to send updates about the LAN.

- **Link-state advertisement (LSA)**—State information about a link or network.

- **Hello packets**—Small packets sent periodically out each interface of a router that is participating in OSPF, to indicate that the router is still alive.

- **Dead interval**—The time that a router waits to hear from a neighbor before declaring that the neighbor router is down.

A router running OSPF uses a multicast address to propagate LSAs.

The sequence of events for OSPF convergence when Router C in Figure 1-12 detects the failure of network 1.1.0.0 is as follows:

1  Router C detects the link failure on the Ethernet between Routers A and C. Router C tries to perform a designated router election process on the Ethernet interface but fails to reach any neighbors. Router C deletes the route to network 1.1.0.0 from the routing table, builds a router LSA, and sends it out all other interfaces.

2  Upon receipt of the LSA, Routers B and D copy the advertisement and forward (flood) the LSA packet out all interfaces other than the one upon which it arrived.

3  All routers, including Router C, wait for the built-in delay time (which defaults to 5 seconds) after receiving the LSA and then run the SPF algorithm. After running this algorithm, Router C adds the new route to 1.2.0.0 to the routing table, and Routers D and E update the metric to 1.2.0.0 in their routing tables.

**4** After a period of time, Router A sends an LSA. This is the result of Router A not receiving hello packets from Router C over the Ethernet within the dead interval, which defaults to 40 seconds. (The approximately 24 seconds seen in the debug output in Example 1-5 is the last 24 seconds of the 40-second dead interval.) Router C was originally the DR for the Ethernet; Router A now becomes the DR and sends out an LSA about the Ethernet network, 1.1.0.0. This LSA from Router A is flooded throughout the network; when it gets to Router C, Router C immediately passes it on to Router D, and so on. After 5 seconds, all routers run the SPF algorithm again. As a result of running the SPF algorithm, Router C updates its routing table for 1.1.0.0, to go via Router B.

From Router E's perspective, convergence time is the total of detection time, plus LSA flooding time, plus 5 seconds. The time to converge at Router E is approximately 6 seconds before Router A's LSA is accounted for (and this could be longer, depending on the size of the topology table). When Router A's LSA about network 1.1.0.0 (as a result of the dead interval to Router C expiring) is considered in Router E's convergence time, up to another 40 seconds is added before the network is considered converged.

---

### OSPF Convergence Testing Details

During testing of OSPF convergence, the **debug ip routing, debug ip ospf adj, debug ip ospf events, debug ip ospf lsa-generation, debug ip ospf packet, debug ip ospf spf,** and **show ip route** command outputs shown in Example 1-5 was obtained from Router C in Figure 1-12. Note that comment lines (starting with a ! character) have been added to the output in Example 1-5 and that some of the debug output has been omitted. The shaded lines in Example 1-5 highlight some of the more important events and information for understanding how OSPF converges.

---

**Example 1-5** *Example Debug Output on Router C in Figure 1-12 When Running OSPF*

```
C#
03:49:53: %LINEPROTO-5-UPDOWN: Line protocol on Interface Ethernet0, changed state
to down
03:49:53: OSPF: Interface Ethernet0 going Down
03:49:53: OSPF: 1.4.0.1 address 1.1.0.1 on Ethernet0 is dead, state DOWN
03:49:53: OSPF: Neighbor change Event on interface Ethernet0

!strange to have an election on an interface that just went down!
03:49:53: OSPF: DR/BDR election on Ethernet0
```

**Example 1-5**  *Example Debug Output on Router C in Figure 1-12 When Running OSPF (Continued)*

```
03:49:53: OSPF: 1.2.0.1 address 1.1.0.2 on Ethernet0 is dead, state DOWN
03:49:53: OSPF: Neighbor change Event on interface Ethernet0
03:49:53: RT: interface Ethernet0 removed from routing table

!remove 1.1.0.0 from routing table
03:49:53: RT: del 1.1.0.0/16 via 0.0.0.0, connected metric [0/0]
03:49:53: RT: delete subnet route to 1.1.0.0/16
!remove 1.2.0.0 from routing table
03:49:53: RT: delete route to 1.2.0.0 via 1.1.0.2, Ethernet0
03:49:53: RT: no routes to 1.2.0.0, flushing

03:49:54: OSPF: Build network LSA for Ethernet0, router ID 1.4.0.1
03:49:54: OSPF: We are not DR to build Net Lsa for interface Ethernet0
03:49:54: OSPF: Build router LSA for area 0, router ID 1.4.0.1, seq 0x80000005

!receive updates from Routers B and D
03:49:56: OSPF: rcv. v:2 t:5 l:64 rid:1.3.0.1
          aid:0.0.0.0 chk:F8CF aut:0 auk: from Serial1
03:49:56: OSPF: rcv. v:2 t:5 l:64 rid:1.5.0.1
          aid:0.0.0.0 chk:F8CD aut:0 auk: from Serial0

!run SPF algorithm
03:49:59: OSPF: running SPF for area 0

!add route to 1.2.0.0 via Router B
03:49:59: RT: add 1.2.0.0/16 via 1.3.0.1, ospf metric [110/128]

!receive LSA update from Router A, and run SPF again
03:50:23: OSPF: Detect change in LSA type 1, LSID 1.2.0.1, from 1.2.0.1 area 0
03:50:28: OSPF: running SPF for area 0

! add route to 1.1.0.0 via Router B
03:50:28: RT: add 1.1.0.0/16 via 1.3.0.1, ospf metric [110/138]

C#show ip route
!output omitted
1.0.0.0/16 is subnetted, 5 subnets
O        1.1.0.0 [110/138] via 1.3.0.1, 00:03:29, Serial1
C        1.3.0.0 is directly connected, Serial1
O        1.2.0.0 [110/128] via 1.3.0.1, 00:03:29, Serial1
O        1.5.0.0 [110/74] via 1.4.0.2, 00:03:29, Serial0
C        1.4.0.0 is directly connected, Serial0
```

# Routing Table Analysis

There are two basic ways to update routing information: the distance vector approach and the link-state approach. These are shown in Figure 1-13.

**Figure 1-13** *Routing Updates Are Sent Differently by Distance Vector and Link-State Protocols*

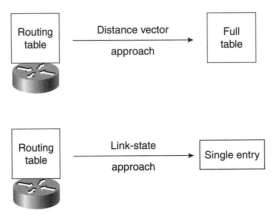

Traditional distance vector protocols use a routine, periodic announcement that contains the entire contents of the routing table. These announcements are usually broadcasts and are propagated only to directly connected devices. The downside of this approach is that considerable bandwidth is consumed at regular intervals on each link, even if there are no topology changes to report.

Link-state protocols use a triggered-update type of announcement. These announcements are generated only when there is a topology change within the network. The link-state announcements contain only information about the link that changed (such as a single route) and are propagated to all devices in the network. Link-state announcements are sent as multicast packets. The flooding of the announcement is required because link-state devices make their route calculations independently; however, those calculations are based upon a common understanding of the network topology. This approach saves bandwidth on each link because the announcements contain less information than a full routing table and are sent only when there is a topology change. In some link-state protocols, a periodic announcement (every 30 minutes, for OSPF) is required to ensure that the topology database is synchronized among all routing devices.

The routing process must maintain a single, loop-free path to each destination network. If equal, lowest-metric paths exist to a destination, then all paths (up to a maximum of six, for IP) will be listed in the routing table. The IP routing process will attempt to load share traffic across equal-metric paths.

An IP routing table display can be requested with the Cisco IOS EXEC command **show ip route**. If you think that the information that is displayed has changed, you can delete the current routes in the routing table and force an update from the neighboring devices by using the privileged EXEC **clear ip route** command. An optional parameter, either an individual network or subnetwork route, or the * (wildcard for all) character, can be used to further identify the routes to be refreshed.

Example 1-6 shows a sample IP routing table on a router. OSPF is the routing protocol used in this network, and it has knowledge of both internal and external routes. The last line represents a default network. The * indicates that this route is the default path, and this is reflected by its selection as the gateway of last resort (as shown in the upper portion of the routing table display).

**Example 1-6** *A Sample IP Routing Table*

```
Backbone_r1#show ip route

Codes:  C - connected, S - static, I - IGRP, R - RIP, M - mobile, B - BGP
    D - EIGRP, EX - EIGRP external, O- OSPF, IA - OSPF inter area
    N1 - OSPF NSSA external type 1, N2 - OSPF NSSA external type 2
    E1 - OSPF external type 1, E2 - OSPF external type 2, E - EGP
    i - IS-IS, L1 - IS-IS level-1, L2 - IS-IS level-2, * - candidate default

Gateway of last resort is 10.5.5.5 to network 0.0.0.0

     172.16.0.0/24 is subnetted, 2 subnets
C       172.16.10.0 is directly connected, Loopback100
C       172.16.11.0 is directly connected, Loopback101
O E2    172.22.0.0/16 [110/20] via 10.3.3.3, 01:03:01, Serial1/2
                      [110/20] via 10.4.4.4, 01:03:01, Serial1/3
                      [110/20] via 10.5.5.5, 01:03:01, Serial1/4
O E2 192.168.4.0/24 [110/20] via 10.4.4.4, 01:03:01, Serial1/3
O E2 192.168.5.0/24 [110/20] via 10.5.5.5, 01:03:01, Serial1/4
     10.0.0.0/24 is subnetted, 4 subnets
C       10.5.5.0 is directly connected, Serial1/4
C       10.4.4.0 is directly connected, Serial1/3
C       10.3.3.0 is directly connected, Serial1/2
C       10.1.1.0 is directly connected, Serial1/0
O E2 192.168.3.0/24 [110/20] via 10.3.3.3, 01:03:02, Serial1/2
S*      0.0.0.0/0 [1/0] via 10.5.5.5
```

**NOTE**    The content of the routing table is limited to the best route to all destinations. If multiple equal-metric paths exist, all paths will be listed in the table, as is the case for the 172.22.0.0/16 network in Example 1-6. Additional detail about a specific route in the table can be displayed by using the **show ip route** *network* command, indicating the specific network.

The entries in a routing table represent each possible logical destination network that is known to the router. The order of the entries may at times look like a random pattern, but the router optimizes the order to facilitate the lookup process based upon length of subnet mask.

# Introduction to the Case Study

Throughout the rest of this book we use a case study of JKL Corporation, as shown in Figure 1-14, to discuss various aspects of scalable routing. The case study sections are used to review key concepts, to discuss critical issues surrounding network operation, and to provide a focus for the configuration exercises.

**Figure 1-14**   *JKL Corporation Is Used in Case Study Sections Throughout the Book*

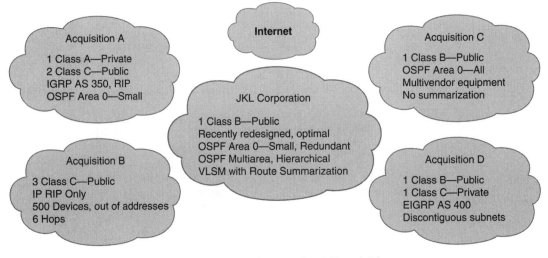

JKL is an enterprise that will be making four acquisitions—A, B, C, and D. JKL's ultimate goal is to integrate the acquisitioned networks with its own network.

JKL has recently redesigned its network and now has a robust design using OSPF, VLSM, and route summarization. JKL has a Class B public address. As we introduce details on various topics throughout the rest of the book, you will see the problems that JKL must overcome as it integrates the networks of the acquisitions with its own OSPF network.

Acquisition A is using a mixture of routing protocols—RIP, IGRP, and OSPF. It has two Class C public addresses and uses a Class A private address.

Acquisition B is using three Class C public addresses and is using only IP RIP as the routing protocol. It has 500 devices and has run out of IP addresses.

Acquisition C has a multivendor environment and is using OSPF and one Class B public address. It is not using route summarization.

Acquisition D has one Class B public address and one Class C private address and discontiguous subnets. It is using EIGRP as the routing protocol.

Each of the acquired companies had a sound business reason for why their networks were implemented in the current configuration. Another complete redesign is not possible at this time, so adjustments will have to be made to both the acquired networks and JKL's corporate structure.

In this book, we elaborate on many issues relating to routing protocols and addressing strategies; the JKL case study provides a mechanism to study a practical application of these concepts.

# Summary

In this chapter, you learned the key information that routers need to route data, the differences between classful and classless routing protocols, the differences between distance vector and link-state protocols, the use of the fields in a routing table, and how routers perform two functions—routing and switching. You also learned how IP routing protocols converge.

Table 1-5 summarizes some of the characteristics exhibited by IP routing protocols. Recall that EIGRP is technically an advanced distance vector protocol, but it demonstrates some link-state features.

**Table 1-5**    *Routing Protocol Comparison Summary*

| Characteristic | RIPv1 | RIPv2 | IGRP | EIGRP | OSPF |
|---|---|---|---|---|---|
| Distance vector | X | X | X | X | |
| Link-state | | | | | X |
| Automatic route summarization | X | X | X | X | |
| VLSM support | | X | | X | X |
| Proprietary | | | X | X | |
| Scalability | Small | Small | Medium | Large | Large |
| Convergence time | Slow | Slow | Slow | Fast | Fast |

Chapter 2, "Extending IP Addresses," discusses many aspects of IP addressing that can be useful in a large network.

# Configuration Exercise: Discovering the Network

**Introduction to the Configuration Exercises**

In this book, Configuration Exercises are used to provide practice in configuring routers with the commands presented. If you have access to real hardware, you can try these exercises on your routers; refer to Appendix H, "Configuration Exercise Equipment Requirements and Backbone Configurations," for a list of recommended equipment and configuration commands for the backbone routers. However, even if you don't have access to any routers, you can go through the exercises and keep a log of your own "running configurations" on separate sheets of paper. Commands used and answers to the configuration exercises are provided at the end of the exercise.

In these exercises, you are in control of a pod of three routers; there are assumed to be 12 pods in the network. The pods are interconnected to a backbone. In most of the exercises, there is only one router in the backbone; in some cases, another router is added to the backbone. Each of the Configuration Exercises in this book assumes that you have completed the previous exercises on your pod.

In this first exercise, you will do a basic configuration on your pod routers.

## Objectives

Given the routers in your pod are properly cabled, your task is to do the following:

- Build a minimum configuration on the three routers within your assigned pod.
- Verify connectivity.

## Visual Objective

Figure 1-15 illustrates the topology used in the network.

## Command List

You should already be familiar with all the Cisco IOS commands used in this configuration exercise.

| NOTE | Refer to Appendix C, "Summary of ICND Router Commands," for a listing of the Cisco IOS router commands covered in the Cisco Press *Interconnecting Cisco Network Devices* coursebook, which this book assumes that you are familiar with. |
|---|---|

**Figure 1-15**  *Configuration Exercise Topology*

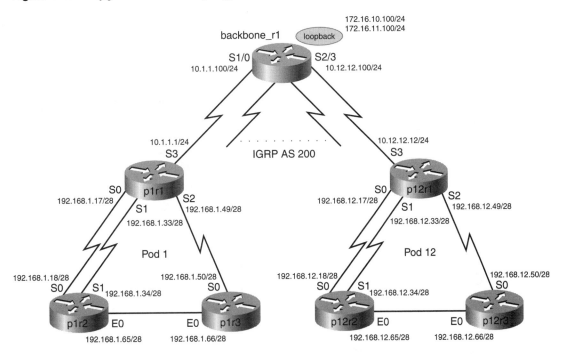

## Setup

Table 1-6 provides the IP networks that you will use in the configuration exercises.

**Table 1-6**  *IP Network Numbers Used in Configuration Exercises*

| Pod | Network Number |
|---|---|
| Pod 1 | 192.168.1.0 |
| Pod 2 | 192.168.2.0 |
| Pod 3 | 192.168.3.0 |
| Pod 4 | 192.168.4.0 |
| Pod 5 | 192.168.5.0 |

*continues*

**Table 1-6** *IP Network Numbers Used in Configuration Exercises (Continued)*

| Pod | Network Number |
|-----|----------------|
| Pod 6 | 192.168.6.0 |
| Pod 7 | 192.168.7.0 |
| Pod 8 | 192.168.8.0 |
| Pod 9 | 192.168.9.0 |
| Pod 10 | 192.168.10.0 |
| Pod 11 | 192.168.11.0 |
| Pod 12 | 192.168.12.0 |

Table 1-7 provides the IP addresses that you will use on each of the interfaces of each router in your pod in the configuration exercises.

**NOTE**     In this and subsequent tables, $x$ is used to refer to the pod numbers 1, 2, 3 and so on, up to 12. Your pod Class C IP address will be subnetted with a 28-bit mask.

**Table 1-7** *IP Addresses Used for Routers in Pods 1 to 12 in the Configuration Exercises*

| Router | Interface | IP Address | Subnet Mask |
|--------|-----------|------------|-------------|
| p$x$r1 | S0 | 192.168.$x$.17 | 255.255.255.240 |
| p$x$r1 | S1 | 192.168.$x$.33 | 255.255.255.240 |
| p$x$r1 | S2 | 192.168.$x$.49 | 255.255.255.240 |
| p$x$r1 | S3 | 10.$x$.$x$.$x$ | 255.255.255.0 |
| p$x$r2 | S0 | 192.168.$x$.18 | 255.255.255.240 |
| p$x$r2 | S1 | 192.168.$x$.34 | 255.255.255.240 |
| p$x$r2 | E0 | 192.168.$x$.65 | 255.255.255.240 |
| p$x$r3 | S0 | 192.168.$x$.50 | 255.255.255.240 |
| p$x$r3 | E0 | 192.168.$x$.66 | 255.255.255.240 |

## Task: Basic Router Setup

Your pod number is _____.

**Step 1**   Set the host name on all the routers in your pod. The host names should be set to p*x*r1, p*x*r2, and p*x*r3, respectively, where *x* is your pod number. Which command will you use to do this step?

**NOTE**   If you are using setup made to do your configuration on a router with Cisco IOS Release 12.0 or later software, answer **no** to the question "Would you like to enter basic management setup? [yes/no]."

**Step 2**   Set the passwords on all the routers in your pod. The passwords should be set to:

— Secret password: cisco

— Enable password: sanfran

— Vty password: cisco

Which commands will you use to do this step?

**Step 3**   Configure the IP addresses shown in the table on the router interfaces within your pod. Which commands will you use to do this step?

All other interfaces are not used at this time.

From the given IP address and subnet mask, determine the subnet address, and complete the last column in the table.

| Router | Interface | IP Address | Subnet Mask | Subnet Address |
|--------|-----------|------------|-------------|----------------|
| p*x*r1 | S0 | 192.168.*x*.17 | 255.255.255.240 | |
| p*x*r1 | S1 | 192.168.*x*.33 | 255.255.255.240 | |
| p*x*r1 | S2 | 192.168.*x*.49 | 255.255.255.240 | |
| p*x*r1 | S3 | 10.*x.x.x* | 255.255.255.0 | |
| p*x*r2 | S0 | 192.168.*x*.18 | 255.255.255.240 | |
| p*x*r2 | S1 | 192.168.*x*.34 | 255.255.255.240 | |
| p*x*r2 | E0 | 192.168.*x*.65 | 255.255.255.240 | |
| p*x*r3 | S0 | 192.168.*x*.50 | 255.255.255.240 | |
| p*x*r3 | E0 | 192.168.*x*.66 | 255.255.255.240 | |

**Step 4** Enable IGRP on all the routers in your pod, using autonomous system (AS) number 200. Which commands will you use to enable IGRP?

---

Recall from ICND that an AS is a collection of networks under a common administration sharing a common routing strategy.

---

What **network** command (or commands) are required on the routers?

On pxr1:

On pxr2:

On pxr3:

**Step 5** Determine which serial interfaces on the routers have a DCE cable attached to them. Which Cisco IOS command should you use to perform this task?

Set a clock rate of 64 kbps on all DCE serial interfaces. Which command will you use to do this step?

Set the bandwidth of all the serial interfaces to 64 kbps. Which command will you use to do this step?

**Step 6** Enable the following interfaces, and then verify connectivity within your pod. Which command will you use to enable an interface?

Place a check mark next to the interface when it comes up to the "up/up" state.

pxr1: S0 ___ S1 ___ S2 ___ S3 ___

pxr2: S0 ___ S1 ___ E0 ___

pxr3: S0 ___ E0 ___

---

**NOTE** The pxr3 Serial1 interface should remain shut down until a later configuration exercise.

---

**Step 7** Create an IP host table in each of your routers, with an entry for each of the other routers in your pod and for the backbone_r1 router. Which command will you use to create an entry in the host table?

**Step 8**   Add the **no ip domain-lookup** command to your routers. What does this command do?

**Step 9**   Using the Cisco Discovery Protocol (CDP), do the following:

Use the proper CDP command to verify that all the routers within your pod can see all their connected neighbors. Which command should you use?

Fill in the blanks that follow using the CDP output from each of the routers within your pod.

From pxr1:

| Device Identifier (ID) | Local Interface |
|---|---|
|  |  |
|  |  |
|  |  |
|  |  |

From pxr2:

| Device Identifier (ID) | Local Interface |
|---|---|
|  |  |
|  |  |
|  |  |

From pxr3:

| Device Identifier (ID) | Local Interface |
|---|---|
|  |  |
|  |  |

Which CDP commands can you use to verify the IP address configuration on your neighbor router?

What is the default CDP holdtime?

What is the purpose of the holdtime?

**Step 10** Display the IP routing table on each of the routers in your pod, and verify that you have full connectivity within your pod. Which command will you use to display the routing table?

Make sure you can successfully **ping** all the other routers within your pod.

**Step 11** Display the routing table on each of the routers in your pod, and verify that you have valid routes and connectivity to backbone_r1 router. (Note that if you have configured other pods, you will also see routes to those other pods).

**Step 12** Examine the pxr1 routing table, and use the **show ip protocols** command to answer the following questions:

What is the administrative distance of IGRP?

What is the purpose of the administrative distance?

How often are the IGRP routing updates sent by default?

How many paths are in the routing table to the 192.168.x.64 subnet? Why are there multiple paths to that subnet?

By default, IGRP calculates the routing metric based on what two factors?

**Step 13** Examine the pxr3 routing table. What information does pxr3 know about network 10.0.0.0? Is this different from what pxr1 knows about network 10.0.0.0? Why?

**Step 14** On the pxr1 router, issue the **debug ip igrp transactions** command to capture the IGRP routing updates. Examine the routing updates sent by the pxr1 router to the backbone_r1 router over the Serial 3 interface. What update is the pxr1 router sending to the backbone_r1 router?

Is IGRP a classless or a classful routing protocol?

IGRP performs autosummarization across what boundary?

What is the function of the **ip classless** command?

**Step 15** What is the Cisco IOS version and router type used within your pod? Which command will you use to determine this information?

Fill in the blanks that follow with the information you obtained.

| Router | Cisco IOS Version | Router Type |
|--------|-------------------|-------------|
| p*x*r1 | | |
| p*x*r2 | | |
| p*x*r3 | | |

**Step 16** You may also wish to add the **exec-timeout 0 0** and the **logging synchronous** commands to the line console 0 configuration on all the routers in your pod. What is the function of these commands?

**Step 17** Save the current configurations of all the routers within your pod. Which command will you use to save your configuration?

## Completion Criteria

You have successfully completed this Configuration Exercise if you correctly supplied the commands required to perform the task, and if you were able to correctly answer the questions in the exercises. At the end of this exercise, all the routers should have full connectivity to each other. All the routers will be in autonomous system 200 running the IGRP routing protocol.

# Answers to Configuration Exercise: Discovering the Network

This section provides the answers to the questions in the Configuration Exercise. The answers are in **bold**.

## Answers to Task: Basic Router Setup

Your pod number is _____.

**The answers are provided for the routers in pod 1.**

**Step 1** Set the hostname on all the routers in your pod. The hostnames should be set to p*x*r1, p*x*r2, and p*x*r3, respectively, where *x* is your pod number. Which command will you use to do this step?

---

**NOTE**     If you are using setup made to do your configuration on a router with Cisco IOS Release 12.0 or later software, answer **no** to the question "Would you like to enter basic management setup? [yes/no]."

---

**The following shows how to set the hostname on the p1r1 router:**

```
Router#conf t
Enter configuration commands, one per line.  End with CNTL/Z.
Router(config)#hostname p1r1
```

**Step 2**   Set the passwords on all the routers in your pod. The passwords should be set to:

—   Secret password: cisco

—   Enable password: sanfran

—   Vty password: cisco

Which commands will you use to do this step?

**The following shows how to set the passwords on the p1r1 router:**

```
p1r1#conf t
Enter configuration commands, one per line.  End with CNTL/Z.
p1r1(config)#enable secret cisco
p1r1(config)#enable password sanfran
p1r1(config)#line vty 0 4
p1r1(config-line)#login
p1r1(config-line)#password cisco
```

**Step 3**   Configure the IP addresses shown in the table on the router interfaces within your pod. Which commands will you use to do this step?

**The following shows how to set the IP addresses on the p1r1 router:**

```
p1r1#conf t
Enter configuration commands, one per line.  End with CNTL/Z.
p1r1(config)#int s0
p1r1(config-if)#ip address 192.168.1.17 255.255.255.240
p1r1(config-if)#int s1
p1r1(config-if)#ip address 192.168.1.33 255.255.255.240
p1r1(config-if)#int s2
p1r1(config-if)#ip address 192.168.1.49 255.255.255.240
p1r1(config-if)#int s3
p1r1(config-if)#ip address 10.1.1.1 255.255.255.0
```

All other interfaces are not used at this time.

From the given IP address and subnet mask, determine the subnet address, and complete the last column in the table.

**The following subnet addresses are for the Pod 1 routers:**

| Router | Interface | IP Address | Subnet Mask | Subnet Address |
|--------|-----------|------------|-------------|----------------|
| p*x*r1 | S0 | 192.168.*x*.17 | 255.255.255.240 | **192.168.1.16** |
| p*x*r1 | S1 | 192.168.*x*.33 | 255.255.255.240 | **192.168.1.32** |
| p*x*r1 | S2 | 192.168.*x*.49 | 255.255.255.240 | **192.168.1.48** |
| p*x*r1 | S3 | 10.*x.x.x* | 255.255.255.0 | **10.1.1.0** |
| p*x*r2 | S0 | 192.168.*x*.18 | 255.255.255.240 | **192.168.1.16** |
| p*x*r2 | S1 | 192.168.*x*.34 | 255.255.255.240 | **192.168.1.32** |
| p*x*r2 | E0 | 192.168.*x*.65 | 255.255.255.240 | **192.168.1.64** |
| p*x*r3 | S0 | 192.168.*x*.50 | 255.255.255.240 | **192.168.1.48** |
| p*x*r3 | E0 | 192.168.*x*.66 | 255.255.255.240 | **192.168.1.64** |

**Step 4**   Enable IGRP on all the routers in your pod, using autonomous system (AS) number 200. Which commands will you use to enable IGRP?

**NOTE**   Recall from ICND that an AS is a collection of networks under a common administration sharing a common routing strategy.

**The following shows how to configure IGRP in AS 200 on the p1r1 router:**

```
p1r1#conf t
Enter configuration commands, one per line.  End with CNTL/Z.
p1r1(config)#router igrp 200
p1r1(config-router)#network 192.168.1.0
p1r1(config-router)#network 10.0.0.0
```

What **network** command (or commands) are required on the routers?

On p*x*r1:

**On p1r1, the network 192.168.1.0 and network 10.0.0.0 commands are required.**

On p*x*r2:

**On p1r2, the network 192.168.1.0 command is required.**

On p*x*r3:

**On p1r3, the network 192.168.1.0 command is required.**

**Step 5** Determine which serial interfaces on the routers have a DCE cable attached to them. Which Cisco IOS command should you use to perform this task?

**The following example shows how to determine which serial interfaces on the p1r1 router have a DCE cable attached:**

```
p1r1#show controller s 0
HD unit 0, idb = 0x121CD4, driver structure at 0x127148
buffer size 1524  HD unit 0, V.35 DCE cable
<output omitted>
```

**By using the show controller command, you should determine that the p1r1 S0, S1, and S2 interfaces have a DCE cable attached. All other interfaces on all the routers in your pod should have DTE cables attached.**

Set a clock rate of 64 kbps on all DCE serial interfaces. Which command will you use to do this step?

**The following shows how to configure a clock rate on the DCE serial interfaces on the p1r1 router:**

```
p1r1#conf t
Enter configuration commands, one per line.  End with CNTL/Z.
p1r1(config)#int s0
p1r1(config-if)#clock rate 64000
p1r1(config-if)#int s1
p1r1(config-if)#clock rate 64000
p1r1(config-if)#int s2
p1r1(config-if)#clock rate 64000
```

Set the bandwidth of all the serial interfaces to 64 kbps. Which command will you use to do this step?

**The following shows how to configure the bandwidth on all the serial interfaces on the p1r1 router:**

```
p1r1#conf t
Enter configuration commands, one per line.  End with CNTL/Z.
p1r1(config)#int s0
p1r1(config-if)#bandwidth 64
p1r1(config-if)#int s1
p1r1(config-if)#bandwidth 64
p1r1(config-if)#int s2
p1r1(config-if)#bandwidth 64
p1r1(config-if)#int s3
p1r1(config-if)#bandwidth 64
```

**Step 6** Enable the following interfaces, and then verify connectivity within your pod. Which command will you use to enable an interface?

Place a check mark next to the interface when it comes up to the "up/up" state.

p*x*r1: S0 ____ S1 ____ S2 ____ S3 ____

p*x*r2: S0 ____ S1 ____ E0 ____

p*x*r3: S0 ____ E0 ____

---

**NOTE**    The p*x*r3 Serial 1 interface should remain shut down until a later configuration exercise.

---

**The following shows how to enable the interfaces on the p1r1 router. The output generated by the router is also shown (note that the p1r1 router was the first one in the pod to have its interfaces enabled):**

```
p1r1#conf t
Enter configuration commands, one per line.  End with CNTL/Z.
p1r1(config)#int s0
p1r1(config-if)#no shutdown
p1r1(config-if)#
00:11:39: %LINK-3-UPDOWN: Interface Serial0, changed state to down
p1r1(config-if)#int s1
p1r1(config-if)#no shutdown
p1r1(config-if)#
00:11:48: %LINK-3-UPDOWN: Interface Serial1, changed state to down
p1r1(config-if)#int s2
p1r1(config-if)#no shutdown
p1r1(config-if)#
00:11:56: %LINK-3-UPDOWN: Interface Serial2, changed state to down
p1r1(config-if)#int s3
p1r1(config-if)#no shutdown
p1r1(config-if)#
00:12:04: %LINK-3-UPDOWN: Interface Serial3, changed state to up
00:12:05: %LINEPROTO-5-UPDOWN: Line protocol on Interface Serial3,
    changed state to up
```

**When all the configured interfaces on all the routers in your pod have had the no shutdown command applied, then they will all be in the "up/up" state. The following shows the status of the serial 3 interface on p1r1:**

```
p1r1#show interfaces s3
Serial3 is up, line protocol is up
  Hardware is CD2430 in sync mode
<output omitted>
```

**Step 7**    Create an IP host table in each of your routers, with an entry for each of the other routers in your pod and for the backbone_r1 router. Which command will you use to create an entry in the host table?

The following shows how to create the IP host table on the p1r1 router:

```
p1r1#conf t
Enter configuration commands, one per line.  End with CNTL/Z.
p1r1(config)#ip host p1r1 192.168.1.17 192.168.1.33 192.168.1.49 10.1.1.1
p1r1(config)#ip host p1r2 192.168.1.65 192.168.1.18 192.168.1.34
p1r1(config)#ip host p1r3 192.168.1.66 192.168.1.50
p1r1(config)#ip host bbr1 10.1.1.100
```

**Step 8**    Add the **no ip domain-lookup** command to your routers. What does this command do?

**The no ip domain-lookup command disables the IP Domain Naming System (DNS)-based host name-to-address translation. The following shows how configure this command on the p1r1 router:**

```
p1r1#conf t
Enter configuration commands, one per line.  End with CNTL/Z.
p1r1(config)#no ip domain-lookup
```

**Step 9**    Using the Cisco Discovery Protocol (CDP), do the following:

Use the proper CDP command to verify that all the routers within your pod can see all their connected neighbors. Which command should you use?

Fill in the blanks that follow using the CDP output from each of the routers within your pod.

**The following shows the use of the show cdp neighbors command on the p1r1 router:**

```
p1r1#show cdp neighbors
Capability Codes: R - Router, T - Trans Bridge, B - Source Route Bridge
                  S - Switch, H - Host, I - IGMP, r - Repeater

Device ID        Local Interface     Holdtme     Capability  Platform  Port ID
p1r3                Ser 2            141            R           2500     Ser 0
p1r2                Ser 1            134            R           2500     Ser 1
p1r2                Ser 0            134            R           2500     Ser 0
backbone_r1         Ser 3            135            R           3640     Ser 1/0
p1r1#
```

**The information that follows was obtained by using the show cdp neighbors command on each of the routers in pod 1.**

From p*x*r1:

| Device Identifier (ID) | Local Interface |
|---|---|
| p1r3 | Ser 2 |
| p1r2 | Ser 1 |
| p1r2 | Ser 0 |
| Backbone_r1 | Ser 3 |

From p*x*r2:

| Device Identifier (ID) | Local Interface |
|---|---|
| p1r3 | Eth 0 |
| p1r1 | Ser 0 |
| p1r1 | Ser 1 |

From p*x*r3:

| Device Identifier (ID) | Local Interface |
|---|---|
| p1r2 | Eth 0 |
| p1r1 | Ser 0 |

Which CDP commands can you use to verify the IP address configuration on your neighbor router?

**The following shows the use of the show cdp neighbors detail command on the p1r1 router to verify the IP address configuration of p1r1's neighbor routers:**

```
p1r1#show cdp neighbors detail
-------------------------
Device ID: p1r3
Entry address(es):
  IP address: 192.168.1.50
Platform: cisco 2500,  Capabilities: Router
Interface: Serial2,  Port ID (outgoing port): Serial0
Holdtime : 144 sec

Version :
Cisco Internetwork Operating System Software
IOS (tm) 2500 Software (C2500-JS-L), Version 12.0(3), RELEASE SOFTWARE (fc1)
Copyright  1986-1999 by cisco Systems, Inc.
Compiled Mon 08-Feb-99 18:18 by phanguye

-------------------------
Device ID: p1r2
Entry address(es):
  IP address: 192.168.1.34
Platform: cisco 2500,  Capabilities: Router
```

```
Interface: Serial1,  Port ID (outgoing port): Serial1
Holdtime : 137 sec

Version :
Cisco Internetwork Operating System Software
IOS (tm) 2500 Software (C2500-JS-L), Version 12.0(3), RELEASE SOFTWARE (fc1)
Copyright  1986-1999 by cisco Systems, Inc.
Compiled Mon 08-Feb-99 18:18 by phanguye

-------------------------
Device ID: p1r2
Entry address(es):
  IP address: 192.168.1.18
Platform: cisco 2500,  Capabilities: Router
Interface: Serial0,  Port ID (outgoing port): Serial0
Holdtime : 130 sec

Version :
Cisco Internetwork Operating System Software
IOS (tm) 2500 Software (C2500-JS-L), Version 12.0(3), RELEASE SOFTWARE (fc1)
Copyright  1986-1999 by cisco Systems, Inc.
Compiled Mon 08-Feb-99 18:18 by phanguye

-------------------------
Device ID: backbone_r1
Entry address(es):
  IP address: 10.1.1.100
Platform: cisco 3640,  Capabilities: Router
Interface: Serial3,  Port ID (outgoing port): Serial1/0
Holdtime : 130 sec

Version :
Cisco Internetwork Operating System Software
IOS (tm) 3600 Software (C3640-JS-M), Version 12.0(5)T1,  RELEASE SOFTWARE (fc1)
Copyright  1986-1999 by cisco Systems, Inc.
Compiled Tue 17-Aug-99 22:32 by cmong
```

What is the default CDP holdtime?

**The default CDP holdtime is 180 seconds, as shown in the following partial output of the show cdp interface command on the p1r1 router:**

```
p1r1#show cdp interface
<output omitted>
Serial0 is up, line protocol is up
  Encapsulation HDLC
  Sending CDP packets every 60 seconds
  Holdtime is 180 seconds
<output omitted>
```

What is the purpose of the holdtime?

**The CDP holdtime specifies the amount of time that the receiving device should hold a CDP packet from your router before discarding it.**

**Step 10** Display the IP routing table on each of the routers in your pod, and verify that you have full connectivity within your pod. Which command will you use to display the routing table?

**The following shows the use of the show ip route command on the p1r1 router to display the IP routing table:**

```
p1r1#show ip route
Codes: C - connected, S - static, I - IGRP, R - RIP, M - mobile, B - BGP
       D - EIGRP, EX - EIGRP external, O - OSPF, IA - OSPF inter area
       N1 - OSPF NSSA external type 1, N2 - OSPF NSSA external type 2
       E1 - OSPF external type 1, E2 - OSPF external type 2, E - EGP
       i - IS-IS, L1 - IS-IS level-1, L2 - IS-IS level-2, * - candidate default
       U - per-user static route, o - ODR
       T - traffic engineered route

Gateway of last resort is not set

I    172.16.0.0/16 [100/158750] via 10.1.1.100, 00:01:16, Serial3
     10.0.0.0/24 is subnetted, 1 subnets
C       10.1.1.0 is directly connected, Serial3
     192.168.1.0/28 is subnetted, 4 subnets
I       192.168.1.64 [100/158350] via 192.168.1.50, 00:00:42, Serial2
                     [100/158350] via 192.168.1.18, 00:00:00, Serial0
                     [100/158350] via 192.168.1.34, 00:00:00, Serial1
C       192.168.1.32 is directly connected, Serial1
C       192.168.1.48 is directly connected, Serial2
C       192.168.1.16 is directly connected, Serial0
```

Make sure that you can successfully **ping** all the other routers within your pod.

**The following shows the use of the ping command on the p1r1 router to verify connectivity to the p1r2 and p1r3 routers:**

```
p1r1#ping p1r2

Type escape sequence to abort.
Sending 5, 100-byte ICMP Echos to 192.168.1.65, timeout is 2 seconds:
!!!!!
Success rate is 100 percent (5/5), round-trip min/avg/max = 28/32/36 ms
p1r1#ping p1r3

Type escape sequence to abort.
Sending 5, 100-byte ICMP Echos to 192.168.1.66, timeout is 2 seconds:
!!!!!
Success rate is 100 percent (5/5), round-trip min/avg/max = 32/32/36 ms
```

**Step 11** Display the routing table on each of the routers in your pod, and verify that you have valid routes and connectivity to backbone_r1 router. (Note that if you have configured other pods, you will also see routes to those other pods).

The following shows partial output from the show ip route command on the p1r1 router, indicating valid routes to the backbone_r1 router. The results of the ping command to the backbone_r1 router are also shown.

```
p1r1#show ip route
<output omitted>
I    172.16.0.0/16 [100/158750] via 10.1.1.100, 00:00:19, Serial3
     10.0.0.0/24 is subnetted, 1 subnets
C       10.1.1.0 is directly connected, Serial3
     192.168.1.0/28 is subnetted, 4 subnets
I       192.168.1.64 [100/158350] via 192.168.1.50, 00:01:11, Serial2
                     [100/158350] via 192.168.1.18, 00:00:28, Serial0
                     [100/158350] via 192.168.1.34, 00:00:27, Serial1
C       192.168.1.32 is directly connected, Serial1
C       192.168.1.48 is directly connected, Serial2
<output omitted>

p1r1#ping bbr1

Type escape sequence to abort.
Sending 5, 100-byte ICMP Echos to 10.1.1.100, timeout is 2 seconds:
!!!!!
Success rate is 100 percent (5/5), round-trip min/avg/max = 32/32/32 ms
```

**Step 12** Examine the p.xr1 routing table, and use the **show ip protocols** command to answer the following questions.

The following shows output from the show ip protocols command on the p1r1 router:

```
p1r1#show ip protocols
Routing Protocol is "igrp 200"
  Sending updates every 90 seconds, next due in 49 seconds
  Invalid after 270 seconds, hold down 280, flushed after 630
  Outgoing update filter list for all interfaces is
  Incoming update filter list for all interfaces is
  Default networks flagged in outgoing updates
  Default networks accepted from incoming updates
  IGRP metric weight K1=1, K2=0, K3=1, K4=0, K5=0
  IGRP maximum hopcount 100
  IGRP maximum metric variance 1
  Redistributing: igrp 200
  Routing for Networks:
    10.0.0.0
    192.168.1.0
  Routing Information Sources:
    Gateway         Distance       Last Update
    192.168.1.34         100       00:00:12
    192.168.1.50         100       00:00:43
    10.1.1.100           100       00:01:05
    192.168.1.18         100       00:00:12
  Distance: (default is 100)
```

**The following shows partial output from the show ip route command on the p1r1 router:**

```
p1r1#show ip route
<output omitted>
I    172.16.0.0/16 [100/158750] via 10.1.1.100, 00:00:33, Serial3
     10.0.0.0/24 is subnetted, 1 subnets
C       10.1.1.0 is directly connected, Serial3
     192.168.1.0/28 is subnetted, 4 subnets
I       192.168.1.64 [100/158350] via 192.168.1.50, 00:00:08, Serial2
                     [100/158350] via 192.168.1.18, 00:01:02, Serial0
                     [100/158350] via 192.168.1.34, 00:01:02, Serial1
C       192.168.1.32 is directly connected, Serial1
C       192.168.1.48 is directly connected, Serial2
C       192.168.1.16 is directly connected, Serial0
```

What is the administrative distance of IGRP?

**The default administrative distance of IGRP is 100.**

What is the purpose of the administrative distance?

**The administrative distance is used as a measure of the *trustworthiness* of the source of the IP routing information. It is important only when a router learns about a destination route from more than one source.**

How often are the IGRP routing updates sent by default?

**The IGRP routing updates are sent every 90 seconds, by default.**

How many paths are in the routing table to the 192.168.x.64 subnet? Why are there multiple paths to that subnet?

**There are three routes to the 192.168.1.64 subnet in the routing table. There are multiple paths in the routing table because they are all of equal metric (in this case, the metric is 158350).**

By default, IGRP calculates the routing metric based on what two factors?

**By default, IGRP calculates the routing metric based on bandwidth and delay.**

**Step 13**  Examine the p*x*r3 routing table. What information does p*x*r3 know about network 10.0.0.0? Is this different from what p*x*r1 knows about network 10.0.0.0? Why?

The following shows partial outputs from the show ip route command on the
p1r3 and p1r1 routers.

```
p1r3#show ip route
<output omitted>
I     172.16.0.0/16 [100/160750] via 192.168.1.49, 00:01:12, Serial0
I     10.0.0.0/8 [100/160250] via 192.168.1.49, 00:01:13, Serial0
      192.168.1.0/28 is subnetted, 4 subnets
C        192.168.1.64 is directly connected, Ethernet0
I        192.168.1.32 [100/158350] via 192.168.1.65, 00:00:48, Ethernet0
C        192.168.1.48 is directly connected, Serial0
I        192.168.1.16 [100/158350] via 192.168.1.65, 00:00:48, Ethernet0
p1r3#


p1r1#show ip route
<output omitted>
I     172.16.0.0/16 [100/158750] via 10.1.1.100, 00:00:33, Serial3
      10.0.0.0/24 is subnetted, 1 subnets
C        10.1.1.0 is directly connected, Serial3
      192.168.1.0/28 is subnetted, 4 subnets
I        192.168.1.64 [100/158350] via 192.168.1.50, 00:00:08, Serial2
                      [100/158350] via 192.168.1.18, 00:01:02, Serial0
                      [100/158350] via 192.168.1.34, 00:01:02, Serial1
C        192.168.1.32 is directly connected, Serial1
C        192.168.1.48 is directly connected, Serial2
C        192.168.1.16 is directly connected, Serial0
```

The p1r3 router knows about only the Class A network 10.0.0.0, while the
p1r1 router knows the subnets of the 10.0.0.0 network—in this case, only
subnet 10.1.1.0. This is because the p1r1 router has an interface directly
connected to the 10.1.1.0 subnet and therefore will exchange subnet
information with other routers in the 10.0.0.0 network (in this case, with the
backbone_r1 router). Because the network is using a classful routing protocol
IGRP, and because p1r2 and p1r3 do not participate in the 10.0.0.0 network,
p1r1 automatically sends only a classful summary route about network
10.0.0.0 to the other routers in the pod.

**Step 14** On the p.xr1 router, issue the **debug ip igrp transactions** command to
capture the IGRP routing updates. Examine the routing updates sent by
the p.xr1 router to the backbone_r1 router over the Serial 3 interface.
What update is the p.xr1 router sending to the backbone_r1 router?

The following shows the enabling of and partial output from the debug ip igrp
transactions command on the p1r1 router, indicating the updates sent by the
p1r1 router to the backbone_r1 router:

```
p1r1#debug ip igrp transactions
IGRP protocol debugging is on
p1r1#
<output omitted>
01:11:26: IGRP: sending update to 255.255.255.255 via Serial3 (10.1.1.1)
01:11:27:      network 192.168.1.0, metric=158250
<output omitted>
```

**The output shows that the p1r1 router is sending a classful summary route about network 192.168.1.0 to the backbone_r1 router.**

Is IGRP a classless or a classful routing protocol?

**IGRP is a classful routing protocol.**

IGRP performs autosummarization across what boundary?

**IGRP performs autosummarization across the classful network boundary.**

What is the function of the **ip classless** command?

**The ip classless command enables forwarding of a packet destined for an unrecognized subnet of a directly connected attached network, using the supernet or default route.**

**Step 15**  What is the Cisco IOS version and router type used within your pod? Which command will you use to determine this information?

**The following shows partial output from the show version command on the p1r1 router, used to determine the Cisco IOS version and router type.**

```
p1r1#show version
Cisco Internetwork Operating System Software
IOS (tm) 2500 Software (C2500-JS-L), Version 12.0(3), RELEASE SOFTWARE (fc1)
Copyright 1986-1999 by cisco Systems, Inc.
Compiled Mon 08-Feb-99 18:18 by phanguye
Image text-base: 0x03050C84, data-base: 0x00001000

ROM: System Bootstrap, Version 11.0(10c), SOFTWARE
BOOTFLASH: 3000 Bootstrap Software (IGS-BOOT-R), Version 11.0(10c), RELEASE SOFTWARE
(fc1)

p1r1 uptime is 1 hour, 14 minutes
System restarted by power-on
System image file is "flash:/c2500-js-l_120-3.bin"

cisco 2520 (68030) processor (revision M) with 6144K/2048K bytes of memory.
Processor board ID 08308443, with hardware revision 00000003
<output omitted>
```

**The information that follows was determined from the show version command output on the routers in pod 1. Note that your output may differ, depending on the routers you have.**

Fill in the blanks that follow with the information that you obtained.

| Router | Cisco IOS Version | Router Type |
|--------|-------------------|-------------|
| p*x*r1 | 12.0(3) | 2520 |
| p*x*r2 | 12.0(3) | 2500 |
| p*x*r3 | 12.0(3) | 2500 |

**Step 16** You may also wish to add the **exec-timeout 0 0** and the **logging synchronous** commands to the line console 0 configuration on all the routers in your pod. What is the function of these commands?

**The following shows the configuration of these commands on the p1r1 router:**

```
p1r1#conf t
Enter configuration commands, one per line.  End with CNTL/Z.
p1r1(config)#line con 0
p1r1(config-line)# exec-timeout 0 0
p1r1(config-line)# logging synchronous
```

**The exec-timeout 0 0 command ensures that your console session will not time out. When you are typing on the console, the logging synchronous command ensures that any router output will not interfere with your command input.**

**Step 17** Save the current configurations of all the routers within your pod. Which command will you use to save your configuration?

**The following shows how to save the configuration of the p1r1 router, using the copy run start command (this is an abbreviated form of the copy running-config startup-config command):**

```
p1r1#copy run start
Destination filename [startup-config]?
Building configuration...
```

# Review Questions

Answer the following questions, and then refer to Appendix G, "Answers to Review Questions," for the answers.

1 What characteristic defines the difference between classful and classless protocols?

2 What characteristic of distance vector protocols is responsible for their slower convergence?

3 Which field in a routing table entry measures the reachability of the destination network?

**4** Complete the following table by indicating which protocols demonstrate the characteristic shown in the right column. Indicate your choices in the left column by entering one or more of the following routing protocols: **RIPv1, RIPv2, IGRP, EIGRP**, or **OSPF**.

| Protocol | Characteristic |
| --- | --- |
| | Maintains a topology table to assist in rapid convergence |
| | Uses broadcast packets to propagate topology updates |
| | Has an administrative distance of 110 |
| | Supports flooding of updates to avoid routing loops |
| | Requires a hierarchical design to operate correctly |
| | Allows manual route summarization at any location |
| | Can select preferred path based upon bandwidth consideration |
| | Supports variable-length subnet masks |
| | Is a link-state protocol supported by all vendors of routing equipment |

**5** For distance vector protocols, what did Cisco implement as a way to enable routers to become aware of topology changes more quickly?

**6** Which characteristic of OSPF ensures that convergence time will always be greater than 5 seconds?

**7** What function does the **clear ip route 172.16.3.0** command perform?

This chapter discusses various aspects of Internet Protocol (IP) addressing. This chapter covers the following topics:

- Current Challenges in IP Addressing
- IP Addressing Solutions
- Hierarchical Addressing
- Variable-Length Subnet Masks
- Route Summarization
- Classless Interdomain Routing
- Using IP Unnumbered Serial Interfaces
- Using Helper Addresses
- Summary
- Review Questions

# Extending IP Addresses

After reading this chapter, you will be able to use variable-length subnet masks to extend the use of the IP addresses when given an IP address range, explain whether route summarization is possible when given a network plan that includes IP addressing, and configure an IP helper address to manage broadcasts.

## Current Challenges in IP Addressing

IP addressing was first defined in 1981. An IP address consists of a 32-bit number with two components: a network address and a node (host) address. Classes of addresses are also defined—originally, only Classes A, B, and C were defined, and later Classes D and E were added. Since then, the growth of the Internet has been incredible. Two addressing challenges have resulted from this explosion:

- **IP address exhaustion**—This has largely been due to the random allocation of IP addresses by the Network Information Center (NIC). Address exhaustion also has occurred because subnetting with one subnet mask may not be suitable for a typical network topology, as you will see in the "Variable-Length Subnet Masks" section later in this chapter.

- **Routing table growth and manageability**—One source indicates that in 1990, only about 5000 routes were tracked to use the Internet. This number had grown to more than 70,000 routes by the end of 1999. In addition to the exponential growth of the Internet, the random assignment of IP addresses throughout the world has contributed to the exponential growth of routing tables.

Next-generation IP (IP version 6) tries to respond to these problems by introducing a 128-bit address. In the meantime, Internet Requests For Comments (RFCs) have been introduced to enable the current IP addressing scheme to continue to be useful.

## IP Addressing Solutions

Since the 1980s, solutions have been developed to slow the depletion of IP addresses and to reduce the number of Internet route table entries by enabling more hierarchical layers in an IP address. These solutions include the following:

- **Subnet masking**—Covered by RFCs 950 (1985) and 1812 (1995). Developed to add another level of hierarchy to an IP address. This additional level allows for extending the number of network addresses derived from a single IP address. (Subnet masking is reviewed in the "IP Addressing and Subnetting" section in this chapter and in Appendix A, "Job Aids and Supplements"; this subject also is discussed in detail in the Cisco Press *Interconnecting Cisco Network Devices* coursebook and Cisco ICND course.)

---

**NOTE**    RFC 1812 also contains a lot of information on how IP routing protocols should work.

---

- **Address allocation for private internets**—Covered by RFC 1918 (1996). Developed for organizations that do not need much access to the Internet. The only reason to have a NIC-assigned IP address is to interconnect to the Internet. Any and all companies can use the privately assigned IP addresses within their organization rather than using a NIC-assigned IP address unnecessarily. The private addresses are 10.0.0.0 through 10.255.255.255, 172.16.0.0 through 172.31.255.255, and 192.168.0.0 through 192.168.255.255. (Private addresses are discussed in the Cisco Press *Building Cisco Remote Access Networks* coursebook and in the Cisco BCRAN course.)

- **Network address translation (NAT)**—Covered by RFC 1631 (1994). Developed for those companies that use private addressing or use IP addresses not assigned by NIC. This strategy enables an organization to access the Internet with a NIC-assigned address, without having to reassign the private addresses (sometimes called *illegal* addresses) that are already in place. (NAT is discussed in the Cisco Press *Building Cisco Remote Access Networks* coursebook and in the Cisco BCRAN course.)

- **Hierarchical addressing**—Applying a structure to addressing so that multiple addresses share the same left-most bits. Hierarchical addressing is discussed in this chapter in the section "Hierarchical Addressing."

- **Variable-length subnet masks (VLSMs)**—Covered by RFC 1812 (1995). Developed to allow multiple levels of subnetworked IP addresses within a single network. This strategy can be used only when it is supported by the routing protocol in use, such as the Open Shortest Path First (OSPF) protocol and the Enhanced Interior Gateway Routing Protocol (EIGRP). VLSMs are discussed later in this chapter in the section "Variable-Length Subnet Masks."

- **Route summarization**—Covered by RFC 1518 (1993). A way of having a single IP address represent a collection of IP addresses when you employ a hierarchical addressing plan. Route summarization is discussed later in this chapter in the section "Route Summarization."

- **Classless Interdomain Routing (CIDR)**—Covered by RFCs 1518 (1993), 1519 (1993), and 2050 (1996). Developed for Internet service providers (ISPs). This strategy suggests that the remaining IP addresses be allocated to ISPs in contiguous blocks, with geography being a consideration. CIDR is discussed later in this chapter in the section "Classless Interdomain Routing."

# IP Addressing and Subnetting

This section is an overview of IP subnetting and addresses. Appendix A includes a more detailed review of these topics.

When contiguous ones are added to the default mask, making the all-ones field in the mask longer, the definition of the network part of an IP address is extended to include subnets. Adding bits to the network part of an address decreases the number of bits in the host part. Thus, creating additional networks (subnets) is done at the expense of the number of host devices that can occupy each network segment.

The number of bits added to a default routing mask creates a counting range for counting subnets. Each subnet is a unique binary pattern.

The number of subnetworks created is calculated by the formula $2^n$, where $n$ is the number of bits by which the default mask was extended. Subnet 0 (where all the subnet bits are 0) must be explicitly allowed using the **ip subnet-zero** global configuration command in Cisco IOS releases prior to 12.0. In Cisco IOS Release 12.0 and later, subnet zero is enabled by default.

---

**NOTE**    This book describes the formula for obtaining the number of subnets differently than previous Cisco courses and books. Previously, the same formula that was used to count hosts, $2^n - 2$, was used to count subnets. Now $2^n$ subnets and $2^n - 2$ hosts are available. The $2^n$ rule for subnets has been adopted because the all-ones subnet has always been a legal subnet according to the RFC, and subnet zero can be enabled by configuration commands on the Cisco routers (and, in fact, is on by default in Cisco IOS Release 12.0 and later). Note, however, that not all vendor equipment supports the use of subnet zero.

---

The remaining bits in the routing mask form a counting range for hosts. Host addresses are selected from these remaining bits and must be numerically unique from all other hosts on the subnetwork.

The number of hosts created is calculated by the formula $2^n - 2$ where $n$ is the number of bits available in the host portion. In the host counting range, the all 0s bit pattern is reserved as the subnet identifier (sometimes called *the wire*), and the all 1s bit pattern is reserved as a broadcast address, to reach all hosts on that subnet.

Both the IP address and the associated mask contain 32 bits. Routers are similar to computers in that both use the binary numbering scheme to represent addresses. Network administrators, however, typically do not use binary numbers on a daily basis and therefore have adopted other formats to represent 32-bit IP addresses. Some common formats include decimal (base 10) and hexadecimal (base 16) notations.

The generally accepted method of representing IP addresses and masks is to break the 32-bit field into four groups of 8 bits (octets) and to represent those 8-bit fields in a decimal format, separated by decimal points. This is known as 32-bit *dotted decimal notation.*

**NOTE**   Although the dotted decimal notation is commonly accepted, this notation means nothing to the routing device because the device internally uses the 32-bit binary string. All routing decisions are based on the 32-bit binary string.

IP addresses belong to classes, defined by the decimal value represented in the first octet. The class definition is referred to as the *First Octet Rule.* As shown in Table 2-1, Classes A through E are defined. Of the five available addressing spaces, Classes A, B, and C are the best known and most commonly used because they are used to identify devices connected to the Internet.

**Table 2-1**   *Determining IP Address Class by the First Octet Rule*

| First Octet of Address (Decimal) | Address Class |
|---|---|
| 1 to 126 | Class A |
| 128 to 191 | Class B |
| 192 to 223 | Class C |
| 224 to 239 | Class D |
| 240 to 255 | Class E |

**NOTE**   The first octet for Class A ranges from 1 (not 0) to 126 (not 127). The 0 address is a reserved address, meaning *this network*, and can be used only as a source address. The 127 address is reserved for the local loopback address.

Class D addresses are not as widely used. Class D addresses are multicast addresses; some Class D multicast addresses used by routing protocols are as follows:

- **OSPF**—224.0.0.5 and 224.0.0.6
- **Routing Information Protocol version 2 (RIPv2)**—224.0.0.9
- **EIGRP**—224.0.0.10

Videoconferencing and other applications use other Class D multicast addresses. In videoconferencing applications, users subscribe to a group service and are issued a special group address that allows them access to the data created for that special event. This approach enables many users to subscribe and unsubscribe to a service as their needs and schedules permit.

Class E addresses are used for experimental purposes.

# Hierarchical Addressing

This section discusses hierarchical addressing and the benefits of using it. The following topics are covered:

- Planning an IP address hierarchy
- Benefits of hierarchical addressing

## Planning an IP Address Hierarchy

Perhaps the best-known addressing hierarchy is the telephone network. The telephone network uses a hierarchical numbering scheme that includes country codes, area codes, and local exchange numbers. For example, if you are in San Jose, California, and call someone else in San Jose, you dial the San Jose local exchange number, 528, and the person's telephone number—for example, 7777. Upon seeing the number 528, the central office recognizes that the destination telephone is within its area, so it looks for number 7777 and transfers the call.

In another example, as shown in Figure 2-1, to call Aunt Judy in Alexandria, Virginia, from San Jose, you dial 1, then the area code 703, then the Alexandria prefix 555, and then Aunt Judy's local number, 1212. The central office first sees the number 1, indicating a remote call, and then looks up the number 703. The central office immediately routes the call to a central office in Alexandria. The San Jose central office does not know exactly where 555-1212 is in Alexandria, nor does it have to. It needs to know only the area codes, which summarize the local telephone numbers within an area.

**Figure 2-1**    *The Telephone Network Uses an Addressing Hierarchy*

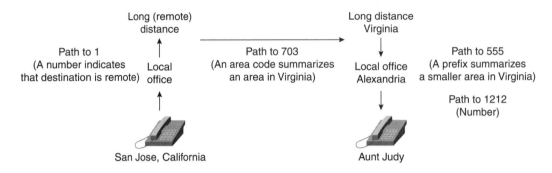

If there were no hierarchical structure, every central office would need to have every telephone number worldwide in its locator table. Instead, the central offices have summary numbers, such as area codes and country codes. A summary number (address) represents a group of numbers. For example, an area code such as 408 is a summary number for the San Jose area. That is, if you dial 1-408 from anywhere in the United States, followed by a seven-digit telephone number, the central office will route the call to a San Jose central office. This is the type of addressing strategy that the Internet gurus are trying to work toward and that you as a network administrator should implement in your own internetwork.

## Benefits of Hierarchical Addressing

Imagine if the telephone network did not use a hierarchy—each central office would need to keep track of all the phone numbers in the phone network. This would obviously be unacceptable. Instead, the telephone network uses the area code and prefix to represent a collection of phone numbers—that is, they *summarize* the phone numbers within an area. Similarly, a routed network can employ a hierarchical addressing scheme to take advantage of those same benefits.

The benefits of hierarchical addressing include these:

- **Reduced number of routing table entries**—Whether it is with your Internet routers or your internal routers, you should try to keep your routing tables as small as possible by using route summarization. Route summarization is a way of having a single IP address represent a collection of IP addresses when you employ a hierarchical addressing plan. By summarizing routes, you can keep your routing table entries manageable, which offers the following benefits:

  — More efficient routing

  — Reduced number of CPU cycles when recalculating a routing table or sorting through the routing table entries to find a match

— Reduced router memory requirements

— Faster convergence after a change in the network

— Easier troubleshooting

- **Efficient allocation of addresses**—Hierarchical addressing enables you to take advantage of all possible addresses because you group them contiguously. With random address assignment, you may end up wasting groups of addresses because of addressing conflicts. For example, recall that classful routing protocols automatically create summary routes at a network boundary. Therefore, these protocols do not support discontiguous addressing (as you will see later in this chapter in the section "Summarizing Routes in a Discontiguous Network"), so some addresses would be unusable if not assigned contiguously.

# Variable-Length Subnet Masks

This section introduces VLSMs, gives some examples, and discusses VLSM use with classless routing protocols. The section covers the following:

- VLSM overview

- Calculating VLSMs

- A working VLSM example

## VLSM Overview

VLSMs provide the capability to include more than one subnet mask within a major network and the capability to subnet an already subnetted network address. The benefits of VLSMs include these:

- **Even more efficient use of IP addresses**—Without the use of VLSMs, companies are locked into implementing a single subnet mask within an entire Class A, B, or C network number.

  For example, consider the 172.16.0.0/16 network address divided into subnets using /24 masking, and one of the subnetworks in this range, 172.16.14.0/24, further divided into smaller subnets with the /27 masking, as shown in Figure 2-2. These smaller subnets range from 172.16.14.0/27 to 172.16.14.224/27. In Figure 2-2, one of these smaller subnets, 172.16.14.128, is further divided with the /30 prefix, creating subnets with only two hosts, to be used on the WAN links. (The details of the subnets used are shown following Figure 2-2.)

- **Greater capability to use route summarization**—VLSMs allow for more hierarchical levels within your addressing plan and thus allow for better route summarization within routing tables. For example, in Figure 2-2, address 172.16.14.0/24 could summarize all the subnets that are further subnets of 172.16.14.0, including those from subnet 172.16.14.0/27 and from 172.16.14.128/30.

**Figure 2-2**   *VLSMs Allow More Than One Subnet Mask Within a Major Network*

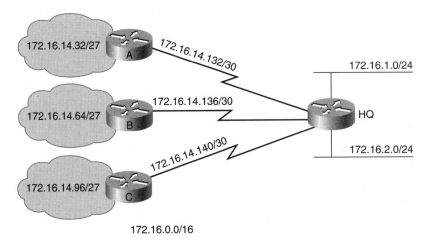

In Figure 2-2, the subnets available are as follows:

| From 172.16.0.0/24: | 172.16.0.0/24 (not used in this example)<br>172.16.1.0/24<br>172.16.2.0/24<br>and so on |
| --- | --- |
| | 172.16.14.0/24 (not used, was further subnetted to 172.16.14.0/27) |
| From 172.16.14.0/27: | 172.16.14.0/27 (not used in this example)<br>172.16.14.32/27<br>172.16.14.64/27<br>172.16.14.96/27<br>and so on |
| | 172.16.14.128/27 (not used, but was further subnetted to 172.16.14.128/30) |
| From 172.16.14.128/30: | 172.16.14.128/30 (not used in this example)<br>172.16.14.132/30<br>172.16.14.136/30<br>172.16.14.140/30<br>and so on |

## Calculating VLSMs

With VLSMs, you can subnet an already subnetted address. Consider, for example, that you have a subnet address 172.16.32.0/20, and you need to assign addresses to a network that has ten hosts. With this subnet address, however, you have $2^{12} - 2 = 4094$ host addresses, so you would be wasting more than 4000 IP addresses. With VLSMs, you can further subnet the address 172.16.32.0/20 to give you more subnetwork addresses and fewer hosts per network, which would work better in this network topology. For example, if you subnet 172.16.32.0/20 to 172.16.32.0/26, you gain 64 ($2^6$) subnets, each of which could support 62 ($2^6 - 2$) hosts.

---

**NOTE**    The "Decimal-to-Binary Conversion Chart" in Appendix A may be helpful when you are calculating VLSMs.

---

To further subnet 172.16.32.0/20 to 172.16.32.0/26, do the following, as illustrated in Figure 2-3:

**Step 1**    Write 172.16.32.0 in binary form.

**Step 2**    Draw a vertical line between the 20th and 21st bits, as shown in Figure 2-3.

**Step 3**    Draw a vertical line between the 26th and 27th bits, as shown in Figure 2-3.

**Step 4**    Calculate the 64 subnet addresses using the bits between the two vertical lines, from lowest to highest in value. Figure 2-3 shows the first five subnets available. If necessary, refer to the "Decimal-to-Binary Conversion Chart," in Appendix A.

**Figure 2-3**    *An Example of Further Subnetting a Subnetted Address*

```
Subnetted Address: 172.16.32.0/20
In Binary 10101100.00010000.00100000.00000000

VLSM Address: 172.16.32.0/26
In Binary 10101100.00010000.00100000.00000000

1st subnet: 10101100  .  00010000  .0010 0000.00  000000=172.16.32.0/26
2nd subnet:   172      .     16     .0010 0000.01  000000=172.16.32.64/26
3rd subnet:   172      .     16     .0010 0000.10  000000=172.16.32.128/26
4th subnet:   172      .     16     .0010 0000.11  000000=172.16.32.192/26
5th subnet:   172      .     16     .0010 0001.00  000000=172.16.33.0/26
                    Network          Subnet  VLSM     Host
                                             subnet
```

| NOTE | VLSM calculators are available on the Web. The following URL is for the one offered by Cisco: www.cisco.com/techtools/ip_addr.html. (Note that you need to have an account to use this calculator; you can see it but cannot use it without logging in.) |
|------|---|

## A Working VLSM Example

VLSMs are commonly used to maximize the number of possible addresses available for a network. For example, because point-to-point serial lines require only two host addresses, you can use a subnetted address that has only two host addresses and therefore will not waste scarce subnet numbers.

In Figure 2-4, the addresses used on the local-area networks (LANs) are those generated in the previous section, "Calculating VLSMs."

**Figure 2-4** *A Working VLSM Example Using Ethernet and Point-to-Point WAN Links*

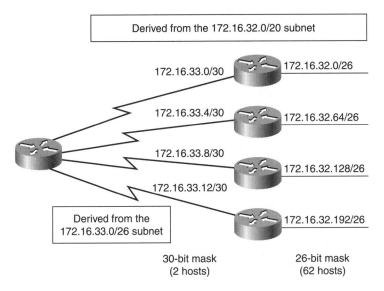

Figure 2-4 illustrates where the addresses can be applied, depending on the number of hosts anticipated at each layer. For example, the wide-area network (WAN) links use addresses with a prefix of /30 (corresponding to a subnet mask of 255.255.255.252). This prefix allows for only two hosts—just enough hosts for a point-to-point connection between a pair of routers. To calculate the addresses used on the WAN links, further subnet one of the unused subnets. In this case, you can further subnet 172.16.33.0/26 with a prefix of /30. This provides 4 more subnet bits and therefore $2^4 = 16$ subnets for the WANs.

The WAN addresses derived from the 172.16.33.0/26 subnet are as follows:

- 172.16.33.00**000000** = 172.16.33.0/30
- 172.16.33.00**000100** = 172.16.33.4/30
- 172.16.33.00**001000** = 172.16.33.8/30
- 172.16.33.00**001100** = 172.16.33.12/30

**NOTE**    It is important to remember that only subnets that are unused can be further subnetted. In other words, if you use any addresses from a subnet, that subnet cannot be further subnetted. In the example in Figure 2-4, four subnet numbers are used on the LANs. Another, as yet unused subnet, 172.16.33.0/26, is further subnetted for use on the WANs.

# Route Summarization

This section describes and gives examples of route summarization, including implementation considerations. This section covers the following topics:

- Route summarization overview
- Summarizing within an Octet
- Summarizing addresses in a VLSM-designed network
- Route summarization implementation
- Route summarization operation in Cisco routers
- Summarizing routes in a discontiguous network
- Route summarization summary

## Route Summarization Overview

In large internetworks, hundreds or even thousands of networks can exist. In these environments, it is often not desirable for routers to maintain all these routes in their routing table. Route summarization (also called *route aggregation* or *supernetting*) can reduce the number of routes that a router must maintain because it is a method of representing a series of network numbers in a single summary address. For example, in Figure 2-5, Router A either can send three routing update entries or can summarize the three addresses into a single network number.

**Figure 2-5**  *Routers Can Summarize to Reduce the Number of Routes*

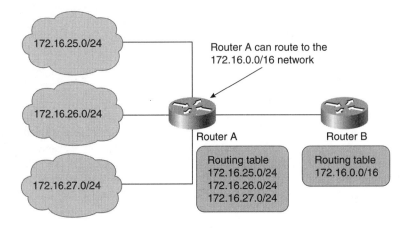

**NOTE**    Router A in Figure 2-5 is advertising that it can route to the network 172.16.0.0/16, including all subnets of that network. However, if there were other subnets of 172.16.0.0 elsewhere in the network (for example, if 172.16.0.0 were discontiguous), summarizing in this way might not be valid. Discontiguous networks and summarization are discussed in the "Summarizing Routes in a Discontiguous Network" section, later in this chapter.

Another advantage to using route summarization in a large, complex network is that it can isolate topology changes from other routers. That is, if a specific link in the 172.16.27.0/24 domain were *flapping* (going down and up rapidly), the summary route would not change, so no router external to the domain would need to keep modifying its routing table due to this flapping activity.

**NOTE**    A summary route will be announced by the summarizing router as long as at least one specific route matches the summary route in its routing table.

Route summarization is most effective and possible only when a proper addressing plan is in place. Route summarization is most effective within a subnetted environment when the network addresses are in contiguous blocks in powers of two. For example, 4, 16, or 512 addresses can be represented by a single routing entry because summary masks are binary masks—just like subnet masks—so summarization must take place on binary boundaries (powers of two). If the number of network addresses is not contiguous or a power of two, you can divide the addresses into groups and try to summarize the groups separately.

Routing protocols summarize or aggregate routes based on shared network numbers within the network. Classless routing protocols—such as OSPF, and EIGRP—support route summarization based on subnet addresses, including VLSM addressing. Classful routing protocols—RIPv1 and IGRP—automatically summarize routes on the classful network boundary and do not support summarization on any other bit boundaries. Classless routing protocols support summarization on any bit boundary.

Summarization is described in RFC 1518, "An Architecture for IP Address Allocation with CIDR."

## Summarizing Within an Octet

Figure 2-5 illustrated a summary route based on a full octet—172.16.25.0/24, 172.16.26.0/24, and 172.16.27.0/24 could be summarized into 172.16.0.0/16. However, this is not always the case.

A router could receive updates for the following routes:

- 172.16.168.0/24
- 172.16.169.0/24
- 172.16.170.0/24
- 172.16.171.0/24
- 172.16.172.0/24
- 172.16.173.0/24
- 172.16.174.0/24
- 172.16.175.0/24

In this case, to determine the summary route, the router determines the number of highest-order (left-most) bits that match in all the addresses. As shown in Figure 2-6, the left-most 21 bits match in all these addresses. Therefore, the best summary route is 172.16.168.0/21 (or 172.16.168.0 255.255.248.0).

To allow the router to aggregate the most IP addresses into a single route summary, your IP addressing plan should be hierarchical in nature. This approach is particularly important when using VLSMs, as illustrated in the next section.

**Figure 2-6** *An Example of Summarizing Within an Octet*

| | | | | |
|---|---|---|---|---|
| 172.16.168.0/24 = | 10101100. | 00010000 . | 10101 | 000 . 00000000 |
| 172.16.169.0/24 = | 172 . | 16 . | 10101 | 001 . 0 |
| 172.16.170.0/24 = | 172 . | 16 . | 10101 | 010 . 0 |
| 172.16.171.0/24 = | 172 . | 16 . | 10101 | 011 . 0 |
| 172.16.172.0/24 = | 172 . | 16 . | 10101 | 100 . 0 |
| 172.16.173.0/24 = | 172 . | 16 . | 10101 | 101 . 0 |
| 172.16.174.0/24 = | 172 . | 16 . | 10101 | 110 . 0 |
| 172.16.175.0/24 = | 172 . | 16 . | 10101 | 111 . 0 |

Number of common bits = 21          Number of
Summary: 172.16.168.0/21          noncommon
                                                  bits = 11

# Summarizing Addresses in a VLSM-Designed Network

A VLSM design allows for maximum use of IP addresses as well as more efficient routing update communication when using hierarchical IP addressing. In Figure 2-7 for example, route summarization occurs at two levels:

- Router C summarizes two routing updates from networks 172.16.32.64/26 and 172.16.32.128/26 into a single update, 172.16.32.0/24.

- Router A receives three different routing updates but summarizes them into a single routing update before propagating it to the corporate network.

# Route Summarization Implementation

Route summarization reduces memory use on routers and routing protocol network traffic, due to less entries in the routing table. For summarization in a network to work correctly, the following requirements must be met:

- Multiple IP addresses must share the same high-order bits.

- Routing protocols must base their routing decisions on a 32-bit IP address and a prefix length that can be up to 32 bits.

- Routing updates must carry the prefix length (the subnet mask) along with the 32-bit IP address.

**Figure 2-7**    *An Example of Summarizing in a Network Using VLSM*

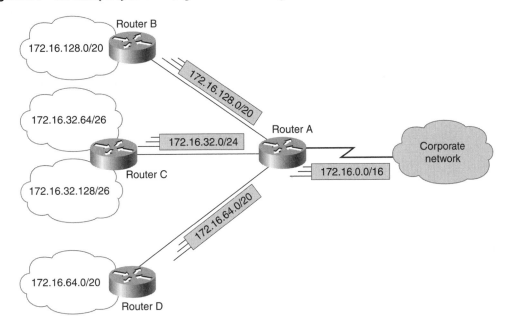

## Route Summarization Operation in Cisco Routers

This section discusses generalities of how Cisco routers handle route summarization. Details about how route summarization operates with a specific protocol are discussed in the specific protocol chapter of this book. For example, route summarization for OSPF is discussed in Chapter 4, "Interconnecting Multiple OSPF Areas."

Cisco routers manage route summarization in two ways:

- **Sending route summaries**—Routing information advertised out an interface is automatically summarized at major (classful) network address boundaries by RIP, IGRP, and EIGRP. Specifically, this automatic summarization occurs for those routes whose classful network address differs from the major network address of the interface to which the advertisement is being sent. For OSPF, you must configure summarization.

  Route summarization is not always a solution. You would not want to use route summarization if you needed to advertise all networks across a boundary, such as when you have discontiguous networks (discussed in the next section). When using EIGRP and RIPv2, you can disable this automatic summarization.

- **Selecting routes from route summaries**—If more than one entry in the routing table matches a particular destination, the longest prefix match in the routing table is used. Several routes might match one destination, but the longest matching prefix is used.

  For example, if a routing table has the paths shown in Figure 2-8, packets addressed to destination 172.16.5.99 would be routed through the 172.16.5.0/24 path because that address has the longest match with the destination address.

**Figure 2-8**  *Routers Will Use the Longest Match When Selecting a Route*

| 172.16.5.33 | /32 | Host |
| 172.16.5.32 | /27 | Subnet |
| 172.16.5.0 | /24 | Network |
| 172.16.0.0 | /16 | Block of networks |
| 0.0.0.0 | /0 | Default |

---

**NOTE**

When running classful protocols (RIPv1 and IGRP), you must enable **ip classless** if you want the router to select a default route when it must route to an unknown subnet of a network for which it knows some subnets. For example, consider a router's routing table that has entries for subnets 10.5.0.0/16 and 10.6.0.0/16, and a default route of 0.0.0.0. If a packet arrives for a destination on the 10.7.0.0/16 subnet, and if **ip classless** is not enabled, then the packet will be dropped. Classful protocols assume that if they know some of the subnets of network 10.0.0.0, then they must know all the existing subnets of that network. Enabling **ip classless** indicates to the router that it should follow the best supernet route or the default route for unknown subnets of known networks, as well as for unknown networks.

Note that **ip classless** is enabled by default in Release 12.0 of the Cisco IOS software; in previous releases, it is disabled by default.

---

## Summarizing Routes in a Discontiguous Network

Discontiguous subnets are subnets of the same major network that are separated by a different major network.

Recall that RIP, IGRP, and EIGRP summarize automatically at network boundaries. This behavior, which cannot be changed with RIPv1 and IGRP, has important results:

- Subnets are not advertised to a different major network.
- Discontiguous subnets are not visible to each other.

In the example shown in Figure 2-9, Routers A and B do not advertise the 172.16.5.0 255.255.255.0 and 172.16.6.0 255.255.255.0 subnets because RIPv1 cannot advertise subnets across a different major network; both Router A and Router B advertise 172.16.0.0. This leads to confusion when routing across network 192.168.14.0. For example, Router C receives routes about 172.16.0.0 from two different directions; therefore, it might not make a correct routing decision.

**Figure 2-9**    *Classful Routing Protocols Do Not Support Discontiguous Subnets*

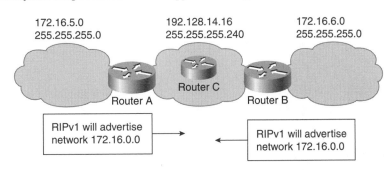

This situation can be resolved by using RIPv2, OSPF, or EIGRP and not using summarization because the subnet routes would be advertised with their actual subnet masks. Advertisements are configurable when using OSPF and EIGRP, but not RIPv2.

The Cisco IOS software also provides an IP unnumbered feature that permits noncontiguous subnets to be separated by an unnumbered link; this feature is discussed in the section "Using IP Unnumbered Serial Interfaces," later in this chapter.

## Route Summarization Cautions in Discontiguous Networks

Be careful when using route summarization in a network that has discontiguous subnets, or if not all the summarized subnets are reachable via the advertising router. If a summarized route indicates that certain subnets are reachable via a router, when those subnets actually are discontiguous or are not reachable via that router, the network may have problems similar to those shown in Figure 2-9 for a RIPv1 network. For example, in Figure 2-10, EIGRP is being used, and both Router A and Router B are advertising a summarized route to 172.16.0.0/16. Therefore, Router C receives two routes to 172.16.0.0/16 and has no knowledge of which subnets are attached to which router.

**Figure 2-10** *Care Is Also Needed When Summarizing with Classless Routing Protocols*

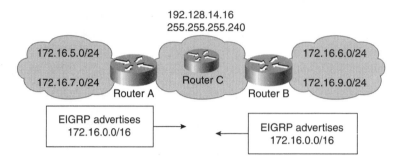

This problem can be resolved if you are using a classless routing protocol because automatic summarization can be turned off (if it is on by default). Because routers running classless routing protocols use the longest prefix match when selecting a route from the routing table, if one of the routers advertised without summarizing, other routers would see subnet routes as well as the summary route. The other routers could then select the longest prefix match and follow the correct path. For example, in Figure 2-10, if Router A continues to summarize to 172.16.0.0/16, and Router B was configured to not summarize, then Router C would receive explicit routes for 172.16.6.0/24 and 172.16.9.0/24 along with the summarized route to 172.16.0.0/16. All traffic for Router B's subnets would then be sent to Router B, while all other traffic for the 172.16.0.0 network would be sent to Router A. This would be true for any other classless protocol.

## Route Summarization Summary

Table 2-2 provides a summary of the route summarization support available in the various IP routing protocols discussed.

**Table 2-2** *Routing Protocol Route Summarization Support*

| Protocol | Automatic Summarization at Classful Network Boundary? | Capability to Turn Off Automatic Summarization? | Capability to Summarize at Other Than Classful Network Boundary? |
|---|---|---|---|
| RIPv1 | Yes | No | No |
| RIPv2 | Yes | Yes | No |
| IGRP | Yes | No | No |
| EIGRP | Yes | Yes | Yes |
| OSPF | No | — | Yes |

# Classless Interdomain Routing

CIDR is a mechanism developed to help alleviate the problem of exhaustion of IP addresses and growth of routing tables. The idea behind CIDR is that blocks of multiple Class C addresses can be combined, or aggregated, to create a larger classless set of IP addresses (that is, with more hosts allowed). Blocks of Class C network numbers are allocated to each network service provider. Organizations using the network service provider for Internet connectivity are allocated subsets of the service provider's address space as required.

These multiple Class C addresses can then be summarized in routing tables, resulting in fewer route advertisements.

CIDR is described further in RFCs 1518 and 1519. RFC 2050, "Internet Registry IP Allocation Guidelines," specifies guidelines for the allocation of IP addresses.

## CIDR Example

Figure 2-11 shows an example of CIDR and route summarization. The Class C network addresses 192.168.8.0/24 through 192.168.15.0/24 are being used and are being advertised to the ISP router. When the ISP router advertises the networks available, it can summarize these into one route instead of separately advertising the eight Class C networks. By advertising 192.168.8.0/21, the ISP router indicates that it can get to all destination addresses that have the first 21 bits the same as the first 21 bits of the address 192.168.8.0.

**Figure 2-11**  *CIDR Allows a Router to Summarize Multiple Class C Addresses*

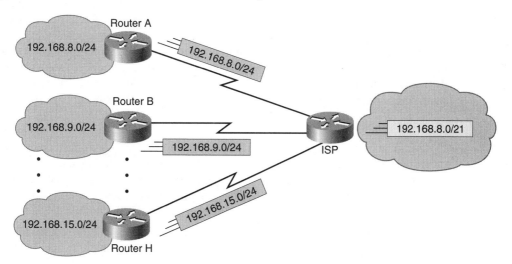

| | |
|---|---|
| **NOTE** | The mechanism used to calculate the summary route to advertise is the same as shown in the "Route Summarization" section, earlier in this chapter. The Class C network addresses 192.168.8.0/24 through 192.168.15.0/24 are being used and are being advertised to the ISP router. To summarize these addresses, find the common bits as shown here: |

192.168.8.0    192.168.**00001**000.00000000
192.168.9.0    192.168.**00001**001.00000000
192.168.10.0   192.168.**00001**010.00000000
. . .
192.168.14.0   192.168.**00001**110.00000000
192.168.15.0   192.168.**00001**111.00000000

The route 192.168.00001*xxx.xxxxxxxx* or 192.168.8.0/21 (also written as 192.168.8.0 255.255.248.0) summarizes these eight routes.

# Using IP Unnumbered Serial Interfaces

To enable IP processing on a serial interface without assigning an explicit IP address to the interface, use the **ip unnumbered** *type number* interface configuration command. In the command, *type number* indicates the type and number of another interface on which the router has an assigned IP address. It cannot be another unnumbered interface. To disable the IP processing on the interface, use the **no** form of this command.

Whenever the unnumbered interface generates a packet (for example, for a routing update), it uses the address of the specified interface as the source address of the IP packet. The router also uses the address of the specified interface in determining which routing processes are sending updates over the unnumbered interface. (For example, if the **network** command configured for the RIP routing protocol indicates that network 10.0.0.0 is running RIP, then all interfaces with an address in network 10.0.0.0 will be running RIP, as will all unnumbered interfaces that specify an interface that has an address in network 10.0.0.0.)

Restrictions on unnumbered interfaces include the following:

- Serial interfaces using High-Level Data Link Control (HDLC); Point-to-Point Protocol (PPP); Link Access Procedure, Balanced (LAPB); and Frame Relay encapsulations, as well as Serial Line Internet Protocol (SLIP) and tunnel interfaces can be unnumbered. It is not possible to use this interface configuration command with X.25 or Switched Multimegabit Data Service (SMDS) interfaces.

- You cannot use the **ping** EXEC command to determine whether the interface is up because the interface has no address. Simple Network Management Protocol (SNMP) can be used to remotely monitor the interface status.

The interface you specify (by the type and number parameters) must be enabled; in other words, it must be listed as up in the **show interfaces** command display.

**NOTE**    Using an unnumbered serial line between different major networks requires special care. If at each end of the link different major networks are assigned to the interfaces you specified as unnumbered, then any routing protocol running across the serial line must not advertise subnet information. (For example, Router A and Router B are connected via an unnumbered serial line. Router A has all its interfaces in network 172.16.0.0, and therefore the serial line specifies an interface in network 172.16.0.0. Router B has all its interfaces in network 172.17.0.0, so the serial line specifies an interface in network 172.17.0.0. If OSPF is configured to run on the unnumbered serial line, it must be configured to summarize the subnet information and not send it across the link.)

In the example network in Figure 2-12, interface Serial 0 uses Ethernet 0's address. The configuration for the router in this figure is provided in Example 2-1.

**Figure 2-12**  *An Example of Using the ip unnumbered Command*

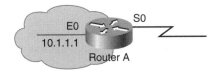

**Example 2-1**  *Configuration of the Router in Figure 2-12*

```
interface Ethernet0
 ip address 10.1.1.1 255.255.255.0
!
interface Serial0
 ip unnumbered Ethernet0
```

A loopback interface is often used as the interface from which unnumbered interfaces get their IP address. Loopback interfaces are virtual interfaces, so after they are defined, they are always active and cannot go down like a real interface.

# Using Helper Addresses

This section covers the use of helper addresses to forward selected broadcasts beyond a router. Routers do not forward broadcasts by default. By doing this, routers prevent broadcast storms—a situation in which a single broadcast triggers an onslaught of other broadcasts, ultimately leading to a disruption in network services. Large, flat networks are notorious for their bouts of broadcast storms.

However, a client might need to reach a server and might not know the server's address. In this situation, the client broadcasts to find the server. If there is a router between the client and server, the broadcast will not get through, by default. Helper addresses facilitate connectivity by forwarding these broadcasts directly to the target server.

Client hosts interact with a variety of network-support servers such as a Domain Name System (DNS) server, a Bootstrap protocol (BOOTP)/Dynamic Host Configuration Protocol (DHCP) server, or a Trivial File Transfer Protocol (TFTP) server. At startup time, the clients often do not know the IP address of the server, so they send broadcast packets to find it. Sometimes the clients do not know their own IP address, so they use BOOTP or DHCP to obtain it. If the client and server are on the same network, the server will respond to the client's broadcast request. From these replies, the client can glean the IP address of the server and use it in subsequent communication.

However, the server might not be on the same physical medium as the client, as shown in Figure 2-13. Remember that a destination IP address of 255.255.255.255 is sent in a link-layer broadcast (FFFFFFFFFFFF). By default, routers will never forward such broadcasts, and you would not want them to. A primary reason for implementing routers is to localize broadcast traffic. However, you do want clients to be capable of reaching the appropriate servers. Use helper addresses for this purpose.

**Figure 2-13**   *Routers Do Not Forward Broadcasts by Default*

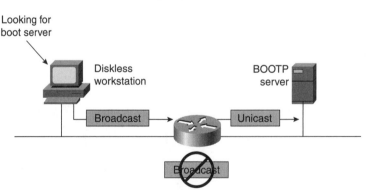

Helper address commands change destination broadcasts addresses to a unicast address (or a directed broadcast—a local broadcast within a particular subnet) so that the broadcast message can be routed to a specific destination rather than everywhere. It is important to note that every broadcast (with the default port numbers, or with the port numbers that you specify) gets sent to all helper addresses, regardless of whether the server will actually be capable of helping for a certain port.

**NOTE**    Helper addresses assist devices in locating necessary services within the network. It is more efficient administratively to allow a client device to broadcast for a service than to hard-code (in the client machines) the IP addresses for devices that may not always be online and available.

## Server Location

It is important to consider how you want to get the broadcast, in a controlled way, to the appropriate servers. Such considerations depend on the location of the servers. In practice, server location is implemented in several ways, as shown in Figure 2-14:

- **A single server on a single remote medium**—Such a medium may be directly connected to the router that blocks the broadcast, or it might be several routing hops away. In any case, the all-ones broadcast needs to be handled at the first router it encounters and then sent to the server.

- **Multiple servers on a single remote medium, sometimes called a server farm**—Different kinds of servers (for example, DNS and TFTP servers used in the automatic install process [AutoInstall] for Cisco routers), could exist on the same medium. Or, perhaps redundant servers of the same type are installed on the same medium. In either case, a directed broadcast can be sent on the server farm subnet so that the multiple devices can see it.

- **Multiple servers on multiple remote media**—In this case, for example, a secondary DNS server could exist on one subnet and the primary DNS server could exist on another subnet. For fault tolerance, client requests need to reach both servers.

**NOTE**    In Cisco IOS Release 12.0 and later, the **no ip directed-broadcast** command is on by default, which means that all received IP directed broadcasts are dropped. To enable the translation of directed broadcasts to physical broadcasts, use the **ip directed broadcast** interface configuration command.

**Figure 2-14** *Servers May Be in Many Locations*

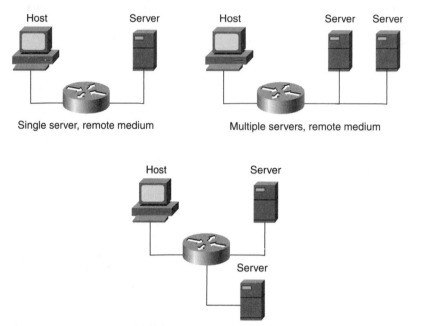

IP Helper Address Configuration

Use the **ip helper-address** *address* interface configuration command to configure an interface on which broadcasts are expected or can be received. In the command, *address* indicates the destination address to be used when forwarding User Datagram Protocol (UDP) broadcasts. The specified address can be the unicast address of a remote server or a directed broadcast address.

If an **ip helper-address** command is defined, forwarding for eight default UDP ports is enabled automatically. The default ports are TFTP (port 69), DNS (port 53), Time (port 37), Network Basic Input/Output System (NetBIOS) name service (port 137), NetBIOS datagram service (port 138), BOOTP server (port 67), BOOTP client (port 68), and Terminal Access Controller Access Control System (TACACS) (port 49).

These same eight UDP ports are automatically forwarded if you define an **ip helper-address** and the **ip forward-protocol udp** command with the same ports specified.

Use the **ip forward-protocol** {**udp** [*port*] | **nd** | **sdns**} global configuration command to specify which type of broadcast packets are forwarded, as described in Table 2-3.

**Table 2-3**    *ip forward-protocol Command Description*

| ip forward-protocol Command | Description |
|---|---|
| **udp** | UDP—the transport layer protocol |
| *port* | (Optional) When **udp** is specified, UDP destination port numbers or port names may be specified |
| **nd** | Network disk; an older protocol used by diskless Sun workstations |
| **sdns** | Network Security Protocol |

To forward only one UDP port (whether a default-forwarded port, another UDP port, or a custom port), you must use **ip forward-protocol udp** *port* command for the ports that you want to forward, and then specify **no ip forward-protocol udp** *port* for the default ports that you do *not* want forwarded.

| NOTE | There is no easy way to forward all UDP broadcasts; you would need to specify all the UDP ports in the **ip forward-protocol** command. |
|---|---|
| | DHCP and BOOTP use the same port—port 68—but it is always referred to as the BOOTP port. |

## IP Helper Address Examples

In the example shown in Figure 2-15, a single server is on a single remote medium. A helper address allows the router to perform the desired function of forwarding a client request to a server.

**Figure 2-15**    *IP Helper Address with a Single Server on a Remote Medium*

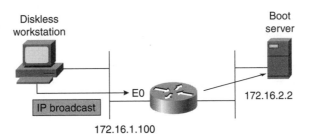

The configuration for the router in this example is shown in Example 2-2.

**Example 2-2** *Configuration of the Router in Figure 2-15*

```
interface ethernet 0
    ip address 172.16.1.100 255.255.255.0
    ip helper-address 172.16.2.2
!
ip forward-protocol udp 3000
no ip forward-protocol udp tftp
```

The **ip helper-address** command must be placed on the router interface that receives the original client broadcast. It causes the router to convert the 255.255.255.255 (all-ones) broadcast to a unicast or a directed broadcast. In Example 2-2, the **ip helper-address** command placed on interface Ethernet 0 would cause the default eight UDP broadcasts sent by all hosts to be converted into unicasts with a destination address of the boot server, 172.16.2.2. These unicasts would then be forwarded to the boot server.

You may not want to forward all default UDP broadcasts to the server, but only those of a protocol type supported on that server. To do this, use the **ip forward-protocol** command followed by the keyword **udp** and a port number or protocol name for those UDP broadcasts that are not automatically forwarded. Turn off any automatically forwarded ports with the **no ip forward-protocol udp** *port* or *port name* command. In Example 2-2, in addition to the default UDP broadcasts, the configuration has enabled the forwarding of a custom application using UDP port 3000. Because the server does not support TFTP requests, the automatic forwarding of TFTP, port 69, is disabled.

---

**NOTE**     Additional helper addresses are not required on any routers in the middle of a series of routers in the path from the client to the server. This is because the first router has modified the destination address. The modification of the destination address from broadcast to unicast or directed broadcast allows the packet to be routed—over several hops, if necessary—to its final destination.

---

To handle forwarding broadcasts to multiple servers on the same remote medium, you can use a directed broadcast into the subnet instead of using several unicast helper addresses. The most general case is where multiple servers are located on different remote media. This case can be handled by a combination of multiple helper statements, some with a unicast and some with a directed-broadcast address. An example of this case is shown in Figure 2-16; the configuration for the router in this figure is shown in Example 2-3.

**Figure 2-16**  *IP Helper Address With Multiple Servers on a Remote Medium*

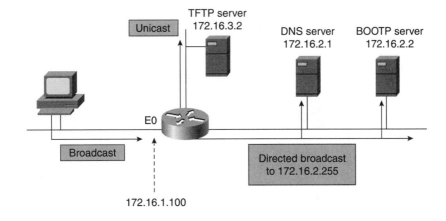

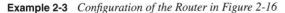

**Example 2-3**  *Configuration of the Router in Figure 2-16*

```
interface ethernet 0
  ip address 172.16.1.100 255.255.255.0
  ip helper-address 172.16.2.255
  ip helper-address 172.16.3.2
```

As Example 2-3 illustrates, a combination of helper addresses can be used on the same interface. Broadcasts arriving on Ethernet 0 will be forwarded to all servers on the 172.16.2.0 subnet and to the designated server (172.16.3.2) on the 172.16.3.0 subnet.

**NOTE**  All broadcast traffic for the specified UDP ports (the default ports in Example 2-3) will be forwarded to both the 172.16.2.0 subnet and the 172.16.3.2 server. This will occur even for traffic that cannot be handled by the servers on that subnet. For example, DNS requests will be sent to the 172.16.3.2 TFTP server. Assuming that the DNS service is not enabled on the 172.16.3.2 device, this DNS request will be ignored and an ICMP "port unreachable" message will be generated. This sequence consumes bandwidth on the network.

# Summary

In this chapter, you learned about IP addressing issues—address exhaustion and routing table growth—and solutions to these problems.

Hierarchical addressing can result in smaller routing tables and efficient allocation of addresses.

Using VLSMs can result in even more efficient use of IP addresses by allowing the use of multiple subnet masks within the same major network. VLSM addresses can then be summarized to reduce the routing table size.

Route summarization is a method of representing a series of network numbers in a single summary address. Summarizing of discontiguous subnets—subnets of the same major network that are separated by a different major network—requires care. Classful routing protocols do not support discontiguous subnets. Classless routing protocols do support discontiguous subnets.

CIDR is a solution developed to allow multiple Class C addresses to be combined into a larger classless set of IP addresses.

The use of an unnumbered interface in IP allows IP processing on a serial interface without using an explicit IP address.

Helper addresses facilitate connectivity on networks by forwarding selected broadcasts to specified servers.

The next section of this book is Part II, "Scalable Routing Protocols." Part II discusses details of the OSPF, EIGRP, and BGP routing protocols.

# Review Questions

Answer the following questions, and then refer to Appendix G, "Answers to the Review Questions," for the answers.

**1** You are in charge of the network in the following figure. It consists of 5 LANs with 25 users on each LAN, and 5 serial links. You have been assigned the IP address 192.168.49.0/24 to allocate addressing for all links.

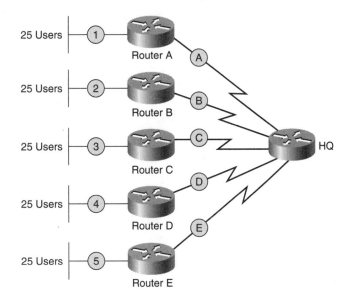

Write the addresses that you would assign to each of the LANs and the serial links in the following spaces.

| LAN 1 | |
|---|---|
| LAN 2 | |
| LAN 3 | |
| LAN 4 | |
| LAN 5 | |
| WAN A | |
| WAN B | |
| WAN C | |
| WAN D | |
| WAN E | |

2   The following figure shows a network with subnets of the 172.16.0.0 network
    configured. Indicate where route summarization can occur in this network and what
    the summarized addresses would be in the spaces that follow.

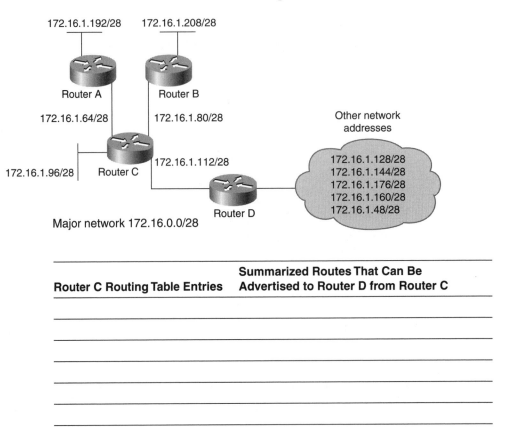

| Router C Routing Table Entries | Summarized Routes That Can Be Advertised to Router D from Router C |
|---|---|
| | |
| | |
| | |
| | |
| | |
| | |

**3** The following figure shows a network with subnets of the 172.16.0.0 network configured. Indicate where route summarization can occur in this network and what the summarized address would be in the spaces that follow.

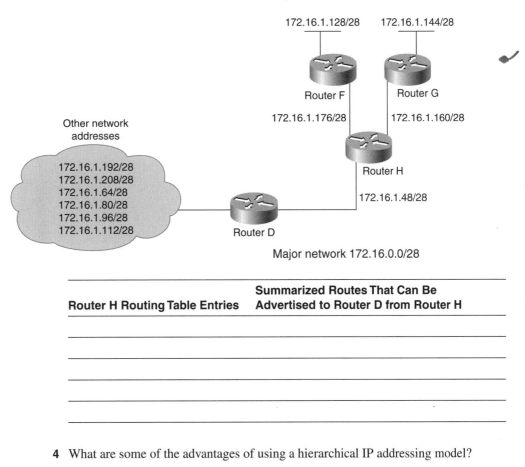

172.16.1.128/28          172.16.1.144/28

Router F          Router G

Other network addresses

172.16.1.176/28          172.16.1.160/28

172.16.1.192/28
172.16.1.208/28
172.16.1.64/28
172.16.1.80/28
172.16.1.96/28
172.16.1.112/28

Router H

172.16.1.48/28

Router D

Major network 172.16.0.0/28

| Router H Routing Table Entries | Summarized Routes That Can Be Advertised to Router D from Router H |
| --- | --- |
|  |  |
|  |  |
|  |  |
|  |  |
|  |  |

**4** What are some of the advantages of using a hierarchical IP addressing model?

**5** Given an address with a prefix of /20, how many additional subnets are gained when subnetting with a prefix of /28?

**6** When selecting a route, which prefix match is used?

# PART II

# Scalable Routing Protocols

This chapter introduces you to the Open Shortest Path First (OSPF) routing protocol. This chapter includes the following sections:

- OSPF Overview
- OSPF Terminology
- OSPF Operation in a Broadcast Multiaccess Topology
- OSPF Operation in a Point-to-Point Topology
- OSPF Operation in an NBMA Topology
- Configuring OSPF in a Single Area
- Verifying OSPF Operation
- Case Study: OSPF in a Single Area
- Summary
- Configuration Exercise #1: Configuring OSPF for a Single Area
- Configuration Exercise #2: Configuring OSPF for a Single Area in an NBMA Environment
- Answers to Configuration Exercise #1: Configuring OSPF for a Single Area
- Answers to Configuration Exercise #2: Configuring OSPF for a Single Area in an NBMA Environment
- Review Questions

CHAPTER 3

# Configuring OSPF in a Single Area

This chapter covers the use, operation, configuration, and verification of OSPF in a single area. After you complete this chapter, you will be able to enumerate the main features of OSPF using the proper related terminology. You will also be able to describe the different modes of operation for both LAN and WAN environments. Finally, you will be able to configure and verify OSPF operations within a single area.

**NOTE**  OSPF was written for large and growing networks. It enables you to segregate the internetwork into smaller areas. This chapter discusses how OSPF operates within an area. Chapter 4, "Interconnecting Multiple OSPF Areas," discusses how the areas interoperate with each other.

## OSPF Overview

OSPF is a link-state technology, as opposed to a distance vector technology such as Routing Information Protocol (RIP). The OSPF protocol performs the two primary functions of every routing protocol algorithm: path selection and path switching. The Internet Engineering Task Force (IETF) developed OSPF in 1988. The most recent version, known as OSPF version 2, is described in RFC 2328. OSPF is an Interior Gateway Protocol (IGP), which means that it distributes routing information between routers belonging to the same autonomous system. OSPF was written to address the needs of large, scalable internetworks that RIP could not. OSPF addresses the following issues:

- **Speed of convergence**—In large networks, RIP convergence can take several minutes as the routing algorithm goes through a holddown and route-aging period. With OSPF, convergence is faster than with RIP because routing changes are flooded immediately and are computed in parallel.

- **Support for variable-length subnet masks (VLSMs)**—OSPF supports subnet masking and VLSMs, as opposed to RIPv1, which supports only fixed-length subnet masking (FLSM). (Note that RIPv2 does support VLSMs.)

- **Network reachability**—A RIP network that spans more than 15 hops (15 routers) is considered unreachable. OSPF has virtually no reachability limitations.

- **Use of bandwidth**—RIP broadcasts complete routing tables to all neighbors every 30 seconds. This operation is especially problematic over slower WAN links. OSPF multicasts link-state updates and sends these updates only when there is a change in the network. (Note that OSPF sends updates every 30 minutes to ensure that all routers are synchronized.)

- **Method for path selection**—RIP has no concept of network delays (interface delays) and link costs. With RIP, routing decisions are based purely on hop count, which could lead to suboptimal path selection so that a longer path (in terms of hop count) might have a higher aggregate link bandwidth and shorter delays. OSPF uses a cost value, which for Cisco routers is based on the speed of the connection. As with RIP and IGRP, OSPF also provides support for equal-cost multipaths.

Note that although OSPF was written for large networks, implementing it requires proper design and planning. This is especially important if your network has more than 50 routers.

OSPF information is carried inside IP packets, using protocol number 89 (decimal), as shown in Figure 3-1.

**Figure 3-1** *OSPF in an IP Packet*

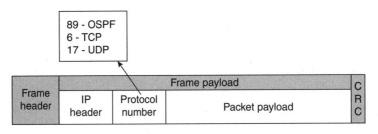

# OSPF Terminology

You will want to be familiar with the following terms related to link-state technology and OSPF before proceeding with the rest of the chapter. These terms are represented in Figure 3-2:

- **Interface**—The connection between the router and one of its attached networks. An interface is sometimes referred to as a *link* in OSPF literature.

- **Link state**—The status of a link between two routers—that is, a router's interface and its relationship to its neighboring routers. The link states are advertised to other routers in special packets called link-state advertisements (LSAs).

- **Cost**—The value assigned to a link. Rather than hops, link-state protocols assign a cost to a link; for OSPF on Cisco routers, the cost is based on the speed of the media. A cost is associated with the output side of each router interface, referred to as interface output cost.

- **Autonomous system**—A group of routers exchanging routing information using a common routing protocol.

- **Area**—A collection of networks and routers that have the same area identification. Each router within an area has the same link-state information. A router within an area is an internal router.

- **Neighbors**—Two routers that have interfaces on a common network. A neighbor relationship is usually discovered and maintained by the Hello protocol.

- **Hello**—Protocol used by OSPF to establish and maintain neighbor relationships.

- **Neighborship database**—A listing of all the neighbors to which a router has established bidirectional communication.

- **Link-state database (also known as a topology database)**—A list of link-state entries of all other routers in the network. It shows the network topology. All routers within an area have identical link-state databases. The link-state database is pieced together from LSAs generated by routers.

- **Routing table (also known as the forwarding database)**—Generated when the shortest path first (SPF) algorithm (also known as the Dijkstra algorithm) is run on the link-state database. The content of each OSPF routing table is unique.

**Figure 3-2** *Link-State and OSPF Components*

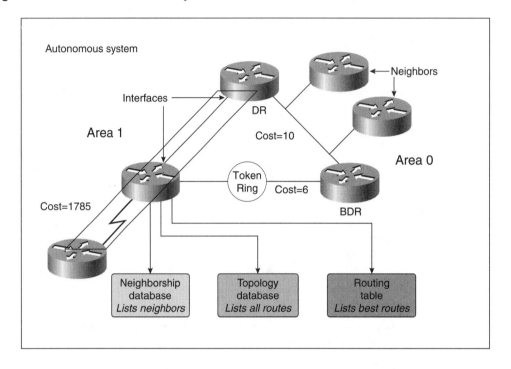

OSPF can run over broadcast networks or over nonbroadcast networks. The topology of a network has an impact on how neighborship is created. Figure 3-3 illustrates the following topologies found in OSPF:

- **Broadcast multiaccess topologies**—Networks supporting more than two routers attached together, with the capability of addressing a single physical message (a broadcast) to all the attached routers. An Ethernet segment is an example of a broadcast multiaccess network.

- **Point-to-point topologies**—A network that joins a single pair of routers. A T1 dedicated serial line is an example of a point-to-point network.

- **Nonbroadcast multiaccess (NBMA) topologies**—Networks supporting many (more than two) routers, but having no broadcast capability. Frame Relay and X.25 are examples of nonbroadcast multiaccess networks.

**Figure 3-3**   *OSPF Topologies*

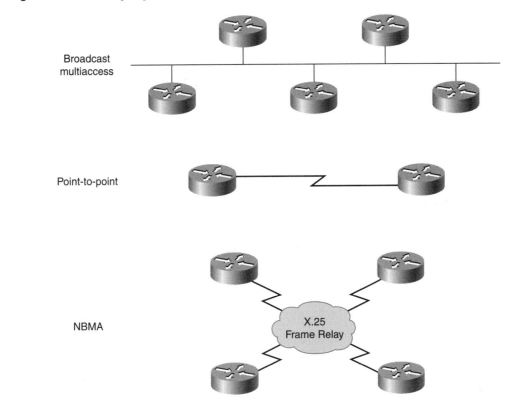

# OSPF Operation in a Broadcast Multiaccess Topology

This section covers OSPF behavior with a broadcast multiaccess topology. The other topologies are covered later in this chapter.

Because OSPF routing is dependent on the status of a link between two routers, neighbor routers must recognize each other on the network before they can share information. This process is done using the Hello protocol. The Hello protocol is responsible for establishing and maintaining neighbor relationships. It ensures that the communication between neighbors is bidirectional—a router sees itself listed in the hello packet that it receives from a neighbor.

Hello packets are sent out periodically from each interface participating in OSPF using IP multicast address 224.0.0.5, which is also known as the AllSPFRouter address.

**OSPF Multicast and MAC Addresses**

OSPF sends all advertisements using multicast addressing. Except for Token Ring, the multicast IP addresses are mapped to MAC-level multicast addresses. The MAC address used for 224.0.0.5 is 010005E 0000005, and the MAC address for 244.0.0.6 is 010005E 0000006. Cisco maps Token Ring multicast IP addressses to MAC-level broadcast addresses.

The information contained in a hello packet, shown in Figure 3-4, is as follows:

- **Router ID**—This 32-bit number uniquely identifies the router within an autonomous system. The highest IP address on an active interface is chosen by default. For example, IP address 172.16.12.1 would be chosen over 172.16.1.1. This identification is important in establishing neighbor relationships and coordinating messages between copies of the SPF algorithm running in the network. Also, the router ID is used to break ties during the designated router (DR) and backup designated router (BDR) election process if the priority values are equal. (DR and BDR are discussed later in this chapter.)

- **Hello and dead intervals**—The hello interval specifies the frequency in seconds that a router sends hellos (10 seconds is the default on multiaccess networks). The dead interval is the time in seconds that a router waits to hear from a neighbor before declaring the neighbor router down (this is four times the hello interval, by default). These timers must be the same on neighboring routers.

- **Neighbors**—These are the neighbors with which a bidirectional communication has been established. Bidirectional communication is indicated when the router sees itself listed in the neighbor's hello packet. A neighbor might have multiple neighbors while connecting to broadcast and NBMA topologies.

- **Area-ID**—To communicate, two routers must share a common segment. Also, their interfaces must belong to the same area on that segment (they must also share the same subnet number and mask). These routers will all have the same link-state information.

- **Router priority**—This 8-bit number indicates the priority of this router when selecting a DR and a BDR. The higher the router priority, the greater the chances are that it will be elected the DR or the BDR. Because each multiaccess link has its own election process, a router priority for that link is set at the interface configuration mode.

- **DR and BDR IP addresses**—These are the IP addresses of the DR and BDR for the specific network, if known (covered in the next section).

- **Authentication password**—If authentication is enabled, two routers must exchange the same password. Authentication does not have to be set, but if it is set, all peer routers must have the same password.
- **Stub area flag**—A stub area is a special area that is discussed in Chapter 4. Two routers must agree on the stub area flag in the hello packets.

**Figure 3-4**  *Contents of an OSPF Hello Packet*

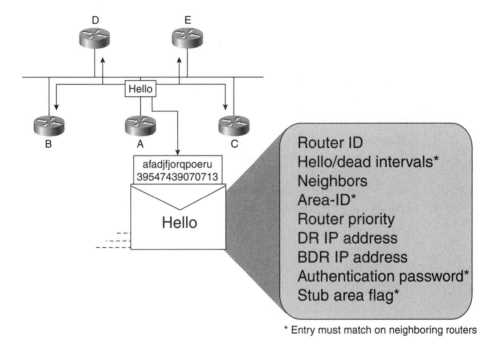

\* Entry must match on neighboring routers

---

### OSPF Packet Header

The following descriptions summarize the header fields of an OSPF packet, as illustrated in Figure 3-5.

- **Version number**—Identifies the OSPF version used.
- **Type**—Identifies the OSPF packet type as one of the following:
    — Hello: Establishes and maintains neighbor relationships.
    — Database description: Describes the contents of the topological database. These messages are exchanged when an adjacency is initialized. (Adjacency is discussed in the following section.)

— Link-state request: Requests portions of the topological database from neighbor routers. These messages are exchanged after a router discovers (by examining database description packets) that parts of its topological database are out-of-date.

— Link-state update: Responds to a link-state request packet. These messages are also used for the regular dispersal of LSAs. Several LSAs can be included within a single link-state update packet.

— Link-state acknowledgment: Acknowledges link-state update packets.

- **Packet length**—Identifies the packet length, including the OSPF header, in bytes.
- **Router ID**—Identifies the source of the packet.
- **Area ID**—Identifies the area to which the packet belongs. All OSPF packets are associated with a single area.
- **Checksum**—Checks the entire packet contents for any damage suffered in transit.
- **Authentication type**—Contains the authentication type. All OSPF protocol exchanges are authenticated. The authentication type is configurable on a per-area basis. Type 0 indicates no authentication. Type 1 indicates a clear-text authentication. Type 2 indicates an MD5 authentication.
- **Authentication**—Contains authentication information.
- **Data**—Contains encapsulated upper-layer information (actual routing information).

**Figure 3-5**  *OSPF Header Format*

| Version number | Type | Packet length | Router ID | Area ID | Checksum | Authentication type | Authentication | Data |
|---|---|---|---|---|---|---|---|---|
| 1 | 1 | 2 | 4 | 4 | 2 | 2 | 8 | Variable |

Field length, in bytes

## Designated Router and Backup Designated Router

The routers on a multiaccess environment, such as an Ethernet segment, must elect a DR and a BDR to represent the network. The BDR does not perform any DR functions when the DR is operating. Instead, it receives all information but allows the DR to perform the forwarding and synchronization tasks. The BDR performs DR tasks only if the DR fails.

The DR and BDR add value to the network in the following ways:

- **Reducing routing update traffic**—The DR and BDR act as a central point of contact for link-state information exchange on a given multiaccess network. Therefore, each router must establish an adjacency with the DR and BDR. Instead of each router exchanging link-state information with every other router on the segment, each router sends the link-state information to the DR and the BDR. The DR represents the multiaccess network in the sense that it sends each router's link-state information to all other routers in the multiaccess network. This flooding process significantly reduces the router-related traffic on a segment.

- **Managing link-state synchronization**—The DR and BDR assure that the other routers on the network have the same link-state information about the internetwork. In this way, the number of routing errors is reduced.

An adjacency is the relationship that exists between a router and its DR and BDR. Adjacent routers will have synchronized link-state databases (as described later in this section). Adjacency is based upon the use of a common media segment, such as two routers connected on the same Ethernet segment. When routers first come up on a network, they perform the hello process (as discussed later in this section) and elect the DR and BDR. The routers then attempt to form adjacencies with the DR and BDR.

---

**NOTE**    After a DR and a BDR are elected, any router added to the network will establish adjacencies only with the DR and the BDR.

---

To elect a DR and a BDR, the routers view each other's priority value during the hello packet exchange process, as shown in Figure 3-6. They then use the following conditions to determine which is elected:

- The router with the highest priority value is the DR.

- The router with the second-highest priority value is the BDR.

- The default for the interface OSPF priority is 1. In case of a tie, the router ID is used. The router with the highest router ID then becomes the DR, and the router with the second-highest router ID then becomes the BDR. (Note that the highest IP address on an active interface is normally used as the router ID, but this can be overridden by configuring an IP address on a loopback interface.)

- A router with a priority set to 0 is ineligible to become a DR or a BDR. A router that is not the DR or the BDR is also referred to as a "Drother."

- If a router with a higher priority value gets added to the network, the DR and BDR do not change. A DR or BDR changes only if one goes down. If the DR goes down, the BDR takes over as the DR, and a new BDR is elected. If the BDR goes down, a new

BDR is elected. To determine whether the DR is down, the BDR sets a timer. This is a reliability feature. If the BDR does not hear the DR forwarding LSAs before the timer expires, then the BDR assumes that the DR is out of service.

**Figure 3-6**    *Election of DR and BDR*

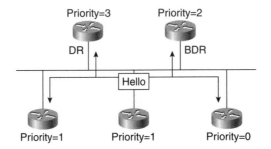

In a multiaccess environment, each network segment will have its own DR and BDR. Therefore, a router that is connected to multiple networks can be a DR on one segment and a regular router on another segment. How neighbors are perceived in other network topologies is discussed later in this chapter in the sections "OSPF Operation in an NBMA Topology" and "OSPF Operation in a Point-to-Point Topology."

Example 3-1 provides sample debug output of the DR/BDR election process performed on an Ethernet segment.

**Example 3-1**    *Broadcast Multiaccess Adjacency Sample **debug** Output*

```
Router#debug ip ospf adj
Ethernet interface coming up: Election
OSPF: 2 Way Communication to 192.168.0.10 on Ethernet0, state 2WAY
OSPF: end of Wait on interface Ethernet0
OSPF: DR/BDR election on Ethernet0
OSPF: Elect BDR 192.168.0.12
OSPF: Elect DR 192.168.0.12
      DR: 192.168.0.12 (Id)    BDR: 192.168.0.12 (Id)
OSPF: Send DBD to 192.168.0.12 on Ethernet0 seq 0x546 opt 0x2 flag 0x7 len 32
<...>
OSPF: DR/BDR election on Ethernet0
OSPF: Elect BDR 192.168.0.11
OSPF: Elect DR 192.168.0.12
      DR: 192.168.0.12 (Id)    BDR: 192.168.0.11 (Id)
```

## OSPF Startup

This section covers the steps involved when routers running OSPF come up on a network.

### Exchange Process

In the first step of OSPF startup, the exchange process takes place using the Hello protocol, as shown in Figure 3-7. The following explains the exchange process, when all routers are coming up on the network at the same time:

**Step 1**   Router A is enabled on the LAN and is in a *down* state because it has not exchanged information with any other router. It begins by sending a hello packet through each of its interfaces participating in OSPF, even though it does not know the identity of any routers, including the DR. The hello packet is sent out using multicast address 224.0.0.5.

**Step 2**   All routers running OSPF receive the hello packet from Router A and add Router A to their list of neighbors. This is the *init* state.

**Step 3**   All routers that received the packet send a unicast reply hello packet to Router A with their corresponding information, as listed in Step 1. The neighbor field includes all other neighboring routers, including Router A.

**Step 4**   When Router A receives these packets, it adds all the routers that had its router ID in their hello packet to its own neighborship database. This is referred to as the *two-way* state. At this point, all routers that have each other in their own list of neighbors have established bidirectional communication.

**Step 5**   The routers determine who the DR and BDR will be, using the process described earlier. This process must occur before routers can begin exchanging link-state information.

**Step 6**   Periodically (every 10 seconds, by default) the routers within a network exchange hello packets to ensure that communication is still working. The hello updates include the DR, the BDR, and the list of routers whose hello packets have been received by the router. Remember that *received* means that the receiving router saw its own router ID as one of the entries in the received hello packet.

**NOTE**   No election will be declared if a new router with a better router ID value joins the multiaccess network.

**Figure 3-7** *OSPF Exchange Process*

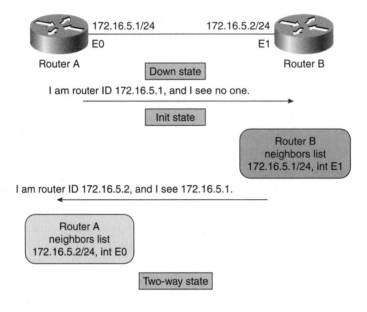

## Discovering Routes

When the DR and BDR have been elected, the routers are considered to be in the *exstart* state and are ready to discover the link-state information about the internetwork and create their link-state databases. The process used to discover the network routes is called the exchange protocol and is performed to get the routers to a *full* state of communication. The first step in this protocol is for the DR and the BDR to establish adjacencies with each of the other routers. When adjacent routers are in a full state, they do not redo the exchange protocol unless the full state changes.

The exchange protocol, as illustrated in Figure 3-8, operates as follows:

**Step 1** In the *exstart* state, the DR and the BDR establish adjacencies with each router in the network. During this process, a master-slave relationship is created between each router and its adjacent DR and BDR. The router that has the higher router ID acts as the master.

Note that link-state information is exchanged and synchronized only between the DR and BDR and the routers to which they have established adjacencies because having the DR represent the network in this capacity reduces the amount of routing update traffic.

**Step 2**    The master and slave routers exchange one or more database description packets (DBDs, sometimes referred to as DDPs). The routers are in the *exchange* state.

A DBD includes the LSA headers (summary) information of the LSA entries that appear in the master router's link-state database. The entries can be about a link or about a network (there are different types of LSAs; these are discussed in Chapter 4). Each LSA header includes such things as a link-state type, the address of the advertising router, and the LSA sequence number. The LSA sequence number is the way a router determines the newness of the received link-state information. The DBD also includes a DBD sequence number to ensure that all the DBDs are received in the database synchronization process. The master defines the DBD sequence numbers.

**Step 3**    When the slave router receives the DBD, it does the following:

— Acknowledges the receipt of the DBD by echoing the DBD sequence numbers in a link-state acknowledgment (LSAck) packet.

— Compares the information it received with the information it has by checking the LSA sequence number in the LSA header. If the DBD has a more up-to-date link-state entry, the slave router sends a link-state request (LSR) to the master router.

— The master router responds with the complete information about the requested entry in a link-state update (LSU) packet. Again, the slave router sends an LSAck when the LSU is received. The process of sending LSRs is referred to as the *loading* state.

**Step 4**    All routers add the new link-state entries into their link-state database.

**Step 5**    When all LSRs have been satisfied for a given router, the adjacent routers are considered synchronized and in a *full* state. The routers must be in a full state before they can route traffic. At this point, the routers should all have identical link-state databases.

# Choosing Routes

When a router has a complete link-state database, it is ready to create its routing table so that it can route traffic, as shown in Figure 3-9. Recall that distance vector protocols such as RIP select the best route to a destination based on a hop-count metric using the Bellman-Ford algorithm. However, link-state protocols use a cost metric to determine the best path to a destination.

**Figure 3-8** *Discovering Routes with OSPF*

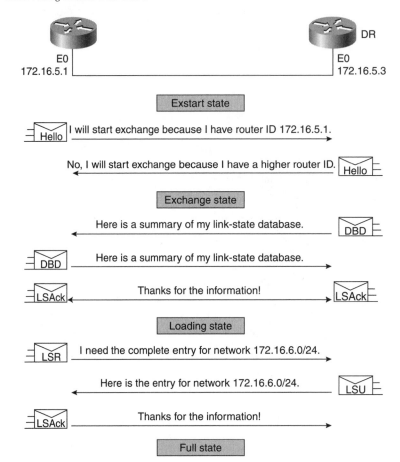

**Figure 3-9**    *Choosing the Best Route to be Inserted in the Routing Table*

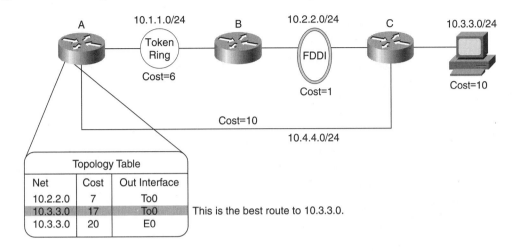

On Cisco routers, the default cost metric is based on media bandwidth. For example, 10-Mbps Ethernet has a lower cost than a 56-kbps line because it is faster.

To calculate the lowest cost to a destination, link-state protocols such as OSPF use the Dijkstra algorithm. Using its link-state database as input, a router runs the Dijkstra algorithm, thus building its routing table step-by-step. In simple terms, the algorithm adds up the total costs between the local router (the root) and each destination network. If there are multiple paths to a destination, the lowest-cost path is preferred. Note that OSPF keeps up to six equal-cost route entries in the routing table for load balancing.

---

### OSPF and Load Balancing

By default, four equally good routes to the same destination are kept in the routing table for load balancing. However, with the **maximum-paths** router configuration command, this value can be increased to up to six equally good routes to the same destination.

---

Sometimes a link, such as a serial line, will go up and down rapidly (called *flapping*), or a link-state change may affect another series of links. In these situations, a series of LSUs could be generated, which would cause routers to repeatedly recompute a new routing table. This flapping could be so serious that the routers would never converge. To minimize this problem, each time an LSU is received, the router waits for a period of time before recalculating its routing table. The default for this time is 5 seconds. The **timers spf** *spf-delay spf-holdtime* router configuration command in the Cisco IOS software allows this value and the minimum time between two consecutive SPF calculations (which has a default of 10 seconds) to be configured.

Refer to the OSPF version 2 RFC 2328 for a detailed description of the Dijkstra algorithm.

## Maintaining Routing Information

In a link-state routing environment, it is very important for all routers' topological databases to stay synchronized. When there is a change in a link state, the routers use a flooding process to notify the other routers in the network of the change, as shown in Figure 3-10. Link-state update packets provide the mechanism for flooding LSAs.

**Figure 3-10** *Link-State Updates Inform Routers of Topology Changes*

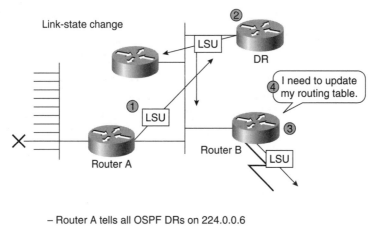

– Router A tells all OSPF DRs on 224.0.0.6
– DR tells others on 224.0.0.5

---

**NOTE**    Although not shown in Figure 3-10, all LSUs are acknowledged.

---

The flooding process on a multiaccess link is as follows:

**Step 1**    A router notices a change in a link state and multicasts an LSU packet that includes the updated LSA entry to 224.0.0.6, which is the address of all OSPF DRs and BDRs. An LSU packet may contain several distinct LSAs.

**Step 2**   The DR acknowledges the receipt of the change and floods the LSU to others on the network using the OSPF multicast address 224.0.0.5. To make the flooding procedure reliable, each LSA must be acknowledged separately. After receiving the LSU, each router responds to the DR with an LSAck.

**Step 3**   If a router is connected to another network, it floods the LSU to other networks by forwarding the LSU to the DR of the multiaccess network, or to the adjacent router if in a point-to-point network. In turn, the DR multicasts the LSU to the other routers in the network.

**Step 4**   When a router receives the LSU that includes the changed LSA, the router updates its link-state database. It then computes the SPF algorithm with the new database to generate a new routing table. After a short delay, it switches over to the new routing table. Remember, as mentioned earlier, each time an LSU is received, the router waits for a period of time before recalculating its routing table to reduce the effects of flapping routes.

OSPF simplifies the synchronization issue by requiring only adjacent routers to remain synchronized.

**NOTE**   In a Cisco router, if a route already exists, the routing table is used at the same time the SPF is calculating. However, if the SPF is calculating a new route, the use of the routing table occurs after the SPF calculation is complete.

Each LSA entry has its own aging timer, carried in the LS age field. The default timer value is 30 minutes (it is expressed in seconds in the LS age field). After an LSA entry ages, the router that originated the entry sends an LSU about the network to verify that the link is still active. This validation method saves on bandwidth compared to distance vector routers, which send their entire routing table to their neighbors.

Figure 3-11 illustrates the following analysis done by a router upon receiving an LSU:

- If the entry does not already exist, the router adds the entry to its link-state database, sends an LSAck to the DR, floods the information to other routers, and updates its routing table.

- If the entry already exists and the received LSU has the same information, the router ignores the LSA entry.

- If the entry already exists but the LSU includes new information, the router adds the entry to its link-state database, sends an LSAck to the DR, floods the information to other routers, and updates its routing table.

- If the entry already exists but the LSU includes older information, the router sends an LSU to the sender with its newer information.

**Figure 3-11** *Analyzing an LSU*

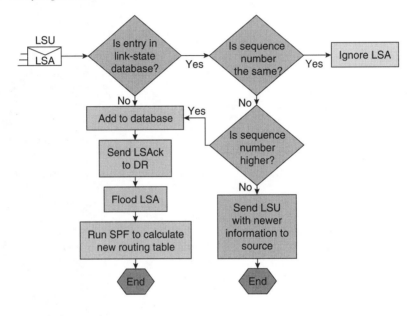

Many different types of LSAs exist. This chapter covers the router link LSA, which is an LSA about a link and its status, and the network LSA, which the DR sends out. The network LSA describes all the routers attached to a multiaccess segment. Chapter 4 discusses other LSA types.

# OSPF Operation in a Point-to-Point Topology

A point-to-point network joins a single pair of routers. A T1 serial line is an example of a point-to-point network.

On point-to-point networks, the router dynamically detects its neighboring routers by sending its hello packets to the multicast address AllSPFRouters, 224.0.0.5. On physical point-to-point networks, neighboring routers become adjacent whenever they can communicate directly. No election is performed, and there is no concept of DR or BDR, as shown in Example 3-2.

**Example 3-2**  *Point-to-Point Topology—Adjacency Election*

```
Router#debug ip ospf adj
Point-to-point interfaces coming up:  No election
OSPF: Interface Serial1 going Up
OSPF: Rcv Hello from 192.168.0.11 area 0 from Serial1 10.1.1.2
OSPF: End of Hello processing
OSPF: Build router LSA for area 0, router ID 192.168.0.10
OSPF: Rcv DBD from 192.168.0.11 on Serial1 seq 0x20C4 opt 0x2 flag 0x7 len 32 state
INIT
OSPF: 2 Way Communication to 192.168.0.11 on Serial1, state 2WAY
OSPF: Send DBD to 192.168.0.11 on Serial1 seq 0x167F opt 0x2 flag 0x7 len 32
OSPF: NBR Negotiation Done. We are the SLAVE
OSPF: Send DBD to 192.168.0.11 on Serial1 seq 0x20C4 opt 0x2 flag 0x2 len 72
```

Usually, the IP source address of an OSPF packet is set to its outgoing interface address. It is possible to use IP unnumbered interfaces with OSPF. On these interfaces, the IP source address will be set to the IP addresses of another interface of the router. (IP unnumbered is discussed in Chapter 2, "Extending IP Addresses.")

The default OSPF hello and dead intervals on point-to-point topologies are 10 seconds and 40 seconds, respectively.

---

### OSPF over Dialup Links—BRI/PRI and Asynchronous

For BRI/PRI connectivity, you should use the **dialer map** command in addition to the normal OSPF configuration commands.

For asynchronous links, you should use the **async default routing** command in addition to the normal OSPF configuration commands on the asynchronous interface. This command enables the router to pass routing updates to other routers over the asynchronous interface. In both cases, when using the **dialer map** command, use the **broadcast** keyword to indicate that broadcasts should be forwarded to the protocol address.

---

# OSPF Operation in an NBMA Topology

NBMA networks are those networks that support many (more than two) routers but have no broadcast capability. When a single interface is used to interconnect multiple sites over an NBMA network, you may have reachability issues because of the nonbroadcast nature of the network. Frame Relay, ATM, and X.25 are examples of NBMA networks. Partially meshed or point-to-multipoint NBMA topologies don't guarantee that routers will receive multicasts or broadcasts from other routers. Also, to provide broadcast capability, the broadcast option must be enabled on VCs. For the purpose of this NBMA discussion, Frame Relay examples are covered.

The default OSPF hello and dead intervals on NBMA topologies are 30 seconds and 120 seconds, respectively.

### Default Hello and Dead Intervals

The following table contains the default hello and dead intervals for the various OSPF environments.

| OSPF Environment | Hello Interval | Dead Interval |
| --- | --- | --- |
| Broadcast | 10 seconds | 40 seconds |
| Point-to-point | 10 seconds | 40 seconds |
| NBMA | 30 seconds | 120 seconds |

With Frame Relay you can interconnect your remote sites in a variety of ways, as shown in Figure 3-12.

Example topologies, as shown in Figure 3-12, include the following:

— A star topology, also known as a hub-and-spoke configuration, is the most popular Frame Relay network topology. In this environment, remote sites are connected to a central site, which generally provides a service or application. This is the least expensive topology because it requires the least number of permanent virtual circuits. In this scenario, the central router provides a multipoint connection because it typically uses a single interface to interconnect multiple permanent virtual circuits.

— In a full-mesh topology, all routers have virtual circuits to all other destinations. This method, although costly, provides direct connections from each site to all other sites and allows for redundancy. For example, when a link to site B goes down, a router at site A can reroute traffic transiting through site B to use site C. As the number of nodes in the full-mesh topology increases, the topology becomes increasingly more expensive.

### PVC Requirements Formula

The formula to calculate the number of PVCs required for a fully meshed topology is $(n(n-1)) \div 2$, where $n$ is the number of sites. Therefore, a fully meshed WAN of 40 sites would require 780 PVCs.

— In a partial-mesh topology, not all sites have direct access to a central site.

**Figure 3-12**  *NBMA Topologies*

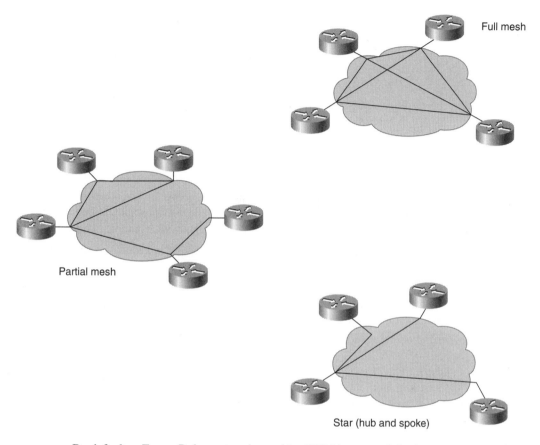

By default, a Frame Relay network provides NBMA connectivity between remote sites. Therefore, routing updates must be replicated by the routers and then distributed to each virtual circuit.

OSPF considers the NBMA environment like any other broadcast media, such as Ethernet. However, NBMA clouds are usually built in a hub-and-spoke topology, where permanent virtual circuits (PVCs) or switched virtual circuits (SVCs) are laid out in a partial mesh. In these cases, the physical topology does not provide the multiaccess that OSPF believes is out there.

The selection of the DR becomes an issue in NBMA topologies because the DR and the BDR need to have full physical connectivity with all routers in the NBMA network. The DR and the BDR also need to have a list of all these other routers so that adjacencies can be established.

# OSPF over NBMA Topology—Modes of Operation

As described in RFC 2328, OSPF runs in one of two official modes in NBMA topologies:

- **Nonbroadcast multiaccess (NBMA)**—Emulates the operation of OSPF in a broadcast network. That is, routers exchange update traffic to identify their neighbors and elect a DR and a BDR. This configuration is usually seen in a fully meshed network. Some configuration, such as defining OSPF neighbors, is necessary on the router for this mode to work properly; this is covered in the section "Configuring OSPF in NBMA Mode," later in this chapter.

  To implement broadcasting, the router replicates the packets to be broadcast and individually sends them to all destinations. This process is CPU- and bandwidth-intensive.

- **Point-to-multipoint**—Treats the nonbroadcast network as a collection of point-to-point links. In this environment, the routers identify their neighbors but do not elect a DR and a BDR. This configuration is used typically with partially meshed networks.

The choice between NBMA mode and point-to-multipoint mode determines the way that the Hello protocol and flooding work over the nonbroadcast network, as discussed in the sections "NBMA Mode Neighborship" and "Point-to-Multipoint Mode Neighborship," later in this chapter.

Additional modes defined by Cisco are point-to-multipoint nonbroadcast (an extension of the RFC mode), broadcast, and point-to-point. These modes are discussed later in this section.

## Subinterfaces

When configuring routers in an NBMA topology, subinterfaces are typically used. A physical interface can be split into multiple logical interfaces, called subinterfaces, with each subinterface being defined as a point-to-point or point-to-multipoint interface. Subinterfaces originally were created to better handle issues caused by split horizon over NBMA and distance vector-based routing protocols. A point-to-point subinterface has the same properties as any physical point-to-point interface.

Subinterfaces are created with the following command:

```
Router(config)#interface serial number.subinterface-number {multipoint | point-to-point}
```

Table 3-1 explains the **interface serial** command.

**Table 3-1**    *The **interface serial** Command*

| interface serial Command | Description |
|---|---|
| *number.subinterface-number* | Interface number and subinterface number. The subinterface number is in the range 1 to 4294967293. The interface number that precedes the period (.) must match the interface number to which this subinterface belongs. |
| **multipoint** | On multipoint subinterface routing IP, all routers are in the same subnet. |
| **point-to-point** | On point-to-point subinterface routing IP, each pair of point-to-point routers is on its own subnet. |

The default OSPF mode on a point-to-point subinterface is point-to-point mode; the default OSPF mode on a point-to-multipoint subinterface is nonbroadcast multiaccess mode.

## NBMA Mode Neighborship

In NBMA mode, OSPF emulates operation over a broadcast network. A DR and a BDR are elected for the NBMA network, and the DR originates an LSA for the network. Note that in this environment, the routers are usually fully meshed for adjacencies to be established among them. (If they are not fully meshed, the DR and the BDR must be selected manually and must have full connectivity to all other routers.) Neighbors must be statically defined to start the DR election process. When using NBMA mode, all routers are on one subnet.

When flooding out a nonbroadcast interface in NBMA mode, the LSA update or LSAck packet is replicated to be sent to each NBMA neighbor listed in the neighborship table.

Assuming that there are not a lot of neighbors in the network, NBMA mode is the most efficient way to run OSPF over nonbroadcast multiaccess networks, both in terms of link-state database size and in terms of the amount of routing protocol traffic. However, consider the following before using this mode:

- **Full mesh and direct communication**—In this mode, all routers attached to the NBMA network are usually fully meshed (or the DR and the BDR selected are capable of communicating directly with all other routers).

- **Stability of the network**—Link-state routing protocols require that, for a multiaccess environment, neighbor adjacencies have been defined for routing updates to be exchanged. In OSPF, the DR and the BDR assure that all the routers on the same segment have the same link-state information regarding the internetwork. If the network is not stable, for example, any time a connection goes down, routers noticing the link-state change multicast an update to the DR and the BDR. The DR acknowledges the update and floods it to other routers. This traffic goes across the NBMA network. Furthermore, any changes made to the link-state database require the forwarding database to be recalculated, thus burdening the router CPU.

Note that if you are using a single PVC on an interface and that PVC goes down, the interface goes down because no keepalives will be received on this interface. This means that a link failure would be recognized. If you are running OSPF over subinterfaces, however, and a subinterface goes down, the physical interface remains up, so the router does not reflect that the link has gone down and that a connectivity problem exists. When a subinterface fails, keepalives will still be arriving from other subinterface, so the main interface will still report that the interface is up and that the line protocol is up.

One DR and one BDR are elected per segment. The intent is to prevent the segment from being overwhelmed with broadcast updates from all the devices on that same segment. However, this does not mean that broadcasts are limited to those devices. When a change occurs, the DR and the BDR handle the change for that segment. The change is then flooded out into the area, which you will see in Chapter 4. It is possible for the Frame Relay cloud to be its own area, therefore isolating its link-state changes from the rest of the network. This is not a rule, however, and it depends on the customer's network and provider.

On nonbroadcast networks where not all routers can communicate directly, you can break the nonbroadcast network into logical subnets using subinterfaces, with the routers on each subnet being capable of communicating directly. Then each separate subnet can be run as an NBMA network or a point-to-point network if each virtual circuit is defined as a separate logical subnet. However, this setting requires quite a bit of administrative overhead and is prone to misconfiguration. It is probably better to run such a nonbroadcast network in point-to-multipoint mode, as described next.

## Point-to-Multipoint Mode Neighborship

Networks in point-to-multipoint mode are designed to work with partial mesh or star topologies. In point-to-multipoint mode, OSPF treats all router-to-router connections over the nonbroadcast network as if they were point-to-point links—that is, no DR or BDR is elected, nor is an LSA generated for the network.

OSPF point-to-multipoint works by exchanging additional link-state updates that contain a number of information elements that describe connectivity to the neighboring routers.

In large networks, using point-to-multipoint mode reduces the number of PVCs necessary for complete connectivity because you are not required to have a fully meshed topology. In addition, not having a fully meshed topology also reduces the number of neighbor entries in your neighbor table.

Point-to-multipoint mode has the following properties:

- **Does not require a fully meshed network**—This environment allows for routing between two routers that are not directly connected but that are connected through a router that has virtual circuits to each of the two routers. The router that interconnects the nonadjacent neighbors is the one configured for point-to-multipoint mode. The other routers, assuming that they have connections to only the target router, could be configured for point-to-point mode. (However, if a spoke router was interconnected to the hub router and another spoke router, it would be configured as point-to-multipoint as well.)

- **Does not require static neighbor configuration**—In a broadcast network, a multicasted OSPF hello packet is used to identify the router's neighbors. In NBMA mode, neighbors are required to be statically defined to start the DR election process and allow routing updates to be exchanged. However, because the point-to-multipoint mode treats the network as a collection of point-to-point links, multicast hello packets discover neighbors dynamically, and statically configuring neighbors is not required. Neighbors—and the cost to each neighbor—can be defined, if desired.

- **Uses one IP subnet**—As in NBMA mode, when using point-to-multipoint mode, all routers are on one IP subnet.

- **Duplicates LSA packets**—Also as in NBMA mode, when flooding out a nonbroadcast interface in point-to-multipoint mode, the LSA update or LSAck packet is replicated to be sent to each of the interfaces' neighbors, as defined in the neighborship table.

## Additional Cisco Neighborship Modes

As mentioned, Cisco has defined additional modes for OSPF neighborship. These are discussed in the following sections.

### Point-to-Multipoint Nonbroadcast Mode

Point-to-multipoint nonbroadcast mode is a Cisco extension of the RFC-compliant point-to-multipoint mode. With this mode, you must statically define neighbors and can modify, if necessary, the cost of the link to the neighbor to reflect the different bandwidths of each link. The RFC point-to-multipoint mode was developed to support underlying point-to-multipoint virtual circuits (VCs) that support multicast and broadcast functions, and, therefore, to allow dynamic neighbor discovery. However, some point-to-multipoint networks use nonbroadcast media (such as classic IP over ATM, or Frame Relay SVCs) and cannot use the RFC mode because the routers cannot dynamically discover their neighbors.

## Broadcast Mode

The broadcast mode is a workaround preventing the static listing of all existing neighbors. The interface will be logically set to broadcast and will behave as if the router were connected to a LAN. DR and BDR election will still be performed, so special care should be taken to assure either a full-mesh topology or a static selection of the DR based on the interface OSPF priority.

## Point-to-Point Mode

The point-to-point mode is used when only two nodes exist on the NBMA network. This mode is typically used only with point-to-point subinterfaces. Each point-to-point connection is one IP subnet. An adjacency is formed over the point-to-point network with no DR or BDR election, as explained earlier in the section "OSPF Operation in a Point-to-Point Topology."

Table 3-2 provides a concise comparison of the different modes of operation for OSPF over NBMA topologies.

**Table 3-2**   *OSPF over NBMA Topology Summary*

| Mode | Preferred Topology | Subnet Address | Adjacency | RFC- or Cisco-defined |
|------|--------------------|----------------|-----------|-----------------------|
| NBMA | Fully meshed | Neighbors must belong to the same subnet number | Manual Configuration<br>DR/BDR elected | RFC |
| Broadcast | Fully meshed | Neighbors must belong to the same subnet number | Automatic<br>DR/BDR elected | Cisco |
| Point-to-multipoint | Partially meshed or star | Neighbors must belong to the same subnet number | Automatic<br>No DR/BDR | RFC |
| Point-to-multipoint nonbroadcast | Partially meshed or star | Neighbors must belong to the same subnet number | Manual configuration<br>No DR/BDR | Cisco |
| Point-to-point | Partially meshed or star, using subinterface | Different subnets for each subinterface | Automatic<br>No DR/BDR | Cisco |

# Configuring OSPF in a Single Area

In this section, you will learn the actual commands required on Cisco routers to enable the OSPF process in a certain area. To configure OSPF, you must perform the following steps:

**Step 1**   Enable OSPF on the router using the **router ospf** *process-id* configuration command. In this command, *process-id* is an internally used number to identify whether you have multiple OSPF processes running within a single router. The process-id need not match process-ids on other routers. Running multiple OSPF processes on the same router is not recommended because it creates multiple database instances that add extra overhead.

**Step 2**   Identify which IP networks on the router are part of the OSPF network using the **network area** router configuration command. For each network, you must identify to which area the networks belong. The network value can vary in that it can be either the network address supported by the router or the specific interface addresses configured. The router knows how to interpret the address by comparing the address to the wildcard mask. Table 3-3 explains the **network area** command.

```
router(config-router)#network address wildcard-mask area area-id
```

**Table 3-3**   *network area Command*

| network area Command | Description |
| --- | --- |
| *address* | Can be the network address, the subnet, or the address of the interface. Instructs the router to know which links to advertise to, which links to use to listen to advertisements, and what networks to advertise. |
| *wildcard-mask* | An inverse mask used to determine how to read the address. The mask has wildcard bits, where 0 is a match and 1 is "don't care." For example, 0.0.255.255 indicates a match in the first 2 bytes. If specifying the interface address, use the mask 0.0.0.0. |
| **area** *area-id* | Specifies the area to be associated with the address. It can be a decimal number or similar to an IP address, A.B.C.D. |

Example 3-3 provides the configuration on OSPF internal Routers A and B in Figure 3-13.

**Example 3-3**   *Configuration on Router A and Router B from Figure 3-13*

```
<Output Omitted>
RouterA(config)#interface Ethernet0
RouterA(config-if)#ip address 10.64.0.1 255.255.255.0
!
<Output Omitted>
```

*continues*

**Example 3-3** *Configuration on Router A and Router B from Figure 3-13 (Continued)*

```
RouterA(config)#router ospf 1
RouterA(config-router)#network 10.0.0.0 0.255.255.255 area 0
. . .
<Output Omitted>
RouterB(config)#interface Ethernet0
RouterB(config-if)#ip address 10.64.0.2 255.255.255.0
!
RouterB(config)#interface Serial0
RouterB(config-if)#ip address 10.2.1.2 255.255.255.0
<Output Omitted>
RouterB(config)#router ospf 50
RouterB(config-router)#network 10.2.1.2 0.0.0.0 area 0
RouterB(config-router)#network 10.64.0.2 0.0.0.0 area 0
```

**Figure 3-13** *Configuring OSPF on Internal Routers*

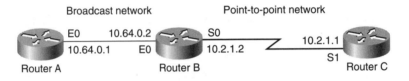

## Optional OSPF Configuration Commands

This section covers commands that can be used to modify OSPF behavior, such as influencing the election process or how OSPF chooses the router ID, and amending the metric calculation.

### Router ID

The highest IP address on an active interface is normally used as the OSPF router ID. This can be overriden by configuring an IP address on a loopback interface. In this case, the highest such loopback IP address becomes the OSPF router ID.

Modifying the OSPF router ID to a loopback address first involves defining a loopback interface:

```
router(config)#interface loopback number
```

**NOTE**     The OSPF router ID of a router will usually change if the interface with that IP address goes down. During testing it was noted, however, that with IOS release 12.0(8), this was no longer the case; the router ID remained as the IP address of the down interface.

OSPF is more reliable if a loopback interface is configured because the interface is always active and cannot go down like a real interface. For this reason, it is recommended that you use the loopback address on key routers. If you plan to publish your loopback address with the **network area** command, you might consider using a private IP address to save on your registered IP addresses. Note that a loopback address requires a different subnet for each router, unless the host address itself is advertised.

Pros and cons exist in using an address that will not be advertised. Using an unadvertised address saves on real IP addresses, but the address does not appear in the OSPF table, so it cannot be pinged. This decision represents a trade-off between the ease of debugging the network and conservation of address space.

To determine the router ID of a router, enter the **show ip ospf interface** command.

## Router Priority

Modifying router priority involves changing the OSPF priority on an interface by using the following interface command:

```
router(config-if)#ip ospf priority number
```

In this command, *number* is a number between 0 and 255. The default is 1. A priority value of 0 indicates that an interface cannot be elected as a DR or a BDR. The router with the highest priority value is the DR. The router with the second-highest priority value becomes the BDR.

---

### Election and Router Priority

If a router with a higher priority value gets added to the network, the DR and the BDR do not change. A DR and a BDR change only if one goes down. If the DR goes down, the BDR takes over as the DR and a new BDR is elected. If the BDR goes down, a new BDR is elected.

---

## Link Cost

Modifying the link cost requires overriding the default cost value assigned to an OSPF interface using the **ip ospf cost** *cost* command. In this command, *cost* is a number from 1 to 65535 that indicates the metric assigned to the interface. The path cost is the total of the costs assigned to all interfaces that forward traffic along the path to the destination.

Cisco's OSPF default cost assignment is based on the bandwidth of the link. Other vendors might use a different mechanism to assign OSPF cost to a link, so you may have to change the default cost because all interfaces connected to the same link must agree on the link's cost.

In general, the path cost in Cisco routers is calculated using the formula: $10^8 \div$ bandwidth (in bps). Using this formula, the following are some example default costs:

- **56-kbps serial link**—Default cost is 1785
- **T1 (1.544-Mbps serial link)**—Default cost is 64
- **Ethernet**—Default cost is 10
- **16-Mbps Token Ring**—Default cost is 6

On serial lines, the default bandwidth is 1.544 Mbps. If the line is a slower speed, use the **bandwidth** command to specify the real link speed. The cost of the link will then change to correspond to the bandwidth that you configured.

## Cost Modification

To control how OSPF calculates default metrics (cost) for the interface, use the **auto-cost reference-bandwidth** router configuration command to change the numerator of the OSPF cost formula.

As mentioned earlier, the OSPF metric is calculated as reference bandwidth divided by bandwidth, with the reference bandwidth equal to 100 bps or, if you prefer, $10^8$ bps. The bandwidth is determined by the **bandwidth** command. For example, a 64-kbps link will get a metric of 1562 because the formula is: $10^8 \div 64,000$. A T1 link will have a metric of 64. The calculation gives FDDI a metric of 1.

If you have multiple links with high bandwidth (such as FDDI or ATM), you might want to use a larger number to differentiate the cost on those links. As an example, you may want to use the **auto-cost reference-bandwidth** command when dealing with a very high-speed link, such as with Sonet OC-12, which runs at 622 Mbps. The standard metric formula would be $10^8 \div 622,000,000$ bps, which would produce a cost of 0.16.

---

**NOTE**     Changing the bandwidth on interfaces or the reference bandwidth under **router ospf** will cause SPF calculations on all routers.

---

In the following command, *reference-bandwidth* is a number in Mbps. The range is 1 to 4294967; the default is 100 Mbps ($10^8$ bps).

```
router(config-router)#auto-cost reference-bandwidth reference-bandwidth
```

Any change using this command must be done on all routers in the AS so that they are all using the same formula to calculate cost. The value set by the **ip ospf cost** command overrides the calculated cost resulting from the **auto-cost** command.

| NOTE | In the Cisco IOS documentation, the **auto-cost** command is documented as **ospf auto-cost**. However, **auto-cost** is the actual command in the Cisco IOS, as tested with IOS 12.0. |
|------|----------------------------------------------------------------------------------------------------------------------------------------------------------------------------|

## Configuring OSPF over NBMA Topology

In the section "OSPF Operation in an NBMA Topology," earlier in this chapter, you saw that OSPF over NBMA topologies can be configured in different modes, as follows:

- RFC-compliant modes:
  - NBMA mode
  - Point-to-multipoint mode
- Cisco-defined modes:
  - Point-to-multipoint nonbroadcast mode
  - Broadcast mode
  - Point-to-point mode

The **ip ospf network** command, typed under the interface configuration mode, is used to specify the OSPF network mode configuration (note that this is not necessarily the physical interface configuration). The possible modes are listed in Table 3-4.

**Table 3-4**    *ip ospf network Command Modes*

| Mode | Description |
|------|-------------|
| **nonbroadcast** | Sets the network mode to nonbroadcast multiaccess mode (also known as the NBMA mode). This is the default mode for NBMA interfaces and point-to-multipoint subinterfaces. |
| **point-to-multipoint** | Sets the network mode to point-to-multipoint. |
| **point-to-multipoint nonbroadcast** | Sets the network mode to point-to-multipoint nonbroadcast. |
| **broadcast** | Sets the network mode to broadcast. This is the default mode for broadcast multiaccess networks, such as Ethernet. |
| **point-to-point** | Sets the network mode to point-to-point. This is the default mode for point-to-point interfaces and subinterfaces. |

## Configuring OSPF in NBMA Mode

In NBMA mode, the selection of the DR is an issue because the DR and BDR need to have full physical connectivity with all routers connected to the cloud. Also, because of the lack of broadcast capabilities, the DR and the BDR need to have a static list of all other routers attached to the cloud—that is, a list of their OSPF neighbors. This is achieved with the use of the **neighbor** command.

---

**NOTE**    The **neighbor** command became somewhat obsolete with the introduction of the capability to configure other network modes for the interface, regardless of the underlying physical topology.

---

The **neighbor** command, as follows, is used to configure OSPF routers interconnecting to nonbroadcast networks. The different options used with the **neighbor** command are explained in Table 3-5.

```
Router(config-router)#neighbor ip-address [priority number]
    [poll-interval sec] [cost number]
```

**Table 3-5**    *neighbor* Command

| Command | Description |
| --- | --- |
| *ip-address* | Interface IP address of the neighbor |
| **priority** *number* | (Optional) An 8-bit number indicating the router priority value of the nonbroadcast neighbor associated with the IP address specified. The default is 0. This keyword does not apply to point-to-multipoint mode interfaces. |
| **poll-interval** *sec* | (Optional) Unsigned integer value reflecting the poll interval. RFC 1247 recommends that this value be much larger than the hello interval. The default is 120 seconds. This keyword does not apply to point-to-multipoint mode interfaces. |
| | If a neighboring router has become inactive (hello packets have not been seen for the router dead interval period), it may still be necessary to send hello packets to the dead neighbor. These hello packets will be sent at a reduced rate called a poll interval. |
| **cost** *number* | (Optional) A cost assigned to the neighbor, in the form of an integer from 1 to 65535. Neighbors with no specific cost configured will assume the cost of the interface, based on the bandwidth or the **ip ospf cost** command. On point-to-multipoint mode interfaces, this is the only keyword and argument that make sense. This keyword does not apply to NBMA mode networks. |

Example 3-4 shows the use of the **neighbor** command.

**Example 3-4**    *Configuring OSPF in NBMA Mode Using the **neighbor** Command*

```
R1(config)#interface Serial0
R1(config-if)#ip address 10.1.1.1 255.255.255.0
R1(config-if)#encapsulation frame-relay
R1(config-if)#ip ospf network non-broadcast
R1(config)#router ospf 1
R1(config-router)#network 10.1.1.0 0.0.0.255 area 0
R1(config-router)#neighbor 10.1.1.2
R1(config-router)#neighbor 10.1.1.3
R1(config-router)#neighbor 10.1.1.4
```

**NOTE**    NBMA mode is used by default, so there is no need for the **ip ospf network non-broadcast** command. However, neighbor statements are necessary.

## Configuring OSPF in Point-to-Multipoint Mode

An OSPF point-to-multipoint interface is seen as one or more numbered point-to-point interfaces. The WAN cloud is configured as one subnet.

Example 3-5 provides a sample of the configuration necessary when using the OSPF in point-to-multipoint mode (point-to-multipoint broadcast mode because the keyword **non-broadcast** is not specified).

**Example 3-5**    *OSPF in Point-to-Multipoint Mode Configuration*

```
R1(config)#interface Serial0
R1(config-if)#ip address 10.1.1.1 255.255.255.0
R1(config-if)#encapsulation frame-relay
R1(config-if)#ip ospf network point-to-multipoint
R1(config)#router ospf 1
R1(config-router)#network 10.1.1.0 0.0.0.255 area 0
```

**NOTE**    The point-to-multipoint **non-broadcast** keyword is a new feature related to point-to-multipoint networks with Cisco IOS Release 11.3a. You can find more information on the subject by searching CCO (cisco.com) with these keywords: OSPF point-to-multipoint network with separate costs per neighbor.

Without the **non-broadcast** keyword, the point-to-multipoint network is considered to be a broadcast network, and the mode is compliant with the RFC. There is no need to specify neighbors. However, you can specify neighbors with the **neighbor** command, in which case you should specify a cost to each neighbor.

With the **non-broadcast** keyword, the point-to-multipoint network is considered to be a nonbroadcast network, and the mode is a Cisco extension. The **neighbor** command is required to identify neighbors. Assigning a cost to a neighbor is optional.

## Configuring OSPF in Broadcast Mode

Configuring broadcast mode is a workaround for using the **neighbor** command, where the administrator must hard code all existing neighbors. This broadcast mode works best with a fully meshed network. Example 3-6 shows a typical configuration of OSPF in broadcast mode.

**Example 3-6**   *Configuration Example of OSPF in Broadcast Mode*

```
R1(config)#interface Serial0
R1(config-if)#ip address 10.1.1.1 255.255.255.0
R1(config-if)#encapsulation frame-relay
R1(config-if)#ip ospf network broadcast
R1(config)#router ospf 1
R1(config-router)#network 10.1.1.0 0.0.0.255 area 0
```

## Configuring OSPF in Point-to-Point Mode

In point-to-point mode, OSPF considers each subinterface as a physical point-to-point network, so the adjacency is automatic.

The following steps explain how to configure OSPF point-to-point mode on subinterfaces, as shown in Example 3-7:

**Step 1**   Go into the interface configuration mode of the interface on which you will create subinterface.

**Step 2**   It is recommended that you remove any network layer address assigned to the physical interface, and assign the network layer address to the subinterface.

**Step 3**   Configure Frame Relay encapsulation.

**Step 4**   Configure the subinterfaces as discussed earlier in the "OSPF over NBMA Topology—Modes of Operation" section.

**Step 5**   Configure network layer addresses and Frame Relay data-link connection identifier (DLCI) numbers on the subinterface.

**Step 6**   Point-to-point mode is the default OSPF mode for point-to-point subinterfaces, so no further configuration is required.

**Example 3-7**  *Example of a Configuration of OSPF in Point-to-Point Mode*

```
R1(config)#interface Serial0
R1(config-if)#no ip address
R1(config-if)#encapsulation frame-relay
R1(config)#interface Serial0.1 point-to-point
R1(config-subif)#ip address 10.1.1.1 255.255.255.0
R1(config-subif)#frame-relay interface-dlci 51
R1(config)#interface Serial0.2 point-to-point
R1(config-subif)#ip address 10.1.2.1 255.255.255.0
R1(config-subif)#frame-relay interface-dlci 52
R1(config)#router ospf 1
R1(config-router)#network 10.1.0.0 0.0.255.255 area 0
```

# Verifying OSPF Operation

The commands covered in this section can be used to verify OSPF operation and statistics.

The **show ip protocols** command, shown in Example 3-8, displays parameters about timers, filters, metrics, networks, and other information for the entire router.

**Example 3-8**  *show ip protocols Command Output*

```
Router#show ip protocols
Routing Protocol is "ospf 200"
  Sending updates every 0 seconds
  Invalid after 0 seconds, hold down 0, flushed after 0
  Outgoing update filter list for all interfaces is
  Incoming update filter list for all interfaces is
  Redistributing: ospf 200
  Routing for Networks:
    192.168.1.0
  Routing Information Sources:
    Gateway         Distance       Last Update
    192.168.1.66        110        00:09:40
    192.168.1.49        110        00:09:13
    172.16.11.100       110        00:09:50
  Distance: (default is 110)
```

The **show ip route** command, shown in Example 3-9, displays the routes known to the router and how they were learned. This is one of the best ways to determine connectivity between the local router and the rest of the internetwork.

**Example 3-9**  *show ip route Command Output*

```
p1r1#show ip route
Codes: C - connected, S - static, I - IGRP, R - RIP, M - mobile, B - BGP
       D - EIGRP, EX - EIGRP external, O - OSPF, IA - OSPF inter area
       N1 - OSPF NSSA external type 1, N2 - OSPF NSSA external type 2
       E1 - OSPF external type 1, E2 - OSPF external type 2, E - EGP
       i - IS-IS, L1 - IS-IS level-1, L2 - IS-IS level-2, * - candidate default
       U - per-user static route, o - ODR
```

*continues*

**Example 3-9** *show ip route Command Output (Continued)*

```
         T - traffic engineered route

Gateway of last resort is not set

     192.168.1.0/28 is subnetted, 4 subnets
O       192.168.1.64 [110/1572] via 192.168.1.50, 00:06:28, Serial2
                      [110/1572] via 192.168.1.34, 00:06:28, Serial1
                      [110/1572] via 192.168.1.18, 00:06:28, Serial0
C       192.168.1.32 is directly connected, Serial1
C       192.168.1.48 is directly connected, Serial2
C       192.168.1.16 is directly connected, Serial0
```

The **show ip route ospf** command, shown in Example 3-10, displays strictly OSPF routes.

**Example 3-10** *show ip route ospf Command Output*

```
p1r1#show ip route ospf
     192.168.1.0/28 is subnetted, 4 subnets
O       192.168.1.64 [110/1572] via 192.168.1.50, 00:06:33, Serial2
                      [110/1572] via 192.168.1.34, 00:06:33, Serial1
                      [110/1572] via 192.168.1.18, 00:06:33, Serial0
```

The **show ip ospf interface** command verifies that interfaces have been configured in the intended areas. If no loopback address is specified, the interface with the highest address is taken as the router ID. It also gives the timer intervals, including the hello interval, and shows the neighbor adjacencies. The **show ip ospf interface** [*type number*] command displays OSPF-related interface information, as shown in Example 3-11. In this command, *type* is an option to set the interface type, and *number* is an option to set the interface number.

**Example 3-11** *show ip ospf interface Command Output*

```
R2#show ip ospf interface e0
Ethernet0 is up, line protocol is up
  Internet Address 192.168.0.12/24, Area 0
  Process ID 1, Router ID 192.168.0.12, Network Type BROADCAST, Cost: 10
  Transmit Delay is 1 sec, State DROTHER, Priority 1
  Designated Router (ID) 192.168.0.11, Interface address 192.168.0.11
  Backup Designated router (ID) 192.168.0.13, Interface address 192.168.0.13
  Timer intervals configured, Hello 10, Dead 40, Wait 40, Retransmit 5
    Hello due in 00:00:04
  Neighbor Count is 3, Adjacent neighbor count is 2
    Adjacent with neighbor 192.168.0.13  (Backup Designated Router)
    Adjacent with neighbor 192.168.0.11  (Designated Router)
  Suppress Hello for 0 neighbor(s)
```

The **show ip ospf** command, shown in Example 3-12, displays the number of times the SPF algorithm has been executed.

**Example 3-12** *show ip ospf Command Output*

```
p1r3#show ip ospf
 Routing Process "ospf 200" with ID 172.26.1.49
 Supports only single TOS(TOS0) routes
 SPF schedule delay 5 secs, Hold time between two SPFs 10 secs
 Minimum LSA interval 5 secs. Minimum LSA arrival 1 secs
 Number of external LSA 0. Checksum Sum 0x0
 Number of DCbitless external LSA 0
 Number of DoNotAge external LSA 0
 Number of areas in this router is 1. 0 normal 1 stub 0 nssa
    Area 1
        Number of interfaces in this area is 2
        It is a stub area
        Area has no authentication
        SPF algorithm executed 6 times
        Area ranges are
        Number of LSA 7. Checksum Sum 0x25804
        Number of DCbitless LSA 0
        Number of indication LSA 0
        Number of DoNotAge LSA 0
```

The **show ip ospf neighbor** command displays OSPF neighbor information on a per-interface basis.

```
Router>show ip ospf neighbor [type number] [neighbor-id] [detail]
```

Table 3-6 explains this command.

**Table 3-6**    *show ip ospf neighbor Command*

| show ip ospf neighbor Command | Description |
| --- | --- |
| *type* | (Optional) Interface type |
| *number* | (Optional) Interface number |
| *neighbor-id* | (Optional) Neighbor's ID |
| *detail* | (Optional) Display of all neighbors in detail (lists all neighbors) |

Example 3-13 provides an output of this command in an Ethernet environment, where a DR and a BDR are elected. Other routers which are just neighbors (not DR or BDR) are referred to as 2WAY/DROTHER.

In Example 3-13, OSPF over Ethernet, a state of 2WAY/DROTHER indicates that this router has reached the two-way state with its neighbor. We can also observe that the router with router ID 192.168.0.12 is the DR for this Ethernet segment.

**Example 3-13** *show ip ospf neighbor Command in an Ethernet Topology*

```
Router>show ip ospf neighbor
Neighbor ID    Pri    State          Dead Time      Address         Interface
192.168.0.13    1    2WAY/DROTHER    00:00:31       192.168.0.13    Ethernet0
192.168.0.14    1    FULL/BDR        00:00:38       192.168.0.14    Ethernet0
192.168.0.11    1    2WAY/DROTHER    00:00:36       192.168.0.11    Ethernet0
192.168.0.12    1    FULL/DR         00:00:38       192.168.0.12    Ethernet0
```

Example 3-14 provides an output of the **show ip ospf neighbor** command for OSPF over a point-to-point network. A state of FULL/ – indicates that this router has reached the full state with its neighbor, and that there is no DR on this segment (because it is a point-to-point network).

**Example 3-14** *show ip ospf neighbor Command in a Point-to-Point Network*

```
Router>show ip ospf neighbor
Neighbor ID    Pri    State      Dead Time    Address       Interface
192.168.0.11    1     FULL/  -   00:00:39     10.1.1.2      Serial1
```

In Example 3-15, using NBMA mode, although not visible, the neighbor statement was used under the **router ospf** command so that adjacencies could be established. Example 3-15 provides an output of the **show ip ospf neighbor** command. The router that this example was taken from is the DR; its neighbor with ID 192.168.0.11 is the BDR.

**Example 3-15** *show ip ospf neighbor Command in an NBMA Mode Using the Neighbor Statements*

```
Router>show ip ospf neighbor
Neighbor ID    Pri    State          Dead Time    Address       Interface
192.168.0.12    1     FULL/DROTHER   0:01:56      10.1.1.2      Serial0
192.168.0.13    0     FULL/DROTHER   0:01:34      10.1.1.3      Serial0
192.168.0.11    1     FULL/BDR       0:01:56      10.1.1.1      Serial0
```

In Example 3-16, OSPF broadcast mode was configured in a fully meshed network. This example was performed on the BDR; the neighbor with ID 192.168.0.14 is the DR.

**Example 3-16** *show ip ospf neighbor Command on a Frame Relay Network Configured for Broadcast Mode*

```
Router>show ip ospf neighbor
Neighbor ID    Pri    State          Dead Time    Address       Interface
192.168.0.14    1     FULL/DR        00:00:30     10.1.1.4      Serial0
192.168.0.13    1     FULL/DROTHER   00:00:36     10.1.1.3      Serial0
192.168.0.12    1     FULL/DROTHER   00:00:39     10.1.1.2      Serial0
```

The **show ip ospf neighbor detail** command, shown in Example 3-17, displays a detailed list of neighbors, their priorities, and their state (for example, INIT, EXSTART, or FULL).

**Example 3-17** *show ip ospf neighbor detail* *Command Output*

```
Router#show ip ospf neighbor detail

Neighbor 160.89.96.54, interface address 160.89.96.54
    In the area 0.0.0.3 via interface Ethernet0
    Neighbor priority is 1, State is FULL
    Options 2
    Dead timer due in 0:00:38
 Neighbor 160.89.103.52, interface address 160.89.103.52
    In the area 0.0.0.0 via interface Serial0
    Neighbor priority is 1, State is FULL
    Options 2
    Dead timer due in 0:00:31
```

The **show ip ospf database** command displays the contents of the topological database. The command also shows the router ID and the OSPF process ID. When entered with the optional keywords **router**, **network**, **summary**, **asb-summary**, and **external**, different displays result. The **show ip ospf database** command can be used when you wish to confirm that your router is aware of all segments in your area.

In Example 3-18, you see the router advertising the links (the ADV router) and the link count. The link count shown for the router link states in Area 0 indicates the number of links that each of the routers has in that area. (Note that, in some cases, the link count may be larger than the number of physical interfaces in the area because some interface types—such as point-to-point interfaces—generate two links in the OSPF database.)

**Example 3-18** *show ip ospf database* *Command*

```
R2#show ip ospf database
        OSPF Router with ID (192.168.0.12) (Process ID 1)

                Router Link States (Area 0)
Link ID         ADV Router      Age    Seq#        Checksum  Link count
192.168.0.10    192.168.0.10    817    0x80000003  0xFF56    1
192.168.0.11    192.168.0.11    817    0x80000003  0xFD55    1
192.168.0.12    192.168.0.12    816    0x80000003  0xFB54    1
192.168.0.13    192.168.0.13    816    0x80000003  0xF953    1
192.168.0.14    192.168.0.14    817    0x80000003  0xD990    1
                Net Link States (Area 0)
Link ID         ADV Router      Age    Seq#        Checksum
192.168.0.14    192.168.0.14    812    0x80000002  0x4AC8
```

**NOTE**    Cisco has an OSPF Design Guide document that includes, in its Appendix A, a detailed example of interpreting the OSPF database. This document can be found by searching www.cisco.com with the keywords "OSPF Design Guide".

The remaining commands in this section and their associated options can be used when troubleshooting OSPF.

The **clear ip route** command is used to reset the IP routing table. The available options are displayed in the following output:

```
p2r2#clear ip route ?
  *          Delete all routes
  A.B.C.D    Destination network route to delete
```

Note that performing a **clear ip route** * causes the router to clear and then recalculate its entire routing table, but it does not affect the neighborship database or the topology database.

The **debug ip ospf** command is used to debug a variety of OSPF operations. The following debug options are available:

```
p2r2#debug ip ospf ?
  adj               OSPF adjacency events
  events            OSPF events
  flood             OSPF flooding
  lsa-generation    OSPF lsa generation
  packet            OSPF packets
  retransmission    OSPF retransmission events
  spf               OSPF spf
  tree              OSPF database tree
```

The **debug ip ospf adj** command can be used when you wish to monitor the election of the DR and BDR, as shown in Example 3-19.

---

**NOTE**   The last parameter in this command is really **adj**, *not* **adjacency**.

---

**Example 3-19** *debug ip ospf adj Example*

```
192.168.0.14 on Ethernet0, state 2WAY
OSPF: end of Wait on interface Ethernet0
OSPF: DR/BDR election on Ethernet0
OSPF: Elect BDR 192.168.0.14
OSPF: Elect DR 192.168.0.14
      DR: 192.168.0.14 (Id)    BDR: 192.168.0.14 (Id)
OSPF: Send DBD to 192.168.0.14 on Ethernet0 seq 0x11DB opt 0x2 flag 0x7 len 32
OSPF: Build router LSA for area 0, router ID 192.168.0.11
OSPF: Neighbor change Event on interface Ethernet0
OSPF: Rcv DBD from 192.168.0.14 on Ethernet0 seq 0x1598 opt 0x2 flag 0x7 len 32
      state EXSTART
OSPF: NBR Negotiation Done. We are the SLAVE
OSPF: Send DBD to 192.168.0.14 on Ethernet0 seq 0x1598 opt 0x2 flag 0x2 len 52
OSPF: Rcv DBD from 192.168.0.14 on Ethernet0 seq 0x1599 opt 0x2 flag 0x3 len 92
      state EXCHANGE
OSPF: Exchange Done with 192.168.0.14 on Ethernet0
```

**Example 3-19** *debug ip ospf adj Example (Continued)*

```
OSPF: Send DBD to 192.168.0.14 on Ethernet0 seq 0x159A opt 0x2 flag 0x0 len 32
OSPF: Synchronized with 192.168.0.14 on Ethernet0, state FULL
OSPF: Build router LSA for area 0, router ID 192.168.0.11
OSPF: Neighbor change Event on interface Ethernet0
OSPF: DR/BDR election on Ethernet0
OSPF: Elect BDR 192.168.0.13
OSPF: Elect DR 192.168.0.14
      DR: 192.168.0.14 (Id)    BDR: 192.168.0.13 (Id)
```

# Case Study: OSPF in a Single Area

Refer to Chapter 1, "Routing Principles," for introductory information on the running case study.

Link-state routing protocols such as OSPF are commonly deployed in medium- to large-scale networks. Implementation of OSPF usually begins with the creation of Area 0, the core of the network. In Figure 3-14, which shows JKL's acquisition C, OSPF was selected because different vendor's equipment is in use and a nonproprietary routing protocol is required. There are fewer than 20 routers in the network, and all routers are part of Area 0 core.

---

**NOTE**    If a network has only one area, it does not have to be configured as Area 0.

---

While looking at Figure 3-14, analyze the following:

- Topology considerations
- Metric limitations
- Routing update traffic
- Convergence time
- Ease of configuration and management

**Figure 3-14** *Case Study Topology—OSPF Single Area*

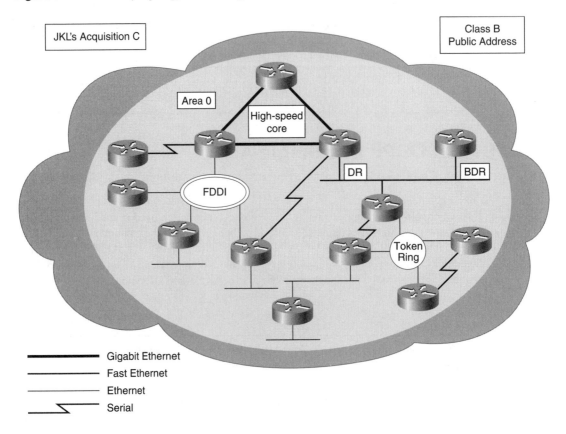

## Case Study Solution

Acquisition C's network has been in place for a number of years, and the infrastructure reflects different technologies that were selected because they offered the highest available bandwidth at the time of their inception. The management of Acquisition C always had speed as a primary concern and, as a result, selected a link-state routing protocol (OSPF) because of its rapid convergence. In an attempt to control costs while deploying the most current technology, management has purchased equipment from many different vendors.

The use of multivendor equipment and high-speed links may require the OSPF interface costs to be adjusted.

The growth of C's single-campus network has been done in an ad hoc fashion rather than by design. This random growth might have caused subnet addresses to be arbitrarily distributed throughout the network. Therefore, due to the noncontiguous subnet address space of this network, route summarization might be impossible. Moreover, because all routers are in Area 0 (and therefore, no hierarchy exists), there are no area border routers (ABRs) at which to configure summarization.

The lack of route summarization means that the routing tables are larger than necessary. The random growth has also precluded any thought of creating a hierarchical topology with routers deployed based upon functionality.

The failure of any link causes a disruption of traffic in all parts of the network and could consume a significant portion of the bandwidth. Attempts to increase reliability by creating redundant paths through the network have been only partially successful. The speed of the alternate paths is dramatically different than the primary links, and this means that link-state advertisements can arrive out of order.

Also, this network might be more difficult than necessary to manage because of its multivendor environment and the lack of hierarchy.

## Summary

In this chapter, you have learned why OSPF, a link-state routing protocol, is better than RIP, a distance vector routing protocol, in a large internetwork. You saw how OSPF discovers its neighbors using the Hello protocol. You also saw how OSPF builds a topology database, on which it applies the SPF algorithm to choose the best routes and build its routing table. You also learned how OSPF maintains routes when a topological change happens on the network.

Also in this chapter, you learned how to configure Cisco routers to operate in a single-area OSPF network, whether in a broadcast or a nonbroadcast environment. Finally, you learned how to verify OSPF operation in a single area.

# Configuration Exercise #1: Configuring OSPF for a Single Area

---

**Configuration Exercises**

In this book, Configuration Exercises are used to provide practice in configuring routers with the commands presented. If you have access to real hardware, you can try these exercises on your routers; refer to Appendix H, "Configuration Exercise Equipment Requirements and Backbone Configurations," for a list of recommended equipment and configuration commands for the backbone routers. However, even if you don't have access to any routers, you can go through the exercises and keep a log of your own "running configurations" on separate sheets of paper. Commands used and answers to the Configuration Exercises are provided at the end of the exercise.

In these exercises, you are in control of a pod of three routers; there are assumed to be 12 pods in the network. The pods are interconnected to a backbone. In most of the exercises, there is only one router in the backbone; in some cases, another router is added to the backbone. Each of the Configuration Exercises in this book assumes that you have completed the previous exercises on your pod.

---

Complete the following exercise to configure OSPF for a single area.

## Objectives

In this Configuration Exercise, you will practice how to configure routers to be in OSPF Area 0, verify the connectivity within your pod, and verify the connectivity to external routes sourced from the backbone_r1 router. You will also use **show** and **debug** commands to verify OSPF operations.

## Visual Objective

Figure 3-15 illustrates the topology used for this single-area OSPF Configuration Exercise.

**Figure 3-15**  *Topology for Configuring OSPF for a Single Area*

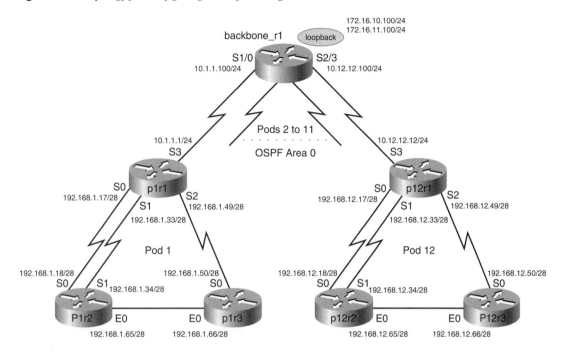

## Command List

In this Configuration Exercise, you will use the commands listed in Table 3-7. Refer to this list if you need configuration command assistance during this exercise.

**Table 3-7**  *Commands Used in Configuration Exercise #1*

| Command | Description |
|---|---|
| **no router igrp 200** | Disables IGRP. |
| **router ospf 200** | Enables OSPF with a process ID of 200. |
| **network 10.0.0.0 0.255.255.255 area 0** | Specifies interfaces on which to run OSPF, and specifies their areas. |
| **show ip ospf** | Displays general information about the OSPF routing process. |
| **show ip ospf neighbor** | Displays information about OSPF neighbors. |
| **show ip ospf database** | Displays the entries in the OSPF link-state database. |

*continues*

**Table 3-7** *Commands Used in Configuration Exercise #1 (Continued)*

| Command | Description |
| --- | --- |
| **show ip ospf interface** | Displays OSPF-specific information about an interface. |
| **debug ip ospf adj** | Shows the events involved in the building or breaking of an OSPF adjacency. |

# Task 1: Enabling OSPF Within Your Pod

Complete the following steps:

**Step 1**   Shut the p*x*r1 S3 interface that connects to the backbone_r1 router. What command do you type to shut down this interface?

Type the command to disable IGRP on all the routers within your assigned pod.

Which routing protocol has a better administrative distance: IGRP or OSPF?

**Step 2**   Enable OSPF with process ID 200 on all the routers within your pod. What command do you use to do this?

**Step 3**   Enable all the interfaces within your pod to run OSPF, and set their area to Area 0. Can you use a mask of 0.0.0.255 on the OSPF network command to accomplish this task?

**Step 4**   Display the routing table and verify that you have full connectivity within your pod. What command is used to display the routing table? Make sure that you can successfully ping all the other routers within your pod.

**Step 5**   Examine the p*x*r1 routing table, and answer the following:

Does OSPF load balance by default? What is the OSPF routing metric based on? What is the default administrative distance of OSPF?

**Step 6**   What is the OSPF router ID of p*x*r2?

What is the OSPF router ID of p*x*r3?

From the p*x*r3 router, issue the command to show the OSPF neighbor state.

Is the neighbor state of p*x*r2 and p*x*r1 in the full state?

Which router is the DR on the Ethernet connection between p*x*r2 and p*x*r3? Why?

Is there a DR/BDR on a serial interface with HDLC encapsulation? What is the default OSPF router priority?

Shut the E0 interface at p*x*r2 and p*x*r3.

At the router that was the BDR, change its E0 interface OSPF router priority to 2, and then no shut the E0 interface at router p*x*r2 and p*x*r3. Which router is the DR now?

**Step 7**    From the p*x*r2 router, issue the **debug ip ospf adj** command.

Shut and no shut the p*x*r2 E0 interface, and observe the OSPF adjacency debug messages.

What command can be typed to disable the debug?

**Step 8**    From any router in your pod, issue the command to display the OSPF database.

What are the two types of link-state advertisements that you see in the OSPF database?

For the router link states, why is the link count 5 for router p*x*r2, 6 for router p*x*r1, and 3 for router p*x*r3?

**Step 9**    From the p*x*r2 or p*x*r3 router, issue the command to display OSPF information about the interfaces.

What is the OSPF network type on the Ethernet interface?

What is the OSPF network type on the serial interface?

What is the OSPF hello interval on the Ethernet and serial (HDLC) interface?

**Step 10** Save the current configurations of all the routers within your pod to NVRAM.

## Task 2: Enabling OSPF Connectivity to the backbone_r1 Router

**Step 1**    From the p*x*r1 router, no shut the S3 interface that connects to the backbone_r1 router.

**Step 2**    Enable the p*x*r1 S3 interface to run OSPF, and set its area to Area 0. Can you use a mask of 0.255.255.255 on the OSPF **network** command to accomplish this task? Display the routing table. Do you see the backbone's loopback interface subnet addresses in your routing table? (Note that you may also see routes from other pods.)

When you were running IGRP, did you see the backbone's loopback interface subnet addresses (or subnets from other pods) in your routing table? Explain your answer.

**Step 3**   Save the current configurations of all the routers within your pod to NVRAM.

## Bonus Task

**Step 1**   From the p*x*r3 and p*x*r2 router, shut the E0 interface.

**Step 2**   Change p*x*r3 E0 interface from Area 0 to Area 99. The p*x*r2 E0 interface remains in Area 0.

---

**NOTE**   The OSPF network statements are matched from top to bottom. Therefore, the most specific statements should be at the top, and the least specific statements should be at the bottom.

---

**Step 3**   No shut the p*x*r3 E0 interface.

**Step 4**   Enter the **debug** command to display the OSPF adjacency information at p*x*r2. What would this command be?

**Step 5**   No shut the p*x*r2 E0 interface.

Are there error messages on the console regarding mismatch area ID?

**Step 6**   Disable the debug.

What is the neighbor status between p*x*r2 and p*x*r3?

**Step 7**   Change the p*x*r3 E0 interface back to Area 0.

## Completion Criteria

You have successfully completed this Configuration Exercise if you correctly supplied the commands required to configure and to verify a single-area OSPF network, and if you were able to correctly answer the questions in the Configuration Exercise. At the end of this exercise, all routers will be running the OSPF protocol in Area 0. The answers to this Configuration Exercise can be found later in this chapter.

# Configuration Exercise #2: Configuring OSPF for a Single Area in an NBMA Environment

Complete the following exercise to configure OSPF over Frame Relay.

## Objectives

In this Configuration Exercise, you will configure the pxr1 router as the Frame Relay switch for the pxr2 and pxr3 routers. You will then configure the pxr2 and pxr3 router serial interface (S0) with Frame Relay encapsulation. When you have verified connectivity between pxr2 and pxr3, you will be asked to configure OSPF over NBMA using the main interface and then using a point-to-point subinterface. You will use the **show** commands to verify OSPF operations.

In this Configuration Exercise, your pxr1 router will act as the Frame Relay switch between your pxr2 and pxr3 routers.

## Visual Objective

Figure 3-16 and Figure 3-17 provide the topologies used in this Configuration Exercise.

**Figure 3-16**  *Configuring OSPF for a Single Area in NBMA Environment Using Main Interface*

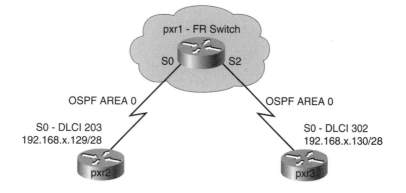

**Figure 3-17** *Configuring OSPF for a Single Area in NBMA Environment Using Point-to-Point Subinterface*

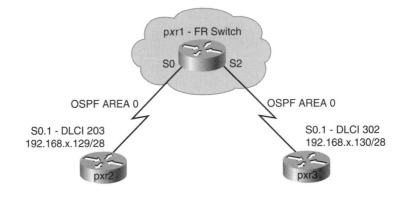

## Command List

In this Configuration Exercise, you will use the commands listed in Table 3-8 in logical order. Refer to this list if you need configuration command assistance during the Configuration Exercise.

**Table 3-8** *Commands Used in Configuring OSPF for a Single Area in an NBMA Environment*

| Command | Description |
|---|---|
| **router ospf 200** | Enables OSPF with a process ID of 200. |
| **network 192.168.*x*.129 0.0.0.0 area 0** | Specifies interfaces on which to run OSPF, and specifies their areas. |
| **neighbor 192.168.*x*.129** | Manually informs a router of its neighbor on a nonbroadcast network. |
| **ip ospf priority 0** | Sets the router priority of an interface for use in the DR/BDR election process. |
| **show ip ospf** | Displays general information about the OSPF routing process. |
| **show ip ospf neighbor** | Displays information about OSPF neighbors. |
| **show ip ospf database** | Displays the entries in the OSPF link-state database. |
| **show ip ospf Interface** | Displays OSPF-specific information about an interface. |
| **encapsulation frame-relay** | Enables Frame Relay frames on an interface. |
| **show frame-relay map** | Displays a mapping between DLCI and IP addresses, and shows traffic forwarding characteristics. |

## Setup

To set up, do the following:

**Step 1**   On pxr1, shut down the Serial 1 and Serial 3 interfaces. Turn off OSPF.

**Step 2**   On pxr2, shut down the Ethernet 0, Serial 0, and Serial 1 interfaces. Reconfigure the Serial 0 IP address to 192.168.x.129/28.

**Step 3**   On pxr3, shut down the Ethernet 0 and Serial 0 interfaces. Reconfigure the Serial 0 IP address to 192.168.x.130/28.

## Task 1: Creating the Frame Relay Switch

Complete the following steps:

**Step 1**   Enable your pxr1 router. Provide the commands necessary for turning a router into a Frame Relay switch. Interface Serial 0, a DCE interface, will switch frames to Serial 2 interface (from Serial 0 DLCI 203 to Serial 2 DLCI 302). Interface Serial 2, also a DCE interface, will switch frames to Serial 0 interface (from Serial 2 DLCI 302 to Serial 0 DLCI 203).

**Step 2**   Enable Frame Relay encapsulation on the S0 interface of your pxr2 and pxr3 routers, and verify that your pxr2 and pxr3 routers' S0 IP addresses are as follows from setup:

| Router | S0 IP Address |
|--------|---------------|
| pxr2   | 192.168.x.129/28 |
| pxr3   | 192.168.x.130/28 |

Enable the Serial 0 interfaces on pxr2 and pxr3.

From pxr2, ping the pxr3 Serial 0 interface to ensure connectivity. What command would you use to achieve this?

## Task 2: Enabling OSPF over NBMA Network Using Main Interface

**Step 1**   Verify that your pxr2 and pxr3 router S0 interfaces are configured for OSPF (in Area 0).

**Step 2**   From pxr2, enter the **show ip ospf interface** command.

What is the network type of S0?

What are the hello and dead intervals of S0?

**Step 3** From p*x*r2, enter the **show ip ospf neighbor** command.

Do you see p*x*r3 as the neighbor? Why or why not?

**Step 4** At the p*x*r2 router, set the OSPF router priority to 0 on the S0 interface.

**Step 5** At the p*x*r3 router, use the **neighbor** statement to manually create a neighbor relationship with the p*x*r2 router.

---

**NOTE** Although you are putting a **neighbor** statement on only one of the routers in this Configuration Exercise, it is good practice to put a **neighbor** statement on both routers.

---

**Step 6** Verify that the neighbor status between your p*x*r2 and p*x*r3 routers is now in the full state.

Which router is the DR, and why?

## Bonus Task

**Step 1** Remove the **neighbor** statement from the p*x*r3 router, and remove the **ip ospf priority 0** statement from the p*x*r2 router. Shut down the p*x*r2 S0 interface; leave it down for more than 2 minutes, and then bring it back up.

**Step 2** Use the **ip ospf network point-to-multipoint** command on the S0 interface of the p*x*r2 and p*x*r3 routers.

**Step 3** What is the OSPF neighbor status between your p*x*r2 and p*x*r3 routers now?

Is there a DR/BDR election using the point-to-multipoint OSPF network type?

**Step 4** Save the current configurations of all the routers within your pod to NVRAM.

## Task 3: Enabling OSPF over NBMA Network Using Point-to-Point Subinterface

Complete the following steps:

**Step 1** On the p*x*r2 and p*x*r3 router S0 interfaces, remove the IP address.

**Step 2**  Create a point-to-point subinterface (S0.1), and assign an IP address and a DLCI to the subinterface. The IP addresses are as follows; use the **frame-relay interface-dlci** *dlci* command to assign the DLCI:

| Router | S0.1 IP Address | S0.1 DLCI |
|--------|-----------------|-----------|
| p*x*r2 | 192.168.*x*.129/28 | 203 |
| p*x*r3 | 192.168.*x*.130/28 | 302 |

**Step 3**  From p*x*r2, ping the p*x*r3 S0.1 interface to ensure connectivity.

**Step 4**  Remove the **neighbor** statement, the **ip ospf priority 0** statement, and the **ip ospf network point-to-multipoint** statement from the respective p*x*r2 and p*x*r3 routers (if they are in your configuration from the previous task).

**Step 5**  At the p*x*r2 router, enter the command **show ip ospf interface S0.1**.

What is the network type of S0.1?

What are the hello and dead intervals of S0.1?

**Step 6**  What is the OSPF neighbor status between your p*x*r2 and p*x*r3 routers?

Is there a DR/BDR election over the point-to-point subinterface?

**Step 7**  Save the current configurations of all the routers within your pod to NVRAM.

**Step 8**  (Bonus question)

What is the main advantage of using a point-to-point subinterface when configuring OSPF over Frame Relay?

## Completion Criteria

You have successfully completed this Configuration Exercise if you correctly supplied the commands required to configure and to verify a single-area OSPF network over an NBMA environment using both the main interface and the point-to-point subinterface, and if you were able to correctly answer the questions in the exercises. At the end of this exercise, your p*x*r2 and p*x*r3 routers will be running OSPF in a single area over Frame Relay. The answers to this Configuration Exercise can be found in the next section of this chapter.

# Answers to Configuration Exercise #1: Configuring OSPF for a Single Area

This section provides the answers to the questions in Configuration Exercise #1. The answers are in **bold**.

## Answers to Task 1: Enabling OSPF Within Your Pod

**Step 1**  Shut down the p*x*r1 S3 interface that connects to the backbone_r1 router. What command do you type to shut down this interface?

```
p1r1(config)#int s3
p1r1(config-if)#shutdown
```

Type the command to disable IGRP on all the routers within your assigned pod.

```
p1r1(config)#no router igrp 200
```

Which routing protocol has a better administrative distance, IGRP or OSPF?

**IGRP, with an AD of 100. OSPF has an AD of 110.**

**Step 2**  Enable OSPF with process ID 200 on all the routers within your pod. What command do you use to do this?

```
p1r1(config)#router ospf 200
```

```
p1r2(config)#router ospf 200
```

```
p1r3(config)#router ospf 200
```

**Step 3**  Enable all the interfaces within your pod to run OSPF, and set their area to Area 0. Can you use a mask of 0.0.0.255 on the OSPF network command to accomplish this task?

```
p1r1(config-router)#network 192.168.1.0 0.0.0.255 area 0
```

```
p1r2(config-router)#network 192.168.1.0 0.0.0.255 area 0
```

```
p1r3(config-router)#network 192.168.1.0 0.0.0.255 area 0
```

**Step 4**  Display the routing table and verify that you have full connectivity within your pod. What command is used to display the routing table? Make sure that you can successfully ping all the other routers within your pod.

```
p1r1#show ip route
Codes: C - connected, S - static, I - IGRP, R - RIP, M - mobile, B - BGP
       D - EIGRP, EX - EIGRP external, O - OSPF, IA - OSPF inter area
       N1 - OSPF NSSA external type 1, N2 - OSPF NSSA external type 2
       E1 - OSPF external type 1, E2 - OSPF external type 2, E - EGP
       i - IS-IS, L1 - IS-IS level-1, L2 - IS-IS level-2, * - candidate default
       U - per-user static route, o - ODR
       T - traffic engineered route

Gateway of last resort is not set

     192.168.1.0/28 is subnetted, 4 subnets
O        192.168.1.64 [110/1572] via 192.168.1.34, 00:00:39, Serial1
                      [110/1572] via 192.168.1.18, 00:00:39, Serial0
                      [110/1572] via 192.168.1.50, 00:00:39, Serial2
C        192.168.1.32 is directly connected, Serial1
C        192.168.1.48 is directly connected, Serial2
C        192.168.1.16 is directly connected, Serial0

p1r1#ping p1r2

Type escape sequence to abort.
Sending 5, 100-byte ICMP Echos to 192.168.1.65, timeout is 2 seconds:
!!!!!
Success rate is 100 percent (5/5), round-trip min/avg/max = 28/31/36 ms
p1r1#ping p1r3

Type escape sequence to abort.
Sending 5, 100-byte ICMP Echos to 192.168.1.66, timeout is 2 seconds:
!!!!!
Success rate is 100 percent (5/5), round-trip min/avg/max = 28/30/32 ms


p1r2#show ip route
Codes: C - connected, S - static, I - IGRP, R - RIP, M - mobile, B - BGP
       D - EIGRP, EX - EIGRP external, O - OSPF, IA - OSPF inter area
       N1 - OSPF NSSA external type 1, N2 - OSPF NSSA external type 2
       E1 - OSPF external type 1, E2 - OSPF external type 2, E - EGP
       i - IS-IS, L1 - IS-IS level-1, L2 - IS-IS level-2, * - candidate default
       U - per-user static route, o - ODR
       T - traffic engineered route

Gateway of last resort is not set

     192.168.1.0/28 is subnetted, 4 subnets
C        192.168.1.64 is directly connected, Ethernet0
C        192.168.1.32 is directly connected, Serial1
O        192.168.1.48 [110/1572] via 192.168.1.66, 00:00:52, Ethernet0
C        192.168.1.16 is directly connected, Serial0
p1r2#ping p1r1

Type escape sequence to abort.
Sending 5, 100-byte ICMP Echos to 192.168.1.17, timeout is 2 seconds:
!!!!!
Success rate is 100 percent (5/5), round-trip min/avg/max = 28/31/32 ms

p1r2#ping p1r3

Type escape sequence to abort.
Sending 5, 100-byte ICMP Echos to 192.168.1.66, timeout is 2 seconds:
!!!!!
Success rate is 100 percent (5/5), round-trip min/avg/max = 4/4/4 ms


p1r3#show ip route
```

```
Codes: C - connected, S - static, I - IGRP, R - RIP, M - mobile, B - BGP
       D - EIGRP, EX - EIGRP external, O - OSPF, IA - OSPF inter area
       N1 - OSPF NSSA external type 1, N2 - OSPF NSSA external type 2
       E1 - OSPF external type 1, E2 - OSPF external type 2, E - EGP
       i - IS-IS, L1 - IS-IS level-1, L2 - IS-IS level-2, * - candidate default
       U - per-user static route, o - ODR
       T - traffic engineered route

Gateway of last resort is not set

     192.168.1.0/28 is subnetted, 4 subnets
C       192.168.1.64 is directly connected, Ethernet0
O       192.168.1.32 [110/1572] via 192.168.1.65, 00:01:02, Ethernet0
C       192.168.1.48 is directly connected, Serial0
O       192.168.1.16 [110/1572] via 192.168.1.65, 00:01:02, Ethernet0
p1r3#ping p1r1

Type escape sequence to abort.
Sending 5, 100-byte ICMP Echos to 192.168.1.17, timeout is 2 seconds:
!!!!!
Success rate is 100 percent (5/5), round-trip min/avg/max = 32/32/36 ms
p1r3#ping p1r2

Type escape sequence to abort.
Sending 5, 100-byte ICMP Echos to 192.168.1.65, timeout is 2 seconds:
!!!!!
Success rate is 100 percent (5/5), round-trip min/avg/max = 4/4/4 ms
p1r3#
```

**Step 5**   Examine the p*x*r1 routing table, and answer the following:

```
p1r1#show ip route
Codes: C - connected, S - static, I - IGRP, R - RIP, M - mobile, B - BGP
       D - EIGRP, EX - EIGRP external, O - OSPF, IA - OSPF inter area
       N1 - OSPF NSSA external type 1, N2 - OSPF NSSA external type 2
       E1 - OSPF external type 1, E2 - OSPF external type 2, E - EGP
       i - IS-IS, L1 - IS-IS level-1, L2 - IS-IS level-2, * - candidate default
       U - per-user static route, o - ODR
       T - traffic engineered route

Gateway of last resort is not set

     192.168.1.0/28 is subnetted, 4 subnets
O       192.168.1.64 [110/1572] via 192.168.1.34, 00:02:03, Serial1
                     [110/1572] via 192.168.1.18, 00:02:03, Serial0
                     [110/1572] via 192.168.1.50, 00:02:03, Serial2
C       192.168.1.32 is directly connected, Serial1
C       192.168.1.48 is directly connected, Serial2
C       192.168.1.16 is directly connected, Serial0
p1r1#
```

Does OSPF load balance by default?

**Yes, as an example for subnet 192.168.1.64.**

What is the OSPF routing metric based on?

**Cost, which is based on bandwidth.**

What is the default administrative distance of OSPF?

**110**

**Step 6**   What is the OSPF router ID of p*x*r2?

**The router ID of p*x*r2 is 192.168.1.65.**

```
p1r1#show ip ospf neighbor

Neighbor ID     Pri   State         Dead Time   Address        Interface
192.168.1.65     1    FULL/  -      00:00:31    192.168.1.18   Serial0
192.168.1.65     1    FULL/  -      00:00:31    192.168.1.34   Serial1
192.168.1.66     1    FULL/  -      00:00:34    192.168.1.50   Serial2
p1r1#
```

What is the OSPF router ID of p*x*r3?

**192.168.1.66**

From the p*x*r3 router, issue the command to show the OSPF neighbor state.

```
p1r3#show ip ospf neighbor

Neighbor ID     Pri   State         Dead Time   Address        Interface
192.168.1.65     1    FULL/BDR      00:00:36    192.168.1.65   Ethernet0
192.168.1.49     1    FULL/  -      00:00:35    192.168.1.49   Serial0
p1r3#
```

Is the neighbor state of p*x*r2 and p*x*r1 in the full state?

**Yes.**

Which router is the DR on the Ethernet connection between p*x*r2 and p*x*r3? Why?

**In this case, p1r3. According to the previous output of the show ip ospf neighbor command, p1r3 has only one neighbor on its Ethernet0 interface, and that neighbor is listed as the BDR. Therefore, p1r3 must be the DR. plr3 has the higher router ID and, therefore, was elected as the DR. Note that if plr2 was enabled for OSPF first, and plr3 was not running OSPF within 40 seconds of plr2 running OSPF, then plr2 would have elected itself as the DR.**

Is there a DR/BDR on a serial interface with HDLC encapsulation?

**No.**

What is the default OSPF router priority?

**1**

Shut the E0 interface at pxr2 and pxr3.

```
p1r2(config)#int eo
p1r2(config-if)#shutdown
p1r3(config)#int e0
p1r3(config-if)#shutdown
```

At the router that was the BDR, change its E0 interface OSPF router priority to 2, then no shut the E0 interface at router pxr2 and pxr3. Which router is the DR now?

```
p1r2(config)#int e0
p1r2(config-if)#shutdown
p1r2(config-if)#ip ospf priority 2
p1r2(config-if)#no shutdown

p1r3(config)#int e0
p1r3(config-if)#no shutdown

p1r3#show ip ospf neighbor

Neighbor ID     Pri   State        Dead Time   Address        Interface
192.168.1.34     2    FULL/DR      00:00:30    192.168.1.65   Ethernet0
192.168.1.49     1    FULL/  -     00:00:31    192.168.1.49   Serial0
```

**In this case, p1r2 is the DR now. It now has router ID 192.168.1.34.**

**Step 7** From the pxr2 router, issue the **debug ip ospf adj** command.

```
p1r2#debug ip ospf adj
OSPF adjacency events debugging is on
p1r2#
```

Shut and no shut the pxr2 E0 interface, and observe the OSPF adjacency debug messages.

```
p1r2(config)#int e0
p1r2(config-if)#shutdown
p1r2(config-if)#
03:23:23: OSPF: Rcv hello from 192.168.1.50 area 0 from Ethernet0 192.168.1.66
03:23:23: OSPF: End of hello processing
03:23:23: OSPF: Interface Ethernet0 going Down
03:23:23: OSPF: 192.168.1.34 address 192.168.1.65 on Ethernet0 is dead,
    state DOWN
03:23:23: OSPF: Neighbor change Event on interface Ethernet0
03:23:23: OSPF: DR/BDR election on Ethernet0
03:23:23: OSPF: Elect BDR 192.168.1.50
03:23:23: OSPF: Elect DR 192.168.1.50
03:23:23: OSPF: Elect BDR 192.168.1.50
03:23:23: OSPF: Elect DR 192.168.1.50
03:23:23:       DR: 192.168.1.50 (Id)    BDR: 192.168.1.50 (Id)
```

```
03:23:23: OSPF: Flush network LSA immediately
03:23:23: OSPF: Remember old DR 192.168.1.34 (id)
03:23:23: OSPF: 192.168.1.50 address 192.168.1.66 on Ethernet0 is dead,
   state DOWN
03:23:23: OSPF: Neighbor change Event on interface Ethernet0
03:23:23: OSPF: DR/BDR election on Ethernet0
03:23:23: OSPF: Elect BDR 0.0.0.0
03:23:23: OSPF: Elect DR 0.0.0.0
03:23:23:         DR: none     BDR: none
03:23:23: OSPF: Remember old DR 192.168.1.50 (id)
03:23:23: OSPF: Build network LSA for Ethernet0, router ID 192.168.1.34
03:23:23: OSPF: We are not DR to build Net Lsa for interface Ethernet0
03:23:23: OSPF: Build router LSA for area 0, router ID 192.168.1.34,
   seq 0x80000005
p1r2(config-if)#
03:23:25: %LINK-5-CHANGED: Interface Ethernet0, changed state to
   administratively down
03:23:26: %LINEPROTO-5-UPDOWN: Line protocol on Interface Ethernet0,
   changed state to down
p1r2(config-if)#
03:23:26: OSPF: Rcv hello from 192.168.1.49 area 0 from Serial0 192.168.1.17
03:23:26: OSPF: End of hello processing
03:23:26: OSPF: Rcv hello from 192.168.1.49 area 0 from Serial1 192.168.1.33
03:23:26: OSPF: End of hello processing
p1r2(config-if)#
p1r2(config-if)#no shut
p1r2(config-if)#
03:23:33: OSPF: Interface Ethernet0 going Up
03:23:34: OSPF: Build router LSA for area 0, router ID 192.168.1.34,
   seq 0x80000006
p1r2(config-if)#
03:23:35: %LINK-3-UPDOWN: Interface Ethernet0, changed state to up
03:23:36: OSPF: Rcv hello from 192.168.1.49 area 0 from Serial0 192.168.1.17
03:23:36: OSPF: End of hello processing
03:23:36: OSPF: Rcv hello from 192.168.1.49 area 0 from Serial1 192.168.1.33
03:23:36: OSPF: End of hello processing
p1r2(config-if)#
03:23:36: %LINEPROTO-5-UPDOWN: Line protocol on Interface Ethernet0,
   changed state to up
p1r2(config-if)#
03:23:43: OSPF: Rcv hello from 192.168.1.50 area 0 from Ethernet0 192.168.1.66
03:23:43: OSPF: 2 Way Communication to 192.168.1.50 on Ethernet0, state 2WAY
03:23:43: OSPF: Backup seen Event before WAIT timer on Ethernet0
03:23:43: OSPF: DR/BDR election on Ethernet0
03:23:43: OSPF: Elect BDR 192.168.1.34
03:23:43: OSPF: Elect DR 192.168.1.50
03:23:43: OSPF: Elect BDR 192.168.1.34
03:23:43: OSPF: Elect DR 192.168.1.50
03:23:43:         DR: 192.168.1.50 (Id)   BDR: 192.168.1.34 (Id)
03:23:43: OSPF: Send DBD to 192.168.1.50 on Ethernet0 seq 0x1106 opt
   0x2 flag 0x7 len 32
03:23:43: OSPF: End of hello processing
p1r2(config-if)#
03:23:46: OSPF: Rcv DBD from 192.168.1.50 on Ethernet0 seq 0xBD7 opt
   0x2 flag 0x7 len 32   mtu 1500 state EXSTART
03:23:46: OSPF: NBR Negotiation Done. We are the SLAVE
03:23:46: OSPF: Send DBD to 192.168.1.50 on Ethernet0 seq 0xBD7 opt
   0x2 flag 0x2 len 92
03:23:46: OSPF: Rcv DBD from 192.168.1.50 on Ethernet0 seq 0xBD8 opt
   0x2 flag 0x3 len 92   mtu 1500 state EXCHANGE
03:23:46: OSPF: Send DBD to 192.168.1.50 on Ethernet0 seq 0xBD8 opt
   0x2 flag 0x0 len 32
03:23:46: OSPF: Rcv DBD from 192.168.1.50 on Ethernet0 seq 0xBD9 opt
   0x2 flag 0x1 len 32   mtu 1500 state EXCHANGE
03:23:46: OSPF: Exchange Done with 192.168.1.50 on Ethernet0
```

```
03:23:46: OSPF: Synchronized with 192.168.1.50 on Ethernet0, state FULL
03:23:46: OSPF: Send DBD to 192.168.1.50 on Ethernet0 seq 0xBD9 opt
    0x2 flag 0x0 len 32
03:23:46: OSPF: Rcv hello from 192.168.1.49 area 0 from Serial0 192.168.1.17
03:23:46: OSPF: End of hello processing
03:23:46: OSPF: Rcv hello from 192.168.1.49 area 0 from Serial1 192.168.1.33
03:23:46: OSPF: End of hello processing
03:23:47: OSPF: Build router LSA for area 0, router ID 192.168.1.34,
    seq 0x80000007
03:23:53: OSPF: Rcv hello from 192.168.1.50 area 0 from Ethernet0 192.168.1.66
03:23:53: OSPF: Neighbor change Event on interface Ethernet0
03:23:53: OSPF: DR/BDR election on Ethernet0
03:23:53: OSPF: Elect BDR 192.168.1.34
03:23:53: OSPF: Elect DR 192.168.1.50
03:23:53:         DR: 192.168.1.50 (Id)    BDR: 192.168.1.34 (Id)
03:23:53: OSPF: End of hello processing
03:23:56: OSPF: Rcv hello from 192.168.1.49 area 0 from Serial0 192.168.1.17
03:23:56: OSPF: End of hello processing
03:23:56: OSPF: Rcv hello from 192.168.1.49 area 0 from Serial1 192.168.1.33
03:23:56: OSPF: End of hello processing
```

What command can be typed to disable the debug?

```
p1r2#no debug all
All possible debugging has been turned off
```

**Step 8**  From any router in your pod, issue the command to display the OSPF
database.

```
p1r1#show ip ospf database

    OSPF Router with ID (192.168.1.49) (Process ID 200)


            Router Link States (Area 0)

Link ID          ADV Router       Age     Seq#        Checksum Link count
192.168.1.34     192.168.1.34     128     0x80000007 0xCEFF    5
192.168.1.49     192.168.1.49     140     0x80000006 0x918     6
192.168.1.50     192.168.1.50     128     0x80000006 0x5917    3

            Net Link States (Area 0)

Link ID          ADV Router       Age     Seq#        Checksum
192.168.1.66     192.168.1.50     128     0x80000001 0x5680


p1r2#show ip ospf database

    OSPF Router with ID (192.168.1.34) (Process ID 200)


            Router Link States (Area 0)

Link ID          ADV Router       Age     Seq#        Checksum Link count
192.168.1.34     192.168.1.34     134     0x80000007 0xCEFF    5
192.168.1.49     192.168.1.49     149     0x80000006 0x918     6
```

```
192.168.1.50      192.168.1.50    135        0x80000006 0x5917   3

                  Net Link States (Area 0)

Link ID           ADV Router      Age        Seq#       Checksum
192.168.1.66      192.168.1.50    135        0x80000001 0x5680


p1r3#show ip ospf database

      OSPF Router with ID (192.168.1.50) (Process ID 200)


                  Router Link States (Area 0)

Link ID           ADV Router      Age        Seq#       Checksum Link count
192.168.1.34      192.168.1.34    143        0x80000007 0xCEFF   5
192.168.1.49      192.168.1.49    157        0x80000006 0x918    6
192.168.1.50      192.168.1.50    142        0x80000006 0x5917   3

                  Net Link States (Area 0)

Link ID           ADV Router      Age        Seq#       Checksum
192.168.1.66      192.168.1.50    142        0x80000001 0x5680
p1r3#
```

What are the two types of link-state advertisements that you see in the OSPF database?

**Router LSAs (Type 1) and network LSAs (Type 2).**


For the router link states, why is the link count 5 for router p*x*r2, 6 for router p*x*r1, and 3 for router p*x*r3?

**The link count indicates the number of links that each of the routers has in that area. In all cases that the link count is larger than the number of physical interfaces in the area point-to-point interfaces, generate two links in the OSPF database.**

**Pxr1 has three serial interfaces participating in OSPF Area 0, so the link count of 6 (interface Serial 3 is shut down and therefore does not have any link participating in Area 0.)**

**Pxr2 has two serial interfaces and one Ethernet interface, so the link count is 5.**

**Pxr3 has one serial interface and one Ethernet interface, so the link count is 3.**

**Step 9**    From the p*x*r2 or p*x*r3 router, issue the command to display OSPF
information about the interfaces.

```
p1r2#show ip ospf interface
Ethernet0 is up, line protocol is up
  Internet Address 192.168.1.65/28, Area 0
  Process ID 200, Router ID 192.168.1.34, Network Type BROADCAST, Cost: 10
  Transmit Delay is 1 sec, State BDR, Priority 2
  Designated Router (ID) 192.168.1.50, Interface address 192.168.1.66
  Backup Designated router (ID) 192.168.1.34, Interface address 192.168.1.65
  Timer intervals configured, Hello 10, Dead 40, Wait 40, Retransmit 5
    Hello due in 00:00:08
  Neighbor Count is 1, Adjacent neighbor count is 1
    Adjacent with neighbor 192.168.1.50  (Designated Router)
  Suppress hello for 0 neighbor(s)
Serial0 is up, line protocol is up
  Internet Address 192.168.1.18/28, Area 0
  Process ID 200, Router ID 192.168.1.34, Network Type POINT_TO_POINT, Cost: 1562
  Transmit Delay is 1 sec, State POINT_TO_POINT,
  Timer intervals configured, Hello 10, Dead 40, Wait 40, Retransmit 5
    Hello due in 00:00:07
  Neighbor Count is 1, Adjacent neighbor count is 1
    Adjacent with neighbor 192.168.1.49
  Suppress hello for 0 neighbor(s)
Serial1 is up, line protocol is up
  Internet Address 192.168.1.34/28, Area 0
  Process ID 200, Router ID 192.168.1.34, Network Type POINT_TO_POINT, Cost: 1562
  Transmit Delay is 1 sec, State POINT_TO_POINT,
  Timer intervals configured, Hello 10, Dead 40, Wait 40, Retransmit 5
    Hello due in 00:00:05
  Neighbor Count is 1, Adjacent neighbor count is 1
    Adjacent with neighbor 192.168.1.49
  Suppress hello for 0 neighbor(s)


p1r3#show ip ospf interface
Ethernet0 is up, line protocol is up
  Internet Address 192.168.1.66/28, Area 0
  Process ID 200, Router ID 192.168.1.50, Network Type BROADCAST, Cost: 10
  Transmit Delay is 1 sec, State DR, Priority 1
  Designated Router (ID) 192.168.1.50, Interface address 192.168.1.66
  Backup Designated router (ID) 192.168.1.34, Interface address 192.168.1.65
  Timer intervals configured, Hello 10, Dead 40, Wait 40, Retransmit 5
    Hello due in 00:00:04
  Neighbor Count is 1, Adjacent neighbor count is 1
    Adjacent with neighbor 192.168.1.34  (Backup Designated Router)
  Suppress hello for 0 neighbor(s)
Serial0 is up, line protocol is up
  Internet Address 192.168.1.50/28, Area 0
  Process ID 200, Router ID 192.168.1.50, Network Type POINT_TO_POINT, Cost: 1562
  Transmit Delay is 1 sec, State POINT_TO_POINT,
  Timer intervals configured, Hello 10, Dead 40, Wait 40, Retransmit 5
    Hello due in 00:00:03
  Neighbor Count is 1, Adjacent neighbor count is 1
    Adjacent with neighbor 192.168.1.49
  Suppress hello for 0 neighbor(s)
```

What is the OSPF network type on the Ethernet interface?

**Broadcast**

What is the OSPF network type on the serial interface?

**Point-to-point**

What is the OSPF hello interval on the Ethernet and serial (HDLC) interface?

**10 seconds**

**Step 10**  Save the current configurations of all the routers within your pod to NVRAM.

```
p1r1#copy run start
Destination filename [startup-config]?
Building configuration...

p1r1#
p1r2#copy run start
Destination filename [startup-config]?
Building configuration...

p1r2#
p1r3#copy run start
Destination filename [startup-config]?
Building configuration...
```

# Answers to Task 2: Enabling OSPF Connectivity to the backbone_r1 Router

**Step 1**  From the p*x*r1 router, no shut the S3 interface that connects to the backbone_r1 router.

```
p1r1(config)#int s3
p1r1(config-if)#no shutdown
```

**Step 2**  Enable the p*x*r1 S3 interface to run OSPF, and set its area to Area 0. Can you use a mask of 0.255.255.255 on the OSPF network command to accomplish this task?

**Yes**

```
p1r1(config)#router ospf 200
p1r1(config-router)#network 10.0.0.0 0.255.255.255 area 0
```

**Step 3**  Display the routing table. Do you see the backbone's loopback interface subnet addresses in your routing table? (Note that you may also see routes from other pods.)

**Yes**

```
p1r1#show ip route
Codes: C - connected, S - static, I - IGRP, R - RIP, M - mobile, B - BGP
       D - EIGRP, EX - EIGRP external, O - OSPF, IA - OSPF inter area
       N1 - OSPF NSSA external type 1, N2 - OSPF NSSA external type 2
       E1 - OSPF external type 1, E2 - OSPF external type 2, E - EGP
       i - IS-IS, L1 - IS-IS level-1, L2 - IS-IS level-2, * - candidate default
       U - per-user static route, o - ODR
       T - traffic engineered route

Gateway of last resort is not set

     172.16.0.0/24 is subnetted, 2 subnets
O E2    172.16.10.0 [110/20] via 10.1.1.100, 00:00:08, Serial3
O E2    172.16.11.0 [110/20] via 10.1.1.100, 00:00:08, Serial3
     10.0.0.0/24 is subnetted, 2 subnets
O       10.2.2.0 [110/3124] via 10.1.1.100, 00:00:08, Serial3
C       10.1.1.0 is directly connected, Serial3
     192.168.1.0/28 is subnetted, 4 subnets
O       192.168.1.64 [110/1572] via 192.168.1.50, 00:00:08, Serial2
                     [110/1572] via 192.168.1.34, 00:00:08, Serial1
                     [110/1572] via 192.168.1.18, 00:00:08, Serial0
C       192.168.1.32 is directly connected, Serial1
C       192.168.1.48 is directly connected, Serial2
C       192.168.1.16 is directly connected, Serial0
p1r1#
```

When you were running IGRP, did you see the backbone's loopback interface subnet addresses (or subnets from other pods) in your routing table? Explain your answer.

**During the Configuration Exercise in Chapter 1, you should not see actual subnets; you should see only major network numbers because IGRP is a classful routing protocol and therefore automatically summarizes to the major network number.**

**Step 4**  Save the current configurations of all the routers within your pod to NVRAM.

```
p1r1#copy run start
Destination filename [startup-config]?
Building configuration...

p1r2#copy run start
Destination filename [startup-config]?
Building configuration...

p1r3#copy run start
Destination filename [startup-config]?
Building configuration...
```

## Bonus Task

**Step 1**   From the p*x*r3 and p*x*r2 routers, shut the E0 interface.

```
p1r2(config)#int e0
p1r2(config-if)#shutdown
```

**Step 2**   Change p*x*r3 E0 interface from Area 0 to Area 99. The p*x*r2 E0 interface remains in Area 0.

---

**NOTE**   The OSPF network statements are matched from top to bottom. Therefore, the most specific statements should be at the top, and the least specific statements should be at the bottom.

---

```
p1r3(config)#int e0
p1r3(config-if)#shutdown
p1r3(config-if)#exit
p1r3(config)#router ospf 200
p1r3(config-router)#no network 192.168.1.0 0.0.0.255 area 0
p1r3(config-router)#network 192.168.1.66 0.0.0.0 area 99
p1r3(config-router)#network 192.168.1.0 0.0.0.255 area 0
```

**Step 3**   No shut the p*x*r3 E0 interface.

```
p1r3(config)#int e0
p1r3(config-if)#no shut
```

**Step 4**   Enter the **debug** command to display the OSPF adjacency information at p*x*r2. What would this command be?

```
p1r2#debug ip ospf adj
OSPF adjacency events debugging is on
```

**Step 5**   No shut the p*x*r2 E0 interface.

```
p1r2(config)#int e0
p1r2(config-if)#no shut
```

Are there error messages on the console regarding mismatch area ID?

**Yes**

```
03:38:33: OSPF: Interface Ethernet0 going Up
03:38:34: OSPF: Build router LSA for area 0, router ID 192.168.1.34, seq 0x80000
009
p1r2#
03:38:34: %SYS-5-CONFIG_I: Configured from console by console
p1r2#
03:38:35: %LINK-3-UPDOWN: Interface Ethernet0, changed state to up
```

```
03:38:36: OSPF: Rcv pkt from 192.168.1.66, Ethernet0, area 0.0.0.0
    mismatch area 0.0.0.99 in the header
03:38:36: OSPF: Rcv hello from 192.168.1.49 area 0 from Serial0 192.168.1.17
03:38:36: OSPF: End of hello processing
03:38:36: %LINEPROTO-5-UPDOWN: Line protocol on Interface Ethernet0,
    changed state to up
03:38:36: OSPF: Rcv hello from 192.168.1.49 area 0 from Serial1 192.168.1.33
03:38:36: OSPF: End of hello processing
03:38:46: OSPF: Rcv pkt from 192.168.1.66, Ethernet0, area 0.0.0.0
    mismatch area 0.0.0.99 in the header
03:38:46: OSPF: Rcv hello from 192.168.1.49 area 0 from Serial0 192.168.1.17
03:38:46: OSPF: End of hello processing
03:38:46: OSPF: Rcv hello from 192.168.1.49 area 0 from Serial1 192.168.1.33
03:38:46: OSPF: End of hello processing
03:38:56: OSPF: Rcv pkt from 192.168.1.66, Ethernet0, area 0.0.0.0
    mismatch area 0.0.0.99 in the header
03:38:56: OSPF: Rcv hello from 192.168.1.49 area 0 from Serial0 192.168.1.17
03:38:56: OSPF: End of hello processing
03:38:56: OSPF: Rcv hello from 192.168.1.49 area 0 from Serial1 192.168.1.33
03:38:56: OSPF: End of hello processing
```

**Step 6**  Disable the debug.

```
p1r2#no debug all
All possible debugging has been turned off
```

What is the neighbor status between p*x*r2 and p*x*r3?

**According to the show ip ospf neighbor command, p1r2 does not see p1r3 as its neighbor.**

```
p1r2#show ip ospf neighbor

Neighbor ID     Pri   State        Dead Time   Address        Interface
192.168.1.49     1    FULL/  -     00:00:30    192.168.1.17   Serial0
192.168.1.49     1    FULL/  -     00:00:30    192.168.1.33   Serial1
```

**Step 7**  Change the p*x*r3 E0 interface back to Area 0.

```
p1r3(config)#no router ospf 200
p1r3(config)#router ospf 200
p1r3(config-router)#network 192.168.1.0 0.0.0.255 area 0


p1r3#show ip ospf neighbor

Neighbor ID     Pri   State        Dead Time   Address        Interface
192.168.1.34     2    FULL/DR      00:00:31    192.168.1.65   Ethernet0
192.168.1.49     1    FULL/  -     00:00:31    192.168.1.49   Serial0
p1r3#
```

| NOTE | During lab testing, performing the no network 192.168.1.66 0.0.0.0 area 99 on p1r3 was not successful at having p1r2 and p1r3 becoming neighbors again, although both running configurations appeared fine. Therefore, the no router ospf 200 command was issued to remove all reference to an OSPF routing process, and the router ospf 200 and network 192.168.1.0 0.0.0.255 area 0 commands were reissued to the p1r3. |
|------|---|

# Answers to Configuration Exercise #2: Configuring OSPF for a Single Area in an NBMA Environment

This section provides the answers to the questions in Configuration Exercise #2. The answers are in **bold**.

## Answers to Setup

**Step 1**  On p*x*r1, shut down the Serial 1 and Serial 3 interfaces. Turn off OSPF.

```
p1r1(config)#int s1
p1r1(config-if)#shutdown
p1r1(config-if)#exit
p1r1(config)#int s3
p1r1(config-if)#shutdown
p1r1(config-if)#exit
p1r1(config)#no router ospf 200
```

**Step 2**  On p*x*r2, shut down the Ethernet 0, Serial 0, and Serial 1 interfaces. Reconfigure the Serial 0 IP address to 192.168.*x*.129/28.

```
p1r2(config)#int e0
p1r2(config-if)#shutdown
p1r2(config-if)#int s0
p1r2(config-if)#shutdown
p1r2(config-if)#ip address 192.168.1.129 255.255.255.240
p1r2(config-if)#int s1
p1r2(config-if)#shutdown
```

**Step 3**  On p*x*r3, shut down the Ethernet 0 and Serial 0 interfaces. Reconfigure the Serial 0 IP address to 192.168.*x*.130/28.

```
p1r3(config)#int e0
p1r3(config-if)#shutdown
p1r3(config-if)#int s0
p1r3(config-if)#shutdown
p1r3(config-if)#ip address 192.168.1.130 255.255.255.240
```

# Answers to Task 1: Creating the Frame Relay Switch

**Step 1**   Enable your p*x*r1 router. Provide the commands necessary for turning a router into a Frame Relay switch. Interface Serial 0, a DCE interface, will switch frames to Serial 2 interface (from Serial 0 DLCI 203 to Serial 2 DLCI 302). Interface Serial 2, also a DCE interface, will switch frames to Serial 0 interface (from Serial 2 DLCI 302 to Serial 0 DLCI 203).

```
p1r1(config)#frame-relay switching
p1r1(config)#int s0
p1r1(config-if)#encapsulation frame-relay
p1r1(config-if)#frame-relay intf-type dce
p1r1(config-if)#frame-relay route 203 interface serial2 302
p1r1(config-if)#exit
p1r1(config)#int s2
p1r1(config-if)#encapsulation frame-relay
p1r1(config-if)#frame-relay intf-type dce
p1r1(config-if)#frame-relay route 302 interface serial0 203
```

**Step 2**   Enable Frame Relay encapsulation on the S0 interface of your p*x*r2 and p*x*r3 router, and verify that your p*x*r2 and p*x*r3 routers' S0 IP addresses are as follows from setup:

| Router | S0 IP Address |
| --- | --- |
| p*x*r2 | 192.168.*x*.129/28 |
| p*x*r3 | 192.168.*x*.130/28 |

```
p1r2(config)#int s0
p1r2(config-if)#encapsulation frame-relay
```

```
p1r3(config)#int s0
p1r3(config-if)#encapsulation frame-relay
```

Enable the Serial 0 interfaces on p*x*r2 and p*x*r3.

```
p1r2(config)#int s0
p1r2(config-if)#no shutdown
```

```
p1r3(config)#int s0
p1r3(config-if)#no shutdown
```

From p*x*r2, ping the p*x*r3 Serial 0 interface to ensure connectivity. What command would you use to achieve this?

```
p1r2#ping 192.168.1.130

Type escape sequence to abort.
Sending 5, 100-byte ICMP Echos to 192.168.1.130, timeout is 2 seconds:
!!!!!
Success rate is 100 percent (5/5), round-trip min/avg/max = 56/59/60 ms
```

# Answers to Task 2: Enabling OSPF over NBMA Network Using Main Interface

**Step 1**   Verify that your pxr2 and pxr3 router S0 interfaces are configured for OSPF (in Area 0).

```
p1r2#sh ip protocols
Routing Protocol is "ospf 200"
  Sending updates every 0 seconds
  Invalid after 0 seconds, hold down 0, flushed after 0
  Outgoing update filter list for all interfaces is
  Incoming update filter list for all interfaces is
  Redistributing: ospf 200
  Routing for Networks:
    192.168.1.0
  Routing Information Sources:
    Gateway          Distance      Last Update
    192.168.1.66          110      00:09:40
    192.168.1.49          110      00:09:13
    172.16.11.100         110      00:09:50
  Distance: (default is 110)


p1r3#show ip protocols
Routing Protocol is "ospf 200"
  Sending updates every 0 seconds
  Invalid after 0 seconds, hold down 0, flushed after 0
  Outgoing update filter list for all interfaces is
  Incoming update filter list for all interfaces is
  Redistributing: ospf 200
  Routing for Networks:
    192.168.1.0
  Routing Information Sources:
    Gateway          Distance      Last Update
    192.168.1.34          110      00:09:04
    192.168.1.49          110      00:09:59
    172.16.11.100         110      00:09:59
  Distance: (default is 110)
```

**Step 2**   From pxr2, enter the **show ip ospf interface** command.

```
p1r2#show ip ospf interface
Ethernet0 is administratively down, line protocol is down
  Internet Address 192.168.1.65/28, Area 0
  Process ID 200, Router ID 192.168.1.129, Network Type BROADCAST, Cost: 10
  Transmit Delay is 1 sec, State DOWN, Priority 2
  No designated router on this network
  No backup designated router on this network
  Timer intervals configured, Hello 10, Dead 40, Wait 40, Retransmit 5
Serial0 is up, line protocol is up
  Internet Address 192.168.1.129/28, Area 0
  Process ID 200, Router ID 192.168.1.129, Network Type NON_BROADCAST, Cost: 1562
  Transmit Delay is 1 sec, State DR, Priority 1
  Designated Router (ID) 192.168.1.129, Interface address 192.168.1.129
  No backup designated router on this network
  Timer intervals configured, Hello 30, Dead 120, Wait 120, Retransmit 5
    Hello due in 00:00:08
  Neighbor Count is 0, Adjacent neighbor count is 0
  Suppress hello for 0 neighbor(s)
Serial1 is administratively down, line protocol is down
  Internet Address 192.168.1.34/28, Area 0
```

```
Process ID 200, Router ID 192.168.1.129, Network Type POINT_TO_POINT, Cost:1562
Transmit Delay is 1 sec, State DOWN,
Timer intervals configured, Hello 10, Dead 40, Wait 40, Retransmit 5
```

What is the network type of S0?

**Nonbroadcast.**

What are the hello and dead intervals of S0?

**Hello 30 seconds, dead 120 seconds.**

**Step 3**   From p*x*r2, enter the **show ip ospf neighbor** command.

```
p1r2#show ip ospf neighbor
p1r2#
```

Do you see p*x*r3 as the neighbor? Why or why not?

**No. In an NBMA environment, the default mode is nonbroadcast. Therefore, the neighbor statement must be used to manually define neighbors.**

**Step 4**   At the p*x*r2 router, set the OSPF router priority to 0 on the S0 interface.

```
p1r2(config)#int s0
p1r2(config-if)#ip ospf priority 0
```

**Step 5**   At the p*x*r3 router, use the **neighbor** statement to manually create a neighbor relationship with the p*x*r2 router.

```
p1r3(config)#router ospf 200
p1r3(config-router)#neighbor 192.168.1.129
```

**NOTE**   Although you are putting a **neighbor** statement on only one of the routers in this Configuration Exercise, it is good practice to put a **neighbor** statement on both routers.

**Step 6**   Verify that the neighbor status between your p*x*r2 and p*x*r3 routers is now in the full state.

```
p1r2#show ip ospf neighbor

Neighbor ID     Pri  State       Dead Time   Address         Interface
192.168.1.130     1  FULL/DR     00:01:30    192.168.1.130   Serial0
p1r2#
```

```
p1r3#show ip ospf neighbor

Neighbor ID      Pri   State          Dead Time   Address         Interface
192.168.1.129     0    FULL/DROTHER   00:01:32    192.168.1.129   Serial0
p1r3#
```

Which router is the DR and why?

**p1r3 is the DR. p1r2 can't be elected because its OSPF priority is set to 0.**

# Answers to Bonus Task

**Step 1**   Remove the **neighbor** statement from the p*x*r3 router, and remove the **ip
ospf priority 0** statement from the p*x*r2 router. Shut down the p*x*r2 S0
interface; leave it down for 2 minutes, the dead interval, and then bring it
back up.

```
p1r3(config)#router ospf 200
p1r3(config-router)#no neighbor 192.168.1.129

p1r2(config)#int s0
p1r2(config-if)#no ip ospf priority 0
```

**Step 2**   Use the **ip ospf network point-to-multipoint** command on the S0
interface of the p*x*r2 and p*x*r3 routers.

```
p1r2(config)#int s0
p1r2(config-if)#ip ospf network point-to-multipoint

p1r3(config)#int s0
p1r3(config-if)#ip ospf network point-to-multipoint
```

**Step 3**   What is the OSPF neighbor status between your p*x*r2 and p*x*r3 routers
now?

```
p1r3#show ip ospf neighbor

Neighbor ID      Pri   State       Dead Time   Address         Interface
192.168.1.129     1    FULL/  -    00:01:37    192.168.1.129   Serial0

p1r2#show ip ospf neighbor

Neighbor ID      Pri   State       Dead Time   Address         Interface
192.168.1.130     1    FULL/  -    00:01:49    192.168.1.130   Serial0
```

**p1r2 and p1r3 are in FULL state.**

Is there a DR/BDR election using the point-to-multipoint OSPF network
type?

**No.**

**Step 4** Save the current configurations of all the routers within your pod to
NVRAM.

```
p1r1#copy run start
Destination filename [startup-config]?
Building configuration...

p1r2#copy run start
Destination filename [startup-config]?
Building configuration...

p1r2#copy run start
Destination filename [startup-config]?
Building configuration...
```

# Answers to Task 3: Enabling OSPF over NBMA Network Using Point-to-Point Subinterface

**Step 1** On the p*x*r2 and p*x*r3 router S0 interface, remove the IP address.

```
p1r2(config)#int s0
p1r2(config-if)#no ip address

p1r3(config)#int s0
p1r3(config-if)#no ip address
```

**Step 2** Create a point-to-point subinterface (S0.1), and assign an IP address and
a DLCI to the subinterface. The IP addresses are as follows; use the
**frame-relay interface-dlci** *dlci* command to assign the DLCI:

| Router | S0.1 IP Address | S0.1 DLCI |
| --- | --- | --- |
| p*x*r2 | 192.168.*x*.129/28 | 203 |
| p*x*r3 | 192.168.*x*.130/28 | 302 |

```
p1r2(config)#int s0.1 point-to-point
p1r2(config-subif)#ip address 192.168.1.129 255.255.255.240
p1r2(config-subif)#frame-relay interface-dlci 203

p1r3(config)#int s0.1 point-to-point
p1r3(config-subif)#ip address 192.168.1.130 255.255.255.240
p1r3(config-subif)#frame-relay interface-dlci 302
```

**Step 3** From p*x*r2, ping the p*x*r3 S0.1 interface to ensure connectivity.

```
p1r2#ping 192.168.1.130

Type escape sequence to abort.
Sending 5, 100-byte ICMP Echos to 192.168.1.130, timeout is 2 seconds:
!!!!!
Success rate is 100 percent (5/5), round-trip min/avg/max = 60/71/92 ms
```

**Step 4**  Remove the **neighbor** statement, the **ip ospf priority 0** statement, and
the **ip ospf network point-to-multipoint** statement from the respective
pxr2 and pxr3 routers (if they are in your configuration from the previous
task).

```
p1r2(config)#int s0
p1r2(config-if)#no ip ospf network point-to-multipoint

p1r3(config)#int s0
p1r3(config-if)#no ip ospf network point-to-multipoint
```

**Step 5**  At the pxr2 router, enter the command **show ip ospf interface S0.1**.

```
p1r2#show ip ospf interface s0.1
Serial0.1 is up, line protocol is up
  Internet Address 192.168.1.129/28, Area 0
  Process ID 200, Router ID 192.168.1.129, Network Type POINT_TO_POINT, Cost:1562
  Transmit Delay is 1 sec, State POINT_TO_POINT,
  Timer intervals configured, Hello 10, Dead 40, Wait 40, Retransmit 5
    Hello due in 00:00:04
  Neighbor Count is 1, Adjacent neighbor count is 1
    Adjacent with neighbor 192.168.1.130
  Suppress hello for 0 neighbor(s)
p1r2#
```

What is the network type of S0.1?

**Point-to-point.**

What are the hello and dead intervals of S0.1?

**Hello 10 seconds, dead 40 seconds.**

**Step 6**  What is the OSPF neighbor status between your pxr2 and pxr3 routers?

```
p1r2#show ip ospf neighbor

Neighbor ID      Pri   State       Dead Time   Address        Interface
192.168.1.130     1    FULL/  -    00:00:33    192.168.1.130  Serial0.1
p1r2#
```

**plr2 and plr3 are in FULL state.**

Is there a DR/BDR election over the point-to-point subinterface?

**No.**

**Step 7**    Save the current configurations of all the routers within your pod to
              NVRAM.

```
p1r1#copy run start
Destination filename [startup-config]?
Building configuration...

p1r2#copy run start
Destination filename [startup-config]?
Building configuration...

p1r3#copy run start
Destination filename [startup-config]?
Building configuration...
```

**Step 8**    (Bonus question) What is the main advantage of using a point-to-point
              subinterface when configuring OSPF over Frame Relay?

              **Each point-to-point connection is treated  like a separate connection,
              eliminating the need for OSPF neighbor configuration or OSPF network-
              type configuration.**

# Review Questions

Answer the following questions, and then refer to Appendix G, "Answers to the Review
Questions," for the answers.

1    List three reasons why OSPF operates better than RIP in a large internetwork.

2    What does a router do when it receives an LSU?

3    Identify when the exchange protocol and the flooding process are used, and describe
     how each operates.

4    Write a brief description of the following:

     — Internal router

     — LSU

     — DBD

     — Hello packet

**5** Match the term in the table with the statement most closely describing it:

A. Indicates the router responsible for route synchronization

B. Indicates routers that can route information

C. Indicates that routers can discover link-state information

D. A collection of routers and networks

| Term | Answer |
| --- | --- |
| Area | |
| Full state | |
| DR | |
| Exchange state | |

**6** Name the two RFC-compliant modes for OSPF over nonbroadcast multiaccess networks. Name the additional Cisco modes for OSPF over NBMA.

**7** How many subnets are there when OSPF is used in an NBMA environment with nonbroadcast multiaccess mode?

**8** What command should be used to run OSPF on all interfaces on a router?

**9** What command is used to configure OSPF in broadcast mode?

**10** How do you configure OSPF point-to-point mode on a point-to-point subinterface?

This chapter introduces you to multiple OSPF areas. It includes the following sections:

- Multiple OSPF Areas
- OSPF Operation Across Multiple Areas
- Using and Configuring OSPF Multiarea Components
- Verifying OSPF Operation
- Case Study: OSPF Multiarea
- Summary
- Configuration Exercise: Configuring a Multiarea OSPF Network
- Answers to Configuration Exercise: Configuring a Multiarea OSPF Network
- Review Questions

# CHAPTER 4

# Interconnecting Multiple OSPF Areas

This chapter introduces readers to the use, operation, configuration, and verification of Open Shortest Path First (OSPF) in multiple areas. After completing this chapter, you will be able to describe issues related to interconnecting multiple areas. You will see the differences among the possible types of areas and how OSPF supports the use of VLSM. At the end of this chapter, you should be able to explain how OSPF supports the use of route summarization in multiple areas and how it operates in a multiple-area NBMA environment.

---

**NOTE**  This chapter covers OSPF capabilities. OSPF design is covered in the Cisco Press book *OSPF Network Design Solutions* (ISBN 1-57870-046-9).

---

## Multiple OSPF Areas

In the previous chapter, you learned how OSPF operates within a single area. Now it is time to consider what would happen if this single area ballooned into, say, 400 networks. The following issues, at a minimum, need to be addressed to understand OSPF in multiple areas:

- **Frequent calculations of the shortest path first (SPF) algorithm**—With such a large number of segments, network changes are inevitable. The routers would have to spend many more CPU cycles recalculating the routing tables because they would receive every update generated within the area.

- **Large routing table**—Each router would need to maintain at least one entry for every network—in this previous example, that would be at least 400 networks. Assuming that alternative paths would exist for 25 percent of these 400 networks, routing tables would have an additional 100 entries.

- **Large link-state table**—Because the link-state table includes the complete topology of the network, each router would need to maintain an entry for every network in the area, even if routes are not selected for the routing table.

In light of these issues, OSPF was designed to allow large areas to be separated into smaller, more manageable areas that can still exchange routing information.

OSPF's capability to separate a large internetwork into multiple areas is also referred to as hierarchical routing. Hierarchical routing enables you to separate a large internetwork (autonomous system) into smaller internetworks that are called areas, as shown in Figure 4-1. With this technique, routing still occurs between the areas (called interarea routing), but many of the internal routing operations, such as recalculating the database, are kept within an area. In Figure 4-1, for example, if Area 1 is having problems with a link going up and down, routers in other areas need not continually run their SPF calculation because they are isolated from the Area 1 problem.

**Figure 4-1** *OSPF Hierarchical Routing*

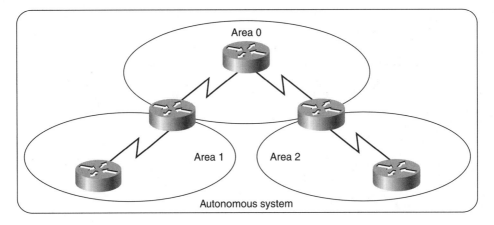

The hierarchical topology of OSPF has the following advantages:

- **Reduced frequency of SPF calculations**—Because detailed route information is kept within each area, it is not necessary to flood all link-state changes to every area. Thus, not all routers need to run the SPF calculation when a topological change happens. Only those affected by the change will need to recompute routes.

- **Smaller routing tables**—When using multiple areas, detailed route entries for interarea networks are kept within the area. Instead of advertising these explicit routes outside the area, these routes can be summarized into one or more summary addresses. Advertising these summaries reduces the number of link-state advertisements (LSAs) propagated between areas, while keeping all networks reachable.

- **Reduced link-state update (LSU) overhead**—LSUs can contain a variety of LSA types, including link-state information and summary information. Rather than sending an LSU about each network within an area, you can advertise a single or a few summarized routes between areas, thus reducing the overhead associated with link-state updates passed to other areas.

Hierarchical routing enables efficient routing because it enables you to control the types of routing information that you allow in and out of an area. OSPF enables different types of routing updates by assigning characteristics to each area and the routers connecting the areas. Area and router characteristics govern how they process routing information, including what types of LSUs a router can create, receive, and send. This section provides an overview of the following OSPF multiarea components, and their usage and configuration:

- Types of routers
- Types of LSAs
- Types of areas

---

**OSPF Design Guidelines**

Studies and real-world implementations have led to the following OSPF design guidelines, as documented in *OSPF Network Design Solutions*:

| | | | |
|---|---|---|---|
| **Routers in a Domain** | Minimum 20 | Mean 510 | Maximum 1000 |
| **Routers per Single Area** | Minimum 20 | Mean 160 | Maximum 350 |
| **Areas per Domain** | Minimum 1 | Mean 23 | Maximum 60 |

---

# Types of Routers

Different types of OSPF routers, shown in Figure 4-2, control differently how traffic is passed to and from areas. The router types are as follows:

- **Internal router**—Routers that have all interfaces in the same area are internal routers. Internal routers within the same area have identical link-state databases.

- **Backbone router**—Routers that sit in the backbone area. They have at least one interface connected to Area 0. These routers maintain OSPF routing information using the same procedures and algorithms as internal routers. Area 0 serves as the transit area between other OSPF areas.

- **Area Border Router (ABR)**—Routers that have interfaces attached to multiple areas. These routers maintain separate link-state databases for each area to which they are connected, and route traffic destined for or arriving from other areas. ABRs are exit points for the area, which means that routing information destined for another area can get there only via the local area's ABR. ABRs may summarize information from their link-state databases of their attached areas and distribute the information into the backbone area. The backbone ABRs then forward the information to all other connected areas. An area can have one or more ABRs.

- **Autonomous System Boundary Router (ASBR)**—Routers that have at least one interface into an external internetwork (another autonomous system), such as a non-OSPF network and another interface within OSPF. These routers can import (referred to as redistribution) non-OSPF network information to the OSPF network, and vice versa.

**Figure 4-2** *Types of Routers*

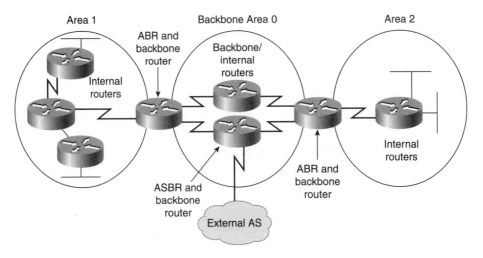

A router can be more than one router type. For example, if a router connects to Area 0 and Area 1, as well as to a non-OSPF network, it would be considered an ABR, an ASBR, and a backbone router.

A router has a separate link-state database for each area it is connected to. Therefore, an ABR would have a link-state database for Area 0 and another link-state database for the other area it participates in. Two routers belonging to the same area have, for that one area, identical area link-state databases.

Remember that a link-state database is synchronized between pairs of adjacent routers, meaning that it is synchronized between a router and its designated router (DR) and backup designated router (BDR).

## Types of Link-State Advertisements

Table 4-1 shows the types of LSAs included in an LSU. The Name column in Table 4-1 provides the official name of the LSA. Contained in the first set of parentheses is the nomenclature used in the routing table for that specific LSA. The second set of parentheses shows how the LSA type is indicated in the OSPF database. Example 4-1 provides a sample OSPF database.

**Table 4-1**    *Types of LSAs*

| LSA Type | Name | Description |
|---|---|---|
| 1 | Router link entry (record)<br>(O—OSPF)<br>(Router Link States) | Generated by each router for each area it belongs to. Describes the states of the router's link to the area. These are flooded only within a particular area. The link status and cost are two of the descriptors provided. |
| 2 | Network link entry<br>(O—OSPF)<br>(Net Link States) | Generated by DRs in multiaccess networks. Describes the set of routers attached to a particular network. These are flooded within the area that contains the network only. |
| 3 or 4 | Summary link entry<br>(IA—OSPF interarea)<br>(Summary Net Link States and Summary ASB Link States) | Originated by ABRs. Describes the links between the ABR and the internal routers of a local area. These entries are flooded throughout the backbone area to the other ABRs. Type 3 LSAs describe routes to networks within the local area and are sent to the backbone area. Type 4 LSAs describe reachability to ASBRs. These link entries are not flooded through totally stubby areas. |
| 5 | Autonomous system external link entry<br>(E1—OSPF external type 1)<br>(E2—OSPF external type 2)<br>(AS External Link States) | Originated by the ASBR. Describes routes to destinations external to the autonomous system. They are flooded throughout an OSPF autonomous system except for stub, totally stubby, and not-so-stubby areas. |
| 7 | Not-so-stubby area (NSSA) autonomous system external link entry<br>(N1—OSPF NSSA external type 1)<br>(N2—OSPF NSSA external type 2) | Originated by the ASBR in an NSSA. These LSAs are similar to type 5 LSAs, except that they are flooded only within the NSSA. At the area border router, selected type 7 LSAs are translated into type 5 LSAs and are flooded into the backbone. See Appendix A, "Job Aids and Supplements," for further information on NSSAs. |

**NOTE**    Type 3 and 4 LSAs are *summary* LSAs; they may or may not be *summarized.*

LSAs type 6 do not appear in Table 4-1 because they are not supported by Cisco Routers.

**NOTE**    All LSA types, except the autonomous system external link entry LSAs (type 5), are
flooded throughout a single area only.

**NOTE**    Only LSA types 1 through 5 are covered in this chapter. Types 6 and 7 LSAs are beyond
the scope of this chapter. Type 7 LSAs are discussed in Appendix A. Type 6 LSAs are
covered in RFC 1584.

**Example 4-1**    *OSPF Database Output*

```
p1r3#show ip ospf database
        OSPF Router with ID (10.64.0.1) (Process ID 1)


             Router Link States (Area 1)
Link ID         ADV Router      Age         Seq#         Checksum Link count
10.1.2.1        10.1.2.1        651         0x80000005 0xD482    4

             Net Link States (Area 1)
Link ID         ADV Router      Age         Seq#         Checksum
10.64.0.1       10.64.0.1       538         0x80000002 0xAD9A

             Summary Net Link States (Area 1)
Link ID         ADV Router      Age         Seq#         Checksum
10.2.1.0        10.2.1.2        439         0x80000002 0xE6F8
```

Figure 4-3 provides a representation of the different types of LSAs flooded in an OSPF
network. The router link states are type 1 LSAs, the network link states are type 2 LSAs,
and the summary link states are type 3 LSAs. The external link states are type 5 LSAs.

**Figure 4-3**    *Examples of LSAs Flooded in a Network*

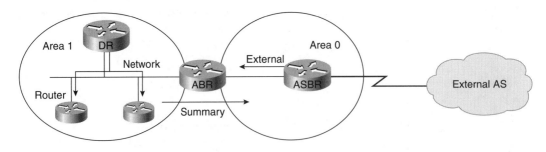

## Cost Associated with Summary Routes

The cost of a summary route is the smallest cost of a given interarea route that appears in the summary, plus the cost of the ABR link to the backbone. For example, if the cost of the ABR link to the backbone were 50, and if the ABR had an interarea route of 49, the total cost associated with the summary route would be 99. This calculation is done automatically for each summary route.

## Calculating the Cost of External Routes

The cost of an external route differs depending on the external type configured on the ASBR. You configure the router to generate one of the following external packet types:

- **Type 1 (E1)**—If a packet is an E1, then the metric is calculated by adding the external cost to the internal cost of each link that the packet crosses. Use this packet type when you have multiple ASBRs advertising a route to the same autonomous system.

- **Type 2 (E2)**—This is the default type. If a packet is an E2, then it will always have only the external cost assigned, no matter where in the area it crosses. Use this packet type if only one router is advertising a route to the external autonomous system. Type 2 routes are preferred over type 1 routes unless two same-cost routes exist to the destination.

| | |
|---|---|
| **NOTE** | The process of different routing protocols exchanging routing information is referred to as redistribution. Redistribution is discussed in Chapter 8, "Optimizing Routing Update Operation." |

Figure 4-4 provides a graphical example of how type 1 external routes are calculated.

# Types of Areas

The characteristics that you assign an area control the type of route information that it receives. The possible area types include the following:

- **Standard area**—An area that operates as discussed in Chapter 3, "Configuring OSPF in a Single Area." This area can accept (intra-area) link updates, (interarea) route summaries, and external routes.

- **Backbone area (transit area)**—When interconnecting multiple areas, the backbone area is the central entity to which all other areas connect. The backbone area is always labeled Area 0. All other areas must connect to this area to exchange and route information. The OSPF backbone has all the properties of a standard OSPF area.

**Figure 4-4** *External Routes Calculations*

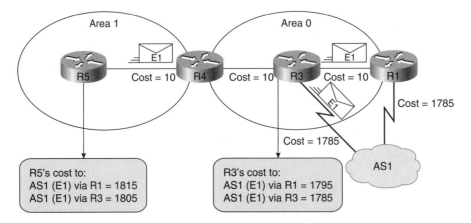

- **Stub area**—This refers to an area that does not accept information about routes external to the autonomous system (that is, the OSPF internetwork), such as routes from non-OSPF sources. If routers need to route to networks outside the autonomous system, they use a default route. A default route is noted as 0.0.0.0.

- **Totally stubby area**—This is an area that does not accept external autonomous system (AS) routes or summary routes from other areas internal to the autonomous system. Instead, if the router needs to send a packet to a network external to the area, it sends it using a default route. Totally stubby areas are Cisco proprietary.

- **Not-so-stubby-area**—A not-so-stubby area imports a limited number of external routes. The number of routes is limited to only those required to provide connectivity between areas. NSSAs are discussed in Appendix A.

## Routing Table Results with Different Areas

Example 4-2, Example 4-3, and Example 4-4 provide a comparison of routing tables that result when using summarization, stub areas, and totally stubby areas, respectively.

**Example 4-2** *IP Routing Table Without Any Special OSPF Capabilities: Route Summaries Without Route Summarization*

```
p1r3#show ip route
<Output Omitted>
      10.0.0.0/24 is subnetted, 15 subnets
O IA   10.3.1.0 [110/148] via 10.64.0.2, 00:03:12, Ethernet0
C      10.1.3.0 is directly connected, Serial0
O IA   10.2.1.0 [110/74] via 10.64.0.2, 00:31:46, Ethernet0
```

**Example 4-2**  *IP Routing Table Without Any Special OSPF Capabilities: Route Summaries Without Route Summarization (Continued)*

```
C       10.1.2.0 is directly connected, Serial1
O IA    10.3.3.0 [110/148] via 10.64.0.2, 00:03:12, Ethernet0
O IA    10.2.2.0 [110/138] via 10.64.0.2, 00:31:46, Ethernet0
O       10.1.1.0 [110/128] via 10.1.3.1, 00:31:46, Serial0
                 [110/128] via 10.1.2.1, 00:31:46, Serial
O IA    10.3.2.0 [110/212] via 10.64.0.2, 00:03:12, Ethernet0
O IA    10.2.3.0 [110/74] via 10.64.0.2, 00:31:46, Ethernet0
O IA    10.4.2.0 [110/286] via 10.64.0.2, 00:02:50, Ethernet0
O IA    10.4.3.0 [110/222] via 10.64.0.2, 00:02:50, Ethernet0
O IA    10.4.1.0 [110/222] via 10.64.0.2, 00:02:50, Ethernet0
O IA    10.66.0.0 [110/158] via 10.64.0.2, 00:02:51, Ethernet0
C       10.64.0.0 is directly connected, Ethernet0
O IA    10.65.0.0 [110/84] via 10.64.0.2, 00:03:19, Ethernet0
p1r3#
```

**Example 4-3**  *IP Routing Table with Route Summarization and Stub Capabilities Enabled*

```
p1r3#show ip route
<Output Omitted>
Gateway of last resort is 10.64.0.2 to network 0.0.0.0
     10.0.0.0/8 is variably subnetted, 9 subnets, 2 masks
O IA    10.2.0.0/16 [110/74] via 10.64.0.2, 00:11:11, Ethernet0
C       10.1.3.0/24 is directly connected, Serial0
O IA    10.3.0.0/16 [110/148] via 10.64.0.2, 00:07:59, Ethernet0
C       10.1.2.0/24 is directly connected, Serial1
O       10.1.1.0/24 [110/128] via 10.1.3.1, 00:16:51, Serial0
                    [110/128] via 10.1.2.1, 00:16:51, Serial1
O IA    10.4.0.0/16 [110/222] via 10.64.0.2, 00:09:13, Ethernet0
O IA    10.66.0.0/24 [110/158] via 10.64.0.2, 00:16:51, Ethernet0
C       10.64.0.0/24 is directly connected, Ethernet0
O IA    10.65.0.0/24 [110/84] via 10.64.0.2, 00:16:51, Ethernet0
O*IA 0.0.0.0/0 [110/11] via 10.64.0.2, 00:16:51, Ethernet0
p1r3#
```

**Example 4-4**  *IP Routing Table with Route Summarization and Totally Stub Capabilities Enabled*

```
p4r2#show ip route
Gateway of last resort is 10.66.0.1 to network 0.0.0.0
     10.0.0.0/24 is subnetted, 4 subnets
O       10.4.2.0 [110/128] via 10.4.3.2, 00:20:43, Serial1
                 [110/128] via 10.4.1.1, 00:20:43, Serial0
C       10.4.3.0 is directly connected, Serial1
C       10.4.1.0 is directly connected, Serial0
C       10.66.0.0 is directly connected, Ethernet0
O*IA 0.0.0.0/0 [110/11] via 10.66.0.1, 00:20:43, Ethernet0
```

**NOTE**    Example 4-4 was taken from a different router than Examples 4-2 and 4-3.

# OSPF Operation Across Multiple Areas

This section summarizes how routers generate link information, flood information, and build their routing tables when operating within a multiarea environment.

| | |
|---|---|
| **NOTE** | OSPF router operation is complex and accounts for numerous possible scenarios based on the nature of the network. This section provides a basic overview; refer to the OSPF version 2 RFC for more detailed information. |

Before reviewing how ABRs and other router types process route information, you should know how a packet makes its way across multiple areas. In general, the path a packet must take is as follows:

- If the packet is destined for a network within an area, then it is forwarded from the internal router, through the area to the destination internal router.

- If the packet is destined for a network outside the area, it must go through the following path:

  — The packet goes from the source network to an ABR.

  — The ABR sends the packet through the backbone area to the ABR of the destination network.

  — The destination ABR then forwards the packet through the area to the destination network.

## Flooding LSUs in Multiple Areas

ABRs are responsible for generating routing information about each area to which they are connected and flooding the information through the backbone area to the other areas to which they are connected. Figure 4-5 provides a graphical representation of the different LSA types exchanged in a multiple-area environment. The general process for flooding is as follows:

**Step 1**   The intra-area routing process occurs, as discussed in Chapter 3. Note that the entire intra-area must be synchronized before the ABR can begin sending summary LSAs.

**Step 2**   The ABR reviews the resulting link-state database and generates summary LSAs.

By default, the ABR sends summary LSAs for each network that it knows about. To reduce the number of summary LSA entries, you can configure route summarization so that a single IP address can represent multiple networks. To use route summarization, your areas must use contiguous IP addressing, as discussed in Chapter 2, "Extending IP Addresses." A good IP address plan will lower the number of summary LSA entries that an ABR needs to advertise.

**Step 3**    The summary LSAs (types 3 and 4) are placed in an LSU and are distributed through all ABR interfaces that are not in the local area, with the following exceptions:

— If the interface is connected to a neighboring router that is in a state below the exchange state, then the summary LSA is not forwarded.

— If the interface is connected to a totally stubby area, then the summary LSA is not forwarded.

— If the summary LSA includes a type 5 (external) route and the interface is connected to a stubby or totally stubby area, then the LSA is not sent to that area.

**Step 4**    When an ABR or ASBR receives summary LSAs, it adds them to its link-state database and floods them to its local area. The internal routers then assimilate the information into their databases.

Note that to reduce the number of route entries maintained by internal routers, you may define the area as a form of stub area.

**Figure 4-5**    *Flooding LSUs to Multiple Areas*

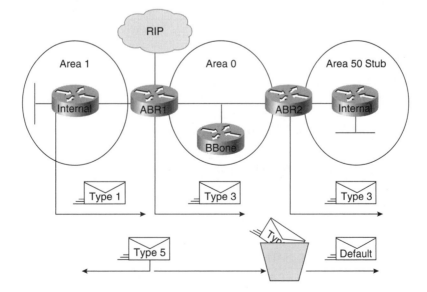

After all router types receive the routing updates, they must add them to their link-state databases and recalculate their routing tables. The order in which paths are calculated is as follows:

**Step 1**    All routers first calculate the paths to destinations within their area and add these entries into the routing table. These are the type 1 and type 2 LSAs.

**Step 2**    All routers, unless they are in a totally stubby area, then calculate the paths to the other areas within the internetwork. These paths are the interarea route entries, or type 3 and type 4 LSAs. If a router has an interarea route to a destination and an intra-area route to the same destination, the intra-area route is kept.

**Step 3**    All routers, except those that are in a form of stub area, then calculate the paths to the AS external (type 5) destinations.

At this point, a router can get to any network within or outside the OSPF autonomous system.

---

**NOTE**    According to RFC 2328, the order of preference for OSPF routes is as follows:

Intra-area routes, O
Interarea routes, O IA
External routes type 1, O E1
External routes type 2, O E2

---

## Virtual Links Overview

OSPF has certain restrictions when multiple areas are configured. One area must be defined as Area 0, the backbone area. It is called the backbone area because all communication must go through it—that is, all areas should be physically connected to Area 0 so that the routing information injected into Area 0 can be disseminated to other areas.

In some situations, however, a new area is added after the OSPF internetwork has been designed and configured, and it is not possible to provide that new area with direct access to the backbone. In these cases, a virtual link can be defined to provide the needed connectivity to the backbone area, as shown in Figure 4-6. The virtual link provides the disconnected area with a logical path to the backbone. The virtual link has two requirements, as follows:

- It must be established between two ABRs that share a common area.
- One of these two ABRs must be connected to the backbone area.

**Figure 4-6**    *Backbone Area Requirement Met Through Virtual Links*

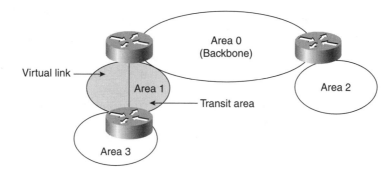

When virtual links are used, they require special processing during the SPF calculation. That is, the true next-hop router must be determined so that the true cost to get to a destination across the backbone can be calculated.

Virtual links serve the following purposes:

- Linking an area that does not have a physical connection to the backbone, as shown in Figure 4-6. This linking could occur when two organizations merge, for example.

- Patching the backbone in case discontinuity of Area 0 occurs.

Figure 4-7 illustrates the second purpose. Discontinuity of the backbone might occur, for example, if two companies, each running OSPF, are trying to merge the two separate networks into one with a common Area 0. The alternative would be to redesign the entire OSPF network and create a unified backbone.

**Figure 4-7**    *Discontiguous Area 0*

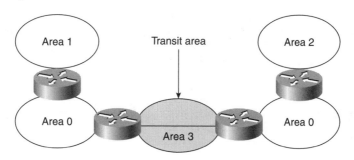

Another reason for creating a virtual link would be to provide redundancy in cases where a router failure causes the backbone to be split into two portions.

In Figure 4-7, the disconnected Area 0s are linked via a virtual link through the common Area 3. If a common area does not already exist, one can be created to become the transit area.

For adjacency purposes, OSPF treats two routers joined by a virtual link as an unnumbered point-to-point backbone network because they don't share a physical connection and, therefore, the IP address of their connecting interfaces is not on the same IP subnet.

---

**TIP**   When an unnumbered interface is configured, it references another interface on the router. When enabling OSPF on the unnumbered interface with the **network** command, use an *address wildcard-mask* pair that refers to the interface to which the unnumbered interface is pointing.

---

# Using and Configuring OSPF Multiarea Components

No special commands exist to activate the ABR or ASBR functionality on a router. The router takes on this role by virtue of the areas to which it is connected. As a reminder, the basic OSPF configuration steps are as follows:

**Step 1**   Enable OSPF on the router.

```
router(config)#router ospf process-id
```

**Step 2**   Identify which IP networks on the router are part of the OSPF network. For each network, you must identify what area the network belongs to. When configuring multiple OSPF areas, make sure to associate the correct network addresses with the desired area ID, as shown in Figure 4-8 and Example 4-5.

```
router(config-router)#network address wildcard-mask area area-id
```

**Step 3**   (Optional) If the router has at least one interface connected into a non-OSPF network, perform the proper configuration steps. At this point, the router will be acting as an ASBR. How the router exchanges (redistributes) non-OSPF route information with the other OSPF routers is discussed in Chapter 8.

---

**NOTE**   Refer to Chapter 3 for details about basic OSPF configuration commands.

---

Example 4-5 provides the configuration for an internal router (Router A) and for an ABR (Router B), as shown in Figure 4-8.

**Example 4-5**   *Configuring an OSPF Interarea Router and Area Border Router*

```
<Output Omitted>
RouterA(config)#interface Ethernet0
```

**Example 4-5**  *Configuring an OSPF Interarea Router and Area Border Router (Continued)*

```
RouterA(config-if)#ip address 10.64.0.1 255.255.255.0
!
<Output Omitted>
RouterA(config)#router ospf 77
RouterA(config-router)#network 10.0.0.0 0.255.255.255 area 0

<Output Omitted>
RouterB(config)#interface Ethernet0
RouterB(config-if)#ip address 10.64.0.2 255.255.255.0
!
RouterB(config)#interface Serial0
RouterB(config-if)#ip address 10.2.1.2 255.255.255.0
<Output Omitted>
RouterB(config)#router ospf 50
RouterB(config-router)#network 10.2.1.2 0.0.0.0 area 1
RouterB(config-router)#network 10.64.0.2 0.0.0.0 area 0
```

**Figure 4-8**  *Configuring Interarea Routers and ABRs*

## Using Stub and Totally Stubby Areas

RFCs provide for OSPF stub and OSPF NSSA configuration. NSSA is discussed in Appendix A. Totally stubby area is a Cisco proprietary standard. This section is concerned with stub areas and totally stubby areas.

Configuring a stub area reduces the size of the link-state database inside that area, thus reducing the memory requirements on routers. External networks (type 5 LSAs), such as those redistributed from other protocols into OSPF, are not allowed to be flooded into a stub area, as shown in Figure 4-9. Routing from these areas to the outside world is based on a default route (0.0.0.0). ABRs inject the default route (0.0.0.0) into the stub area. Having a default route means that if a packet is addressed to a network that is not in an internal router's route table, the router will automatically forward the packet to the ABR that sent a 0.0.0.0 LSA. This allows routers within the stub to reduce the size of their routing tables because a single default route replaces the many external routes.

A stub area is typically created when you have a hub-and-spoke topology, with the spoke being the stub area, such as a branch office. In this case, the branch office does not need to know about every network at the headquarters site; instead, it can use a default route to get there.

**Figure 4-9**    *Flooding LSAs to a Stub Area*

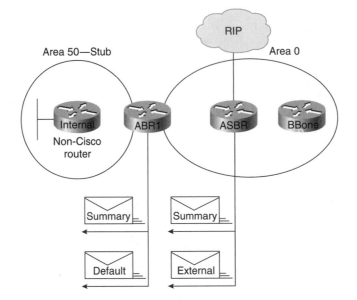

To further reduce the number of routes in a table, you can create a totally stubby area, which is a Cisco-specific feature. A totally stubby area is a stub area that blocks external type 5 LSAs and summary (type 3 and type 4) LSAs (interarea routes) from going into the area, as shown in Figure 4-10. This way, intra-area routes and the default of 0.0.0.0 are the only routes known to the stub area. ABRs inject the default summary link 0.0.0.0 into the totally stubby area. Each router picks the closest ABR as a gateway to everything outside the area.

Totally stubby areas further minimize routing information (as compared to stub areas) and increase stability and scalability of OSPF internetworks. This is typically a better solution than creating stub areas, unless the target area uses a mix of Cisco and non-Cisco routers.

An area could be qualified as a stub or totally stubby when it meets the following criteria:

- There is a single exit point from that area, or, if multiple exits (ABRs) exist, routing to outside the area does not have to take an optimal path. If the area has multiple exits, one or more ABRs will inject a default route into the stub area. In this situation, routing to other areas or autonomous systems could take a suboptimal path in reaching the destination by going out of the area via an exit point that is farther from the destination than other exit points.

- All OSPF routers inside the stub area (ABRs and internal routers) are configured as stub routers so that they will become neighbors and exchange routing information. The configuration commands for creating stub networks are covered in the next section.

- The area is not needed as a transit area for virtual links.

**Figure 4-10** *Flooding LSAs to a Totally Stubby Area*

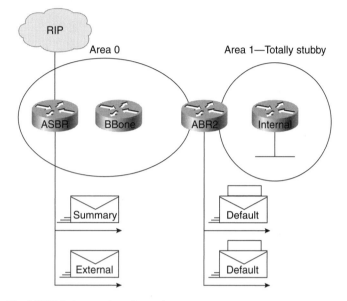

- No ASBR is internal to the stub area.
- The area is not the backbone area (not Area 0).

These restrictions are necessary because a stub or a totally stubby area is mainly configured to carry internal routes and can't have external links injected in that area.

## Configuring Stub and Totally Stubby Areas

To configure an area as stub or totally stubby, do the following:

**Step 1**  Configure OSPF, as described earlier in this chapter.

**Step 2**  Define an area as stub or totally stubby by adding the **area stub** command to all routers within the area, as explained in Table 4-2:

```
router (config-router)#area area-id stub [no-summary]
```

**Table 4-2**  *area stub Command for Configuring Stub and Totally Stubby Areas*

| area stub Command | Description |
| --- | --- |
| *area-id* | Serves as an identifier for the stub or totally stubby area. The identifier can be either a decimal value or an IP address. |
| **no-summary** | (Only for ABRs connected to totally stubby areas.) Prevents an ABR from sending summary link advertisements into the stub area. Use this option for creating a totally stubby area. |

| NOTE | Remember that the stub flag contained in the hello packet must be set on all routers within a stubby area. |
|------|----|

| NOTE | The **no-summary** keyword can be put on non-ABR routers, but it has no effect. |
|------|----|

Step 3    (Optional, for ABRs only.) Define the cost of the default route that is injected in the stub or totally stubby area, using the **area default-cost** command, as explained in Table 4-3.

```
router (config-router)#area area-id default-cost cost
```

**Table 4-3**    *Changing the OSPF Cost*

| area default-cost Command | Description |
|---|---|
| *area-id* | Identifier for the stub area. The identifier can be either a decimal value or an IP address. |
| *cost* | Cost for the default summary route used for a stub or totally stubby area. The cost value is a 24-bit number. The default cost is 1. |

## Stub Area Configuration Example

In Example 4-6, Area 2 is defined as the stub area, as shown in Figure 4-11. No external routes from the external autonomous system will be forwarded into the stub area.

**Example 4-6**    *Configuring a Stub Area*

```
R3#

interface Ethernet 0
ip address 192.168.14.1 255.255.255.0
interface Serial 0
ip address 192.168.15.1 255.255.255.252

router ospf 100
network 192.168.14.0 0.0.0.255 area 0
network 192.168.15.0 0.0.0.255 area 2
area 2 stub

R4#

interface Serial 0
ip address 192.168.15.2 255.255.255.252
```

**Example 4-6**  *Configuring a Stub Area (Continued)*

```
router ospf 15
network 192.168.15.0 0.0.0.255 area 2
area 2 stub
```

The last line in the configuration of each router in Example 4-6, **area 2 stub**, defines the stub area. The area stub default cost has not been configured on R3, so this router advertises 0.0.0.0 (the default route) with a default cost metric of 1 plus any internal costs.

Each router in the stub area must be configured with the **area stub** command.

**Figure 4-11**  *Stub Area Topology*

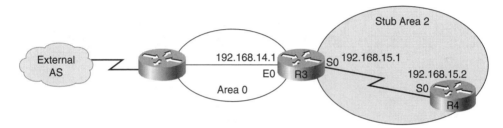

The only routes that will appear in R4's routing table are intra-area routes (designated with an O in the routing table), the default route, and interarea routes (both designated with an IA in the routing table; the default route will also be denoted with an asterisk).

**NOTE**    The **area stub** command determines whether the routers in the stub become neighbors. This command must be included in all routers in the stub if they are to exchange routing information.

## Totally Stubby Area Configuration Example

In Example 4-7, the keyword **no-summary** has been added to the **area stub** command on R3 (the ABR). This keyword causes summary routes (interarea) to also be blocked from the stub area. Each router in the stub area picks the closest ABR as a gateway to everything outside the area, as shown in Figure 4-12.

**Example 4-7**  *Totally Stubby Configuration Example*

```
R3#showrun
<output omitted>
router ospf 100
network 192.168.14.0 0.0.0.255 area 0
network 192.168.15.0 0.0.0.255 area 2
```

**Example 4-7** *Totally Stubby Configuration Example (Continued)*

```
area 2 stub no-summary

R4#showrun
<output omitted>
router ospf 15
network 192.168.15.0 0.0.0.255 area 2
area 2 stub
```

**Figure 4-12** *Totally Stubby Area*

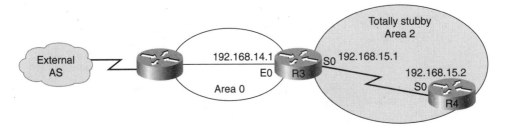

In Example 4-7, the only routes that will appear in R4's routing table are intra-area routes (designated with an O in the routing table) and the default route. No interarea routes (designated with an IA in the routing table) will be included.

Remember that to further reduce the number of link-state advertisements sent into a stub area, you can configure **no-summary** on the ABR (R3) to prevent it from sending summary link advertisements (link-state advertisements type 3) into the stub area—thus, R4 has only intra-area routes.

**NOTE** As shown in Example 4-7, the difference in configuring a stub area and a totally stubby area is the keyword **no-summary** applied on the ABR

### How Does OSPF Generate Default Routes?

The way that OSPF generates default routes (0.0.0.0) varies depending on the type of area into which the default route is being injected— normal areas, stub and totally stubby areas, and NSSAs.

By default, in normal areas, routers don't generate default routes. To have an OSPF router generate a default route, use the **default-information originate** [**always**] [**metric** *metric-value*] [**metric-type** *type-value*] [**route-map** *map-name*] router configuration command. This generates an external type 2 link (by default) with link-state ID 0.0.0.0 and network mask 0.0.0.0, which makes the router an Autonomous System Boundary Router (ASBR).

There are two ways to inject a default route into a normal area. If the ASBR already has the default route, you can advertise 0.0.0.0 into the area. If the ASBR doesn't have the route, you can add the keyword **always** to the **default-information originate** command, which will then advertise 0.0.0.0.

For stub and totally stubby areas, the ABR to the stub area generates a summary LSA with the link-state ID 0.0.0.0. This is true even if the ABR doesn't have a default route. In this scenario, you don't need to use the **default-information originate** command.

The ABR for the NSSA generates the default route, but not by default. To force the ABR to generate the default route, use the **area** *area-id* **nssa default-information-originate** command. The ABR generates a type 7 LSA with the link-state ID 0.0.0.0. If you want to import routes only into the normal areas, but not into the NSSA area, you can use the **no-redistribution** option on the NSSA ABR.

## Multiple-Area NBMA Environment

Multiple areas can be used within nonbroadcast multiaccess (NBMA) OSPF environments. In Figure 4-13, the networks located at the corporate headquarters are in Area 0, while the fully meshed Frame Relay network and each of the regional site networks are assigned to Area 1. Area 1 is a stub area. One benefit of this design is that it eliminates the flooding of external LSAs into the Frame Relay network because OSPF does not flood external LSAs into stub areas—in this case, Area 1. Router R1 functions as an ABR, which keeps topology changes in Area 0 from causing a topological recalculation in Area 1. With this topology, the remote LAN segments must participate in Area 1, or virtual links would need to be configured so the LAN segment's areas would connect to the backbone area.

Another possible OSPF area configuration involves putting all the Frame Relay interfaces in Area 0, as shown in Figure 4-14. This permits the location of stub or transit areas at each remote site and at the headquarters, but it causes summary LSAs to be flooded throughout the Frame Relay network and results in a larger number of routers performing recalculation if any topology change takes place in Area 0.

## Supporting Route Summarization

Summarizing is the consolidation of multiple routes into a single advertisement. The operation and benefits of route summarization are discussed in Chapter 2 . At this point, however, you should realize the importance of proper summarization in a network. Route summarization directly affects the amount of bandwidth, CPU, and memory resources consumed by the OSPF process.

If summarization is not used, every specific-link LSA will be propagated into the OSPF backbone and beyond, causing unnecessary network traffic and router overhead. Whenever an LSA is sent, all affected OSPF routers will have to recompute their LSA databases and routes using the SPF algorithm.

With summarization, only summarized routes will propagate into the backbone (Area 0). This process is very important because it prevents every router from having to rerun the SPF algorithm, increases the network's stability, and reduces unnecessary traffic. Also with summarization, if a network link fails, the topology change will not be propagated into the backbone (and other areas by way of the backbone). As such, flooding outside the area will not occur.

**Figure 4-13** *Multiple OSPF Area with Frame Relay*

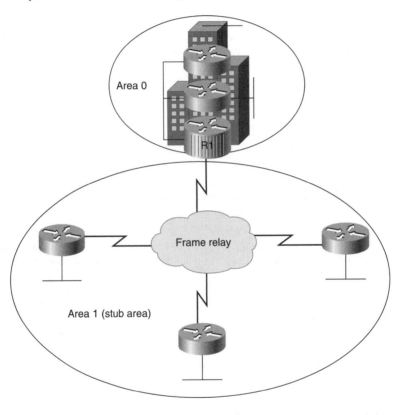

| NOTE | Be careful with the terminology: summary LSAs (type 3 and type 4) may or may not contain summarized routes. |
|------|--------------------------------------------------------------------------------------------------------------|

**Figure 4-14**  *Multiple OSPF Area in Frame Relay with a Centralized Area 0*

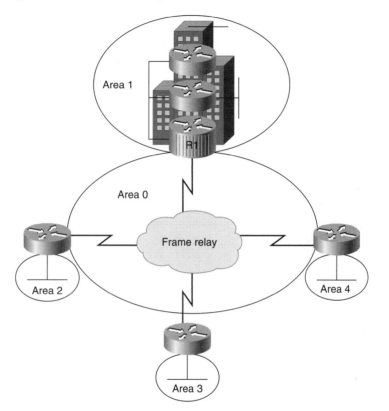

Two types of summarization exist, as follows:

- **Interarea route summarization**—Interarea route summarization is done on ABRs and applies to routes from within each area. It does not apply to external routes injected into OSPF via redistribution. To take advantage of summarization, network numbers within areas should be assigned in a contiguous way to be capable of consolidating these addresses into one range.

- **External route summarization**—External route summarization is specific to external routes that are injected into OSPF via redistribution. Here again, it is important to ensure that the external address ranges that are being summarized are contiguous. Summarizing overlapping ranges from two different routers could cause packets to be sent to the wrong destination. Usually only ASBRs summarize external routes, but ABRs can also do this.

## Variable-Length Subnet Masking

Variable-length subnet masking (VLSM) is discussed in Chapter 2.

OSPF carries subnet mask information and therefore supports multiple subnet masks for the same major network. Discontiguous subnets are also supported by OSPF because subnet masks are part of the link-state database. However, other protocols such as Routing Information Protocol version 1 (RIPv1) and Interior Gateway Routing Protocol (IGRP) do not support VLSM or discontiguous subnets. If the same major network crosses the boundaries of an OSPF and RIP or IGRP domain, VLSM information redistributed into RIP or IGRP will be lost and static routes will have to be configured in the RIP or IGRP domains.

Because OSPF supports VLSM, it is possible to develop a true hierarchical addressing scheme. This hierarchical addressing results in very efficient summarization of routes throughout the network.

## Using Route Summarization

To take advantage of summarization, as discussed in Chapter 2, network numbers in areas should be assigned in a contiguous way, thus enabling the grouping of addresses into one range, as shown in Figure 4-15.

In Figure 4-15, the list of six networks in Router B's routing table can be summarized into two summary address advertisements.

**Figure 4-15** *Summarization Between Two Areas*

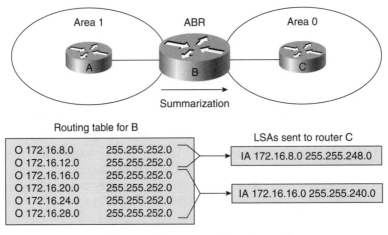

– Interarea (IA) summary link carries mask
– One entry can represent several subnets

The third octet of each address is shown in binary in Table 4-4, to illustrate which addresses can be summarized.

**Table 4-4**    *Binary Calculation of the Summarization on Router B*

| Bit Value | 128 | 64 | 32 | 16 | 8 | 4 | 2 | 1 | Decimal Value of Octet |
|---|---|---|---|---|---|---|---|---|---|
| The first two addresses can be summarized using a /21 prefix | 0 | 0 | 0 | 0 | 1 | 0 | 0 | 0 | 8 |
| | 0 | 0 | 0 | 0 | 1 | 1 | 0 | 0 | 12 |
| The last four addresses can be summarized using a /20 prefix | 0 | 0 | 0 | 1 | 0 | 0 | 0 | 0 | 16 |
| | 0 | 0 | 0 | 1 | 0 | 1 | 0 | 0 | 20 |
| | 0 | 0 | 0 | 1 | 1 | 0 | 0 | 0 | 24 |
| | 0 | 0 | 0 | 1 | 1 | 1 | 0 | 0 | 28 |

**Actual mask is /22 (255.255.252.0)**

## Configuring Route Summarization

In OSPF, summarization is off by default. To configure route summarization on the ABR, do the following:

**Step 1**    Configure OSPF, as discussed earlier in this section.

**Step 2**    Instruct the ABR to summarize routes for a specific area before injecting them into a different area, using the following **area range** command. This command is defined in Table 4-5.

```
router(config-router)#area area-id range address mask
```

**Table 4-5**    *area range Command*

| area range Command | Description |
|---|---|
| *area-id* | Identifier of the area about which routes are to be summarized |
| *address* | Summary address designated for a range of addresses |
| *mask* | IP subnet mask used for the summary route |

To configure route summarization on an ASBR to summarize external routes, do the following:

**Step 1** Configure OSPF, as discussed earlier in this section.

**Step 2** Instruct the ASBR to summarize external routes before injecting them into the OSPF domain, using the **summary-address** command, explained in Table 4-6.

```
router(config-router)#summary-address address mask [prefix mask][not-
advertise] [tag tag]
```

**Table 4-6** *summary-address Command*

| summary-address Command | Description |
| --- | --- |
| *address* | Summary address designated for a range of addresses |
| *mask* | IP subnet mask used for the summary route |
| *prefix* | IP route prefix for the destination |
| *mask* | IP subnet mask used for the summary route |
| **not-advertise** | (Optional) Used to suppress routes that match the prefix/mask pair |
| *tag* | (Optional) Tag value that can be used as a match value for controlling redistribution via route maps, or other routing protocols such as EIGRP and BGP |

**NOTE** The OSPF **summary-address** command summarizes only external routes. This command is usually used on the ASBR that is injecting the external routes into OSPF, but may also be used on an ABR. Use the **area range** command for summarization of routes between OSPF areas (in other words, for summarization of IA routes).

Figure 4-16 provides the graphical representation of Example 4-8, where route summarization can occur in both directions.

**Figure 4-16** *Summarization on Multiple Areas*

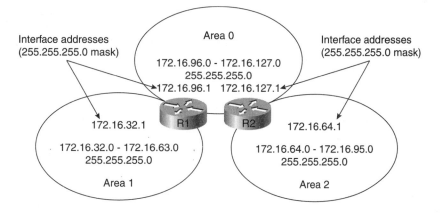

**Example 4-8** *Summarization Configuration on ABRs*

```
R1#
router ospf 100
  network 172.16.32.1  0.0.0.0 area 1
  network 172.16.96.1  0.0.0.0 area 0
  area 0 range 172.16.96.0  255.255.224.0
  area 1 range 172.16.32.0  255.255.224.0

R2#
router ospf 100
  network 172.16.64.1 0.0.0.0 area 2
  network 172.16.127.1 0.0.0.0 area 0
  area 0 range 172.16.96.0  255.255.224.0
  area 2 range 172.16.64.0  255.255.224.0
```

In the configuration on router R1, the following is true:

- **area 0 range 172.16.96.0 255.255.224.0**—Identifies Area 0 as the area containing the range of networks to be summarized into Area 1. The ABR R1 is summarizing the range of subnets from 172.16.96.0 to 172.16.127.0 into one range: 172.16.96.0 255.255.224.0. This summarization is achieved by masking the first 3 left-most bits of subnet 96 using the mask 255.255.224.0.

- **area 1 range 172.16.32.0 255.255.224.0**—Identifies Area 1 as the area containing the range of networks to be summarized into Area 0. The ABR R1 is summarizing the range of subnets from 172.16.32.0 to 172.16.63.0 into one range: 172.16.32.0 255.255.224.0.

The configuration on router R2 works exactly the same way.

Note that, depending on your network topology, you may not want to summarize Area 0 networks. For example, if you have more than one ABR between an area and the backbone area, sending a summary LSA with the explicit network information will ensure that the shortest path is selected. If you summarize the addresses, a suboptimal path selection may occur.

## Configuring Virtual Links

To configure a virtual link, do the following:

**Step 1** Configure OSPF, as described earlier in this section.

**Step 2** On each router that will make the virtual link, create the virtual link using the **area virtual-link** command, as explained in Table 4-7. The routers that make the links are the ABR that connects the remote area to the transit area and the ABR that connects the transit area to the backbone area.

```
router(config-router)#area area-id virtual-link router-id
```

**Table 4-7** *area virtual-link Configuration Command*

| area virtual-link Command | Description |
| --- | --- |
| *area-id* | Area ID assigned to the transit area for the virtual link (decimal or dotted decimal format). There is no default. |
| *router-id* | Router ID of the virtual link neighbor. |

If you do not know the neighbor's router ID, you can Telnet to it and enter the **show ip ospf interface** command, as displayed in Example 4-9.

**Example 4-9** *show ip ospf interface Command Output*

```
remoterouter#show ip ospf interface ethernet 0
Ethernet0 is up, line protocol is up
  Internet Address 10.64.0.2/24, Area 0
  Process ID 1, Router ID 10.64.0.2, Network Type BROADCAST, Cost: 10
  Transmit Delay is 1 sec, State DR, Priority 1
  Designated Router (ID) 10.64.0.2, Interface address 10.64.0.2
  Backup Designated router (ID) 10.64.0.1, Interface address 10.64.0.1
```

In Figure 4-17, Area 3 does not have a direct physical connection to the backbone (Area 0), which is an OSPF requirement because the backbone is a collection point for LSAs. ABRs forward summary LSAs to the backbone, which in turn forwards the traffic to all areas. All interarea traffic transits the backbone.

**Figure 4-17**  *Need for a Virtual Link*

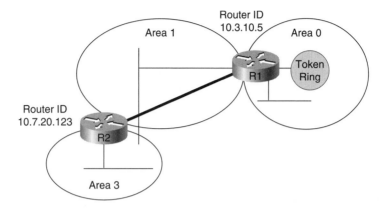

To provide connectivity to the backbone, a virtual link must be configured between R2 and R1. Area 1 will be the transit area, and R1 will be the entry point into Area 0. R2 will have a logical connection to the backbone through the transit area.

In Figure 4-17, both sides of the virtual link must be configured. Example 4-10 shows the configuration of R1 and R2; in these configurations:

- R2 has the command **area 1 virtual-link 10.3.10.5**. With this command, Area 1 is defined to be the transit area, and the router ID of the other side of the virtual link is configured.

- R1 has the command **area 1 virtual-link 10.7.20.123**. With this command, Area 1 is defined to be the transit area, and the router ID of the other side of the virtual link is configured.

**Example 4-10**  *Virtual Link Configuration on Routers R1 and R2*

```
R1#showrun
<output omitted>
router ospf 100
network 10.2.3.0 0.0.0.255 area 0
network 10.3.2.0 0.0.0.255 area 1
area 1 virtual-link 10.7.20.123

R2#showrun
<output omitted>
router ospf 63
 network 10.3.0.0 0.0.0.255 area 1
 network 10.7.0.0 0.0.0.255 area 3
area 1 virtual-link 10.3.10.5
```

# Verifying OSPF Operation

The same **show** commands listed in Chapter 3 can be used to verify OSPF operation in multiple areas. Some additional commands include the following:

- **show ip ospf border-routers**—Displays the internal OSPF routing table entries to ABRs and ASBRs.

- **show ip ospf virtual-links**—Displays parameters about the current state of OSPF virtual links.

- **show ip ospf process-id**—Displays information about each area to which the router is connected, and indicates whether the router is an ABR, an ASBR, or both.

- **show ip ospf** [*process-id area-id*] **database** [*keyword*]—Displays the contents of the topological database maintained by the router. Several keywords can be used with this command to get specific information about links:

  — **network**—Displays network link-state information.

  — **summary**—Displays summary information about router link states.

  — **asbr-summary**—Displays information about ASBR link states.

  — **external**—Displays information about autonomous system external link states.

  — **database-summary**—Displays database summary information and totals.

# Case Study: OSPF Multiarea

Refer to Chapter 1, "Routing Principles," for introductory information on the running case study.

This section provides an overview of JKL's recently redesigned corporate network, as shown in Figure 4-18. This topology embodies many of the characteristics that a properly addressed hierarchical network should exhibit.

**Figure 4-18** *JKL's Enterprise Redesigned Network*

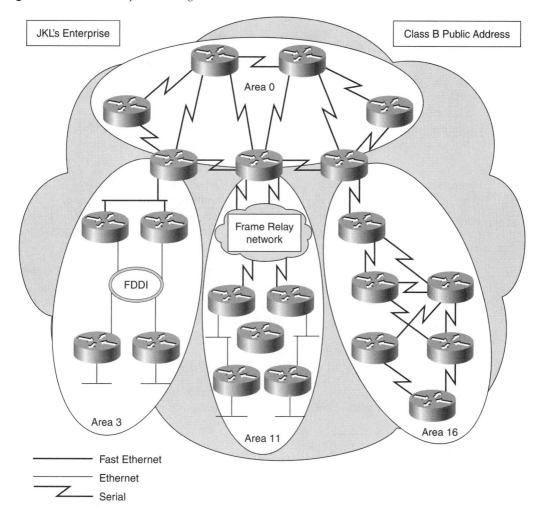

Following are some issues to consider when analyzing Figure 4-18:

- Requirements for a hierarchical topology
- Address allocation with route summarization
- Limits for routing update traffic
- Elements that affect convergence time
- Effects of an NBMA topology
- Ease of configuration and management

## Case Study Solution

Over the past few years, JKL Corporation had experienced continuous growth in all of its business sectors. In some areas, the growth was very rapid and business needs overshadowed good design principles. These growth spikes caused the address space to become fragmented and caused the size of the topology tables and routing tables to increase dramatically. Management was alerted to the fact that the network was no longer easily scalable and that continued growth would only compound the problems. Rather than wait for the scaling issues to dramatically affect their ability to do business, management ordered a complete overhaul and upgrade of the network. For more than a year, portions of the network were readdressed and reconfigured to form a hierarchical topology that emphasized proper address allocation, summary routes, and ease of troubleshooting.

Proper design allowed Area 0 to be small, redundant, and free of host devices. Thanks to proper address allocation, individual areas pass summary routes into Area 0 that enable traffic between areas to be forwarded efficiently (because of the small number of entries in the Area 0 routing tables) through the backbone. Area 0 design employed redundant links to assist in rapid convergence in case of a link failure in the core of the network.

Although the backbone area must be numbered as zero, the numbers for the other areas can be chosen arbitrarily. In Figure 4-18, three areas are shown, although more areas exist in the actual network. These three areas were selected because they demonstrate different technologies and topologies that OSPF supports. This multiarea topology demonstrates the different router types (internal router, backbone router, Area Border Router, and Autonomous System Border Router). This topology also offers an opportunity to reinforce where the different types of LSAs (router, summary, default, and so on) are used.

Area 3 demonstrates a purely LAN-based topology. Therefore, the neighbor relationships will be done automatically following DR/BDR elections.

Area 11 shows a partial-mesh (hub-and-spoke) switched network topology. In this area, the neighbor either will be acquired dynamically or will be, preferably, manually configured. Also, you must remember to use the **broadcast** keyword on the frame-relay map commands to allow routing updates to pass through the switched portion of the network.

Area 16 is an example of a WAN-based, point-to-point topology. In this area, no DRs/DBRs are elected and the neighborship is automatic. This area offers a favorable topology in which an effective use of VLSM would help with address allocation.

A hierarchical topology in this case offers several benefits:

- Route summarization is available
- Area 0 routing table is small and efficient
- Link-state changes are localized to one area
- Convergence within an area is rapid

This case study gives you a chance to confirm that proper network design, especially of large networks, provides numerous advantages when it comes to controlling the types and frequency of routing information allowed in and out of areas.

# Summary

After reading this chapter, you should be able to describe the issues with interconnecting multiple areas, understand how OSPF addresses each of these issues, and explain the differences among the possible types of areas, routers, and LSAs. You should also be able to show how OSPF supports the use of VLSM, how it applies route summarization in multiple areas, and how it operates in a multiple-area NBMA environment.

Finally, you should be able to configure a multiarea OSPF network and verify OSPF operations in multiple areas.

# Configuration Exercise: Configuring a Multiarea OSPF Network

Complete the following exercise to configure OSPF with multiple areas.

---

### Configuration Exercises

In this book, Configuration Exercises are used to provide practice in configuring routers with the commands presented. If you have access to real hardware, you can try these exercises on your routers; refer to Appendix H, "Configuration Exercise Equipment Requirements and Backbone Configurations," for a list of recommended equipment and configuration commands for the backbone routers. However, even if you don't have access to any routers, you can go through the exercises and keep a log of your own "running configurations" on separate sheets of paper. Commands used and answers to the Configuration Exercises are provided at the end of the exercise.

In these exercises, you are in control of a pod of three routers; there are assumed to be 12 pods in the network. The pods are interconnected to a backbone. In most of the exercises, there is only one router in the backbone; in some cases, another router is added to the backbone. Each of the Configuration Exercises in this book assumes that you have completed the previous exercises on your pod.

---

## Objectives

In this Configuration Exercise, you will configure the pxr1 router serial interface S3 to be in OSPF Area 0. Then you will configure all other router serial interfaces to be part of a specific OSPF area, other than 0. You will then verify connectivity to the backbone_r1 router, summarize the subnets in your OSPF area, and check again for connectivity to backbone_r1 router.

When the previous tasks will have been completed, you will reconfigure your OSPF area to be a stub area and then a totally stubby area, and verify connectivity to the backbone_r1 router.

As an additional exercise, you may want to reconfigure your OSPF area to be a not-so-stubby area (NSSA) and verify connectivity to the backbone_r1 router. You will use loopback interfaces to simulate type 7 external routes into your NSSA. You will then summarize the simulated type 7 external routes into Area 0.

Also as an optional practice, you can configure an OSPF virtual link to support an OSPF area not directly connected to Area 0.

You will use the **show** and **debug** commands to verify OSPF operations of all these exercises.

## Visual Objective

Figure 4-19 illustrates the topology used for this multiarea OSPF Configuration Exercise.

**Figure 4-19** *Configuration of Multiarea OSPF Network*

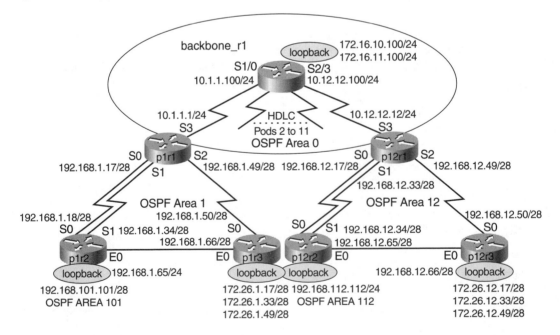

## Command List

In this Configuration Exercise, you will use the commands listed in Table 4-8 in logical order. Refer to this list if you need configuration command assistance during the Configuration Exercise.

**Table 4-8**    *Commands Used in the Configuration Exercise*

| Command | Description |
|---|---|
| **router ospf 200** | Enables OSPF with a process ID of 200 |
| **network 10.x.x.x 0.0.0.0 area 0** | Specifies the interfaces on which to run OSPF, and their areas |
| **area x range 192.168.x.0 255.255.255.0** | Summarizes addresses |
| **area x stub [no-summary]** | Configures an area as a stub or totally stubby area |
| **area x virtual-link 192.168.x.49** | Creates an OSPF virtual link |
| **area x nssa** | Configures an area as a not-so-stubby-area (NSSA) |
| **summary-address 172.16.0.0 255.255.0.0** | Summarizes external addresses into OSPF |
| **show ip ospf** | Displays general information about the OSPF routing process |
| **show ip ospf neighbor** | Displays information about OSPF neighbors |
| **show ip ospf database** | Displays the entries in the OSPF link-state database |
| **show ip ospf interface** | Displays OSPF-specific information about an interface |
| **show ip ospf virtual-links** | Displays the status of the OSPF virtual links |
| **debug ip ospf adj** | Shows the events involved in the building or breaking of an OSPF adjacency |

## Setup

Setup is as follows:

**Step 1**    On pxr1, disable Frame Relay switching.

Reconfigure the pxr1 serial interfaces (S0, S1, S2, and S3) to be running HDLC encapsulation. Change the pxr1 serial interface S0, S1, S2, and S3 to the correct IP address configuration:

| | |
|---|---|
| pxr1 S0 | 192.168.x.17/28 |
| pxr1 S1 | 192.168.x.33/28 |
| pxr1 S2 | 192.168.x.49/28 |
| pxr1 S3 | 10.x.x.x/24 |

Apply the **no shut** command to Serial 1 and Serial 3 interfaces on your p*x*r1 router.

**Step 2**   On p*x*r2, remove the S0.1 subinterface.

```
p1r2(config)#no interface s0.1 point-to-point
```

Change the p*x*r2 S0 interface encapsulation back to HDLC. Reconfigure the IP address on your p*x*r2 S0 to 192.168.*x*.18/28. Apply the **no shut** command to Ethernet 0 and Serial 1 interfaces on p*x*r2.

**Step 3**   On p*x*r3, remove the S0.1 subinterface.

```
p1r3(config)#no interface s0.1 point-to-point
```

Change the p*x*r3 S0 interface encapsulation back to HDLC. Reconfigure the IP address on your p*x*r3 S0 to 192.168.*x*.50/28. Apply the **no shut** command to Ethernet 0 and interface on p*x*r3.

**Step 4**   On your p*x*r2 router, create a loopback interface (loopback 10) with the following IP address:

| Pod | pxr2 Loopback10 Interface IP Address |
| --- | --- |
| 1 | 192.168.101.101/24 |
| 2 | 192.168.102.102/24 |
| 3 | 192.168.103.103/24 |
| 4 | 192.168.104.104/24 |
| 5 | 192.168.105.105/24 |
| 6 | 192.168.106.106/24 |
| 7 | 192.168.107.107/24 |
| 8 | 192.168.108.108/24 |
| 9 | 192.168.109.109/24 |
| 10 | 192.168.110.110/24 |
| 11 | 192.168.111.111/24 |
| 12 | 192.168.112.112/24 |

Create three loopback interfaces on your p*x*r3 router using the following IP addresses:

| Router | Int Loopback11 | Int Loopback12 | Int Loopback13 |
| --- | --- | --- | --- |
| p1r3 | 172.26.1.17/28 | 172.26.1.33/28 | 172.26.1.49/28 |
| p2r3 | 172.26.2.17/28 | 172.26.2.33/28 | 172.26.2.49/28 |
| p3r3 | 172.26.3.17/28 | 172.26.3.33/28 | 172.26.3.49/28 |

| Router | Int Loopback11 | Int Loopback12 | Int Loopback13 |
|--------|----------------|----------------|----------------|
| p4r3 | 172.26.4.17/28 | 172.26.4.33/28 | 172.26.4.49/28 |
| p5r3 | 172.26.5.17/28 | 172.26.5.33/28 | 172.26.5.49/28 |
| p6r3 | 172.26.6.17/28 | 172.26.6.33/28 | 172.26.6.49/28 |
| p7r3 | 172.26.7.17/28 | 172.26.7.33/28 | 172.26.7.49/28 |
| p8r3 | 172.26.8.17/28 | 172.26.8.33/28 | 172.26.8.49/28 |
| p9r3 | 172.26.9.17/28 | 172.26.9.33/28 | 172.26.9.49/28 |
| p10r3 | 172.26.10.17/28 | 172.26.10.33/28 | 172.26.10.49/28 |
| p11r3 | 172.26.11.17/28 | 172.26.11.33/28 | 172.26.11.49/28 |
| p12r3 | 172.26.12.17/28 | 172.26.12.33/28 | 172.26.12.49/28 |

## Task 1: Enabling OSPF with Multiple Areas and Area Summarization

Complete the following steps:

**Step 1**  Type in the command to configure the p$x$r1 router to run OSPF, with the S3 interface as the only interface within your pod to be in Area 0.

**Step 2**  What commands would you type to configure all the 192.168.$x.y$/28 interfaces on all routers in your pod to be in area $x$, where $x$ = your pod number?

| Pod | OSPF Area Number |
|-----|------------------|
| 1 | Area 1 |
| 2 | Area 2 |
| 3 | Area 3 |
| 4 | Area 4 |
| 5 | Area 5 |
| 6 | Area 6 |
| 7 | Area 7 |
| 8 | Area 8 |
| 9 | Area 9 |
| 10 | Area 10 |
| 11 | Area 11 |
| 12 | Area 12 |

**Step 3**   Verify you have full connectivity within your pod.

**Step 4**   Telnet to the backbone_r1 router; the password is cisco. Display its routing table. Do you see your pod's subnets as O IA routes in the backbone_r1 routing table? What type of routes are O IA routes?

Exit the Telnet to the backbone_r1 router.

**Step 5**   Display the pxr1 routing table. Which types of OSPF routes are in the routing table? (If there is another pod configured for OSPF, you should see three types; otherwise, you should see two types.)

Display the pxr2 routing table. Which three types of OSPF routes are in the routing table?

Which router within your pod is the Area Border Router (ABR)?

At the ABR, summarize all the 192.168.*x*.y/28 subnets in your area (area *x*) into a single summarized route of 192.168.*x*.0/24.

Telnet to the backbone_r1 router; the password is cisco. Display the backbone_r1 router's routing table to verify that your subnets are summarized properly. Exit the Telnet to the backbone_r1 router.

**Step 6**   Save the current configurations of all the routers within your pod to NVRAM.

## Task 2: Enabling OSPF Stub Area

Complete the following steps:

**Step 1**   Configure your pod's OSPF area (area *x*) into a stub area. For this step, on which router(s) do you need to configure?

**Step 2**   Do you still see the O IA routes in the pxr2 and pxr3 routing table?

Do you still see the O E2 route in the pxr2 and pxr3 routing table? Explain your answer.

Do you see any additional routes in the pxr2 and pxr3 routing table that were not there before?

**Step 3**   Use the **show ip ospf** command to verify that your OSPF area *x* is a stub area.

**Step 4**   Verify you have full connectivity within your pod and to the backbone_r1 router loopback interfaces (you may also see routes to the other pods).

**Step 5**   Save the current configurations of all the routers within your pod to NVRAM.

## Task 3: Enabling OSPF Totally Stubby Area

Complete the following steps:

**Step 1**    Configure your pod's OSPF area into a totally stubby area. For this step, on which router(s) do you need to configure?

Do you still see the O IA routes in the p*x*r2 and p*x*r3 routing table? Please explain your answer.

**Step 2**    Verify that you have full connectivity within your pod and to the backbone_r1 router loopback interfaces (you may also see routes to the other pods).

**Step 3**    Save the current configurations of all the routers within your pod to NVRAM.

## Task 4: Enabling OSPF Not-So-Stubby Area (Optional)

**Step 1**    Remove the totally stubby area configuration commands and then reconfigure your pod's OSPF area into an NSSA area. For this step, which router(s) do you need to configure? (On the p*x*r1 router, use the **default-information-originate** option when configuring NSSA.)

---

**NOTE**    On p*x*r1, you must remove the totally stubby area configuration command and then remove the stub area configuration command to completely remove any stub characteristics before configuring NSSA.

---

**Step 2**    Do you see any O IA routes in the p*x*r2 and p*x*r3 routing table?

Do you see any O*N2 route in the p*x*r2 and p*x*r3 routing table?

What type of route is the O*N2 route?

**Step 3**    Verify that you have full connectivity within your pod and to the backbone_r1 router (you may also see routes to the other pods).

**Step 4**    Save the current configurations of all the routers within your pod to NVRAM.

**Step 5**    The loopback interfaces that you created on p*x*r3 in setup are used to simulate type 7 external routes into your NSSA. Use the **redistribute** command at your p*x*r3 routers to redistribute only the loopback interfaces into your NSSA. Route redistribution will be discussed in Chapter 8. For now, just enter the following commands to perform the redistribution at the p*x*r3 router:

```
router ospf 200
redistribute connected metric-type 1 subnets route-map passlb
route-map passlb
match ip address 1
access-list 1 permit 172.26.x.0 0.0.0.255
```

*x* is your pod number.

**Step 6** Do you see any O N1 routes in the routing table of p*x*r1? What type of routes are those?

Telnet to the backbone_r1 router. Do you see your 172.26.*x*.0 routes in the backbone_r1 routing table? What type of routes are those? Exit the Telnet session to the backbone_r1 router when you're done.

**Step 7** At your p*x*r1 router, summarize the three external loopback interface addresses into a single summarized route of 172.26.*x*.0 255.255.255.0, where *x* = your pod number.

Telnet to the backbone_r1 router; the password is cisco. Display the backbone_r1 router's routing table to verify that your external routes are summarized properly. Exit the Telnet session to the backbone_r1 router.

**Step 8** Save the current configurations of all the routers within your pod to NVRAM.

**Step 9** (Bonus step) Currently, your pod's external summarized route shows up as O E1 type route at the backbone_r1 router and at any other pods that are configured. Change it so that it shows up as O E2 type route at the backbone_r1 router and any other pods.

## Bonus Questions

How is the OSPF cost metric calculated on Cisco routers?

Which type of external OSPF route will have its metric incremented as it is distributed into the OSPF domain, type 1 or type 2?

Summarize the following subnet address range into the minimum number of routes: 172.25.168.0/24 to 172.25.175.0/24

## Task 5: Enabling OSPF Virtual Link to Support an OSPF Area Not Connected to Area 0 (Optional)

Complete the following steps:

**Step 1**    In this task, you will be setting up virtual links. Virtual links do not support stub areas, so before you can perform the next task, you need to remove the stub area commands.

Do not remove the loopback interfaces on any of your routers. You will need to use them again in the later Configuration Exercises.

At your pxr1 router, remove any **area stub** or **area nssa** commands. Save the current configuration of pxr1 to NVRAM. Note: if you have configured NSSA, you must remove the **area x nssa default-information-originate** command and then remove the **area x nssa** command to completely remove any NSSA characteristics. Otherwise, you must remove the totally stubby area configuration command and then remove the stub area configuration command to completely remove any stub characteristics.

At your pxr2 router, remove any **area stub** or **area nssa** commands from your pxr2 router. Save the current configuration of pxr2 to NVRAM.

At your pxr3 router, remove any **area stub** or **area nssa** commands. Save the current configuration of pxr3 to NVRAM.

**Step 2**    At your pxr2 router, place that loopback interface you created in setup into the following assigned OSPF area:

| Pod | pxr2 loopback10 Interface IP Address | OSPF Area |
|-----|--------------------------------------|-----------|
| 1 | 192.168.101.101/24 | 101 |
| 2 | 192.168.102.102/24 | 102 |
| 3 | 192.168.103.103/24 | 103 |
| 4 | 192.168.104.104/24 | 104 |
| 5 | 192.168.105.105/24 | 105 |
| 6 | 192.168.106.106/24 | 106 |
| 7 | 192.168.107.107/24 | 107 |
| 8 | 192.168.108.108/24 | 108 |
| 9 | 192.168.109.109/24 | 109 |
| 10 | 192.168.110.110/24 | 110 |
| 11 | 192.168.111.111/24 | 111 |
| 12 | 192.168.112.112/24 | 112 |

**Step 3**  Enter the command to check the OSPF router ID of your pxr2 router.

What is the current OSPF router ID of pxr2?

**Step 4**  Create an OSPF virtual link to support the OSPF area (10x) that you created in Step 1. At which routers do you need to configure the virtual link?

**Step 5**  Use the **show ip ospf virtual-links** command to verify that your virtual link is up.

**Step 6**  Verify that the pxr1 routing table shows your pxr2 loopback interface as an O IA route.

From pxr1, ping your pxr2 loopback interface. Was the ping successful?

**Step 7**  (Challenge step) Telnet to the backbone_r1 router; the password is cisco. Display its routing table. Notice that your area summarization from Task 1 is no longer working. You should see all your 192.168.x.y subnets in the backbone_r1 router now. Why?

Hint: Enter the **show ip ospf** command at your pxr2 router. What type of OSPF router is pxr2 now with the virtual link defined?

At the pxr2 router, summarize all the 192.168.x.y/28 subnets in your area (area x) into a single summarized route of 192.168.x.0/24.

Telnet to the backbone_r1 router; the password is cisco. Display the backbone_r1 router's routing table to verify that your subnets are summarized properly.

**Step 8**  Save the current configurations of all the routers within your pod to NVRAM.

## Completion Criteria

You have successfully completed this Configuration Exercise if you correctly supplied the commands required to configure and to verify a multiple-area OSPF network, and if you were able to correctly answer the questions in the Configuration Exercises. At the end of this exercise, all the routers should have full connectivity to each other; each pod will be running OSPF in its own area, and the pxr1 routers will be ABRs to Area 0.

# Answers to Configuration Exercise: Configuring a Multiarea OSPF Network

This section provides the answers to the questions in the Configuration Exercise. The answers are in **bold**.

## Answers to Setup

**Step 1**   On p*x*r1, disable Frame Relay switching.

Reconfigure the p*x*r1 serial interfaces (S0, S1, S2, and S3) to be running HDLC encapsulation. Change the p*x*r1 serial interface S0, S1, S2, and S3 to the correct IP address configuration:

| | |
|---|---|
| p*x*r1 S0 | 192.168.*x*.17/28 |
| p*x*r1 S1 | 192.168.*x*.33/28 |
| p*x*r1 S2 | 192.168.*x*.49/28 |
| p*x*r1 S3 | 10.*x.x.x*/24 |

Apply the **no shut** command to Serial 1 and Serial 3 interfaces on your p*x*r1 router.

```
p1r1(config)#no frame-relay switching
p1r1(config)#int s0
p1r1(config-if)#encapsulation hdlc
p1r1(config-if)#ip address 192.168.1.17 255.255.255.240
p1r1(config-if)#exit
p1r1(config)#int s1
p1r1(config-if)#encapsulation hdlc
p1r1(config-if)#ip address 192.168.1.33 255.255.255.240
p1r1(config-if)#no shut
p1r1(config-if)#exit
p1r1(config)#int s2
p1r1(config-if)#encapsulation hdlc
p1r1(config-if)#ip address 192.168.1.49 255.255.255.240
p1r1(config-if)#no shut
p1r1(config-if)#exit
p1r1(config)#int s3
p1r1(config-if)#encapsulation hdlc
p1r1(config-if)#ip address 10.1.1.1 255.255.255.0
p1r1(config-if)#no shut
```

**Step 2**   On p*x*r2, remove the S0.1 subinterface.

```
p1r2(config)#no interface s0.1 point-to-point
```

Change the p*x*r2 S0 interface encapsulation back to HDLC. Reconfigure the IP address on your p*x*r2 S0 to 192.168.*x*.18/28. Apply the **no shut** command to Ethernet 0 and Serial 1 interfaces on p*x*r2.

```
p1r2(config)#int s0
p1r2(config-if)#encapsulation hdlc
p1r2(config-if)#ip address 192.168.1.18 255.255.255.240
p1r2(config-if)#exit
p1r2(config)#int s1
p1r2(config-if)#no shutdown
p1r2(config-if)#exit
p1r2(config)#int e0
p1r2(config-if)#no shutdown
```

**Step 3**   On p*x*r3, remove the S0.1 subinterface.

```
p1r3(config)#no interface s0.1 point-to-point
```

Change the p*x*r3 S0 interface encapsulation back to HDLC. Reconfigure the IP address on your p*x*r3 S0 to 192.168.*x*.50/28. Apply the **no shut** command to Ethernet 0 and interface on p*x*r3.

```
p1r3(config)#int s0
p1r3(config-if)#encapsulation hdlc
p1r3(config-if)#ip address 192.168.1.50 255.255.255.240
p1r3(config-if)#exit
p1r3(config)#int e0
p1r3(config-if)#no shutdown
```

**Step 4**   On your p*x*r2 router, create a loopback interface (loopback 10) with the following IP address:

| Pod | pxr2 Loopback10 Interface IP Address |
| --- | --- |
| 1 | 192.168.101.101/24 |
| 2 | 192.168.102.102/24 |
| 3 | 192.168.103.103/24 |
| 4 | 192.168.104.104/24 |
| 5 | 192.168.105.105/24 |
| 6 | 192.168.106.106/24 |
| 7 | 192.168.107.107/24 |
| 8 | 192.168.108.108/24 |
| 9 | 192.168.109.109/24 |
| 10 | 192.168.110.110/24 |
| 11 | 192.168.111.111/24 |
| 12 | 192.168.112.112/24 |

```
p1r2(config)#int loopback 10
p1r2(config-if)#ip address 192.168.101.101 255.255.255.0
```

Create three loopback interfaces on your p*x*r3 router using the following IP addresses:

| Router | Int Loopback11 | Int Loopback12 | Int Loopback13 |
| --- | --- | --- | --- |
| p1r3 | 172.26.1.17/28 | 172.26.1.33/28 | 172.26.1.49/28 |
| p2r3 | 172.26.2.17/28 | 172.26.2.33/28 | 172.26.2.49/28 |
| p3r3 | 172.26.3.17/28 | 172.26.3.33/28 | 172.26.3.49/28 |
| p4r3 | 172.26.4.17/28 | 172.26.4.33/28 | 172.26.4.49/28 |

*(Continued)*

| Router | Int Loopback11 | Int Loopback12 | Int Loopback13 |
|--------|----------------|----------------|----------------|
| p5r3 | 172.26.5.17/28 | 172.26.5.33/28 | 172.26.5.49/28 |
| p6r3 | 172.26.6.17/28 | 172.26.6.33/28 | 172.26.6.49/28 |
| p7r3 | 172.26.7.17/28 | 172.26.7.33/28 | 172.26.7.49/28 |
| p8r3 | 172.26.8.17/28 | 172.26.8.33/28 | 172.26.8.49/28 |
| p9r3 | 172.26.9.17/28 | 172.26.9.33/28 | 172.26.9.49/28 |
| p10r3 | 172.26.10.17/28 | 172.26.10.33/28 | 172.26.10.49/28 |
| p11r3 | 172.26.11.17/28 | 172.26.11.33/28 | 172.26.11.49/28 |
| p12r3 | 172.26.12.17/28 | 172.26.12.33/28 | 172.26.12.49/28 |

```
p1r3(config)#int loopback 11
p1r3(config-if)#ip address 172.26.1.17 255.255.255.240
p1r3(config-if)#int loopback 12
p1r3(config-if)#ip address 172.26.1.33 255.255.255.240
p1r3(config-if)#int loopback 13
p1r3(config-if)#ip address 172.26.1.49 255.255.255.240
```

## Answers to Task 1: Enabling OSPF with Multiple Areas and Area Summarization

Complete the following steps:

**Step 1**   Type in the command to configure the p*x*r1 router to run OSPF, with the S3 interface as the only interface within your pod to be in Area 0.

```
p1r1(config)#router ospf 200
p1r1(config-router)#network 10.0.0.0 0.255.255.255 area 0
```

**Step 2**   What commands would you type to configure all the 192.168.*x.y*/28 interfaces on all routers in your pod to be in area *x*, where *x* = your pod number?

| Pod | OSPF Area Number |
|-----|------------------|
| 1 | Area 1 |
| 2 | Area 2 |
| 3 | Area 3 |
| 4 | Area 4 |
| 5 | Area 5 |
| 6 | Area 6 |

*continues*

*(Continued)*

| Pod | OSPF Area Number |
|-----|------------------|
| 7 | Area 7 |
| 8 | Area 8 |
| 9 | Area 9 |
| 10 | Area 10 |
| 11 | Area 11 |
| 12 | Area 12 |

```
p1r1(config)#router ospf 200
p1r1(config-router)#network 192.168.1.0 0.0.0.255 area 1

p1r2(config)#router ospf 200
p1r2(config-router)#network 192.168.1.0 0.0.0.255 area 1

p1r3(config)#router ospf 200
p1r3(config-router)#network 192.168.1.0 0.0.0.255 area 1
```

**Step 3** Verify that you have full connectivity within your pod.

```
p1r1#ping p1r2

Type escape sequence to abort.
Sending 5, 100-byte ICMP Echos to 192.168.1.65, timeout is 2 seconds:
!!!!!
Success rate is 100 percent (5/5), round-trip min/avg/max = 32/32/36 ms


p1r1#ping p1r3

Type escape sequence to abort.
Sending 5, 100-byte ICMP Echos to 192.168.1.66, timeout is 2 seconds:
!!!!!
Success rate is 100 percent (5/5), round-trip min/avg/max = 28/31/32 ms


p1r2#ping p1r1

Type escape sequence to abort.
Sending 5, 100-byte ICMP Echos to 192.168.1.17, timeout is 2 seconds:
!!!!!
Success rate is 100 percent (5/5), round-trip min/avg/max = 32/32/32 ms


p1r2#ping p1r3

Type escape sequence to abort.
Sending 5, 100-byte ICMP Echos to 192.168.1.66, timeout is 2 seconds:
!!!!!
```

```
Success rate is 100 percent (5/5), round-trip min/avg/max = 4/4/4 ms


p1r3#ping p1r1

Type escape sequence to abort.
Sending 5, 100-byte ICMP Echos to 192.168.1.17, timeout is 2 seconds:
!!!!!
Success rate is 100 percent (5/5), round-trip min/avg/max = 32/32/32 ms


p1r3#ping p1r2

Type escape sequence to abort.
Sending 5, 100-byte ICMP Echos to 192.168.1.65, timeout is 2 seconds:
!!!!!
Success rate is 100 percent (5/5), round-trip min/avg/max = 1/3/4 ms
```

**Step 4**    Telnet to the backbone_r1 router; the password is cisco. Display its
routing table. Do you see your pod's subnets as O IA routes in the
backbone_r1 routing table? What type of routes are O IA routes?

```
p1r1#telnet bbr1
Trying bbr1 (10.1.1.100)... Open


User Access Verification

Password:
backbone_r1>show ip route
Codes: C - connected, S - static, I - IGRP, R - RIP, M - mobile, B - BGP
       D - EIGRP, EX - EIGRP external, O - OSPF, IA - OSPF inter area
       N1 - OSPF NSSA external type 1, N2 - OSPF NSSA external type 2
       E1 - OSPF external type 1, E2 - OSPF external type 2, E - EGP
       i - IS-IS, L1 - IS-IS level-1, L2 - IS-IS level-2, ia - IS-IS inter area
       * - candidate default, U - per-user static route, o - ODR
       P - periodic downloaded static route

Gateway of last resort is not set

     172.16.0.0/24 is subnetted, 2 subnets
C       172.16.10.0 is directly connected, Loopback100
C       172.16.11.0 is directly connected, Loopback101
     10.0.0.0/24 is subnetted, 2 subnets
C       10.1.1.0 is directly connected, Serial1/0
C       10.2.2.0 is directly connected, Serial1/1
     192.168.1.0/28 is subnetted, 4 subnets
O IA    192.168.1.64 [110/3134] via 10.1.1.1, 00:01:15, Serial1/0
O IA    192.168.1.32 [110/3124] via 10.1.1.1, 00:03:08, Serial1/0
O IA    192.168.1.48 [110/3124] via 10.1.1.1, 00:03:08, Serial1/0
O IA    192.168.1.16 [110/3124] via 10.1.1.1, 00:03:08, Serial1/0
backbone_r1>
```

**Yes, the backbone_r1 router has OIA routes. The OIA routes are interarea routes.**

Exit the Telnet to the backbone_r1 router.

```
backbone_r1>exit

[Connection to bbr1 closed by foreign host]
p1r1#
```

**Step 5**    Display the p*x*r1 routing table. Which types of OSPF routes are in the routing table? (If there is another pod configured for OSPF, you should see three types; otherwise, you should see two types.)

**Intra-area (O) routes and external type 2 (O E2) routes can be seen. If there was another pod configured, interarea (OIA) routes would also be seen.**

```
p1r1#show ip route
Codes: C - connected, S - static, I - IGRP, R - RIP, M - mobile, B - BGP
       D - EIGRP, EX - EIGRP external, O - OSPF, IA - OSPF inter area
       N1 - OSPF NSSA external type 1, N2 - OSPF NSSA external type 2
       E1 - OSPF external type 1, E2 - OSPF external type 2, E - EGP
       i - IS-IS, L1 - IS-IS level-1, L2 - IS-IS level-2, * - candidate default
       U - per-user static route, o - ODR
       T - traffic engineered route

Gateway of last resort is not set

     172.16.0.0/24 is subnetted, 2 subnets
O E2    172.16.10.0 [110/20] via 10.1.1.100, 00:02:30, Serial3
O E2    172.16.11.0 [110/20] via 10.1.1.100, 00:02:30, Serial3
     10.0.0.0/24 is subnetted, 2 subnets
O       10.2.2.0 [110/3124] via 10.1.1.100, 00:04:17, Serial3
C       10.1.1.0 is directly connected, Serial3
     192.168.1.0/28 is subnetted, 4 subnets
O       192.168.1.64 [110/1572] via 192.168.1.34, 00:02:30, Serial1
                     [110/1572] via 192.168.1.18, 00:02:30, Serial0
                     [110/1572] via 192.168.1.50, 00:02:30, Serial2
C       192.168.1.32 is directly connected, Serial1
C       192.168.1.48 is directly connected, Serial2
C       192.168.1.16 is directly connected, Serial0
p1r1#
```

Display the p*x*r2 routing table. Which three types of OSPF routes are in the routing table?

```
p1r2#show ip route
Codes: C - connected, S - static, I - IGRP, R - RIP, M - mobile, B - BGP
       D - EIGRP, EX - EIGRP external, O - OSPF, IA - OSPF inter area
```

```
     N1 - OSPF NSSA external type 1, N2 - OSPF NSSA external type 2
     E1 - OSPF external type 1, E2 - OSPF external type 2, E - EGP
     i - IS-IS, L1 - IS-IS level-1, L2 - IS-IS level-2, * - candidate default
     U - per-user static route, o - ODR
     T - traffic engineered route

Gateway of last resort is not set

     172.16.0.0/24 is subnetted, 2 subnets
O E2    172.16.10.0 [110/20] via 192.168.1.17, 00:02:47, Serial0
                    [110/20] via 192.168.1.33, 00:02:47, Serial1
O E2    172.16.11.0 [110/20] via 192.168.1.17, 00:02:47, Serial0
                    [110/20] via 192.168.1.33, 00:02:47, Serial1
     10.0.0.0/24 is subnetted, 2 subnets
O IA    10.2.2.0 [110/4686] via 192.168.1.33, 00:02:47, Serial1
                 [110/4686] via 192.168.1.17, 00:02:47, Serial0
O IA    10.1.1.0 [110/3124] via 192.168.1.33, 00:02:47, Serial1
                 [110/3124] via 192.168.1.17, 00:02:47, Serial0
     192.168.1.0/28 is subnetted, 4 subnets
C       192.168.1.64 is directly connected, Ethernet0
C       192.168.1.32 is directly connected, Serial1
O       192.168.1.48 [110/1572] via 192.168.1.66, 00:02:49, Ethernet0
C       192.168.1.16 is directly connected, Serial0
C    192.168.101.0/24 is directly connected, Loopback10
p1r2#
```

Which router within your pod is the Area Border Router (ABR)?

**Router p*x*r1 is the ABR.**

At the ABR, summarize all the 192.168.*x*.y/28 subnets in your area (area *x*) into a single summarized route of 192.168.*x*.0/24.

```
p1r1(config)#router ospf 200
p1r1(config-router)#area 1 range 192.168.1.0 255.255.255.0
```

Telnet to the backbone_r1 router; the password is cisco. Display the backbone_r1 router's routing table to verify that your subnets are summarized properly. Exit the Telnet to the backbone_r1 router.

```
p1r1#telnet bbr1
Trying bbr1 (10.1.1.100)... Open


User Access Verification

Password:
backbone_r1>show ip route
Codes: C - connected, S - static, I - IGRP, R - RIP, M - mobile, B - BGP
       D - EIGRP, EX - EIGRP external, O - OSPF, IA - OSPF inter area
       N1 - OSPF NSSA external type 1, N2 - OSPF NSSA external type 2
```

```
          E1 - OSPF external type 1, E2 - OSPF external type 2, E - EGP
          i - IS-IS, L1 - IS-IS level-1, L2 - IS-IS level-2, ia - IS-IS inter area
          * - candidate default, U - per-user static route, o - ODR
          P - periodic downloaded static route

Gateway of last resort is not set

     172.16.0.0/24 is subnetted, 2 subnets
C        172.16.10.0 is directly connected, Loopback100
C        172.16.11.0 is directly connected, Loopback101
     10.0.0.0/24 is subnetted, 2 subnets
C        10.1.1.0 is directly connected, Serial1/0
C        10.2.2.0 is directly connected, Serial1/1
O IA 192.168.1.0/24 [110/3134] via 10.1.1.1, 00:00:30, Serial1/0
backbone_r1>
backbone_r1>exit

[Connection to bbr1 closed by foreign host]
p1r1#
```

**Step 6**   Save the current configurations of all the routers within your pod to NVRAM.

```
p1r1#copy run start
Destination filename [startup-config]?
Building configuration...


p1r2#copy run start
Destination filename [startup-config]?
Building configuration...


p1r3#copy run start
Destination filename [startup-config]?
Building configuration...
```

# Answers to Task 2: Enabling OSPF Stub Area

Complete the following steps:

**Step 1**   Configure your pod's OSPF area (area *x*) into a stub area. For this step, on which router(s) do you need to configure?

```
p1r1(config)#router ospf 200
p1r1(config-router)#area 1 stub

p1r2(config)#router ospf 200
p1r2(config-router)#area 1 stub

p1r3(config)#router ospf 200
p1r3(config-router)#area 1 stub
```

**Step 2**   Do you still see the O IA routes in the p*x*r2 and p*x*r3 routing table?

Yes

```
p1r2#show ip route
Codes: C - connected, S - static, I - IGRP, R - RIP, M - mobile, B - BGP
       D - EIGRP, EX - EIGRP external, O - OSPF, IA - OSPF inter area
       N1 - OSPF NSSA external type 1, N2 - OSPF NSSA external type 2
       E1 - OSPF external type 1, E2 - OSPF external type 2, E - EGP
       i - IS-IS, L1 - IS-IS level-1, L2 - IS-IS level-2, * - candidate default
       U - per-user static route, o - ODR
       T - traffic engineered route

Gateway of last resort is 192.168.1.33 to network 0.0.0.0

     10.0.0.0/24 is subnetted, 2 subnets
O IA    10.2.2.0 [110/4686] via 192.168.1.33, 00:00:14, Serial1
                 [110/4686] via 192.168.1.17, 00:00:14, Serial0
O IA    10.1.1.0 [110/3124] via 192.168.1.33, 00:00:14, Serial1
                 [110/3124] via 192.168.1.17, 00:00:14, Serial0
     192.168.1.0/28 is subnetted, 4 subnets
C       192.168.1.64 is directly connected, Ethernet0
C       192.168.1.32 is directly connected, Serial1
O       192.168.1.48 [110/1572] via 192.168.1.66, 00:00:14, Ethernet0
C       192.168.1.16 is directly connected, Serial0
C    192.168.101.0/24 is directly connected, Loopback10
O*IA 0.0.0.0/0 [110/1563] via 192.168.1.33, 00:00:15, Serial1
                [110/1563] via 192.168.1.17, 00:00:15, Serial0


p1r3#show ip route
Codes: C - connected, S - static, I - IGRP, R - RIP, M - mobile, B - BGP
       D - EIGRP, EX - EIGRP external, O - OSPF, IA - OSPF inter area
       N1 - OSPF NSSA external type 1, N2 - OSPF NSSA external type 2
       E1 - OSPF external type 1, E2 - OSPF external type 2, E - EGP
       i - IS-IS, L1 - IS-IS level-1, L2 - IS-IS level-2, * - candidate default
       U - per-user static route, o - ODR
       T - traffic engineered route

Gateway of last resort is 192.168.1.49 to network 0.0.0.0

     172.26.0.0/28 is subnetted, 3 subnets
C       172.26.1.48 is directly connected, Loopback13
C       172.26.1.32 is directly connected, Loopback12
C       172.26.1.16 is directly connected, Loopback11
     10.0.0.0/24 is subnetted, 2 subnets
O IA    10.2.2.0 [110/4686] via 192.168.1.49, 00:00:19, Serial0
O IA    10.1.1.0 [110/3124] via 192.168.1.49, 00:00:19, Serial0
     192.168.1.0/28 is subnetted, 4 subnets
C       192.168.1.64 is directly connected, Ethernet0
O       192.168.1.32 [110/1572] via 192.168.1.65, 00:00:19, Ethernet0
C       192.168.1.48 is directly connected, Serial0
O       192.168.1.16 [110/1572] via 192.168.1.65, 00:00:20, Ethernet0
O*IA 0.0.0.0/0 [110/1563] via 192.168.1.49, 00:00:20, Serial0
p1r3#
```

Do you still see the O E2 route in the p*x*r2 and p*x*r3 routing table? Explain your answer.

**No. All the area routers are configured as stub, so the ABR, p*x*r1, does not pass any external routes within its OSPF updates.**

Do you see any additional routes in the p*x*r2 and p*x*r3 routing table that were not there before?

**Router p*x*r2 and router p*x*r3 now have a default route pointing to the ABR, p*x*r1.**

**Step 3**  Use the **show ip ospf** command to verify that your OSPF area *x* is a stub area.

```
p1r2#show ip ospf
 Routing Process "ospf 200" with ID 192.168.101.101
 Supports only single TOS(TOS0) routes
 SPF schedule delay 5 secs, Hold time between two SPFs 10 secs
 Minimum LSA interval 5 secs. Minimum LSA arrival 1 secs
 Number of external LSA 0. Checksum Sum 0x0
 Number of DCbitless external LSA 0
 Number of DoNotAge external LSA 0
 Number of areas in this router is 1. 0 normal 1 stub 0 nssa
    Area 1
        Number of interfaces in this area is 3
        It is a stub area
        Area has no authentication
        SPF algorithm executed 8 times
        Area ranges are
        Number of LSA 8. Checksum Sum 0x29602
        Number of DCbitless LSA 0
        Number of indication LSA 0
        Number of DoNotAge LSA 0

p1r3#show ip ospf
 Routing Process "ospf 200" with ID 172.26.1.49
 Supports only single TOS(TOS0) routes
 SPF schedule delay 5 secs, Hold time between two SPFs 10 secs
 Minimum LSA interval 5 secs. Minimum LSA arrival 1 secs
 Number of external LSA 0. Checksum Sum 0x0
 Number of DCbitless external LSA 0
 Number of DoNotAge external LSA 0
 Number of areas in this router is 1. 0 normal 1 stub 0 nssa
    Area 1
        Number of interfaces in this area is 2
        It is a stub area
        Area has no authentication
        SPF algorithm executed 6 times
        Area ranges are
        Number of LSA 7. Checksum Sum 0x25804
```

```
Number of DCbitless LSA 0
Number of indication LSA 0
Number of DoNotAge LSA 0
```

**Step 4**   Verify that you have full connectivity within your pod and to the backbone_r1 router loopback interfaces (you may also see routes to the other pods).

```
p1r1#ping 172.16.10.100

Type escape sequence to abort.
Sending 5, 100-byte ICMP Echos to 172.16.10.100, timeout is 2 seconds:
!!!!!
Success rate is 100 percent (5/5), round-trip min/avg/max = 28/30/32 ms

p1r1#ping 172.16.11.100

Type escape sequence to abort.
Sending 5, 100-byte ICMP Echos to 172.16.11.100, timeout is 2 seconds:
!!!!!
Success rate is 100 percent (5/5), round-trip min/avg/max = 32/32/32 ms


p1r2#ping 172.16.10.100

Type escape sequence to abort.
Sending 5, 100-byte ICMP Echos to 172.16.10.100, timeout is 2 seconds:
!!!!!
Success rate is 100 percent (5/5), round-trip min/avg/max = 56/58/64 ms

p1r2#ping 172.16.11.100

Type escape sequence to abort.
Sending 5, 100-byte ICMP Echos to 172.16.11.100, timeout is 2 seconds:
!!!!!
Success rate is 100 percent (5/5), round-trip min/avg/max = 56/58/60 ms


p1r3#ping 172.16.10.100

Type escape sequence to abort.
Sending 5, 100-byte ICMP Echos to 172.16.10.100, timeout is 2 seconds:
!!!!!
Success rate is 100 percent (5/5), round-trip min/avg/max = 60/60/64 ms


p1r3#ping 172.16.11.100

Type escape sequence to abort.
Sending 5, 100-byte ICMP Echos to 172.16.11.100, timeout is 2 seconds:
!!!!!
Success rate is 100 percent (5/5), round-trip min/avg/max = 60/60/60 ms
p1r3#
```

**Step 5** Save the current configurations of all the routers within your pod to NVRAM.

```
p1r1#copy run start
Destination filename [startup-config]?
Building configuration...

p1r2#copy run start
Destination filename [startup-config]?
Building configuration...

p1r3#copy run start
Destination filename [startup-config]?
Building configuration...
```

# Answers to Task 3: Enabling OSPF Totally Stubby Area

Complete the following steps:

**Step 1** Configure your pod's OSPF area into a totally stubby area. For this step, on which router(s) do you need to configure?

**Add the no-summary option to the ABR, p*x*r1.**

```
p1r1(config)#router ospf 200
p1r1(config-router)#area 1 stub no-summary
```

Do you still see the O IA routes in the p*x*r2 and p*x*r3 routing table? Please explain your answer.

**No, you have only a default route pointing at the ABR. The ABR does not pass interarea or external routes to p*x*r2 and p*x*r3.**

```
p1r2#show ip route
Codes: C - connected, S - static, I - IGRP, R - RIP, M - mobile, B - BGP
       D - EIGRP, EX - EIGRP external, O - OSPF, IA - OSPF inter area
       N1 - OSPF NSSA external type 1, N2 - OSPF NSSA external type 2
       E1 - OSPF external type 1, E2 - OSPF external type 2, E - EGP
       i - IS-IS, L1 - IS-IS level-1, L2 - IS-IS level-2, * - candidate default
       U - per-user static route, o - ODR
       T - traffic engineered route

Gateway of last resort is 192.168.1.66 to network 0.0.0.0

     192.168.1.0/28 is subnetted, 4 subnets
C       192.168.1.64 is directly connected, Ethernet0
C       192.168.1.32 is directly connected, Serial1
O       192.168.1.48 [110/1572] via 192.168.1.66, 00:00:05, Ethernet0
C       192.168.1.16 is directly connected, Serial0
C    192.168.101.0/24 is directly connected, Loopback10
O*IA 0.0.0.0/0 [110/1573] via 192.168.1.66, 00:00:05, Ethernet0
p1r2#
```

```
p1r3#show ip route
Codes: C - connected, S - static, I - IGRP, R - RIP, M - mobile, B - BGP
       D - EIGRP, EX - EIGRP external, O - OSPF, IA - OSPF inter area
       N1 - OSPF NSSA external type 1, N2 - OSPF NSSA external type 2
       E1 - OSPF external type 1, E2 - OSPF external type 2, E - EGP
       i - IS-IS, L1 - IS-IS level-1, L2 - IS-IS level-2, * - candidate default
       U - per-user static route, o - ODR
       T - traffic engineered route

Gateway of last resort is 192.168.1.49 to network 0.0.0.0

     172.26.0.0/28 is subnetted, 3 subnets
C       172.26.1.48 is directly connected, Loopback13
C       172.26.1.32 is directly connected, Loopback12
C       172.26.1.16 is directly connected, Loopback11
     192.168.1.0/28 is subnetted, 4 subnets
C       192.168.1.64 is directly connected, Ethernet0
O       192.168.1.32 [110/1572] via 192.168.1.65, 00:00:01, Ethernet0
C       192.168.1.48 is directly connected, Serial0
O       192.168.1.16 [110/1572] via 192.168.1.65, 00:00:02, Ethernet0
O*IA 0.0.0.0/0 [110/1563] via 192.168.1.49, 00:00:02, Serial0
p1r3#
```

**Step 2**   Verify that you have full connectivity within your pod and to the
backbone_r1 router loopback interfaces (you may also see routes to the
other pods).

```
p1r1#ping 172.16.10.100

Type escape sequence to abort.
Sending 5, 100-byte ICMP Echos to 172.16.10.100, timeout is 2 seconds:
!!!!!
Success rate is 100 percent (5/5), round-trip min/avg/max = 28/28/28 ms
p1r1#ping 172.16.11.100

Type escape sequence to abort.
Sending 5, 100-byte ICMP Echos to 172.16.11.100, timeout is 2 seconds:
!!!!!
Success rate is 100 percent (5/5), round-trip min/avg/max = 32/32/32 ms
p1r1#

p1r2#ping 172.16.10.100

Type escape sequence to abort.
Sending 5, 100-byte ICMP Echos to 172.16.10.100, timeout is 2 seconds:
!!!!!
Success rate is 100 percent (5/5), round-trip min/avg/max = 56/59/60 ms
p1r2#ping 172.16.11.100

Type escape sequence to abort.
Sending 5, 100-byte ICMP Echos to 172.16.11.100, timeout is 2 seconds:
!!!!!
Success rate is 100 percent (5/5), round-trip min/avg/max = 56/59/60 ms
p1r2#

p1r3#ping 172.16.10.100
```

```
Type escape sequence to abort.
Sending 5, 100-byte ICMP Echos to 172.16.10.100, timeout is 2 seconds:
!!!!!
Success rate is 100 percent (5/5), round-trip min/avg/max = 60/60/60 ms
p1r3#ping 172.16.11.100

Type escape sequence to abort.
Sending 5, 100-byte ICMP Echos to 172.16.11.100, timeout is 2 seconds:
!!!!!
Success rate is 100 percent (5/5), round-trip min/avg/max = 60/60/60 ms
p1r3#
```

**Step 3**    Save the current configurations of all the routers within your pod to
NVRAM.

```
p1r1#copy run start
Destination filename [startup-config]?
Building configuration...


p1r2#copy run start
Destination filename [startup-config]?
Building configuration...


p1r3#copy run start
Destination filename [startup-config]?
Building configuration...
```

# Answers to Task 4: Enabling OSPF Not-So-Stubby Area (Optional)

**Step 1**    Remove the totally stubby area configuration commands and then
reconfigure your pod's OSPF area into an NSSA area. For this step,
which router(s) do you need to configure? (On the p*x*r1 router, use the
**default-information-originate** option when configuring NSSA.)

---

**NOTE**    On p*x*r1, you must remove the totally stubby area configuration command and then remove
the stub area configuration command to completely remove any stub characteristics before
configuring NSSA.

---

**All routers in the area require the configuration.**

```
p1r1(config)#router ospf 200
plrl(config-router)#no area 1 stub no-summary
p1r1(config-router)#no area 1 stub
p1r1(config-router)#area 1 nssa default-information-originate


p1r2(config)#router ospf 200
p1r2(config-router)#no area 1 stub
```

```
p1r2(config-router)#area 1 nssa
```

```
p1r3(config)#router ospf 200
p1r3(config-router)#no area 1 stub
p1r3(config-router)#area 1 nssa
```

**Step 2**    Do you see any O IA routes in the p*x*r2 and p*x*r3 routing table?

**Yes**

```
p1r2#show ip route
Codes: C - connected, S - static, I - IGRP, R - RIP, M - mobile, B - BGP
       D - EIGRP, EX - EIGRP external, O - OSPF, IA - OSPF inter area
       N1 - OSPF NSSA external type 1, N2 - OSPF NSSA external type 2
       E1 - OSPF external type 1, E2 - OSPF external type 2, E - EGP
       i - IS-IS, L1 - IS-IS level-1, L2 - IS-IS level-2, * - candidate default
       U - per-user static route, o - ODR
       T - traffic engineered route

Gateway of last resort is 192.168.1.33 to network 0.0.0.0

     10.0.0.0/24 is subnetted, 2 subnets
O IA    10.2.2.0 [110/4686] via 192.168.1.33, 00:00:33, Serial1
                 [110/4686] via 192.168.1.17, 00:00:33, Serial0
O IA    10.1.1.0 [110/3124] via 192.168.1.33, 00:00:33, Serial1
                 [110/3124] via 192.168.1.17, 00:00:33, Serial0
     192.168.1.0/28 is subnetted, 4 subnets
C       192.168.1.64 is directly connected, Ethernet0
C       192.168.1.32 is directly connected, Serial1
O       192.168.1.48 [110/1572] via 192.168.1.66, 00:00:33, Ethernet0
C       192.168.1.16 is directly connected, Serial0
C    192.168.101.0/24 is directly connected, Loopback10
O*N2 0.0.0.0/0 [110/1] via 192.168.1.33, 00:00:34, Serial1
               [110/1] via 192.168.1.17, 00:00:34, Serial0
```

```
p1r3#show ip route
Codes: C - connected, S - static, I - IGRP, R - RIP, M - mobile, B - BGP
       D - EIGRP, EX - EIGRP external, O - OSPF, IA - OSPF inter area
       N1 - OSPF NSSA external type 1, N2 - OSPF NSSA external type 2
       E1 - OSPF external type 1, E2 - OSPF external type 2, E - EGP
       i - IS-IS, L1 - IS-IS level-1, L2 - IS-IS level-2, * - candidate default
       U - per-user static route, o - ODR
       T - traffic engineered route

Gateway of last resort is 192.168.1.49 to network 0.0.0.0

     172.26.0.0/28 is subnetted, 3 subnets
C       172.26.1.48 is directly connected, Loopback13
C       172.26.1.32 is directly connected, Loopback12
C       172.26.1.16 is directly connected, Loopback11
     10.0.0.0/24 is subnetted, 2 subnets
O IA    10.2.2.0 [110/4686] via 192.168.1.49, 00:00:49, Serial0
O IA    10.1.1.0 [110/3124] via 192.168.1.49, 00:00:49, Serial0
```

```
     192.168.1.0/28 is subnetted, 4 subnets
C        192.168.1.64 is directly connected, Ethernet0
O        192.168.1.32 [110/1572] via 192.168.1.65, 00:00:49, Ethernet0
C        192.168.1.48 is directly connected, Serial0
O        192.168.1.16 [110/1572] via 192.168.1.65, 00:00:50, Ethernet0
O*N2 0.0.0.0/0 [110/1] via 192.168.1.49, 00:00:50, Serial0
p1r3#
```

Do you see any O*N2 route in the p*x*r2 and p*x*r3 routing table?

**Yes**

What type of route is the O*N2 route?

**Default route, NSSA (LSA type 7), external route type 2**

**Step 3**    Verify that you have full connectivity within your pod and to the
            backbone_r1 router (you may also see routes to the other pods).

```
p1r1#ping p1r2

Type escape sequence to abort.
Sending 5, 100-byte ICMP Echos to 192.168.1.65, timeout is 2 seconds:
!!!!!
Success rate is 100 percent (5/5), round-trip min/avg/max = 32/33/36 ms
p1r1#ping p1r3

Type escape sequence to abort.
Sending 5, 100-byte ICMP Echos to 192.168.1.66, timeout is 2 seconds:
!!!!!
Success rate is 100 percent (5/5), round-trip min/avg/max = 32/32/36 ms
p1r1#ping bbr1

Type escape sequence to abort.
Sending 5, 100-byte ICMP Echos to 10.1.1.100, timeout is 2 seconds:
!!!!!
Success rate is 100 percent (5/5), round-trip min/avg/max = 28/30/32 ms
p1r1#


p1r2#ping p1r1

Type escape sequence to abort.
Sending 5, 100-byte ICMP Echos to 192.168.1.17, timeout is 2 seconds:
!!!!!
Success rate is 100 percent (5/5), round-trip min/avg/max = 32/32/32 ms
p1r2#ping p1r3

Type escape sequence to abort.
Sending 5, 100-byte ICMP Echos to 192.168.1.66, timeout is 2 seconds:
!!!!!
Success rate is 100 percent (5/5), round-trip min/avg/max = 4/4/4 ms
p1r2#ping bbr1

Type escape sequence to abort.
Sending 5, 100-byte ICMP Echos to 10.1.1.100, timeout is 2 seconds:
!!!!!
```

```
Success rate is 100 percent (5/5), round-trip min/avg/max = 60/60/60 ms
p1r2#


p1r3#ping p1r1

Type escape sequence to abort.
Sending 5, 100-byte ICMP Echos to 192.168.1.17, timeout is 2 seconds:
!!!!!
Success rate is 100 percent (5/5), round-trip min/avg/max = 28/34/48 ms
p1r3#ping p1r2

Type escape sequence to abort.
Sending 5, 100-byte ICMP Echos to 192.168.1.65, timeout is 2 seconds:
!!!!!
Success rate is 100 percent (5/5), round-trip min/avg/max = 1/3/4 ms
p1r3#ping bbr1

Type escape sequence to abort.
Sending 5, 100-byte ICMP Echos to 10.1.1.100, timeout is 2 seconds:
!!!!!
Success rate is 100 percent (5/5), round-trip min/avg/max = 56/57/60 ms
p1r3#
```

**Step 4**    Save the current configurations of all the routers within your pod to
NVRAM.

```
p1r1#copy run start
Destination filename [startup-config]?
Building configuration...


p1r2#copy run start
Destination filename [startup-config]?
Building configuration...


p1r3#copy run start
Destination filename [startup-config]?
Building configuration...
```

**Step 5**    The loopback interfaces that you created on p$x$r3 in setup are used to
simulate type 7 external routes into your NSSA. Use the **redistribute**
command at your p$x$r3 routers to redistribute only the loopback interfaces
into your NSSA. Route redistribution will be discussed in Chapter 8. For
now, just enter the following commands to perform the redistribution at
the p$x$r3 router:

```
router ospf 200
redistribute connected metric-type 1 subnets route-map passlb
route-map passlb
match ip address 1
access-list 1 permit 172.26.x.0 0.0.0.255
```

$x$ is your pod number.

**For Pod 1:**

```
p1r3(config)#router ospf 200
p1r3(config-router)#redistribute connected metric-type 1 subnets route-map passlb
p1r3(config-router)#route-map passlb
p1r3(config-route-map)#match ip address 1
p1r3(config-route-map)#access-list 1 permit 172.26.1.0 0.0.0.255
```

**Step 6** Do you see any O N1 routes in the routing table of p*x*r1? What type of routes are those?

**Yes. N1—OSPF NSSA external type 1.**

```
p1r1#show ip route
Codes: C - connected, S - static, I - IGRP, R - RIP, M - mobile, B - BGP
       D - EIGRP, EX - EIGRP external, O - OSPF, IA - OSPF inter area
       N1 - OSPF NSSA external type 1, N2 - OSPF NSSA external type 2
       i - IS-IS, L1 - IS-IS level-1, L2 - IS-IS level-2, * - candidate default
       U - per-user static route, o - ODR
       T - traffic engineered route

Gateway of last resort is not set

     172.16.0.0/24 is subnetted, 2 subnets
O E2    172.16.10.0 [110/20] via 10.1.1.100, 00:01:34, Serial3
O E2    172.16.11.0 [110/20] via 10.1.1.100, 00:01:34, Serial3
     172.26.0.0/28 is subnetted, 3 subnets
O N1    172.26.1.48 [110/1582] via 192.168.1.50, 00:01:34, Serial2
O N1    172.26.1.32 [110/1582] via 192.168.1.50, 00:01:34, Serial2
O N1    172.26.1.16 [110/1582] via 192.168.1.50, 00:01:34, Serial2
     10.0.0.0/24 is subnetted, 2 subnets
O       10.2.2.0 [110/3124] via 10.1.1.100, 00:06:41, Serial3
C       10.1.1.0 is directly connected, Serial3
     192.168.1.0/28 is subnetted, 4 subnets
O       192.168.1.64 [110/1572] via 192.168.1.50, 00:01:35, Serial2
                     [110/1572] via 192.168.1.34, 00:01:35, Serial1
                     [110/1572] via 192.168.1.18, 00:01:35, Serial0
C       192.168.1.32 is directly connected, Serial1
C       192.168.1.48 is directly connected, Serial2
C       192.168.1.16 is directly connected, Serial0
p1r1#
```

Telnet to the backbone_r1 router. Do you see your 172.26.*x*.0 routes in the backbone_r1 routing table? What type of routes are those? Exit the Telnet session to the backbone_r1 router when you're done.

```
p1r1#bbr1
Trying bbr1 (10.1.1.100)... Open


User Access Verification

Password:
backbone_r1>show ip route
```

```
Codes: C - connected, S - static, I - IGRP, R - RIP, M - mobile, B - BGP
       D - EIGRP, EX - EIGRP external, O - OSPF, IA - OSPF inter area
       N1 - OSPF NSSA external type 1, N2 - OSPF NSSA external type 2
       E1 - OSPF external type 1, E2 - OSPF external type 2, E - EGP
       i - IS-IS, L1 - IS-IS level-1, L2 - IS-IS level-2, ia - IS-IS inter area
       * - candidate default, U - per-user static route, o - ODR
       P - periodic downloaded static route

Gateway of last resort is not set

     172.16.0.0/24 is subnetted, 2 subnets
C        172.16.10.0 is directly connected, Loopback100
C        172.16.11.0 is directly connected, Loopback101
     172.26.0.0/28 is subnetted, 3 subnets
O E1     172.26.1.48 [110/3154] via 10.1.1.1, 00:02:06, Serial1/0
O E1     172.26.1.32 [110/3154] via 10.1.1.1, 00:02:06, Serial1/0
O E1     172.26.1.16 [110/3154] via 10.1.1.1, 00:02:06, Serial1/0
     10.0.0.0/24 is subnetted, 2 subnets
C        10.1.1.0 is directly connected, Serial1/0
C        10.2.2.0 is directly connected, Serial1/1
O IA 192.168.1.0/24 [110/3134] via 10.1.1.1, 00:06:35, Serial1/0
backbone_r1>
backbone_r1>exit

[Connection to bbr1 closed by foreign host]
p1r1#
```

### The routes are OE1-OSPF external type 1.

**Step 7**  At your p*x*r1 router, summarize the three external loopback interface
addresses into a single summarized route of 172.26.*x*.0 255.255.255.0,
where *x* = your pod number.

```
p1r1(config)#router ospf 200
p1r1(config-router)#summary-address 172.26.1.0 255.255.255.0
```

Telnet to the backbone_r1 router; the password is cisco. Display the
backbone_r1 router's routing table to verify that your external routes are
summarized properly. Exit the Telnet session to the backbone_r1 router.

```
p1r1#telnet bbr1
Trying bbr1 (10.1.1.100)... Open


User Access Verification

Password:
backbone_r1>show ip route
Codes: C - connected, S - static, I - IGRP, R - RIP, M - mobile, B - BGP
       D - EIGRP, EX - EIGRP external, O - OSPF, IA - OSPF inter area
       N1 - OSPF NSSA external type 1, N2 - OSPF NSSA external type 2
```

```
       E1 - OSPF external type 1, E2 - OSPF external type 2, E - EGP
       i - IS-IS, L1 - IS-IS level-1, L2 - IS-IS level-2, ia - IS-IS inter area
       * - candidate default, U - per-user static route, o - ODR
       P - periodic downloaded static route

Gateway of last resort is not set

     172.16.0.0/24 is subnetted, 2 subnets
C        172.16.10.0 is directly connected, Loopback100
C        172.16.11.0 is directly connected, Loopback101
     172.26.0.0/24 is subnetted, 1 subnets
O E1     172.26.1.0 [110/1582] via 10.1.1.1, 00:00:13, Serial1/0
     10.0.0.0/24 is subnetted, 2 subnets
C        10.1.1.0 is directly connected, Serial1/0
C        10.2.2.0 is directly connected, Serial1/1
O IA 192.168.1.0/24 [110/3134] via 10.1.1.1, 00:10:46, Serial1/0
backbone_r1>exit

[Connection to bbr1 closed by foreign host]
p1r1#
```

**Step 8**   Save the current configurations of all the routers within your pod to NVRAM.

```
p1r1#copy run start
Destination filename [startup-config]?
Building configuration...


p1r2#copy run start
Destination filename [startup-config]?
Building configuration...


p1r3#copy run start
Destination filename [startup-config]?
Building configuration...
```

**Step 9**   (Bonus step) Currently, your pod's external summarized route shows up as O E1 type route at the backbone_r1 router and at any other pods that are configured. Change it so that it shows up as O E2 type route at the backbone_r1 router and at any other pods.

```
p1r3(config)#router ospf 200
p1r3(config-router)#no redistribute connected metric-type 1 subnets route-map pass1b
p1r3(config-router)#redistribute connected metric-type 2 subnets route-map pass1b
```

## Answers to Bonus Questions

How is the OSPF cost metric calculated on Cisco routers?

**The metric is a factor of the bandwdith: $10^8 \div$ bandwidth**

Which type of external OSPF route will have its metric incremented as it is distributed into the OSPF domain, type 1 or type 2?

**Type 1**

Summarize the following subnet address range into the minimum number of routes: 172.25.168.0/24 to 172.25.175.0/24

**Summarized:  172.25.168.0/21**

## Answers to Task 5: Enabling OSPF Virtual Link to Support an OSPF Area Not Connected to Area 0 (Optional)

Complete the following steps:

**Step 1**    In this task, you will be setting up virtual links. Virtual links do not support stub areas, so before you can perform the next task, you need to remove the stub area commands.

Do not remove the loopback interfaces on any of your routers. You will need to use them again in the later Configuration Exercises.

At your p*x*r1 router, remove any **area stub** or **area nssa** commands. Save the current configuration of p*x*r1 to NVRAM. Note: if you have configured NSSA, you must remove the **area x nssa default-information-originate** command and then remove the **area x nssa** command to completely remove any NSSA characteristics. Otherwise, you must remove the totally stubby area configuration command and then remove the stub area configuration command to completely remove any stub characteristics.

```
p1r1(config)#router ospf 200
p1r1(config-router)#no area 1 nssa default-information-originate
plrl(config-router)#no area 1 nssa

p1r1#copy run start
Destination filename [startup-config]?
Building configuration...
```

At your p*x*r2 router, remove any **area stub** or **area nssa** commands. Save the current configuration of p*x*r2 to NVRAM.

```
p1r2(config)#router ospf 200
p1r2(config-router)#no area 1 nssa

p1r2#copy run start
Destination filename [startup-config]?
Building configuration...
```

At your p*x*r3 router, remove any **area stub** or **area nssa** commands. Save the current configuration of p*x*r3 to NVRAM.

```
p1r3(config)#router ospf 200
p1r3(config-router)#no area 1 nssa

p1r3#copy run start
Destination filename [startup-config]?
Building configuration...
```

**Step 2**    At your p*x*r2 router, place that loopback interface you created in setup into the following assigned OSPF area:

| Pod | pxr2 loopback10 Interface IP Address | OSPF Area |
|-----|--------------------------------------|-----------|
| 1 | 192.168.101.101/24 | 101 |
| 2 | 192.168.102.102/24 | 102 |
| 3 | 192.168.103.103/24 | 103 |
| 4 | 192.168.104.104/24 | 104 |
| 5 | 192.168.105.105/24 | 105 |
| 6 | 192.168.106.106/24 | 106 |
| 7 | 192.168.107.107/24 | 107 |
| 8 | 192.168.108.108/24 | 108 |
| 9 | 192.168.109.109/24 | 109 |
| 10 | 192.168.110.110/24 | 110 |
| 11 | 192.168.111.111/24 | 111 |
| 12 | 192.168.112.112/24 | 112 |

```
p1r2(config)#router ospf 200
p1r2(config-router)#network 192.168.101.101 0.0.0.0 area 101
```

**Step 3**    Enter the command to check the OSPF router ID of your p*x*r2 router.

```
p1r2#show ip ospf interface
Ethernet0 is up, line protocol is up
  Internet Address 192.168.1.65/28, Area 1
  Process ID 200, Router ID 192.168.101.101, Network Type BROADCAST, Cost: 10
  Transmit Delay is 1 sec, State DR, Priority 2
  Designated Router (ID) 192.168.101.101, Interface address 192.168.1.65
  Backup Designated router (ID) 172.26.1.49, Interface address 192.168.1.66
  Timer intervals configured, Hello 10, Dead 40, Wait 40, Retransmit 5
    Hello due in 00:00:07
  Neighbor Count is 1, Adjacent neighbor count is 1
    Adjacent with neighbor 172.26.1.49  (Backup Designated Router)
  Suppress hello for 0 neighbor(s)
```

```
Loopback10 is up, line protocol is up
  Internet Address 192.168.101.101/24, Area 101
  Process ID 200, Router ID 192.168.101.101, Network Type LOOPBACK, Cost: 1
  Loopback interface is treated as a stub Host
Serial0 is up, line protocol is up
  Internet Address 192.168.1.18/28, Area 1
  Process ID 200, Router ID 192.168.101.101, Network Type POINT_TO_POINT, Cost:
1562
  Transmit Delay is 1 sec, State POINT_TO_POINT,
  Timer intervals configured, Hello 10, Dead 40, Wait 40, Retransmit 5
    Hello due in 00:00:04
  Neighbor Count is 0, Adjacent neighbor count is 0
  Suppress hello for 0 neighbor(s)
Serial1 is up, line protocol is up
  Internet Address 192.168.1.34/28, Area 1
  Process ID 200, Router ID 192.168.101.101, Network Type POINT_TO_POINT, Cost:
1562
  Transmit Delay is 1 sec, State POINT_TO_POINT,
  Timer intervals configured, Hello 10, Dead 40, Wait 40, Retransmit 5
    Hello due in 00:00:03
  Neighbor Count is 0, Adjacent neighbor count is 0
  Suppress hello for 0 neighbor(s)
p1r2#
```

What is the current OSPF router ID of p*x*r2?

**For p1r2, during this Configuration Exercise: Router ID 192.168.101.101**

**Step 4**   Create an OSPF virtual link to support the OSPF area (10*x*) that you created in Step 1. At which routers do you need to configure the virtual link?

```
p1r1(config)#router ospf 200
p1r1(config-router)#area 1 virtual-link 192.168.101.101

p1r2(config)#router ospf 200
p1r2(config-router)#area 1 virtual-link 192.168.1.49
```

**Step 5**   Use the **show ip ospf virtual-links** command to verify that your virtual link is up.

```
p1r2#show ip ospf virtual-links
Virtual Link OSPF_VL0 to router 192.168.1.49 is up
  Run as demand circuit
  DoNotAge LSA allowed.
  Transit area 1, via interface Serial0, Cost of using 1562
  Transmit Delay is 1 sec, State POINT_TO_POINT,
  Timer intervals configured, Hello 10, Dead 40, Wait 40, Retransmit 5
    Hello due in 00:00:08
    Adjacency State FULL (Hello suppressed)
p1r2#
```

```
p1r1#show ip ospf virtual-links
Virtual Link OSPF_VL0 to router 192.168.101.101 is up
  Run as demand circuit
  DoNotAge LSA allowed.
  Transit area 1, via interface Serial0, Cost of using 1562
  Transmit Delay is 1 sec, State POINT_TO_POINT,
  Timer intervals configured, Hello 10, Dead 40, Wait 40, Retransmit 5
    Hello due in 00:00:05
    Adjacency State FULL (Hello suppressed)
p1r1#
```

**Step 6**  Verify that the p*x*r1 routing table shows your p*x*r2 loopback interface as
an O IA route.

```
p1r1#show ip route
Codes: C - connected, S - static, I - IGRP, R - RIP, M - mobile, B - BGP
       D - EIGRP, EX - EIGRP external, O - OSPF, IA - OSPF inter area
       N1 - OSPF NSSA external type 1, N2 - OSPF NSSA external type 2
       E1 - OSPF external type 1, E2 - OSPF external type 2, E - EGP
       i - IS-IS, L1 - IS-IS level-1, L2 - IS-IS level-2, * - candidate default
       U - per-user static route, o - ODR
       T - traffic engineered route

Gateway of last resort is not set

     172.16.0.0/24 is subnetted, 2 subnets
O E2    172.16.10.0 [110/20] via 10.1.1.100, 00:01:22, Serial3
O E2    172.16.11.0 [110/20] via 10.1.1.100, 00:01:22, Serial3
     172.26.0.0/28 is subnetted, 3 subnets
O E2    172.26.1.48 [110/20] via 192.168.1.50, 00:01:22, Serial2
O E2    172.26.1.32 [110/20] via 192.168.1.50, 00:01:22, Serial2
O E2    172.26.1.16 [110/20] via 192.168.1.50, 00:01:22, Serial2
     10.0.0.0/24 is subnetted, 2 subnets
O       10.2.2.0 [110/3124] via 10.1.1.100, 00:01:22, Serial3
C       10.1.1.0 is directly connected, Serial3
     192.168.1.0/28 is subnetted, 4 subnets
O       192.168.1.64 [110/1572] via 192.168.1.50, 00:01:33, Serial2
                     [110/1572] via 192.168.1.34, 00:01:33, Serial1
                     [110/1572] via 192.168.1.18, 00:01:33, Serial0
C       192.168.1.32 is directly connected, Serial1
C       192.168.1.48 is directly connected, Serial2
C       192.168.1.16 is directly connected, Serial0
     192.168.101.0/32 is subnetted, 1 subnets
O IA    192.168.101.101 [110/1563] via 192.168.1.34, 00:01:30, Serial1
```

From p*x*r1, ping your p*x*r2 loopback interface. Was the ping successful?

```
p1r1#ping 192.168.101.101

Type escape sequence to abort.
Sending 5, 100-byte ICMP Echos to 192.168.101.101, timeout is 2 seconds:
!!!!!
Success rate is 100 percent (5/5), round-trip min/avg/max = 32/32/32 ms
p1r1#
```

**Step 7**   (Challenge step) Telnet to the backbone_r1 router; the password is cisco. Display its routing table. Notice that your area summarization from Task 1 is no longer working. You should see all your 192.168.*x.y* subnets in the backbone_r1 router now. Why?

```
p1r1#telnet bbr1
Trying bbr1 (10.1.1.100)... Open


User Access Verification

Password:
backbone_r1>show ip route
Codes: C - connected, S - static, I - IGRP, R - RIP, M - mobile, B - BGP
       D - EIGRP, EX - EIGRP external, O - OSPF, IA - OSPF inter area
       N1 - OSPF NSSA external type 1, N2 - OSPF NSSA external type 2
       E1 - OSPF external type 1, E2 - OSPF external type 2, E - EGP
       i - IS-IS, L1 - IS-IS level-1, L2 - IS-IS level-2, ia - IS-IS inter area
       * - candidate default, U - per-user static route, o - ODR
       P - periodic downloaded static route

Gateway of last resort is not set

     172.16.0.0/24 is subnetted, 2 subnets
C       172.16.10.0 is directly connected, Loopback100
C       172.16.11.0 is directly connected, Loopback101
     172.26.0.0/28 is subnetted, 3 subnets
O E2    172.26.1.48 [110/20] via 10.1.1.1, 00:02:22, Serial1/0
O E2    172.26.1.32 [110/20] via 10.1.1.1, 00:02:22, Serial1/0
O E2    172.26.1.16 [110/20] via 10.1.1.1, 00:02:22, Serial1/0
     10.0.0.0/24 is subnetted, 2 subnets
C       10.1.1.0 is directly connected, Serial1/0
C       10.2.2.0 is directly connected, Serial1/1
     192.168.1.0/24 is variably subnetted, 5 subnets, 2 masks
O IA    192.168.1.64/28 [110/3134] via 10.1.1.1, 00:02:22, Serial1/0
O IA    192.168.1.32/28 [110/4686] via 10.1.1.1, 00:02:22, Serial1/0
O IA    192.168.1.48/28 [110/4696] via 10.1.1.1, 00:02:25, Serial1/0
O IA    192.168.1.0/24 [110/3134] via 10.1.1.1, 00:02:25, Serial1/0
O IA    192.168.1.16/28 [110/4686] via 10.1.1.1, 00:02:25, Serial1/0
     192.168.101.0/32 is subnetted, 1 subnets
O IA    192.168.101.101 [110/3125] via 10.1.1.1, 00:02:25, Serial1/0
```

Hint: Enter the **show ip ospf** command at your p*x*r2 router. What type of OSPF router is p*x*r2 now with the virtual link defined?

```
p1r2#show ip ospf
 Routing Process "ospf 200" with ID 192.168.101.101
 Supports only single TOS(TOS0) routes
 It is an area border router
 SPF schedule delay 5 secs, Hold time between two SPFs 10 secs
 Minimum LSA interval 5 secs. Minimum LSA arrival 1 secs
 Number of external LSA 5. Checksum Sum 0x2F1CC
 Number of DCbitless external LSA 0
 Number of DoNotAge external LSA 0
 Number of areas in this router is 3. 3 normal 0 stub 0 nssa
    Area BACKBONE(0)
        Number of interfaces in this area is 1
        Area has no authentication
        SPF algorithm executed 2 times
        Area ranges are
        Number of LSA 11. Checksum Sum 0x5EC4A
        Number of DCbitless LSA 0
        Number of indication LSA 0
        Number of DoNotAge LSA 4
    Area 1
        Number of interfaces in this area is 3
        Area has no authentication
        SPF algorithm executed 28 times
        Area ranges are
        Number of LSA 16. Checksum Sum 0x6A13D
        Number of DCbitless LSA 0
        Number of indication LSA 0
        Number of DoNotAge LSA 0
    Area 101
        Number of interfaces in this area is 1
        Area has no authentication
        SPF algorithm executed 3 times
        Area ranges are
        Number of LSA 10. Checksum Sum 0x59BE0
        Number of DCbitless LSA 0
        Number of indication LSA 0
        Number of DoNotAge LSA 0


p1r1#show ip ospf
 Routing Process "ospf 200" with ID 192.168.1.49
 Supports only single TOS(TOS0) routes
 It is an area border router
 SPF schedule delay 5 secs, Hold time between two SPFs 10 secs
 Minimum LSA interval 5 secs. Minimum LSA arrival 1 secs
 Number of external LSA 5. Checksum Sum 0x2F1CC
 Number of DCbitless external LSA 0
 Number of DoNotAge external LSA 0
 Number of areas in this router is 2. 2 normal 0 stub 0 nssa
```

```
Area BACKBONE(0)
    Number of interfaces in this area is 2
    Area has no authentication
    SPF algorithm executed 15 times
    Area ranges are
    Number of LSA 11. Checksum Sum 0x5EC4A
    Number of DCbitless LSA 0
    Number of indication LSA 0
    Number of DoNotAge LSA 7
Area 1
    Number of interfaces in this area is 3
    Area has no authentication
    SPF algorithm executed 34 times
    Area ranges are
        192.168.1.0/24 Active(1572) Advertise
    Number of LSA 13. Checksum Sum 0x53104
    Number of DCbitless LSA 0
    Number of indication LSA 0
    Number of DoNotAge LSA 0
```

**Both p*x*r1 and p*x*r2 are ABRs, but only p*x*r1 is summarizing. p*x*r2 sends the subnet route information to the backbone_r1.**

At the p*x*r2 router, summarize all the 192.168.*x.y*/28 subnets in your area (area *x*) into a single summarized route of 192.168.*x*.0/24.

```
p1r2(config)#router ospf 200
p1r2(config-router)#area 1 range 192.168.1.0 255.255.255.0
```

Telnet to the backbone_r1 router; the password is cisco. Display the backbone_r1 router's routing table to verify that your subnets are summarized properly.

```
p1r2#telnet bbr1
Trying bbr1 (10.1.1.100)... Open


User Access Verification

Password:
backbone_r1>show ip route
Codes: C - connected, S - static, I - IGRP, R - RIP, M - mobile, B - BGP
       D - EIGRP, EX - EIGRP external, O - OSPF, IA - OSPF inter area
       N1 - OSPF NSSA external type 1, N2 - OSPF NSSA external type 2
       E1 - OSPF external type 1, E2 - OSPF external type 2, E - EGP
       i - IS-IS, L1 - IS-IS level-1, L2 - IS-IS level-2, ia - IS-IS inter area
       * - candidate default, U - per-user static route, o - ODR
       P - periodic downloaded static route

Gateway of last resort is not set
```

```
      172.16.0.0/24 is subnetted, 2 subnets
C        172.16.10.0 is directly connected, Loopback100
C        172.16.11.0 is directly connected, Loopback101
      172.26.0.0/28 is subnetted, 3 subnets
O E2     172.26.1.48 [110/20] via 10.1.1.1, 00:05:12, Serial1/0
O E2     172.26.1.32 [110/20] via 10.1.1.1, 00:05:12, Serial1/0
O E2     172.26.1.16 [110/20] via 10.1.1.1, 00:05:12, Serial1/0
      10.0.0.0/24 is subnetted, 2 subnets
C        10.1.1.0 is directly connected, Serial1/0
C        10.2.2.0 is directly connected, Serial1/1
O IA 192.168.1.0/24 [110/3134] via 10.1.1.1, 00:00:11, Serial1/0
      192.168.101.0/32 is subnetted, 1 subnets
O IA     192.168.101.101 [110/3125] via 10.1.1.1, 00:05:12, Serial1/0
backbone_r1>exit

[Connection to bbr1 closed by foreign host]
p1r2#
```

**Step 8**   Save the current configurations of all the routers within your pod to NVRAM.

```
p1r1#copy run start
Destination filename [startup-config]?
Building configuration...


p1r2#copy run start
Destination filename [startup-config]?
Building configuration...


p1r3#copy run start
Destination filename [startup-config]?
Building configuration...
```

# Review Questions

Answer the following questions, and then refer to Appendix G, "Answers to the Review Questions," for the answers.

1   Define hierarchical routing and explain what internetwork problems it solves.

2   An internal router will receive type 5 LSAs if it is what type of area?

3   What area types are connected to the backbone area?

4   The backbone must be configured as what area?

**5** Write a brief description of the following LSA types:

Type 1: Router link entry (record)

Type 2: Network link entry

Type 3 or 4: Summary link entry

Type 5: Autonomous system external link entry

**6** Describe the path a packet must take to get from one area to another.

**7** When is a default route injected into an area?

**8** What are the four types of OSPF routers?

**9** Which router generates a type 2 LSA?

**10** What are the advantages of configuring a totally stubby area?

**11** What command is used on an ABR to summarize routes for a specific area?

This chapter introduces students to the Enhanced Interior Gateway Routing Protocol (EIGRP). This chapter includes the following sections:

- EIGRP Overview
- EIGRP Operation
- Configuring EIGRP
- Case Study: EIGRP
- Summary
- Configuration Exercise #1: Configuring EIGRP
- Configuration Exercise #2: Configuring EIGRP in an NBMA Environment
- Answers to Configuration Exercise #1: Configuring EIGRP
- Answers to Configuration Exercise #2: Configuring EIGRP in an NBMA Environment
- Review Questions

# CHAPTER 5

# Configuring EIGRP

After completing this chapter, you will be able to describe Enhanced Interior Gateway Routing Protocol (EIGRP) features and operation; explain how EIGRP discovers, chooses, and maintains routes; explain how EIGRP supports the use of variable-length subnet mask (VLSM); explain how EIGRP operates in an NBMA environment; explain how EIGRP supports the use of route summarization; and describe how EIGRP supports large networks. You will also be able to configure EIGRP, verify EIGRP operation, and, given a set of network requirements, configure an EIGRP environment and verify proper operation (within described guidelines) of your routers. Also, given a set of network requirements, you will be able to configure EIGRP in an NBMA environment and verify proper operation (within described guidelines) of your routers.

## EIGRP Overview

EIGRP is a Cisco proprietary protocol that combines the advantages of link-state and distance vector routing protocols. This hybrid protocol provides the following features:

- **Rapid convergence**—EIGRP uses the Diffusing Update Algorithm (DUAL) to achieve rapid convergence. A router running EIGRP stores backup routes, when available, for destinations so that it can quickly adapt to alternate routes. If no appropriate route or backup route exists in the local routing table, EIGRP queries its neighbors to discover an alternative route. These queries are propagated until an alternate route is found.

- **Reduced bandwidth usage**—EIGRP does not send periodic updates. Instead, it uses partial updates when the path or the metric to a destination changes. When the route information changes, DUAL sends an update about only that link rather than the entire routing table. In addition, the information is passed only to routers that require it, in contrast to link-state protocol operation, which sends a change update to all routers within an area.

- **Multiple network layer support**—EIGRP supports AppleTalk, IP, and Novell NetWare using protocol-dependent modules (PDMs).

EIGRP has its roots as a distance vector routing. Like its predecessor IGRP, EIGRP is easy to configure and is adaptable to a wide variety of network topologies. What makes EIGRP an advanced distance vector protocol is its addition of several link-state features, such as dynamic neighbor discovery.

Although EIGRP is compatible with IGRP, it offers superior performance thanks to a rapid convergence and the guarantee of a loop-free topology at all times. Partial routing updates are generated only upon topology changes. Distribution of partial updates is bounded so that only routers that need the information are updated. As a classless routing protocol, EIGRP advertises a routing mask for each destination network. This feature enables support of discontiguous subnetworks and VLSM.

An additional feature of EIGRP is its capability to support IPX and AppleTalk protocols as well as IP. The EIGRP rapid convergence and sophisticated metric offer superior performance and stability when implemented in IPX and AppleTalk networks.

To summarize, the following are the key features of EIGRP:

- Rapid convergence
- Reduced bandwidth usage
- Support for multiple network layer protocols
- Advanced distance vector capabilities
- 100% loop-free
- Easy configuration
- Incremental updates
- Support for VLSM, discontiguous networks, and classless routing
- Compatibility with IGRP

## Advantages of EIGRP

EIGRP offers many advantages over traditional distance vector routing protocols. One of the most significant advantages is in the area of bandwidth utilization. With EIGRP, operational traffic is primarily multicast rather than broadcast. As a result, end stations are unaffected by routing updates or queries.

EIGRP uses the IGRP algorithm for metric calculation, although the value is represented in 32-bit format, providing an additional granularity for route selection. The EIGRP metric is the IGRP metric multiplied by 256. A significant advantage of EIGRP is its support for unequal metric load balancing that allows administrators to better distribute traffic flow in their networks.

Some of the EIGRP operational characteristics are borrowed from link-state protocols. For example, EIGRP allows administrators to create summary routes at any bit position within the network rather than the traditional distance vector approach of performing classful summarization at major network number boundaries. EIGRP also supports route redistribution from other routing protocols.

Like all TCP/IP routing protocols, EIGRP relies on IP packets to deliver routing information. The EIGRP routing process is a transport layer function of the OSI model. IP packets carrying EIGRP information use protocol number 88 in their IP header. Figure 5-1 shows the format of an IP packet and values used to designate the packet payload.

**Figure 5-1**    *Frame and IP Packet*

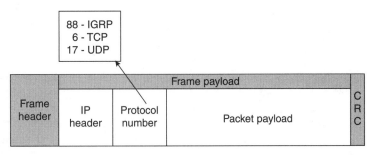

EIGRP was designed to operate in both LAN and WAN environments. In multiaccess topologies, such as Ethernet and Token Ring, neighbor relationships are formed and maintained using reliable multicasting. EIGRP supports all WAN topologies: dedicated links, point-to-point links, and nonbroadcast multiaccess (NBMA) topology.

EIGRP supports both hierarchical and nonhierarchical IP addressing. EIGRP also supports VLSM, thus promoting efficient allocation of IP addresses. Secondary addresses can be applied to interfaces to solve particular addressing issues, although all routing overhead traffic will be generated through the primary interface address.

By default, EIGRP performs route summarization at major network boundaries, as shown in Figure 5-2. Also, administrators can configure manual summarization on arbitrary bit boundaries to shrink the size of the routing table. EIGRP supports the creation of supernets or aggregated blocks of addresses (networks).

**Figure 5-2** *Route Summarization Example*

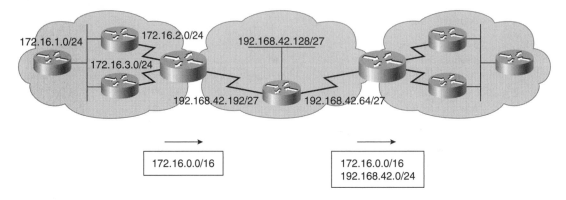

# EIGRP Terminology

This section introduces terms related to EIGRP:

- **Neighbor table**—Each EIGRP router maintains a neighbor table that lists adjacent routers. This table is comparable to the neighborship (adjacency) database used by OSPF. It serves the same purpose, to ensure bidirectional communication between each of the directly connected neighbors. EIGRP keeps a neighbor table for each network protocol supported, such as an IP neighbor table, an IPX neighbor table, and an AppleTalk neighbor table.

- **Topology table**—An EIGRP router maintains a topology table for each network protocol configured: IP, IPX, and AppleTalk. All learned routes to a destination are maintained in the topology table.

- **Routing table**—EIGRP chooses the best routes to a destination from the topology table and places these routes in the routing table. The router maintains one routing table for each network protocol.

- **Successor**—This is the primary route used to reach a destination. Successors are kept in the routing table.

- **Feasible successor**—This is a neighbor that is downstream with respect to the destination, but it is not the least-cost path and thus is not used for forwarding data. In other words, this is a backup route to the destination. These routes are selected at the same time as successors, but are kept in the topology table. The topology table can maintain multiple feasible successors for a destination.

# EIGRP Operation

This section discusses elements of EIGRP operations:

- EIGRP packets
- EIGRP neighbor relationship

## EIGRP Packets

EIGRP uses the following five types of packets:

- **Hello**—Hello packets are used for neighbor discovery. They are sent as multicasts and carry a 0 acknowledgment number.

- **Update**—An update is sent to communicate the routes that a particular router has used to converge. These updates are sent as multicasts when a new route is discovered and when convergence is completed (when the route becomes passive). To synchronize topology tables, updates are sent as unicasts to neighbors during their EIGRP startup sequence. Updates are sent reliably.

- **Queries**—When a router is performing route computation and can't find a feasible successor, it sends a query packet to its neighbors asking if they have a feasible successor to the destination. Queries are always multicast and are sent reliably.

- **Replies**—A reply packet is sent in response to a query packet. Replies are unicasts to the originator of the query and are sent reliably.

- **ACK**—The ACK is used for acknowledging updates, queries, and replies. ACKs are hello packets sent as unicasts and contain a nonzero acknowledgment number.

### EIGRP Reliability

EIGRP's reliability mechanism ensures delivery of critical route information to neighboring routers. This information is required to allow EIGRP to maintain a loop-free topology. All packets carrying routing information (update, query, and reply) are sent reliably. Assigning a sequence number to each reliable packet, and requiring an explicit acknowledgment for that sequence number, provides reliability.

The Reliable Transport Protocol (RTP) is responsible for guaranteed, ordered delivery of EIGRP packets to all neighbors. It supports intermixed transmission of multicast or unicast packets. For efficiency, only certain EIGRP packets are transmitted reliably. On a multiaccess network that has multicast capabilities, such as Ethernet, it is not necessary to send hello packets reliably to all neighbors individually. For that reason, EIGRP sends a single multicast hello packet containing an indicator that informs the receivers that the packet need not be acknowledged. Other types of packets, such as updates, indicate in the packet that acknowledgment is required. RTP contains a provision for sending multicast packets quickly when unacknowledged packets are pending, which helps ensure that convergence time remains low in the presence of varying speed links.

RTP ensures that ongoing communication is maintained between neighboring routers. As such, a retransmission list is maintained for each neighbor. This list indicates packets not yet acknowledged by a neighbor. Unacknowledged reliable packets are retransmitted up to 16 times or up to the hold time, whichever is longer.

---

### Hold Time

The length of time, in seconds, that the router will wait to hear from the peer before declaring it down is the hold time. The default hold time is set to three times the hello interval. The hold time value can be seen with the **show ip eigrp neighbors** command.

---

The use of reliable multicast packets is efficient. A potential delay exists on multiaccess media where multiple neighbors reside. The next reliable multicast packet cannot be transmitted until all peers have acknowledged the previous multicast. If one or more peers are slow to respond, this adversely affects all peers by delaying the next transmission. RTP is designed to handle such exceptions. Neighbors that are slow to respond to multicasts have the unacknowledged multicast packets retransmitted as unicasts. This allows the reliable multicast operation to proceed without delaying communication with other peers.

## EIGRP Neighbor Relationship

The router sends hello packets out of interfaces configured for EIGRP. The EIGRP multicast address used is 224.0.0.10. When an EIGRP router receives a hello packet from a router belonging to the same autonomous system, it establishes a neighbor relationship (adjacency).

The time interval of Hello packets varies depending on the media. Hello packets are released every 5 seconds on a LAN link such as Ethernet, Token Ring, and FDDI. The default interval is also set to 5 seconds for point-to-point links such as Point-to-Point Protocol (PPP), High-Level Data Link Control (HDLC), point-to-point Frame Relay, ATM subinterfaces, and for multipoint circuits with bandwidth greater than T1, including ISDN Primary Rate Interface (PRI), Switched Multimegabit Data Service (SMDS), and Frame Relay. Hello packets are sent out less frequently on lower-speed links, such as multipoint serial interfaces and ISDN Basic Rate Interfaces (BRI). Hellos are generated at 60-second intervals on these types of interfaces.

Through the Hello protocol, an EIGRP router dynamically discovers other routers directly connected to it. Information learned about neighbors, such as address and interface used by neighbors, is maintained in the neighbor table. The neighbor table also maintains the hold time. The hold time is the amount of time a router considers a neighbor up, without receiving a hello or some other EIGRP packet from that neighbor. Hello packets report the hold time value.

If a packet is not received before the expiration of the hold time, then a topology change is detected. The neighbor adjacency is deleted, and all topology table entries learned from that neighbor are removed, as if the neighbor had sent an update stating that all the routes are unreachable. This enables the routes to quickly reconverge if an alternate feasible route is available. A route is considered passive when the router is not performing recomputation on that route. The route is active when it is undergoing recomputation.

The rate at which hello packets are sent, called the hello interval, can be adjusted per interface with the **ip eigrp hello-interval** command. The hold time interval is set by default to three times the hello interval. Therefore, the default hold time value is 15 seconds on LAN and fast WAN interfaces, and 180 seconds on slower WAN interfaces. The hold time can also be adjusted with the **ip eigrp hold-time** command.

| NOTE | If you change the hello interval, you must manually adjust the hold time to reflect the configured hello interval. |
|------|------|

It is possible for two routers to become EIGRP neighbors even though the hello and hold time values do not match; this means that the hello interval and hold time values can be set independently on different routers.

EIGRP will not build peer relationships over secondary addresses because all EIGRP traffic uses the primary address of the interface. In addition, peer relationships will not be formed if the neighbor resides in a different autonomous system or if the metric-calculation mechanism constants (the K-values) are misaligned on that link. K-values are discussed later in this section.

## Neighbor Table

Like OSPF, EIGRP routers multicast hello packets to discover neighbors and to exchange route updates. In Chapter 3, "Configuring OSPF in a Single Area," you learned that only adjacent routers will exchange routing information. Each router builds a neighbor table from hello packets that it receives from adjacent EIGRP routers running the same network layer protocol. The IP neighbor table can be looked at with the **show ip eigrp neighbors** command, as shown in Example 5-1.

**Example 5-1**  *Output of the **show ip eigrp neighbors** command*

```
p2r2#show ip eigrp neighbors
IP-EIGRP neighbors for process 400
H Address        Interface  Hold Uptime   SRTT  RTO Q  Seq
                            (sec)         (ms)      Cnt Num
1 172.68.2.2     To0        13 02:15:30    8   200 0  9
0 172.68.16.2    Se1        10 02:38:29   29   200 0  6
```

EIGRP maintains a neighbor table for each configured network layer protocol. The table includes the following key elements:

- **H (handle)**—A number used internally by the Cisco IOS to track a neighbor.

- **Neighbor address**—The network layer address of the neighbor.

- **Interface**—The interface on this router by which the neighbor can be reached.

- **HoldTime**—The maximum time to wait without receiving anything from a neighbor before considering the link unavailable. Originally, the expected packet was a hello packet, but in current Cisco IOS software releases, any EIGRP packets received after the first hello from that neighbor will reset the timer.

- **Uptime**—Elapsed time, in hours, minutes, and seconds, since the local router first heard from this neighbor.

- **Smooth Round Trip Timer (SRTT)**—The number of milliseconds it takes for an EIGRP packet to be sent to this neighbor and for the local router to receive an acknowledgment of that packet. This timer is used to determine the retransmit interval, also known as the retransmit timeout (RTO).

- **RTO**—The amount of time, in milliseconds, that the software waits before retransmitting a packet from the retransmission queue to a neighbor.

- **Queue count**—The number of packets waiting in queue to be sent out. If this value is constantly higher than 0, there may be a congestion problem.

- **Seq Num**—Sequence number of the last update, query, or reply packet that was received from this neighbor.

## Topology Table

When the router dynamically discovers a new neighbor, it sends an update about the routes that it knows to its new neighbor and receives the same from the new neighbor. These updates populate what is known as the topology table. The topology table contains all destinations advertised by neighboring routers. The **show ip eigrp topology all-links** command displays all the IP entries in the topology table. The **show ip eigrp topology** command displays only the successor and feasible successor for IP routes. It is important to note that if a neighbor is advertising a destination, then it must be using that route to forward packets. This rule must be strictly followed by all distance vector protocols.

The topology table also maintains the metric that the neighbors advertise for each destination and the metric that this router uses to reach the destination. The metric used by this router is the sum of the best-advertised metric from all neighbors, plus the cost of this router to reach the best neighbor. The topology table is also updated when a directly connected route or interface changes, or when a neighboring router reports a change to a route.

## Initial Route Discovery

EIGRP combines in one step the process of discovering neighbors and learning routes. Figure 5-3 illustrates the initial route discovery process.

**Figure 5-3**   *Initial Route Discovery*

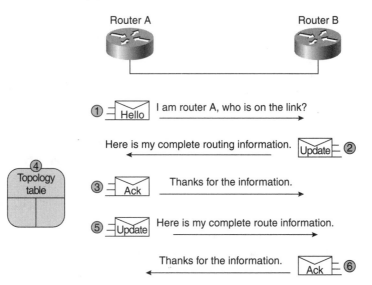

The following is a description of the initial route discovery process:

1   A new router (Router A) comes up on the link and sends out a hello packet through all its interfaces.

2   Routers receiving the hello on one interface (Router B, in Figure 5-3) reply with update packets that contain all the routes that they have in their routing table, except those learned through that interface (split horizon). Unlike OSPF operation, Router B does not send a hello packet back to Router A. Instead, the update packet establishes a neighbor relationship between the communicating devices. As such,

these update packets have the Init bit set, indicating that this is the initialization process. An update packet contains information about the routes that a neighbor is aware of, including the metric that the neighbor is advertising for each destination.

3   Router A replies to each neighbor with an ACK packet, indicating that it received the update information.

4   Router A inserts update packet information in its topology table. The topology table includes all destinations advertised by neighboring (adjacent) routers. It is organized so that each destination is listed, along with all the neighbors that can get to the destination and their associated metric.

5   Router A then exchanges update packets with each of its neighbors.

6   Upon receiving the update packets, each router sends an ACK packet to Router A. When all updates are received, the router is ready to choose the primary and backup routes to keep in the topology table.

---

### Split Horizon

Split horizon controls the sending of IP EIGRP update and query packets. When split horizon is enabled on an interface, these packets are not sent for destinations for which this interface is the next hop. This reduces the possibility of routing loops. By default, split horizon is enabled on all interfaces.

Split horizon blocks information about routes from being advertised by a router out any interface from which that information originated. This behavior usually optimizes communications among multiple routers, particularly when links are broken.

---

## Route Selection

EIGRP route selection process works differently than other routing protocols. EIGRP's route selection key characteristics are as follows:

• EIGRP selects primary and backup routes and injects those into the topology table (up to six per destination). The primary routes are then moved to the routing table.

Similarly to OSPF, EIGRP supports several types of routes: internal, external (that is, non-EIGRP), and summary routes. Internal routes are routes that originate within the EIGRP AS. External routes are learned from another routing protocol or from another EIGRP AS. Summary routes are routes encompassing multiple subnets.

• The EIGRP metric is the IGRP metric multiplied by 256. The metric calculation can use the following five variables:

— **Bandwidth**—The smallest bandwidth between the source and destination

— **Delay**—Cumulative interface delay along the path

The following criteria, although available, are not commonly used because they typically result in frequent recalculation of the topology table:

— **Reliability**—Worst reliability between source and destination based on keepalives

— **Loading**—Worst load on a link between source and destination based on bits per second

— **Maximum transmission unit (MTU)**—Smallest MTU in path

- EIGRP uses DUAL to calculate the best route to a destination. DUAL selects routes based on the composite metric and assures that the selected routes are loop-free.

EIGRP calculates the metric by adding together weighted values of different variables of the link to the network in question. The default constant values are K1 = K3 = 1, and K2 = K4 = K5 = 0, where weights are attributed to the variables: K1 = bandwidth, K2 = load, K3 = delay, K4 = reliability, and K5 = MTU.

In EIGRP metric calculations when KS is equal to 0, variables (bandwidth, bandwidth divided by load, and delay) are weighted with the constants K1, K2, and K3. The following is the formula used:

Metric = K1 × bandwidth + [(K2 × bandwidth) / (256 − load)] + K3 × delay

If these K-values are equal to their defaults, the formula becomes:

Metric = 1 × bandwidth + [(0 × bandwidth) / (256 − load)] + 1 × delay
Metric = bandwidth + [0] + delay
Metric = bandwidth + delay

If K5 is not equal to 0, an additional operation is performed:

Metric = Metric × [K5 / (reliability + K4)]

K-values are carried in hello packets. Mismatched K-values can cause a neighbor to be reset. (Only K1 and K3 are used, by default, in metric compilation). These K-values should be modified only after careful planning. Changing these values can prevent your network from converging.

---

**NOTE**    The format of the delay and bandwidth values is different than those displayed by the **show interfaces** command. The EIGRP delay value is the sum of the delays in the path, in tens of microseconds, multiplied by 256. The **show interfaces** command displays delay in microseconds.

The bandwidth is calculated using the minimum bandwidth link along the path, represented in kilobits per second. This value is divided into $10^7$ and then multiplied by 256.

---

EIGRP represents its metrics in a 32-bit format instead of the 24-bit representation used by IGRP. This representation allows a more granular decision to be made when calculating successor and feasible successor. When integrating IGRP routes into an EIGRP domain, multiply the IGRP metric by 256 to get the EIGRP-equivalent metric.

## Routing Table and the EIGRP Diffusing Update Algorithm (DUAL)

DUAL is the finite-state machine that selects which information will be stored in the topology table. As such, DUAL embodies the decision process for all route computations. It tracks all routes advertised by all neighbors. DUAL uses the distance information, known as a metric, to select an efficient, loop-free path to each destination and inserts that choice in the routing table. The lowest-cost route is calculated by adding the cost between the next-hop router and the destination (referred to as the advertised distance [AD]) to the cost between the local router and the next-hop router. (The total is referred to as the feasible distance [FD].) A successor is a neighboring router used for packet forwarding that has a least-cost path to a destination that is guaranteed not to be part of a routing loop. Multiple successors can exist if they have the same feasible distance. All successors are added to the routing table. The routing table is essentially a subset of the topology table. The topology table contains more detailed information about each route, backup routes, and information used exclusively by DUAL.

The next-hop router(s) for the backup path is referred to as the feasible successor (FS). When the router loses a route, it looks at the topology table for an FS. If one is available, the route will not go into an active state; rather, the best feasible successor will be promoted as the successor and will be installed in the routing table. When there are not feasible successors, a route will go into active state, and route computation occurs.

To qualify as a feasible successor, a next-hop router must have an advertised distance less than the feasible distance of the current successor route. More than one feasible successor can be kept at one time.

When there are no feasible successors but neighbors are advertising the destination, a recompilation must occur. Through this process, a new successor is determined. The amount of time that it takes to recalculate the route affects the convergence time.

### DUAL Example

In the following example, you will examine partial entries (for Network [a]) of the topology tables for Router C, Router D, and Router E to get a better understanding of EIGRP behavior. The partial topology tables shown in Figure 5-4 indicate the following:

- **FD or fd (feasible distance)**—Equal to the sum of the costs of the links to reach Network (a).

- **AD (advertised distance )**—The link cost of the path to Network (a) as advertised by neighboring routers.

- **Successor**—Forwarding path to Network (a); path cost equal to fd.

- **fs (feasible successor)**—An alternate path.

The sample network is stable and converged.

**Figure 5-4**    *DUAL Example Step 1*

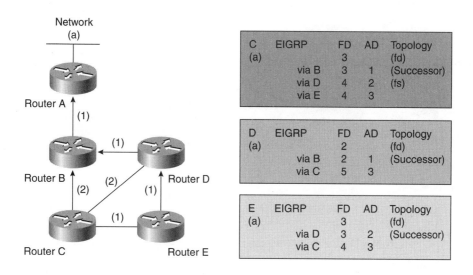

| C (a) | EIGRP | FD | AD | Topology |
|---|---|---|---|---|
| | | 3 | | (fd) |
| | via B | 3 | 1 | (Successor) |
| | via D | 4 | 2 | (fs) |
| | via E | 4 | 3 | |

| D (a) | EIGRP | FD | AD | Topology |
|---|---|---|---|---|
| | | 2 | | (fd) |
| | via B | 2 | 1 | (Successor) |
| | via C | 5 | 3 | |

| E (a) | EIGRP | FD | AD | Topology |
|---|---|---|---|---|
| | | 3 | | (fd) |
| | via D | 3 | 2 | (Successor) |
| | via C | 4 | 3 | |

**NOTE**    EIGRP implements the split-horizon technique. For example, Router E will not pass its route for Network (a) to Router D because Router E uses Router D as its next hop to Network (a).

In Figure 5-5, Routers B and D detect the link failure. Upon notification of the link failure, DUAL performs the following step in Figure 5-5:

- At Router D: Marks the path to Network (a) through Router B as unusable.

**Figure 5-5** *DUAL Example Step 2*

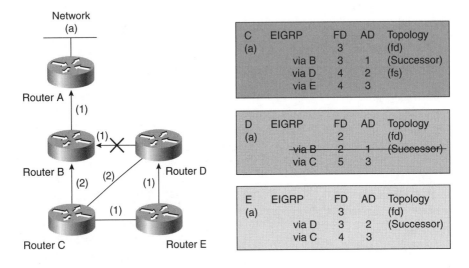

The following steps occur in Figure 5-6:

- At Router D: Has no feasible successor to Network (a) because the AD via C (3) is greater than the FD via B (2).

  — Sets the metric to Network (a) as unreachable (–1 is unreachable).

  — Goes active on Network (a).

  — Sends a query to Routers C and E for an alternate path.

  — Marks Routers C and E as having a query pending (q).

- At Router E: Marks the path to Network (a) through Router D as unusable.

The following steps occur in Figure 5-7:

- At Router D: Receives reply from Router C; no change to path to Network (a).

  — Removes query flag from Router C.

  — Stays active on Network (a), awaiting reply from Router E (q).

- At Router E: Has no feasible successor to Network (a) because the AD from Router C (3) is not less than the original FD (also 3).

  — Generates a query to Router C.

  — Marks Router C as query pending (q).

**Figure 5-6**   *DUAL Example Step 3*

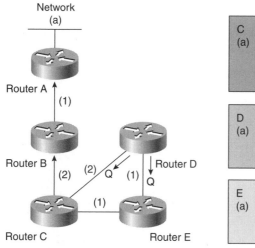

| C<br>(a) | EIGRP | FD | AD | Topology |
|---|---|---|---|---|
| | | 3 | | (fd) |
| | via B | 3 | 1 | (Successor) |
| | via D | | | |
| | via E | 4 | 3 | |

| D<br>(a) | EIGRP<br>**ACTIVE** | FD<br>−1 | AD | Topology<br>(fd) |
|---|---|---|---|---|
| | via E | | | (q) |
| | via C | 5 | 3 | (q) |

| E<br>(a) | EIGRP | FD | AD | Topology |
|---|---|---|---|---|
| | | 3 | | (fd) |
| | ~~via D~~ | ~~3~~ | ~~2~~ | ~~(Successor)~~ |
| | via C | 4 | 3 | |

**Figure 5-7**   *DUAL Example Step 4*

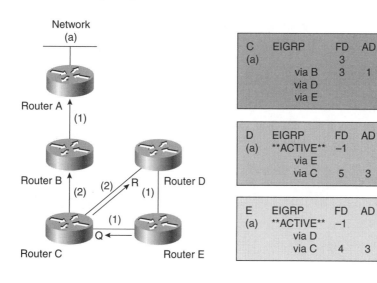

| C<br>(a) | EIGRP | FD | AD | Topology |
|---|---|---|---|---|
| | | 3 | | (fd) |
| | via B | 3 | 1 | (Successor) |
| | via D | | | |
| | via E | | | |

| D<br>(a) | EIGRP<br>**ACTIVE** | FD<br>−1 | AD | Topology<br>(fd) |
|---|---|---|---|---|
| | via E | | | (q) |
| | via C | 5 | 3 | |

| E<br>(a) | EIGRP<br>**ACTIVE** | FD<br>−1 | AD | Topology<br>(fd) |
|---|---|---|---|---|
| | via D | | | |
| | via C | 4 | 3 | (q) |

The following steps occur in Figure 5-8:

- At Router D: Stays active on Network (a), awaiting reply from Router E (q).
- At Router E: Receives reply from Router C indicating no change.
  - — Removes query flag from Router C.
  - — Calculates new FD and installs new successor route in table.

**Figure 5-8**   *DUAL Example Step 5*

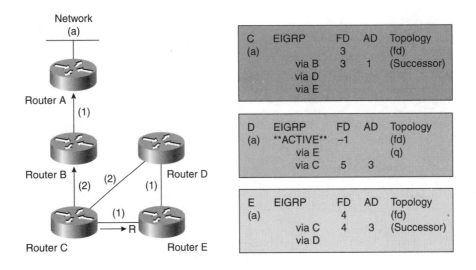

The following steps occur in Figure 5-9:

- At Router D: Receives reply from Router E.
  - — Removes query flag from Router E.
  - — Calculates new FD.
  - — Installs new successor routes in table. Two routes match the FD, and both are marked as successors.

**Figure 5-9** *DUAL Example Step 6*

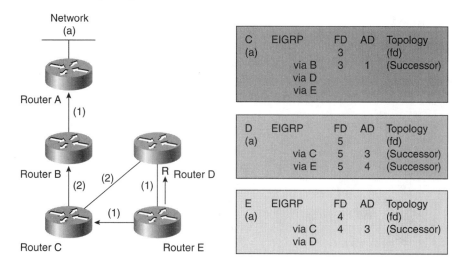

The following steps occur in Figure 5-10:

- At Router D: Two successor routes in the topology table for Network (a). Both successor routes should be listed in the routing table, and equal-cost load balancing should be in effect.

The network is stable and converged.

In Figure 5-4, the original topology (before the link failure) shows traffic from Router E passing through Routers D and B. In Figure 5-10, the new topology shows traffic from Routers D and E going through Routers C and B.

---

**NOTE**    When DUAL decides that a packet needs to be transmitted to a neighbor, the packets are not actually generated until the moment of transmission. The transmit queues instead contain small, fixed-size structures that indicate which parts of the topology table to include in the packet when it is finally transmitted. This means that the queues will not consume large amounts of memory. It also means that only the latest information will be transmitted in each packet. If a route changes state several times, only the last state will be transmitted in the packet, thus reducing link utilization.

---

**Figure 5-10** *DUAL Example Step 7*

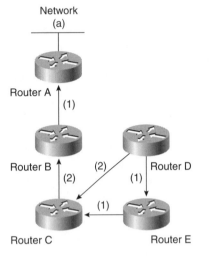

| C (a) | EIGRP | FD | AD | Topology |
|---|---|---|---|---|
| | | 3 | | (fd) |
| | via B | 3 | 1 | (Successor) |
| | via D | | | |
| | via E | | | |

| D (a) | EIGRP | FD | AD | Topology |
|---|---|---|---|---|
| | | 5 | | (fd) |
| | via C | 5 | 3 | (Successor) |
| | via E | 5 | 4 | (Successor) |

| E (a) | EIGRP | FD | AD | Topology |
|---|---|---|---|---|
| | | 4 | | (fd) |
| | via C | 4 | 3 | (Successor) |
| | via D | | | |

# Configuring EIGRP

This section covers the following topics:

- Steps for configuring EIGRP
- Route summarization
- EIGRP load balancing
- EIGRP and WAN links
- Using EIGRP in a scalable internetwork
- Verifying EIGRP operation

## Steps for Configuring EIGRP

Perform the following steps to configure EIGRP for IP:

**Step 1** Enable EIGRP, and define the autonomous system.

```
router(config)#router eigrp autonomous-system-number
```

*autonomous-system-number* is the number that identifies the autonomous system. It is used to indicate all routers that belong within the internetwork. This value must match on all routers within the internetwork.

**Step 2**    Indicate which networks are parts of the EIGRP autonomous system.

> `router(config-router)#`**`network`** `network-number`

network-number entries determine which interfaces of the router are participating in EIGRP and to which networks the router advertises.

**Step 3**    If using serial links, especially for Frame Relay or SMDS, define the bandwidth of a link for the purposes of sending routing update traffic on the link. If you do not change the bandwidth value for these interfaces, EIGRP assumes that the bandwidth on the link is of T1 speed. If the link is slower, the router may not be capable of converging, or routing updates might become lost.

> `router(config-if)#`**`bandwidth`** `kilobits`

kilobits indicates the intended bandwidth in kilobits per second. With point-to-point topology, such as PPP or HDLC, set the bandwidth to match the line speed. For Frame Relay point-to-point interfaces, set the bandwidth to the committed information rate (CIR). For multipoint connections, set it to the sum of all CIRs.

# Route Summarization

Some EIGRP features have distance vector characteristics, such as summarizing routes at a major network boundary—this is an example of traditional distance vector behavior. Traditional distance vector protocols, which are classful routing protocols, cannot presume the mask for networks that are not directly connected because masks are not exchanged by the routing updates.

Summarizing routes at major boundaries (classful) creates smaller routing tables. Smaller routing tables, in turn, make the routing update process less bandwidth-intensive. Cisco distance vector routing protocols have autosummarization enabled by default. As mentioned earlier, EIGRP has its roots in IGRP and, therefore, summarizes at the network boundary by default. EIGRP does autosummarization by default, but it can be turned off.

The inability to create summary routes at arbitrary boundaries with a major network has been a drawback of distance vector protocols since their inception. EIGRP has the added functionality to allow administrators to turn off autosummarization and to create one or more summary routes within a network.

When summarization is configured on an interface, a summary route is added to the routing table with a reference to Null0, a directly connected, software-only interface. The use of the Null0 interface prevents the router from trying to forward traffic to other routers in search of a more precise match.

For effective summarization, blocks of contiguous addresses (subnets) should funnel back to a common router so that a single summary route can be created and then advertised. The number of subnets that can be represented by a summary route is directly related to the number of bits by which the subnet mask has been pulled back toward the major network (natural) mask. The formula of $2^n$, where $n$ equals the number of bits by which the subnet mask has been reduced, indicates how many subnets can be represented by a single summary route. For example, if the summary mask contains 3 fewer bits than the subnet mask, then eight subnets can be aggregated into one advertisement ($2^3 = 8$).

When creating summary routes, the administrator needs to specify only the IP address of the summary route and the routing mask. The Cisco IOS handles the details surrounding proper implementation, such as metrics, loop prevention, and removal of the route from the routing table when the summary route is no longer valid.

## Configuring Summarization

EIGRP automatically summarizes routes at the classful boundary, but in some cases, you may want to turn off this feature, such as if you have discontiguous subnets. This scenario is discussed in Example 5-2. However, an EIGRP router will not perform an automatic summarization of networks in which it does not participate.

To turn off automatic summarization, initiate the following command:

```
router(config-router)#no auto-summary
```

Use the following interface command to manually create a summary route at an arbitrary network boundary or for networks in which your router does not participate:

```
router(config-if)#ip summary-address eigrp as-number address mask
```

Table 5-1 summarizes this command.

**Table 5-1**    **ip summary-address eigrp** *Command*

| ip summary-address eigrp Command | Description |
| --- | --- |
| *as-number* | EIGRP autonomous system number. |
| *address* | The IP address being advertised as the summary address. This address does not need to be aligned on Class A, B, or C boundaries. |
| *mask* | The IP mask being used to create the summary address. |

Figure 5-11 shows a discontiguous network 172.16.0.0. By default, both Routers A and B summarize routes at the classful boundary. In this example, Router C will have two equally good routes to network 172.16.0.0 and will perform load balancing between Router A and Router B.

**Figure 5-11** *Summarizing EIGRP Routes*

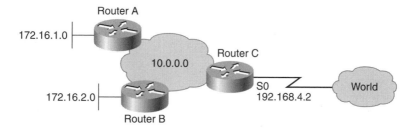

As shown on Example 5-2, you can disable this feature to eliminate route summarization so that Router C knows precisely that 172.16.1.0 is reached via Router A and that 172.16.2.0 is reached only via Router B.

**Example 5-2**  *Turning Off EIGRP Autosummarization on Router A and Router B*

```
router eigrp 1
  network 10.0.0.0
  network 172.16.0.0
  no auto-summary
```

An EIGRP router autosummarizes routes for only networks to which it is attached. If a network was not autosummarized at the major network boundary (as in Router A and Router B because autosummary was turned off), then all the subnet routes will be carried into the routing table of Router C. In turn, Router C will be sending routing information about 172.16.1.0 subnet and 172.16.2.0 subnet out to the WAN.

Forcing a summary route out of Router C's interface s0, as shown in Example 5-3, will help reduce route advertisements about network 172.16.0.0 to the world.

The following are the steps for forcing summarization:

**Step 1**    Select the interface that will propagate the route summary.

**Step 2**    Specify the format of the route summary and the autonomous system of the routes being summarized.

**Example 5-3**  *Forcing Summarization*

```
router eigrp 1
  network 10.0.0.0
  network 192.168.4.0
!
int s0
  ip address 192.168.4.2 255.255.255.0
  ip summary-address eigrp 1 172.16.0.0 255.255.0.0
```

**NOTE**    For manual summarization, the summary is advertised only if a component (an entry that is represented in the summary) of the summary is present in the routing table. Also, IP EIGRP summary routes are given an administrative distance value of 5. Standard EIGRP routes receive an administrative distance of 90, and external EIGRP routes receive an administrative distance of 170.

You will notice the EIGRP summary route with an administrative distance of 5 only on the local router performing the summarization with the **summary-address** command. You can see this administrative distance on the router doing the summarization using the **show ip route** *network* command, where the *network* is the specified summarized route.

# EIGRP Load Balancing

Load balancing is the capability of a router to distribute traffic over all its network ports that are the same distance from the destination address. Good load-balancing algorithms use both line speed and reliability information. Load balancing increases the utilization of network segments, thus increasing effective network bandwidth.

By default, the Cisco IOS will balance between a maximum of four equal-cost paths. Using the router configuration command **maximum-paths**, you can request that up to six equally good routes be kept in the routing table. When a packet is process switched, load balancing over equal-cost paths occurs on a per-packet basis. When packets are fast switched, load balancing over equal-cost paths is on a per-destination basis.

EIGRP can balance traffic across multiple routes that have different metrics. The amount of load balancing that is performed can be controlled by the **variance** router configuration command.

The multiplier is a variance value, between 1 and 128, used for load balancing. The default is 1, which means equal-cost load balancing. The multiplier defines the range of metric values that will be accepted for load balancing. In Figure 5-12, the variance is 2 and the range of the metric values (the feasible distances) for Router E to get to Network Z is 20 through 45. This range of values is used in the procedure for determining the feasibility of a potential route. A route is feasible if the next router in the path is closer to the destination than the current router and if the metric for the entire path is within the variance. Only paths that are feasible can be used for load balancing. The two feasibility conditions are listed here:

- The local best metric (the current feasible distance) must be greater than the next router best metric (the advertised distance) learned from the next router.

- The variance × the local best metric (the current feasible distance) must be greater than the metric (the advertised distance) through the next router.

If both of these conditions are met, the route is called feasible and can be added to the routing table.

**Figure 5-12**  *EIGRP Load Balancing with a Variance of 2*

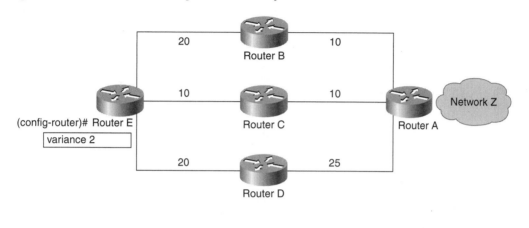

## Traffic Sharing

To control how traffic is distributed among routes when there are multiple routes for the same destination network that have different costs, use the **traffic-share** router configuration command. With the keyword **balanced**, the router distributes traffic proportionately to the ratios of the metrics associated with the different routes. With the keyword **min**, the router uses routes that have minimum costs.

## Example of EIGRP Load Balancing

In Figure 5-12, Router E will use Router C as the successor because its feasible distance is lowest (20). With the **variance** command applied to Router E, the path through Router B meets the criteria for load balancing. In this case, the feasible distance through Router B is less than twice the feasible distance for the successor (Router C). Router D will not be considered for load balancing because the feasible distance through Router D is greater than twice the feasible distance for the successor (Router C). Also, because Router D's AD of 25 is greater than Router E's FD of 20, Router D is not considered closer to the destination then Router E.

Example 5-4 is another example of unequal load balancing where four different paths to a destination have different metric.

**Example 5-4**  *Unequal Load-Balancing Example*

```
Path 1: 1100
Path 2: 1100
Path 3: 2000
Path 4: 4000
```

By default, the router will route to the destination using both paths 1 and 2. To load-balance over paths 1, 2, and 3, you would use the **variance 2** command because $1100 \times 2 = 2200$, which is greater than the metric through path 3. Similarly, to also include path 4, you would issue the **variance 4** command under the routing protocol configuration mode.

# EIGRP and WAN Links

EIGRP is scalable on both point-to-point links and NBMA multipoint and point-to-point links. Because of the inherent differences in operational characteristics of links, default configuration of WAN connections may not be optimal. A solid understanding of EIGRP operation coupled with knowledge of link speeds can yield an efficient, reliable, and scalable router configuration.

## EIGRP Link Utilization

By default, EIGRP will use up to 50 percent of the bandwidth declared on an interface or subinterface. This percentage can be adjusted on an interface or subinterface with the following interface command:

```
Router(config-if)#ip bandwidth-percent eigrp as-number percent
```

The *percent* parameter can be set to a value greater than 100. This is useful if the bandwidth is configured artificially low for routing policy reasons. Example 5-5 shows a configuration that allows EIGRP to use 40 kbps (200 percent of the configured bandwidth) on the interface. It is essential to make sure that the line is provisioned to handle the configured capacity.

**Example 5-5** *Adjusting the EIGRP Link Utilization*

```
interface serial0
bandwidth 20
ip bandwidth-percent eigrp 1 200
```

The Cisco IOS treats point-to-point Frame Relay subinterfaces in the same manner as any serial interface when it comes to bandwidth. The IOS presumes that those serial interfaces and subinterfaces are operating at full T1 link speed. In many implementations, however, only fractional T1 speeds are available. Therefore, when configuring these types of interfaces, set the bandwidth to match the contracted CIR.

When configuring multipoint interfaces (especially for Frame Relay) remember that the bandwidth is shared equally by all neighbors. That is, EIGRP uses the **bandwidth** statement of the physical interface divided by the number of Frame Relay neighbors connected on that physical interface to get the bandwidth attributed to each neighbor. EIGRP configuration should reflect the correct percentage of the actual available bandwidth on the line.

Each installation has a unique topology, and with that comes unique configurations. Differing CIR values often require a hybrid configuration that blends the characteristics of point-to-point circuits with multipoint circuits. When configuring multipoint interfaces, configure the bandwidth to represent the minimum CIR times the number of circuits. This approach may not fully utilize the higher-speed circuits, but it ensures that the circuits with the lowest CIR will not be overdriven. If the topology has a small number of very low-speed circuits, these interfaces should be defined as point-to-point so that their bandwidth can be set to match the provisioned CIR.

In Figure 5-13, the interface has been configured for a bandwidth of 224 kbps. In a pure multipoint topology, each circuit will be allocated one-quarter of the configured bandwidth on the interface, and this 56 kbps allocation matches the provisioned CIR of each circuit.

**Figure 5-13**  *Frame-Relay Multipoint in Which All VCs Share the Bandwidth Evenly*

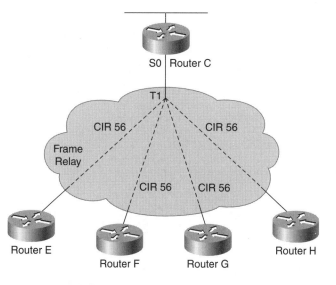

• All VCs share bandwidth evenly: 4 x 56 = 224

Example 5-6 shows the configuration for the interface Serial 0 of Router C:

**Example 5-6**  *Adjusting the **bandwidth** command on an interface*

```
interface serial 0
encapsulation frame-relay
  bandwidth 224
```

In Figure 5-14, one of the circuits has been provisioned for a 56-kbps CIR, while the other circuits have a higher CIR. This interface has been configured for a bandwidth that represents the lowest CIR multiplied by the number of circuits being supported ($56 \times 4 = 224$). This configuration protects against overwhelming the slowest speed circuit in the topology.

**Figure 5-14** *Frame-Relay Multipoint in Which VCs Have Different CIRs*

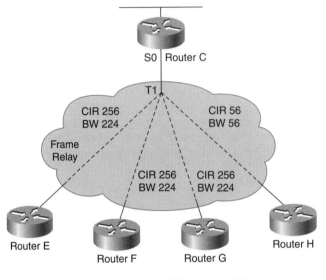

- Lowest CIR x # of VC: 56 x 4 = 224

In Figure 5-15, a hybrid solution is presented. There is only one low-speed circuit and other VCs are provisioned for a higher CIR.

**Figure 5-15** *Frame-Relay Multipoint and Point-to-Point*

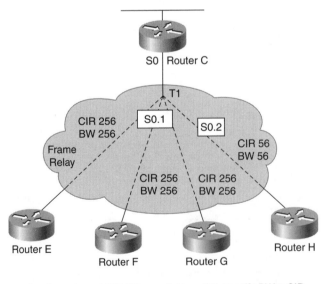

- Configure lowest CIR VC as point-to-point, specify BW = CIR
- Configure higher CIR VCs as multipoint, combine CIRs

Example 5-7 shows the configuration applied to Router C in Figure 5-15.

**Example 5-7**  *Adjusting the Bandwidth for a Frame-Relay Subinterface*

```
interface serial 0.1 multipoint
  bandwidth 768

interface serial 0.2 point-to-point
  bandwidth 56
```

Example 5-7 shows the low-speed circuit configured as point-to-point. The remaining circuits are designated as multipoint, and their respective CIRs are added up to set the bandwidth for the interface.

Figure 5-16 illustrates a common hub-and-spoke oversubscribed topology with ten virtual circuits out to the remotes.

**Figure 5-16**  *Frame Relay Hub-and-Spoke Topology*

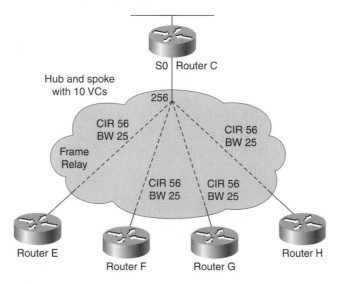

• Configure each VC as point-to-point, specify BW = 1/10 of link capacity
• Increase EIGRP utilization to 50% of actual VC capacity

The circuits are provisioned as 56-kbps links, though there is not sufficient bandwidth at the interface to support the allocation. In a point-to-point topology, all VCs are treated equally and are configured for exactly one tenth (25 kbps) of the available link speed.

By default, EIGRP utilizes 50 percent of the configured bandwidth on a circuit. In an attempt to ensure that EIGRP packets are delivered through the Frame Relay network in Figure 5-16, each subinterface has the EIGRP allocation percentage raised to 110 percent of the specified bandwidth. This adjustment results in EIGRP packets receiving approximately 28 kbps of the provisioned 56 kbps on each circuit. This extra configuration restores the 50-50 ratio that was tampered with when the bandwidth was set to an artificially low value.

Example 5-8 shows the configuration used on Router C and Router G of Figure 5-16.

**Example 5-8**  *EIGRP WAN Configuration—Point-to-Point Links*

```
RouterC(config)#interface serial 0.1 point-to-point
RouterC(config-subif)#bandwidth 25
RouterC(config-subif)#ip bandwidth-percent eigrp 63 110
<output omitted>
RouterC(config)#interface serial 0.10 point-to-point
RouterC(config-subif)#bandwidth 25
RouterC(config-subif)#ip bandwidth-percent eigrp 63 110


RouterG(config)#interface serial 0
RouterG(config-if)#bandwidth 25
RouterG(config-if)#ip bandwidth-percent eigrp 63 110
```

**NOTE**    Suppressing ACKs also saves bandwidth. An ACK will not be sent if a unicast data packet is ready for transmission. The ACK field in any reliable unicast packet (RTP packet) is sufficient to acknowledge the neighbor's packet, so the ACK packet is suppressed to save bandwidth. This is a significant feature for point-to-point links and NBMA networks because on those media, all data packets are sent as unicasts and thus are capable of carrying an acknowledgment themselves. In that instance, there is no need for another packet known as an ACK packet.

## Using EIGRP in a Scalable Internetwork

The following are some of the many variables that impact network scalability:

- **The amount of information exchanged between neighbors**—Too much information exchanged between EIGRP neighbors causes unnecessary compilation work during routing startup and topology changes.

- **A topology change**—When a topology change occurs, the amount of resources consumed by EIGRP will be directly related to the number of routers that must be involved in the change.

- **The depth of the topology**—The depth of the topology can impact the convergence time. Depth refers to the number of hops that information must travel to reach all routers.

- **The number of alternative paths through the network**—A network should provide alternative paths to avoid single points of failure. At the same time, however, too many alternative paths can create problems with EIGRP convergence.

As an advanced distance vector routing protocol, EIGRP relies on its neighbors to provide routing information. If a route is lost and no feasible successor is available, EIGRP will query its neighbors regarding the lost route.

When a router loses a route and does not have a feasible successor in its topology table, it looks for an alternative path to the destination. This is known as going active on a route. (A route is considered passive when a router is not performing recompilation on that route.) Recompilation of a route involves sending query packets to all neighbors on interfaces other than the one used to reach the previous successor (*split horizon*), inquiring whether they have a route to the given destination. If a router has an alternate route, it will answer the query and not propagate it further. If a neighbor does not have an alternative route, it will query each of its own neighbors for an alternative path. The queries will then propagate out through the network, thus creating an expanding tree of queries. When a router answers to a query, it will stop the spread of the query through that branch of the network.

Because of the reliable multicast approach used by EIGRP when searching for an alternate to a lost route, it is imperative that a reply be received for each query generated in the network. In other words, when a route goes active and queries are initiated, the only way that this route can come out of the active state is by receiving a reply for every generated query. Therefore, a route will transition from active state to passive state when the router receives a reply for every generated query.

If the router does not receive a reply to all the outstanding queries within 3 minutes, the route goes to the stuck in active (SIA) state. The router then resets the neighbors that fail to reply by going active on all routes known through that neighbor, and it readvertises all routes to that neighbor. Limiting the scope of query propagation through the network (the *query range*), also known as *query scoping*, helps reduce incidences of SIA.

---

**NOTE**    The active-state time limit can be changed from it's default of 3 minutes using the **timers active-time** [*time-limit* | **disabled**] router configuration command. The *time-limit* is in minutes.

---

**NOTE**    Use the **eigrp log-neighbor-changes** command to enable the logging of neighbor adjacency changes to monitor the stability of the routing system and to help detect problems related to SIA.

Many networks have been implemented using multiple EIGRP autonomous systems to somewhat simulate OSPF areas with mutual redistribution between the different autonomous systems. Although this approach does change the way the network behaves, it does not always achieve the results intended.

One erroneous approach for decreasing the chances of a stuck-in-active route is to use multiple EIGRP autonomous systems, thus bounding the query range. If a query reaches the edge of the AS (where routes are redistributed into another AS), the original query will be answered. Then a new query will be initiated in the other AS by the edge router. However, the query process has not been stopped because the querying continues in the other AS, where the route can potentially go in SIA.

| NOTE | Stuck in active mode lasts for a maximum of 3 minutes by default, at which point DUAL resets the neighbor relationship with the neighbor that failed to respond to the query. |
|------|------|

The best solution to control queries is to reduce their reach in the internetwork. This is done by summarization. However, the query range is not a common reason for stuck-in-active routes being reported. The most common reasons for this are as follows:

- **The router is too busy**—The router is too busy to answer the query (generally because of high CPU utilization).

- **The router is having memory problems**—The router cannot allocate the memory to process the query or build the reply packet.

- **Packets are lost between the routers because of circuit problems**—Enough packets are getting through to keep the neighbor relationship up, but some queries or replies are not getting through.

- **The router is using unidirectional links**—This is a link on which traffic can flow in only one direction due to failure.

Remote routers rarely need to know all the routes advertised in an entire network. Therefore, it is the network manager's responsibility to look at what information is necessary to properly route user traffic, and maybe consider the use of a default route.

Examples of mechanisms used to limit what information is provided to other routers include filters on routing updates and the **ip summary-address** command on the router's outbound interfaces.

In Figure 5-17, Router B notices the loss of network 10.1.8.0 and sends a query to Routers A, C, D, and E. In turn, these routers send queries to their neighbors requesting a feasible successor for 10.1.8.0. When the query process starts, each path receives duplicate queries due to the topology. Therefore, not only are the remote routers required to respond to queries from the head office, but they also continue the search by reflecting the queries back toward the head office's other router. This significantly complicates the convergence process on the network.

**Figure 5-17** *Effect of the EIGRP Update and Query Process*

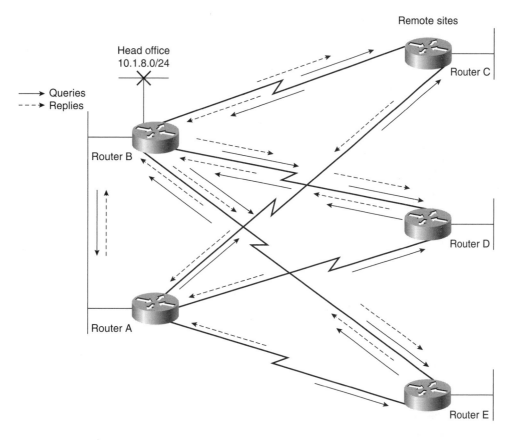

In Figure 5-17, the architect provided redundancy with dual links from the head office to remote sites. The architect did not mean for the traffic to go from the head office to the remote office and back to the head office, but unfortunately this is the situation. The design of the network in Figure 5-17 is sound, but because of EIGRP behavior, remote routers are involved in the convergence process.

The **ip summary-address** command judiciously placed on Router A and Router B will prevent some route components from being forwarded to remote routers, as shown in Figure 5-18, thus reducing queries back to the head office.

**Figure 5-18** *Limiting Updates and Queries Using Summarization*

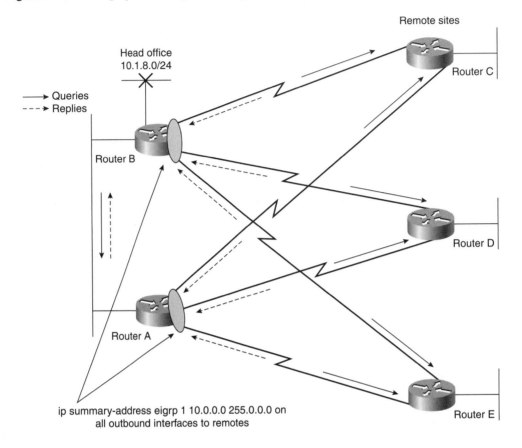

Another approach would be to install route filters to limit advertisements to the remote routers. Having proper filtering would cause the remote routers to reply to the head office routers that the head office LANs are unreachable. A combination of summarization and filtering could be used for best results.

## EIGRP Scalability Rules

EIGRP has many features that allow for the creation of very large internetworks. Solid design principles are the foundation upon which the network infrastructure rests.

Route summarization is most effective with a sound address allocation. Having a two- or three-layer hierarchy, with routers positioned by function rather than by geography, greatly assists traffic flow and route distribution.

Figure 5-19 shows the topology of a nonscalable internetwork in which addresses (subnets) are randomly assigned. In this example, multiple subnets from different major networks are located in each cloud, requiring many subnet routes to be injected into the core. In addition, because of the random assignment of addresses, query traffic cannot be localized to any portion of the network, thus increasing convergence time.

**Figure 5-19** *Example of a Nonscalable Internetwork*

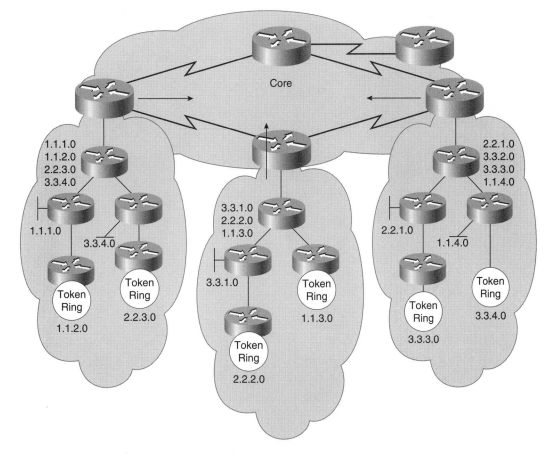

Figure 5-20 illustrates a better-designed network. Subnet addresses from individual major networks are localized within each cloud. This allows for summary routes to be injected into the core. As an added benefit, the summary routes act as a boundary for the queries generated by a topology change.

**Figure 5-20**   *Example of a Scalable Internetwork*

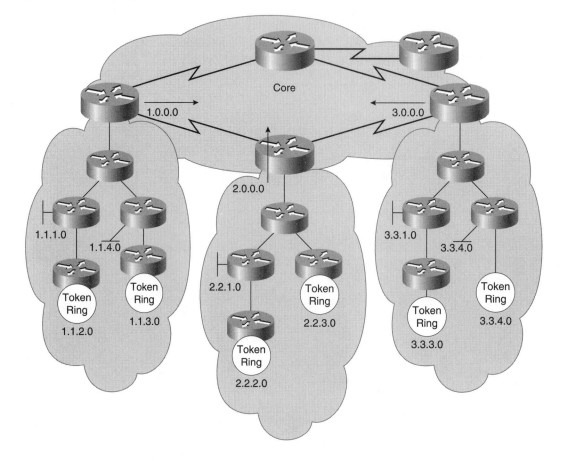

## Tiered Network Design

A tiered network model, as shown in Figure 5-21, provides benefits at all layers of the hierarchical model:

- **At the core**—Summarized routes reduce the size of the routing table held by core routers. These smaller tables make for efficient lookups, thus providing a fast-switching core.

- **At the regional head office**—Summarized routes at the regional head office help in the selection of the most efficient path by reducing the number of entries to be checked.

- **At the remote office**—Proper allocation of blocks of addresses to remote offices enables local traffic to remain local and not to unnecessarily burden other portions of the network.

**Figure 5-21**  *Tiered Network Topology*

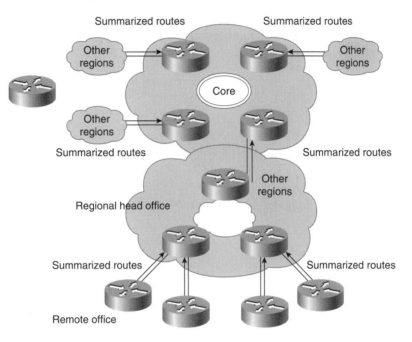

Some common design principles should be followed for proper operation of EIGRP. Routers located at convergence points within the network need sufficient memory to buffer a large number of packets and to support numerous processes related to routing large volumes of traffic.

On WAN links, and especially with the hub-and-spoke topology, enough bandwidth should be provided to prevent router overhead traffic from interfering with normal user-generated traffic. In this respect, the impact of EIGRP packets being lost because of contention for bandwidth might be greater than application delays experienced by some users.

Multiple autonomous systems can share route information through the redistribution process discussed in Chapter 8, "Optimizing Routing Update Operation." Proper implementation of redistribution requires route filters to prevent feedback loops. It is strongly recommended that you implement route filters when redistributing between routing protocols or multiple autonomous systems.

## Verifying EIGRP Operation

This section discusses commands to use for verifying EIGRP operation.

Table 5-2 describes commands used to verify EIGRP operation.

**Table 5-2**    *Verifying EIGRP Operation Commands*

| Command | Description |
|---|---|
| **show ip eigrp neighbors** | Displays neighbors discovered by EIGRP. |
| **show ip eigrp topology** | Displays the EIGRP topology table. This command shows the topology table, the active or passive state of routes, the number of successors, and the feasible distance to the destination. |
| **show ip route eigrp** | Displays the current EIGRP entries in the routing table. |
| **show ip protocols** | Displays the parameters and current state of the active routing protocol process. This command shows the EIGRP autonomous system number. It also displays filtering and redistribution numbers, as well as neighbors and distance information. |
| **show ip eigrp traffic** | Displays the number of EIGRP packets sent and received. This command displays statistics on hello packets, updates, queries, replies, and acknowledgments. |

Table 5-3 shows **debug** commands used to verify EIGRP operation.

**Table 5-3**    *debug eigrp Commands*

| Command | Description |
|---|---|
| **debug eigrp packets** | Displays the types of EIGRP packets sent and received. A maximum of 11 packet types can be selected for individual or group display. |
| **debug eigrp neighbors** | Displays neighbors discovered by EIGRP and the contents of the hello packets. |

**Table 5-3**    *debug eigrp Commands (Continued)*

| Command | Description |
| --- | --- |
| **debug ip eigrp** | Displays packets that are sent and received on an interface. Because the **debug ip eigrp** command generates large amounts of output, use it only when traffic on the network is light. |
| **debug ip eigrp summary** | Displays a summarized version of EIGRP activity. It also displays filtering and redistribution numbers, as well as neighbors and distance information. |

# Case Study: EIGRP

Refer to Chapter 1, "Routing Principles," for introductory information on the running case study.

Link-state routing protocols, such as EIGRP, are commonly deployed in medium- to large-scale networks. In Figure 5-22, EIGRP was selected by Acquisition D because of its ease of implementation and management. There are fewer than 20 routers in the network, and all WAN routers participate in the partially meshed Frame Relay network.

While looking at Figure 5-22, analyze how the following points are treated advantageously by EIGRP over other routing protocols:

- Support for VLSM and discontiguous subnets
- Automatic route summarization at major network boundaries
- Manual route summarization at arbitrary network boundaries
- Support for various WAN topologies, including NBMA
- Efficient bandwidth utilization for overhead routing operations
- Support for hierarchical designs
- Route information exchanged by only routers within the same AS

**Figure 5-22** *EIGRP Case Study—JKL's Topology*

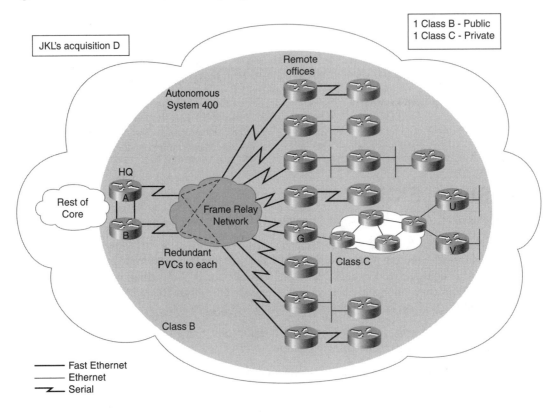

## Case Study Solution

Acquisition D's network is reasonably new and represents a redundant approach to support the company's business units at different remote locations. Although some communication is required between the business units, each remote office primarily sends sales orders to headquarters via the Frame Relay network.

Network designers applied a hierarchical design to assist in proper address allocation of D's public registered Class B address space. VLSM conserves addresses to allow for future growth. The network administrators have already researched the possibility of using **ip unnumbered** on the serial links to free up additional addresses if necessary.

One of the business units required a large number of users at its location, and a private Class C address was deployed to provide the necessary support. Fortunately, some default distance vector characteristicsof EIGRP (such as, automatic route summarization and no discontiguous subnets) could be handled by additional router configuration commands. Routers U and V have a **no eigrp auto-summary** command applied. This command allows the subnets of U and V (discontiguous subnets) to pass through the Class C network and to be advertised with the rest of the Class B subnets that make up AS400. To honor their registered network advertisement to the Internet, a route filter is required on the HQ routers to block the private Class C address from being advertised. With EIGRP, manual summary routes can be applied at selected locations within the network as needed.

One of the reasons that Router D's administrators selected EIGRP as the routing protocol is for its rapid convergence. With a redundant NBMA topology like this one, convergence could be slowed while waiting for query replies from all remote routers. Network administrators have solved the convergence issue by applying a manual summary route about the core network on the interface of the two HQ routers (on the left side of the graphic) touching the Frame Relay cloud. The summarized route restricts the queries from being propagated to all remote routers during the convergence process. This is an example of query scoping, the mechanism by which the scope of the query packets is restricted to encourage rapid convergence.

Remember that a migration to EIGRP will require all routers to be Cisco devices.

# Summary

In this chapter, you learned about Cisco's own EIGRP, an advanced routing protocol that uses the DUAL algorithm to make decisions.

You learned about how EIGRP differs from OSPF, such as how EIGRP combines in one step the discovering of neighbors and route learning process. Other features of EIGRP that you learned about include its supports for VLSM and its autosummarization feature. You saw that EIGRP is well suited for both LAN and WAN traffic, including an NBMA environment.

# Configuration Exercise #1: Configuring EIGRP

---

**Configuration Exercises**

In this book, Configuration Exercises are used to provide practice in configuring routers with the commands presented. If you have access to real hardware, you can try these exercises on your routers; refer to Appendix H, "Configuration Exercise Equipment Requirements and Backbone Configurations," for a list of recommended equipment and configuration commands for the backbone routers. However, even if you don't have access to any routers, you can go through the exercises and keep a log of your own "running configurations" on separate sheets of paper. Commands used and answers to the Configuration Exercises are provided at the end of the exercise.

In these exercises, you are in control of a pod of three routers; there are assumed to be 12 pods in the network. The pods are interconnected to a backbone. In most of the exercises, there is only one router in the backbone; in some cases, another router is added to the backbone. Each of the Configuration Exercises in this book assumes that you have completed the previous exercises on your pod.

---

Complete the following Configuration Exercise to configure EIGRP.

## Objectives

In the following Configuration Exercise, you will practice how to configure the routers with EIGRP. You will also practice disabling EIGRP autosummarization and enabling manual EIGRP route summarization. In addition, you will see the commands used to verify EIGRP operations.

Assuming that the routers in your pod are properly cabled, your task is to do the following:

- Enable EIGRP on all routers within your assigned pods.
- Verify connectivity within your pod.
- Verify connectivity to the other pods.

## Visual Objective

Figure 5-23 illustrates the topology used for this EIGRP Configuration Exercise.

**Figure 5-23**  *EIGRP Configuration Exercise Topology*

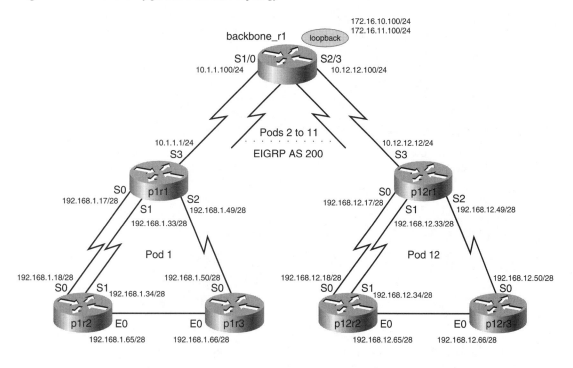

## Command List

In this Configuration Exercise, you will use the commands listed in Table 5-4. Refer to this list if you need configuration command assistance during this exercise.

**Table 5-4**  *Commands Used in Configuration Exercise #1*

| Command | Description |
| --- | --- |
| **router eigrp 200** | Enables EIGRP with an AS number of 200 |
| **network 10.0.0.0** | Specifies interfaces on which to run EIGRP |
| **show ip eigrp neighbors** | Displays information about EIGRP neighbors |
| **show ip eigrp topology** | Displays the entries in the EIGRP topology table |
| **no auto-summary** | Disables EIGRP autosummarization |
| **ip summary-address eigrp 200 192.168.x.0 255.255.255.128** | Performs manual route summarization |
| **debug eigrp packets** | Debugs EIGRP packets |

## Setup

To prepare your equipment prior to starting this Configuration Exercise, you will need to perform the following steps:

**Step 1**   Shut the p*x*r1 S3 interface.

**Step 2**   Disable OSPF on all the routers within your pod.

## Task 1: Enabling EIGRP Within Your Pod

Now enter commands that will activate EIGRP within your pod. Use the following steps to guide you in this task.

**Step 1**   Enable EIGRP on all interfaces in the 192.168.*x*.0 network on all routers within your pod. The AS number is 200.

**Step 2**   Verify that you have full connectivity within your pod.

**Step 3**   Examine the routing tables of p*x*r1, p*x*r2, and p*x*r3.

What is the administrative distance for EIGRP?

How is the EIGRP metric different than the IGRP metric?

Does EIGRP support load balancing by default?

**Step 4**   From the p*x*r1 router, issue the command to display information about the EIGRP neighbors. What would that command be?

How many entries do you see in the p*x*r1 EIGRP neighbors table?

**Step 5**   From the p*x*r1 router, what would be the command to display the EIGRP topology table?

How many successor routes are available from p*x*r1 to subnet 192.168.*x*.64/28?

What is the FD from p*x*r1 to subnet 192.168.*x*.64/28?

What is the AD to subnet 192.168.*x*.64/28 via S0?

What is the AD to subnet 192.168.*x*.64/28 via S1?

What is the AD to subnet 192.168.*x*.64/28 via S2?

**Step 6**   Which command would save the current configurations of all the routers within your pod to NVRAM?

## Task 2: Enabling EIGRP Connectivity to the backbone_r1 Router

Complete the following steps.

**Step 1**   Which command would you type to reactivate the p*x*r1 S3 interface?

**Step 2**   Which command would you use to enable EIGRP on the S3 interface of your p*x*r1 router?

**Step 3**   What command would you type to verify that you have full connectivity to the backbone router loopback interfaces?

**Step 4**   Examine the routing table of p*x*r1.

Do you see the external EIGRP routes sourced from the backbone_r1 router?

What is the administrative distance of the external EIGRP routes?

From your p*x*r3 router, ping 172.16.10.100 and 172.16.11.100.

Were the pings successful?

**Step 5**   Telnet to the backbone_r1 router; the password is cisco. Do you see an entry for your pod's 192.168.*x*.0 network?

Does EIGRP perform autosummarization across the network boundary by default?

**Step 6**   Exit the Telnet to the backbone_r1 router.

**Step 7**   At your p*x*r1 router, disable autosummarization. Which command is used to achieve this?

**Step 8**   Telnet to the backbone_r1 router; the password is cisco. Do you see an entry for each of your pod's 192.168.*x*.0 subnets?

From your p*x*r3 router, ping 172.16.10.100 and 172.16.11.100.

Were the pings successful?

**Step 9**   At your p*x*r1 router, create a manual summarization statement to summarize all the subnets in your pod to a single summarized route of 192.168.*x*.0/25 (where *x* = your pod number). What is the command that you used?

**Step 10**   Telnet to the backbone_r1 router; the password is cisco. Do you see your summarized route?

**Step 11**   Exit the Telnet to the backbone_r1 router.

**Step 12**   From your p*x*r3 router, ping 172.16.10.100 and 172.16.11.100.

Were the pings successful?

**Step 13** Enter the **debug eigrp packets** command at one of the routers within your pod.

How often are the EIGRP hello packets sent out on the serial interfaces?

| | |
|---|---|
| **Note** | You may want to put the **service timestamps debug datetime** configuration command on the router so that debug messages will be timestamped. |

**Step 14** Turn off debug on your router.

**Step 15** Save the current configurations of all the routers within your pod to NVRAM.

## Completion Criteria

You have successfully completed this Configuration Exercise if you correctly supplied the commands required to configure and to verify EIGRP on your pod routers, and if you were able to correctly answer the questions in the exercises. At the end of this Configuration Exercise, all the routers should have full connectivity to each other running EIGRP, including connectivity to the backbone router. The answers to this Configuration Exercise can be found later in this chapter.

# Configuration Exercise #2: Configuring EIGRP in an NBMA Environment

Complete the following exercise to configure EIGRP over Frame Relay.

## Objectives

In the following Configuration Exercise, you will configure the pxr1 router as the Frame Relay switch for the pxr2 and pxr3 routers. You also will be required to configure the pxr2 and pxr3 routers' serial interface (S0) with Frame Relay encapsulation. When you have verified the connectivity between pxr2 and pxr3, you will configure EIGRP over NBMA using the main interface. Using the **show** commands, you will verify EIGRP operations.

In this exercise, your pxr1 router will act as the Frame Relay switch between your pxr2 and pxr3 routers.

## Visual Objective

Figure 5-24 provides the topology used for this EIGRP in NBMA Configuration Exercise.

**Figure 5-24**  *Configuring EIGRP in an NBMA Environment Using Main Interface*

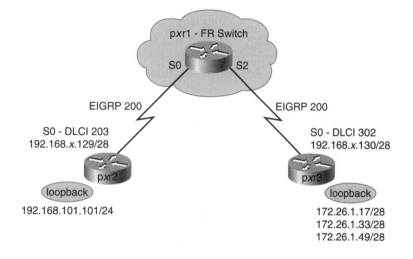

## Command List

In this Configuration Exercise, you will use the commands listed in Table 5-5. Refer to this list if you need configuration command assistance during the Configuration Exercise.

**Table 5-5**  *Commands Used in Configuration Exercise #2*

| Command | Description |
| --- | --- |
| **encapsulation frame-relay** | Enables Frame Relay frames on an interface. |
| **router eigrp 200** | Enables EIGRP with an AS number of 200. |
| **network 10.0.0.0** | Specifies the interfaces on which to run EIGRP. |
| **show ip eigrp neighbors** | Displays information about OSPF neighbors. |
| **show frame-relay map** | Displays a mapping between DLCI and IP addresses, and shows traffic forwarding characteristics. |
| **ip bandwidth-percent eigrp** | Specifies the maximum percentage of the bandwidth that EIGRP will use. |

## Setup

**Step 1** On your pxr1 router, shut down the Serial 1 and Serial 3 interfaces. Disable EIGRP 200 on your pxr1 router.

**Step 2** On your pxr2 router, shut down the Ethernet 0, Serial 0, and Serial 1 interfaces. Reconfigure your pxr2 Serial 0 IP address to be 192.168.x.129/28.

**Step 3** On your pxr3 router, shut down the Ethernet 0 and Serial 0 interfaces. Reconfigure your pxr3 Serial 0 IP address to be 192.168.x.130/28.

## Task 1: Creating a Frame Relay Switch

Complete the following steps:

**Step 1** Enable your pxr1 router as the Frame Relay switch.

Which command do you use to activate the Frame Relay switch?

Which command do you use to set your router as a Frame Relay DCE device?

Which command do you type on pxr1, S0 interface, to perform switching from pxr2 to pxr3?

Which command do you use on pxr1, S2 interface, to perform switching from pxr3 to pxr2?

**Step 2** Enable Frame Relay encapsulation on the S0 interface of your pxr2 and pxr3 router.

Verify that your pxr2 and pxr3 router S0 IP addresses are as follows:

— Router pxr2: S0 IP address 192.168.x.129/28

— Router pxr3: S0 IP address 192.168.x.130/28

Enable the Serial 0 interfaces on pxr2 and pxr3. What command is used to achieve this?

**Step 3** From pxr2, ping the pxr3 Serial 0 interface to ensure connectivity.

## Task 2: Enabling EIGRP over NBMA Network Using Main Interface

Complete the following steps:

**Step 1** Which command would you use to verify that the pxr2 and pxr3 Serial 0 interfaces are running EIGRP in AS 200?

**Step 2**    On pxr2, type in the command to start advertising the loopback 10 network in EIGRP.

**Step 3**    On pxr3, ping the pxr2 loopback address to verify connectivity. (Note: it may take a while for the ping to work)

**Step 4**    On pxr2, enter the **show ip eigrp neighbors** command. Do you see your neighbor pxr3 router?

**Step 5**    EIGRP sends hello packets to establish a neighbor relationship using the multicast address of 224.0.0.10. Is your Frame Relay interface enabled to send broadcast (which includes multicast) traffic?

**Step 6**    Enter the command to enable EIGRP to use only 20 percent of your Frame Relay interface bandwidth on your pxr2 router.

**Step 7**    Save the current configurations of all the routers within your pod to NVRAM.

**Step 8**    Bonus Question: What is the EIGRP interface configuration command to disable IP split horizon on an NBMA interface? (Use AS number 200.)

## Completion Criteria

You have successfully completed this Configuration Exercise if you correctly supplied the commands required to configure and to verify an EIGRP network over an NBMA environment using a main interface, and if you were able to correctly answer the questions in the exercises. At the end of this exercise, your pxr2 and pxr3 routers will be running EIGRP over Frame Relay.

# Answers to Configuration Exercise #1: Configuring EIGRP

This section provides the answers to the questions in Configuration Exercise #1. The answers are in **bold**.

## Answers to Setup

**Step 1**    Shut the pxr1 S3 interface.

```
p1r1(config)#interface s3
p1r1(config-if)#shutdown
02:50:31: %LINK-5-CHANGED: Interface Serial3, changed state to administratively down
02:50:32: %LINEPROTO-5-UPDOWN: Line protocol on Interface Serial3, changed state to
down
```

Step 2   Disable OSPF on all the routers within your pod.

```
p1r1(config)#no router ospf 200
p1r1(config)#

p1r2(config)#no router ospf 200
p1r2(config)#

p1r3(config)#no router ospf 200
p1r3(config)#
```

## Answers to Task 1: Enabling EIGRP Within Your Pod

Step 1   Enable EIGRP on all interfaces in the 192.168.x.0 network on all routers within your pod. The AS number is 200.

```
p1r1(config)#router eigrp 200
p1r1(config-router)#network 192.168.1.0

p1r2(config)#router eigrp 200
p1r2(config-router)#network 192.168.1.0

p1r3(config)#router eigrp 200
p1r3(config-router)#network 192.168.1.0
```

Step 2   Verify that you have full connectivity within your pod.

```
p1r1#ping p1r2
Type escape sequence to abort.
Sending 5, 100-byte ICMP Echos to 192.168.1.65, timeout is 2 seconds:
!!!!!
Success rate is 100 percent (5/5), round-trip min/avg/max = 28/32/36 ms

p1r1#ping p1r3
Type escape sequence to abort.
Sending 5, 100-byte ICMP Echos to 192.168.1.66, timeout is 2 seconds:
!!!!!
Success rate is 100 percent (5/5), round-trip min/avg/max = 32/32/36 ms
p1r1#

p1r2#ping p1r1
Type escape sequence to abort.
Sending 5, 100-byte ICMP Echos to 192.168.1.17, timeout is 2 seconds:
!!!!!
Success rate is 100 percent (5/5), round-trip min/avg/max = 32/32/32 ms

p1r2#ping p1r3
Type escape sequence to abort.
Sending 5, 100-byte ICMP Echos to 192.168.1.66, timeout is 2 seconds:
!!!!!
Success rate is 100 percent (5/5), round-trip min/avg/max = 4/5/12 ms

p1r3#ping p1r1
Type escape sequence to abort.
Sending 5, 100-byte ICMP Echos to 192.168.1.17, timeout is 2 seconds:
!!!!!
Success rate is 100 percent (5/5), round-trip min/avg/max = 32/32/36 ms

p1r3#ping p1r2
Type escape sequence to abort.
```

```
Sending 5, 100-byte ICMP Echos to 192.168.1.65, timeout is 2 seconds:
!!!!!
Success rate is 100 percent (5/5), round-trip min/avg/max = 4/4/4 ms
```

**Step 3**   Examine the routing tables of p*x*r1, p*x*r2, and p*x*r3.

```
p1r1#show ip route
Codes: C - connected, S - static, I - IGRP, R - RIP, M - mobile, B - BGP
       D - EIGRP, EX - EIGRP external, O - OSPF, IA - OSPF inter area
       N1 - OSPF NSSA external type 1, N2 - OSPF NSSA external type 2
       E1 - OSPF external type 1, E2 - OSPF external type 2, E - EGP
       i - IS-IS, L1 - IS-IS level-1, L2 - IS-IS level-2, * - candidate default
       U - per-user static route, o - ODR
       T - traffic engineered route

Gateway of last resort is not set

     192.168.1.0/28 is subnetted, 4 subnets
D       192.168.1.64 [90/40537600] via 192.168.1.34, 00:01:19, Serial1
                     [90/40537600] via 192.168.1.18, 00:01:19, Serial0
                     [90/40537600] via 192.168.1.50, 00:01:19, Serial2
C       192.168.1.32 is directly connected, Serial1
C       192.168.1.48 is directly connected, Serial2
C       192.168.1.16 is directly connected, Serial0
p1r1#


p1r2#show ip route
Codes: C - connected, S - static, I - IGRP, R - RIP, M - mobile, B - BGP
       D - EIGRP, EX - EIGRP external, O - OSPF, IA - OSPF inter area
       N1 - OSPF NSSA external type 1, N2 - OSPF NSSA external type 2
       E1 - OSPF external type 1, E2 - OSPF external type 2, E - EGP
       i - IS-IS, L1 - IS-IS level-1, L2 - IS-IS level-2, * - candidate default
       U - per-user static route, o - ODR
       T - traffic engineered route

Gateway of last resort is not set

     192.168.1.0/28 is subnetted, 4 subnets
C       192.168.1.64 is directly connected, Ethernet0
C       192.168.1.32 is directly connected, Serial1
D       192.168.1.48 [90/40537600] via 192.168.1.66, 00:01:25, Ethernet0
C       192.168.1.16 is directly connected, Serial0
C    192.168.101.0/24 is directly connected, Loopback10
p1r2#


p1r3#show ip route
Codes: C - connected, S - static, I - IGRP, R - RIP, M - mobile, B - BGP
       D - EIGRP, EX - EIGRP external, O - OSPF, IA - OSPF inter area
       N1 - OSPF NSSA external type 1, N2 - OSPF NSSA external type 2
       E1 - OSPF external type 1, E2 - OSPF external type 2, E - EGP
       i - IS-IS, L1 - IS-IS level-1, L2 - IS-IS level-2, * - candidate default
       U - per-user static route, o - ODR
       T - traffic engineered route

Gateway of last resort is not set

     172.26.0.0/28 is subnetted, 3 subnets
C       172.26.1.48 is directly connected, Loopback13
C       172.26.1.32 is directly connected, Loopback12
C       172.26.1.16 is directly connected, Loopback11
     192.168.1.0/28 is subnetted, 4 subnets
C       192.168.1.64 is directly connected, Ethernet0
D       192.168.1.32 [90/40537600] via 192.168.1.65, 00:01:27, Ethernet0
C       192.168.1.48 is directly connected, Serial0
D       192.168.1.16 [90/40537600] via 192.168.1.65, 00:01:27, Ethernet0
p1r3#
```

What is the administrative distance for EIGRP?

**EIGRP AD is 90.**

How is the EIGRP metric different than the IGRP metric?

**It is a much larger number; it is 256 times the IGRP metric.**

Does EIGRP support load balancing by default?

**Yes. As an example, the show ip route output of p1r1 shows three equally good routes for subnet 192.168.1.64.**

**Step 4**   From the p*x*r1 router, issue the command to display information about the EIGRP neighbors. What would that command be?

```
p1r1#show ip eigrp neighbors
IP-EIGRP neighbors for process 200
H    Address                 Interface    Hold Uptime    SRTT    RTO   Q  Seq
                                          (sec)          (ms)          Cnt Num
2    192.168.1.50            Se2            13 00:02:25    28    2280   0  3
1    192.168.1.34            Se1            10 00:02:37    29    2280   0  9
0    192.168.1.18            Se0            14 00:02:37    26    2280   0  8
```

How many entries do you see in the p*x*r1 EIGRP neighbors table?

**Three**

**Step 5**   From the p*x*r1 router, what would be the command to display the EIGRP topology table?

```
p1r1#show ip eigrp topology
IP-EIGRP Topology Table for process 200

Codes: P - Passive, A - Active, U - Update, Q - Query, R - Reply,
       r - Reply status

P 192.168.1.64/28, 3 successors, FD is 40537600
        via 192.168.1.50 (40537600/281600), Serial2
        via 192.168.1.18 (40537600/281600), Serial0
        via 192.168.1.34 (40537600/281600), Serial1
P 192.168.1.32/28, 1 successors, FD is 40512000
        via Connected, Serial1
P 192.168.1.48/28, 1 successors, FD is 40512000
        via Connected, Serial2
P 192.168.1.16/28, 1 successors, FD is 40512000
        via Connected, Serial0
p1r1#
```

How many successor routes are available from p*x*r1 to subnet 192.168.*x*.64/28?

**Three successor routes are available.**

What is the FD from p*x*r1 to subnet 192.168.*x*.64/28?

**FD is 40537600.**

What is the AD to subnet 192.168.*x*.64/28 via S0?

**AD is 281600.**

What is the AD to subnet 192.168.*x*.64/28 via S1?

**AD is 281600.**

What is the AD to subnet 192.168.*x*.64/28 via S2?

**AD is 281600.**

**Step 6**   Which command would save the current configurations of all the routers within your pod to NVRAM?

```
p1r1#copy run start
Destination filename [startup-config]?
Building configuration...


p1r2#copy run start
Destination filename [startup-config]?
Building configuration...


p1r3#copy run start
Destination filename [startup-config]?
Building configuration...
```

# Answers to Task 2: Enabling EIGRP Connectivity to the backbone_r1 Router

**Step 1**   Which command would you type to reactivate the p*x*r1 S3 interface?

```
p1r1(config)#int s3
p1r1(config-if)#no shutdown
```

**Step 2**   Which command would you use to enable EIGRP on the S3 interface of
your p*x*r1 router?

```
p1r1(config-if)#router eigrp 200
p1r1(config-router)#network 10.0.0.0
```

**Step 3**   What command would you type to verify that you have full connectivity
to the backbone router loopback interfaces?

```
p1r1#ping 172.16.10.100
Type escape sequence to abort.
Sending 5, 100-byte ICMP Echos to 172.16.10.100, timeout is 2 seconds:
!!!!!
Success rate is 100 percent (5/5), round-trip min/avg/max = 28/28/32 ms

p1r1#ping 172.16.11.100
Type escape sequence to abort.
Sending 5, 100-byte ICMP Echos to 172.16.11.100, timeout is 2 seconds:
!!!!!
Success rate is 100 percent (5/5), round-trip min/avg/max = 32/32/32 ms

p1r2#ping 172.16.10.100
Type escape sequence to abort.
Sending 5, 100-byte ICMP Echos to 172.16.10.100, timeout is 2 seconds:
!!!!!
Success rate is 100 percent (5/5), round-trip min/avg/max = 56/59/60 ms

p1r2#ping 172.16.11.100
Type escape sequence to abort.
Sending 5, 100-byte ICMP Echos to 172.16.11.100, timeout is 2 seconds:
!!!!!
Success rate is 100 percent (5/5), round-trip min/avg/max = 56/58/60 ms

p1r3#ping 172.16.10.100
Type escape sequence to abort.
Sending 5, 100-byte ICMP Echos to 172.16.10.100, timeout is 2 seconds:
!!!!!
Success rate is 100 percent (5/5), round-trip min/avg/max = 60/60/60 ms

p1r3#ping 172.16.11.100
Type escape sequence to abort.
Sending 5, 100-byte ICMP Echos to 172.16.11.100, timeout is 2 seconds:
!!!!!
Success rate is 100 percent (5/5), round-trip min/avg/max = 60/60/60 ms
```

Note: It may take a while for the ping to work.

**Step 4**   Examine the routing table of p*x*r1.

```
p1r1#show ip route
Codes: C - connected, S - static, I - IGRP, R - RIP, M - mobile, B - BGP
       D - EIGRP, EX - EIGRP external, O - OSPF, IA - OSPF inter area
       N1 - OSPF NSSA external type 1, N2 - OSPF NSSA external type 2
       E1 - OSPF external type 1, E2 - OSPF external type 2, E - EGP
       i - IS-IS, L1 - IS-IS level-1, L2 - IS-IS level-2, * - candidate default
       U - per-user static route, o - ODR
       T - traffic engineered route
```

```
Gateway of last resort is not set

     172.16.0.0/24 is subnetted, 2 subnets
D EX    172.16.10.0 [170/40537600] via 10.1.1.100, 00:00:26, Serial3
D EX    172.16.11.0 [170/40537600] via 10.1.1.100, 00:00:26, Serial3
     10.0.0.0/8 is variably subnetted, 3 subnets, 2 masks
D       10.2.2.0/24 [90/41024000] via 10.1.1.100, 00:00:28, Serial3
D       10.0.0.0/8 is a summary, 00:00:26, Null0
C       10.1.1.0/24 is directly connected, Serial3
     192.168.1.0/24 is variably subnetted, 5 subnets, 2 masks
D       192.168.1.64/28 [90/40537600] via 192.168.1.18, 00:00:27, Serial0
                        [90/40537600] via 192.168.1.50, 00:00:27, Serial2
                        [90/40537600] via 192.168.1.34, 00:00:27, Serial1
C       192.168.1.32/28 is directly connected, Serial1
C       192.168.1.48/28 is directly connected, Serial2
D       192.168.1.0/24 is a summary, 00:00:34, Null0
C       192.168.1.16/28 is directly connected, Serial0
```

Do you see the external EIGRP routes sourced from the backbone_r1
router?

**Yes.**

```
D EX    172.16.10.0 [170/40537600] via 10.1.1.100, 00:00:26, Serial3
D EX    172.16.11.0 [170/40537600] via 10.1.1.100, 00:00:26, Serial3
```

What is the administrative distance of the external EIGRP routes?

**170**

From your p*x*r3 router, ping 172.16.10.100 and 172.16.11.100.

```
p1r3#ping 172.16.10.100
Type escape sequence to abort.
Sending 5, 100-byte ICMP Echos to 172.16.10.100, timeout is 2 seconds:
!!!!!
Success rate is 100 percent (5/5), round-trip min/avg/max = 60/60/60 ms

p1r3#ping 172.16.11.100
Type escape sequence to abort.
Sending 5, 100-byte ICMP Echos to 172.16.11.100, timeout is 2 seconds:
!!!!!
Success rate is 100 percent (5/5), round-trip min/avg/max = 60/60/60 ms
```

Were the pings successful?

**Yes.**

**Step 5**   Telnet to the backbone_r1 router; the password is cisco. Do you see an
entry for your pod's 192.168.x.0 network?

```
p1r1#telnet bbr1
Trying bbr1 (10.1.1.100)... Open

User Access Verification

Password:
backbone_r1>show ip route
Codes: C - connected, S - static, I - IGRP, R - RIP, M - mobile, B - BGP
       D - EIGRP, EX - EIGRP external, O - OSPF, IA - OSPF inter area
       N1 - OSPF NSSA external type 1, N2 - OSPF NSSA external type 2
       E1 - OSPF external type 1, E2 - OSPF external type 2, E - EGP
       i - IS-IS, L1 - IS-IS level-1, L2 - IS-IS level-2, ia - IS-IS inter area
       * - candidate default, U - per-user static route, o - ODR
       P - periodic downloaded static route

Gateway of last resort is not set

     172.16.0.0/24 is subnetted, 2 subnets
C       172.16.10.0 is directly connected, Loopback100
C       172.16.11.0 is directly connected, Loopback101
     10.0.0.0/8 is variably subnetted, 3 subnets, 2 masks
C       10.1.1.0/24 is directly connected, Serial1/0
D       10.0.0.0/8 is a summary, 00:11:06, Null0
C       10.2.2.0/24 is directly connected, Serial1/1
D    192.168.1.0/24 [90/41024000] via 10.1.1.1, 00:03:07, Serial1/0
backbone_r1>
```

Does EIGRP perform autosummarization across the network boundary
by default?

**Yes. EIGRP autosummarized routes 192.168.1.*x* advertised by p1r1.**

**Step 6**   Exit the Telnet to the backbone_r1 router.

```
backbone_r1>exit

[Connection to bbr1 closed by foreign host]
p1r1#
```

**Step 7**   At your p*x*r1 router, disable autosummarization. Which command is used
to achieve this?

```
p1r1(config)#router eigrp 200
p1r1(config-router)#no auto-summary
```

**Step 8**   Telnet to the backbone_r1 router; the password is cisco. Do you see an entry for each of your pod's 192.168.*x*.0 subnets?

```
p1r1#telnet bbr1
Trying bbr1 (10.1.1.100)... Open

User Access Verification

Password:
backbone_r1>show ip route
Codes: C - connected, S - static, I - IGRP, R - RIP, M - mobile, B - BGP
       D - EIGRP, EX - EIGRP external, O - OSPF, IA - OSPF inter area
       N1 - OSPF NSSA external type 1, N2 - OSPF NSSA external type 2
       E1 - OSPF external type 1, E2 - OSPF external type 2, E - EGP
       i - IS-IS, L1 - IS-IS level-1, L2 - IS-IS level-2, ia - IS-IS inter area
       * - candidate default, U - per-user static route, o - ODR
       P - periodic downloaded static route

Gateway of last resort is not set

     172.16.0.0/24 is subnetted, 2 subnets
C       172.16.10.0 is directly connected, Loopback100
C       172.16.11.0 is directly connected, Loopback101
     10.0.0.0/8 is variably subnetted, 3 subnets, 2 masks
C       10.1.1.0/24 is directly connected, Serial1/0
D       10.0.0.0/8 is a summary, 00:00:05, Null0
C       10.2.2.0/24 is directly connected, Serial1/1
     192.168.1.0/28 is subnetted, 4 subnets
D       192.168.1.64 [90/41049600] via 10.1.1.1, 00:00:05, Serial1/0
D       192.168.1.32 [90/41024000] via 10.1.1.1, 00:00:05, Serial1/0
D       192.168.1.48 [90/41024000] via 10.1.1.1, 00:00:05, Serial1/0
D       192.168.1.16 [90/41024000] via 10.1.1.1, 00:00:05, Serial1/0
backbone_r1>exit

[Connection to bbr1 closed by foreign host]
p1r1#
```

From your p*x*r3 router, ping 172.16.10.100 and 172.16.11.100.

```
p1r3#ping 172.16.10.100

Type escape sequence to abort.
Sending 5, 100-byte ICMP Echos to 172.16.10.100, timeout is 2 seconds:
!!!!!
Success rate is 100 percent (5/5), round-trip min/avg/max = 56/59/60 ms
p1r3#ping 172.16.11.100

Type escape sequence to abort.
Sending 5, 100-byte ICMP Echos to 172.16.11.100, timeout is 2 seconds:
!!!!!
Success rate is 100 percent (5/5), round-trip min/avg/max = 56/58/60 ms
p1r3#
```

Were the pings successful?

**Yes.**

**Step 9** At your p.xr1 router, create a manual summarization statement to summarize all the subnets in your pod to a single summarized route of 192.168.x.0/25 (where x = your pod number). What is the command that you used?

```
p1r1(config)#int s3
p1r1(config-if)#ip summary-address eigrp 200 192.168.1.0 255.255.255.128
```

**Step 10** Telnet to the backbone_r1 router; the password is cisco. Do you see your summarized route?

**Yes.**

```
p1r1#telnet bbr1
Trying bbr1 (10.1.1.100)... Open


User Access Verification

Password:
backbone_r1>show ip route
Codes: C - connected, S - static, I - IGRP, R - RIP, M - mobile, B - BGP
       D - EIGRP, EX - EIGRP external, O - OSPF, IA - OSPF inter area
       N1 - OSPF NSSA external type 1, N2 - OSPF NSSA external type 2
       E1 - OSPF external type 1, E2 - OSPF external type 2, E - EGP
       i - IS-IS, L1 - IS-IS level-1, L2 - IS-IS level-2, ia - IS-IS inter area
       * - candidate default, U - per-user static route, o - ODR
       P - periodic downloaded static route

Gateway of last resort is not set

     172.16.0.0/24 is subnetted, 2 subnets
C       172.16.10.0 is directly connected, Loopback100
C       172.16.11.0 is directly connected, Loopback101
     10.0.0.0/8 is variably subnetted, 3 subnets, 2 masks
C       10.1.1.0/24 is directly connected, Serial1/0
D       10.0.0.0/8 is a summary, 00:04:11, Null0
C       10.2.2.0/24 is directly connected, Serial1/1
     192.168.1.0/25 is subnetted, 1 subnets
D       192.168.1.0 [90/41024000] via 10.1.1.1, 00:00:06, Serial1/0
backbone_r1>exit

[Connection to bbr1 closed by foreign host]
p1r1#
```

**Step 11** Exit the Telnet to the backbone_r1 router.

```
backbone_r1>exit

[Connection to bbr1 closed by foreign host]
p1r1#
```

**Step 12** From your p*x*r3 router, ping 172.16.10.100 and 172.16.11.100.

```
p1r3#ping 172.16.10.100

Type escape sequence to abort.
Sending 5, 100-byte ICMP Echos to 172.16.10.100, timeout is 2 seconds:
!!!!!
Success rate is 100 percent (5/5), round-trip min/avg/max = 60/60/60 ms
p1r3#ping 172.16.11.100

Type escape sequence to abort.
Sending 5, 100-byte ICMP Echos to 172.16.11.100, timeout is 2 seconds:
!!!!!
Success rate is 100 percent (5/5), round-trip min/avg/max = 60/60/60 ms
p1r3#
```

Were the pings successful?

**Yes.**

**Step 13** Enter the **debug eigrp packets** command at one of the routers within
your pod.

```
p1r3#debug eigrp packets
EIGRP Packets debugging is on
    (UPDATE, REQUEST, QUERY, REPLY, HELLO, IPXSAP, PROBE, ACK)
```

How often are the EIGRP hello packets sent out on the serial interfaces?

---

**Note**        You may want to put the **service timestamps debug datetime**
configuration command on the router so that debug messages
will be timestamped.

---

```
p1r3#
03:06:45: EIGRP: Sending HELLO on Ethernet0
03:06:45:   AS 200, Flags 0x0, Seq 0/0 idbQ 0/0 iidbQ un/rely 0/0
03:06:46: EIGRP: Sending HELLO on Serial0
03:06:46:   AS 200, Flags 0x0, Seq 0/0 idbQ 0/0 iidbQ un/rely 0/0
p1r3#
03:06:47: EIGRP: Received HELLO on Ethernet0 nbr 192.168.1.65
03:06:47:   AS 200, Flags 0x0, Seq 0/0 idbQ 0/0 iidbQ un/rely 0/0 peerQ un/rely 0/0
p1r3#
03:06:48: EIGRP: Received HELLO on Serial0 nbr 192.168.1.49
03:06:48:   AS 200, Flags 0x0, Seq 0/0 idbQ 0/0 iidbQ un/rely 0/0 peerQ un/rely 0/0
p1r3#
03:06:50: EIGRP: Sending HELLO on Ethernet0
03:06:50:   AS 200, Flags 0x0, Seq 0/0 idbQ 0/0 iidbQ un/rely 0/0
03:06:50: EIGRP: Sending HELLO on Serial0
03:06:50:   AS 200, Flags 0x0, Seq 0/0 idbQ 0/0 iidbQ un/rely 0/0
p1r3#
03:06:51: EIGRP: Received HELLO on Ethernet0 nbr 192.168.1.65
03:06:51:   AS 200, Flags 0x0, Seq 0/0 idbQ 0/0 iidbQ un/rely 0/0 peerQ un/rely 0/0
```

```
p1r3#
03:06:53: EIGRP: Received HELLO on Serial0 nbr 192.168.1.49
03:06:53:   AS 200, Flags 0x0, Seq 0/0 idbQ 0/0 iidbQ un/rely 0/0 peerQ un/rely 0/0
p1r3#
03:06:55: EIGRP: Sending HELLO on Ethernet0
03:06:55:   AS 200, Flags 0x0, Seq 0/0 idbQ 0/0 iidbQ un/rely 0/0
03:06:55: EIGRP: Sending HELLO on Serial0
03:06:55:   AS 200, Flags 0x0, Seq 0/0 idbQ 0/0 iidbQ un/rely 0/0
p1r3#
03:06:56: EIGRP: Received HELLO on Ethernet0 nbr 192.168.1.65
03:06:56:   AS 200, Flags 0x0, Seq 0/0 idbQ 0/0 iidbQ un/rely 0/0 peerQ un/rely 0/0
p1r3#
03:06:57: EIGRP: Received HELLO on Serial0 nbr 192.168.1.49
03:06:57:   AS 200, Flags 0x0, Seq 0/0 idbQ 0/0 iidbQ un/rely 0/0 peerQ un/rely 0/0
```

**Hellos are sent out every 5 seconds on Serial 0 interface.**

**Step 14**  Turn off debug on your router.

```
p1r3#no debug all
All possible debugging has been turned off
p1r3#
```

**Step 15**  Save the current configurations of all the routers within your pod to
NVRAM.

```
p1r1#copy run start
Destination filename [startup-config]?
Building configuration...

p1r2#copy run start
Destination filename [startup-config]?
Building configuration...

p1r3#copy run start
Destination filename [startup-config]?
Building configuration...
```

# Answers to Configuration Exercise #2: Configuring EIGRP in an NBMA Environment

This section provides the answers to the questions in Configuration Exercise #2.
The answers are in **bold**.

## Answers to Setup

**Step 1**  On your p*x*r1 router, shut down the Serial 1 and Serial 3 interfaces.
Disable EIGRP 200 on your p*x*r1 router.

```
p1r1(config)#int s1
p1r1(config-if)#shutdown
p1r1(config-if)#exit
```

```
p1r1(config)#int s3
p1r1(config-if)#shutdown
p1r1(config-if)#exit
p1r1(config)#no router eigrp 200
```

**Step 2**    On your p*x*r2 router, shut down the Ethernet 0, Serial 0, and Serial 1 interfaces. Reconfigure your p*x*r2 Serial 0 IP address to be 192.168.*x*.129/28.

```
p1r2(config)#int e0
p1r2(config-if)#shutdown
p1r2(config-if)#exit
p1r2(config)#int s0
p1r2(config-if)#shutdown
p1r2(config-if)#exit
p1r2(config)#int s1
p1r2(config-if)#shutdown
p1r2(config-if)#exit
p1r2(config)#int s0
p1r2(config-if)#ip address 192.168.1.129 255.255.255.240
```

**Step 3**    On your p*x*r3 router, shut down the Ethernet 0 and Serial 0 interfaces. Reconfigure your p*x*r3 Serial 0 IP address to be 192.168.*x*.130/28.

```
p1r3(config)#int e0
p1r3(config-if)#shutdown
p1r3(config-if)#exit
p1r3(config)#int s0
p1r3(config-if)#shutdown
p1r3(config-if)#ip address 192.168.1.130 255.255.255.240
```

# Answers to Task 1: Creating a Frame Relay Switch

**Step 1**    Enable your p*x*r1 router as the Frame Relay switch.

Which command do you use to activate the Frame Relay switch?

```
p1r1(config)#frame-relay switching
```

Which command do you use to set your router as a Frame Relay DCE device?

```
p1r1(config)#int s0
p1r1(config-if)#encapsulation frame-relay
p1r1(config-if)#frame-relay intf-type dce
```

Which command do you type on p*x*r1, S0 interface, to perform switching from p*x*r2 to p*x*r3?

```
p1r1(config-if)#frame-relay route 203 interface s 2 302
```

Which command do you use on p*x*r1, S2 interface, to perform switching from p*x*r3 to p*x*r2?

```
p1r1(config)#int s2
p1r1(config-if)#encapsulation frame-relay
p1r1(config-if)#frame-relay intf-type dce
p1r1(config-if)#frame-relay route 302 interface s 0 203
```

**Step 2**   Enable Frame Relay encapsulation on the S0 interface of your p*x*r2 and p*x*r3 routers.

```
p1r2(config)#int s0
p1r2(config-if)#encapsulation frame-relay
p1r2(config-if)#no shutdown

p1r3(config)#int s0
p1r3(config-if)#encapsulation frame-relay
p1r3(config-if)#no shutdown
```

Verify that your p*x*r2 and p*x*r3 routers' S0 IP addresses are as follows:

**Router p*x*r2: S0 IP address 192.168.*x*.129/28**
**Router p*x*r3: S0 IP address 192.168.*x*.130/28**

Enable the Serial 0 interfaces on p*x*r2 and p*x*r3. What command is used to achieve this?

```
p1r2(config)#int s0
p1r2(config-if)#no shutdown

p1r3(config)#int s0
p1r3(config-if)#no shutdown
```

**Step 3**   From p*x*r2, ping the p*x*r3 Serial 0 interface to ensure connectivity.

```
p1r2#ping 192.168.1.130

Type escape sequence to abort.
Sending 5, 100-byte ICMP Echos to 192.168.1.130, timeout is 2 seconds:
!!!!!
Success rate is 100 percent (5/5), round-trip min/avg/max = 56/59/60 ms
```

# Answers to Task 2: Enabling EIGRP over NBMA Network Using Main Interface

**Step 1**   Which command would you use to verify that the p*x*r2 and p*x*r3 Serial 0 interfaces are running EIGRP in AS 200?

```
p1r2#show ip protocols
Routing Protocol is "eigrp 200"
  Outgoing update filter list for all interfaces is
```

```
      Incoming update filter list for all interfaces is
      Default networks flagged in outgoing updates
      Default networks accepted from incoming updates
      EIGRP metric weight K1=1, K2=0, K3=1, K4=0, K5=0
      EIGRP maximum hopcount 100
      EIGRP maximum metric variance 1
      Redistributing: eigrp 200
      Automatic network summarization is in effect
      Routing for Networks:
        192.168.1.0
      Routing Information Sources:
        Gateway          Distance      Last Update
        192.168.1.66        90         00:05:45
        192.168.1.33        90         00:12:35
        192.168.1.17        90         00:05:27
      Distance: internal 90 external 170

  p1r3#show ip protocols
  Routing Protocol is "eigrp 200"
      Outgoing update filter list for all interfaces is
      Incoming update filter list for all interfaces is
      Default networks flagged in outgoing updates
      Default networks accepted from incoming updates
      EIGRP metric weight K1=1, K2=0, K3=1, K4=0, K5=0
      EIGRP maximum hopcount 100
      EIGRP maximum metric variance 1
      Redistributing: eigrp 200
      Automatic network summarization is in effect
      Routing for Networks:
        192.168.1.0
      Routing Information Sources:
        Gateway          Distance      Last Update
        192.168.1.65        90         00:05:57
        192.168.1.49        90         00:06:17
      Distance: internal 90 external 170
```

**Step 2**   On pxr2, type in the command to start advertising the loopback 10
network in EIGRP.

```
p1r2(config)#router eigrp 200
p1r2(config-router)#network 192.168.101.0
```

**Step 3**   On pxr3, ping the pxr2 loopback address to verify connectivity.

```
p1r3#ping 192.168.101.101

Type escape sequence to abort.
Sending 5, 100-byte ICMP Echos to 192.168.101.101, timeout is 2 seconds:
!!!!!
Success rate is 100 percent (5/5), round-trip min/avg/max = 56/59/60 ms
```

**Step 4**   On pxr2, enter the **show ip eigrp neighbors** command. Do you see your
neighbor pxr3 router?

```
p1r2#show ip eigrp neighbors
IP-EIGRP neighbors for process 200
H   Address                 Interface   Hold Uptime   SRTT   RTO  Q   Seq
                                        (sec)         (ms)        Cnt Num
0   192.168.1.130           Se0          148 00:06:09    0   5000  0   40
```

**Step 5** EIGRP sends hello packets to establish neighbor relationship using the multicast address of 224.0.0.10. Is your Frame Relay interface enabled to send broadcast (which includes multicast) traffic?

```
p1r2#show frame-relay map
Serial0 (up): ip 192.168.1.130 dlci 203(0xCB,0x30B0), dynamic,
         broadcast,, status defined, active

p1r3#show frame-relay map
Serial0 (up): ip 192.168.1.129 dlci 302(0x12E,0x48E0), dynamic,
         broadcast,, status defined, active
```

**Step 6** Enter the command to enable EIGRP to use only 20 percent of your Frame Relay interface bandwidth on your p*x*r2 router.

```
p1r2(config)#int s0
p1r2(config-if)#ip bandwidth-percent eigrp 200 20
```

**Step 7** Save the current configurations of all the routers within your pod to NVRAM.

```
p1r1#copy run start
Destination filename [startup-config]?
Building configuration…

p1r2#copy run start
Destination filename [startup-config]?
Building configuration...

p1r3#copy run start
Destination filename [startup-config]?
Building configuration...
```

**Step 8** Bonus Question: What is the EIGRP interface configuration command to disable IP split horizon on an NBMA interface? (Use AS number 200.)

```
p1r2(config)#int s0
p1r2(config-if)#no ip split-horizon eigrp 200
```

# Review Questions

Answer the following questions, and then refer to Appendix G, "Answers to the Review Questions," for the answers.

1 How are IGRP and EIGRP different in their metric calculation?

2 Why are EIGRP routing updates described as reliable?

3 What does it mean when a route is marked as a feasible successor?

4 What is the recommended practice for configuring bandwidth on a Frame Relay point-to-point subinterface?

**5**  In this exercise, you can test your understanding of EIGRP by matching terms with statements. Place the letter of the description in front of the term that the statement describes. A statement may describe more than one term.

Statements:

— A. A network protocol that EIGRP supports

— B. A table that contains feasible successor information

— C. Administrative distance to determine routing information that is included in this table

— D. A neighbor router that has the best path to a table destination

— E. A neighbor router that has the best alternative path to a destination

— F. An algorithm used by EIGRP that assures fast convergence

— G. A multicast packet used to discover neighbors

— H. A packet sent by EIGRP routers when a new neighbor is discovered and when a change occurs

| Answer | Term |
|--------|------|
|        | Successor |
|        | Feasible successor |
|        | Hello |
|        | Topology table |
|        | IP |
|        | Update |
|        | AppleTalk |
|        | Routing table |
|        | DUAL |
|        | IPX |

**6**  Answer true or false for the following statements:

— EIGRP performs autosummarization.

— Autosummarization can't be turned off.

— EIGRP supports VLSM.

— EIGRP could maintain three independent routing tables.

— The hello interval is an unchangeable fixed value.

This chapter introduces the Border Gateway Protocol (BGP), including the fundamentals of BGP operation. This chapter includes the following sections:

- BGP Overview
- When to Use BGP
- When Not to Use BGP
- BGP Terminology and Concepts
- BGP Operation
- Configuring BGP
- Verifying BGP
- Summary
- Configuration Exercise: Configuring BGP
- Answers to Configuration Exercise: Configuring BGP
- Review Questions

# CHAPTER 6

# Configuring Basic Border Gateway Protocol

When you finish this chapter, you will be able to describe BGP features and operation, BGP communities and peer groups, BGP synchronization, and how to connect to another autonomous system (AS) using an alternative to BGP—static routes. You will be able to explain how BGP policy-based routing functions within an AS, and how BGP peering functions. You will be able to describe and configure external and internal BGPs. Given a set of network requirements, you will be able to configure a BGP environment and verify proper operation (within described guidelines) of your routers.

## BGP Overview

This section provides an overview of BGP. Understanding BGP first requires an understanding of autonomous systems.

## Autonomous Systems

One way to categorize routing protocols is by whether they are interior or exterior. Two types of routing protocols are as follows:

- **Interior Gateway Protocol (IGP)**—Routing protocol used to exchange routing information *within* an autonomous system. The Routing Information Protocol (RIP), Interior Gateway Routing Protocol (IGRP), Open Shortest Path First (OSPF), and Enhanced Interior Gateway Routing Protocol (EIGRP) are examples of IGPs.

- **Exterior Gateway Protocol (EGP)**—Routing protocol used to connect *between* autonomous systems. The Border Gateway Protocol (BGP) is an example of an EGP.

This concept is illustrated in Figure 6-1.

**Figure 6-1** *IGPs Operate Within an Autonomous System, and EGPs Operate Between Autonomous Systems*

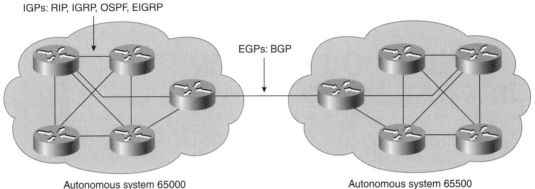

BGP is an interdomain routing protocol, which is also known as an EGP. All the routing protocols you have seen so far in this book are interior routing protocols, also known as IGPs.

BGP version 4, BGP-4, is the latest version of BGP and is defined in Requests For Comments (RFC) 1771. As noted in this RFC, the classic definition of an *autonomous system* is "a set of routers under a single technical administration, using an Interior Gateway Protocol and common metrics to route packets within the AS, and using an Exterior Gateway Protocol to route packets to other [autonomous systems]."

Today, autonomous systems may use more than one IGP, with potentially several sets of metrics. The important characteristic of an AS from the BGP point of view is that the AS appears to other autonomous systems to have a single coherent interior routing plan and presents a consistent picture of which destinations are reachable through it. All parts of the AS must be connected to each other.

The Internet Assigned Numbers Authority (IANA) is the umbrella organization responsible for allocating autonomous system numbers. Specifically, the American Registry for Internet Numbers (ARIN) has the jurisdiction for assigning numbers for the Americas, the Caribbean, and Africa. Reseaux IP Europeennes-Network Information Center (RIPE-NIC) administers the numbers for Europe, and the Asia Pacific-NIC (AP-NIC) administers the autonomous system numbers for the Asia-Pacific region.

This autonomous system designator is a 16-bit number, with a range of 1 to 65535. RFC 1930 provides guidelines for the use of AS numbers. A range of AS numbers, 64512 through 65535, is reserved for private use, much like the private Internet Protocol (IP) addresses. All the examples and exercises in this book use private AS numbers.

## BGP Use

BGP is used between autonomous systems, as illustrated in Figure 6-2. The main goal of
BGP is to provide an interdomain routing system that guarantees the loop-free exchange of
routing information between autonomous systems. BGP routers exchange information
about paths to destination networks.

**Figure 6-2**    *BGP-4 Is Used Between Autonomous Systems on the Internet*

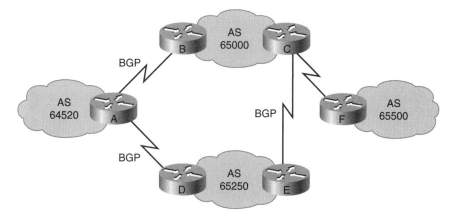

BGP is a successor to EGP, the Exterior Gateway Protocol. (Note the dual use of the EGP
acronym). The EGP protocol was developed to isolate networks from each other at the early
stages of the Internet.

The use of the term *autonomous system* in connection with BGP stresses the fact that the
administration of an autonomous system appears to other autonomous systems to have a
single coherent interior routing plan, and presents a consistent picture of those networks
that are reachable through it. There is also a distinction between an ordinary autonomous
system and one that has been configured with BGP for implementing a transit policy; the
latter is called an Internet service provider (ISP), or simply a service provider.

Many RFCs relate to BGP-4, including those listed in Table 6-1.

**Table 6-1** *RFCs Relating to BGP-4*

| RFC Number | RFC Title |
|---|---|
| RFC 1771 | A Border Gateway Protocol 4 (BGP-4) |
| RFC 1772 | An Application of BGP in the Internet |
| RFC 1773 | Experience with the BGP-4 Protocol |
| RFC 1774 | BGP-4 Protocol Analysis |
| RFC 1863 | A BGP/IDRP (Interdomain Routing Protocol) Route Server Alternative to a Full-Mesh Routing |
| RFC 1930 | Guidelines for Creation, Selection, and Registration of an Autonomous System (AS) |
| RFC 1965 | AS Confederations for BGP |
| RFC 1966 | BGP Route Reflection—An Alternative to Full-Mesh IBGP |
| RFC 1997 | BGP Communities Attribute |
| RFC 1998 | Application of the BGP Community Attribute in Multihome Routing |
| RFC 2042 | Registering New BGP Attribute Types |
| RFC 2283 | Multiprotocol Extensions for BGP-4 |
| RFC 2385 | Protection of BGP Sessions via TCP MD5 Signature Option |
| RFC 2439 | BGP Route Flap Damping |

**NOTE**    For BGP technical tips, see the following URL on Cisco's web site: www.cisco.com/warp/customer/459/18.html#I00. (Access to this information requires you to have an account on Cisco's web site.)

BGP-4 has many enhancements over earlier protocols. It is used extensively in the Internet today to connect ISPs and to interconnect enterprises to ISPs.

## Comparison with Other Scalable Routing Protocols

Table 6-2 compares some of the key characteristics of BGP to the other scalable routing protocols discussed in this book.

**Table 6-2**    *Comparison of Scalable Routing Protocols*

| Protocol | Interior or Exterior | Distance Vector or Link-State | Hierarchy Required | Metric |
|---|---|---|---|---|
| OSPF | Interior | Link-state | Yes | Cost |
| EIGRP | Interior | Advanced distance vector | No | Composite |
| BGP | Exterior | Advanced distance vector | No | Path vectors or attributes |

As shown in Table 6-2, OSPF and EIGRP are interior protocols, whereas BGP is an exterior protocol.

Chapter 1, "Routing Principles," discusses the characteristics of distance vector and link-state routing protocols. OSPF is a link-state protocol, whereas EIGRP is an advanced distance vector protocol. BGP is also a distance vector protocol, with many enhancements.

Most link-state routing protocols, including OSPF, require a hierarchical design, especially to support proper address summarization. OSPF enables you to separate a large internetwork into smaller internetworks that are called areas. EIGRP and BGP do not require a hierarchical topology.

OSPF uses cost, which on Cisco routers is based on bandwidth, as its metric. EIGRP uses a composite metric, similar to the IGRP metric. Routers running BGP exchange network reachability information, called path vectors or attributes, that include a list of the full path (of BGP AS numbers) that a route should take to reach a destination network.

# When to Use BGP

BGP use in an AS is most appropriate when the effects of BGP are well understood and at least one of the following conditions exist:

- The AS allows packets to transit through it to reach other autonomous systems (for example, a service provider).
- The AS has multiple connections to other autonomous systems.
- The flow of traffic entering and leaving the AS must be manipulated.

A policy decision that must differentiate between traffic from an AS and its ISP means that the AS will have to connect to its ISP with BGP (rather than with a static route).

BGP was designed to allow ISPs to communicate and exchange packets. These ISPs have multiple connections to one another and have agreements to exchange updates. BGP is the protocol that is used to implement these agreements between two or more autonomous systems.

If BGP is not properly controlled and filtered, it has the potential to allow an outside AS to affect your routing decisions. This chapter and the next focus on how BGP operates and how to configure it properly so that you can prevent this from happening.

## How Big Is the Internet?

To give you an idea of the size of tables that a BGP router in an ISP must deal with consider that a BGP router in the Internet may have the following knowledge:

* A routing table that uses more than 30 megabytes (MB) and has knowledge of more than 70,000 routes.

* That routing table also has knowledge of more than 6,500 AS numbers.

These numbers represent a snapshot of the size of the Internet. Note that because the Internet is constantly growing, these numbers are constantly changing (increasing).

# When Not to Use BGP

This section discusses when BGP is not appropriate for use in a network and covers the use of the alternative, static routes.

BGP is not always the appropriate solution to interconnect autonomous systems. For example, if only one path exists, a default or static route would be appropriate; using BGP would not accomplish anything except to use router CPU resources and memory. If the routing policy that will be implemented in an AS is consistent with the policy implemented in the ISP AS, it is not necessary or even desirable to configure BGP in that AS. The only time it would be required is when the local policy differs from the ISP policy.

Do not use BGP if you have one or more of the following conditions:

* A single connection to the Internet or another AS
* No concern for routing policy and route selection
* Lack of memory or processor power on routers to handle constant BGP updates
* A limited understanding of route filtering and BGP path selection process
* Low bandwidth between autonomous systems

In these cases, use static routes instead.

The use of static routes to connect to another AS is reviewed in the following section.

# Static Routes

Use the **ip route** *prefix mask* {*address | interface*} [*distance*] global configuration command to define a static route entry in the IP routing table, as described in Table 6-3.

**Table 6-3**    *ip route Command Description*

| ip route Command | Description |
| --- | --- |
| *prefix mask* | IP route prefix and mask for the destination to be entered into the IP routing table |
| *address* | IP address of the next-hop router to be used to reach the destination network |
| *interface* | The local router outbound interface to be used to reach the destination network |
| *distance* | (Optional) Administrative distance |

As discussed in Chapter 1, if there is more than one route to a destination, the administrative distance determines which one will be put in the routing table, with the lower administrative distance preferred. By default, the administrative distance of a static route specified with the *next-hop address* parameter is set to 1. The default administrative distance of a static route specified with the *interface* parameter is set to 0.

You can establish a *floating static route* by using an administrative distance that is larger than the default administrative distance of the dynamic routing protocol in use in your network. A floating static route is a statically configured route that can be overridden by dynamically learned routing information. Thus, a floating static route can be used to create a *path of last resort* that is used only when no dynamic information is available.

---

### ip route Command Parameters

The **ip route** command has two configuration options: specifying the destination by adjacent router IP address or specifying the destination by the local router interface name. There are a few differences in these two methods for configuring a static route. As mentioned, in the case of the IP address parameter, the default administrative distance is 1; in the case of the interface format, the default administrative distance is 0. The distinction is that using the *next-hop address* parameter makes the route look like a standard statically defined route, but under certain conditions, using the *interface* parameter treats the link as if it is locally attached to the router.

You must use the next-hop address in the **ip route** command if using multiaccess media (for example, on local-area networks [LANs], Frame Relay, X.25, Integrated Services Digital Network [ISDN], and so on) so that the router knows exactly where to go to reach the destination, not just which interface to go out of. (An exception to this is when using a dial-on-demand interface, such as ISDN, and using a **dialer string** command on the interface, so that the interface only knows how to get to one place.) You can use the *interface* syntax if the adjacent router interface is part of a serial unnumbered link and therefore has no IP address (unnumbered interfaces are discussed in Chapter 2, "Extending IP Addresses"). The *interface* syntax is also a very quick way to establish connectivity when trying to recover from routing problems in a network because you do not have to know the IP addresses on the link that you want to traverse.

## Static Route Examples

The sample network in Figure 6-3 illustrates a network running RIP and using a default static route. The configuration for Router A in Figure 6-3 is provided in Example 6-1.

**Figure 6-3**   *An Example of Using RIP and a Default Static Route*

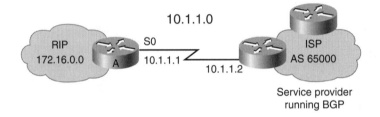

Service provider
running BGP

**Example 6-1**   *Configuration of Router A in Figure 6-3*

```
ip route 0.0.0.0 0.0.0.0 S0
!
router rip
  network 172.16.0.0
```

The route 0.0.0.0 is a default route that will be included in the IP routing table of Router A. If there is no matching route for the destination IP address in the routing table, then the 0.0.0.0 matches the address and causes the packet to be routed out interface serial 0. The default route will be automatically propagated into the RIP domain.

---

**A Caution About Default Routes**

The default route 0.0.0.0 matches only networks that the router knows *nothing* about. When using classful routing protocols such as RIP or IGRP, use the **ip classless** command if you want it to also match unknown subnets of known networks. Note that **ip classless** is on by default in Cisco IOS Release 12.0 and later (it is off by default in earlier releases).

---

The sample network in Figure 6-4 illustrates a network running OSPF and using a default static route. The configuration for Router A in Figure 6-4 is provided in Example 6-2.

**Figure 6-4**    *An Example of Using OSPF and a Default Static Route*

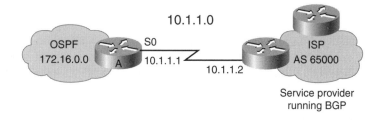

**Example 6-2**    *Configuration of Router A in Figure 6-4*

```
ip route 0.0.0.0 0.0.0.0 S0
!
router ospf 111
  network 172.16.0.0 0.0.255.255 area 0
  default-information originate always
```

The **default-information originate always** command in OSPF propagates a default route into the OSPF routing domain. The configuration in this example has an effect similar to the RIP example. The **always** keyword causes the default route to always be advertised, whether or not the router has a default route. This ensures that the default route will get advertised into OSPF, even if the path to the default route (in this case, interface serial 0) goes down.

# BGP Terminology and Concepts

BGP has many concepts that become clearer if you understand the terminology. This section discusses BGP characteristics, concepts of BGP neighbors, internal and external BGP, policy-based routing, and BGP attributes.

## BGP Characteristics

What type of protocol is BGP? Chapter 1 covers the characteristics of distance vector and link-state routing protocols. BGP is a distance vector protocol, but it has many differences from the likes of RIP.

---

<table>
<tr><td>**NOTE**</td><td>The *distance vector* for BGP is more a *path vector*. Many attributes describing a path are sent with the network information; these attributes are discussed in the "BGP Attributes" section later in this chapter.</td></tr>
</table>

---

BGP uses the Transmission Control Protocol (TCP) as its transport protocol, which provides connection-oriented reliable delivery. In this way, BGP assumes that its communication is reliable and therefore doesn't have to implement any retransmission or error-recovery mechanisms. BGP uses TCP port 179. Two routers speaking BGP establish a TCP connection with one another and exchange messages to open and confirm the connection parameters. These two routers are called peer routers, or neighbors.

When the connection is made, full routing tables are exchanged. However, because the connection is reliable, BGP routers need send only changes (incremental updates) after that. Periodic routing updates are also not required on a reliable link, so triggered updates are used. BGP sends keepalive messages, similar to the hello messages sent by OSPF and EIGRP.

BGP routers exchange network reachability information, called path vectors, made up of path attributes, including a list of the full path (of BGP AS numbers) that a route should take to reach a destination network. This path information is used in constructing a graph of autonomous systems that is loop-free. The path is loop-free because a router running BGP will not accept a routing update that already includes its AS number in the path list; this would mean that the update has already passed through its AS, and accepting it again would result in a routing loop. Routing policies can also be applied to the path of BGP AS numbers to enforce some restrictions on the routing behavior.

BGP is designed to scale to huge internetworks—the Internet, for example.

## BGP Inside IP Packets

BGP information is carried inside TCP segments using protocol number 179; these segments are carried inside IP packets. Figure 6-5 illustrates this concept.

## BGP Tables

As shown in Figure 6-6, a router running BGP keeps its own table for storing BGP information received from and sent to other routers. This table is separate from the IP routing table in the router. The router can be configured to share information between the two tables.

**Figure 6-5**    *BGP Is Carried Inside TCP Segments, Which Are Inside IP Packets*

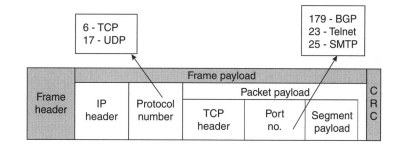

**Figure 6-6**    *A Router Running BGP Keeps a BGP Table, Separate from the IP Routing Table*

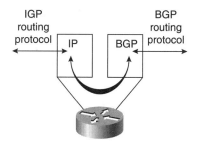

# BGP Peers or Neighbors

Any two routers that have formed a TCP connection to exchange BGP routing information—in other words, that have formed a BGP connection—are called peers or neighbors. BGP peers can be either internal to the AS or external to the AS.

When BGP is running between routers within one AS, this is called internal BGP (IBGP). IBGP is run within an AS to exchange BGP information within the AS so that it can be passed to other autonomous systems. Routers running IBGP do not have to be directly connected to each other, as long as they can reach each other (for example, when an IGP is running within the AS).

When BGP is running between routers in different autonomous systems, this is called external BGP (EBGP). Routers running EBGP are usually directly connected to each other.

IBGP and EBGP neighbors are illustrated in Figure 6-7.

**Figure 6-7** *Routers That Have Formed a BGP Connection Are BGP Peers or Neighbors, Either External or Internal*

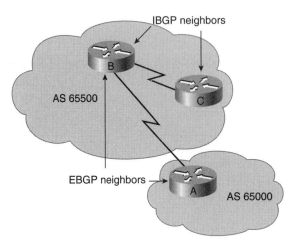

## Policy-Based Routing

BGP allows policy decisions at the AS level to be enforced. This setting of policies or rules for routing is known as *policy-based routing*.

BGP allows policies to be defined for how data will flow through the AS. These policies are based on the attributes carried in the routing information and configured on the routers.

BGP specifies that a BGP router can advertise to its peers in neighboring autonomous systems only those routes that it itself uses. This rule reflects the hop-by-hop routing paradigm generally used throughout the current Internet.

Some policies cannot be supported by the hop-by-hop routing paradigm and thus require techniques such as source routing to enforce. For example, BGP does not allow one AS to send traffic to a neighboring AS, intending that the traffic take a different route from that taken by traffic originating in that neighboring AS. However, BGP can support any policy conforming to the hop-by-hop routing paradigm. In other words, you cannot influence how the neighbor AS will route your traffic, but you can influence how your traffic gets to a neighbor AS.

Because the current Internet uses only the hop-by-hop routing paradigm, and because BGP can support any policy that conforms to that paradigm, BGP is highly applicable as an inter-AS routing protocol for the current Internet.

# BGP Attributes

Routers send BGP update messages about destination networks. These update messages include information about BGP metrics, which are called path attributes. Following are some terms defining how these attributes are implemented:

- An attribute is either well-known or optional, mandatory or discretionary, and transitive or nontransitive. An attribute may also be partial.

- Not all combinations of these characteristics are valid. In fact, path attributes fall into four separate categories:

  — Well-known, mandatory

  — Well-known, discretionary

  — Optional, transitive

  — Optional, nontransitive

- Only optional transitive attributes may be marked as partial.

These characteristics are described in the following sections.

---

### BGP Update Message Contents

A BGP update message includes a variable-length sequence of path attributes describing the route. A path attribute is of variable length and consists of three fields, as follows:

- Attribute type, which consists of a 1-byte attribute flags field and a 1-byte attribute type code field

- Attribute length

- Attribute value

The first bit of the attribute flags field indicates whether the attribute is optional or well-known. The second bit indicates whether an optional attribute is transitive or nontransitive. The third bit indicates whether a transitive attribute is partial or complete. The fourth bit indicates whether the attribute length field is 1 or 2 bytes. The rest of the flag bits are unused and are set to 0.

---

## Well-Known Attributes

A well-known attribute is one that all BGP implementations must recognize. These attributes are propagated to BGP neighbors.

A well-known mandatory attribute must appear in the description of a route. A well-known discretionary attribute does not need to appear in a route description.

## Optional Attributes

An optional attribute need not be supported by all BGP implementations; it could be a private attribute. If it is supported, it may be propagated to BGP neighbors.

An optional transitive attribute that is not implemented in a router should be passed to other BGP routers untouched. In this case, the attribute is marked as partial.

An optional nontransitive attribute must be deleted by a router that has not implemented the attribute.

## Defined BGP Attributes

The attributes defined by BGP include the following:

- Well-known, mandatory attributes:
    - AS-path
    - Next-hop
    - Origin
- Well-known, discretionary attributes:
    - Local preference
    - Atomic aggregate
- Optional, transitive attributes:
    - Aggregator
    - Community
- Optional, nontransitive attribute:
    - Multi-exit-discriminator (MED)

In addition, Cisco has defined a weight attribute for BGP.

The AS-path, next-hop, local preference, MED, origin, community, and weight attributes are expanded upon in the following sections. The other attributes are explained in later sections in this chapter or in the following chapter.

---

### BGP Attribute Type Codes

Attribute type codes used by Cisco are these:

- Origin, type code 1
- AS-path, type code 2
- Next-hop, type code 3
- MED, type code 4

- Local-preference, type code 5
- Atomic-aggregate, type code 6
- Aggregator, type code 7
- Community, type code 8 (Cisco-defined)
- Originator-ID, type code 9 (Cisco-defined)
- Cluster list, type code 10 (Cisco-defined)

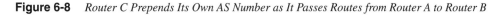

## AS-Path Attribute

The AS-path attribute is a well-known mandatory attribute. Whenever a route update passes through an AS, the AS number is *prepended* to that update (in other words, it is put at the beginning of the list). The AS-path attribute is actually the list of AS numbers that a route has traversed to reach a destination, with the AS number of the AS that originated the route at the end of the list.

In Figure 6-8, network 192.168.1.0 is advertised by Router A in AS 64520. When that route traverses AS 65500, Router C prepends its own AS number to it. When 192.168.1.0 reaches Router B, it has two AS numbers attached to it. From Router B's perspective, the path to reach 192.168.1.0 is (65500, 64520).

**Figure 6-8**    *Router C Prepends Its Own AS Number as It Passes Routes from Router A to Router B*

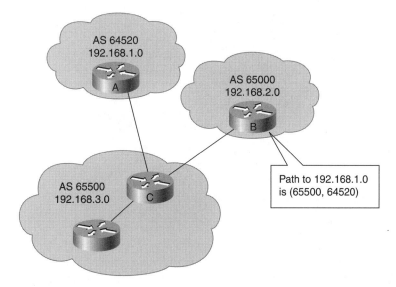

The same applies for 192.168.2.0 and 192.168.3.0. Router A's path to 192.168.2.0 will be (65500, 65000)—traverse AS 65500 and then AS 65000. Router C will have to traverse path (65000) to reach 192.168.2.0 and path (64520) to reach 192.168.1.0.

The AS-path attribute is used by BGP routers to ensure a loop-free environment. If a BGP router receives a route in which its own AS is part of the AS-path attribute, it will not accept the route.

AS numbers are prepended only by routers advertising routes to EBGP neighbors. Routers advertising routes to IBGP neighbors do not change the AS-path attribute.

### Next-Hop Attribute

The BGP next-hop attribute is a well-known mandatory attribute that indicates the next-hop IP address that is to be used to reach a destination.

For EBGP, the next hop is the IP address of the neighbor that sent the update. In Figure 6-9, Router A will advertise 172.16.0.0 to Router B, with a next hop of 10.10.10.3, and Router B will advertise 172.20.0.0 to Router A, with a next hop of 10.10.10.1. Therefore, Router A uses 10.10.10.1 as the next-hop attribute to get to 172.20.0.0, and Router B uses 10.10.10.3 as the next-hop attribute to get to 172.16.0.0.

**Figure 6-9**   *The BGP Next-Hop Attribute*

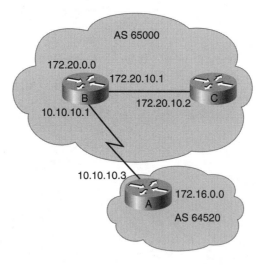

For IBGP, the protocol states that *the next hop advertised by EBGP should be carried into IBGP.* Because of that rule, Router B will advertise 172.16.0.0 to its IBGP peer Router C, with a next hop of 10.10.10.3 (Router A's address). Therefore, Router C knows that the next hop to reach 172.16.0.0 is 10.10.10.3, not 172.20.10.1, as you might expect.

It is very important, therefore, that Router C knows how to reach the 10.10.10.0 subnet, either via an IGP or a static route; otherwise, it will drop packets destined to 172.16.0.0 because it will not be capable of getting to the next-hop address for that network.

When running BGP over a multiaccess network such as Ethernet, a BGP router will use the appropriate address as the next-hop address (by changing the next-hop attribute), to avoid inserting additional hops into the network. This feature is sometimes called a *third-party next hop*.

For example, in Figure 6-10, assume that Routers B and C in AS 65000 are running an IGP. Router B can reach network 172.30.0.0 via 10.10.10.2. Router B is running BGP with Router A. When Router B sends a BGP update to Router A regarding 172.30.0.0, it will use 10.10.10.2 as the next hop, not its own IP address (10.10.10.1). This is because the network among the three routers is a multiaccess network, and it makes more sense for Router A to use Router C as a next hop to reach 172.30.0.0 rather than making an extra hop via Router B.

**Figure 6-10**  *Multiaccess Network—Router A Has 10.10.10.2 as the Next-Hop Attribute to Reach 172.30.0.0*

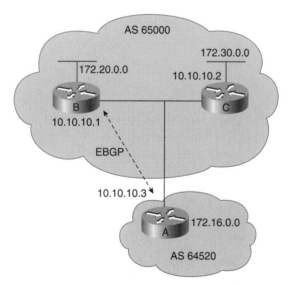

However, if the common media between routers is a nonbroadcast multiaccess (NBMA) media, complications may occur.

For example, in Figure 6-11, the last example was changed so that the three routers are connected by Frame Relay. Router B can still reach network 172.30.0.0 via 10.10.10.2. When Router B sends a BGP update to Router A regarding 172.30.0.0, it will use 10.10.10.2 as the next hop, not its own IP address (10.10.10.1). A problem will arise if Router A and Router C do not know how to communicate directly—in other words, if

Routers A and C do not have a map to each other. Router A will not know how to reach the next-hop address on Router C.

**Figure 6-11** *Nonbroadcast Multiaccess (NBMA) Media—Router A Has 10.10.10.2 as the Next-Hop Attribute to Reach 172.30.0.0, But It May Be Unreachable*

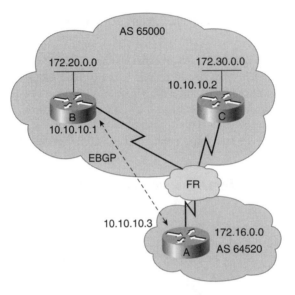

This behavior can be overridden in Router B by configuring it to advertise *itself* as the next-hop address for routes sent to Router A.

## Local Preference Attribute

Local preference is a well-known discretionary attribute that provides an indication to routers in the AS about which path is preferred to exit the AS. A path with a *higher* local preference is preferred.

The local preference is an attribute that is configured on a router and exchanged only among routers within the same AS. The default value for local preference on a Cisco router is 100.

---

**NOTE**      The term *local* refers to *inside the AS*. The local preference attribute is sent only to internal BGP neighbors; it is not passed to EBGP peers.

---

For example, in Figure 6-12, AS 64520 is receiving updates about network 172.16.0.0 from two directions. Assume that the local preference on Router A for network 172.16.0.0

is set to 200 and that the local preference on Router B for network 172.16.0.0 is set to 150. Because the local preference information is exchanged within AS 64520, all traffic in AS 64520 addressed to network 172.16.0.0 will be sent to Router A as an exit point from AS 64520.

**Figure 6-12**  *Local Preference Attribute—Router A Is the Preferred Router to Get to 172.16.0.0*

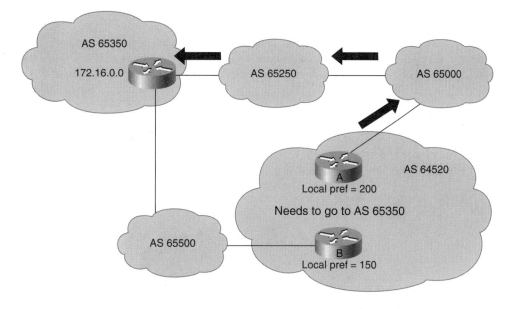

| NOTE | Configuring the BGP local preference is discussed in the "Multihoming" section in Chapter 7, "Implementing BGP in Scalable Networks." |
|---|---|

## MED Attribute

The Multi-exit-discriminator (MED) attribute, also called the metric, is an optional nontransitive attribute. The MED was known as the inter-AS attribute in BGP-3.

| NOTE | In **show** command outputs the MED attribute is called the *metric*. |
|---|---|

The MED is an indication to *external* neighbors about the preferred path into an AS. This is a dynamic way for an AS to try to influence another AS on which way it should choose to reach a certain route, if there are multiple entry points into an AS.

A *lower* value of a metric is preferred.

By using the MED attribute, BGP is the only protocol that can try to affect how routes are sent *into* an AS.

Unlike local preference, the MED is exchanged between autonomous systems. The MED is carried into an AS and is used there, but is not passed on to the next AS. When the same update is passed on to another AS, the metric will be set back to the default of 0.

By default, a router will compare the MED attribute only for paths from neighbors in the same AS.

For example, in Figure 6-13, Router B has set the MED attribute to 150, and Router C has set the MED attribute to 200. When Router A receives updates from Routers B and C, it picks Router B as the best next hop to get to AS 65500 because 150 is less than 200.

**Figure 6-13** *MED Attribute—Router B Is the Best Next Hop to Get to AS 65500*

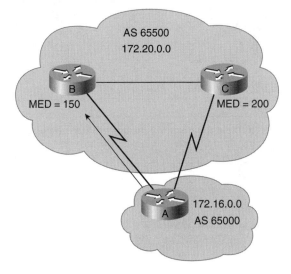

**NOTE** By default, the MED comparison is done only if the neighboring autonomous system is the same for all routes considered. For the router to compare metrics from neighbors coming from different autonomous systems, the **bgp always-compare-med** command must be configured on the router.

## Origin Attribute

The origin is a well-known mandatory attribute that defines the origin of the path information. The origin attribute can be one of three values, as follows:

- **IGP**—The route is interior to the originating AS. This normally happens when the **network** command (discussed later in this chapter) is used to advertise the route via BGP. An origin of IGP is indicated with an "i" in the BGP table.

- **EGP**—The route is learned via the Exterior Gateway Protocol. This is indicated with an "e" in the BGP table.

- **Incomplete**—The origin of the route is unknown or is learned via some other means. This usually occurs when a route is redistributed into BGP (redistribution is discussed in Chapter 7 and Chapter 8, "Optimizing Routing Update Operation"). An incomplete origin is indicated with a "?" in the BGP table.

## Community Attribute

BGP communities are one way to filter incoming or outgoing routes. BGP communities allow routers to *tag* routes with an indicator (the *community*) and allow other routers to make decisions based upon that tag. Any BGP router can tag routes in incoming and outgoing routing updates, or when doing redistribution. Any BGP router can filter routes in incoming or outgoing updates or can select preferred routes, based on communities (the tag).

BGP communities are used for destinations (routes) that share some common properties and therefore share common policies; routers thus act on the community rather than on individual routes. Communities are not restricted to one network or one AS, and they have no physical boundaries.

Communities are optional transitive attributes. If a router does not understand the concept of communities, it will defer to the next router. However, if the router does understand the concept, then it must be configured to propagate the community; otherwise, communities are dropped by default.

---

**NOTE**    BGP community configuration is detailed in Appendix A, "Job Aids and Supplements."

---

## Weight Attribute (Cisco Only)

The weight attribute is a Cisco-defined attribute used for the path selection process. The weight is configured locally to a router, on a per-neighbor basis. The weight attribute provides local routing policy only and is *not* propagated to *any* BGP neighbors.

The weight can have a value from 0 to 65535. Paths that the router originates have a weight of 32768 by default, and other paths have a weight of 0 by default.

Routes with a *higher* weight are preferred when multiple routes exist to the same destination.

In Figure 6-14, Routers B and C learn about network 172.20.0.0 from AS 65250 and will propagate the update to Router A. Router A has two ways to reach 172.20.0.0 and must decide which way to go. In the example, Router A sets the weight of updates coming from Router B to 200, and the weight of those coming from Router C to 150. Because the weight for Router B is higher than the weight for Router C, Router A is forced to use Router B as a next hop to reach 172.20.0.0.

**Figure 6-14** *Weight Attribute—Router A Will Use Router B as the Next Hop to Reach 172.20.0.0*

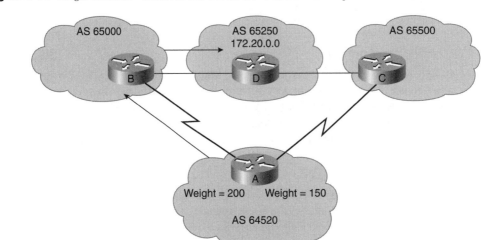

## BGP Synchronization

The BGP synchronization rule states that a BGP router should not use or advertise to an external neighbor a route learned by IBGP, unless that route is local or is learned from the IGP. If your autonomous system is passing traffic from one AS to another AS, BGP should not advertise a route before all routers in your AS have learned about the route via IGP.

A router learning a route via IBGP will wait until the IGP has propagated the route within the AS and then will advertise it to external peers. This is done so that all routers in the AS are synchronized and will be capable of routing traffic that the AS advertises to other autonomous systems that it is capable of routing. The BGP synchronization rule also ensures consistency of information throughout the AS and avoids *black holes* (for example, advertising a destination to an external neighbor when all routers within the AS cannot reach the destination) within the AS.

BGP synchronization is on by default in current IOS releases. Only if all routers in the transit path in the AS (in other words, in the path between the BGP border routers) are running BGP is it safe to turn synchronization off. (Indications are that in future IOS releases, BGP synchronization will be off by default, because most ISPs run BGP on all routers.)

In the example in Figure 6-15, Routers A, B, C, and D are all running BGP with each other (full mesh IBGP). There are no matching IGP routers for the BGP routes.

**Figure 6-15** *A BGP Synchronization Example*

All routers in AS 65500 are running BGP; there are no matching IGP is routes

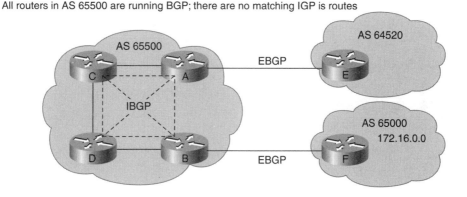

If synchronization is on (the default) in AS 65500 in Figure 6-15, then the following would happen:

- Router B would advertise the route to 172.16.0.0 to the other routers in AS 65500 using IBGP.

- Router B would use the route to 172.16.0.0 and install it in its routing table.

- Routers A, C, and D would not use or advertise the route to 172.16.0.0 until they received the matching route via an IGP. Because there is no IGP running, these routers would never use or advertise the route.

- Router E would not hear about 172.16.0.0. If Router E received traffic destined for network 172.16.0.0, it would not have a route for that network and would not be capable of forwarding the traffic.

If synchronization is turned off in AS 65500 in Figure 6-15, then the following would happen:

- Routers A, C, and D would use and advertise the route to 172.16.0.0 that they receive via IBGP, and would install it in their routing tables (assuming, of course, that Routers A, C, and D can reach the next-hop address for 172.16.0.0).

- Router E would hear about 172.16.0.0. Router E would have a route to 172.16.0.0 and could send traffic destined for that network.

- If Router E sends traffic for 172.16.0.0, Routers A, C, and D would route the packets correctly to Router B. Router E would send the packets to Router A, and Router A would forward them to Router C. Router C has learned a route to 172.16.0.0 via IBGP and therefore would forward the packets to Router D. Router D would forward the packets to Router B. Router B would forward the packets to Router F for network 172.16.0.0.

# BGP Operation

This section describes the operation of the BGP protocol. The following topics are covered:

- BGP message types
- Route selection decision process
- CIDR and aggregate addresses

## BGP Message Types

BGP defines the following message types:

- Open
- Keepalive
- Update
- Notification

After a TCP connection is established, the first message sent by each side is an open message. If the open message is acceptable, a keepalive message confirming the open is sent back. When the open is confirmed, the BGP connection is established, and update, keepalive, and notification messages may be exchanged.

BGP peers will initially exchange their full BGP routing tables. From then on, incremental updates are sent as the routing table changes. Keepalive packets are sent to ensure that the connection is alive between the BGP peers, and notification packets are sent in response to errors or special conditions.

An open message includes the following information:

- **Version**—This 8-bit field indicates the BGP protocol version number of the message. The current BGP version number is 4.

- **My Autonomous System**—This 16-bit field indicates the autonomous system number of the sender.

- **Hold time**—This 16-bit field indicates the maximum number of seconds that may elapse between the receipt of successive keepalive or update messages by the sender. Upon receipt of an open message, the router calculates the value of the hold timer to use by using the smaller of its configured hold time and the hold time received in the open message.

- **BGP identifier (router ID)**—This 32-bit field indicates the BGP identifier of the sender. The BGP identifier is an IP address assigned to that router and is determined on startup. The BGP router ID is chosen the same way that the OSPF router ID is chosen—it is the highest active IP address on the router, unless a loopback interface with an IP address exists, in which case it is the highest such loopback IP address.

- **Optional parameters**—A length field indicates the total length of the optional parameters field in octets. The optional parameters field may contain a list of optional parameters (currently, only authentication is defined).

BGP does not use any transport protocol-based keepalive mechanism to determine whether peers are reachable. Instead, keepalive messages are exchanged between peers often enough to not cause the hold timer to expire. If the negotiated hold time interval is zero, then periodic keepalive messages will not be sent.

An update message has information on one path only; multiple paths require multiple messages. All the attributes in the message refer to that path, and the networks are those that can be reached through it. An update message may include the following fields:

- **Withdrawn routes**—A list of IP address prefixes for routes that are being withdrawn from service, if any.

- **Path attributes**—These path attributes are the AS-path, origin, local preference, and the like, discussed earlier in this chapter in the section "BGP Attributes." Each path attribute includes the attribute type, attribute length, and attribute value. The attribute type consists of the attribute flags, followed by the attribute type code.

- **Network layer reachability information**—This field contains a list of IP address prefixes that can be reached by this path.

A notification message is sent when an error condition is detected. The BGP connection is closed immediately after this is sent. Notification messages include an error code, an error subcode, and data related to the error.

---

### BGP Neighbor States

The BGP protocol is a state machine, which takes a router through the following states with its neighbors:

- Idle
- Connect
- Active
- OpenSent
- OpenConfirm
- Established

Only when the connection is in the Established state are update, keepalive, and notification messages exchanged.

| NOTE | Keepalive messages consist of only a message header and have a length of 19 bytes; they are sent every 60 seconds by default. Other messages may be between 19 bytes and 4096 bytes long. The default hold time is 180 seconds. |
|------|---|

## Route Selection Decision Process

After BGP receives updates about different destinations from different autonomous systems, the protocol decides which path to choose to reach a specific destination. BGP chooses only a single path to reach a specific destination.

The decision process is based on the attributes discussed earlier in this chapter in the section "BGP Attributes." When faced with multiple routes to the same destination, BGP chooses the best route for routing traffic toward the destination. The following process summarizes how BGP on a Cisco router chooses the best route:

**Step 1**   If the path is internal, synchronization is on, and the route is not synchronized (in other words, the route is not in the IGP routing table), do not consider it.

**Step 2**   If the next-hop address of a route is not reachable, do not consider it.

**Step 3**   Prefer the route with the highest weight. (Recall that the weight is Cisco-proprietary and is local to the router only.)

**Step 4**   If multiple routes have the same weight, prefer the route with the highest local preference. (Recall that the local preference is used within an AS.)

**Step 5**   If multiple routes have the same local preference, prefer the route that was originated by the local router.

**Step 6**   If multiple routes have the same local preference, or if no route was originated by the local router, prefer the route with the shortest AS-path.

**Step 7**   If the AS-path length is the same, prefer the lowest origin code (IGP < EGP < incomplete).

**Step 8**   If all origin codes are the same, prefer the path with the lowest MED. (Recall that the MED is sent from other autonomous systems.)

The MED comparison is done only if the neighboring autonomous system is the same for all routes considered, unless the **bgp always-compare-med** command is enabled.

| Note | The most recent Internet Engineering Task Force (IETF) decision regarding BGP MED assigns a value of infinity to a missing MED, making a route lacking the MED variable the least preferred. The default behavior of BGP routers running Cisco IOS software is to treat routes without the MED attribute as having a MED of 0, making a route lacking the MED variable the most preferred. To configure the router to conform to the IETF standard, use the **bgp bestpath missing-as-worst** command. |
|---|---|

**Step 9**   If the routes have the same MED, prefer external paths (EBGP) over internal paths (IBGP).

**Step 10**   If synchronization is disabled and only internal paths remain, prefer the path through the closest IGP neighbor. This means that the router will prefer the shortest internal path within the AS to reach the destination (the shortest path to the BGP next hop).

**Step 11**   For EBGP paths, select the oldest route, to minimize the effect of routes going up and down (flapping).

**Step 12**   Prefer the route with the lowest neighbor BGP router ID value.

**Step 13**   If the BGP router IDs are the same, prefer the route with the lowest neighbor IP address.

The path is put in the routing table and is propagated to the router's BGP neighbors.

| NOTE | The route selection decision process summarized here does not cover all cases, but it is sufficient for a basic understanding of how BGP selects routes. |
|---|---|
| | Step 11 in the decision process, to prefer the oldest route for EBGP paths, is not found in any of the BGP documentation; it came from Cisco's Technical Assistance Center (TAC). You will be able to see this if you perform the multihomed BGP Configuration Exercise in the next chapter with more than one pod. You will see that the backbone routers chose the best path based on whichever pod came up first; in other words, they will choose the oldest route because all other parameters will be equal. |

## Multiple Path Selection

BGP chooses only a single path for each destination.

The **maximum-paths** router configuration command for BGP works if your router has two parallel paths to two different routers in same remote AS. For example, consider three routers: p1r1 is in AS 65201, and both p1r2 and p1r3 are in AS 65301. p1r1 is running EBGP to p1r2 and p1r3. p1r2 and p1r3 are advertising network 10.0.0.0. Without the **maximum-paths** command under the **router bgp 65201** command on p1r1, there will not be two paths in p1r1's routing table. After the **maximum-paths 2** command is added to the p1r1 bgp configuration, both paths appear in the routing table, as shown in the output in Example 6-3. However, as also shown in Example 6-3, there is still only one path selected as the best in the BGP table (as indicated by the ">" symbol).

**Example 6-3** *Output from Testing of the **maximum-paths** Command for BGP*

```
p1r1#show ip route bgp
B    10.0.0.0/8 [20/0] via 192.168.1.18, 00:00:41
                [20/0] via 192.168.1.50, 00:00:41

p1r1#show ip bgp
BGP table version is 3, local router ID is 192.168.1.49
Status codes: s suppressed, d damped, h history, * valid, > best, i ->internal
Origin codes: i - IGP, e - EGP, ? - incomplete

   Network          Next Hop          Metric LocPrf Weight Path
*> 10.0.0.0         192.168.1.18           0             0 65301 i
*                   192.168.1.50           0             0 65301 i
```

# CIDR and Aggregate Addresses

As discussed in Chapter 2, classless interdomain routing (CIDR) is a mechanism developed to help alleviate the problem of exhaustion of IP addresses and the growth of routing tables. The idea behind CIDR is that blocks of multiple Class C addresses can be combined, or aggregated, to create a larger classless set of IP addresses. These multiple Class C addresses can then be summarized in routing tables, resulting in fewer route advertisements.

Earlier versions of BGP did not support CIDR; BGP-4 does. BGP-4 support includes the following:

- The BGP update message includes both the prefix and the prefix length. Previous versions included only the prefix; the length was assumed from the address class.

- Addresses can be aggregated when advertised by a BGP router.

- The AS-path attribute can include a combined unordered list of all autonomous systems that all the aggregated routes have passed through. This combined list should be considered to ensure that the route is loop-free.

As an example, in Figure 6-16, Router C is advertising network 192.168.2.0/24, and Router D is advertising network 192.168.1.0/24. Router A could pass those advertisements to Router B; however, Router A could reduce the size of the routing tables by aggregating the two routes into one, for example, 192.168.0.0/16.

**Figure 6-16** *An Example of Using CIDR with BGP*

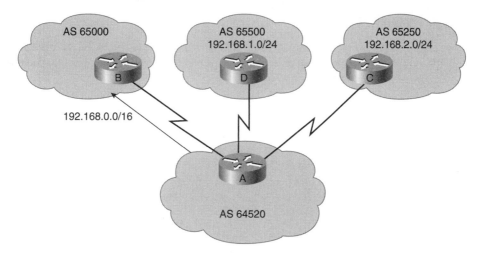

Two BGP attributes are related to aggregate addressing. The well-known discretionary attribute *atomic aggregate* informs the neighbor AS that the originating router has aggregated the routes. The optional transitive attribute *aggregator* specifies the BGP router ID and AS number of the router that performed the route aggregation.

By default, the aggregate route will be advertised as coming from the autonomous system that did the aggregation and will have the atomic aggregate attribute set to show that information might be missing. The AS numbers from the nonaggregated routes are not listed. The router can be configured to include the unordered list of all autonomous systems contained in all paths that are being summarized.

---

**NOTE**    Indications are that aggregate addresses are not used in the Internet as much as they could be because autonomous systems that are multihomed (connected to more than one ISP) want to make sure that their routes are advertised, without being aggregated into a summarized route.

---

In Figure 6-16, by default, the aggregated route 192.168.0.0/16 would have an AS-path attribute of (64520). If Router A was configured to include the combined unordered list, it would include the set of {65250, 65500} as well as (64520) in the AS-path attribute.

| NOTE | In the example in Figure 6-16, the aggregate route that Router A is sending covers more than the two routes from Routers C and D. The example assumes that Router A also has jurisdiction over all the other routes covered by this aggregate route. |
|---|---|

# Configuring BGP

This section covers the commands used to configure some of the BGP features discussed in this chapter. First, the concept of peer groups is described because peer groups appear in many of the configuration commands.

## Peer Groups

In BGP, many neighbors are often configured with the same update policies (for example, they have the same filtering applied). On a Cisco router, neighbors with the same update policies can be grouped into peer groups to simplify configuration and, more importantly, to make updating more efficient. When you have many peers, this approach is highly recommended.

A BGP peer group is a group of BGP neighbors of the router being configured that all have the same update policies. Instead of separately defining the same policies for each neighbor, a peer group can be defined with these policies assigned to the peer group. Individual neighbors are then made members of the peer group. The policies of the peer group are similar to a template; the template is then applied to the individual members of the peer group.

Members of the peer group inherit all the configuration options of the peer group. The router can also be configured to override these options for some members of the peer group if these options do not affect outbound updates; in other words, only options that affect the inbound updates can be overridden.

| NOTE | All EBGP neighbors in a peer group must be reachable over the same interface. This is because the next-hop attribute would be different for EBGP neighbors accessible on different interfaces. You can get around this restriction by configuring a loopback source address for EBGP peers. |
|---|---|

Peer groups are useful to simplify configurations when many neighbors have the same policy. They are also more efficient because updates are generated only once per peer group rather than once for each neighbor.

The peer group name is local only to the router it is configured on; it is not passed to any other router.

---

**NOTE**    BGP peer group configuration is detailed in Appendix A.

## Basic BGP Commands

Basic BGP commands are covered in this section.

---

**NOTE**    The syntax of basic BGP configuration commands is similar to the syntax of commands used for configuring internal routing protocols. However, there are significant differences in the way that an external protocol functions.

---

Use the **router bgp** *autonomous-system* global configuration command to activate the BGP protocol and identify the local autonomous system. In the command, *autonomous-system* identifies the local autonomous system.

Use the **neighbor** {*ip-address* | *peer-group-name*} **remote-as** *autonomous-system* router configuration command to identify a peer router with which the local router will establish a session, as described in Table 6-4.

**Table 6-4**    *neighbor remote-as Command Description*

| neighbor remote-as Command | Description |
|---|---|
| *ip-address* | Identifies the peer router. |
| *peer-group-name* | Gives the name of a BGP peer group. |
| *autonomous-system* | Identifies the autonomous system of the peer router. |

The value placed in the autonomous system field of the **neighbor remote-as** command determines whether the communication with the neighbor is an EBGP or an IBGP session. If the autonomous system field configured in the **router bgp** command is identical to the field in the **neighbor remote-as** command, then BGP will initiate an internal session. If the field values are different, then BGP will initiate an external session.

### Other BGP Commands

To disable an existing BGP neighbor or neighbor peer group, use the **neighbor** {*ip-address* | *peer-group-name*} **shutdown** router configuration command. To enable a previously existing neighbor or neighbor peer group that had been disabled using the **neighbor shutdown** command, use the **no neighbor** {*ip-address* | *peer-group-name*} **shutdown** router configuration command.

EBGP assumes a Time To Live (TTL) of 1. The **neighbor** {*ip-address* | *peer-group-name*} **ebgp-multihop** [*ttl*] command must be used if the EBGP neighbors are not directly connected. Whenever the EBGP neighbors are more than one hop away (which includes connections to loopback interfaces), the **neighbor ebgp-multihop** command will by default set the TTL to 255. This will allow BGP to create an inter-AS connection. Note that IBGP already assumes a TTL of 255.

Using a loopback interface to define neighbors is commonly used with IBGP (rather than EBGP). Normally the loopback interface is used to make sure that the IP address of the neighbor stays up and is independent of hardware that might be flaky. If the IP address of a loopback interface is used in the **neighbor** command, some extra configuration must be done on the neighbor router. The neighbor router needs to tell BGP that it is using a loopback interface rather than a physical interface to initiate the BGP neighbor TCP connection. Use the **neighbor** {*ip-address* | *peer-group-name}* **update-source loopback** *interface-number* command to cause the router to use its loopback interface for BGP connections to its neighbors.

If you have multiple physical connections between EBGP neighbors, using a loopback interface and static routes to the loopback interface allows you to load balance the traffic between the multiple connections.

Use the **network** *network-number* [**mask** *network-mask*] router configuration command to permit BGP to advertise a network if it is present in the IP routing table, as described in Table 6-5.

**Table 6-5**   *network Command Description*

| Network Command | Description |
|---|---|
| *network-number* | Identifies an IP network to be advertised by BGP. |
| *network-mask* | (Optional) Identifies the subnet mask to be advertised by BGP. If the network mask is not specified, the default mask will be the classful mask. |

The **network** command controls which networks are originated by this router. This is a different concept from what you are used to when configuring IGPs. The **network** command does not start up BGP on certain interfaces; rather, it indicates to BGP which networks it should originate from this router. The **mask** parameter is used because BGP-4 can handle subnetting and supernetting. The list of **network** commands must include all networks in your AS that you want to advertise, not just those locally connected to your router.

The **network** command allows classless prefixes; the router can advertise individual subnets, networks, or supernets. Note that the prefix must exactly match (address and mask) an entry in the IP routing table. A static route to null 0 may be used to create a supernet entry in the IP routing table; this is discussed in the "Redistribution with IGPs" section in the next chapter.

Prior to Cisco IOS Release 12.0, there was a limit of 200 **network** commands per BGP router; this limit has now been removed. The router's resources, such as the configured nonvolatile random-access memory (NVRAM) or random-access memory (RAM), determine the maximum number of **network** commands that you can now use.

## Basic BGP Commands Example

Figure 6-17 shows an example BGP network. Example 6-4 provides the configuration of Router A in Figure 6-17, and Example 6-5 provides the configuration of Router B in Figure 6-17.

**Figure 6-17**  *An Example BGP Network*

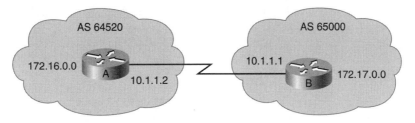

**Example 6-4**  *Configuration of Router A in Figure 6-17*

```
RtrA(config)#router bgp 64520
RtrA(config-router)# neighbor 10.1.1.1 remote-as 65000
RtrA(config-router)# network 172.16.0.0
```

**Example 6-5**  *Configuration of Router B in Figure 6-17*

```
RtrB(config)#router bgp 65000
RtrB(config-router)# neighbor 10.1.1.2 remote-as 64520
RtrB(config-router)# network 172.17.0.0
```

In this example, Routers A and B define each other as BGP neighbors and will start an EBGP session. Router A will advertise the network 172.16.0.0/16, while Router B will advertise the network 172.17.0.0/16.

## Changing the Next-Hop Attribute

It is sometimes necessary—for example, in an NBMA environment—to override the default behavior of a router and force it to advertise itself as the next-hop address for routes sent to a neighbor.

The **neighbor** {*ip-address* | *peer-group-name*} **next-hop-self** router configuration command is used to force BGP to use its own IP address as the next hop rather than letting the protocol choose the next-hop address to use, as described in Table 6-6.

**Table 6-6** *neighbor next-hop-self Command Description*

| neighbor next-hop-self Command | Description |
| --- | --- |
| *ip-address* | Identifies the peer router to which advertisements will be sent, with this router identified as the next hop. |
| *peer-group-name* | Gives the name of a BGP peer group to which advertisements wil be sent, wtih this router identified as the next hop. |

**NOTE**     This command is useful in NBMA environments, but it should be used only where there is a single path to the peer AS, or else a suboptimal path to the AS may be chosen.

## Disabling BGP Synchronization

In some cases you do not need BGP synchronization. If you will not be passing traffic from a different autonomous system through your AS (in other words, if your AS is not a transit AS), or if all routers in the BGP transit path in your AS will be running BGP, you can disable synchronization. Disabling this feature can allow you to carry fewer routes in your IGP and allow BGP to converge more quickly. Use synchronization if some routers in the BGP transit path in the AS are not running BGP.

Synchronization is on by default; use the **no synchronization** router configuration command to disable it. This command will allow a router to use and advertise to an external BGP neighbor routes learned by IBGP before learning them in an IGP.

## Creating a Summary Address in the BGP Table

The **aggregate-address** *ip-address mask* [**summary-only**] [**as-set**] router configuration command is used to create an aggregate, or summary, entry in the BGP table, as described in Table 6-7.

**Table 6-7** *aggregate-address Command Description*

| aggregate-address Command | Description |
|---|---|
| *ip-address* | Gives the aggregate address to be created. |
| *mask* | Gives the mask of the aggregate address to be created. |
| **summary-only** | (Optional) Causes the router to advertise only the aggregated route; the default is to advertise both the aggregate and the more specific routes. |
| **as-set** | (Optional) Generates AS path information with the aggregate route to include all the AS numbers listed in all the paths of the more specific routes. The default for the aggregate route is to list only the AS number of the router that generated the aggregate route. |

**NOTE**     The **aggregate-address** command applies to networks already in the BGP table. This is different from the requirement for advertising summaries with the BGP **network** command. In that case, the network must exist in the IP routing table; in this case, the networks being aggregated must exist in the BGP table.

When you use this command without the **as-set** keyword, the aggregate route will be advertised as coming from your autonomous system and will have the atomic aggregate attribute set to show that information might be missing. The atomic aggregate attribute is set unless you specify the **as-set** keyword.

### aggregate-address Command Keywords

Without the **summary-only** keyword, the router will still advertise the individual networks. This can be useful for redundant ISP links. For example, if one ISP is advertising only summaries, while the other is advertising a summary plus the more specific routes, then the more specific routes will be followed. However, if the ISP advertising the more specific routes becomes inaccessible, then the other ISP advertising only the summary will be followed.

If you use only the **summary-only** keyword on the **aggregate-address** command, the summary route is advertised and the path indicates only the AS that summarized (all other path information is missing). If you use only the **as-set** keyword on the **aggregate-address** command, the set of AS numbers is included in the path information (and the command with the **summary-only** keyword is deleted if it existed). However, you may use *both* keywords on one command; this will result in the summary address only being sent and all the autonomous systems being listed in the path information.

## Resetting BGP

Use the **clear ip bgp** {* | *address*} [**soft** [**in** | **out**]] privileged EXEC command to remove entries from the BGP table and reset BGP sessions, as described in Table 6-8. Use this command after every configuration change to ensure that the change is activated and that peer routers are informed.

**Table 6-8**    *clear ip bgp Command Description*

| clear ip bgp Command | Description |
| --- | --- |
| * | Resets all current BGP sessions. |
| *address* | Identifies the address of a specific neighbor for which the BGP sessions will be reset. |
| **soft** | (Optional) Does a soft reconfiguration, as explained in the following paragraph. |
| **in** | **out** | (Optional) Triggers inbound or outbound soft reconfiguration. If the **in** or **out** option is not specified, both inbound and outbound soft reconfigurations are triggered. |

If you specify BGP soft reconfiguration by including the **soft** keyword, the BGP sessions are not reset and the router sends all routing updates again. To generate new inbound updates without resetting the BGP session, the local BGP speaker would have to store all received updates without modification, regardless of whether it is accepted by the inbound policy, using the **neighbor soft-reconfiguration** router configuration command. (After configuring the **neighbor soft-reconfiguration** command for the first time, clear all current BGP sessions so that all updates will be resent by all neighbors and can then be stored in the local router.) This process is memory-intensive and should be avoided if possible. Outbound BGP soft configuration does not have any memory overhead. You can trigger an outbound reconfiguration on the other side of the BGP session to make the new inbound policy take effect.

---

**WARNING**    Clearing the BGP table and resetting BGP sessions will disrupt routing, so do not use this command unless you have to.

---

NOTE    The Cisco IOS documentation says that the **clear ip bgp** command can have {* | *address* | *peer-group-name*} parameters. However, the command for peer groups is actually **clear ip bgp peer-group** *peer-group-name*.

## Another BGP Example

Figure 6-18 shows an example BGP network. Example 6-6 provides the configuration of Router B in Figure 6-18.

**Figure 6-18**  *A Sample Network for Using BGP Configuration Commands*

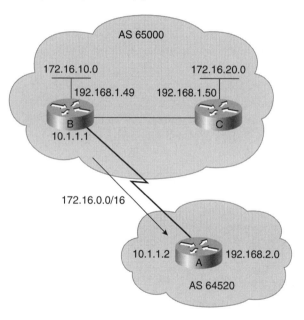

NOTE    There is no IGP running in this example.

**Example 6-6**  *Configuration of Router B in Figure 6-18*

```
RtrB(config)#router bgp 65000
RtrB(config-router)# neighbor 10.1.1.2 remote-as 64520
RtrB(config-router)# neighbor 192.168.1.50 remote-as 65000
RtrB(config-router)# network 172.16.10.0 mask 255.255.255.0
RtrB(config-router)# network 192.168.1.0 mask 255.255.255.0
RtrB(config-router)# no synchronization
RtrB(config-router)# neighbor 192.168.1.50 next-hop-self
RtrB(config-router)# aggregate-address 172.16.0.0 255.255.0.0 summary-only
```

In Example 6-6, the first two commands under the **router bgp 65000** command establish that Router B has two BGP neighbors: Router A in AS 64520 and Router C in AS 65000. The next two commands allow Router B to advertise networks 172.16.10.0 and 192.168.1.0 to its BGP neighbors.

Assuming that Router C is advertising 172.16.20.0 in BGP, Router B would receive that route via IBGP but would not pass it to Router A until the **no synchronization** command is added to both Routers B and C because there is no IGP running in this example. This command can be used here because all the routers in the AS are running BGP. The **clear ip bgp \*** command would be required on Routers B and C to reset the BGP sessions after the synchronization has been turned off.

By default, Router B will pass the BGP advertisement from Router A about network 192.168.2.0 to Router C, with the next-hop address left as 10.1.1.2. However, Router C does not know how to get to 10.1.1.2, so it will not install the route. The **neighbor 192.168.1.50 next-hop-self** command will force Router B to send advertisements to Router C with its own (Router B) address as the next-hop address. Router C will then be capable of reaching 192.168.2.0.

By default, Router A would learn about both subnets 172.16.10.0 and 172.16.20.0. However, when the **aggregate-address 172.16.0.0 255.255.0.0 summary-only** command is added to Router B, Router B will summarize the subnets and send only the 172.16.0.0/16 route to Router A.

# Verifying BGP

Verifying BGP operation can be accomplished using the following **show** EXEC commands:

- **show ip bgp**—Displays entries in the BGP routing table. Specify a network number to get more specific information about a particular network.
- **show ip bgp summary**—Displays the status on all BGP connections.
- **show ip bgp neighbors**—Displays information about the TCP and BGP connections to neighbors.

Other BGP **show** commands can be found in the BGP documentation on Cisco's web site (www.cisco.com) or on the Documentation CD-ROM. Use the **show ip bgp ?** command on a router to see other BGP **show** commands.

Debug commands display events as they are happening on the router. For BGP, the **debug ip bgp** privileged EXEC command has the following options:

- **dampening**—BGP dampening
- **events**—BGP events

- **keepalives**—BGP keepalives
- **updates**—BGP updates

## show ip bgp Command Output Example

The example output of the **show ip bgp** command shown in Example 6-7 is taken from Router A in the BGP example in Figure 6-18.

**Example 6-7**  *show ip bgp Command Output from Router A in Figure 6-18*

```
RTRA#show ip bgp
BGP table version is 5, local router ID is 192.168.2.1
Status codes:s suppressed,d damped,h history,* valid,> best,i - internal
Origin codes: i - IGP, e - EGP, ? - incomplete

   Network          Next Hop          Metric LocPrf Weight Path
*> 172.16.0.0       10.1.1.1                          0 65000 i
*> 192.168.1.0      10.1.1.1          0                0 65000 i
*> 192.168.2.0      0.0.0.0           0            32768 i
```

The status codes are shown at the beginning of each line of output, and the origin codes are shown at the end of each line of output. From the example output, you can see that Router A learned about two networks from 10.1.1.1: 172.16.0.0 and 192.168.1.0. The path Router A will use to get to these networks is via AS 65000, and the routes have origin codes of IGP (shown as "i" in the output). Note the aggregated route to 172.16.0.0 in this output.

An example of the additional information displayed when a network is specified in the **show ip bgp** command is provided in Example 6-8. (Note that this example is not from the network in Figure 6-18.)

**Example 6-8**  *show ip bgp network Command Output*

```
p1r1#show ip bgp 172.31.20.0/24
BGP routing table entry for 172.31.20.0/24, version 211
Paths: (1 available, best #1)
  Advertised to non peer-group peers:
    192.168.1.18 192.168.1.34 192.168.1.50
  65200 65106 65201
    10.1.1.100 from 10.1.1.100 (172.16.11.100)
      Origin IGP, localpref 100, valid, external, best, ref 2
p1r1#exit
```

## show ip bgp summary Command Output Example

The example output of the **show ip bgp summary** command shown in Example 6-9 is taken from Router A in the BGP example in Figure 6-18.

**Example 6-9** *show ip bgp summary Output from Router A in Figure 6-18*

```
RTRA#show ip bgp summary
BGP table version is 5, main routing table version 5
3 network entries and 3 paths using 363 bytes of memory
3 BGP path attribute entries using 372 bytes of memory
BGP activity 3/0 prefixes, 3/0 paths
0 prefixes revised.

Neighbor    V    AS MsgRcvd MsgSent    TblVer  InQ OutQ Up/Down   State/PfxRcd
10.1.1.1    4 65000      14       13        5    0    0 00:08:03           2
```

In this example output, you can see that Router A has one neighbor, 10.1.1.1. It speaks BGP-4 with that neighbor, which is in AS 65000. Router A has received 14 messages from and has sent 13 messages to 10.1.1.1. The TblVer is the last version of the BGP database that was sent to that neighbor. There are no messages in either the input or the output queue. The BGP session has been established for 8 minutes and 3 seconds. The State field is blank, indicating that the state of the neighbor router is Established. Router A has received two prefixes from neighbor 10.1.1.1.

---

**NOTE**     If the state field of the **show ip bgp summary** command indicates *Active*, the router is attempting to create a TCP connection to that neighbor.

---

## show ip bgp neighbors Command Output Example

The example output of the **show ip bgp neighbors** command shown in Example 6-10 is taken from Router A in the BGP example in Figure 6-18.

**Example 6-10** *show ip bgp neighbors Output from Router A in Figure 6-18*

```
RTRA#show ip bgp neighbors
BGP neighbor is 10.1.1.1,  remote AS 65000, external link
  Index 1, Offset 0, Mask 0x2
  BGP version 4, remote router ID 172.16.10.1
  BGP state = Established, table version = 5, up for 00:10:47
  Last read 00:00:48, hold time is 180, keepalive interval is 60 seconds
  Minimum time between advertisement runs is 30 seconds
  Received 16 messages, 0 notifications, 0 in queue
  Sent 15 messages, 1 notifications, 0 in queue
  Prefix advertised 1, suppressed 0, withdrawn 0
  Connections established 1; dropped 0
  Last reset 00:16:35, due to Peer closed the session
```

**Example 6-10** *show ip bgp neighbors Output from Router A in Figure 6-18 (Continued)*

```
 2 accepted prefixes consume 64 bytes
 0 history paths consume 0 bytes
--More--
```

This command is used to display information about the BGP connections to neighbors. In the example output, the BGP state is Established, which means that the neighbors have established a TCP connection and that the two peers have agreed to speak BGP with each other.

| | |
|---|---|
| **NOTE** | Refer to the Command Reference documentation on the Cisco Documentation CD-ROM or in the technical documents section on Cisco's web site (www.cisco.com) for a complete description of the fields in the output of this command. |

## debug ip bgp updates Command Output Example

The example output of the **debug ip bgp updates** command shown in Example 6-11 is taken from Router A in the BGP example in Figure 6-18. The **clear ip bgp *** command was used to force Router A to reset all its BGP connections.

**Example 6-11** *debug ip bgp updates Output from Router A in Figure 6-18*

```
RTRA#debug ip bgp updates
BGP updates debugging is on
RTRA#clear ip bgp *
3w5d: BGP: 10.1.1.1 computing updates, neighbor version 0, table
version 1, starting at 0.0.0.0
3w5d: BGP: 10.1.1.1 update run completed, ran for 0ms, neighbor
version 0, start version 1, throttled to 1, check point net 0.0.0.0
3w5d: BGP: 10.1.1.1 rcv UPDATE w/ attr: nexthop 10.1.1.1, origin i,
aggregated by 65000 172.16.10.1, path 65000
3w5d: BGP: 10.1.1.1 rcv UPDATE about 172.16.0.0/16
3w5d: BGP: nettable_walker 172.16.0.0/16 calling revise_route
3w5d: BGP: revise route installing 172.16.0.0/16 -> 10.1.1.1
3w5d: BGP: 10.1.1.1 rcv UPDATE w/ attr: nexthop 10.1.1.1, origin i,
metric 0, path 65000
3w5d: BGP: 10.1.1.1 rcv UPDATE about 192.168.1.0/24
3w5d: BGP: nettable_walker 192.168.1.0/24 calling revise_route
3w5d: BGP: revise route installing 192.168.1.0/24 -> 10.1.1.1
3w5d: BGP: 10.1.1.1 computing updates, neighbor version 1, table version 3,
starting at 0.0.0.0
3w5d: BGP: 10.1.1.1 update run completed, ran for 0ms, neighbor version 1,
start version 3, throttled to 3, check point net 0.0.0.0
3w5d: BGP: nettable_walker 192.168.2.0/24 route sourced locally
3w5d: BGP: 10.1.1.1 computing updates, neighbor version 3, table version 4,
starting at 0.0.0.0
```

*continues*

**Example 6-11** *debug ip bgp updates Output from Router A in Figure 6-18 (Continued)*

```
3w5d: BGP: 10.1.1.1 send UPDATE 192.168.2.0/24, next 10.1.1.2, metric 0,
path 64520
3w5d: BGP: 10.1.1.1 1 updates enqueued (average=52, maximum=52)
3w5d: BGP: 10.1.1.1 update run completed, ran for 0ms, neighbor version 3,
start version 4, throttled to 4, check point net 0.0.0.0
```

The output in Example 6-11 shows update messages being received from and being sent to neighbor 10.1.1.1.

**NOTE**     Debugging uses router resources and therefore should be turned on only when necessary.

# Summary

In this chapter, you learned the basics of the BGP protocol.

BGP is an exterior routing protocol used to route between autonomous systems. BGP-4 is the latest version of BGP and is used throughout the Internet. BGP is an advanced distance vector protocol that uses TCP as its transport protocol. The BGP metrics are path attributes that indicate a variety of information about a route.

The BGP route selection decision process is to consider only (synchronized) routes with no AS loops and a valid next hop, and then to prefer the following characteristics:

- Highest weight (local to router)
- Highest local preference (global within AS)
- Route originated by the local router
- Shortest AS-path
- Lowest origin code (IGP < EGP < incomplete)
- Lowest MED (from other AS)
- EBGP path over IBGP path
- Path through the closest IGP neighbor
- Oldest route for EBGP paths
- Path with the lowest neighbor BGP router ID
- Path with lowest neighbor IP address

The next chapter discusses problems that can result when scaling IBGP and gives various solutions to those problems.

# Configuration Exercise: Configuring BGP

---

**Configuration Exercises**

In this book, Configuration Exercises are used to provide practice in configuring routers with the commands presented. If you have access to real hardware, you can try these exercises on your routers; refer to Appendix H, "Configuration Exercise Equipment Requirements and Backbone Configurations," for a list of recommended equipment and configuration commands for the backbone routers. However, even if you don't have access to any routers, you can go through the exercises and keep a log of your own "running configurations" on separate sheets of paper. Commands used and answers to the configuration exercises are provided at the end of the exercise.

In these exercises, you are in control of a pod of three routers; there are assumed to be 12 pods in the network. The pods are interconnected to a backbone. In most of the exercises, there is only one router in the backbone; in some cases, another router is added to the backbone. Each of the Configuration Exercises in this book assumes that you have completed the previous exercises on your pod.

---

In this exercise, you will configure IBGP within your pod and EBGP to the backbone_r1 router.

## Objectives

In the following configuration exercise, you will do the following:

- Disable EIGRP on all the routers in your pod.
- Configure EBGP between your p*x*r1 router and the backbone_r1 router. (The backbone_r1 router should be configured before you start the exercise; refer to Appendix H for the backbone_r1 configuration.)
- Configure IBGP in your pod (full mesh between p*x*r1, p*x*r2, and p*x*r3).
- During the configuration of IBGP, you will configure:
    — Next-hop-self
    — Disabling synchronization
    — Route aggregation
- Verify connectivity within your pod and to the backbone_r1 router.
- Use **show** and **debug** commands to verify BGP operations.

## Visual Objective

Figure 6-19 illustrates the topology used in the network.

**Figure 6-19** *Configuration Exercise Topology*

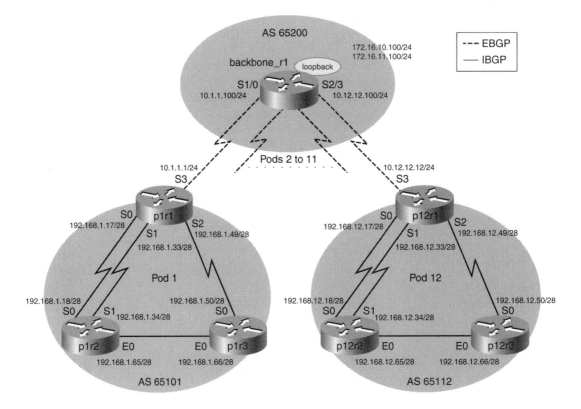

## Command List

In this exercise, you will use commands in Table 6-9, listed in logical order. Refer to this list if you need configuration command assistance during the exercise.

**Table 6-9** *Configuration Exercise Command List*

| Command | Description |
| --- | --- |
| **no router eigrp 200** | Disables EIGRP. |
| **router bgp 6510x** | Enables BGP with an AS number of 6510x. |
| **network 192.168.x.0 [mask 255.255.255.0]** | Specifies the network to be advertised. |

**Table 6-9**    *Configuration Exercise Command List (Continued)*

| Command | Description |
|---|---|
| **neighbor 192.168.x.18 remote-as 6510x** | Establishes a BGP neighbor relationship. |
| **neighbor 192.168.x.18 next-hop-self** | Allows modification of the next-hop router to itself. |
| **aggregate-address 192.168.x.0 255.255.255.0 summary-only** | Allows only the summarized route to be advertised. |
| **no synchronization** | Turns off BGP synchronization. |
| **clear ip bgp \*** | Resets all BGP connections. |
| **show ip bgp** | Shows BGP information. |
| **show ip bgp summary** | Shows summary BGP neighbor status. |
| **show ip bgp neighbors** | Shows detailed BGP neighbor status. |
| **debug ip bgp updates** | Displays BGP updates. |

# Setup

Setup is as follows:

**Step 1**    On your pxr1 router, disable Frame Relay switching. Change the pxr1 Serial 0 and Serial 2 interfaces back to running HDLC encapsulation.

Ensure that the pxr1 serial interfaces S0, S1, S2, and S3 have the correct IP address configuration, as follows:

| | |
|---|---|
| pxr1 S0 | 192.168.x.17/28 |
| pxr1 S1 | 192.168.x.33/28 |
| pxr1 S2 | 192.168.x.49/28 |
| pxr1 S3 | 10.x.x.x/24 |

No shut the Serial 1 and Serial 3 interfaces on your pxr1 router.

**Step 2**    On your pxr2 router, disable EIGRP. Shut down the Serial 0 interface on your pxr2 router. Change the pxr2 Serial 0 interface encapsulation back to HDLC. Reconfigure the IP address on your pxr2 Serial 0 to 192.168.x. 18/28.

No shut the Ethernet 0, Serial 0, and Serial 1 interfaces on your pxr2 router.

**Step 3** On your pxr3 router, disable EIGRP. Shut down the Serial 0 interface on your pxr3 router. Change the pxr3 Serial 0 interface encapsulation back to HDLC. Reconfigure the IP address on your pxr3 Serial 0 to 192.168.x.50/28.

No shut the Ethernet 0 and Serial 0 interfaces on your pxr3 router.

## Task 1: Enabling EBGP

Complete the following steps:

**Step 1** At your pxr1 router, enable BGP using the AS number in Table 6-10.

**Table 6-10** *Autonomous System Numbers to Configure on Routers in Pod x*

| Pod | AS Number |
|-----|-----------|
| 1 | 65101 |
| 2 | 65102 |
| 3 | 65103 |
| 4 | 65104 |
| 5 | 65105 |
| 6 | 65106 |
| 7 | 65107 |
| 8 | 65108 |
| 9 | 65109 |
| 10 | 65110 |
| 11 | 65111 |
| 12 | 65112 |

**NOTE** The backbone_r1 router is in AS 65200.

**Step 2** At your pxr1 router, use a **neighbor** statement to establish the backbone_r1 router as an EBGP neighbor.

**Step 3** At the pxr1 router, use a **network** statement to allow advertisement of the 192.168.x.0/24 network to AS 65200 (where *x* is your pod number).

**Step 4** At the pxr1 router, enter the **show ip bgp summary** and the **show ip bgp neighbors** commands.

What is the neighbor state of the backbone_r1 router?

What is the BGP state of the backbone_r1 router?

What is the BGP version?

**Step 5**  At the pxr1 router, enter the **show ip bgp** command.

List some of the BGP routes that you see. List the following for each route:

- — Network

- — Next hop

- — Metric

- — LocPrf

- — Weight

- — Path

**Step 6**  At the pxr1 router, enter the **show ip route** command.

List some of the BGP routes that you see.

Notice that at the pxr1 router now, you will not see a route to your 192.168.x.64/28 subnet in your pod because you have not enabled an IGP routing protocol between the routers within your pod.

**Step 7**  From your pxr1 router, ping 172.16.10.100 and 172.16.11.100.

Were the pings successful?

**Step 8**  From your pxr1 router, enter the **show ip bgp** command.

If another pod is configured, list the AS path for accessing your neighbor pod.

**Step 9**  Save the current configurations of all the routers within your pod to NVRAM.

## Task 2: Enabling Full-Mesh IBGP Within Your Pod (AS)

Complete the following steps:

**Step 1**  Configure the pxr1, pxr2, and pxr3 routers within your pod to provide full-mesh IBGP connectivity. To have a full-mesh IBGP, the following must be true:

pxr1 should have three IBGP neighbor configuration statements. List them.

p*x*r2 should have three IBGP neighbor configuration statements. List them.

p*x*r3 should have two IBGP neighbor configuration statements. List them.

At your p*x*r2 and p*x*r3 router, enter the **network** command to allow advertisement of the 192.168.*x*.64/28 prefix.

At your p*x*r1 router, enter the **show ip bgp** command. Do you see multiple paths to your 192.168.*x*.64/28 subnet? (Note that it may take a while for the routes to appear.)

At your p*x*r1 router, ping 192.168.*x*.65 and 192.168.*x*.66.

Were the pings successful? Why or why not?

(Hint: At your p*x*r1 router, look at your IP routing table.)

**Step 2**   Verify that you have full IBGP neighbor relationships between the routers within your pod.

**Step 3**   Issue the **show ip bgp** command on your p*x*r2 and p*x*r3 routers.

Do you see a route to networks 172.16.10.0 and 172.16.11.0?

What is the next hop to reach networks 172.16.10.0 and 172.16.11.0?

**Step 4**   Use the **next-hop-self** option. At your p*x*r1 router, enter the commands to cause p*x*r1 to announce itself as the next-hop router for p*x*r2 and p*x*r3.

**Step 5**   At your p*x*r1 router, enter the **clear ip bgp \*** command to reset all its BGP neighbor relationships. (Note: Use the **clear ip bgp** *address* command to clear the relationship to only a particular neighbor.)

**Step 6**   Issue the **show ip bgp** command again on your p*x*r2 and p*x*r3 routers, and compare this result with the result from Step 3. (Note that it may take a minute or so for the changes to appear.)

Do you see a route to networks 172.16.10.0 and 172.16.11.0?

What is the next hop to reach networks 172.16.10.0 and 172.16.11.0?

**Step 7**   Examine the IP routing table of p*x*r2 and p*x*r3. Do you see any BGP routes? Please explain your answer.

**Step 8**   Disable BGP synchronization.

On your p*x*r1, p*x*r2, and p*x*r3 routers, enter the command to disable BGP synchronization.

At your p*x*r1 router, enter the **clear ip bgp \*** command to reset all its BGP neighbor relationships.

**Step 9**    Examine the IP routing table of p*x*r2 and p*x*r3.

Do you see a BGP route to 172.16.10.0 and 172.16.11.0 now?

**Step 10**    From your p*x*r2 and p*x*r3 routers, ping 172.16.10.100 and 172.16.11.100.

Were the pings successful?

**Step 11**    Telnet to the backbone_r1 router, using the password cisco. Display its routing table. Do you see the 192.168.*x*.0/24 and the 192.168.*x*.64/28 routes?

Do not continue to the next step if your answer is no. If your answer is no, review and correct your configuration. You can refer to the answers at the end of this exercise, if necessary.

**Step 12**    Exit the Telnet to the backbone_r1 router.

**Step 13**    Enable route aggregation.

At your p*x*r1 router, enter the BGP command to allow only the 192.168.*x*.0/24 route to appear in the backbone_r1 router.

**Step 14**    At your p*x*r1 router, enter the **show ip bgp** command. Is the IBGP route 192.168.*x*.64/28 being suppressed by performing Step 13?

At your p*x*r1 router, ping 192.168.*x*.65 and 192.168.*x*.66.

Were the pings successful?

**Step 15**    Telnet to the backbone_r1 router, using the password cisco. Display its routing table. Do you still see both the 192.168.*x*.0/24 and 192.168.*x*.64/28 routes?

From the backbone_r1 router, ping the router interfaces in your 192.168.*x*.64/28 subnet.

Were the pings successful?

**Step 16**    Exit the Telnet to the backbone_r1 router.

**Step 17**    Save the current configurations of all the routers within your pod to NVRAM.

## Bonus Questions

1    What is the administrative distance for IBGP routes?

2    What is the administrative distance for EBGP routes?

3    If the next hop to a route is inaccessible, will BGP publish the route in the routing table?

## Completion Criteria

You have successfully completed this configuration exercise if you correctly supplied the commands required to configure EBGP from your pod to the backbone_r1 router and to configure IBGP within your pod, and if you were able to correctly answer the questions in the exercises. At the end of this exercise, all the routers should have full connectivity to each other; each pod will be running IBGP internally and will have EBGP connectivity to the backbone router.

# Answers to Configuration Exercise: Configuring BGP

This section provides the answers to the questions in the Configuration Exercise. The answers are in **bold**.

## Answers to Setup

**Step 1**   On your p*x*r1 router, disable Frame Relay switching. Change the p*x*r1 Serial 0 and Serial 2 interfaces back to running HDLC encapsulation.

Ensure that the p*x*r1 serial interfaces S0, S1, S2, and S3 have the correct IP address configuration, as follows:

| | |
|---|---|
| p*x*r1 S0 | 192.168.*x*.17/28 |
| p*x*r1 S1 | 192.168.*x*.33/28 |
| p*x*r1 S2 | 192.168.*x*.49/28 |
| p*x*r1 S3 | 10.*x.x.x*/24 |

No shut the Serial 1 and Serial 3 interfaces on your p*x*r1 router.

**The following shows how to perform the required setup on the p1r1 router. The router output as a result of this configuration is also displayed.**

```
p1r1#conf t
Enter configuration commands, one per line.  End with CNTL/Z.
p1r1(config)#no frame-relay switching
p1r1(config)#int s0
p1r1(config-if)#encapsulation hdlc
04:15:11: %LINEPROTO-5-UPDOWN: Line protocol on Interface Serial0,
changed state to down
04:15:12: %LINK-3-UPDOWN: Interface Serial0, changed state to up
04:15:13: %LINEPROTO-5-UPDOWN: Line protocol on Interface Serial0,
changed state to up
04:15:16: %FR-5-DLCICHANGE: Interface Serial2
- DLCI 302 state changed to INACTIVE
p1r1(config-if)#ip address 192.168.1.17 255.255.255.240
p1r1(config-if)#int s2
04:15:27: %LINEPROTO-5-UPDOWN: Line protocol on Interface Serial2,
changed state to down
```

```
p1r1(config-if)#encapsulation hdlc
04:15:40: %LINEPROTO-5-UPDOWN: Line protocol on Interface Serial0,
changed state to down
p1r1(config-if)#ip address 192.168.1.49 255.255.255.240
p1r1(config-if)#int s1
p1r1(config-if)#no shutdown
04:16:03: %LINK-3-UPDOWN: Interface Serial1, changed state to down
p1r1(config-if)#int s3
p1r1(config-if)#no shutdown
04:16:13: %LINK-3-UPDOWN: Interface Serial3, changed state to up
04:16:14: %LINEPROTO-5-UPDOWN: Line protocol on Interface Serial3,
changed state to up
```

**Step 2**   On your p*xr*2 router, disable EIGRP. Shut down the Serial 0 interface
on your p*xr*2 router. Change the p*xr*2 Serial 0 interface encapsulation
back to HDLC. Reconfigure the IP address on your p*xr*2 Serial 0 to
192.168.*x*.18/28.

No shut the Ethernet 0, Serial 0, and Serial 1 interfaces on your p*xr*2
router.

**The following shows how to perform the required setup on the p1r2 router.
The router output as a result of this configuration is also displayed.**

```
p1r2#conf t
Enter configuration commands, one per line.  End with CNTL/Z.
p1r2(config)#no router eigrp 200
p1r2(config)#int s0
p1r2(config-if)#shutdown
04:17:56: %LINK-5-CHANGED: Interface Serial0, changed state to
administratively down
p1r2(config-if)#encapsulation hdlc
p1r2(config-if)#ip address 192.168.1.18 255.255.255.240
p1r2(config-if)#no shutdown
04:18:26: %LINK-3-UPDOWN: Interface Serial0, changed state to up
04:18:27: %LINEPROTO-5-UPDOWN: Line protocol on Interface Serial0,
changed state to up
p1r2(config-if)#int e0
p1r2(config-if)#no shutdown
04:18:34: %LINK-3-UPDOWN: Interface Ethernet0, changed state to up
04:18:35: %LINEPROTO-5-UPDOWN: Line protocol on Interface Ethernet0,
changed state to up
p1r2(config-if)#int s1
p1r2(config-if)#no shutdown
04:18:42: %LINK-3-UPDOWN: Interface Serial1, changed state to up
p1r2(config-if)#
04:18:43: %LINEPROTO-5-UPDOWN: Line protocol on Interface Serial1,

changed state to up
```

**Step 3**   On your p*xr*3 router, disable EIGRP. Shut down the Serial 0 interface
on your p*xr*3 router. Change the p*xr*3 Serial 0 interface encapsulation
back to HDLC. Reconfigure the IP address on your p*xr*3 Serial 0 to
192.168.*x*.50/28.

No shut the Ethernet 0 and Serial 0 interfaces on your p*xr*3 router.

The following shows how to perform the required setup on the p1r2 router.
The router output as a result of this configuration is also displayed.

```
p1r3#conf t
Enter configuration commands, one per line.  End with CNTL/Z.
p1r3(config)#no router eigrp 200
p1r3(config)#int s0
p1r3(config-if)#shutdown
04:19:19: %LINK-5-CHANGED: Interface Serial0, changed state to
administratively down
p1r3(config-if)#encapsulation hdlc
p1r3(config-if)#ip address 192.168.1.50 255.255.255.240
p1r3(config-if)#no shutdown
04:19:42: %LINK-3-UPDOWN: Interface Serial0, changed state to up
04:19:43: %LINEPROTO-5-UPDOWN: Line protocol on Interface Serial0,
changed state to up
p1r3(config-if)#int e0
p1r3(config-if)#no shutdown
04:19:53: %LINK-3-UPDOWN: Interface Ethernet0, changed state to up
04:19:54: %LINEPROTO-5-UPDOWN: Line protocol on Interface Ethernet0,
changed state to up
```

## Answers to Task 1: Enabling EBGP

Complete the following steps:

**Step 1**    At your p*x*r1 router, enable BGP using the AS number in Table 6-11.

**Table 6-11**    *Autonomous System Numbers to Configure on Routers in Pod x*

| Pod | AS Number |
| --- | --- |
| 1 | 65101 |
| 2 | 65102 |
| 3 | 65103 |
| 4 | 65104 |
| 5 | 65105 |
| 6 | 65106 |
| 7 | 65107 |
| 8 | 65108 |
| 9 | 65109 |
| 10 | 65110 |
| 11 | 65111 |
| 12 | 65112 |

**NOTE**    The backbone_r1 router is in AS 65200.

**The following shows how to enable BGP on the p1r1 router:**

```
p1r1#conf t
Enter configuration commands, one per line.  End with CNTL/Z.
p1r1(config)#router bgp 65101
```

**Step 2**  At your p*x*r1 router, use a **neighbor** statement to establish the backbone_r1 router as an EBGP neighbor.

**The following shows how to establish the backbone_r1 router as an EBGP neighbor of the p1r1 router:**

```
p1r1#conf t
Enter configuration commands, one per line.  End with CNTL/Z.
p1r1(config)#router bgp 65101
p1r1(config-router)#neighbor 10.1.1.100 remote-as 65200
```

**Step 3**  At the p*x*r1 router, use a **network** statement to allow advertisement of the 192.168.*x*.0/24 network to AS 65200 (where *x* is your pod number).

**The following shows how to advertise the required network on the p1r1 router:**

```
p1r1#conf t
Enter configuration commands, one per line.  End with CNTL/Z.
p1r1(config)#router bgp 65101
p1r1(config-router)#network 192.168.1.0 mask 255.255.255.0
```

**Step 4**  At the p*x*r1 router, enter the **show ip bgp summary** and the **show ip bgp neighbors** commands.

What is the neighbor state of the backbone_r1 router?

What is the BGP state of the backbone_r1 router?

What is the BGP version?

**The following output is from the p1r1 router:**

```
p1r1#show ip bgp summary
BGP table version is 4, main routing table version 4
3 network entries and 3 paths using 363 bytes of memory
1 BGP path attribute entries using 96 bytes of memory
BGP activity 3/0 prefixes, 3/0 paths
0 prefixes revised.
```

| Neighbor | V | AS | MsgRcvd | MsgSent | TblVer | InQ | OutQ | Up/Down | State/PfxRcd |
|----------|---|-----|---------|---------|--------|-----|------|----------|--------------|
| 10.1.1.100 | 4 | 65200 | 6 | 3 | 4 | 0 | 0 | 00:00:58 | 3 |

```
p1r1#show ip bgp neighbors
BGP neighbor is 10.1.1.100,  remote AS 65200, external link
  Index 1, Offset 0, Mask 0x2
   BGP version 4, remote router ID 172.16.11.100
```

```
BGP state = Established, table version = 5, up for 00:01:03
 Last read 00:00:04, hold time is 180, keepalive interval is 60 seconds
 Minimum time between advertisement runs is 30 seconds
 Received 7 messages, 0 notifications, 0 in queue
 Sent 5 messages, 0 notifications, 0 in queue
 Prefix advertised 1, suppressed 0, withdrawn 0
 Connections established 1; dropped 0
 Last reset never
 3 accepted prefixes consume 96 bytes
 0 history paths consume 0 bytes
Connection state is ESTAB, I/O status: 1, unread input bytes: 0
Local host: 10.1.1.1, Local port: 179
Foreign host: 10.1.1.100, Foreign port: 11004

<output omitted>
```

In the show ip bgp summary output, the State field is blank, indicating that the neighbor state of the backbone_r1 (10.1.1.100) router is Established; three prefixes have been received from the backbone_r1 router. This command also indicates in the V field that the BGP version is 4.

The show ip bgp neighbors output indicates that the BGP state of the backbone_r1 router is Established.

**Step 5** At the p*x*r1 router, enter the **show ip bgp** command.

List some of the BGP routes that you see. List the following for each route:

— Network

— Next hop

— Metric

— LocPrf

— Weight

— Path

The following output is from p1r1 router, indicating the BGP routes:

```
p1r1#show ip bgp
BGP table version is 5, local router ID is 192.168.1.49
Status codes: s suppressed, d damped, h history, * valid, > best, i - internal
Origin codes: i - IGP, e - EGP, ? - incomplete

   Network          Next Hop            Metric LocPrf Weight Path
*> 10.0.0.0         10.1.1.100               0             0 65200 i
*> 172.16.10.0/24   10.1.1.100               0             0 65200 i
*> 172.16.11.0/24   10.1.1.100               0             0 65200 i
*> 192.168.1.0      0.0.0.0                  0         32768 i
p1r1#
```

**Step 6**   At the p*x*r1 router, enter the **show ip route** command.

List some of the BGP routes that you see.

Notice that at the p*x*r1 router now, you will not see a route to your 192.168.*x*.64/28 subnet in your pod because you have not enabled an IGP routing protocol between the routers within your pod.

**The following output is from p1r1 router, showing all routes known to p1r1, including those learned by BGP:**

```
p1r1#show ip route
<output omitted>

     172.16.0.0/24 is subnetted, 2 subnets
B       172.16.10.0 [20/0] via 10.1.1.100, 00:03:38
B       172.16.11.0 [20/0] via 10.1.1.100, 00:03:38
     10.0.0.0/8 is variably subnetted, 2 subnets, 2 masks
B       10.0.0.0/8 [20/0] via 10.1.1.100, 00:03:39
C       10.1.1.0/24 is directly connected, Serial3
     192.168.1.0/28 is subnetted, 3 subnets
C       192.168.1.32 is directly connected, Serial1
C       192.168.1.48 is directly connected, Serial2
C       192.168.1.16 is directly connected, Serial0
p1r1#
```

**As noted, there is no route to the 192.168.1.64/28 subnet in p1r1's routing table.**

**Step 7**   From your p*x*r1 router, ping 172.16.10.100 and 172.16.11.100.

Were the pings successful?

**The results of the ping command to the loopback interfaces on the backbone_r1 router are shown in the following output. Both pings are successful.**

```
p1r1#ping 172.16.10.100

Type escape sequence to abort.
Sending 5, 100-byte ICMP Echos to 172.16.10.100, timeout is 2 seconds:
!!!!!
Success rate is 100 percent (5/5), round-trip min/avg/max = 32/32/32 ms

p1r1#ping 172.16.11.100

Type escape sequence to abort.
Sending 5, 100-byte ICMP Echos to 172.16.11.100, timeout is 2 seconds:
!!!!!
Success rate is 100 percent (5/5), round-trip min/avg/max = 32/32/32 ms
```

**Step 8**   From your p*x*r1 router, enter the **show ip bgp** command.

If another pod is configured, list the AS path for accessing your neighbor pod.

**Pod 2 is configured, up to the same point as pod 1 in the Configuration Exercise. The following output is from the p1r1 router:**

```
p1r1#show ip bgp
BGP table version is 6, local router ID is 192.168.1.49
Status codes: s suppressed, d damped, h history, * valid, > best, i - internal
Origin codes: i - IGP, e - EGP, ? - incomplete

   Network          Next Hop         Metric LocPrf Weight Path
*> 10.0.0.0         10.1.1.100            0             0 65200 i
*> 172.16.10.0/24   10.1.1.100            0             0 65200 i
*> 172.16.11.0/24   10.1.1.100            0             0 65200 i
*> 192.168.1.0      0.0.0.0              0         32768 i
*> 192.168.2.0      10.1.1.100                         0 65200 65102 i
p1r1#
```

**From this output, the AS path for accessing the pod 2 network, 192.168.2.0, is {65200, 65102}.**

**Step 9** Save the current configurations of all the routers within your pod to NVRAM.

**The following shows how to save the configuration of the p1r1 router, using the copy run start command (this is an abbreviated form of the copy running-config startup-config command):**

```
p1r1#copy run start
Destination filename [startup-config]?
Building configuration...
```

# Answers to Task 2: Enabling Full-Mesh IBGP Within Your Pod (AS)

Complete the following steps:

**Step 1** Configure the p*x*r1, p*x*r2, and p*x*r3 routers within your pod to provide full-mesh IBGP connectivity. To have a full-mesh IBGP, the following must be true:

p*x*r1 should have three IBGP neighbor configuration statements. List them.

**The following shows the configuration of the IBGP neighbors on the p1r1 router:**

```
p1r1#conf t
Enter configuration commands, one per line.  End with CNTL/Z.
p1r1(config)#router bgp 65101
p1r1(config-router)#neighbor 192.168.1.18 remote-as 65101
p1r1(config-router)#neighbor 192.168.1.34 remote-as 65101
p1r1(config-router)#neighbor 192.168.1.50 remote-as 65101
```

p*x*r2 should have three IBGP neighbor configuration statements. List them.

**The following shows the configuration of the IBGP neighbors on the p1r2 router:**

```
p1r2#conf t
Enter configuration commands, one per line.  End with CNTL/Z.
p1r2(config)#router bgp 65101
p1r2(config-router)#neighbor 192.168.1.17 remote-as 65101
p1r2(config-router)#neighbor 192.168.1.33 remote-as 65101
p1r2(config-router)#neighbor 192.168.1.66 remote-as 65101
```

p*x*r3 should have two IBGP neighbor configuration statements. List them.

**The following shows the configuration of the IBGP neighbors on the p1r3 router:**

```
p1r3#conf t
Enter configuration commands, one per line.  End with CNTL/Z.
p1r3(config)#router bgp 65101
p1r3(config-router)#neighbor 192.168.1.49 remote-as 65101
p1r3(config-router)#neighbor 192.168.1.65 remote-as 65101
```

At your p*x*r2 and p*x*r3 routers, enter the **network** command to allow advertisement of the 192.168.*x*.64/28 prefix.

**The following shows the configuration of the network command on the p1r2 and p1r3 routers:**

```
p1r2#conf t
Enter configuration commands, one per line.  End with CNTL/Z.
p1r2(config)#router bgp 65101
p1r2(config-router)#network 192.168.1.64 mask 255.255.255.240

p1r3#conf t
Enter configuration commands, one per line.  End with CNTL/Z.
p1r3(config)#router bgp 65101
p1r3(config-router)#network 192.168.1.64 mask 255.255.255.240
```

At your p*x*r1 router, enter the **show ip bgp** command. Do you see multiple paths to your 192.168.*x*.64/28 subnet? (Note that it may take a while for the routes to appear.)

**The following shows the show ip bgp output on the p1r1 router:**

```
p1r1#show ip bgp
BGP table version is 6, local router ID is 192.168.1.49
Status codes: s suppressed, d damped, h history, * valid, > best, i - internal
Origin codes: i - IGP, e - EGP, ? - incomplete

   Network          Next Hop          Metric LocPrf Weight Path
*> 10.0.0.0         10.1.1.100             0             0 65200 i
*> 172.16.10.0/24   10.1.1.100             0             0 65200 i
```

```
*> 172.16.11.0/24   10.1.1.100              0               0 65200 i
*> 192.168.1.0      0.0.0.0                 0           32768 i
* i192.168.1.64/28  192.168.1.34            0     100     0 i
* i                 192.168.1.18            0     100     0 i
* i                 192.168.1.50            0     100     0 i
*> 192.168.2.0      10.1.1.100                              0 65200 65102 i
p1r1#
```

From this output, you can see that there are three paths to the 192.168.1.64/28 subnet in the BGP table.

At your pxr1 router, ping 192.168.x.65 and 192.168.x.66.

Were the pings successful? Why or why not?

(Hint: At your pxr1 router, look at your IP routing table.)

The following shows the use of the ping command on the p1r1 router:

```
p1r1#ping 192.168.1.65

Type escape sequence to abort.
Sending 5, 100-byte ICMP Echos to 192.168.1.65, timeout is 2 seconds:
.....
Success rate is 0 percent (0/5)

p1r1#ping 192.168.1.66

Type escape sequence to abort.
Sending 5, 100-byte ICMP Echos to 192.168.1.66, timeout is 2 seconds:
.....
Success rate is 0 percent (0/5)
```

The pings were not successful. From the routing table that follows, you can see that the p1r1 router does not have a route to the 192.168.1.64/28 subnet in its routing table, even though it has multiple routes in its BGP table.

```
p1r1#show ip route
<output omitted>
     172.16.0.0/24 is subnetted, 2 subnets
B       172.16.10.0 [20/0] via 10.1.1.100, 02:27:32
B       172.16.11.0 [20/0] via 10.1.1.100, 02:27:32
     10.0.0.0/8 is variably subnetted, 2 subnets, 2 masks
B       10.0.0.0/8 [20/0] via 10.1.1.100, 02:27:32
C       10.1.1.0/24 is directly connected, Serial3
     192.168.1.0/28 is subnetted, 3 subnets
C       192.168.1.32 is directly connected, Serial1
C       192.168.1.48 is directly connected, Serial2
C       192.168.1.16 is directly connected, Serial0
B    192.168.2.0/24 [20/0] via 10.1.1.100, 00:17:30
p1r1#
```

Step 2   Verify you have full IBGP neighbor relationships between the routers within your pod.

The following shows the results of the show ip bgp summary command on the p1r1 router. From this output, you can see that p1r1 has a full IBGP

**relationship with p1r2 (192.168.1.18 and 192.168.1.34) and p1r3 (192.168.1.50).**

```
p1r1#show ip bgp summary
BGP table version is 6, main routing table version 6
6 network entries and 8 paths using 790 bytes of memory
4 BGP path attribute entries using 436 bytes of memory
BGP activity 6/0 prefixes, 8/0 paths
0 prefixes revised.

Neighbor        V     AS MsgRcvd MsgSent  TblVer  InQ OutQ Up/Down  State/PfxRcd
10.1.1.100      4 65200     155     152       6    0    0 02:28:08       4
192.168.1.18    4 65101       9      11       6    0    0 00:05:49       1
192.168.1.34    4 65101       9      11       6    0    0 00:05:40       1
192.168.1.50    4 65101       9      11       6    0    0 00:05:07       1
p1r1#
```

**Step 3**  Issue the **show ip bgp** command on your p*x*r2 and p*x*r3 routers.

Do you see a route to networks 172.16.10.0 and 172.16.11.0?

What is the next hop to reach networks 172.16.10.0 and 172.16.11.0?

**The following shows the output from the show ip bgp command on the p1r2 and p1r3 routers. From this output, you can see that both routers have routes to 172.16.10.0 and 172.16.11.0, with a next-hop address of 10.1.1.100.**

```
p1r2#show ip bgp
BGP table version is 6, local router ID is 192.168.101.101
Status codes: s suppressed, d damped, h history, * valid, > best, i - internal
Origin codes: i - IGP, e - EGP, ? - incomplete

   Network          Next Hop         Metric LocPrf Weight Path
* i10.0.0.0         10.1.1.100            0    100      0 65200 i
* i                 10.1.1.100            0    100      0 65200 i
* i172.16.10.0/24   10.1.1.100            0    100      0 65200 i
* i                 10.1.1.100            0    100      0 65200 i
* i172.16.11.0/24   10.1.1.100            0    100      0 65200 i
* i                 10.1.1.100            0    100      0 65200 i
* i192.168.1.0      192.168.1.17          0    100      0 i
* i                 192.168.1.33          0    100      0 i
* i192.168.2.0      10.1.1.100                 100      0 65200 65102 i
* i                 10.1.1.100                 100      0 65200 65102 i
p1r2#

p1r3#show ip bgp
BGP table version is 3, local router ID is 172.26.1.49
Status codes: s suppressed, d damped, h history, * valid, > best, i - internal
Origin codes: i - IGP, e - EGP, ? - incomplete

   Network          Next Hop         Metric LocPrf Weight Path
* i10.0.0.0         10.1.1.100            0    100      0 65200 i
* i172.16.10.0/24   10.1.1.100            0    100      0 65200 i
* i172.16.11.0/24   10.1.1.100            0    100      0 65200 i
* i192.168.1.0      192.168.1.49          0    100      0 i
```

```
*> 192.168.1.64/28  0.0.0.0                    0            32768 i
*  i192.168.2.0      10.1.1.100                        100      0 65200 65102 i
p1r3#
```

**Step 4**   Use the **next-hop-self** option. At your pxr1 router, enter the commands
to cause pxr1 to announce itself as the next-hop router for pxr2 and pxr3.

**The following shows the configuration of the p1r1 router to announce itself as
the next-hop router for p1r2 and p1r3:**

```
p1r1#conf t
Enter configuration commands, one per line.  End with CNTL/Z.
p1r1(config)#router bgp 65101
p1r1(config-router)#neighbor 192.168.1.18 next-hop-self
p1r1(config-router)#neighbor 192.168.1.34 next-hop-self
p1r1(config-router)#neighbor 192.168.1.50 next-hop-self
```

**Step 5**   At your pxr1 router, enter the **clear ip bgp *** command to reset all its BGP
neighbor relationships. (Note: Use the **clear ip bgp** *address* command to
clear the relationship to only a particular neighbor.)

**The following shows the use of the clear ip bgp * command on the p1r1
router:**

```
p1r1#clear ip bgp *
p1r1#
```

**Step 6**   Issue the **show ip bgp** command again on your pxr2 and pxr3 routers, and
compare this result with the result from Step 3. (Note that it may take a
minute or so for the changes to appear.)

Do you see a route to networks 172.16.10.0 and 172.16.11.0?

What is the next hop to reach networks 172.16.10.0 and 172.16.11.0?

**The following shows the output from the show ip bgp command on the p1r2
router. From this output, you can see that p1r2 has routes to 172.16.10.0 and
172.16.11.0, with next-hop addresses of 192.168.1.17 and 192.168.1.33, which
are the p1r1 router's addresses. p1r3 has similar routes in its BGP table.**

```
p1r2#show ip bgp
BGP table version is 9, local router ID is 192.168.101.101
Status codes: s suppressed, d damped, h history, * valid, > best, i - internal
Origin codes: i - IGP, e - EGP, ? - incomplete

   Network          Next Hop         Metric LocPrf Weight Path
*  i10.0.0.0         192.168.1.33          0    100      0 65200 i
*  i                 192.168.1.17          0    100      0 65200 i
*  i172.16.10.0/24   192.168.1.17          0    100      0 65200 i
*  i                 192.168.1.33          0    100      0 65200 i
*  i172.16.11.0/24   192.168.1.17          0    100      0 65200 i
*  i                 192.168.1.33          0    100      0 65200 i
*  i192.168.1.0      192.168.1.17          0    100      0 i
```

```
*  i                     192.168.1.33            0    100     0 i
*> 192.168.1.64/28  0.0.0.0                 0           32768 i
*  i192.168.2.0      192.168.1.17                 100     0 65200 65102 i
*  i                     192.168.1.33                 100     0 65200 65102 i
p1r2#
```

**Step 7**    Examine the IP routing table of p*x*r2 and p*x*r3. Do you see any BGP routes? Please explain your answer.

**The following shows the output from the show ip route command on the p1r2 and p1r3 routers. From this output, you can see that neither router has any BGP routes. Even though the routers have learned BGP information and put it in their BGP tables, the routes will not be used in the routing table because although BGP synchronization is on in the pod, there is no IGP running.**

```
p1r2#show ip route
<output omitted>

     192.168.1.0/28 is subnetted, 3 subnets
C       192.168.1.64 is directly connected, Ethernet0
C       192.168.1.32 is directly connected, Serial1
C       192.168.1.16 is directly connected, Serial0
C    192.168.101.0/24 is directly connected, Loopback10
p1r2#

p1r3#show ip route
<output omitted>
     172.26.0.0/28 is subnetted, 3 subnets
C       172.26.1.48 is directly connected, Loopback13
C       172.26.1.32 is directly connected, Loopback12
C       172.26.1.16 is directly connected, Loopback11
     192.168.1.0/28 is subnetted, 2 subnets
C       192.168.1.64 is directly connected, Ethernet0
C       192.168.1.48 is directly connected, Serial0
p1r3#
```

**Step 8**    Disable BGP synchronization.

On your p*x*r1, p*x*r2, and p*x*r3 routers, enter the command to disable BGP synchronization.

At your p*x*r1 router, enter the **clear ip bgp \*** command to reset all its BGP neighbor relationships.

**The following shows the configuration of the p1r1 router to disable BGP synchronization, and the use of the clear ip bgp \* command on that router. The same commands would be entered on the p1r2 and p1r3 routers.**

```
p1r1#conf t
Enter configuration commands, one per line.  End with CNTL/Z.
p1r1(config)#router bgp 65101
p1r1(config-router)#no synchronization

p1r1#clear ip bgp *
p1r1#
```

**Step 9**  Examine the IP routing table of p*x*r2 and p*x*r3.

Do you see a BGP route to 172.16.10.0 and 172.16.11.0 now?

**The following shows the p1r2 and p1r3 routing tables. From this output, you can see BGP routes to the 172.16.10.0 and 172.16.11.0 subnets.**

```
p1r2#show ip route
<output omitted>
     172.16.0.0/24 is subnetted, 2 subnets
B       172.16.10.0 [200/0] via 192.168.1.17, 00:00:11
B       172.16.11.0 [200/0] via 192.168.1.17, 00:00:11
B    10.0.0.0/8 [200/0] via 192.168.1.17, 00:00:11
     192.168.1.0/28 is subnetted, 3 subnets
C       192.168.1.64 is directly connected, Ethernet0
C       192.168.1.32 is directly connected, Serial1
C       192.168.1.16 is directly connected, Serial0
B    192.168.2.0/24 [200/0] via 192.168.1.17, 00:00:12
C    192.168.101.0/24 is directly connected, Loopback10
p1r2#

p1r3#show ip route
<output omitted>
     172.16.0.0/24 is subnetted, 2 subnets
B       172.16.10.0 [200/0] via 192.168.1.49, 00:00:19
B       172.16.11.0 [200/0] via 192.168.1.49, 00:00:20
     172.26.0.0/28 is subnetted, 3 subnets
C       172.26.1.48 is directly connected, Loopback13
C       172.26.1.32 is directly connected, Loopback12
C       172.26.1.16 is directly connected, Loopback11
B    10.0.0.0/8 [200/0] via 192.168.1.49, 00:00:20
     192.168.1.0/28 is subnetted, 2 subnets
C       192.168.1.64 is directly connected, Ethernet0
C       192.168.1.48 is directly connected, Serial0
B    192.168.2.0/24 [200/0] via 192.168.1.49, 00:00:20
p1r3#
```

**Step 10**  From your p*x*r2 and p*x*r3 routers, ping 172.16.10.100 and 172.16.11.100.

Were the pings successful?

**The following shows the use of the ping command on the p1r2 and p1r3 routers. The pings are all successful.**

```
p1r2#ping 172.16.10.100

Type escape sequence to abort.
Sending 5, 100-byte ICMP Echos to 172.16.10.100, timeout is 2 seconds:
!!!!!
Success rate is 100 percent (5/5), round-trip min/avg/max = 56/60/64 ms

p1r2#ping 172.16.11.100

Type escape sequence to abort.
Sending 5, 100-byte ICMP Echos to 172.16.11.100, timeout is 2 seconds:
```

```
!!!!!
Success rate is 100 percent (5/5), round-trip min/avg/max = 56/58/64 ms
p1r2#

p1r3#ping 172.16.10.100

Type escape sequence to abort.
Sending 5, 100-byte ICMP Echos to 172.16.10.100, timeout is 2 seconds:
!!!!!
Success rate is 100 percent (5/5), round-trip min/avg/max = 60/60/60 ms

p1r3#ping 172.16.11.100

Type escape sequence to abort.
Sending 5, 100-byte ICMP Echos to 172.16.11.100, timeout is 2 seconds:
!!!!!
Success rate is 100 percent (5/5), round-trip min/avg/max = 60/60/60 ms
p1r3#
```

**Step 11**  Telnet to the backbone_r1 router, using the password cisco. Display its routing table. Do you see the 192.168.x.0/24 and 192.168.x.64/28 routes?

Do not continue to the next step if your answer is no. If your answer is no, review and correct your configuration. You can refer to the answers at the end of this exercise, if necessary.

**The following shows the routing table of the backbone_r1 router. From this output, you can see routes to 192.168.1.0/24 and 192.168.1.64/28.**

```
p1r3#bbr1
Trying bbr1 (10.1.1.100)... Open


User Access Verification

Password:
backbone_r1>show ip route
<output omitted>
     172.16.0.0/24 is subnetted, 2 subnets
C       172.16.10.0 is directly connected, Loopback100
C       172.16.11.0 is directly connected, Loopback101
     10.0.0.0/24 is subnetted, 2 subnets
C       10.2.2.0 is directly connected, Serial1/1
C       10.1.1.0 is directly connected, Serial1/0
     192.168.1.0/24 is variably subnetted, 2 subnets, 2 masks
B       192.168.1.64/28 [20/0] via 10.1.1.1, 00:02:08
B       192.168.1.0/24 [20/0] via 10.1.1.1, 00:01:14
B    192.168.2.0/24 [20/0] via 10.2.2.2, 00:38:02
backbone_r1>
```

**Step 12**  Exit the Telnet to the backbone_r1 router.

**The following shows how to exit from the backbone_r1 Telnet session.**

```
backbone_r1>exit
```

```
[Connection to bbr1 closed by foreign host]
p1r3#
```

**Step 13** Enable route aggregation.

At your p*x*r1 router, enter the BGP command to allow only the
192.168.*x*.0/24 route to appear in the backbone_r1 router.

**The following shows the route aggregation configuration on the p1r1 router
to allow only the 192.168.1.0/24 route to appear in the backbone_r1 router.**

```
p1r1#conf t
Enter configuration commands, one per line.  End with CNTL/Z.
p1r1(config)#router bgp 65101
p1r1(config-router)#aggregate-address 192.168.1.0 255.255.255.0 summary-only
```

**Step 14** At your p*x*r1 router, enter the **show ip bgp** command. Is the IBGP route
192.168.*x*.64/28 being suppressed by performing Step 13?

**The following shows the BGP table of the p1r1 router. From this output, you
can see that the routes to 192.168.1.64/28 are being suppressed (indicated by
an "s" in the first column of the table beside these routes).**

```
p1r1#show ip bgp
BGP table version is 8, local router ID is 192.168.1.49
Status codes: s suppressed, d damped, h history, * valid, > best, i - internal
Origin codes: i - IGP, e - EGP, ? - incomplete

   Network          Next Hop         Metric LocPrf Weight Path
*> 10.0.0.0         10.1.1.100            0             0 65200 i
*> 172.16.10.0/24   10.1.1.100            0             0 65200 i
*> 172.16.11.0/24   10.1.1.100            0             0 65200 i
*  192.168.1.0      0.0.0.0                         32768 i
*>                  0.0.0.0               0         32768 i
s i192.168.1.64/28  192.168.1.34          0    100     0 i
s i                 192.168.1.18          0    100     0 i
s>i                 192.168.1.50          0    100     0 i
*> 192.168.2.0      10.1.1.100                        0 65200 65102 i
p1r1#
```

At your p*x*r1 router, ping 192.168.*x*.65 and 192.168.*x*.66.

Were the pings successful?

**The following shows the use of the ping command on the p1r1 router. The
pings are successful.**

```
p1r1#ping 192.168.1.65

Type escape sequence to abort.
Sending 5, 100-byte ICMP Echos to 192.168.1.65, timeout is 2 seconds:
```

```
!!!!!
Success rate is 100 percent (5/5), round-trip min/avg/max = 28/32/36 ms

p1r1#ping 192.168.1.66

Type escape sequence to abort.
Sending 5, 100-byte ICMP Echos to 192.168.1.66, timeout is 2 seconds:
!!!!!
Success rate is 100 percent (5/5), round-trip min/avg/max = 32/32/32 ms
p1r1#
```

**Step 15**  Telnet to the backbone_r1 router, using the password cisco. Display its
routing table. Do you still see both the 192.168.x.0/24 and 192.168.x.64/
28 routes?

**The following shows the routing table of the backbone_r1 router. From this
output, you can see a route to 192.168.1.0/24, but the route to 192.168.1.64/28
is no longer there.**

```
p1r1#bbr1
Trying bbr1 (10.1.1.100)... Open


User Access Verification

Password:
backbone_r1>show ip route
<output omitted>
172.16.0.0/24 is subnetted, 2 subnets
C        172.16.10.0 is directly connected, Loopback100
C        172.16.11.0 is directly connected, Loopback101
     10.0.0.0/24 is subnetted, 2 subnets
C        10.2.2.0 is directly connected, Serial1/1
C        10.1.1.0 is directly connected, Serial1/0
B     192.168.1.0/24 [20/0] via 10.1.1.1, 00:04:28
B     192.168.2.0/24 [20/0] via 10.2.2.2, 00:41:16
backbone_r1>
```

From the backbone_r1 router, ping the router interfaces in your
192.168.x.64/28 subnet.

Were the pings successful?

**The following shows the use of the ping command on the backbone_r1 router.
The pings are successful.**

```
backbone_r1>ping 192.168.1.65

Type escape sequence to abort.
Sending 5, 100-byte ICMP Echos to 192.168.1.65, timeout is 2 seconds:
!!!!!
Success rate is 100 percent (5/5), round-trip min/avg/max = 64/78/132 ms

backbone_r1>ping 192.168.1.66
```

```
Type escape sequence to abort.
Sending 5, 100-byte ICMP Echos to 192.168.1.66, timeout is 2 seconds:
!!!!!
Success rate is 100 percent (5/5), round-trip min/avg/max = 64/70/88 ms
backbone_r1>
```

**Step 16** Exit the Telnet to the backbone_r1 router.

**The following shows how to exit from the backbone_r1 telnet session.**

```
backbone_r1>exit

[Connection to bbr1 closed by foreign host]
p1r1#
```

**Step 17** Save the current configurations of all the routers within your pod to NVRAM.

**The following shows how to save the configuration of the p1r1 router, using the copy run start command (this is an abbreviated form of the copy running-config startup-config command):**

```
p1r1#copy run start
Destination filename [startup-config]?
Building configuration...
p1r1#
```

# Answers to Bonus Questions

**1** What is the administrative distance for IBGP routes?

**The administrative distance for IBGP routes is 200.**

**2** What is the administrative distance for EBGP routes?

**The administrative distance for EBGP routes is 20.**

**3** If the next hop to a route is inaccessible, will BGP publish the route in the routing table?

**No.**

# Review Questions

Answer the following questions, and then refer to Appendix G, "Answers to the Review Questions," for the answers.

**1** When would it be appropriate to use static routes to interconnect autonomous systems?

**2** What protocol does BGP use as its transport protocol? What port number does BGP use?

**3** Any two routers that have formed a BGP connection can be referred to as what two terms?

**4** Write a brief description of the following:

— Internal BGP

— External BGP

— Well-known attributes

— Transitive attributes

— BGP synchronization

**5** For an external update advertised by IBGP, where does the value for the next-hop attribute of an update come from?

**6** Describe the complication that an NBMA network can cause for the next-hop attribute of an update.

**7** Complete the table to answer the following questions about these BGP attributes:

— In which order are the attributes preferred (1, 2, or 3)?

— For the attribute, is the highest or lowest value preferred?

— Which other routers, if any, is the attribute sent to?

| Attribute | Order Preferred In | Highest or Lowest Value Preferred? | Sent to Which Other Routers? |
|---|---|---|---|
| Local Preference | | | |
| MED | | | |
| Weight | | | |

**8** How is the BGP router ID chosen?

**9** What command disables BGP synchronization?

**10** What are the four BGP message types?

**11** How does BGP-4 support CIDR?

**12** Which command is used to activate a BGP session with another router?

**13** Which command is used to display information about the BGP connections to neighbors?

This chapter starts with a discussion of problems that may occur when scaling internal Border Gateway Protocol (IBGP) connections. Various solutions, including route reflectors and policy control using prefix lists, are explained. Connecting an autonomous system (AS) with more than one Border Gateway Protocol (BGP) connection is known as multihoming, and different ways to accomplish this are explored. Configuration of all these BGP features is included in this chapter. This chapter includes the following topics:

- Scalability Problems with IBGP

- Route Reflectors

- Policy Control and Prefix Lists

- Multihoming

- Redistribution with IGPs

- Case Study: Multihomed BGP

- Summary

- Configuration Exercise #1: Configuring BGP Route Reflectors and Prefix List Filtering

- Configuration Exercise #2: Configuring Multihomed BGP

- Answers to Configuration Exercise #1: Configuring BGP Route Reflectors and Prefix List Filtering

- Answers to Configuration Exercise #2: Configuring Multihomed BGP

- Review Questions

# CHAPTER 7

# Implementing BGP in Scalable Networks

At the end of this chapter, you will be able to describe the scalability problems associated with internal BGP, list methods to connect to multiple ISPs using BGP, and describe and configure policy control in BGP using prefix lists. You will be able to explain and configure BGP route reflectors and explain the use of redistribution between BGP and Interior Gateway Protocols (IGPs). Given a set of network requirements, you will be able to configure a multihomed BGP environment and verify proper operation (within described guidelines) of your routers.

## Scalability Problems with IBGP

This section discusses scalability problems with IBGP.

### BGP Split Horizon

Chapter 6, "Configuring Basic Border Gateway Protocol," discusses many BGP concepts, including IBGP and external BGP (EBGP).

Another rule governing IBGP behavior is the BGP split horizon rule. This BGP rule specifies that routes learned via IBGP are never propagated to other IBGP peers. BGP split horizon is illustrated in Figure 7-1. In this figure, Router A learns routes from Router B via IBGP but does not propagate these routes to Router C.

**Figure 7-1**  *The BGP Split Horizon Rule Prevents Router A from Propagating Routes Learned from Router B to Router C*

Similar to the distance vector routing protocol split horizon rule, BGP split horizon is necessary to ensure that routing loops are not started within the AS. The result is that a full mesh of IBGP peers is required within an AS.

As Figure 7-2 illustrates, though, a full mesh of IBGP is not scalable. With only 13 routers, 78 IBGP sessions would need to be maintained. As the number of routers increases, so does the number of sessions required, governed by the following formula, in which $n$ is the number of routers:

$$n(n-1) \div 2$$

**Figure 7-2** *Full-Mesh IBGP Requires Many Sessions and Therefore Is Not Scalable*

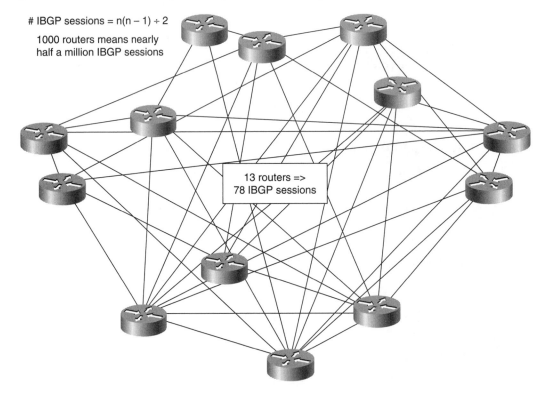

# IBGP sessions = n(n − 1) ÷ 2

1000 routers means nearly half a million IBGP sessions

13 routers => 78 IBGP sessions

In addition to the number of BGP TCP sessions that must be created and maintained, the amount of routing traffic may also be a problem. Depending on the AS topology, traffic may be replicated many times on some links as it travels to each IBGP peer. For example, if the physical topology of a large AS includes some WAN links, the IBGP sessions running over those links may be consuming a significant amount of bandwidth.

A solution to this problem is the use of route reflectors, discussed in the next section.

# Route Reflectors

This section describes what a route reflector is, how it works, and how to configure it.

Route reflectors modify the BGP split horizon rule by allowing the router configured as the route reflector to propagate routes learned by IBGP to other IBGP peers, as illustrated in Figure 7-3.

**Figure 7-3**    *When Router A Is a Route Reflector, It Can Propagate Routes Learned from Router B to Router C*

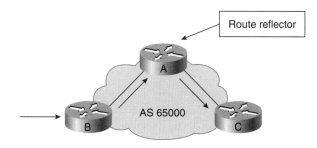

This saves on the number of BGP TCP sessions that must be maintained and also reduces the BGP routing traffic.

## Route Reflector Benefits

With a BGP route reflector configured, a full mesh of IBGP peers is no longer required. The route reflector is allowed to propagate IBGP routes to other IBGP peers. Route reflectors are used mainly by ISPs when the number of internal neighbor statements becomes excessive. Route reflectors reduce the number of BGP neighbor relationships in an AS (thus saving on TCP connections) by having key routers replicate updates to their route reflector clients.

Route reflectors do not affect the paths that IP packets follow; only the path that routing information is distributed on is affected. However, if route reflectors are configured incorrectly, routing loops may result, as shown in the example later in this chapter, in the "Route Reflector Migration Tips" section.

Within an AS there can be multiple route reflectors, both for redundancy and for grouping to further reduce the number of IBGP sessions required.

Migrating to route reflectors involves a minimal configuration and does not have to be done all at once because routers that are not route reflectors can coexist with route reflectors within an AS.

# Route Reflector Terminology

A *route reflector* is a router that is configured to be the router allowed to advertise (or reflect) routes that it learned via IBGP to other IBGP peers. The route reflector will have a partial IBGP peering with other routers, which are called *clients*. Peering between the clients is not needed because the route reflector will pass advertisements between the clients.

The combination of the route reflector and its clients is called a *cluster.*

Other IBGP peers of the route reflector that are not clients are called *nonclients*.

The *originator ID* is an optional, nontransitive BGP attribute that is created by the route reflector. This attribute carries the router ID of the originator of the route in the local AS. If the update comes back to the originator because of poor configuration, the originator ignores it.

Usually a cluster has a single route reflector, in which case the cluster is identified by the router ID of the route reflector. To increase redundancy and avoid single points of failure, a cluster might have more than one route reflector. When this occurs, all the route reflectors in the cluster need to be configured with a *cluster ID*. The cluster ID allows route reflectors to recognize updates from other route reflectors in the same cluster.

---

### Route Reflector Cluster List

A *cluster list* is a sequence of cluster IDs that the route has passed. When a route reflector reflects a route from its clients to nonclients outside the cluster, it appends the local cluster ID to the cluster list. If the update has an empty cluster list, the route reflector will create one. Using this attribute, a route reflector can identify if the routing information is looped back to the same cluster due to poor configuration. If the local cluster ID is found in the cluster list of an advertisement, the advertisement will be ignored.

The originator ID, cluster ID, and cluster list help prevent routing loops in route reflector configurations.

---

# Route Reflector Design

When using route reflectors in an AS, the AS can be divided into multiple clusters, each having at least one route reflector and a few clients. Multiple route reflectors can exist in one cluster for redundancy.

The route reflectors must be fully meshed with IBGP to ensure that all routes learned will be propagated throughout the AS.

An IGP is still used, just as it was before route reflectors were introduced, to carry local routes and next-hop addresses.

## Route Reflector Design Example

Figure 7-4 provides an example of a BGP route reflector design.

**Figure 7-4**    *An Example of a Route Reflector Design*

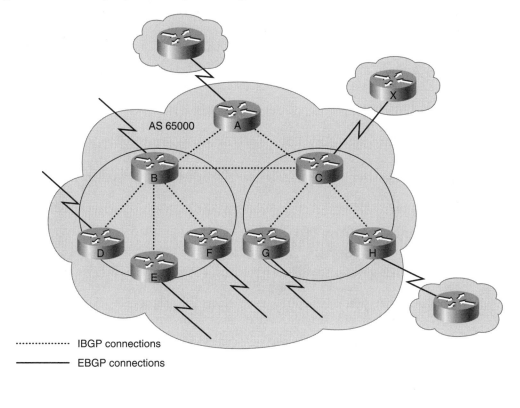

................. IBGP connections
————— EBGP connections

In Figure 7-4, Routers B, D, E, and F form one cluster. Routers C, G, and H form another cluster. Routers B and C are route reflectors. Routers A, B, and C are fully meshed with IBGP. Note that the routers within a cluster are not fully meshed.

## Route Reflector Operation

When a route reflector receives an update, it takes the following actions, depending on the type of peer that sent the update:

- If the update is from a client peer, it sends the update to all nonclient peers and to all client peers (except the originator of the route).
- If the update is from a nonclient peer, it sends the update to all clients in the cluster.
- If the update is from an EBGP peer, it sends the update to all nonclient peers and to all client peers.

For example, in Figure 7-4, the following will happen:

- If Router C receives an update from Router H (a client), it will send it to Router G as well as to routers A and B.
- If Router C receives an update from Router A (a nonclient), it will send it to routers G and H.
- If Router C receives an update from Router X (via EBGP), it will send it to routers G and H as well as to routers A and B.

---

**NOTE**     Routers will also send updatest to their EBGP neighbors, as appropriate.

---

## Route Reflector Migration Tips

When migrating to using route reflectors, the first consideration is which routers should be the reflectors and which should be the clients. Following the physical topology in this design decision will ensure that the packet-forwarding paths will not be affected. Not following the physical topology (for example, configuring route reflector clients that are not physically connected to the route reflector) may result in routing loops.

Figure 7-5 can be used to demonstrate what can happen if route reflectors are configured without following the physical topology. In this figure, the bottom router, Router E, is a route reflector (RR) client for both route reflectors, routers C and D.

In this *bad design*, which does not follow the physical topology, the following will happen:

- Router B would know that the next hop to get to 10.0.0.0 is x (because it would have learned this from its route reflector, Router C).

- Router A would know that the next hop to get to 10.0.0.0 is y (because it would have learned this from its route reflector, Router D).

- For Router B to get to x, the best route may be through Router A, so Router B would send a packet destined for 10.0.0.0 to Router A.

- For Router A to get to y, the best route may be through Router B, so Router A would send a packet destined for 10.0.0.0 to Router B.

- This is a routing loop.

**Figure 7-5**   *A Bad Route Reflector Design*

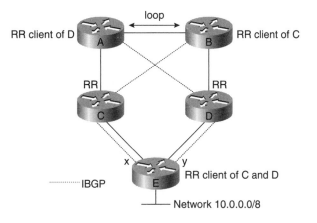

Figure 7-6 shows a better design because it follows the physical topology. Again, in this figure, the bottom router, Router E, is a route reflector client for both route reflectors.

**Figure 7-6**   *A Good Route Reflector Design*

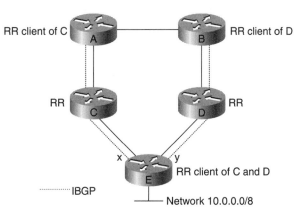

In this *good design*, which does follow the physical topology, the following is true:

- Router B would know that the next hop to get to 10.0.0.0 is y (because it would have learned this from its route reflector, Router D).

- Router A would know that the next hop to get to 10.0.0.0 is x (because it would have learned this from its route reflector, Router C).

- For Router A to get to x, the best route would be through Router C, so Router A w ould send a packet destined for 10.0.0.0 to Router C, and Router C would send it to Router E.

- For Router B to get to y, the best route would be through Router D, so Router B would send a packet destined for 10.0.0.0 to Router D, and Router D would send it to Router E.

- There is not a routing loop.

When migrating to using route reflectors, configure one route reflector at a time, and then delete the redundant IBGP sessions between the clients. It is recommended that you configure one route reflector per cluster.

## Route Reflector Configuration

The **neighbor** *ip-address* **route-reflector-client** router configuration command is used to configure the router as a BGP route reflector and to configure the specified neighbor as its client. This command is described in Table 7-1.

**Table 7-1**    *neighbor route-reflector-client Command Description*

| neighbor route-reflector-client Command | Description |
| --- | --- |
| *ip-address* | IP address of the BGP neighbor being identified as a client |

### Configuring Cluster ID

To configure the cluster ID if the BGP cluster has more than one route reflector, use the **bgp cluster-id** *cluster-id* router configuration command on all the route reflectors in a cluster. You cannot change the cluster ID after the route reflector clients have been configured.

---

### Route Reflector Restrictions

Route reflectors cause some restrictions on other commands, including the following:

- When used on route reflectors, the **neighbor next-hop-self** command will affect only the next hop of EBGP learned routes because the next hop of reflected IBGP routes should not be changed.

- Route reflector clients are not compatible with peer groups. This is because a router configured with a peer group must send any update to *all* members of the peer group. If a route reflector has all its clients in a peer group and then one of these clients sends an update, the route reflector is responsible for sharing that update with all *other* clients. The route reflector must not send the update to the originating client because of the split horizon rule.

---

# Route Reflector Example

The example network in Figure 7-7 illustrates a router configured as a route reflector in AS 65000. The configuration for Router A in this figure is provided in Example 7-1.

**Figure 7-7**    *Router A Is a Route Reflector*

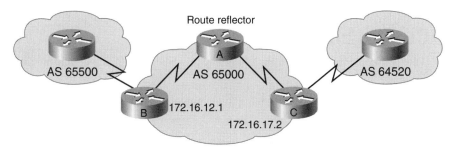

**Example 7-1**    *Configuration of Router A in Figure 7-7*

```
RTRA(config)# router bgp 65000
RTRA(config-router)# neighbor 172.16.12.1 remote-as 65000
RTRA(config-router)# neighbor 172.16.12.1 route-reflector-client
RTRA(config-router)# neighbor 172.16.17.2 remote-as 65000
RTRA(config-router)# neighbor 172.16.17.2 route-reflector-client
```

The **neighbor route-reflector-client** commands are used to configure which neighbors will be route reflector clients. In this example, both routers B and C will be route reflector clients of Router A, the route reflector.

## Verifying Route Reflectors

The **show ip bgp neighbors** command indicates that a particular neighbor is a route reflector client. The example output of this command shown in Example 7-2 is from Router A in the Figure 7-7 and shows that 172.16.12.1 (Router B) is a route reflector client of Router A.

**Example 7-2** *show ip bgp neighbor Output from Router A in Figure 7-7*

```
RTRA#show ip bgp neighbors
BGP neighbor is 172.16.12.1,  remote AS 65000, internal link
 Index 1, Offset 0, Mask 0x2
 Route-Reflector Client
 BGP version 4, remote router ID 192.168.101.101
 BGP state = Established, table version = 1, up for 00:05:42
 Last read 00:00:42, hold time is 180, keepalive interval is 60 seconds
 Minimum time between advertisement runs is 5 seconds
 Received 14 messages, 0 notifications, 0 in queue
 Sent 12 messages, 0 notifications, 0 in queue
 Prefix advertised 0, suppressed 0, withdrawn 0
 Connections established 2; dropped 1
 Last reset 00:05:44, due to User reset
 1 accepted prefixes consume 32 bytes
 0 history paths consume 0 bytes
--More--
```

# Policy Control and Prefix Lists

This section describes how a routing policy is applied to a BGP network using prefix lists.

If you want to restrict the routing information that the Cisco IOS software learns or advertises, you can filter BGP routing updates to and from particular neighbors. To do this, you can define either an access list or a prefix list and then apply it to the updates.

Distribute lists use access lists to specify what routing information is to be filtered. Distribute lists for BGP have been obsoleted by prefix lists in the Cisco IOS.

Prefix lists are available in Cisco IOS Release 12.0 and later.

---

**NOTE**     Distribute lists for BGP are detailed in Appendix A, "Job Aids and Supplements."

---

Figure 7-8 shows an example where prefix lists may be used. In this figure, Router C is advertising network 172.30.0.0 to Router A. If we wanted to stop those updates from propagating to AS 65000 (to Router B), a prefix list could be applied on Router A to filter those updates when Router A is talking to Router B.

# Prefix List Characteristics

Distribute lists make use of access lists to do route filtering. However, access lists were originally designed to do packet filtering.

Prefix lists, available in Cisco IOS Release 12.0 and later, can be used as an alternative to access lists in many BGP route filtering commands. The advantages of using prefix lists include the following:

- A significant performance improvement over access lists in loading and route lookup of large lists.
- Support for incremental modifications. Compared to the normal access list in which one **no** command will erase the whole access list, prefix list entries can be modified incrementally.

**Figure 7-8**    *An Example Where Prefix Lists May Be Used*

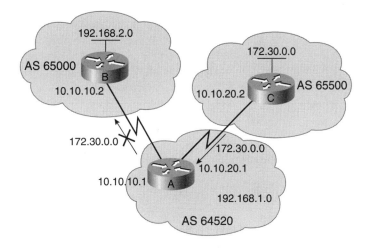

- More user-friendly command-line interface. The command-line interface for using extended access lists to filter BGP updates is difficult to understand and use.
- Greater flexibility.

# Filtering with Prefix Lists

Filtering by prefix list involves matching the prefixes of routes with those listed in the prefix list, similar to using access lists.

Whether a prefix is permitted or denied is based upon the following rules:

- An empty prefix list permits all prefixes.

- If a prefix is permitted, the route is used. If a prefix is denied, the route is not used.

- Prefix lists consist of statements with sequence numbers. The router begins the search for a match at the top of the prefix list, which is the statement with the lowest sequence number.

- When a match occurs, the router does not need to go through the rest of the prefix list. For efficiency, you may want to put the most common matches (permits or denies) near the top of the list by specifying a lower sequence number.

- An implicit deny is assumed if a given prefix does not match any entries of a prefix list.

## Configuring Prefix Lists

| | |
|---|---|
| **NOTE** | Most of the **prefix-list** commands are *not* documented in the Cisco IOS Command Reference manuals for Release 12.0. The only published documentation is in the *BGP Configuration Guide* for Release 12.0. However, all the prefix list commands that are in this book have been tested and do work on Release 12.0. The commands are documented in the Cisco IOS Command Reference manuals for Release 12.1. |

The **ip prefix-list** *list-name* [**seq** *seq-value*] {**deny** | **permit**} *network/len* [**ge** *ge-value*] [**le** *le-value*] global configuration command is used to create a prefix-list, as described in Table 7-2.

**Table 7-2**    *ip prefix-list Command Description*

| ip prefix-list Command | Description |
|---|---|
| *list-name* | Name of the prefix list that will be created. (Note that the list name is case sensitive.) |
| *seq-value* | 32-bit sequence number of the prefix list statement, used to determine the order in which the statements are processed when filtering. Default sequence numbers are in increments of 5 (5, 10, 15, and so on). |
| **deny** | **permit** | The action taken when a match is found. |
| *network/len* | The prefix to be matched and the length of the prefix. The network is a 32-bit address; the length is a decimal number. |
| *ge-value* | The range of the prefix length to be matched for prefixes that are more specific than *network/len*. The range is assumed to be from *ge-value* to 32 if only the **ge** attribute is specified. |

**Table 7-2**    *ip prefix-list Command Description (Continued)*

| | |
|---|---|
| *le-value* | The range of the prefix length to be matched for prefixes that are more specific than *network/len*. The range is assumed to be from *len* to *le-value* if only the **le** attribute is specified. |

Both **ge** and **le** are optional. They can be used to specify the range of the prefix length to be matched for prefixes that are more specific than *network/len*. The value range is:

$len < ge\text{-}value < le\text{-}value <= 32$

An exact match is assumed when neither **ge** nor **le** is specified.

Prefix list entries can be reconfigured incrementally—in other words, an entry can be deleted or added individually.

The **neighbor** {*ip-address* | *peer-group-name*} **prefix-list** *prefix-listname* {**in** | **out**} router configuration command is used to distribute BGP neighbor information as specified in a prefix list, as described in Table 7-3.

**Table 7-3**    *neighbor prefix-list Command Description*

| neighbor prefix-list Command | Description |
|---|---|
| *ip-address* | IP address of the BGP neighbor for which routes will be filtered |
| *peer-group-name* | Name of a BGP peer group |
| *prefix-listname* | Name of the prefix list that will be used to filter the routes |
| **in** | Indication that the prefix list is to be applied to incoming advertisements from the neighbor |
| **out** | Indication that the prefix list is to be applied to outgoing advertisements to the neighbor |

**NOTE**    The **neighbor prefix-list** command can be used as an alternative to the **neighbor distribute-list** command, but you cannot use both commands for configuring the same BGP peer.

### ip prefix-list Command Options

The use of the **ge** and **le** options in the **ip prefix-list** command can be confusing. The following are results of some testing done to understand these keywords.

Three routers were used in this testing: Router B and Router A and its neighbor 10.1.1.1, as illustrated in Figure 7-9.

Before configuring the prefix list, Router A learns the following routes (from Router B):

```
172.16.0.0 subnetted:
    172.16.10.0/24
    172.16.11.0/24
```

Five scenarios were tested, as follows:

**Scenario 1**—In this scenario, the following is configured on Router A:

```
router bgp 65000
    aggregate-address 172.16.0.0 255.255.0.0
    neighbor 10.1.1.1 prefix-list tenonly out
ip prefix-list tenonly permit 172.16.10.0/8 le 24
```

**Figure 7-9** *Network Used in Prefix List Option Testing*

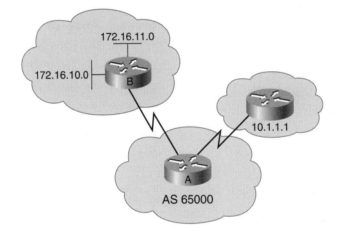

When the router's configuration is viewed with the **show run** command, you see that the router automatically changed the last line of this configuration to the following:

```
ip prefix-list tenonly permit 172.0.0.0/8 le 24
```

Neighbor 10.1.1.1 learned about 172.16.0.0/16, 172.16.10.0/24, and 172.16.11.0/24.

**Scenario 2**—In this scenario, the following is configured on Router A:

```
router bgp 65000
    aggregate-address 172.16.0.0 255.255.0.0
    neighbor 10.1.1.1 prefix-list tenonly out
ip prefix-list tenonly permit 172.0.0.0/8 le 16
```

Neighbor 10.1.1.1 learned about only 172.16.0.0/16.

**Scenario 3**—In this scenario, the following is configured on Router A:

```
router bgp 65000
    aggregate-address 172.16.0.0 255.255.0.0
    neighbor 10.1.1.1 prefix-list tenonly out
ip prefix-list tenonly permit 172.0.0.0/8 ge 17
```

Neighbor 10.1.1.1 learned about only 172.16.10.0/24 and 172.16.11.0/24. (In other words, it ignores the **/8** parameter and treats the command as if it had the parameters **ge 17 le 32**.)

**Scenario 4**—In this scenario, the following is configured on Router A:

```
router bgp 65000
    aggregate-address 172.16.0.0 255.255.0.0
    neighbor 10.1.1.1 prefix-list tenonly out
ip prefix-list tenonly permit 172.0.0.0/8 ge 16 le 24
```

Neighbor 10.1.1.1 learned about 172.16.0.0/16, 172.16.10.0/24, and 172.16.11.0/24. (In other words, it ignores the **/8** parameter and treats the command as if it had the parameters **ge 16 le 24**.)

**Scenario 5**—In this scenario, the following is configured on Router A:

```
router bgp 65000
    aggregate-address 172.16.0.0 255.255.0.0
    neighbor 10.1.1.1 prefix-list tenonly out
ip prefix-list tenonly permit 172.0.0.0/8 ge 17 le 24
```

Neighbor 10.1.1.1 learned about 172.16.10.0/24 and 172.16.11.0/24. (In other words, it ignores the **/8** parameter and treats the command as if it had the parameters **ge 17 le 24**.)

The **no ip prefix-list** *list-name* global configuration command, where *list-name* is the name of a prefix list, is used to delete a prefix list.

The [no] **ip prefix-list** *list-name* **description** *text* global configuration command can be used to add or delete a text description for a prefix list.

## Prefix List Sequence Numbers

Prefix list sequence numbers are generated automatically, unless you disable this automatic generation. If you disable the automatic generation of sequence numbers, you must specify the sequence number for each entry using the *seq-value* argument of the **ip prefix-list** command.

A prefix list is an ordered list. The sequence number is significant when a given prefix is matched by multiple entries of a prefix list, in which case the one with the smallest sequence number is considered the real match.

Regardless of whether the default sequence numbers are used in configuring a prefix list, a sequence number does not need to be specified when removing a configuration entry.

By default, the entries of a prefix list will have sequence values of 5, 10, 15, and so on. In the absence of a specified sequence value, a new entry will be assigned with a sequence number equal to the current maximum sequence number plus 5.

Prefix list **show** commands include the sequence numbers in their output.

The **no ip prefix-list sequence-number** global configuration command is used to disable the automatic generation of sequence numbers of prefix list entries. Use the **ip prefix-list sequence-number** global configuration command to re-enable the automatic generation of sequence numbers.

## Prefix List Example

The example network in Figure 7-10 illustrates the use of a prefix list. In this example, we want Router A to send only the supernet 172.0.0.0/8 to AS 65000; the route to the network 172.30.0.0/16 should not be sent. The configuration for Router A in this figure is provided in Example 7-3.

**Figure 7-10** *A Prefix List Example*

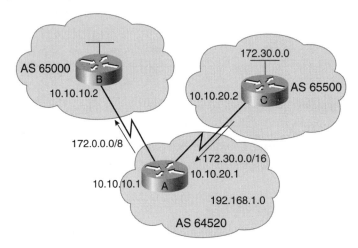

**Example 7-3** *Configuration of Router A in Figure 7-10*

```
RtrA(config)# ip prefix-list superonly permit 172.0.0.0/8
RtrA(config)# ip prefix-list superonly description only permit supernet
RtrA(config)# router bgp 64520
RtrA(config-router)# network 192.168.1.0
RtrA(config-router)# neighbor 10.10.10.2 remote-as 65000
RtrA(config-router)# neighbor 10.10.20.2 remote-as 65500
RtrA(config-router)# aggregate-address 172.0.0.0 255.0.0.0
RtrA(config-router)# neighbor 10.10.10.2 prefix-list superonly out
RtrA(config-router)# exit
```

In this example, Router A has two neighbors: Router B (10.10.10.2 in AS 65000) and Router C (10.10.20.2 in AS 65500). When Router A sends updates to neighbor Router B, the **neighbor prefix-list** statement specifies that it will use the prefix list called superonly to determine which updates are to be sent.

The **ip prefix-list superonly** specifies that only the route 172.0.0.0/8 should be sent (it is permitted in the prefix list). No other routes will be sent to Router B because prefix lists have an implicit deny any at the end.

## Verifying Prefix Lists

The EXEC commands related to prefix lists are described in Table 7-4. Use the **show ip prefix-list ?** command to see all the **show** commands available for prefix lists.

**Table 7-4**    *Commands Used to Verify Prefix Lists*

| Command | Description |
|---|---|
| **show ip prefix-list** [**detail** I **summary**] | Displays information on all prefix lists. Specifying the **detail** keyword includes the description and the hit count (the number of times the entry has matched a route) in the display. |
| **show ip prefix-list** [**detail** I **summary**] *name* | Displays a table showing the entries in a specific prefix list. |
| **show ip prefix-list** *name* [*network/len*] | Displays the policy associated with a specific prefix/len in a prefix list. |
| **show ip prefix-list** *name* [**seq** *seq-num*] | Displays the prefix list entry with a given sequence number. |
| **show ip prefix-list** *name* [*network/len*] **longer** | Displays all entries of a prefix list that are more specific than the given network and length. |
| **show ip prefix-list** *name* [*network/len*] **first-match** | Displays the entry of a prefix list that matches the given prefix (network and length of prefix). |
| **clear ip prefix-list** *name* [*network/len*] | Resets the hit count shown on prefix list entries. |

## Verifying Prefix Lists Example

The example output of the **show ip prefix-list detail** command shown in Example 7-4 is from Router A in Figure 7-10. Router A has a prefix list called superonly, with only one entry (sequence number 5). The hit count of 0 means that no routes have matched this entry.

**Example 7-4** *show ip prefix-list detail Command Output from Router A in Figure 7-10*

```
RtrA #show ip prefix-list detail
Prefix-list with the last deletion/insertion: superonly
ip prefix-list superonly:
    Description: only permit supernet
    count: 1, range entries: 0, sequences: 5 - 5, refcount: 1
    seq 5 permit 172.0.0.0/8 (hit count: 0, refcount: 1)
```

# Multihoming

This section describes multihoming and provides some examples of configuring it.

*Multihoming* is the term used to describe when an AS is connected to more than one ISP. This is usually done for one of two reasons, as follows:

- To increase the reliability of the connection to the Internet so that if one connection fails, another will still be available

- To increase the performance so that better paths can be used to certain destinations

## Types of Multihoming

The configuration of the multiple connections to the ISPs can be classified according to the routes that are provided to the AS from the ISPs. Three common ways of configuring the connections are as follows:

- All ISPs pass only default routes to the AS.

- All ISPs pass default routes and selected specific routes (for example, from customers with whom the AS exchanges a lot of traffic) to the AS.

- All ISPs pass all routes to the AS.

Each of these scenarios is examined in the following sections.

---

**NOTE**     When multihoming, the ISPs you connect to should announce your prefixes to the Internet. For example, if the prefixes assigned to you are part of only one of the ISP address ranges, the other ISPs (which do not own your prefixes) should also advertise your specific prefixes to the Internet.

---

## Default Routes from All Providers

The first scenario is when all ISPs pass only default routes to the AS. This requires the minimum resources (memory and CPU usage) within the routers in the AS because only default routes will have to be processed. The AS will send all its routes to the ISPs, which will process them and pass them on to other autonomous systems, as appropriate.

The ISP that a specific router within the AS uses to reach the Internet will be decided by the Interior Gateway Protocol (IGP) metric used to reach the default route within the AS.

The route that inbound packets take to get to the AS will be decided outside of the AS (within the ISPs and other autonomous systems).

In the example shown in Figure 7-11, AS 65000 and AS 65250 send default routes into AS 65500.

**Figure 7-11** *AS 65500 Is Receiving Default Routes from All Providers*

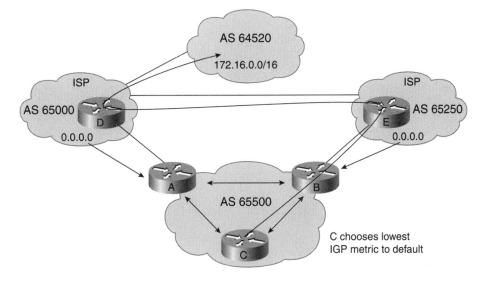

The ISP that a specific router within AS 65500 uses to reach any external address will be decided by the IGP metric used to reach the default route within the AS. For example, if the Routing Information Protocol (RIP) is used within AS 65500, Router C will select the route with the lowest hop count to the default route (to either Router A or Router B) when it wants to send packets to network 172.16.0.0. If Router C chooses the path through Router B, packets will travel to 172.16.0.0 as indicated by the arrow in Figure 7-11.

## Customer and Default Routes from All Providers

The second scenario is when all ISPs pass default routes and selected specific routes (for example, from customers with whom the AS exchanges a lot of traffic) to the AS.

This requires more resources (memory and CPU usage) within the routers in the AS because default routes and some external routes will have to be processed. The AS sends all its routes to the ISPs, which process them and pass them on to other autonomous systems, as appropriate.

The ISP that a specific router within the AS uses to reach the customer networks will usually be the shortest AS path; however this can be overridden. The path to all other external destinations will be decided by the IGP metric used to reach the default route within the AS.

The route that inbound packets take to get to the AS will be decided outside of the AS (within the ISPs and other autonomous systems).

In the example shown in Figure 7-12, AS 65000 and AS 65250 send default routes as well as specific routes to the customer's (AS 64520) network 172.16.0.0, into AS 65500.

**Figure 7-12** *AS 65500 Is Receiving Customer and Default Routes from All Providers*

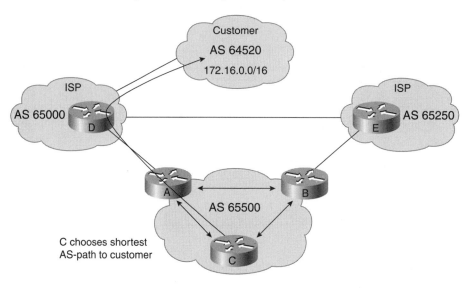

The ISP that a specific router within AS 65500 uses to reach the customer networks will usually be the shortest AS path. The shortest AS path to AS 64520 is via AS 65000 (versus via AS 65250, then AS 65000) through Router A. Router C will select this route when it wants to send packets to network 172.16.0.0, as indicated by the arrow in Figure 7-12.

The routes to other external addresses that are not specifically advertised to AS 65500 will be decided by the IGP metric used to reach the default route within the AS.

In the example shown in Figure 7-13, AS 65000 and AS 65250 send default routes as well as specific routes to the customer's (AS 64520) network 172.16.0.0, into AS 65500. The ISP that a specific router within AS 65500 uses to reach the customer networks will usually be the shortest AS path. However, Router B is configured to change the local preference of routes to 172.16.0.0/16 to 800 from its default of 100. Therefore, Router C will take the path through Router B to get to 172.16.0.0, as indicated by the arrow in Figure 7-13.

**Figure 7-13** *AS 65500 Is Receiving Customer and Default Routes from All Providers and Has Modified the Local Preference*

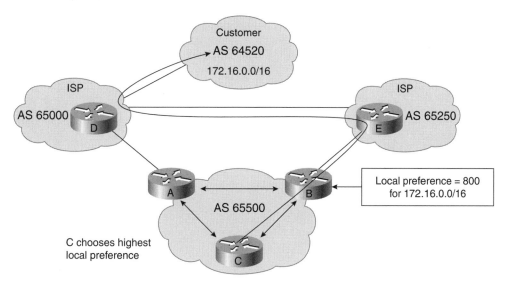

## Configuration of Router B

The configuration of Router B in Figure 7-13 includes the commands shown in Example 7-5.

The use of route maps for BGP is explained in Appendix A.

**Example 7-5** *Part of Configuration of Router B in Figure 7-13*

```
router bgp 65500
  neighbor <Router E ip address> route-map toright in

ip prefix-list customer permit 172.16.0.0/16

route-map toright permit 10
  match ip address prefix-list customer
  set local-preference 800
```

The routes to other external addresses that are not specifically advertised to AS 65500 will be decided by the IGP metric used to reach the default route within the AS.

# Full Routes from All Providers

The third scenario is when all ISPs pass all routes to the AS.

This scenario requires a lot of resources (memory and CPU usage) within the routers in the AS because all external routes will have to be processed. The AS sends all its routes to the ISPs, which process them and pass them on to other autonomous systems, as appropriate.

The ISP that a specific router within the AS uses to reach the external networks will usually be the shortest AS path; however, this can be overridden.

The route that inbound packets take to get to the AS will be decided outside of the AS (within the ISPs and other autonomous systems).

In the example shown in Figure 7-14, AS 65000 and AS 65250 send all routes into AS 65500.

**Figure 7-14** *AS 65500 Is Receiving Full Routes from All Providers*

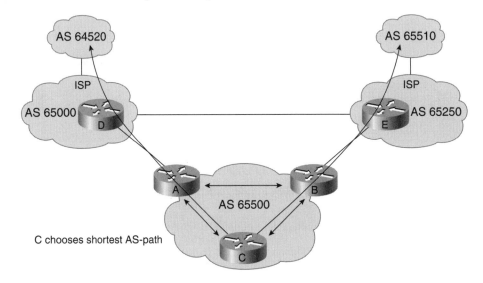

The ISP that a specific router within AS 65500 uses to reach the external networks will usually be the shortest AS path. For example, in Figure 7-14, Router C chooses the path through AS 65000 to get to AS 64520, and it chooses the path through AS 65250 to get to AS 65510, as indicated by the arrows in the figure. However, the routers in AS 65500 could be configured to influence the path that routes to certain networks take. For example, the local preference of certain routes or the weight of a neighbor connection could be changed.

# Configuring Weight and Local Preference

These are some of the commands that can be used to influence the path taken to external routes.

The **neighbor** {*ip-address* | *peer-group-name*} **weight** *weight* router configuration command is used to assign a weight to a neighbor connection, as described in Table 7-5.

**Table 7-5**  *neighbor weight Command Description*

| neighbor weight Command | Description |
|---|---|
| *ip-address* | IP address of the BGP neighbor. |
| *peer-group-name* | Name of a BGP peer group. |
| *weight* | Weight to assign. Acceptable values are 0 to 65535. The default is 32768 for local routes (routes that the router originates); other routes have a weight of 0 by default. |

The **bgp default local-preference** *value* router configuration command is used to change the default local preference value, as described in Table 7-6. The default local preference is 100. This command is used to change the local preference on all routes.

**Table 7-6**  *bgp default local-preference Command Description*

| bgp default local-preference Command | Description |
|---|---|
| *value* | Local preference value from 0 to 4294967295. A higher value is preferred. |

**NOTE**

Recall that the term *local* in *local preference* means that it is local to the AS. Local preference is used to select routes with equal weights because the weight attribute is looked at first. Only when all weights are equal is the local preference attribute examined. The weight attribute influences only the local router, whereas the local preference attribute influences other routers within the AS.

The local preference is stripped in outgoing EBGP updates.

There are also other commands to change BGP attributes. (Most of these commands use route maps. The concept of route maps is covered in the next chapter.)

> **NOTE**    To force new parameters with a neighbor to take effect, a new session must be established
> with the neighbor using the **clear ip bgp** command. This is due to the incremental update
> nature of BGP and the fact that the attribute modifiers are applied on input or output
> updates, not on entries that already exist on the router.

## Multihoming Examples

In the example shown in Figure 7-15, AS 64520 is connected to two ISPs: AS 65000 and
AS 65250. Both ISPs are sending full routes to AS 64520.

**Figure 7-15** *AS 64520 Is Multihomed*

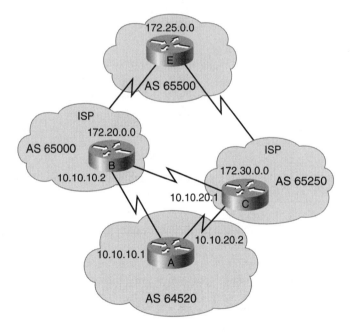

## Multihoming Example with No Special Tuning

In the first example configuration shown in Example 7-6, Router A is configured with two EBGP neighbors: Router B (10.10.10.2) and Router C (10.10.20.1). No special tuning is done to influence the way that AS 64520 gets to the other autonomous systems.

**Example 7-6**    *Configuration of Router A in Figure 7-15, with No Special Tuning*

```
RtrA(config)# router bgp 64520
RtrA(config-router)# network 10.10.10.0 mask 255.255.255.0
RtrA(config-router)# network 10.10.20.0 mask 255.255.255.0
RtrA(config-router)# neighbor 10.10.10.2 remote-as 65000
RtrA(config-router)# neighbor 10.10.20.1 remote-as 65250
```

Example 7-7 provides the **show ip bgp** command output on Router A in the network in Figure 7-15. In this example, Router A selects the route via 10.10.10.2 (Router B) to get to 172.20.0.0 and the route via 10.10.20.1 (Router C) to get to 172.30.0.0 because these paths have the shortest AS path length (of one AS). (Recall that the selected route is indicated with the > symbol in the left-most column of the **show ip bgp** output.)

**Example 7-7**    *show Output from Router A in Figure 7-15, with No Special Tuning*

```
RtrA#show ip bgp
BGP table version is 7, local router ID is 172.16.10.1
Status codes: s suppressed, d damped, h history, * valid, > best, i - internal
Origin codes: i - IGP, e - EGP, ? - incomplete

   Network          Next Hop         Metric LocPrf Weight Path
*> 10.10.10.0/24    0.0.0.0               0        32768 i
*> 10.10.20.0/24    0.0.0.0               0        32768 i
*  172.20.0.0       10.10.20.1                         0 65250 65000 i
*>                  10.10.10.2            0            0 65000 i
*> 172.25.0.0       10.10.10.2                         0 65000 65500 i
*                   10.10.20.1                         0 65250 65500 i
*  172.30.0.0       10.10.10.2                         0 65000 65250 i
*>                  10.10.20.1            0            0 65250 i
```

Router A has two paths to 172.25.0.0, and they both have the same AS path length (there are two autonomous systems in each path). In this case, with all other attributes being equal, Router A will select the oldest path. If we ignore this oldest path criteria for now (because we can't determine which router will send the path to Router A first), Router A will select the path that has the lowest BGP router ID value.

Unfortunately, the BGP router ID values of Routers B and C are not displayed in the output of the **show ip bgp** command. The **show ip bgp neighbors** command or the **show ip bgp 172.25.0.0** command could be used to provide these values. Using these commands, the router ID for Router B was found to be 172.20.0.1, and the router ID for Router C was found to be 172.30.0.1. Router A will select the lowest of these router IDs; Router A therefore chooses the path through Router B (172.20.0.1) to get to 172.25.0.0.

## Multihoming Example with Weight Attributes Changed

In the example configuration for Router A in Figure 7-15 shown in Example 7-8, Router A is configured with two EBGP neighbors: Router B (10.10.10.2) and Router C (10.10.20.1). The weights used for routes from each neighbor have been changed from their default of zero. Routes received from 10.10.10.2 (Router B) will have a weight of 100, and routes received from 10.10.20.1 (Router C) will have a weight of 150.

**Example 7-8**  *Configuration of Router A in Figure 7-15, with Weights Changed*

```
RtrA(config)# router bgp 64520
RtrA(config-router)# network 10.10.10.0 mask 255.255.255.0
RtrA(config-router)# network 10.10.20.0 mask 255.255.255.0
RtrA(config-router)# neighbor 10.10.10.2 remote-as 65000
RtrA(config-router)# neighbor 10.10.10.2 weight 100
RtrA(config-router)# neighbor 10.10.20.1 remote-as 65250
RtrA(config-router)# neighbor 10.10.20.1 weight 150
```

Example 7-9 provides the **show ip bgp** command output on Router A in the network in Figure 7-15, with the weights changed. In this example, because the weight for Router C is higher than the weight for Router B, Router A is forced to use Router C as a next hop to reach all external routes. Recall that the weight attribute is looked at before the AS path length, so the AS path length will be ignored in this case.

**Example 7-9**  *show Output from Router A in Figure 7-15, with Weights Changed*

```
RtrA#show ip bgp
BGP table version is 9, local router ID is 172.16.10.1
Status codes: s suppressed, d damped, h history, * valid, > best, i - internal
Origin codes: i - IGP, e - EGP, ? - incomplete

   Network          Next Hop          Metric LocPrf Weight Path
*> 10.10.10.0/24    0.0.0.0                0          32768 i
*> 10.10.20.0/24    0.0.0.0                0          32768 i
*> 172.20.0.0       10.10.20.1                          150 65250 65000 i
*                   10.10.10.2             0            100 65000 i
*> 172.25.0.0       10.10.20.1                          150 65250 65500 i
*                   10.10.10.2                          100 65000 65500 i
*> 172.30.0.0       10.10.20.1             0            150 65250 i
*                   10.10.10.2                          100 65000 65250 i
```

# Redistribution with IGPs

Chapter 8, "Optimizing Routing Update Operation," discusses route redistribution and how it is configured. Here we examine specifics of when redistribution between BGP and IGPs is appropriate.

As noted earlier, and as shown in Figure 7-16, a router running BGP keeps a table of BGP information, separate from the IP routing table. Information in the tables can be exchanged between the BGP protocol and the IGP protocol running in the routers.

**Figure 7-16**  *A Router Running BGP Keeps Its Own Table, Separate from the IP Routing Table*

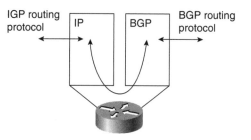

## Advertising Networks into BGP

Route information is sent from an autonomous system *into* BGP in one of the following three ways:

* Using the **network** command. As already discussed, the **network** command allows BGP to advertise a network that is already in the IP table. The list of **network** commands must include all the networks in the AS that you want to advertise.

* Redistributing static routes to null 0 into BGP. Redistribution occurs when a router running different protocols advertises routing information received between the protocols. Static routes in this case are considered to be a protocol, and static information is advertised to BGP. (The use of the null 0 interface is discussed in the following section.)

* Redistributing dynamic IGP routes into BGP. This solution is not recommended because it may cause instability.

The following two sections examine the last two points in more detail.

## Redistributing Static Routes into BGP

Redistribution of static routes configured to the null 0 interface into BGP is done to advertise aggregate routes rather than specific routes from the IP table. An example configuration is shown in Example 7-10.

**Example 7-10** *A Static Route to Null 0 Is Redistributed to Advertise Aggregate Routes*

```
router bgp 64520
  redistribute static
!
ip route 192.168.0.0 255.255.0.0 null 0
```

Any route redistributed into BGP must already be known in the IP table. Using the static route to null 0 is a way of fooling the process into believing that a route actually exists for the aggregate. A static route to null 0 is not necessary if you are using a **network** command with a nonaggregated network—in other words, a network that exists in the IP table.

The use of null 0 may seem strange because a static route to null 0 means to discard any information for this network. This will usually not be a problem because the router doing the redistribution has a more specific route to the destination networks, and these will be used to route any traffic that comes into the router. A problem with using this method of aggregation is that if the router loses access to the more specific routes, it will still be advertising the static aggregate, thus creating a *black hole*.

The preferred method of advertising a summary route is to use the **aggregate-address** command. With this command, as long as a more specific route exists in the BGP table, the aggregate gets sent. If the aggregating router loses all its specific connections to the networks being aggregated, then the aggregate route will disappear from the BGP table and the BGP aggregate will not get sent. For example, consider a router that has knowledge of subnets 172.16.1.0/24 and 172.16.2.0/24, and that advertises the aggregate route 172.16.0.0/16. If the router loses knowledge of only one of these subnets, it will still advertise the aggregate, 172.16.0.0/16. However, if it loses knowledge of both subnets, then it will no longer advertise the aggregate 172.16.0.0/16 because it can no longer get to any part of that network.

## Redistributing Dynamic IGP Routes into BGP

Redistributing from an IGP into BGP is not recommended because any change in the IGP routes—for example, if a link goes down—may cause a BGP update. This method could result in unstable BGP tables.

If redistribution is used, care must be taken that only local routes are redistributed. For example, routes learned from other autonomous systems (that were learned by redistributing BGP into the IGP) must not be sent out again from the IGP, or routing loops could result. Configuring this filtering can be complex.

| NOTE | Using a redistribute command into BGP will result in an incomplete origin attribute for the route; an incomplete origin is indicated with a **?** in the **show ip bgp** command output. |
|------|-----|

# Advertising from BGP into an IGP

Route information may be sent from BGP into an autonomous system by redistribution of the BGP routes into the IGP.

Because BGP is an external routing protocol, care must be taken when exchanging information with internal protocols because of the amount of information in BGP tables.

For ISP autonomous systems, redistributing from BGP is not normally required. Other autonomous systems may use redistribution, but the number of routes will mean that filtering will normally be required.

Each of these situations is examined in the following sections.

## ISP—No Redistribution from BGP into IGP Required

An ISP typically has all routers in the AS (or at least all routers in the transit path within the AS) running BGP. Of course, this would be a full-mesh IBGP environment, and IBGP would be used to carry the EBGP routes across the AS. All the BGP routers in the AS would be configured with the **no synchronization** command because synchronization between IGP and BGP is not required. The BGP information then would not need to be redistributed into the IGP. The IGP would need to route only information local to the AS and routes to the next-hop addresses of the BGP routes.

One advantage of this approach is that the IGP protocol does not have to be concerned with all the BGP routes; BGP will take care of them. BGP will also converge faster in this environment because it does not have to wait for the IGP to advertise the routes.

## Non-ISP—Redistribution from BGP into IGP May Be Required

A non-ISP AS typically would not have all routers in the AS running BGP, and it may not have a full-mesh IBGP environment. If this is the case, and if knowledge of external routes is required inside the AS, then redistribution of BGP into the IGP would be necessary. However, because of the number of routes that would be in the BGP tables, filtering will normally be required.

As discussed earlier in this chapter in the "Multihoming" section, an alternative to receiving full routes from BGP is that the ISP could send only default routes, or default routes and some external routes, to the AS.

NOTE An example of when redistribution into an IGP may be necessary is in an AS that is running BGP only on its border routers and that has other routers in the AS that do not run BGP, but that require knowledge of external routes.

Redistribution between routing protocols is discussed in detail in Chapter 8.

# Case Study: Multihomed BGP

Refer to Chapter 1, "Routing Principles," for introductory information on the JKL case study.

Recall that throughout this book we have been using a case study of JKL Corporation to discuss various aspects of scalable routing. The case studies are used to review key concepts and to discuss critical issues surrounding network operation.

In this case study, you will look at how JKL will connect to the Internet. As shown in Figure 7-17, JKL is AS 65106 and has two ISP connections, to AS 65505 and AS 64573. As you recall, JKL runs the Open Shortest Path First (OSPF) protocol as its IGP. JKL must consider methods to select which ISP handles the bulk of its network traffic at different times of the day.

While looking at Figure 7-17, analyze the following:

- Which topology requirements will determine which routers will run BGP
- Whether synchronization will be required between BGP and the IGP
- The issues associated with redistribution between an IGP and BGP
- The route advertisement method for routes sent to and received from the Internet
- Ease of configuration and management

## Case Study Solution

JKL needs full-time connectivity to the Internet to conduct e-commerce. Two separate routers (located in the core of the corporate network) provide the physical connectivity to the Internet. Each of the routers maintains a connection to a different ISP, and this creates a multihomed BGP topology.

The routers marked A and B run BGP. Routers A and B belong to a registered autonomous system and maintain an EBGP relationship with their respective ISPs.

**Figure 7-17**  *Multihomed BGP Case Study Topology*

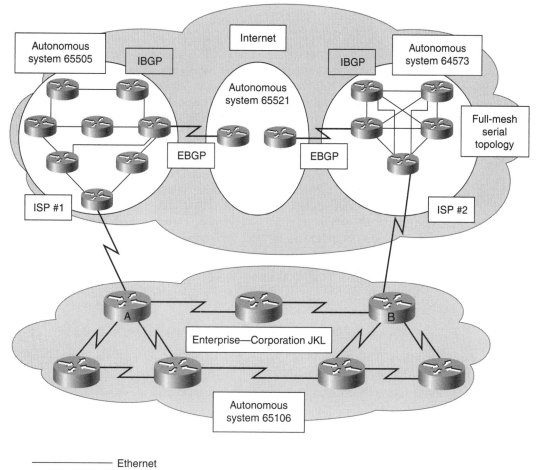

Routers A and B would need to have an IBGP relationship with each other only if the AS was providing a transit path for other autonomous systems. Most likely this would not be the case because then either all the routers in the AS in the path between Routers A and B would need to run BGP or BGP would need to be redistributed into the AS. JKL requested that only default routes be provided from both ISPs.

Routers A and B have been configured with loopback interfaces to provide stability for session establishment with peer routers. As members of JKL's OSPF core, routers A and B must also be configured to run an IGP—in this case, OSPF. The OSPF core uses default routes to direct internal traffic toward the Internet. The strategy of using default routes for outbound traffic means that redistribution of BGP information into OSPF is not a requirement. To reach the Internet, outbound traffic only needs to follow the path already defined by the default route.

It is important to understand some of the issues associated with redistribution between an IGP and BGP. If routers A and B were running IBGP and the BGP routes learned by Router A from ISP 1 were redistributed into the IGP (OSPF, in this case), they would be passed through the AS to Router B. If those routes (and other interior routes) were redistributed from the IGP at Router B into BGP, serious problems could result, including the presence of more than 70,000 routes in the routing table and the loss of AS path and other BGP attributes when those routes enter the IGP.

Routers A and B advertise AS 65106 to both ISPs, which process them and pass them on to other autonomous systems as appropriate. The route that inbound packets take to get to JKL is decided outside of JKL, within the ISPs and other autonomous systems. For the topology shown in Figure 7-17, return traffic would come into JKL through one of the ISPs, determined by the AS path length, if all other parameters were equal. Setting the MED parameter on routers A and B to try to affect the return path in this case would not have an effect. This is because the routers are connected to different ISPs, and the MED attribute is not passed on along with the updates; it would be set back to its default of 0 when updates are passed on.

Some highlights of this case study include these:

- Routers A and B will form an EBGP session with their respective ISPs.

- If a default route policy is used within the JKL core to forward traffic to the ISPs, route redistribution between BGP and OSPF is unnecessary.

- BGP's route selection algorithm checks several criteria, including the following:
    - Highest Cisco weight
    - Highest local preference
    - Locally originated by this router
    - Shortest AS path
    - Lowest origin code
    - Lowest MED value
    - EBGP better than IBGP
    - Shortest internal path inside AS to reach destination
    - Oldest EBGP route
    - Lowest BGP router ID

- The **network** command in BGP operates differently than the **network** command in IGPs.

# Summary

In this chapter, you learned about problems that can occur when scaling IBGP, and you learned about solutions to these problems, including route reflectors and prefix lists. You also learned about three common ways of multihoming connections to the Internet. Redistribution between BGP and an IGP was analyzed as well.

The next chapter discusses route redistribution in detail, including how information between protocols can be controlled. Route maps are also discussed in the next chapter.

# Configuration Exercise #1: Configuring BGP Route Reflectors and Prefix List Filtering

---

### Configuration Exercises

In this book, Configuration Exercises are used to provide practice in configuring routers with the commands presented. If you have access to real hardware, you can try these exercises on your routers; refer to Appendix H, "Configuration Exercise Equipment Requirements and Backbone Configurations," for a list of recommended equipment and configuration commands for the backbone routers. However, even if you don't have access to any routers, you can go through the exercises and keep a log of your own "running configurations" on separate sheets of paper. Commands used and answers to the Configuration Exercises are provided at the end of the exercise.

In these exercises, you are in control of a pod of three routers; there are assumed to be 12 pods in the network. The pods are interconnected to a backbone. In most of the exercises, there is only one router in the backbone; in some cases, another router is added to the backbone. Each of the Configuration Exercises in this book assumes that you have completed the previous chapter's exercises on your pod.

---

In this exercise, you will configure your pxr1 router as a router reflector and enable prefix list filtering.

## Objectives

In this exercise, you will complete the following tasks:

- Disable the Ethernet link between the pxr2 and pxr3 routers.
- Disable IBGP between pxr2 and pxr3.
- Enable pxr1 to be the route reflector for pxr2 and pxr3.

- Enable prefix list filtering on pxr1 to have an inbound prefix list to filter traffic from the backbone_r1 router.
- Verify BGP connectivity.

## Visual Objective

Figure 7-18 illustrates the topology used in the network.

**Figure 7-18**  *Configuring BGP Route Reflectors and Prefix List Filtering Configuration Exercise Visual Objective*

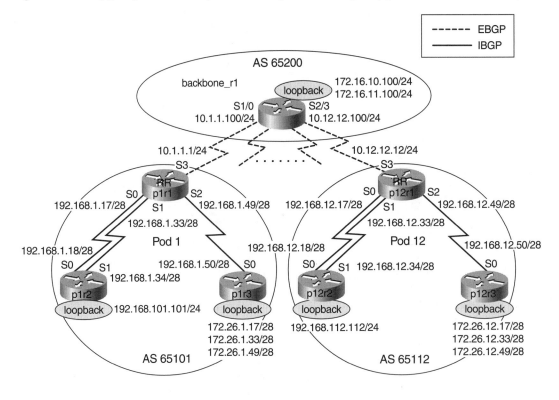

## Command List

In this exercise, you will use the commands in Table 7-7 listed in logical order. Refer to this list if you need configuration command assistance during the exercise.

**Table 7-7**    *Configuring BGP Route Reflectors and Prefix-List Filtering Configuration Exercise Command List*

| Command | Description |
| --- | --- |
| no neighbor 192.168.x.65 remote-as 6510x | Removes a BGP neighbor relationship |
| network 172.26.x.16 mask 255.255.255.240 | Advertises pxr3 loopback interfaces |
| network 172.26.x.32 mask 255.255.255.240 | Advertises pxr3 loopback interfaces |
| network 172.26.x.48 mask 255.255.255.240 | Advertises pxr3 loopback interfaces |
| network 192.168.10x.0  mask 255.255.255.240 | Advertises pxr2 loopback interfaces |
| neighbor 192.168.x.18 route-reflector-client | Enables a route reflector |
| neighbor 10.x.x.100 prefix-list test in | Enables prefix list filtering on incoming updates from the BGP neighbor |
| ip prefix-list test permit 172.16.10.0/24 | Permits routes with the prefix 172.16.10.0/24 |
| clear ip bgp * | Resets all BGP neighbors |
| show ip bgp | Shows BGP information |

## Setup

To set up, do the following:

**Step 1**    At your pxr2 router, shut down the Ethernet 0 interface and remove the IBGP **neighbor** statement to pxr3.

**Step 2**    At your pxr3 router, shut down the Ethernet 0 interface and remove the IBGP **neighbor** statement to pxr2.

## Task 1: Enabling pxr1 to Be the Route Reflector

Complete the following steps:

**Step 1**    At your pxr3 router, enter the **network** statements to allow the advertisement of the following loopback addresses that you created during the OSPF exercise:

—    172.26.x.16/28

—    172.26.x.32/28

—    172.26.x.48/28

(x is your pod number.)

At your p*x*r2 router, enter the **network** statement to allow the advertisement of the following loopback address that you created during the OSPF exercise:

— 192.168.10*x*.0/24

(*x* is your pod number.)

**Step 2**  From the p*x*r1 router, enter the **show ip bgp** command. Do you see the following subnets displayed?

— 172.26.*x*.16/28

— 172.26.*x*.32/28

— 172.26.*x*.48/28

— 192.168.10*x*.0/24

Examine the p*x*r1 IP routing table. Do you see the following subnets displayed?

— 172.26.*x*.16/28

— 172.26.*x*.32/28

— 172.26.*x*.48/28

— 192.168.10*x*.0/24

**Step 3**  From the p*x*r2 router, enter the **show ip bgp** command. Do you see the following subnets displayed?

— 172.26.*x*.16/28

— 172.26.*x*.32/28

— 172.26.*x*.48/28

— 192.168.10*x*.0/24

Examine the p*x*r2 IP routing table. Do you see the following subnets displayed?

— 172.26.*x*.16/28

— 172.26.*x*.32/28

— 172.26.*x*.48/28

— 192.168.10*x*.0/24

**Step 4**   From the p*x*r3 router, enter the **show ip bgp** command. Do you see the following subnets displayed?

— 172.26.*x*.16/28

— 172.26.*x*.32/28

— 172.26.*x*.48/28

— 192.168.10*x*.0/24

Examine the p*x*r3 IP routing table. Do you see the following subnets displayed?

— 172.26.*x*.16/28

— 172.26.*x*.32/28

— 172.26.*x*.48/28

— 192.168.10*x*.0/24

**Step 5**   From Steps 2, 3, and 4, you should be able to determine that because there is no IBGP neighbor relationship between p*x*r2 and p*x*r3, p*x*r1 will not by default propagate the IBGP routes learned from p*x*r2 to p*x*r3 or from p*x*r3 to p*x*r2.

Configure the p*x*r1 router to allow the p*x*r1 router to be a router reflector for p*x*r2 and p*x*r3.

**Step 6**   From the p*x*r2 router, enter the **show ip bgp** command.

Do you see the following subnets displayed?

— 172.26.*x*.16/28

— 172.26.*x*.32/28

— 172.26.*x*.48/28

— 192.168.10*x*.0/24

Examine the p*x*r2 IP routing table. Do you see the following subnets displayed?

— 172.26.*x*.16/28

— 172.26.*x*.32/28

— 172.26.*x*.48/28

— 192.168.10*x*.0/24

(Note that it may take a minute or so for the routes to appear.)

**Step 7**   From the pxr3 router, enter the **show ip bgp** command. Do you see the following subnets displayed?

— 172.26.x.16/28

— 172.26.x.32/28

— 172.26.x.48/28

— 192.168.10x.0/24

Examine the pxr3 IP routing table. Do you see the following subnets displayed?

— 172.26.x.16/28

— 172.26.x.32/28

— 172.26.x.48/28

— 192.168.10x.0/24

**Step 8**   From the pxr3 router, ping 192.168.10x.10x. From the pxr2 router, ping 172.26.x.17, 172.26.x.33, and 172.26.x.49.

Were the pings successful?

**Step 9**   Telnet to the backbone_r1 router, using the password cisco. Ping 192.168.10x.10x, 172.26.x.17, 172.26.x.33, and 172.26.x.49.

Were the pings successful?

**Step 10** Save the current configurations of all the routers within your pod to NVRAM.

## Task 2: Enabling an Inbound Prefix List

Complete the following steps:

**Step 1**   At your pxr1 router, make sure that you can see both the 172.16.10.0 and 172.16.11.0 BGP routes from the backbone_r1 router.

**Step 2**   At your pxr1 router, configure an inbound prefix-list filter to only permit prefix 172.16.10.0/24 to come in from the backbone_r1 router.

**Step 3**   Issue the **clear ip bgp *** command at your pxr1 router.

**Step 4**   Display the routing table of your pxr1 router to verify that your prefix list is working.

**Step 5**   Remove the prefix list configuration.

**Step 6**   Issue the **clear ip bgp** * command on your p*x*r1 router.

**Step 7**   Save the current configurations of all the routers within your pod to NVRAM.

## Completion Criteria

You have successfully completed this exercise if you correctly supplied the commands required to configure your p*x*r1 router to act as the route reflector for your p*x*r2 and p*x*r3 routers, and to configure an inbound prefix list, and if you were able to correctly answer the questions in the exercises. At the end of this exercise, all the routers should have full connectivity to each other; each pod will be running IBGP internally with p*x*r1 as the route reflector and will have EBGP connectivity to the backbone_r1 router.

# Configuration Exercise #2: Configuring Multihomed BGP

Complete the following exercise to configure multihomed BGP.

## Objectives

In this exercise, you will complete the following steps:

* Configure an EBGP connection from your p*x*r3 router to the backbone_r2 router (AS65201).
* Verify connectivity from your pod to AS 65201.

## Visual Objective

Figure 7-19 illustrates the topology used in the network.

---

**NOTE**    Only one pod is shown in Figure 7-19 because of space restrictions.

---

**Figure 7-19** *Configuring Multihomed BGP Configuration Exercise Visual Objective*

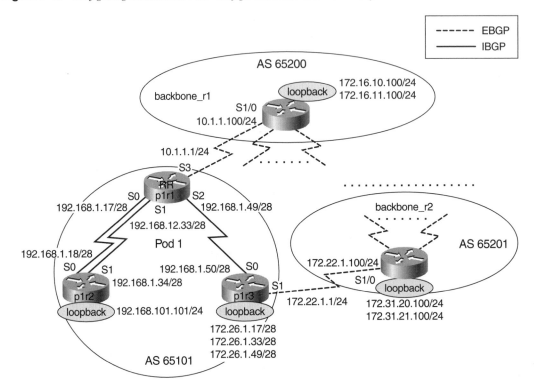

## Command List

In this exercise, you will use the commands listed in Table 7-8 in logical order. Refer to this list if you need configuration command assistance during the exercise.

**Table 7-8** *Configuring Multihomed BGP Configuration Exercise Command List*

| Command | Description |
| --- | --- |
| **neighbor 172.22.x.100 remote-as 65201** | Establishes BGP neighbor relationship |
| **neighbor 192.168.x.49 next-hop-self** | Changes the next hop to be the router itself |
| **show ip bgp** | Shows BGP information |
| **show ip bgp neighbors** | Shows detailed BGP neighbor status |
| **show ip bgp summary** | Shows BGP neighbor status |
| **clear ip bgp \*** | Resets all BGP neighbors |

## Task: Enabling a Second EBGP Connection

Complete the following steps:

**Step 1**   At the p*x*r3 router, no shut the S1 interface that connects to the backbone_r2 router.

Set the p*x*r3 S1 IP address to 172.22.*x.x*/24, where *x* is your pod number, as shown in the following table.

| Pod | p*x*r3 S1 IP Address |
| --- | --- |
| 1 | 172.22.1.1/24 |
| 2 | 172.22.2.2/24 |
| 3 | 172.22.3.3/24 |
| 4 | 172.22.4.4/24 |
| 5 | 172.22.5.5/24 |
| 6 | 172.22.6.6/24 |
| 7 | 172.22.7.7/24 |
| 8 | 172.22.8.8/24 |
| 9 | 172.22.9.9/24 |
| 10 | 172.22.10.10/24 |
| 11 | 172.22.11.11/24 |
| 12 | 172.22.12.12/24 |

From your p*x*r3 router, ping 172.22.*x*.100 to verify connectivity to the backbone_r2 router.

**Step 2**   At the p*x*r3 router, use the **neighbor** statement to establish the backbone_r2 router as an EBGP neighbor. (The backbone_r2 router is in AS 65201.)

**Step 3**   At the p*x*r3 router, enter the **show ip bgp summary** and the **show ip bgp neighbors** commands.

Wait until the neighbor state indicates established.

What is the BGP state of the backbone_r2 router?

How many prefixes have been learned from the backbone_r2 router?

**Step 4**    At your pxr3 router, enter the **show ip bgp** command.

Do you see a route to 172.31.20.0/24 and 172.31.21.0/24? Write down the following information:

— Network

— Next hop

— Metric

— LocPrf

— Weight

— Path

**Step 5**    At your pxr3 router, ping 172.31.20.100 and 172.31.21.100.

Were the pings successful?

**Step 6**    At your pxr1 router, enter the **show ip bgp** command. Do you see a route to 172.31.20.0/24 and 172.31.21.0/24 (in AS 65201) directly from your AS?

What is the next hop to get to 172.31.20.0/24 and 172.31.21.0/24 directly to AS 65201 from your AS?

Examine your pxr1 IP routing table. Do you see a route to 172.31.20.0/ 24 and 172.31.21.0/24 (in AS 65201) directly from your AS?

**Step 7**    Enable the next-hop-self options. At your pxr3 router, enter the BGP configuration command to cause pxr3 to announce itself as the next-hop router to pxr1.

Issue the **clear ip bgp \*** command at pxr3 to reset the BGP sessions.

**Step 8**    At your pxr1 router, enter the **show ip bgp** command again. Do you see a route to 172.31.20.0/24 and 172.31.21.0/24 (in AS 65201) directly from your AS?

What is the next hop to get to 172.31.20.0/24 and 172.31.21.0/24 directly from your AS?

Examine your pxr1 IP routing table. Do you see a route to 172.31.20.0/ 24 and 172.31.21.0/24 (in AS 65201) directly from your AS?

From pxr1, ping 172.31.20.100 and 172.31.21.100.

Were the pings successful?

**Step 9**   Examine your pxr2 IP routing table. Do you see a route to 172.31.20.0/ 24 and 172.31.21.0/24 directly to AS 65201 from your AS?

From pxr2, ping 172.31.20.100 and 172.31.21.100.

Were the pings successful?

**Step 10**   From pxr3, Telnet to the backbone_r2 router, using the password cisco. Enter the **show ip bgp** command.

How many paths are available to subnet 172.16.10.0 and 172.16.11.0? Which path is selected as the best path? (Note: You should see multiple paths if more than one pod is configured properly.)

Display the IP routing table of the backbone_r2 router. In the routing table, do you see only the best path to 172.16.10.0 and 172.16.11.0 published?

Exit the Telnet to the backbone_r2 router.

**Step 11**   If your pxr3 router connection to the backbone_r2 router fails, your pod should still be capable of reaching AS 65201 by going through AS 65200 and AS 6510x (of another pod) if another pod is configured properly. Try shutting down your S1 interface on your pxr3 router, and then try a trace to 172.31.20.100. Which path are the trace probes taking from pxr3 to the backbone_r2 router now?

No shut the S1 interface on your pxr3 router when you are finished.

**Step 12**   Save the current configurations of all the routers within your pod to NVRAM.

Bonus question: What is the order BGP will use to evaluate the following BGP route attributes?

— MED

— Weight

— Shortest AS path

— Local preference

## Completion Criteria

You have successfully completed this exercise if you correctly supplied the commands required to configure EBGP connectivity from your pxr3 router to the backbone_r2 router, and if you were able to correctly answer the questions in the exercises. At the end of this exercise, all of the routers should have full connectivity to each other; each pod will be running IBGP internally with pxr1 as the route reflector and will have EBGP connectivity to both of the backbone routers.

# Answers to Configuration Exercise #1: Configuring BGP Route Reflectors and Prefix List Filtering

This section provides the answers to the questions in Configuration Exercise #1. The answers are in **bold**.

## Answers to Setup

To set up, do the following:

**Step 1**    At your p*x*r2 router, shut down the Ethernet 0 interface and remove the IBGP **neighbor** statement to p*x*r3.

**The following example shows how to perform the required setup on the p1r2 router. The router output as a result of this configuration is also displayed.**

```
p1r2#conf t
Enter configuration commands, one per line.  End with CNTL/Z.
p1r2(config)#int e0
p1r2(config-if)#shutdown
07:36:49: %LINK-5-CHANGED: Interface Ethernet0, changed state to administratively
down
07:36:50: %LINEPROTO-5-UPDOWN: Line protocol on Interface Ethernet0, changed state
to down
p1r2(config-if)#router bgp 65101
p1r2(config-router)#no neighbor 192.168.1.66 remote-as 65101
```

**Step 2**    At your p*x*r3 router, shut down the Ethernet 0 interface and remove the IBGP **neighbor** statement to p*x*r2.

**The following example shows how to perform the required setup on the p1r3 router. The router output as a result of this configuration is also displayed.**

```
p1r3#conf t
Enter configuration commands, one per line.  End with CNTL/Z.
p1r3(config)#int e0
p1r3(config-if)#shutdown
07:38:08: %LINK-5-CHANGED: Interface Ethernet0, changed state to administratively
down
07:38:09: %LINEPROTO-5-UPDOWN: Line protocol on Interface Ethernet0, changed state
to down
p1r3(config-if)#router bgp 65101
p1r3(config-router)#no neighbor 192.168.1.65 remote-as 65101
```

## Answers to Task 1: Enabling p*x*r1 to Be the Route Reflector

Complete the following steps:

**Step 1**  At your p*x*r3 router, enter the **network** statements to allow the advertisement of the following loopback addresses that you created during the OSPF exercise:

— 172.26.*x*.16/28

— 172.26.*x*.32/28

— 172.26.*x*.48/28

(*x* is your pod number.)

**The following example shows how to advertise the loopback addresses on the p1r3 router:**

```
p1r3#conf t
Enter configuration commands, one per line.  End with CNTL/Z.
p1r3(config)#router bgp 65101
p1r3(config-router)#network 172.26.1.16 mask 255.255.255.240
p1r3(config-router)#network 172.26.1.32 mask 255.255.255.240
p1r3(config-router)#network 172.26.1.48 mask 255.255.255.240
```

At your p*x*r2 router, enter the **network** statement to allow the advertisement of the following loopback address that you created during the OSPF exercise:

— 192.168.10*x*.0/24

(*x* is your pod number.)

**The following example shows how to advertise the loopback address on the p1r2 router:**

```
p1r2#conf t
Enter configuration commands, one per line.  End with CNTL/Z.
p1r2(config)#router bgp 65101
p1r2(config-router)#network 192.168.101.0 mask 255.255.255.0
```

**Step 2**  From the p*x*r1 router, enter the **show ip bgp** command. Do you see the following subnets displayed?

— 172.26.*x*.16/28

— 172.26.*x*.32/28

— 172.26.*x*.48/28

— 192.168.10*x*.0/24

The following example output is from the p1r1 router, indicating the BGP routes:

```
p1r1#show ip bgp
BGP table version is 14, local router ID is 192.168.1.49
Status codes: s suppressed, d damped, h history, * valid, > best, i - internal
Origin codes: i - IGP, e - EGP, ? - incomplete

   Network          Next Hop          Metric LocPrf Weight Path
*> 10.0.0.0         10.1.1.100             0             0 65200 i
*> 172.16.10.0/24   10.1.1.100             0             0 65200 i
*> 172.16.11.0/24   10.1.1.100             0             0 65200 i
*>i172.26.1.16/28   192.168.1.50           0    100      0 i
*>i172.26.1.32/28   192.168.1.50           0    100      0 i
*>i172.26.1.48/28   192.168.1.50           0    100      0 i
*> 192.168.1.0      0.0.0.0                0         32768 i
*> 192.168.2.0      10.1.1.100             0             0 65200 65102 i
*> 192.168.2.64/28  10.1.1.100             0             0 65200 65102 i
*  i192.168.101.0   192.168.1.34           0    100      0 i
*>i                 192.168.1.18           0    100      0 I
p1r1#
```

This output does show the 172.26.1.16/28, 172.26.1.32/28, 172.26.1.48/28, and 192.168.101.0/24 routes.

Examine the p*x*r1 IP routing table. Do you see the following subnets displayed?

— 172.26.*x*.16/28

— 172.26.*x*.32/28

— 172.26.*x*.48/28

— 192.168.10*x*.0/24

The following example output is from the p1r1 router, showing the IP routing table:

```
p1r1#show ip route
<output omitted>
Gateway of last resort is not set

     172.16.0.0/24 is subnetted, 2 subnets
B       172.16.10.0 [20/0] via 10.1.1.100, 00:32:42
B       172.16.11.0 [20/0] via 10.1.1.100, 00:32:42
     172.26.0.0/28 is subnetted, 3 subnets
B       172.26.1.48 [200/0] via 192.168.1.50, 00:01:07
B       172.26.1.32 [200/0] via 192.168.1.50, 00:01:07
B       172.26.1.16 [200/0] via 192.168.1.50, 00:01:07
     10.0.0.0/8 is variably subnetted, 2 subnets, 2 masks
B       10.0.0.0/8 [20/0] via 10.1.1.100, 00:32:42
C       10.1.1.0/24 is directly connected, Serial3
```

```
          192.168.1.0/28 is subnetted, 3 subnets
C             192.168.1.32 is directly connected, Serial1
C             192.168.1.48 is directly connected, Serial2
C             192.168.1.16 is directly connected, Serial0
          192.168.2.0/24 is variably subnetted, 2 subnets, 2 masks
B             192.168.2.64/28 [20/0] via 10.1.1.100, 00:08:16
B             192.168.2.0/24 [20/0] via 10.1.1.100, 00:32:46
B         192.168.101.0/24 [200/0] via 192.168.1.18, 00:00:51
p1r1#
```

> **This output does show the 172.26.1.16/28, 172.26.1.32/28, 172.26.1.48/28, and 192.168.101.0/24 routes.**

**Step 3**   From the p*x*r2 router, enter the **show ip bgp** command. Do you see the following subnets displayed?

— 172.26.*x*.16/28

— 172.26.*x*.32/28

— 172.26.*x*.48/28

— 192.168.10*x*.0/24

> **The following example output is from the p1r2 router, indicating the BGP routes:**

```
p1r2#show ip bgp
BGP table version is 21, local router ID is 192.168.101.101
Status codes: s suppressed, d damped, h history, * valid, > best, i - internal
Origin codes: i - IGP, e - EGP, ? - incomplete

   Network          Next Hop         Metric LocPrf Weight Path
 * i10.0.0.0        192.168.1.33          0    100      0 65200 i
 *>i                192.168.1.17          0    100      0 65200 i
 * i172.16.10.0/24  192.168.1.33          0    100      0 65200 i
 *>i                192.168.1.17          0    100      0 65200 i
 * i172.16.11.0/24  192.168.1.33          0    100      0 65200 i
 *>i                192.168.1.17          0    100      0 65200 i
 * i192.168.1.0     192.168.1.33          0    100      0 i
 *>i                192.168.1.17          0    100      0 i
 * i192.168.2.0     192.168.1.33               100      0 65200 65102 i
 *>i                192.168.1.17               100      0 65200 65102 i
 * i192.168.2.64/28 192.168.1.33               100      0 65200 65102 i
 *>i                192.168.1.17               100      0 65200 65102 i
 *> 192.168.101.0   0.0.0.0               0           32768 i
p1r2#
```

> **This output does not show the 172.26.1.16/28, 172.26.1.32/28, or 172.26.1.48/28 routes. It does show the 192.168.101.0/24 route, which is the loopback network on this router.**

Examine the p*x*r2 IP routing table. Do you see the following subnets displayed?

— 172.26.*x*.16/28

— 172.26.*x*.32/28

— 172.26.*x*.48/28

— 192.168.10*x*.0/24

**The following example output is from the p1r2 router, showing the IP routing table:**

```
p1r2#show ip route
<output omitted>

     172.16.0.0/24 is subnetted, 2 subnets
B       172.16.10.0 [200/0] via 192.168.1.17, 00:33:19
B       172.16.11.0 [200/0] via 192.168.1.17, 00:33:19
B    10.0.0.0/8 [200/0] via 192.168.1.17, 00:33:19
     192.168.1.0/24 is variably subnetted, 3 subnets, 2 masks
C       192.168.1.32/28 is directly connected, Serial1
B       192.168.1.0/24 [200/0] via 192.168.1.17, 00:32:50
C       192.168.1.16/28 is directly connected, Serial0
     192.168.2.0/24 is variably subnetted, 2 subnets, 2 masks
B       192.168.2.64/28 [200/0] via 192.168.1.17, 00:08:51
B       192.168.2.0/24 [200/0] via 192.168.1.17, 00:33:20
C    192.168.101.0/24 is directly connected, Loopback10
p1r2#
```

**This output does not show the 172.26.1.16/28, 172.26.1.32/28, or 172.26.1.48/ 28 routes. It does show the 192.168.101.0/24 route, which is the loopback network on this router.**

**Step 4** From the p*x*r3 router, enter the **show ip bgp** command. Do you see the following subnets displayed?

— 172.26.*x*.16/28

— 172.26.*x*.32/28

— 172.26.*x*.48/28

— 192.168.10*x*.0/24

**The following example output is from the p1r3 router, indicating the BGP routes:**

```
p1r3#show ip bgp
BGP table version is 17, local router ID is 172.26.1.49
Status codes: s suppressed, d damped, h history, * valid, > best, i - internal
Origin codes: i - IGP, e - EGP, ? - incomplete

   Network          Next Hop         Metric LocPrf Weight Path
*>i10.0.0.0         192.168.1.49          0    100      0 65200 i
*>i172.16.10.0/24   192.168.1.49          0    100      0 65200 i
*>i172.16.11.0/24   192.168.1.49          0    100      0 65200 i
*>  172.26.1.16/28  0.0.0.0               0         32768 i
*>  172.26.1.32/28  0.0.0.0               0         32768 i
*>  172.26.1.48/28  0.0.0.0               0         32768 i
*>i192.168.1.0      192.168.1.49          0    100      0 i
*>i192.168.2.0      192.168.1.49               100      0 65200 65102 i
*>i192.168.2.64/28  192.168.1.49               100      0 65200 65102 i
p1r3#
```

**This output does show the 172.26.1.16/28, 172.26.1.32/28, and 172.26.1.48/28 routes (they are the loopback subnets on this router) but does not show the 192.168.101.0/24 route.**

Examine the p*x*r3 IP routing table. Do you see the following subnets displayed?

— 172.26.*x*.16/28

— 172.26.*x*.32/28

— 172.26.*x*.48/28

— 192.168.10*x*.0/24

**The following example output is from the p1r3 router, showing the IP routing table:**

```
p1r3#show ip route
<output omitted>

     172.16.0.0/24 is subnetted, 2 subnets
B       172.16.10.0 [200/0] via 192.168.1.49, 00:34:28
B       172.16.11.0 [200/0] via 192.168.1.49, 00:34:28
     172.26.0.0/28 is subnetted, 3 subnets
C       172.26.1.48 is directly connected, Loopback13
C       172.26.1.32 is directly connected, Loopback12
C       172.26.1.16 is directly connected, Loopback11
B    10.0.0.0/8 [200/0] via 192.168.1.49, 00:34:28
     192.168.1.0/24 is variably subnetted, 2 subnets, 2 masks
C       192.168.1.48/28 is directly connected, Serial0
B       192.168.1.0/24 [200/0] via 192.168.1.49, 00:33:58
     192.168.2.0/24 is variably subnetted, 2 subnets, 2 masks
B       192.168.2.64/28 [200/0] via 192.168.1.49, 00:10:00
B       192.168.2.0/24 [200/0] via 192.168.1.49, 00:34:32
p1r3#
```

This output does show the 172.26.1.16/28, 172.26.1.32/28, and 172.26.1.48/28 routes (they are the loopback subnets on this router) but does not show the 192.168.101.0/24 route.

**Step 5** From Steps 2, 3, and 4, you should be able to determine that because there is no IBGP neighbor relationship between pxr2 and pxr3, pxr1 will not by default propagate the IBGP routes learned from pxr2 to pxr3 or from pxr3 to pxr2.

Configure the pxr1 router to allow the pxr1 router to be a router reflector for pxr2 and pxr3.

**The following example shows the configuration of the p1r1 router as a route reflector for p1r2 and p1r3:**

```
p1r1#conf t
Enter configuration commands, one per line.  End with CNTL/Z.
p1r1(config)#router bgp 65101
p1r1(config-router)#neighbor 192.168.1.18 route-reflector-client
p1r1(config-router)#neighbor 192.168.1.34 route-reflector-client
p1r1(config-router)#neighbor 192.168.1.50 route-reflector-client
```

**Step 6** From the pxr2 router, enter the **show ip bgp** command.

Do you see the following subnets displayed?

— 172.26.x.16/28

— 172.26.x.32/28

— 172.26.x.48/28

— 192.168.10x.0/24

**The following example output is from the p1r2 router:**

```
p1r2#show ip bgp
BGP table version is 41, local router ID is 192.168.101.101
Status codes: s suppressed, d damped, h history, * valid, > best, i - internal
Origin codes: i - IGP, e - EGP, ? - incomplete

   Network          Next Hop         Metric LocPrf Weight Path
 * i10.0.0.0         192.168.1.33          0    100      0 65200 i
 *>i                 192.168.1.17          0    100      0 65200 i
 * i172.16.10.0/24   192.168.1.33          0    100      0 65200 i
 *>i                 192.168.1.17          0    100      0 65200 i
 * i172.16.11.0/24   192.168.1.33          0    100      0 65200 i
 *>i                 192.168.1.17          0    100      0 65200 i
 * i172.26.1.16/28   192.168.1.50          0    100      0 i
 * i                 192.168.1.50          0    100      0 i
 * i172.26.1.32/28   192.168.1.50          0    100      0 i
 * i                 192.168.1.50          0    100      0 i
```

```
  * i172.26.1.48/28   192.168.1.50          0    100       0 i
  * i                 192.168.1.50          0    100       0 i
  * i192.168.1.0      192.168.1.33          0    100       0 i
  *>i                 192.168.1.17          0    100       0 i
  * i192.168.2.0      192.168.1.33               100       0 65200 65102 i
  *>i                 192.168.1.17               100       0 65200 65102 i
  * i192.168.2.64/28  192.168.1.33               100       0 65200 65102 i
  *>i                 192.168.1.17               100       0 65200 65102 i
  *> 192.168.101.0    0.0.0.0               0              32768 i
```

> This output does show the 172.26.1.16/28, 172.26.1.32/28, 172.26.1.48/28, and 192.168.101.0/24 routes.

Examine the p*x*r2 IP routing table. Do you see the following subnets displayed?

— 172.26.*x*.16/28

— 172.26.*x*.32/28

— 172.26.*x*.48/28

— 192.168.10*x*.0/24

(Note that it may take a minute or so for the routes to appear.)

> **The following example output is from the p1r2 router:**

```
p1r2#show ip route

     172.16.0.0/24 is subnetted, 2 subnets
B       172.16.10.0 [200/0] via 192.168.1.17, 00:01:34
B       172.16.11.0 [200/0] via 192.168.1.17, 00:01:34
     172.26.0.0/28 is subnetted, 3 subnets
B       172.26.1.48 [200/0] via 192.168.1.50, 00:00:39
B       172.26.1.32 [200/0] via 192.168.1.50, 00:00:39
B       172.26.1.16 [200/0] via 192.168.1.50, 00:00:39
B    10.0.0.0/8 [200/0] via 192.168.1.17, 00:01:34
     192.168.1.0/24 is variably subnetted, 3 subnets, 2 masks
C       192.168.1.32/28 is directly connected, Serial1
B       192.168.1.0/24 [200/0] via 192.168.1.17, 00:01:34
C       192.168.1.16/28 is directly connected, Serial0
     192.168.2.0/24 is variably subnetted, 2 subnets, 2 masks
B       192.168.2.64/28 [200/0] via 192.168.1.17, 00:01:36
B       192.168.2.0/24 [200/0] via 192.168.1.17, 00:01:36
C    192.168.101.0/24 is directly connected, Loopback10
p1r2#
```

> This output does show the 172.26.1.16/28, 172.26.1.32/28, 172.26.1.48/28, and 192.168.101.0/24 routes.

**Step 7** From the p*x*r3 router, enter the **show ip bgp** command. Do you see the following subnets displayed?

- 172.26.*x*.16/28

- 172.26.*x*.32/28

- 172.26.*x*.48/28

- 192.168.10*x*.0/24

**The following example output is from the p1r3 router:**

```
p1r3#show ip bgp
BGP table version is 33, local router ID is 172.26.1.49
Status codes: s suppressed, d damped, h history, * valid, > best, i - internal
Origin codes: i - IGP, e - EGP, ? - incomplete

   Network          Next Hop          Metric LocPrf Weight Path
*>i10.0.0.0         192.168.1.49           0    100      0 65200 i
*>i172.16.10.0/24   192.168.1.49           0    100      0 65200 i
*>i172.16.11.0/24   192.168.1.49           0    100      0 65200 i
*> 172.26.1.16/28   0.0.0.0                0         32768 i
*> 172.26.1.32/28   0.0.0.0                0         32768 i
*> 172.26.1.48/28   0.0.0.0                0         32768 i
*>i192.168.1.0      192.168.1.49           0    100      0 i
*>i192.168.2.0      192.168.1.49                100      0 65200 65102 i
*>i192.168.2.64/28  192.168.1.49                100      0 65200 65102 i
*>i192.168.101.0    192.168.1.18           0    100      0 i
```

**This output does show the 172.26.1.16/28, 172.26.1.32/28, 172.26.1.48/28, and 192.168.101.0/24 routes.**

Examine the p*x*r3 IP routing table. Do you see the following subnets displayed?

- 172.26.*x*.16/28

- 172.26.*x*.32/28

- 172.26.*x*.48/28

- 192.168.10*x*.0/24

**The following example output is from the p1r3 router:**

```
p1r3#show ip route
<output omitted>
172.16.0.0/24 is subnetted, 2 subnets
B      172.16.10.0 [200/0] via 192.168.1.49, 00:04:00
B      172.16.11.0 [200/0] via 192.168.1.49, 00:04:00
   172.26.0.0/28 is subnetted, 3 subnets
C        172.26.1.48 is directly connected, Loopback13
```

```
C       172.26.1.32 is directly connected, Loopback12
C       172.26.1.16 is directly connected, Loopback11
B    10.0.0.0/8 [200/0] via 192.168.1.49, 00:04:00
     192.168.1.0/24 is variably subnetted, 2 subnets, 2 masks
C       192.168.1.48/28 is directly connected, Serial0
B       192.168.1.0/24 [200/0] via 192.168.1.49, 00:04:00
     192.168.2.0/24 is variably subnetted, 2 subnets, 2 masks
B       192.168.2.64/28 [200/0] via 192.168.1.49, 00:04:00
B       192.168.2.0/24 [200/0] via 192.168.1.49, 00:04:13
B    192.168.101.0/24 [200/0] via 192.168.1.18, 00:04:14
p1r3#
```

**This output does show the 172.26.1.16/28, 172.26.1.32/28, 172.26.1.48/28, and 192.168.101.0/24 routes.**

**Step 8**  From the p*x*r3 router, ping 192.168.10*x*.10*x*. From the p*x*r2 router, ping
172.26.*x*.17, 172.26.*x*.33, and 172.26.*x*.49.

Were the pings successful?

**The results of the ping commands to the loopback interfaces on the routers
are shown in the following output. All pings are successful.**

```
p1r3#ping 192.168.101.101

Type escape sequence to abort.
Sending 5, 100-byte ICMP Echos to 192.168.101.101, timeout is 2 seconds:
!!!!!
Success rate is 100 percent (5/5), round-trip min/avg/max = 56/58/60 ms
p1r3#

p1r2#ping 172.26.1.17

Type escape sequence to abort.
Sending 5, 100-byte ICMP Echos to 172.26.1.17, timeout is 2 seconds:
!!!!!
Success rate is 100 percent (5/5), round-trip min/avg/max = 60/60/64 ms
p1r2#ping 172.26.1.33

Type escape sequence to abort.
Sending 5, 100-byte ICMP Echos to 172.26.1.33, timeout is 2 seconds:
!!!!!
Success rate is 100 percent (5/5), round-trip min/avg/max = 56/59/60 ms
p1r2#ping 172.26.1.49

Type escape sequence to abort.
Sending 5, 100-byte ICMP Echos to 172.26.1.49, timeout is 2 seconds:
!!!!!
Success rate is 100 percent (5/5), round-trip min/avg/max = 60/60/60 ms
p1r2#
```

**Step 9** Telnet to the backbone_r1 router, using the password cisco. Ping
192.168.10*x*.10*x*, 172.26.*x*.17, 172.26.*x*.33, and 172.26.*x*.49.

Were the pings successful?

**The following example shows results of the ping command to the loopback
interfaces on the routers from the backbone_r1 router. All pings are
successful.**

```
p1r2#bbr1
Trying bbr1 (10.1.1.100)... Open


User Access Verification

Password:
backbone_r1>ping 192.168.101.101
Type escape sequence to abort.
Sending 5, 100-byte ICMP Echos to 192.168.101.101, timeout is 2 seconds:
!!!!!
Success rate is 100 percent (5/5), round-trip min/avg/max = 64/69/92 ms
backbone_r1>ping 172.26.1.17

Type escape sequence to abort.
Sending 5, 100-byte ICMP Echos to 172.26.1.17, timeout is 2 seconds:
!!!!!
Success rate is 100 percent (5/5), round-trip min/avg/max = 64/68/84 ms
backbone_r1>ping 172.26.1.33

Type escape sequence to abort.
Sending 5, 100-byte ICMP Echos to 172.26.1.33, timeout is 2 seconds:
!!!!!
Success rate is 100 percent (5/5), round-trip min/avg/max = 64/68/84 ms
backbone_r1>ping 172.26.1.49
Type escape sequence to abort.
Sending 5, 100-byte ICMP Echos to 172.26.1.49, timeout is 2 seconds:
!!!!!
Success rate is 100 percent (5/5), round-trip min/avg/max = 64/68/84 ms
backbone_r1>
```

**Step 10** Save the current configurations of all the routers within your pod to
NVRAM.

**The following example shows how to save the configuration of the p1r1
router, using the copy run start command (this is an abbreviated form of the
copy running-config startup-config command):**

```
p1r1#copy run start
Destination filename [startup-config]?
Building configuration...
p1r1#
```

## Answers to Task 2: Enabling an Inbound Prefix List

Complete the following steps:

**Step 1**    At your p*x*r1 router, make sure that you can see both the 172.16.10.0 and 172.16.11.0 BGP routes from the backbone_r1 router.

**The following example output is from the p1r1 router. Both the 172.16.10.0 and 172.16.11.0 BGP routes from the backbone_r1 router are in the p1r1 routing table.**

**NOTE**    **Note that the routers in pod 2 have now also been configured, up to the end of Task 1 in this Configuration Exercise.**

```
p1r1#show ip route
<output omitted>

      172.16.0.0/24 is subnetted, 2 subnets
B       172.16.10.0 [20/0] via 10.1.1.100, 01:02:22
B       172.16.11.0 [20/0] via 10.1.1.100, 01:02:22
      172.26.0.0/28 is subnetted, 6 subnets
B       172.26.2.48 [20/0] via 10.1.1.100, 00:01:48
B       172.26.1.48 [200/0] via 192.168.1.50, 00:26:07
B       172.26.2.32 [20/0] via 10.1.1.100, 00:01:48
B       172.26.1.32 [200/0] via 192.168.1.50, 00:26:07
B       172.26.2.16 [20/0] via 10.1.1.100, 00:01:48
B       172.26.1.16 [200/0] via 192.168.1.50, 00:26:07
      10.0.0.0/8 is variably subnetted, 2 subnets, 2 masks
B       10.0.0.0/8 [20/0] via 10.1.1.100, 01:02:22
C       10.1.1.0/24 is directly connected, Serial3
B     192.168.102.0/24 [20/0] via 10.1.1.100, 00:02:26
      192.168.1.0/28 is subnetted, 3 subnets
C       192.168.1.32 is directly connected, Serial1
C       192.168.1.48 is directly connected, Serial2
C       192.168.1.16 is directly connected, Serial0
B     192.168.2.0/24 [20/0] via 10.1.1.100, 01:02:23
B     192.168.101.0/24 [200/0] via 192.168.1.18, 00:26:23
p1r1#
```

**Step 2**    At your p*x*r1 router, configure an inbound prefix list filter to permit only prefix 172.16.10.0/24 to come in from the backbone_r1 router.

**The following example shows the configuration of an inbound prefix list on the p1r1 router:**

```
p1r1#conf t
Enter configuration commands, one per line.  End with CNTL/Z.
p1r1(config)#router bgp 65101
p1r1(config-router)#neighbor 10.1.1.100 prefix-list test in
p1r1(config-router)#exit
p1r1(config)#ip prefix-list test permit 172.16.10.0/24
```

**Step 3**   Issue the **clear ip bgp** * command at your p*x*r1 router.

**The following example shows the use of the clear ip bgp * command on the p1r1 router:**

```
p1r1#clear ip bgp *
p1r1#
```

**Step 4**   Display the routing table of your p*x*r1 router to verify that your prefix list is working.

**The following example output is from the p1r1 router. Only the 172.16.10.0 subnet, not the 172.16.11.0 subnet, from the backbone_r1 router is in the p1r1 routing table. (Note that the prefix list also filtered out all routes about pod 2 from the backbone_r1 router.)**

```
p1r1#show ip route
<output omitted>
     172.16.0.0/24 is subnetted, 1 subnets
B       172.16.10.0 [20/0] via 10.1.1.100, 00:00:14
     172.26.0.0/28 is subnetted, 3 subnets
B       172.26.1.48 [200/0] via 192.168.1.50, 00:00:30
B       172.26.1.32 [200/0] via 192.168.1.50, 00:00:30
B       172.26.1.16 [200/0] via 192.168.1.50, 00:00:30
     10.0.0.0/24 is subnetted, 1 subnets
C       10.1.1.0 is directly connected, Serial3
     192.168.1.0/28 is subnetted, 3 subnets
C       192.168.1.32 is directly connected, Serial1
C       192.168.1.48 is directly connected, Serial2
C       192.168.1.16 is directly connected, Serial0
B    192.168.101.0/24 [200/0] via 192.168.1.18, 00:00:31
p1r1#
```

**Step 5**   Remove the prefix list configuration.

**The following example shows the removal of the prefix list on the p1r1 router:**

```
p1r1#conf t
Enter configuration commands, one per line.  End with CNTL/Z.
p1r1(config)#router bgp 65101
p1r1(config-router)#no neighbor 10.1.1.100 prefix-list test in
p1r1(config-router)#no ip prefix-list test permit 172.16.10.0/24
```

**Step 6**  Issue the **clear ip bgp** * command on your p*x*r1 router.

**The following example shows the use of the clear ip bgp * command on the p1r1 router:**

```
p1r1#clear ip bgp *
p1r1#
```

**Step 7**  Save the current configurations of all the routers within your pod to NVRAM.

**The following example shows how to save the configuration of the p1r1 router, using the copy run start command (this is an abbreviated form of the copy running-config startup-config command):**

```
p1r1#copy run start
Destination filename [startup-config]?
Building configuration...
p1r1#
```

# Answers to Configuration Exercise #2: Configuring Multihomed BGP

This section provides the answers to the questions in Configuration Exercise #2.

## Answers to Task: Enabling a Second EBGP Connection

Complete the following steps:

**Step 1**  At the p*x*r3 router, no shut the S1 interface that connects to the backbone_r2 router.

Set the p*x*r3 S1 IP address to 172.22.*x.x*/24, where *x* is your pod number, as shown in the following table.

| Pod | P*x*r3 S1 IP Address |
| --- | --- |
| 1 | 172.22.1.1/24 |
| 2 | 172.22.2.2/24 |
| 3 | 172.22.3.3/24 |
| 4 | 172.22.4.4/24 |
| 5 | 172.22.5.5/24 |
| 6 | 172.22.6.6/24 |
| 7 | 172.22.7.7/24 |
| 8 | 172.22.8.8/24 |

*continues*

*(Continued)*

| Pod | P*x*r3 S1 IP Address |
|---|---|
| 9 | 172.22.9.9/24 |
| 10 | 172.22.10.10/24 |
| 11 | 172.22.11.11/24 |
| 12 | 172.22.12.12/24 |

**The following example shows how to configure the required commands on the p1r3 router:**

```
p1r3#conf t
Enter configuration commands, one per line.  End with CNTL/Z.
p1r3(config)#int s1
p1r3(config-if)#no shutdown
08:19:02: %LINK-3-UPDOWN: Interface Serial1, changed state to up
08:19:03: %LINEPROTO-5-UPDOWN: Line protocol on Interface Serial1, changed state to
up
p1r3(config-if)#ip address 172.22.1.1 255.255.255.0
```

From your p*x*r3 router, ping 172.22.*x*.100 to verify connectivity to the backbone_r2 router.

**The result of the ping command to the backbone_r2 router is shown in the following output. The ping is successful.**

```
p1r3#ping 172.22.1.100

Type escape sequence to abort.
Sending 5, 100-byte ICMP Echos to 172.22.1.100, timeout is 2 seconds:
!!!!!
Success rate is 100 percent (5/5), round-trip min/avg/max = 28/29/32 ms
p1r3#
```

**Step 2**   At the p*x*r3 router, use the **neighbor** statement to establish the backbone_r2 router as an EBGP neighbor. (The backbone_r2 router is in AS 65201.)

**The following example shows the configuration of the neighbor statement on the p1r3 router:**

```
p1r3#conf t
Enter configuration commands, one per line.  End with CNTL/Z.
p1r3(config)#router bgp 65101
p1r3(config-router)#neighbor 172.22.1.100 remote-as 65201
```

**Step 3**   At the p*x*r3 router, enter the **show ip bgp summary** and the **show ip bgp neighbors** commands.

Wait until the neighbor state indicates established.

What is the BGP state of the backbone_r2 router?

How many prefixes have been learned from the backbone_r2 router?

**The following example output is from the p1r3 router:**

```
p1r3#show ip bgp summary
BGP table version is 70, main routing table version 70
15 network entries and 15 paths using 1815 bytes of memory
6 BGP path attribute entries using 708 bytes of memory
BGP activity 33/18 prefixes, 49/34 paths
0 prefixes revised.

Neighbor         V    AS MsgRcvd MsgSent   TblVer  InQ OutQ Up/Down  State/PfxRcd
172.22.1.100     4 65201       4       8       70    0    0 00:00:41            2
192.168.1.49     4 65101     137     119       70    0    0 00:07:59           10

p1r3#show ip bgp neighbors
BGP neighbor is 172.22.1.100,   remote AS 65201, external link
 Index 2, Offset 0, Mask 0x4
  BGP version 4, remote router ID 172.31.21.100
  BGP state = Established, table version = 70, up for 00:00:44
  Last read 00:00:43, hold time is 180, keepalive interval is 60 seconds
  Minimum time between advertisement runs is 30 seconds
  Received 4 messages, 0 notifications, 0 in queue
  Sent 8 messages, 0 notifications, 0 in queue
  Prefix advertised 13, suppressed 0, withdrawn 0
  Connections established 1; dropped 0
  Last reset never
  2 accepted prefixes consume 64 bytes
  0 history paths consume 0 bytes
Connection state is ESTAB, I/O status: 1, unread input bytes: 0
Local host: 172.22.1.1, Local port: 11004
Foreign host: 172.22.1.100, Foreign port: 179
<output omitted>
```

In the show ip bgp summary output, the State field is blank, indicating that the neighbor state of the backbone_r2 (172.22.1.100) router is Established. This command also indicates in the PfxRcd field that p1r3 has learned two prefixes from the backbone_r2 router.

The show ip bgp neighbors output indicates that the BGP state of the backbone_r2 router is Established.

**Step 4** At your p*x*r3 router, enter the **show ip bgp** command.

Do you see a route to 172.31.20.0/24 and 172.31.21.0/24? Write down the following information:

— Network

— Next hop

— Metric

— LocPrf

— Weight

— Path

**The following example output is from p1r3 router, indicating the BGP routes:**

```
p1r3#show ip bgp
BGP table version is 70, local router ID is 172.26.1.49
Status codes: s suppressed, d damped, h history, * valid, > best, i - internal
Origin codes: i - IGP, e - EGP, ? - incomplete

   Network          Next Hop         Metric LocPrf Weight Path
*>i10.0.0.0         192.168.1.49          0    100      0 65200 i
*>i172.16.10.0/24   192.168.1.49          0    100      0 65200 i
*>i172.16.11.0/24   192.168.1.49          0    100      0 65200 i
*> 172.26.1.16/28   0.0.0.0               0         32768 i
*> 172.26.1.32/28   0.0.0.0               0         32768 i
*> 172.26.1.48/28   0.0.0.0               0         32768 i
*>i172.26.2.16/28   192.168.1.49               100      0 65200 65102 i
*>i172.26.2.32/28   192.168.1.49               100      0 65200 65102 i
*>i172.26.2.48/28   192.168.1.49               100      0 65200 65102 i
*> 172.31.20.0/24   172.22.1.100          0              0 65201 i
*> 172.31.21.0/24   172.22.1.100          0              0 65201 i
*>i192.168.1.0      192.168.1.49          0    100      0 i
*>i192.168.2.0      192.168.1.49               100      0 65200 65102 i
*>i192.168.101.0    192.168.1.18          0    100      0 i
*>i192.168.102.0    192.168.1.49               100      0 65200 65102 i
p1r3#
```

**Routes to 172.31.20.0/24 and 172.31.21.0/24 are in the BGP table on p1r3.**

**Step 5** At your p*x*r3 router, ping 172.31.20.100 and 172.31.21.100.

Were the pings successful?

**The following example shows results of the ping command to the loopback interfaces on the backbone_r2 router. Both pings are successful.**

```
p1r3#ping 172.31.20.100
```

```
Type escape sequence to abort.
Sending 5, 100-byte ICMP Echos to 172.31.20.100, timeout is 2 seconds:
!!!!!
Success rate is 100 percent (5/5), round-trip min/avg/max = 32/32/32 ms
p1r3#ping 172.31.21.100

Type escape sequence to abort.
Sending 5, 100-byte ICMP Echos to 172.31.21.100, timeout is 2 seconds:
!!!!!
Success rate is 100 percent (5/5), round-trip min/avg/max = 32/32/32 ms
p1r3#
```

**Step 6**   At your p*x*r1 router, enter the **show ip bgp** command. Do you see a route
to 172.31.20.0/24 and 172.31.21.0/24 (in AS 65201) directly from your
AS?

What is the next hop to get to 172.31.20.0/24 and 172.31.21.0/24 directly
to AS 65201 from your AS?

**The following example output is from the p1r1 router. Routes to 172.31.20.0/
24 and 172.31.21.0/24 (in AS 65201) are shown, directly from the pod 1 AS.
The next hop to get to both of these routes is 172.22.1.100 (the address of the
backbone_r2 router).**

**NOTE**   **Note that the routers in pod 2 have now also been configured, up to this point in this
Configuration Exercise.**

```
p1r1#show ip bgp
BGP table version is 14, local router ID is 192.168.1.49
Status codes: s suppressed, d damped, h history, * valid, > best, i - internal
Origin codes: i - IGP, e - EGP, ? - incomplete

   Network          Next Hop         Metric LocPrf Weight Path
*> 10.0.0.0         10.1.1.100            0           0 65200 i
*> 172.16.10.0/24   10.1.1.100            0           0 65200 i
*> 172.16.11.0/24   10.1.1.100            0           0 65200 i
*>i172.26.1.16/28   192.168.1.50         0    100     0 i
*>i172.26.1.32/28   192.168.1.50         0    100     0 i
*>i172.26.1.48/28   192.168.1.50         0    100     0 i
* i172.26.2.16/28   172.22.1.100              100     0 65201 65102 i
*>                  10.1.1.100                         0 65200 65102 i
* i172.26.2.32/28   172.22.1.100              100     0 65201 65102 i
*>                  10.1.1.100                         0 65200 65102 i
* i172.26.2.48/28   172.22.1.100              100     0 65201 65102 i
*>                  10.1.1.100                         0 65200 65102 i
* i172.31.20.0/24   172.22.1.100         0    100     0 65201 i
* i172.31.21.0/24   172.22.1.100         0    100     0 65201 i
*> 192.168.1.0      0.0.0.0              0         32768 i
* i192.168.2.0      172.22.1.100              100     0 65201 65102 i
```

```
*>                    10.1.1.100                                    0 65200 65102 i
* i192.168.2.64/28   172.22.1.100                      100         0 65201 65102 i
  Network            Next Hop             Metric LocPrf Weight Path
* i192.168.101.0     192.168.1.34              0    100      0 i
*>i                  192.168.1.18              0    100      0 i
* i192.168.102.0     172.22.1.100                   100      0 65201 65102 i
*>                   10.1.1.100                               0 65200 65102 i
p1r1#
```

---

**NOTE**    You can use the show ip bgp 172.31.20.0/24 longer-prefix command to see only the
172.31.20.0/24 part of the BGP table.

---

Examine your p*x*r1 IP routing table. Do you see a route to 172.31.20.0/
24 and 172.31.21.0/24 (in AS 65201) directly from your AS?

**The following example output is from the p1r1 router. No routes to
172.31.20.0/24 or 172.31.21.0/24 exist in the p1r1 outing table.**

```
p1r1#show ip route
<output omitted>

     172.16.0.0/24 is subnetted, 2 subnets
B       172.16.10.0 [20/0] via 10.1.1.100, 00:16:55
B       172.16.11.0 [20/0] via 10.1.1.100, 00:16:55
     172.26.0.0/28 is subnetted, 6 subnets
B       172.26.2.48 [20/0] via 10.1.1.100, 00:16:55
B       172.26.1.48 [200/0] via 192.168.1.50, 00:17:12
B       172.26.2.32 [20/0] via 10.1.1.100, 00:16:55
B       172.26.1.32 [200/0] via 192.168.1.50, 00:17:12
B       172.26.2.16 [20/0] via 10.1.1.100, 00:16:55
B       172.26.1.16 [200/0] via 192.168.1.50, 00:17:12
     10.0.0.0/8 is variably subnetted, 2 subnets, 2 masks
B       10.0.0.0/8 [20/0] via 10.1.1.100, 00:16:55
C       10.1.1.0/24 is directly connected, Serial3
B    192.168.102.0/24 [20/0] via 10.1.1.100, 00:16:56
     192.168.1.0/28 is subnetted, 3 subnets
C       192.168.1.32 is directly connected, Serial1
C       192.168.1.48 is directly connected, Serial2
C       192.168.1.16 is directly connected, Serial0
B    192.168.2.0/24 [20/0] via 10.1.1.100, 00:16:56
B    192.168.101.0/24 [200/0] via 192.168.1.18, 00:17:16
p1r1#
```

**Step 7**    Enable the next-hop-self options. At your p*x*r3 router, enter the BGP
configuration command to cause p*x*r3 to announce itself as the next-hop
router to p*x*r1.

**The following example shows the configuration of the next-hop-self option on
the p1r3 router:**

```
p1r3#conf t
Enter configuration commands, one per line.  End with CNTL/Z.
p1r3(config)#router bgp 65101
p1r3(config-router)#neighbor 192.168.1.49 next-hop-self
```

Issue the **clear ip bgp** * command at p*x*r3 to reset the BGP sessions.

**The following example shows the use of the clear ip bgp * command on the p1r3 router:**

```
p1r3#clear ip bgp *
p1r3#
```

**Step 8**  At your p*x*r1 router, enter the **show ip bgp** command again. Do you see a route to 172.31.20.0/24 and 172.31.21.0/24 (in AS 65201) directly from your AS?

What is the next hop to get to 172.31.20.0/24 and 172.31.21.0/24 directly from your AS?

**The following example output is from the p1r1 router. Routes to 172.31.20.0/ 24 and 172.31.21.0/24 are shown, with a next-hop address of 192.168.1.50 (the address of p1r3).**

```
p1r1#show ip bgp
BGP table version is 35, local router ID is 192.168.1.49
Status codes: s suppressed, d damped, h history, * valid, > best, i - internal
Origin codes: i - IGP, e - EGP, ? - incomplete

   Network          Next Hop         Metric LocPrf Weight Path
*> 10.0.0.0         10.1.1.100            0             0 65200 i
*> 172.16.10.0/24   10.1.1.100            0             0 65200 i
*> 172.16.11.0/24   10.1.1.100            0             0 65200 i
*>i172.26.1.16/28   192.168.1.50         0    100      0 i
*>i172.26.1.32/28   192.168.1.50         0    100      0 i
*>i172.26.1.48/28   192.168.1.50         0    100      0 i
*> 172.26.2.16/28   10.1.1.100                          0 65200 65102 i
*> 172.26.2.32/28   10.1.1.100                          0 65200 65102 i
*> 172.26.2.48/28   10.1.1.100                          0 65200 65102 i
*>i172.31.20.0/24   192.168.1.50         0    100      0 65201 i
*>i172.31.21.0/24   192.168.1.50         0    100      0 65201 i
*> 192.168.1.0      0.0.0.0              0         32768 i
*  i192.168.2.0     192.168.1.50              100      0 65201 65102 i
*>                  10.1.1.100                          0 65200 65102 i
*>i192.168.2.64/28  192.168.1.50              100      0 65201 65102 i
*  i192.168.101.0   192.168.1.34         0    100      0 i
*>i                 192.168.1.18         0    100      0 i
*  i192.168.102.0   192.168.1.50              100      0 65201 65102 i
*>                  10.1.1.100                          0 65200 65102 i
```

Examine your p*x*r1 IP routing table. Do you see a route to 172.31.20.0/ 24 and 172.31.21.0/24 (in AS 65201) directly from your AS?

The following example output is from the p1r1 router. Routes to 172.31.20.0/24 and 172.31.21.0/24 are shown in the routing table.

```
p1r1#show ip route
<output omitted>

        172.16.0.0/24 is subnetted, 2 subnets
B         172.16.10.0 [20/0] via 10.1.1.100, 00:19:49
B         172.16.11.0 [20/0] via 10.1.1.100, 00:19:49
        172.26.0.0/28 is subnetted, 6 subnets
B         172.26.2.48 [20/0] via 10.1.1.100, 00:00:35
B         172.26.1.48 [200/0] via 192.168.1.50, 00:01:24
B         172.26.2.32 [20/0] via 10.1.1.100, 00:00:35
B         172.26.1.32 [200/0] via 192.168.1.50, 00:01:24
B         172.26.2.16 [20/0] via 10.1.1.100, 00:00:35
B         172.26.1.16 [200/0] via 192.168.1.50, 00:01:24
        172.31.0.0/24 is subnetted, 2 subnets
B         172.31.21.0 [200/0] via 192.168.1.50, 00:01:14
B         172.31.20.0 [200/0] via 192.168.1.50, 00:01:14
        10.0.0.0/8 is variably subnetted, 2 subnets, 2 masks
B         10.0.0.0/8 [20/0] via 10.1.1.100, 00:19:51
C         10.1.1.0/24 is directly connected, Serial3
B       192.168.102.0/24 [20/0] via 10.1.1.100, 00:19:51
        192.168.1.0/28 is subnetted, 3 subnets
C         192.168.1.32 is directly connected, Serial1
C         192.168.1.48 is directly connected, Serial2
C         192.168.1.16 is directly connected, Serial0
        192.168.2.0/24 is variably subnetted, 2 subnets, 2 masks
B         192.168.2.64/28 [200/0] via 192.168.1.50, 00:00:32
B         192.168.2.0/24 [20/0] via 10.1.1.100, 00:19:51
B       192.168.101.0/24 [200/0] via 192.168.1.18, 00:20:10
```

From p*x*r1, ping 172.31.20.100 and 172.31.21.100.

Were the pings successful?

The following example shows results of the ping command to the loopback interfaces on the backbone_r2 router. Both pings are successful.

```
p1r1#ping 172.31.20.100

Type escape sequence to abort.
Sending 5, 100-byte ICMP Echos to 172.31.20.100, timeout is 2 seconds:
!!!!!
Success rate is 100 percent (5/5), round-trip min/avg/max = 56/56/60 ms
p1r1#ping 172.31.21.100

Type escape sequence to abort.
Sending 5, 100-byte ICMP Echos to 172.31.21.100, timeout is 2 seconds:
!!!!!
Success rate is 100 percent (5/5), round-trip min/avg/max = 60/60/64 ms
p1r1#
```

**Step 9**  Examine your p*x*r2 IP routing table. Do you see a route to 172.31.20.0/24 and 172.31.21.0/24 directly to AS 65201 from your AS?

The following example output is from the p1r2 router. Routes to 172.31.20.0/24 and 172.31.21.0/24 are shown, via p1r3.

```
p1r2#show ip route
<output omitted>

     172.16.0.0/24 is subnetted, 2 subnets
B       172.16.10.0 [200/0] via 192.168.1.17, 00:20:51
B       172.16.11.0 [200/0] via 192.168.1.17, 00:20:51
     172.26.0.0/28 is subnetted, 6 subnets
B       172.26.2.48 [200/0] via 192.168.1.17, 00:01:37
B       172.26.1.48 [200/0] via 192.168.1.50, 00:02:26
B       172.26.2.32 [200/0] via 192.168.1.17, 00:01:37
B       172.26.1.32 [200/0] via 192.168.1.50, 00:02:26
B       172.26.2.16 [200/0] via 192.168.1.17, 00:01:37
B       172.26.1.16 [200/0] via 192.168.1.50, 00:02:26
     172.31.0.0/24 is subnetted, 2 subnets
B       172.31.21.0 [200/0] via 192.168.1.50, 00:02:10
B       172.31.20.0 [200/0] via 192.168.1.50, 00:02:10
B    10.0.0.0/8 [200/0] via 192.168.1.17, 00:20:52
B    192.168.102.0/24 [200/0] via 192.168.1.17, 00:20:52
     192.168.1.0/24 is variably subnetted, 3 subnets, 2 masks
C       192.168.1.32/28 is directly connected, Serial1
B       192.168.1.0/24 [200/0] via 192.168.1.17, 00:20:38
C       192.168.1.16/28 is directly connected, Serial0
     192.168.2.0/24 is variably subnetted, 2 subnets, 2 masks
B       192.168.2.64/28 [200/0] via 192.168.1.50, 00:01:33
B       192.168.2.0/24 [200/0] via 192.168.1.17, 00:20:53
C    192.168.101.0/24 is directly connected, Loopback10
```

From p*x*r2, ping 172.31.20.100 and 172.31.21.100.

Were the pings successful?

The results of the ping command to the loopback interfaces on the backbone_r2 router are shown in the following output. Both pings are successful.

```
p1r2#ping 172.31.20.100

Type escape sequence to abort.
Sending 5, 100-byte ICMP Echos to 172.31.20.100, timeout is 2 seconds:
!!!!!
Success rate is 100 percent (5/5), round-trip min/avg/max = 84/87/92 ms
p1r2#ping 172.31.21.100

Type escape sequence to abort.
Sending 5, 100-byte ICMP Echos to 172.31.21.100, timeout is 2 seconds:
!!!!!
Success rate is 100 percent (5/5), round-trip min/avg/max = 84/86/92 ms
p1r2#
```

**Step 10**    From p*x*r3, Telnet to the backbone_r2 router, using the password cisco.
Enter the **show ip bgp** command.

How many paths are available to subnet 172.16.10.0 and 172.16.11.0?
Which path is selected as the best path? (Note: You should see multiple
paths if more than one pod is configured properly.)

**The following example output is from the backbone_r2 router. Two paths are
available to both 172.16.10.0 and 172.16.11.0. The selected best path to each
subnet is via pod 1, with a next-hop address of 172.22.1.1 (the address of
p1r3).**

```
p1r3#172.22.1.100
Trying 172.22.1.100 ... Open


User Access Verification

Password:
backbone_r2>show ip bgp
BGP table version is 63, local router ID is 172.31.21.100
Status codes: s suppressed, d damped, h history, * valid, > best, i - internal
Origin codes: i - IGP, e - EGP, ? - incomplete

     Network          Next Hop         Metric LocPrf Weight Path
 *   10.0.0.0         172.22.2.2                         0 65102 65200 i
 *>                   172.22.1.1                         0 65101 65200 i
 *   172.16.10.0/24   172.22.2.2                         0 65102 65200 i
 *>                   172.22.1.1                         0 65101 65200 i
 *   172.16.11.0/24   172.22.2.2                         0 65102 65200 i
 *>                   172.22.1.1                         0 65101 65200 i
 *>  172.26.1.16/28   172.22.1.1            0             0 65101 i
 *>  172.26.1.32/28   172.22.1.1            0             0 65101 i
 *>  172.26.1.48/28   172.22.1.1            0             0 65101 i
 *>  172.26.2.16/28   172.22.2.2            0             0 65102 i
 *>  172.26.2.32/28   172.22.2.2            0             0 65102 i
 *>  172.26.2.48/28   172.22.2.2            0             0 65102 i
 *>  172.31.20.0/24   0.0.0.0              0         32768 i
 *>  172.31.21.0/24   0.0.0.0              0         32768 i
 *>  192.168.1.0      172.22.1.1                         0 65101 i
 *>  192.168.2.0      172.22.2.2                         0 65102 i
 *>  192.168.2.64/28  172.22.2.2           0             0 65102 i
 *>  192.168.101.0    172.22.1.1                         0 65101 i
     Network          Next Hop         Metric LocPrf Weight Path
 *>  192.168.102.0    172.22.2.2                         0 65102 i
```

Display the IP routing table of the backbone_r2 router. In the routing
table, do you see only the best path to 172.16.10.0 and 172.16.11.0
published?

The following example output is from the backbone_r2 router. Only the
selected best path to both 172.16.10.0 and 172.16.11.0 appears in the routing
table.

```
backbone_r2>show ip route
<output omitted>

B     10.0.0.0/8 [20/0] via 172.22.1.1, 00:04:01
B     192.168.101.0/24 [20/0] via 172.22.1.1, 00:03:04
B     192.168.102.0/24 [20/0] via 172.22.2.2, 00:03:35
B     192.168.1.0/24 [20/0] via 172.22.1.1, 00:04:01
      192.168.2.0/24 is variably subnetted, 2 subnets, 2 masks
B        192.168.2.64/28 [20/0] via 172.22.2.2, 00:03:35
B        192.168.2.0/24 [20/0] via 172.22.2.2, 00:03:35
      172.31.0.0/24 is subnetted, 2 subnets
C        172.31.21.0 is directly connected, Loopback101
C        172.31.20.0 is directly connected, Loopback100
      172.26.0.0/28 is subnetted, 6 subnets
B        172.26.2.48 [20/0] via 172.22.2.2, 00:03:05
B        172.26.1.48 [20/0] via 172.22.1.1, 00:04:01
B        172.26.2.32 [20/0] via 172.22.2.2, 00:03:05
B        172.26.1.32 [20/0] via 172.22.1.1, 00:04:04
B        172.26.2.16 [20/0] via 172.22.2.2, 00:03:08
B        172.26.1.16 [20/0] via 172.22.1.1, 00:04:04
      172.22.0.0/24 is subnetted, 2 subnets
C        172.22.2.0 is directly connected, Serial0/1
C        172.22.1.0 is directly connected, Serial0/0
      172.16.0.0/24 is subnetted, 2 subnets
B        172.16.10.0 [20/0] via 172.22.1.1, 00:04:03
B        172.16.11.0 [20/0] via 172.22.1.1, 00:04:03
```

Exit the Telnet to the backbone_r2 router.

**The following example shows how to exit from the backbone_r2 Telnet
session.**

```
backbone_r2>exit

[Connection to 172.22.1.100 closed by foreign host]
p1r3#
```

**Step 11** If your pxr3 router connection to the backbone_r2 router fails, your pod
should still be capable of reaching AS 65201 by going through AS 65200
and AS 6510x (of another pod) if another pod is configured properly. Try
shutting down your S1 interface on your pxr3 router, and then try a trace
to 172.31.20.100. Which path are the trace probes taking from pxr3 to the
backbone_r2 router now?

**The following example shows how to shut down the serial 1 interface on the
p1r3 router:**

```
p1r3#conf t
Enter configuration commands, one per line.  End with CNTL/Z.
p1r3(config)#int s1
p1r3(config-if)#shutdown
08:38:27: %LINK-5-CHANGED: Interface Serial1, changed state to administratively
down
08:38:28: %LINEPROTO-5-UPDOWN: Line protocol on Interface Serial1, changed state
 to down
```

The following output shows the results of the trace to 172.31.20.100 from the p1r3 router. This output indicates that packets from p1r3 can still reach 172.31.20.100 (in AS 65201) by going through AS 65200 (the backbone_r1 router, bbr1) and AS 65102 (pod 2).

```
p1r3#trace 172.31.20.100

Type escape sequence to abort.
Tracing the route to 172.31.20.100

  1 p1r1 (192.168.1.49) 16 msec 20 msec 16 msec
  2 bbr1 (10.1.1.100) [AS 65200] 32 msec 32 msec 32 msec
  3 10.2.2.2 [AS 65200] 48 msec 44 msec 44 msec
  4 192.168.2.50 [AS 65102] 64 msec 56 msec 56 msec
  5 172.22.2.100 76 msec * 72 msec
p1r3#
```

The following output shows how to bring up the serial 1 interface on the p1r3 router:

```
p1r3#conf t
Enter configuration commands, one per line.  End with CNTL/Z.
p1r3(config)#int s1
p1r3(config-if)#no shutdown
08:38:27: %LINK-3-UPDOWN: Interface Serial1, changed state to up
08:38:28: %LINEPROTO-5-UPDOWN: Line protocol on Interface Serial1, changed state  to
up
```

**Step 12**   Save the current configurations of all the routers within your pod to NVRAM.

The following example shows how to save the configuration of the p1r1 router, using the copy run start command (this is an abbreviated form of the copy running-config startup-config command):

```
p1r1#copy run start
Destination filename [startup-config]?
Building configuration...
p1r1#
```

Bonus question: What is the order BGP will use to evaluate the following BGP route attributes?

— MED

— Weight

— Shortest AS path

— Local preference

BGP will evaluate these route attributes in the following order:

— Weight

— Local preference

— Shortest AS path

— MED

# Review Questions

Answer the following questions, and then refer to Appendix G, "Answers to the Review Questions," for the answers.

1  Describe the BGP split horizon rule.

2  What effect do route reflectors have on the BGP split horizon rule?

3  Write a brief description of the following:

— Route reflector

— Route reflector client

— Route reflector cluster

4  Routers configured as route reflectors do not have to be fully meshed with IBGP. True or false?

5  When a route reflector receives an update from a client, it sends it to where?

6  What is the command used to configure a router as a BGP route reflector?

7  Describe the advantages of using prefix lists rather than access lists for BGP route filtering.

8  In a prefix list, what is the sequence number used for?

9  What command is used to clear the hit count of the prefix list entries?

10  What is BGP multihoming?

11  What command is used to assign a weight to a BGP neighbor connection?

12  What is the preferred method to use to advertise an aggregated route from an AS into BGP?

# Controlling Scalable Internetworks

This chapter discusses different ways to control routing update information. It includes the following sections:

- Redistribution Among Multiple Routing Protocols
- Configuring Redistribution
- Controlling Routing Update Traffic
- Verifying Redistribution Operation
- Policy-Based Routing Using Route Maps
- Verifying Policy-Based Routing
- Case Study: Redistribution
- Summary
- Configuration Exercise #1: Configuring Policy-Based Routing
- Configuration Exercise #2: Configuring Route Redistribution Between OSPF and EIGRP
- Configuration Exercise #1 Answers: Configuring Policy-Based Routing
- Configuration Exercise #2 Answers: Configuring Route Redistribution Between OSPF and EIGRP
- Review Questions

# Optimizing Routing Update Operation

This chapter covers how to use route redistribution to interconnect networks that use multiple routing protocols. After completing this chapter, you will be able to select and configure different ways to control route update traffic, configure route redistribution in networks that do and do not have redundant paths, resolve path selection problems, and verify route redistribution. You will also be able to elaborate on policy-based routing using route maps. Given a set of network requirements, you will be able to configure redistribution between different routing domains, configure policy-based routing, and verify proper operation (within described guidelines) of your routers.

## Redistribution Among Multiple Routing Protocols

Thus far in this book, you have seen networks that use a single routing protocol. Sometimes, however, you will need to use multiple routing protocols. The following are possible reasons why you may need multiple protocols:

- You are migrating from an older Interior Gateway Protocol (IGP) to a new IGP. Multiple redistribution boundaries may exist until the new protocol has displaced the old protocol completely.

- You want to use another protocol but need to keep the old protocol because of the needs of host systems.

- Different departments might not want to upgrade their routers, or they might not implement a sufficiently strict filtering policy. In these cases, you can protect yourself by terminating the other routing protocol on one of your routers.

- If you have a mixed-router vendor environment, you can use a Cisco-specific protocol in the Cisco portion of the network, and then use a common protocol to communicate with non-Cisco devices.

## What Is Redistribution?

When any of the previous situations arise, Cisco routers allow internetworks using different routing protocols (referred to as autonomous systems) to exchange routing information through a feature called route redistribution. Redistribution is defined as the capability for boundary routers connecting different autonomous systems to exchange and advertise routing information received from one autonomous system to the other autonomous system.

**NOTE**    The term *autonomous system* as used here denotes internetworks using different routing protocols. These routing protocols may be IGPs and/or Exterior Gateway Protocol (EGPs). This is a different use of the term autonomous system than when discussing the Border Gateway Protocol (BGP).

Within each autonomous system, the internal routers have complete knowledge about their network. The router interconnecting autonomous systems is called a boundary router.

In Figure 8-1, AS 200 is running the Interior Gateway Routing Protocol (IGRP), and AS 300 is running the Enhanced Interior Gateway Routing Protocol (EIGRP). The internal routers within each autonomous system have complete knowledge about their networks. Router A is the boundary router. Router A has both IGRP and EIGRP processes active, and is responsible for advertising routes learned from one autonomous system into the other autonomous system.

Router A learns about network 192.168.5.0 from Router B via the EIGRP protocol running on its S0 interface. It passes (redistributes) that information to Router C on its S1 interface via IGRP. Routing information is also passed (redistributed) the other way, from IGRP into EIGRP.

**Figure 8-1**    *Redistribution Between an IGRP AS and an EIGRP AS*

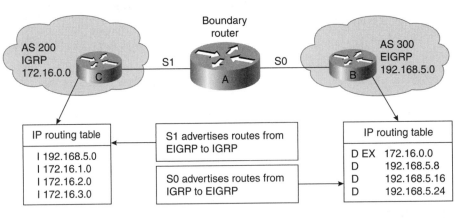

Router B's routing table shows that it has learned about network 172.16.0.0 via EIGRP (as indicated by the "D" in the routing table) and that the route is external to this autonomous system (as indicated by the "EX" in the routing table). Router C's routing table shows that it has learned about network 192.168.5.0 via IGRP (as indicated by the "I" in the routing table). Note that, unlike EIGRP, there is no indication in IGRP of whether the route is external or internal to the autonomous system.

Note that, in this case, the routes that are exchanged are summarized on the network class boundary. Recall from the route summarization discussion in Chapter 1, "Routing Principles," and Chapter 2, "Extending IP Addresses," that EIGRP and IGRP automatically summarize routes on the network class boundary.

# Redistribution Considerations

Redistribution, although powerful, increases the complexity and potential for routing confusion, so it should be used only when absolutely necessary. The key issues that arise when using redistribution are as follows:

- **Routing feedback (loops)**—Depending on how you employ redistribution—for example, if more than one boundary router is performing route redistribution—routers can send routing information received from one autonomous system back into that same autonomous system. The feedback is similar to the routing loop problem that occurs in distance vector technologies.

- **Incompatible routing information**—Because each routing protocol uses different metrics to determine the best path—for example, the Routing Information Protocol (RIP) uses hops, and Open Shortest Path First (OSPF) uses cost—path selection using the redistributed route information may not be optimal. Because the metric information about a route cannot be translated exactly into a different protocol, the path that a router chooses may not be the best.

- **Inconsistent convergence time**—Different routing protocols converge at different rates. For example, RIP converges more slowly than EIGRP, so if a link goes down, the EIGRP network will learn about it before the RIP network.

To understand why some of these problems may occur, you must first understand how Cisco routers select the best path when more than one routing protocol is running, and how they convert the metrics used when importing routes from one autonomous system into another. These topics are discussed in the following sections.

## Selecting the Best Route

Most routing protocols have metric structures and algorithms that are not compatible with other protocols. In a network in which multiple routing protocols are present, the exchange of route information and the capability to select the best path across the multiple protocols is critical. For routers to select the best path when they learn two or more routes to the same destination from different routing protocols, Cisco uses the following two parameters:

- **Administrative distance**—As covered in Chapter 1, administrative distance is used to rate the believability of a routing protocol. Each routing protocol is prioritized in order of most to least believable (or reliable or trustworthy) using a value called administrative distance. This criterion is the first that a router uses to determine which routing protocol to believe if more than one protocol provides route information for the same destination.
- **Routing metric**—The metric is a value representing the path between the local router and the destination network. The metric is usually a hop or cost value, depending on the protocol being used.

## Administrative Distance

Table 8-1 lists the default believability (administrative distance) of protocols supported by Cisco. For example, if a router received a route to network 10.0.0.0 from IGRP and then received a route to the same network from OSPF, the router would use the administrative distance to determine that IGRP is more believable and would add the IGRP version of the route to the routing table.

**Table 8-1**    *Default Administrative Distances of Routing Protocols*

| Routing Protocols | Administrative Distance Value |
|---|---|
| Connected interface | 0 |
| Static route out an interface | 0 |
| Static route to a next hop | 1 |
| EIGRP summary route | 5 |
| External BGP | 20 |
| Internal EIGRP | 90 |
| IGRP | 100 |
| OSPF | 110 |
| IS-IS | 115 |
| RIP version 1, version 2 | 120 |
| EGP | 140 |
| External EIGRP | 170 |
| Internal BGP | 200 |
| Unknown | 255 |

When using route redistribution, you may occasionally need to modify the administrative distance of a protocol so that it will be preferred. For example, if you want the router to select RIP-learned routers rather than IGRP-learned routes to the same destination, you must increase the administrative distance for IGRP or decrease the administrative distance for RIP.

Modifying the administrative distance is discussed in the section "Controlling Routing Update Traffic," later in this chapter.

## Seed Metric

After the most believable protocol is determined for each destination and the routes are added to the routing table, a router may advertise the routing information to other protocols, if configured to do so. If the router was advertising a link directly connected to one of its interfaces, the initial or seed metric used would be derived from the characteristics of that interface, and the metric would increment as the routing information passed to other routers.

However, redistributed routes are not physically connected to a router, they are learned from other protocols. If a boundary router wants to redistribute information between routing protocols, it must be capable of translating the metric of the received route from the source routing protocol into the other routing protocol. For example, if a boundary router receives a RIP route, the route will have hop count as a metric. To redistribute the route into OSPF, the router must translate the hop count into a cost metric that will be understood by other OSPF routers. This cost metric, referred to as the seed or default metric, is defined during configuration.

When the seed metric for a redistributed route is established, the metric will increment normally within the autonomous system. (The exception to this is OSPF E2 routes, as discussed in Chapter 4, "Interconnecting Multiple OSPF Areas," which hold their default metric regardless of how far they are propagated across an autonomous system.)

When configuring a default metric for redistributed routes, the metric should be set to a value larger than the largest metric within the receiving autonomous system to help prevent routing loops.

Configuring default metrics is discussed in the section "Controlling Routing Update Traffic," later in this chapter.

## Protocol Support for Redistribution

All protocols are supported by redistribution. Before implementing redistribution, consider the following points:

- You can redistribute only protocols that support the same routed protocol stack. For example, you can redistribute between IP RIP and OSPF because they both support the TCP/IP stack. However, you cannot redistribute between Internetwork Packet Exchange (IPX) RIP and OSPF because IPX RIP supports the IPX/Sequenced Packet Exchange (SPX) stack and OSPF does not.

- How you configure redistribution varies among protocols and among combinations of protocols. For example, redistribution occurs automatically between IGRP and EIGRP when they have the same autonomous system number, but it must be configured between EIGRP and RIP.

Because EIGRP supports multiple routing protocols, it can be used to redistribute with IP, IPX, and AppleTalk routing protocols (within the same routed protocol stack). Consider the following when redistributing EIGRP with these protocols:

- In the IP environment, IGRP and EIGRP have a similar metric structure, so redistribution is straightforward. For migration purposes, when IGRP and EIGRP are both running in the same autonomous system, redistribution is automatic. When redistributing between different autonomous systems, redistribution must be configured for EIGRP, just as it is required for IGRP.

- All other IP routing protocols, both internal and external, require that redistribution be configured to communicate with EIGRP.

- By design, EIGRP automatically redistributes route information with Novell RIP. Beginning with Cisco IOS Release 11.1, EIGRP can be configured to redistribute route information with the NetWare Link Services Protocol (NLSP).

- By design, EIGRP also automatically redistributes route information with AppleTalk RTMP.

# Configuring Redistribution

Configuring route redistribution can be very simple or very complex, depending on the mix of protocols that you want to redistribute. The commands used to enable redistribution and assign metrics vary slightly depending on the protocols being redistributed. The following steps are generic enough to apply to virtually all protocol combinations. However, the commands used to implement the steps may vary. It is highly recommended that you review the Cisco IOS documentation for the configuration commands that apply to the specific protocols that you want to redistribute.

---

**NOTE**    In this section, the terms *core* and *edge* are generic terms used to simplify the discussion about redistribution.

---

**Step 1**    Locate the boundary router(s) on which redistribution needs to be configured.

**Step 2**    Determine which routing protocol is the core or backbone protocol. Usually this is OSPF or EIGRP.

**Step 3**    Determine which routing protocol is the edge or short-term (if you are migrating) protocol.

**Step 4**    Access the routing process into which you want routes redistributed. Typically, you start with the backbone routing process. For example, to access OSPF, do the following:

```
router(config)#router ospf process-id
```

**Step 5**    Configure the router to redistribute routing updates from the edge protocol into the backbone protocol. This command varies, depending on the protocols.

# Redistributing into OSPF

The following command, explained in Table 8-2, is used for redistributing updates into OSPF:

```
router(config-router)#redistribute protocol [process-id] [metric metric-value]
[metric-type type-value] [route-map map-tag] [subnets] [tag tag-value]
```

**Table 8-2**    *redistribute Command Options for OSPF*

| Command | Description |
| --- | --- |
| *protocol* | Source protocol from which routes are being redistributed. It can be one of the following keywords: **connected, bgp, eigrp, egp, igrp, isis, iso-igrp, mobile, odr, ospf, static,** or **rip**. |
| *process-id* | For BGP, EGP, EIGRP, or IGRP, this is an autonomous system number. For OSPF, this is an OSPF process ID. |
| *metric-value* | Optional parameter used to specify the metric used for the redistributed route. When redistributing into OSPF, the default metric is 20. Use a value consistent with the destination protocol—in this case, the OSPF cost. |
| *type-value* | Optional OSPF parameter that specifies the external link type associated with the default route advertised into the OSPF routing domain. This value can be **1** for type 1 external routes, or **2** for type 2 external routes. The default is 2. |
| *map-tag* | Optional identifier of a configured route map to be interrogated to filter the importation of routes from this source routing protocol to the current routing protocol. Route maps are covered later in this chapter in the section "Policy-Based Routing Using Route Maps." |
| **subnets** | Optional OSPF parameter that specifies that subnetted routes should also be redistributed. Only routes that are not subnetted are redistributed if the **subnets** keyword is not specified. |
| *tag-value* | Optional 32-bit decimal value attached to each external route. This is not used by the OSPF protocol itself. It may be used to communicate information between autonomous system boundary routers. |

## Redistributing into EIGRP

The following command, explained in Table 8-3, is used for redistributing updates into EIGRP:

```
router(config-router)#redistribute protocol [process-id]
[match {internal ¦ external 1 ¦ external 2}]
[metric metric-value] [route-map map-tag]
```

**Table 8-3**    *Redistribute Command Options for EIGRP*

| Command | Description |
|---------|-------------|
| *protocol* | Source protocol from which routes are being redistributed. It can be one of the following keywords: **connected**, **bgp**, **eigrp**, **egp**, **igrp**, **isis**, **iso-igrp**, **mobile**, **odr**, **ospf**, **static**, or **rip**. |
| *process-id* | For BGP, EGP, EIGRP or IGRP, this is an autonomous system number. For OSPF, this is an OSPF process ID. |
| **match** | For OSPF, the optional criteria by which OSPF routes are redistributed into other routing domains. It can be one of the following: |
| | **internal**: Redistribute routes that are internal to a specific autonomous system. |
| | **external 1**: Redistribute routes that are external to the autonomous system but that are imported into OSPF as a type 1 external route. |
| | **external 2**: Redistribute routes that are external to the autonomous system but that are imported into OSPF as a type 2 external route. |
| *metric-value* | Optional parameter used to specify the metric used for the redistributed route. When redistributing into protocols other than OSPF (including this case into EIGRP), if this value is not specified and no value is specified using the **default-metric** router configuration command, the default metric is 0 and routes may not be redistributed. Use a value consistent with the destination protocol (see the description of the default metric command in this section for a description of the EIGRP metric). |
| *map-tag* | Optional identifier of a configured route map to be interrogated to filter the importation of routes from this source routing protocol to the current routing protocol. Route maps are covered later in this chapter in the section "Policy-Based Routing Using Route Maps." |

## Defining the Default Metric

You can affect how routes are redistributed by changing the default metric associated with a protocol. Perform the following steps to change the default metric:

**Step 1**    Define the default seed metric that the router uses when redistributing routes into a routing protocol.

When redistributing into IGRP or EIGRP, use the following command, explained in Table 8-4, to set the seed metric:

```
Router(config-router)#default-metric bandwidth delay reliability
loading mtu
```

You can specify the default metric with the **default-metric** command, or use the **metric** parameters in the **redistribute** command.

If you use the **default-metric** command, the default metric that you specified will apply to all protocols being redistributed in.

If you use the **default-metric** parameters in the **redistribute** command, you can set a different default metric for each protocol being redistributed in.

**Table 8-4**    *default-metric Command for IGRP and EIGRP*

| Command | Description |
|---|---|
| *bandwidth* | Minimum bandwidth of the route, in kilobits per second (kbps). |
| *delay* | Route delay, in tens of microseconds. |
| *reliability* | Likelihood of successful packet transmission expressed in a number from 0 to 255, where 255 means that the route is 100-percent reliable. |
| *loading* | Effective loading of the route expressed in a number from 1 to 255, where 255 means that the route is 100-percent loaded. |
| *mtu* | Maximum transmission unit (MTU). The maximum packet size along the route in bytes; an integer greater than or equal to 1. |

When redistributing into OSPF, RIP, EGP, and BGP, use the following command for setting the seed metric, as explained in Table 8-5.

```
Router(config-router)#default-metric number
```

**Table 8-5**    *default-metric Command for OSPF, RIP, EGP, and BGP*

| Command | Description |
|---|---|
| *number* | The value of the metric, such as the number of hops for RIP |

**Step 2**    Exit the routing process.

## Cofiguring Redistribution into Edge Protocol

**Step 1** Enter configuration mode for the other routing process, usually the edge or short-term process.

**Step 2** Depending on your network, this configuration will vary because you want to employ some techniques to reduce routing loops. For example, you may do any of the following:

— Redistribute a default route about the core autonomous system into the edge autonomous system.

— Redistribute multiple static routes about the core autonomous system into the edge autonomous system.

— Redistribute all routes from the core autonomous system into the edge autonomous system, and then assign a distribution filter to filter out inappropriate routes.

— Redistribute all routes from the core autonomous system into the edge autonomous system, and then modify the administrative distance associated with the received routes so that they are not the selected routes when multiple routes exist for the same destination. In some cases, the route learned by the native protocol is better but may have a less believable administrative distance. Refer to the section "Redistribution Example Using the **distance** Command," later in this chapter, for an example of this scenario.

Redistribution of static and default information is discussed in the following sections. Filtering and changing the administrative distance are discussed in the section "Controlling Routing Update Traffic," later in this chapter.

## The passive-interface Command

The **passive-interface** command can be used in conjunction with redistribution. It prevents all routing updates for a given routing protocol from being sent into a network, but it does not prevent the specified interface from receiving updates.

When using the **passive-interface** command in a network using a link-state routing protocol or EIGRP, the command prevents the router from establishing a neighbor adjacency with other routers connected to the same link as the one specified in the command. An adjacency cannot be established because the Hello protocol is used to verify bidirectional communication between routers. If a router is configured to not send updates, it cannot participate in bidirectional communication.

| NOTE | During testing with **debug** commands, it was found that OSPF does send Hello and DBD packets on passive interfaces, but does not send LSUs. EIGRP does not send anything on passive interfaces. |
|---|---|

To configure a passive interface, regardless of the routing protocol, do the following:

**Step 1**  Select the router and routing protocol that requires the passive interface.

**Step 2**  Determine which interfaces you do not want routing update traffic to be sent through.

**Step 3**  Configure using the **passive-interface** command, as shown in Table 8-6.

```
router(config-router)#passive-interface type number
```

**Table 8-6**   *passive-interface Command*

| Command | Description |
|---|---|
| *type number* | Type of interface and interface number that will not send routing updates |

| NOTE | This capability is typically used in conjunction with other capabilities, as you will see later in this chapter. |
|---|---|

## Static and Default Routes

Static routes are routes that you can manually configure on the router. Static routes are used most often to do the following:

- Define specific routes to use when two autonomous systems must exchange routing information, rather than having entire routing tables exchanged

- Define routes to destinations over a WAN link to eliminate the need for a dynamic routing protocol—that is, when you do not want routing updates to enable or cross the link

The commands to configure static routes for IP and their use are discussed in the following steps:

**Step 1**  Determine which networks you want defined as static. For example, if you are configuring static routes on a WAN router that is connecting to a branch office, you probably want to select the networks at the branch office.

**Step 2** Determine the next-hop router to the destination networks, or the local router's interface that connects to the remote router.

**Step 3** Configure the static route on each router. For IP, use the **ip route** command, as explained in Table 8-7.

```
router(config)#ip route prefix mask {address|interface} [distance ]
[tag tag] [permanent]
```

**Table 8-7**  *ip route Command to Configure Static Routes*

| Command | Description |
|---------|-------------|
| *prefix* | The route prefix for the destination. |
| *mask* | The prefix mask for the destination. |
| *address* | The IP address of the next-hop router that can be used to reach that network. |
| *interface* | The network interface to use to get to the destination network. |
| *distance* | Optional administrative distance to assign to this route. (Recall that administrative distance refers to how believable the routing protocol is.) |
| *tag* | Optional value that can be used as a match value in route maps. |
| **permanent** | Specification that the route will not be removed even if the interface associated with the route goes down. |

**NOTE**  Static routes pointing to an interface should be used only on point-to-point interfaces because on other interfaces the router will not know the specific address to which to send the information. On point-to-point interfaces, the information will be sent to the only other device on the network.

Example 8-1 demonstrates a static route configured on Router p1r2, shown in Figure 8-2. Router p1r2 will use its interface serial 1 to get to network 172.16.0.0/16. As shown in the routing table for Router p1r2 of Example 8-1, static routes pointing to an interface are treated as directly connected networks.

**Figure 8-2** *Redistribution Scenario*

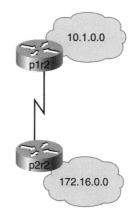

**Example 8-1** *Static Route Configuration on p1r2 in Figure 8-2*

```
router rip
 passive-interface Serial1
 network 10.0.0.0
!
ip route 172.16.0.0 255.255.0.0 Serial1


p1r2#sh ip route
<Output Omitted>
Gateway of last resort is not set

     10.0.0.0 255.255.255.0 is subnetted, 2 subnets
C       10.1.3.0 is directly connected, Serial1
C       10.1.1.0 is directly connected, Serial0
S    172.16.0.0 is directly connected, Serial1
<Output Omitted>
```

When configuring static routes, keep in mind the following considerations:

- When using static routes instead of dynamic routing updates, all participating routers must have static routes defined so that they can advertise their remote networks. Static route entries must be defined for all routes for which a router is responsible. To reduce the number of static route entries, you can define a default static route—for example, **ip route 0.0.0.0 0.0.0.0 s1**. When using RIP, default static routes (0.0.0.0 0.0.0.0) are advertised (redistributed) automatically.

- If you want a router to advertise a static route in a routing protocol, you may need to redistribute it.

Cisco lets you configure default routes for protocols. For example, when you create a default route on a router running RIP, the router advertises an address of 0.0.0.0. When a router receives this default route, it will forward any packets destined for a destination that does not appear in its routing table to the default route you configured.

You can also configure a default route by using the **ip default-network** command, explained in Table 8-8. An example of the use of the **default-network** command on a router running RIP is shown in Figure 8-3 and in Examples 8-2 and 8-3. With the **ip default-network** command, you designate an actual network currently available in the routing table as the default path to use.

**Figure 8-3**    *Using the default-network Command*

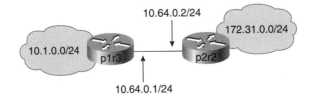

In Examples 8-2 and 8-3, the p2r2 router has a directly connected interface onto the network specified in the **ip default-network** *network-number* command. RIP will generate (or source) a default route, which will appear as a 0.0.0.0 0.0.0.0 route to its RIP neighbor routers.

**Example 8-2**    *Configuration on Router p2r2*

```
router rip
 network 10.0.0.0
 network 172.31.0.0
 !
ip classless
ip default-network 10.0.0.0
```

**Example 8-3**    *Routing Table of p1r3*

```
<Output Omitted>
Gateway of last resort is 10.64.0.2 to network 0.0.0.0
     10.0.0.0/8 is variably subnetted, 7 subnets, 2 masks
<Output Omitted>
R       10.2.3.0/24 [120/1] via 10.64.0.2, 00:00:05, Ethernet0
C       10.64.0.0/24 is directly connected, Ethernet0
R    172.31.0.0/16 [120/1] via 10.64.0.2, 00:00:16, Ethernet0
R*   0.0.0.0/0 [120/1] via 10.64.0.2, 00:00:05, Ethernet0
```

**Table 8-8**    *ip default-network Command*

| Command | Description |
|---|---|
| *network-number* | The number of the destination network |

**NOTE**    The **ip default-network** command is used as a method of distributing default route information to other routers. This command provides no functionality for the router on which it is configured.

Other protocols behave differently than RIP with the **ip route 0.0.0.0 0.0.0.0** and **ip default-network** commands. For example, EIGRP will not redistribute the 0.0.0.0 0.0.0.0 default route by default. However, if the **network 0.0.0.0** command is added to the EIGRP configuration, it will redistribute a default route as the result of the **ip route 0.0.0.0 0.0.0.0** command, but not as the result of the **ip default-network** command. Refer to the Cisco IOS documentation for further information.

### ip default-network Usage

The **ip default-network** command is used when routers do not know how to get to the outside world. This command is configured at the router that connects to the outside world, and this router goes through a different major network to reach the outside world. If your environment is all one major network address, you would probably not want to use the **default-network** command, but rather a static route to 0.0.0.0 via a border router.

The **ip route 0.0.0.0** command is used on routers with IP routing enabled that point to the outside world for Internet connectivity. This route is advertised as "gateway of last resort" if running RIP. The router that is directly connected to the border of the outside world would be the preferred router with the static route pointing to 0.0.0.0.

The **ip default-gateway** command is used on routers or communication servers that have IP routing turned off. The router or communication server acts just like a host on the network.

The following is an example of how you can redistribute in one direction and use a default route in the other direction instead of redistributing in both directions.

Figure 8-4 illustrates an internetwork that uses three autonomous systems. In this case, OSPF is the core protocol and RIP is the edge protocol. This section illustrates how to do the following:

- Allow the OSPF backbone to know all the routes in each autonomous system. This is done by configuring redistribution on the boundary routers so that all RIP routes are redistributed into OSPF.

- Allow the RIP autonomous systems to know only about their internal routes, and use a default route to the external networks. This is done by configuring a default route on the boundary routers. The boundary routers will advertise the default route into the RIP. The boundary routers are running both RIP and OSPF, and are redistributing RIP routes into OSPF. They will have all the RIP and OSPF routes in their routing table.

---

**NOTE**   This redistribution example shows one way to configure redistribution. Many other ways exist, so you must understand your network topology and requirements to choose the best solution.

---

**Figure 8-4**   *OSPF as the Core Routing Protocol and RIP as the Edge*

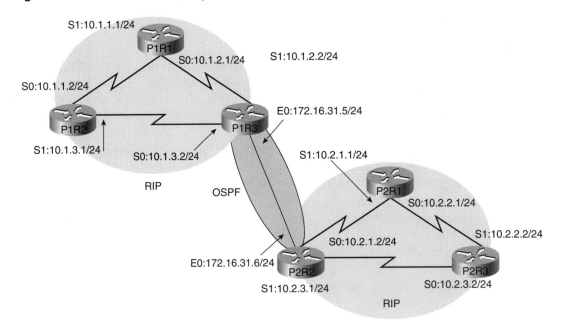

Example 8-4 and Example 8-5 illustrate the configurations of a RIP internal router and of a boundary router, as shown in Figure 8-4. Points about each configuration are as follows:

- **Internal RIP router (p1r1), Example 8-4**—No redistribution configuration is necessary because this router is only running the RIP protocol. The intent is not to have this router learn about external routes.

  The **ip classless** command is required on all RIP/IGRP routers that must use a default route to get to other subnets of network 10.0.0.0 (for example, for p1r1 to get to the 10.2.x.0 subnets). This command allows the IOS to forward packets that are destined for unrecognized subnets of directly connected networks to the best supernet route, which may be the default route. When this feature is disabled, the software discards the packets if the router receives packets for a subnet that numerically falls within its subnetwork addressing scheme, but there is no such subnet number in the routing table.

**Example 8-4**    *Configuration of Internal Router p1r1*

```
interface Serial0
 ip address 10.1.2.1 255.255.255.0
 bandwidth 64
!
interface Serial1
 ip address 10.1.1.1 255.255.255.0
 clockrate 56000
!
<Output Omitted>
!
router rip
 network 10.0.0.0
!
ip classless
<Output Omitted>
```

**NOTE**    The **ip classless** command is on by default in Cisco IOS Release 12.0; it is off by default in earlier releases.

- **Boundary router (p1r3), Example 8-5**—When redistributing into OSPF, you need the **subnets** keyword so that subnetted networks (along with nonsubnetted networks) will be redistributed into OSPF.

  Define the default network to be advertised to the edge protocols.

  The **ip classless** command is not needed on the boundary router because it is running OSPF. The command is shown in the configuration because it is on by default in Cisco IOS Release 12.0

**Example 8-5** *Configuration of Boundary Router p1r3*

```
<Output Omitted>
!
router ospf 200
 redistribute rip metric 30 subnets
 network 172.6.31.5 0.0.0.0 area 0
!
router rip
 network 10.0.0.0
!
ip classless
ip default-network 10.0.0.0
!
<Output Omitted>
```

For comparison's sake, Example 8-6 shows the routing table of the p1r3 boundary router before redistribution.

**Example 8-6** *Routing Table of Boundary Router Before Redistribution*

```
P1R3#show ip route
<Output Omitted>

     10.0.0.0/24 is subnetted, 3 subnets
C       10.1.3.0 is directly connected, Serial0
C       10.1.2.0 is directly connected, Serial1
R       10.1.1.0 [120/1] via 10.1.3.1, 00:00:16, Serial0
                 [120/1] via 10.1.2.1, 00:00:28, Serial1
     172.16.0.0/24 is subnetted, 1 subnets
C       172.16.31.0 is directly connected, Ethernet0
```

Notice that in this routing table output, the 10.2.x.0/24 subnetworks do not appear. They appear after redistribution is configured on p2r2 (the other boundary router).

Example 8-7 illustrates p1r3 after redistribution was enabled on both boundary routers.

**Example 8-7** *Routing Table of Boundary Router After Redistribution*

```
P1R3#show ip route

*    10.0.0.0/24 is subnetted, 6 subnets
C       10.1.3.0 is directly connected, Serial0
O E2    10.2.1.0 [110/30] via 172.6.31.6, 00:44:56, Ethernet0
C       10.1.2.0 is directly connected, Serial1
R       10.1.1.0 [120/1] via 10.1.3.1, 00:00:05, Serial0
                 [120/1] via 10.1.2.1, 00:00:17, Serial1
O E2    10.2.2.0 [110/30] via 172.16.31.6, 00:44:56, Ethernet0
O E2    10.2.3.0 [110/30] via 172.16.31.6, 00:44:56, Ethernet0
     172.16.0.0/24 is subnetted, 1 subnets
C       172.16.31.0 is directly connected, Ethernet0
```

Example 8-8 illustrates one of the internal routing tables after the default route was configured on the boundary router using the **ip default-network** command.

**Example 8-8**  *Routing Table of Internal Router After Redistribution*

```
P1R1#show ip route
<Output Omitted>

     10.0.0.0/24 is subnetted, 3 subnets
R        10.1.3.0 [120/1] via 10.1.1.2, 00:00:24, Serial1
                  [120/1] via 10.1.2.2, 00:00:10, Serial0
C        10.1.2.0 is directly connected, Serial0
C        10.1.1.0 is directly connected, Serial1
R*  0.0.0.0/0 [120/1] via 10.1.2.2, 00:00:10, Serial0
```

Using the default route shown in Example 8-8, p1r1 can successfully ping any network in the other RIP autonomous system, as shown in Example 8-9.

**Example 8-9**  *Internal Router Pinging a Destination in Another Autonomous System*

```
P1R1#ping 10.2.2.1

Type escape sequence to abort.
Sending 5, 100-byte ICMP Echos to 10.2.2.1, timeout is 2 seconds:
!!!!!
Success rate is 100 percent (5/5), round-trip min/avg/max = 68/68/68 ms
P1R1#
```

# Controlling Routing Update Traffic

At a high level, Cisco recommends that you consider employing the following guidelines when using redistribution:

- **Be familiar with your network and your network traffic**—This is the overriding recommendation. There are many ways to implement redistribution, so knowing your network will enable you to make the best decision.

- **Do not overlap routing protocols**—Do not run two different protocols in the same internetwork. Instead, have distinct boundaries between networks that use different protocols.

- **One-way redistribution**—To avoid routing loops and problems with varying convergence time, allow routes to be exchanged in only one direction, not both directions. In the other direction, you should consider using a default route.

- **Two-way redistribution**—If you must allow two-way redistribution, enable a mechanism to reduce the chances of routing loops. Examples of mechanisms covered in this chapter are default routes, route filters, and modification of the metrics advertised. With these types of mechanisms, you can reduce the chances of routes imported from one autonomous system being reinjected into the same autonomous system as new route information if more than one boundary router is performing two-way redistribution.

Thus far, you have seen a variety of routing protocols and how they propagate routing information throughout an internetwork. Sometimes, however, you do not want routing information propagated, for example:

- **When using an on-demand WAN link**—You may want to minimize, or stop entirely, the exchange of routing update information across this type of link. Otherwise, the link will remain up constantly.

- **When you want to prevent routing loops**—Many companies have large enough networks that redundant paths are prominent. In some cases, for example, when a path to the same destination is learned from two different routing protocols, you may want to filter the propagation of one of the paths.

This section discusses two ways that you can control or prevent routing update exchange and propagation, as follows:

- **Route update filtering**—Use access lists to filter route update traffic about specific networks.

- **Changing administrative distance**—Change the administrative distance to affect which protocol the router believes.

Other methods of controlling traffic were presented earlier:

- **Passive interface**—Prevents all routing updates from being sent through an interface.

- **Default routes**—Instructs the router that if it does not have a route for a given destination, it should send the packet to the default route.

- **Static routes**—Serves as a route to a destination that you configured in the router.

## Using Route Filters

The Cisco IOS software can filter incoming and outgoing routing updates by using access lists, as demonstrated in Figure 8-5. In general, the process used by the router is as follows:

**Step 1**   The router receives a routing update or is getting ready to send an update about one or more networks.

**Step 2**   The router looks at the interface involved in the process. For example, if it is an incoming update, then the interface on which it arrived is checked. If it is an update that must be advertised, the interface out of which it should be advertised is checked.

**Step 3**   The router determines whether a filter is associated with the interface.

**Step 4**   If a route filter is associated with the interface, the router views the access list to learn whether there is a match for the given routing update.

If a route filter is not associated with the interface, the routing update packet is processed as normal.

**Step 5**   If there is a match, the route entry is processed as configured (either permitted or denied).

**Step 6**   If no match is found in the access list, the implicit **deny any** at the end of the access list will cause the update to be dropped.

**Figure 8-5**   *Data Flow of Routing Updates When Using Route Filters*

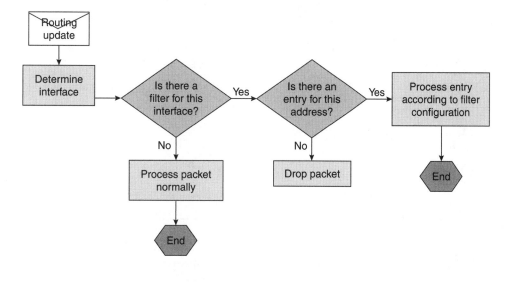

**NOTE**   Filtering routing updates is also discussed in Chapter 7, "Implementing BGP in Scalable Networks," for the Border Gateway Protocol (BGP). The ideas here are the same, although the commands used are different than those used for BGP.

You can filter routing update traffic for any protocol by defining an access list and applying it to a specific routing protocol. To configure a filter, do the following:

**Step 1**  Identify the network addresses that you want to filter, and create an access list.

**Step 2**  Determine whether you want to filter them on an incoming or outgoing interface.

**Step 3**  To assign the access list to filter outgoing routing updates, use the **distribute-list out** command, as detailed in Table 8-9.

```
router(config-router)#distribute-list {access-list-number ¦ name } out
[interface-name  ¦ routing-process [autonomous-system-number]
```

**Table 8-9**  *distribute-list out* Command

| Command | Description |
|---|---|
| *access-list-number* \| *name* | Gives the standard access list number or name. |
| **out** | Applies the access list to outgoing routing updates. |
| *interface-name* | Gives the optional interface name out which updates will be filtered. |
| *routing-process* | Gives the optional name of the routing process, or the keywords **static** or **connected**, from which updates will be filtered. |
| *autonomous-system-number* | Gives the optional autonomous system number of the routing process. |

**NOTE**  OSPF outgoing updates cannot be filtered out of an interface.

To assign the access list to filter incoming routing updates, use the **distribute-list in** command, as explained in Table 8-10.

```
router(config-router)#distribute-list {access-list-number ¦ name }
in [type number]
```

**Table 8-10**  *distribute-list in* Command

| Command | Description |
|---|---|
| *access-list-number* \| *name* | Gives the standard access list number or name. |
| **in** | Applies the access list to incoming routing updates. |
| *type number* | Gives the optional interface type and number from which updates will be filtered. |

## IP Route Filtering Configuration Example

Figure 8-6 provides the topology of a WAN in which network 10.0.0.0 must be hidden from network 192.168.5.0.

**Figure 8-6**    *Network 10.0.0.0 Needs to Be Hidden from Network 192.168.5.0*

Example 8-10 shows that the **distribute-list out** command applies access list 7 to outbound packets. The access list allows only routing information about network 172.16.0.0 to be distributed out the S0 interface of Router B. As a result, network 10.0.0.0 is hidden.

**Example 8-10** *Filtering Out Network 10.0.0.0 on Router B in Figure 8-6*

```
router eigrp 1
  network 172.16.0.0
  network 192.168.5.0
  distribute-list 7 out s0
!
access-list 7 permit 172.16.0.0  0.0.255.255
```

**NOTE**    Another way of achieving the filtering out of network 10.0.0.0 would have been by denying network 10.0.0.0 and permitting any other networks. This method would have been particularly efficient if the routing information contained multiple networks, but only network 10.0.0.0 needed filtering out.

Table 8-11 describes some of the commands shown in Example 8-10.

**Table 8-11**    *Redistribution Commands*

| Command | Description |
| --- | --- |
| **distribute-list 7 out s0** | Applies access list 7 as a route redistribution filter on EIGRP routing updates sent on interface serial 0. |
| **access-list 7 permit 172.16.0.0 0.0.255.255** | |
| **access list 7** | Gives the access list number. |
| **permit** | Enables routes matching the parameters to be forwarded. |
| **172.16.0.0 0.0.255.255** | Gives the network number and wildcard mask used to qualify source addresses. The first two address octets must match, and the rest are masked. |

## IP Static Route Filtering Configuration Example

Figure 8-7 provides the topology used to demonstrate IP static route filtering in Example 8-11.

**Figure 8-7** *IP Static Route Filtering*

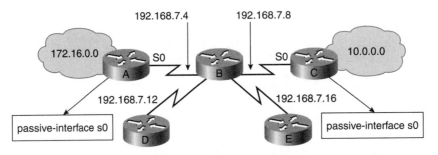

Example 8-11 shows a static route being redistributed and filtered into EIGRP. The 10.0.0.0 route is passed to Routers D and E. The static route to 172.16.0.0 is filtered (denied by the implicit deny at the end of the access list). In Figure 8-7, network 192.168.7.0 is subnetted with 30 bits (255.255.255.252)—subnets 192.168.7.16, 192.168.7.12, 192.168.7.8, and 192.168.7.4. Also, Router A and Router C have their serial interfaces set as passive interfaces, so no dynamic routing updates are sent out. Therefore Router B will use its static routes to reach networks 10.0.0.0 and 172.16.0.0.

**Example 8-11** *Configuration of Router B*

```
ip route 10.0.0.0 255.0.0.0 192.168.7.9
ip route 172.16.0.0 255.255.0.0 192.168.7.5
!
router eigrp 1
  network 192.168.7.0
  default-metric 10000 100 255 1 1500
  redistribute static
  distribute-list 3 out static
!
access-list 3 permit 10.0.0.0 0.255.255.255
```

Table 8-12 describes some of the commands shown in Example 8-11.

**Table 8-12** *Commands Used in Example 8-11*

| Command | Description |
| --- | --- |
| **ip route 10.0.0.0 255.0.0.0 192.168.7.9** | |
| **10.0.0.0 255.0.0.0** | Defines the IP address and subnet mask of the destination network. |

**Table 8-12**    *Commands Used in Example 8-11 (Continued)*

| Command | Description |
| --- | --- |
| **192.168.7.9** | Defines the next-hop address to use to reach the destination (in this case, Router C's S0 interface). |
| **redistribute static** | Assigns routes learned from static entries in the routing table to be redistributed into EIGRP. |
| **distribute-list 3 out static** | Filters routes learned from static entries by using access list 3, before those routes are passed to the EIGRP process. |
| **access-list 3 permit 10.0.0.0 0.255.255.255** | |
| **access-list 3** | Shows that the access list is list number 3. |
| **permit** | Enables routes that match the parameters to be advertised. |
| **10.0.0.0 0.255.255.255** | Enables packets about IP addresses that match the first octet of 10.0.0.0 to be forwarded. |

**NOTE**    Configure static route redistribution on one router only to eliminate the possibility of routing loops created by static route redistribution on routers with parallel routes between networks.

## Modifying Administrative Distance

In some cases, you will find that a router will select a suboptimal path because it believes that a routing protocol has a poorer route, even though it has a better administrative distance. One way to make sure that routes from the desired routing protocol are selected is to give the undesired route(s) from a routing protocol a larger administrative distance.

For all protocols except EIGRP and BGP, use the **distance** command, as explained in Table 8-13, to change the default administrative distances:

```
router(config-router)#distance weight [address mask
[access-list-number ¦ name ]] [ ip ]
```

**Table 8-13**    *Administrative Distance Command (Except for EIGRP and BGP)*

| Command | Description |
| --- | --- |
| *weight* | Administrative distance, an integer from 10 to 255. (The values 0 to 9 are reserved for internal use.) |
| *address* | Optional IP address. Allows filtering of networks according to the IP address of the router supplying the routing information. |

*continues*

**Table 8-13** *Administrative Distance Command (Except for EIGRP and BGP) (Continued)*

| Command | Description |
|---------|-------------|
| *mask* | Optional wildcard mask for IP address. A bit set to 1 in the mask argument instructs the software to ignore the corresponding bit in the address value. |
| *access-list-number* \| *name* | Optional number or name of standard access list to be applied to the incoming routing updates. Allows filtering of the networks being advertised. |
| **ip** | Optional; specification of IP-derived routes for Intermediate System-to-Intermediate System (IS-IS). |

For EIGRP, use the following command, as explained in Table 8-14:

```
router(config-router)#distance eigrp internal-distance external-distance
```

**Table 8-14** *EIGRP Administrative Distance Command*

| Command | Description |
|---------|-------------|
| *internal-distance* | Administrative distance for EIGRP internal routes. Internal routes are those that are learned from another entity within the same autonomous system. |
| *external-distance* | Administrative distance for EIGRP external routes. External routes are those for which the best path is learned from a neighbor external to the autonomous system. |

### Modifying BGP Administrative Distance

For BGP, use the **distance bgp** command to change the administrative distances:

```
router(config-router)#distance bgp external-distance
internal-distance local-distance
```

| Command | Description |
|---------|-------------|
| *external-distance* | Administrative distance for BGP external routes. External routes are routes for which the best path is learned from a neighbor external to the autonomous system. Acceptable values are from 1 to 255. The default is 20. Routes with a distance of 255 are not installed in the routing table. |
| *internal-distance* | Administrative distance for BGP internal routes. Internal routes are those routes that are learned from another BGP entity within the same autonomous system. Acceptable values are from 1 to 255. The default is 200. Routes with a distance of 255 are not installed in the routing table. |

| Command | Description |
|---------|-------------|
| *local-distance* | Administrative distance for BGP local routes. Local routes are those networks listed with a **network** router configuration command, often as back doors, for that router or for networks that are being redistributed from another process. Acceptable values are from 1 to 255. The default is 200. Routes with a distance of 255 are not installed in the routing table. |

# Redistribution Example Using the distance Command

The following example uses RIP and IGRP to illustrate how a router can make a poor path selection because of the default administrative distance values given to RIP and IGRP in a redundant network. The example also illustrates one possible way of correcting the problem.

Figure 8-8 illustrates the network before using multiple routing protocols. The R200 and Cen routers are the primary focus of this example, as are networks 172.16.6.0, 172.16.9.0, and 172.16.10.0. The configuration output and routing tables appear on the following pages.

**Figure 8-8**    *Single Routing Protocol Network*

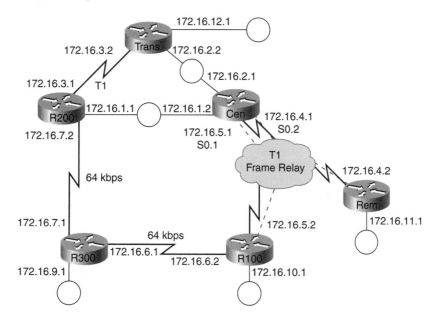

| NOTE | This example uses RIP and IGRP for simplicity. These and other protocol combinations can have the same problems occur, depending on the network topology. This is one reason why Cisco highly recommends that you study your network topology before implementing redistribution and that you monitor it after it is enabled. |
|------|---|

| NOTE | There are a number of ways to correct path selection problems in a redistribution environment. The purpose of this example is to show how a problem can occur, where it appears, and one possible way of resolving it. |
|------|---|

First, you have only IGRP running in all the routers in the network. Example 8-12 shows the complete IP routing table for the Cen router.

**Example 8-12** *Routing Table of Cen When IGRP Is the Only Routing Protocol*

```
Cen#show ip route
<Output Omitted>

     172.16.0.0/24 is subnetted, 11 subnets
I       172.16.12.0 [100/1188] via 172.16.2.2, 00:00:02, TokenRing0
I       172.16.9.0 [100/158813] via 172.16.1.1, 00:00:02, TokenRing1
I       172.16.10.0 [100/8976] via 172.16.5.2, 00:00:02, Serial0.1
I       172.16.11.0 [100/8976] via 172.16.4.2, 00:00:02, Serial0.2
C       172.16.4.0 is directly connected, Serial0.2
C       172.16.5.0 is directly connected, Serial0.1
I       172.16.6.0 [100/160250] via 172.16.5.2, 00:00:02, Serial0.1
I       172.16.7.0 [100/158313] via 172.16.1.1, 00:00:02, TokenRing1
C       172.16.1.0 is directly connected, TokenRing1
C       172.16.2.0 is directly connected, TokenRing0
I       172.16.3.0 [100/8539] via 172.16.2.2, 00:00:02, TokenRing0
                   [100/8539] via 172.16.1.1, 00:00:03, TokenRing1
```

Note the administrative distance and the composite metrics for each learned link. Administrative distance refers to how believable the routing protocol is, and the composite metric is the value assigned to the link.

Now consider that you want to split the network into two autonomous systems—IGRP and RIP, as shown in Figure 8-9. Note that IGRP is more believable than RIP because it has an administrative distance of 100 and RIP has an administrative distance of 120.

**Figure 8-9**    *Running RIP and IGRP in One Network*

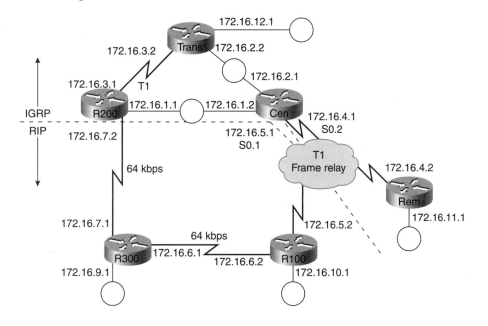

The configuration for Router Cen is shown in Example 8-13.

**Example 8-13** *Router Cen Is Configured for Both RIP and IGRP*

```
router rip
 redistribute igrp 1
 passive-interface Serial0.2
 passive-interface TokenRing0
 passive-interface TokenRing1
 network 172.16.0.0
 default-metric 3
!
router igrp 1
 redistribute rip
 passive-interface Serial0.1
 network 172.16.0.0
 default-metric 10 100 255 1 1500
```

The configuration for Router R200 is shown in Example 8-14.

**Example 8-14** *Router R200 Is Configured for Both RIP and IGRP*

```
router rip
 redistribute igrp 1
 passive-interface Serial0
 passive-interface TokenRing0
```

*continues*

**Example 8-14** *Router R200 Is Configured for Both RIP and IGRP (Continued)*

```
 network 172.16.0.0
 default-metric 3
 !
router igrp 1
 redistribute rip
 passive-interface Serial1
 network 172.16.0.0
 default-metric 10 100 255 1 1500
```

The passive interface commands are used to prevent routes from a particular routing protocol from being forwarded needlessly on links when the remote router cannot understand or is not using that protocol.

Note in these configurations that RIP is being redistributed into IGRP, and IGRP is being redistributed into RIP on both routers.

The table shown in Example 8-15 lists the routes that are relevant to the discussion in this section. Notice that the Cen router learned RIP and IGRP routes. You can use Figure 8-9 to trace some of the routes.

**Example 8-15** *Router Cen's Resulting Routing Table when Running RIP and IGRP*

```
Cen#show ip route
<Output Omitted>

 172.16.0.0/24 is subnetted, 11 subnets
R   172.16.9.0 [120/2] via 172.16.5.2, 00:00:01, Serial0.1
R   172.16.10.0 [120/1] via 172.16.5.2, 00:00:02, Serial0.1
I   172.16.11.0 [100/8976] via 172.16.4.2, 00:00:02, Serial0.2
C   172.16.4.0 is directly connected, Serial0.2
C   172.16.5.0 is directly connected, Serial0.1
R   172.16.6.0 [120/1] via 172.16.5.2, 00:00:02, Serial0.1
I   172.16.3.0 [100/8539] via 172.16.2.2, 00:00:02, TokenRing0
               [100/8539] via 172.16.1.1, 00:00:02, TokenRing1
```

Example 8-16 shows the resulting routing table on the R200 router. The routing table lists the routes that are relevant to the discussion in this section. Notice that all the routes are learned from IGRP, even though Router R200 is also connected to a RIP network. Notice, too, that if you trace some of the routes, such as to network 172.16.9.0, the router uses the long way, via Router Cen rather than via Router R300.

**Example 8-16** *Router R200's Resulting Routing Table when Running RIP and IGRP*

```
R200#show ip route
<Output Omitted>

Gateway of last resort is not set

 172.16.0.0/24 is subnetted, 11 subnets
I   172.16.9.0 [100/1000163] via 172.16.1.2, 00:00:37, TokenRing0
```

**Example 8-16** *Router R200's Resulting Routing Table when Running RIP and IGRP (Continued)*

```
I  172.16.10.0 [100/1000163] via 172.16.1.2, 00:00:37, TokenRing0
I  172.16.11.0 [100/9039] via 172.16.1.2, 00:00:37, TokenRing0
I  172.16.4.0 [100/8539] via 172.16.1.2, 00:00:37, TokenRing0
I  172.16.5.0 [100/8539] via 172.16.1.2, 00:00:37, TokenRing0
I  172.16.6.0 [100/1000163] via 172.16.1.2, 00:00:37, TokenRing0
C  172.16.3.0 is directly connected, Serial0
```

As shown in the routing table of Example 8-16, Router R200 selected the poor paths because IGRP has a better administrative distance than RIP. To make sure that Router R200 selects the RIP routes, you can change the administrative distance, as shown in Example 8-17.

**Example 8-17** *Redistribution Example Using the **distance** Command*

```
Router Cen
router rip
 redistribute igrp 1
<Output Omitted>
 network 172.16.0.0
 default-metric 3
!
router igrp 1
 redistribute rip
 <Output Omitted>
 network 172.16.0.0
 default-metric 10 100 255 1 1500
 distance 130 0.0.0.0 255.255.255.255 1
!
access-list 1 permit 172.16.9.0
access-list 1 permit 172.16.10.0
access-list 1 permit 172.16.6.0


Router R200
router rip
 redistribute igrp 1
<Output Omitted>
 network 172.16.0.0
 default-metric 3
!
router igrp 1
 redistribute rip
 <Output Omitted>
 network 172.16.0.0
 default-metric 10 100 255 1 1500
 distance 130 0.0.0.0 255.255.255.255 1
!
access-list 1 permit 172.16.9.0
access-list 1 permit 172.16.10.0
access-list 1 permit 172.16.6.0
```

Table 8-15 describes some of the commands shown in Example 8-17.

**Table 8-15**   *distance Command Used in Example 8-17*

| Command | Description |
|---------|-------------|
| **distance 130 0.0.0.0 255.255.255.255 1** | |
| **130** | Defines the administrative distance that specified routes will be assigned. |
| **0.0.0.0 255.255.255.255** | Defines the source address of the router supplying the routing information—in this case, any router. |
| **1** | Defines the access list to be used to filter incoming routing updates to determine which will have their administrative distance changed. |
| **access-list 1 permit 172.16.9.0** | |
| **1** | Gives the access list number. |
| **permit** | Allows all networks that match the address to be permitted—in this case, to have their administrative distance changed. |
| **172.16.9.0** | Shows a network to be permitted—in this case to have its administrative distance changed. |

Router R200, for example, is configured to assign an administrative distance of 130 to IGRP routes to networks 172.16.9.0, 172.16.10.0, and 172.16.6.0. In this way, when the router learns about these networks from RIP, the RIP-learned routes (with a lower administrative distance of 120) will be selected and put in the routing table. Note that the **distance** command is for IGRP-learned routes because it is part of the IGRP routing process configuration.

The output in Example 8-18 shows that Router R200 now has retained the better (more optimal) route to some of the networks by using the RIP routes.

**Example 8-18** *Router R200 Learns Some RIP Routes After the **distance** Command Is Added*

```
R200#show ip route
<Output Omitted>

  172.16.0.0/24 is subnetted, 11 subnets
R    172.16.9.0 [120/1] via 172.16.7.1, 00:00:19, Serial1
R    172.16.10.0 [120/2] via 172.16.7.1, 00:00:19, Serial1
I    172.16.11.0 [100/9039] via 172.16.1.2, 00:00:49, TokenRing0
I    172.16.4.0 [100/8539] via 172.16.1.2, 00:00:49, TokenRing0
I    172.16.5.0 [100/8539] via 172.16.1.2, 00:00:49, TokenRing0
R    172.16.6.0 [120/1] via 172.16.7.1, 00:00:19, Serial1
C    172.16.3.0 is directly connected, Serial0
```

With this configuration, given the actual bandwidths involved, the IGRP path would have been better for the 172.16.10.0 network, so it may have made sense to not include 172.16.10.0 in the access list.

This example illustrates the importance of not only knowing your network before implementing redistribution, but also demonstrates that you should view which routes the routers are selecting after redistribution is enabled. You should pay particular attention to routers that can select from a number of possible redundant paths to a network because they are more likely to select suboptimal paths.

# Verifying Redistribution Operation

The best way to verify redistribution operation is to do the following:

- Know your network topology, particularly where redundant routes exist.
- Show the routing table of the appropriate routing protocol on a variety of routers in the internetwork. For example, check the routing table on the boundary router, as well as some of the internal routers in each autonomous system using the following command:

    ```
    router#show ip route [ip-address]
    ```

- Perform a **traceroute** on some of the routes that go across the autonomous systems to verify that the shortest path is being used for routing. Make sure that you especially run traces to networks for which redundant routes exist using the following command:

    ```
    router#traceroute [ip-address]
    ```

---

**NOTE**    The **traceroute** command appears in the Cisco IOS documentation as **trace**; on the routers, however **traceroute** is the full command.

---

- If you do encounter routing problems, use the **traceroute** and **debug** commands to observe the routing update traffic on the boundary routers and on the internal routers.

---

**NOTE**    Running **debug** requires extra processing by the router, so if the router is already overloaded, initiating **debug** is not recommended.

---

# Policy-Based Routing Using Route Maps

Route maps are complex access lists that allow some conditions to be tested against a packet or route in question using **match** commands. If the conditions match, some actions can be taken to modify attributes of the packet or route. These actions are specified by **set** commands.

A collection of route map statements that have the same route map name are considered one route map. Within a route map, each route map statement is numbered and therefore can be edited individually.

The statements in a route map correspond to the lines of an access list. Specifying the match conditions in a route map is similar to specifying the source and destination addresses and masks in an access list.

One big difference between route maps and access lists is that route maps can modify the route by using **set** commands.

The **route-map** command can be used to define the conditions for policy routing. The following command is explained in detail in Table 8-16:

```
router(config)#route-map map-tag [permit | deny] [sequence-number]
```

**Table 8-16**    *route-map Command*

| Command | Description |
| --- | --- |
| *map-tag* | Name of the route map |
| **permit | deny** | The action to be taken if the route map match conditions are met |
| *sequence-number* | Sequence number that indicates the position that a new route map statement will have in the list of route map statements already configured with the same name |

### Route Map Sequence Numbering

The default for the **route-map** command is permit, with a sequence number of 10. If you leave out the sequence number when configuring all statements for the same route map name, the router will assume that you are editing and adding to the first statement, sequence number 10. Route map sequence numbers do not automatically increment!

A route map may be made up of multiple route map statements. The statements are processed top-down, similar to an access list. The first match found for a route is applied. The sequence number is used for inserting or deleting specific route map statements in a specific place in the route map.

The **match** route map configuration commands are used to define the conditions to be checked. The **set** route map configuration commands are used to define the actions to be followed if there is a match.

```
router(config-route-map)#match {condition}
router(config-route-map)#set {condition}
```

A single match statement may contain multiple conditions. At least one condition in the match statement must be true for that match statement to be considered a match. A route map statement may contain multiple match statements. All match statements in the route map statement must be considered true for the route map statement to be considered matched.

---

**NOTE**    Only one match condition listed on the same line must match for the entire line to be considered a match.

---

The *sequence-number* specifies the order in which conditions are checked. For example, if there are two statements in a route map named MYMAP, one with sequence 10 and the other with sequence 20, sequence 10 will be checked first. If the match conditions in sequence 10 are not met, then sequence 20 will be checked.

Like an access list, there is an implicit deny any at the end of a route map. The consequences of this deny depend on how the route map is being used. The specifics for policy-based routing are discussed later in this section.

Another way to explain how a route map works is to use a simple example and see how a router would interpret it. Example 8-19 provides example syntax of a route map. (Note that on a router, all the conditions and actions shown would be replaced with specific conditions and actions, depending on the exact match and set commands used.)

**Example 8-19** *Route Map Demonstration—Simple Example*

```
route-map demo permit 10
  match x y z
  match a
  set b
  set c
route-map demo permit 20
  match q
  set r
route-map demo permit 30
```

The route map named **demo** is interpreted as follows:

If {(x or y or z) and a match} then {set b and c}
Else
    If q matches then set r
    Else
        Set nothing

# Policy-Based Routing

In today's high-performance internetworks, organizations need the freedom to implement packet forwarding and routing according to their own defined policies in a way that goes beyond traditional routing protocol concerns. By using policy-based routing, introduced in Cisco IOS Release 11.0, policies that selectively cause packets to take different paths can be implemented.

Policy-based routing also provides a mechanism to mark packets with different types of service (TOS). This feature can be used in conjunction with Cisco IOS queuing techniques so that certain kinds of traffic can receive preferential service.

The benefits that can be achieved by implementing policy-based routing in networks include the following:

- **Source-based transit provider selection**—Internet service providers and other organizations can use policy-based routing to route traffic originating from different sets of users through different Internet connections, across policy routers.

- **Quality of service (QoS)**—Organizations can provide QoS to differentiated traffic by setting the precedence or TOS values in the IP packet headers in routers at the periphery of the network and leveraging queuing mechanisms to prioritize traffic in the core or backbone of the network. This setup improves network performance by eliminating the need to classify the traffic explicitly at each WAN interface in the core or backbone of the network.

- **Cost savings**—An organization can direct the bulk traffic associated with a specific activity to use a higher-bandwidth, high-cost link for a short time and to continue basic connectivity over a lower-bandwidth, low-cost link for interactive traffic. For example, a dial-on-demand ISDN line could be brought up in response to traffic to a finance server for file transfers selected by policy routing.

- **Load sharing**—In addition to the dynamic load-sharing capabilities offered by destination-based routing that the Cisco IOS software has always supported, network managers can now implement policies to distribute traffic among multiple paths based on the traffic characteristics.

Policy-based routing is applied to incoming packets. All packets received on an interface with policy-based routing enabled are considered for policy-based routing. The router passes the packets through a route map. Based on the criteria defined in the route map, packets are forwarded to the appropriate next hop.

Routers normally forward packets to the destination addresses based on information in their routing tables. Instead of routing by the destination address, policy-based routing allows network administrators to determine and implement routing policies to allow or deny paths based on the following:

- The identity of a source system
- The application being run
- The protocol in use
- The size of packets

The route map statements used for policy-based routing can be marked as permit or deny. If the statement is marked as deny, a packet meeting the match criteria is sent through the normal forwarding channels (in other words, destination-based routing is performed). Only if the statement is marked as permit and the packet meets all the match criteria are the **set** commands applied. If no match is found in the route map, then the packet is forwarded through the normal routing channel. If it is desired not to revert to normal forwarding and to drop a packet that does not match the specified criteria, then a **set** statement to route the packets to interface null 0 should be specified as the last entry in the route map.

## Configuring Policy-Based Routing

IP standard or extended access lists can be used to establish policy-based routing match criteria using the **match ip address** command explained in Table 8-17. A standard IP access list can be used to specify match criteria for the source address of a packet; extended access lists can be used to specify match criteria based on source and destination addresses, application, protocol type, TOS, and precedence.

```
router(config-route-map)#match ip address {access-list-number ¦ name}
[...access-list-number ¦ name]
```

**Table 8-17**    *match ip address* Command

| match ip address Command | Description |
| --- | --- |
| *access-list-number | name* | Number or name of a standard or extended access list to be used to test incoming packets. If multiple access lists are specified, matching any one will result in a match. |

The **match length** command, explained in Table 8-18, can be used to establish criteria based on the packet length between specified minimum and maximum values. For example, a network administrator could use the match length as the criterion that distinguishes between interactive and file transfer traffic because file transfer traffic usually has larger packet sizes.

```
router(config-route-map)#match length min max
```

**Table 8-18**  *match length Command*

| match length Command | Description |
|---|---|
| *min* | Minimum Layer 3 length of the packet, inclusive, allowed for a match |
| *max* | Maximum Layer 3 length of the packet, inclusive, allowed for a match |

If the match statements are satisfied, one or more of the following **set** statements can be used to specify the criteria for forwarding packets through the router:

- The **set ip next-hop** command provides a list of IP addresses used to specify the adjacent next-hop router in the path toward the destination to which the packets should be forwarded. If more than one IP address is specified, the first IP address associated with a currently up connected interface will be used to route the packets. The **set ip next-hop** command is explained in Table 8-19.

  ```
  router(config-route-map)#set ip next-hop ip-address [...ip-address]
  ```

**NOTE**  This **set** command affects all packet types and is always used if configured.

**Table 8-19**  *set ip next-hop Command*

| Command | Description |
|---|---|
| *ip-address* | IP address of the next hop to which packets are output. It must be the address of an adjacent router. |

- The **set interface** command provides a list of interfaces through which the packets can be routed. If more than one interface is specified, the first interface that is found to be up will be used for forwarding the packets. The following command is explained in Table 8-20:

  ```
  router(config-route-map)#set interface type number [...type number]
  ```

**NOTE**  If there is no explicit route for the destination address of the packet in the routing table (for example, if the packet is a broadcast or is destined to an unknown address), the **set interface** command has no effect and is ignored.

**Table 8-20**    *set interface Command*

| Command | Description |
|---------|-------------|
| *type number* | Interface type and number to which packets are output |

The **set ip default next-hop** command provides a list of default next-hop IP addresses. If more than one IP address is specified, the first next hop specified that appears to be adjacent to the router is used. The optional specified IP addresses are tried in turn. Table 8-21 provides information on the **set ip default next-hop** command.

```
router(config-route-map)#set ip default next-hop ip-address [...ip-address]
```

**NOTE**    A packet is routed to the next hop specified by this **set** command only if there is no explicit route for the packet's destination address in the routing table.

**Table 8-21**    *set ip default next-hop Command*

| Command | Description |
|---------|-------------|
| *ip-address* | IP address of the next hop to which packets are output. It must be the address of an adjacent router. |

The **set default interface** command provides a list of default interfaces. If there is no explicit route available to the destination address of the packet being considered for policy routing, it will be routed to the first up interface in the list of specified default interfaces. Table 8-22 provides information about the **set default interface** command.

```
router(config-route-map)#set default interface type number [...type number]
```

**NOTE**    A packet is routed to the next hop specified by this **set** command only if there is no explicit route for the packet's destination address in the routing table.

**Table 8-22**    *set default interface Command*

| Command | Description |
|---------|-------------|
| *type number* | Interface type and number, to which packets are output |

## Using the set Commands

The router evaluates the first four **set** commands for policy-based routing, shown here in the order they are presented. When a destination address or interface has been chosen, other **set** commands for changing the destination address or interface are ignored. Note, however, that some of these commands affect only packets for which there is an explicit route in the routing table, while others affect only packets for which there is *no* explicit route in the routing table. A packet that is not affected by any of the **set** commands in a route map statement that it has matched will not be policy routed and will be forwarded normally (in other words, destination-based routing will be performed).

The **set ip tos** command is used to set the IP TOS value in the IP packets. The TOS field is 8 bits long in the IP header, with 5 bits for setting the Class of Service (COS) and 3 bits for the IP precedence. The **set ip tos** command is used to set the 5 COS bits.

The 5 COS bits are for setting the delay, throughput, reliability, and cost, with 1 of the bits reserved. Table 8-23 provides information on the **set ip tos** command.

```
router(config-route-map)#set ip tos [number ¦ name ]
```

**Table 8-23**    *set ip tos Command*

| Variable: *number* or *name* | Description |
|---|---|
| **0-15** | Type of service value |
| *max-reliability* | Set max reliable TOS (2) |
| *max-throughput* | Set max throughput TOS (4) |
| *min-delay* | Set min delay TOS (8) |
| *min-monetary-cost* | Set min-monetary-cost TOS (1) |
| *normal* | Set normal TOS (0) |

The **set ip precedence** command is used to set the IP precedence bits in the IP packets. With 3 bits, there are eight possible values for the IP precedence. This command is used when implementing quality of service (QoS) and can be used by other QoS services such as weighted fair queuing (WFQ) and weighted random early detection (WRED). Table 8-24 provides information on the **set ip precedence** command.

```
router(config-route-map)#set ip precedence [number ¦ name ]
```

**Table 8-24**    *set ip precedence Command*

| Variable: *number* or *name* | Description |
|---|---|
| **0-7** | Precedence value |
| *critical* | Set critical precedence (5) |

**Table 8-24**   *set ip precedence Command (Continued)*

| Variable: *number* or *name* | Description |
|---|---|
| *flash* | Set flash precedence (3) |
| *flash-override* | Set flash override precedence (4) |
| *immediate* | Set immediate precedence (2) |
| *Internet* | Set internetwork control precedence (6) |
| *network* | Set network control precedence (7) |
| *priority* | Set priority precedence (1) |
| *routine* | Set routine precedence (0) |

The **set** commands can be used in conjunction with each other.

To identify a route map to use for policy routing on an interface, use the **ip policy route-map** interface configuration command, explained in Table 8-25.

```
router(config-if)#ip policy route-map map-tag
```

**Table 8-25**   *ip policy route-map Command*

| Command | Description |
|---|---|
| *map-tag* | Name of the route map to use for policy routing. Must match a map tag specified by a **route-map** command. |

**NOTE**    Policy-based routing is specified on the interface that receives the packets, not on the interface from which the packets are sent.

Since Cisco IOS Release 11.2F, IP policy routing can now be fast-switched. Prior to this feature, policy routing could be only process-switched, which meant that on most platforms, the switching rate was approximately 1,000 to 10,000 packets per second. This was not fast enough for many applications. Users who need policy routing to occur at faster speeds can now implement policy routing without slowing down the router.

Policy routing must be configured before you configure fast-switched policy routing. Fast switching of policy routing is disabled by default. To have policy routing be fast-switched, use the **ip route-cache policy** command in interface configuration mode.

```
router(config-if)#ip route-cache policy
```

Fast-switched policy routing supports all the **match** commands and most of the **set** commands, except for the following restrictions:

- The **set ip default** command is not supported.

- The **set interface** command is supported only over point-to-point links, unless a route-cache entry exists using the same interface specified in the **set interface** command in the route map. Also, at the process level, the routing table is consulted to determine whether the interface is on a reasonable path to the destination. During fast switching, the software does not make this check. Instead, if the packet matches, the software blindly forwards the packet to the specified interface.

## Policy-Based Routing Example

In Figure 8-10, Router A has a policy that packets from 192.168.2.1 should go out to Router C's interface serial 1. All other packets should be routed according to their destination address. The configuration for Router A is shown in Example 8-20.

**Figure 8-10** *Router A Has a Policy That Packets from 192.168.2.1 Go to Router C's Interface S1*

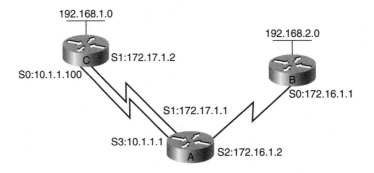

Router A's serial 2 interface, where packets from 192.168.2.1 go into Router A, is configured to do policy routing with the **ip policy route-map** command. The route map test is used for this policy routing. It tests the IP addresses in packets against access list 1 to determine which packets will be policy-routed.

**Example 8-20** *Router A's Configuration*

```
RouterA(config)# interface Serial2
RouterA(config-if)# ip address 172.16.1.2 255.255.255.0
RouterA(config-if)# ip policy route-map test
RouterA(config)#route-map test permit 10
RouterA(config-route-map)#match ip address 1
RouterA(config-route-map)#set ip next-hop 172.17.1.2
RouterA(config-route-map)#exit
RouterA(config)#access-list 1 permit 192.168.2.1 0.0.0.0
```

Access list 1 specifies that packets with a source address of 192.168.2.1 will be policy-routed. Packets that match access list 1 will be sent to the next-hop address 172.17.1.2, which is Router C's serial 1 interface. All other packets will be forwarded normally, according to their destination address. (Recall that access lists have an implicit deny any at the end, so no other packets will be permitted by access list 1.)

# Verifying Policy-Based Routing

To display the route maps used for policy routing on the router's interfaces, use the **show ip policy** EXEC command.

To display configured route maps, use the **show route-map** EXEC command, as shown in Table 8-26.

```
router#show route-map [map-name]
```

**Table 8-26**   *show route-map Command*

| Command | Description |
|---------|-------------|
| *map-name* | Optional name of a specific route map |

Use the **debug ip policy** EXEC command to display IP policy routing packet activity. This command helps you determine what policy routing is doing. It displays information about whether a packet matches the criteria and, if so, the resulting routing information for the packet.

Because the **debug ip policy** command generates a significant amount of output, use it only when traffic on the IP network is low so that other activity on the system is not adversely affected.

To discover the routes that the packets follow when traveling to their destination from the router, use the **traceroute** privileged EXEC command. To change the default parameters and invoke an extended traceroute test, enter the command without a destination argument. You will be stepped through a dialog to select the desired parameters.

To check host reachability and network connectivity, use the **ping** (IP packet Internet groper function) privileged EXEC command. You can use the extended command mode of the **ping** command to specify the supported header options by entering the command without any arguments.

The output shown in Examples 8-21, 8-22, and 8-23 are from Router A in Example 8-20.

Example 8-21 provides an example of the **show ip policy** command. It indicates that the route map called test is used for policy routing on the router's interface serial 2.

**Example 8-21** *show ip policy Output*

```
RouterA#show ip policy
Interface      Route map
Serial2        test
```

The **show route-map** command, shown in Example 8-22, indicates that three packets have matched sequence 10 of the test route map.

**Example 8-22** *show route-map Output*

```
RouterA#show route-map
route-map test, permit, sequence 10
  Match clauses:
    ip address (access-lists): 1
  Set clauses:
    ip next-hop 172.17.1.2
  Policy routing matches: 3 packets, 168 bytes
```

Example 8-23 provides an example of the output of the **debug ip policy** command. The output indicates that a packet from 172.16.1.1 destined for 192.168.1.1 was received on interface serial 2 and that it was rejected by the policy on that interface. The packet is routed normally (by destination).

Another packet, from 192.168.2.1 destined for 192.168.1.1, was later received on the same interface serial 2. This packet matched the policy on that interface and was therefore policy-routed and sent out interface Serial 1 to 172.17.1.2.

**Example 8-23** *Example of debug ip policy*

```
RouterA#debug ip policy
Policy routing debugging is on

...
11:50:51: IP: s=172.16.1.1 (Serial2), d=192.168.1.1 (Serial3), len 100,
policy rejected -- normal forwarding
...
11:51:25: IP: s=192.168.2.1 (Serial2), d=192.168.1.1, len 100, policy match
11:51:25: IP: route map test, item 10, permit
11:51:25: IP: s=192.168.2.1 (Serial2), d=192.168.1.1 (Serial1), len 100,
policyrouted
11:51:25: IP: Serial2 to Serial1 172.17.1.2
```

# Case Study: Redistribution

Refer to Chapter 1 for introductory information on the running case study.

Recall that throughout this book we have been using a case study of JKL Corporation to discuss various aspects of scalable routing. The case studies are used to review key concepts and to discuss critical issues surrounding network operation.

In this case study, you will look at how JKL's Acquisition A will implement its routing protocols. Recall that Acquisition A is running a mixture of protocols: IGRP, RIP, and OSPF. It has two Class C public addresses and uses a Class A private address. As shown in Figure 8-11, each of the three protocol domains is connected to the other two.

**Figure 8-11**  *Topology of JKL After the Acquisition of A*

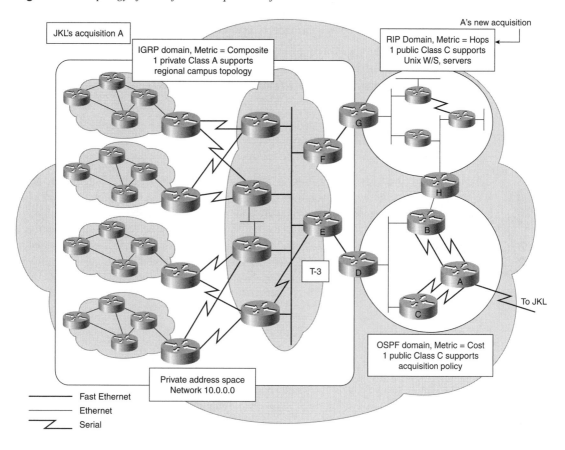

While looking at Figure 8-11, analyze the following:

- Limitations on the size of a routing domain
- Use of administrative distance as a learning mechanism
- Possibilities for suboptimal routes in the routing table
- Protection against feedback loops, especially those caused by topology changes
- Requirement for appropriate seed metrics when passing routes between different protocols

# Case Study Solution

Acquisitions A's network was originally a RIP implementation until it grew too large. IGRP and private addressing were selected to handle the largest portion of the network because

IGRP has a maximum default hop count of 100 and the number of nodes far exceeded the available Class C addressing space. The IGRP domain is a hierarchical regional campus network with route summarization in effect at routers D and G.

The RIP domain at the upper right of Figure 8-11 represents a concentration of UNIX workstations and servers that are not under A's administrative control. The Class C address space from the RIP domain is summarized to a classful boundary at Router G and at Router H.

The OSPF domain was also originally a RIP domain, but it has been converted to OSPF in anticipation of the consolidation into JKL's enterprise network. The Internet connection is currently through Router A, although Router A will eventually link the entire network to JKL.

The administrative distances for IGRP, OSPF, and RIP are 100, 110, and 120, respectively. If two-way redistribution for each domain occurred at Routers D, G, and H, suboptimal paths could be propagated because the administrative distance for IGRP is lowest. In a potentially looping topology, such as shown in Figure 8-11, care must be taken to apply route filters to prevent the feedback of routes learned via redistribution. Routes learned via redistribution start with a seed metric specified by the **redistribute** command. Suboptimal routes might have a bad metric (indicating a less than desirable route) but are still the preferred path because the route was learned by a routing protocol with a superior administrative distance.

As you remember from previous discussions, there is a significant difference between the administrative distance value, which is a preference factor about how routes are learned, and the metric value, which is a preference factor for selecting routes to forward traffic.

Alternatives to potentially dangerous redistribution can be a combination of static routes, default routes, and passive interface statements. In lieu of full redistribution for the RIP domain, consider using a static route to network 10.0.0.0, and default routes in each router pointing toward the OSPF domain (via router H) as a jump-off point to the Internet.

Some points to remember when considering redistribution include the following:

- Redistribution is required when routes having different metric structures need to be exchanged.
- Proper configuration for redistributing routes requires a default-metric statement to establish a seed metric.
- Redundant topologies can create feedback loops that lead to suboptimal paths being propagated.
- Route filtering is one way to control feedback loops.
- Full, two-way redistribution is not the only way to establish connectivity between dissimilar routing domains.
- Administrative distance indicates the router's preference for how a route is learned, whereas the metric value is a measure of a route's reachability.

This case study gave you a chance to reexamine concepts learned in the chapter regarding redistribution and ways to control looping by using route filtering or adjusting the administrative distance of routing protocols.

# Summary

In this chapter, you have learned how to select and configure the different ways to control route update traffic and how to apply judicious route redistribution between dissimilar routing processes. You have also learned how to resolve path selection problems that result in a redistributed network and how to confirm the proper route redistribution.

In the last section of this chapter, you learned how to configure policy-based routing using route maps.

# Configuration Exercise #1: Configuring Policy-Based Routing

Complete the following exercise to configure policy-based routing.

---

### Configuration Exercises

In this book, Configuration Exercises are used to provide practice in configuring routers with the commands presented. If you have access to real hardware, you can try these exercises on your routers; refer to Appendix H, "Configuration Exercise Equipment Requirements and Backbone Configurations," for a list of recommended equipment and configuration commands for the backbone routers. However, even if you don't have access to any routers, you can go through the exercises and keep a log of your own "running configurations" on separate sheets of paper. Commands used and answers to the Configuration Exercises are provided at the end of the exercise.

In these exercises, you are in control of a pod of three routers; there are assumed to be 12 pods in the network. The pods are interconnected to a backbone. In most of the exercises, there is only one router in the backbone; in some cases, another router is added to the backbone. Each of the Configuration Exercises in this book assumes that you have completed the previous chapter's exercises on your pod.

---

## Objectives

In this Configuration Exercise, you will configure p*x*r1 to policy-route the packets coming in from p*x*r3.

## Visual Objective

Figure 8-12 illustrates the topology used for this policy-routing Configuration Exercise.

**Figure 8-12**  *Policy Routing on pxr1*

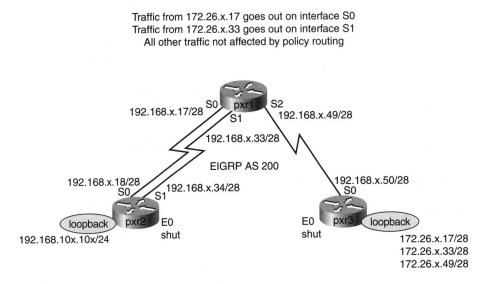

Traffic from 172.26.x.17 goes out on interface S0
Traffic from 172.26.x.33 goes out on interface S1
All other traffic not affected by policy routing

## Command List

In this Configuration Exercise, you will use the commands listed in Table 8-27. Refer to this list if you need configuration command assistance during this exercise.

**Table 8-27**  *Commands Used in Configuration Exercise #1*

| Command | Description |
| --- | --- |
| **ip policy route-map** *mapname* | Enables IP policy routing on an interface using route map. |
| **route-map** *mapname* **permit 10** | Creates a route map. |
| **match IP address 1** | Matches IP address in access list 1. |
| **set interface S0** | Sets outgoing interface to S0. |
| **show IP policy** | Shows IP policy routing-enabled interfaces. |
| **show route-map** | Shows your route map configuration. |
| **debug IP policy** | Debugs IP policy routing events. |
| **trace** | Performs an extended trace so that you can set the source IP address. |

**Table 8-27**    *Commands Used in Configuration Exercise #1 (Continued)*

| Command | Description |
| --- | --- |
| **ping** | Performs an extended ping so that you can set the source IP address. |
| **show logging** | Shows buffered console error and debug messages. |

# Setup

Perform the following steps:

**Step 1**    At pxr1, shut the Serial 3 interface, and disable BGP.

**Step 2**    At pxr2, shut the Ethernet 0 interface and disable BGP.

**Step 3**    At pxr3, shut the Serial 1 and Ethernet 0 interfaces and disable BGP.

# Task: Enable IP Policy-Based Routing at pxr1

Complete the following steps:

**Step 1**    Enable EIGRP in AS 200 on pxr1, pxr2, and pxr3, including on the loopback interfaces of pxr2 and pxr3. What commands will you use to achieve this?

**Step 2**    From pxr3, ensure that you can ping the pxr2 loopback interface (192.168.10x.10x).

From pxr2, ensure that you can ping the pxr3 loopback interfaces (172.26.x.17, 172.26.x.33, and 172.26.x.49).

**Step 3**    Examine the routing table of pxr1.

You should see two paths to 192.168.10x.10x. If not, verify that you have identical bandwidth set on the S0 and S1 interfaces and that you have not disabled load balancing (with the **maximum-paths 1** command).

**Step 4**    Configure IP policy-based routing at pxr1 as follows:

All IP traffic sourced from 172.26.x.17 should be forwarded out on the pxr1 S0 interface. Which commands should you type to create this policy?

All IP traffic sourced from 172.26.x.33 should be forwarded out on the pxr1 S1 interface. Which commands should you type to create this policy?

All other traffic should not be policy-routed.

Issue the **show ip policy** command at pxr1 to verify that the route map is associated with the correct interface.

What command could you issue at pxr1 to verify that the route map is configured correctly?

What command could you issue at pxr1 to confirm that your access lists are configured correctly?

**Step 5**   Clear all logging on pxr1. Enable debugging of IP policy-based routing at pxr1. What commands would you type to achieve this?

From pxr3, use the extended **trace** command to perform a trace to 192.168.10x.10x, using a source address of 172.26.x.17 (loopback address of pxr3).

Which command would show you the buffered debug output on pxr1?

Which path did the packets use at pxr1, S0 or S1?

What command could you use to see the matches on the route map that you created?

**Step 6**   Clear the logging on pxr1. From pxr3, use the extended **trace** command to perform a trace to 192.168.10x.10x, using a source address of 172.26.x.33.

On pxr1, what command will you type to show the buffered debug output?

Which path did the packets use at pxr1, S0 or S1?

What command could you use to see the matches on the route map that you created?

**Step 7**   Enter the **clear logging** command on pxr1. From pxr3, use the extended **trace** command to perform a trace to 192.168.10x.10x, using a source address of 172.26.x.49.

On pxr1, show the buffered debug output with the **show logging** command.

Which path did the packets use at pxr1, S0 or S1?

Which command could you type to see a summary of the policy matches for policy routing?

**Step 8**   From pxr3, use the extended **ping** command to perform a ping to 192.168.10x.10x, using a source address of 172.26.x.17 with a count of 100.

At p*x*r1, look at the debug output.

Is the ping packet from 172.26.*x*.17 being policy-routed correctly?

**Step 9**  From p*x*r3, use the extended **ping** command to perform a ping to 192.168.10*x*.10*x*, using a source address of 172.26.*x*.33 with a count of 100.

At p*x*r1, look at the debug output.

Is the ping packet from 172.26.*x*.33 being policy-routed correctly?

**Step 10**  From p*x*r3, use the extended **ping** command to perform a ping to 192.168.10*x*.10*x*, using a source address of 172.26.*x*.49 with a count of 100.

At p*x*r1, look at the debug output.

Is the ping packet from 172.26.*x*.49 being policy-routed?

**Step 11**  Type in the command to save the current configurations of all the routers within your pod to NVRAM.

## Completion Criteria

You have successfully completed this Configuration Exercise if you correctly supplied the commands required to configure policy-based routing at p*x*r1 according to the given requirements, if you were able to see the correct results in the debug output, and if you were able to correctly answer the questions in the Configuration Exercises. At the end of this Configuration Exercise, all the routers in your pod will have EIGRP connectivity to each other, with policy routing configured on p*x*r1.

# Configuration Exercise #2: Configuring Route Redistribution Between OSPF and EIGRP

Complete the following exercise to configure route redistribution at the p*x*r1 router, which is the ASBR.

## Objectives

In the Configuration Exercise, you will do the following:

- Configure OSPF between your p*x*r1 and p*x*r2 routers.
- Configure EIGRP between your p*x*r1 and p*x*r3 routers.
- Configure route redistribution at your p*x*r1 router.

- Configure route redistribution at your *pxr1* router with filtering.
- Verify connectivity within your pod.

## Visual Objective

Figure 8-13 illustrates the topology used for this redistribution exercise.

**Figure 8-13** *Configuring Route Redistribution*

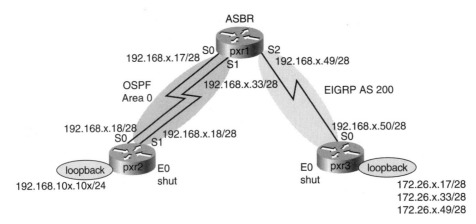

## Command List

In this Configuration Exercise, you will use the commands listed in Table 8-28. Refer to this list if you need configuration command assistance during the Configuration Exercise. You should already be familiar with the EIGRP and OSPF configuration commands from the OSPF and EIGRP Configuration Exercises.

**Table 8-28** *Commands Used for Route Redistribution*

| Command | Description |
| --- | --- |
| **redistribute eigrp 200 subnets metric 1700** | Redistributes EIGRP into OSPF. |
| **redistribute ospf 200 metric 64 100 255 1 1500** | Redistributes OSPF into EIGRP. |
| **distribute-list 10 out eigrp 200** | Enables filtering when redistributing from EIGRP. |
| **access-list 10 permit 172.26.x.16** | Standard access list to only permit route 172.26.*x*.16. |

## Setup

Perform these steps:

**Step 1**    At pxr1, disable EIGRP.

**Step 2**    At pxr2, disable EIGRP.

## Task 1: Enable OSPF Between pxr1 (S0 and S1) and pxr2 (S0 and S1)

Complete the following steps:

**Step 1**    What commands would you use to enable OSPF process ID 200 (area 0) between the S0 and S1 interfaces of pxr1 and pxr2?

**Step 2**    What command would you type to place your loopback interface (192.168.10x.10x/28) of pxr2 into OSPF area 0?

**Step 3**    From pxr1, ping the pxr2 loopback interface to verify OSPF connectivity.

## Task 2: Enable EIGRP Between pxr1 (S2) and pxr3 (S0)

Complete the following steps:

**Step 1**    What commands would you use to enable EIGRP AS 200 between the S2 interface of pxr1 and the S0 interface of pxr3? (Ensure that EIGRP is running only between pxr1 and pxr3.)

**Step 2**    On pxr3, which command could you type to verify that EIGRP is enabled on your loopback interfaces (172.26.x.17/28, 172.26.x.33/28, and 172.26.x.49/28)?

**Step 3**    From pxr1, ping the pxr3 loopback interfaces to verify EIGRP connectivity.

**Step 4**    From pxr3, would a ping to the loopback interface on pxr2 be successful?

Why or why not?

**Step 5**    What command would you type to save the current configurations of all the routers within your pod to NVRAM?

## Task 3: Enable Route Redistribution Between OSPF and EIGRP

Complete the following steps:

**Step 1**   Which router within your pod is the ASBR?

**Step 2**   At your ASBR, what command would you type to redistribute from OSPF into EIGRP?

**Step 3**   At your ASBR, what command would you type to redistribute from EIGRP into OSPF?

**Step 4**   What command would you type to examine the routing tables of pxr2 and pxr3?

Do you see the external EIGRP route at the pxr3 router?

Do you see the external OSPF route at the pxr2 router? What is the metric type?

**Step 5**   From pxr2, ping the loopback interfaces on pxr3.

From pxr3, ping the loopback interface on pxr2.

Were the pings successful?

**Step 6**   Why is your pxr2 router seeing only the 172.26.0.0 summarized route and not the 172.26.x.16/28, 172.26.x.32/28, and 172.26.x.48/32 subnets in its routing table?

**Step 7**   At your pxr3 router, what command would you enter to disable EIGRP autosummarization?

**Step 8**   Re-examine the pxr2 routing table; do you see the 172.26.x.16/28, 172.26.x.32/28, and 172.26.x.48/28 subnets now?

Do not proceed to the next task if you don't see these subnets in your pxr2 routing table. If you don't see the subnets, confirm that the **no auto-summary** command is configured, and be patient because the change will not be instantaneous.

**Step 9**   Save the current configurations of all the routers within your pod to NVRAM.

## Task 4: Enable Route Redistribution from EIGRP to OSPF with Filtering

Complete the following steps:

**Step 1**    Reconfigure your redistribution from EIGRP into OSPF to only allow the 172.26.*x*.16/28 and the 192.168.*x*.48/28 subnets to be redistributed from EIGRP into OSPF. Using the **distribute-list** command to perform this task, list all the commands used.

What command would you use on p*x*r1 to clear the routing table?

**Step 2**    Examine the p*x*r2 routing table. Are the 172.26.*x*.32/28 and 172.26.*x*.48/28 external routes filtered out?

Bonus question: What will happen if we allow only the 172.26.*x*.16/28 subnet and not the 192.168.*x*.48/28 subnet? Will the ping from p*x*r3 to p*x*r2 fail? Why or why not?

**Step 3**    Type the command to remove the distribute list filtering after it is working correctly. Clear the IP routing table on p*x*r1, and then look at the p*x*r2 routing table once more. Which commands would accomplish all this?

**Step 4**    Save the current configurations of all the routers within your pod to NVRAM.

## Bonus Task

Complete the following steps:

**Step 1**    Which commands would you use to repeat Task 4 using a route map instead of a distribute list?

**Step 2**    Remove the route map filtering and clear the IP routing table on p*x*r1.

## Completion Criteria

You have successfully completed this Configuration Exercise if you correctly supplied the commands required to configure your p*x*r1 router, the ASBR, to redistribute OSPF routes into EIGRP AS 200 and redistribute a particular EIGRP route into OSPF, and if you were able to correctly answer the questions in the Configuration Exercises. At the end of this Configuration Exercise, the routers in your pod should have full connectivity to each other, with the exception of the routes that were filtered out.

# Configuration Exercise #1 Answers: Configuring Policy-Based Routing

This section provides the answers to the questions in Configuration Exercise #1. The answers are in **bold**.

## Answers to Setup

Perform the following steps:

**Step 1** At p*x*r1, shut the Serial 3 interface, and disable BGP.

```
p1r1#conf t
Enter configuration commands, one per line.  End with CNTL/Z.
p1r1(config)#int s3
p1r1(config-if)#shutdown
p1r1(config-if)#exit
p1r1(config)#no router bgp 65101
```

**Step 2** At p*x*r2, shut the Ethernet 0 interface and disable BGP.

```
p1r2#conf t
Enter configuration commands, one per line.  End with CNTL/Z.
p1r2(config)#int e0
p1r2(config-if)#shutdown
p1r2(config-if)#exit
p1r2(config)#no router bgp 65101
```

**Step 3** At p*x*r3, shut the Serial 1 and Ethernet 0 interfaces and disable BGP.

```
p1r3#conf t
Enter configuration commands, one per line.  End with CNTL/Z.
p1r3(config)#int s1
p1r3(config-if)#shut
p1r3(config-if)#int e0
p1r3(config-if)#shut
p1r3(config-if)#exit
p1r3(config)#no router bgp 65101
```

## Answers to Task: Enable IP Policy-Based Routing at p*x*r1

Complete the following steps:

**Step 1** Enable EIGRP in AS 200 on p*x*r1, p*x*r2, and p*x*r3, including on the loopback interfaces of p*x*r2 and p*x*r3. What commands will you use to achieve this?

```
p1r1(config)#router eigrp 200
p1r1(config-router)#network 192.168.1.0
p1r1(config-router)#^Z
. . .
p1r2(config)#router eigrp 200
p1r2(config-router)#network 192.168.1.0
p1r2(config-router)#network 192.168.101.0
. . .
p1r3(config)#router eigrp 200
```

```
p1r3(config-router)#network 192.168.1.0
p1r3(config-router)#network 172.26.0.0
```

**Step 2**   From p*x*r3, ensure that you can ping the p*x*r2 loopback interface
(192.168.10*x*.10*x*).

```
p1r3#ping 192.168.101.101

Type escape sequence to abort.
Sending 5, 100-byte ICMP Echos to 192.168.101.101, timeout is 2 seconds:
!!!!!
Success rate is 100 percent (5/5), round-trip min/avg/max = 60/60/64 ms
```

From p*x*r2, ensure that you can ping the p*x*r3 loopback interfaces
(172.26.*x*.17, 172.26.*x*.33, and 172.26.*x*.49).

```
p1r2#ping 172.26.1.33

Type escape sequence to abort.
Sending 5, 100-byte ICMP Echos to 172.26.1.33, timeout is 2 seconds:
!!!!!
Success rate is 100 percent (5/5), round-trip min/avg/max = 56/59/64 ms
p1r2#ping 172.26.1.17

Type escape sequence to abort.
Sending 5, 100-byte ICMP Echos to 172.26.1.17, timeout is 2 seconds:
!!!!!
Success rate is 100 percent (5/5), round-trip min/avg/max = 60/60/64 ms
p1r2#ping 172.26.1.49

Type escape sequence to abort.
Sending 5, 100-byte ICMP Echos to 172.26.1.49, timeout is 2 seconds:
!!!!!
Success rate is 100 percent (5/5), round-trip min/avg/max = 56/57/60 ms
```

**Step 3**   Examine the routing table of p*x*r1.

You should see two paths to 192.168.10*x*.10*x*. If not, verify that you have
identical bandwidth set on the S0 and S1 interfaces and that you have not
disabled load balancing (with the **maximum-paths 1** command).

```
p1r1#show ip route
Codes: C - connected, S - static, I - IGRP, R - RIP, M - mobile, B - BGP
       D - EIGRP, EX - EIGRP external, O - OSPF, IA - OSPF inter area
       N1 - OSPF NSSA external type 1, N2 - OSPF NSSA external type 2
       E1 - OSPF external type 1, E2 - OSPF external type 2, E - EGP
       i - IS-IS, L1 - IS-IS level-1, L2 - IS-IS level-2, * - candidate default
       U - per-user static route, o - ODR
       T - traffic engineered route

Gateway of last resort is not set

D    172.26.0.0/16 [90/40640000] via 192.168.1.50, 00:03:36, Serial2
     192.168.1.0/28 is subnetted, 3 subnets
```

```
C        192.168.1.32 is directly connected, Serial1
C        192.168.1.48 is directly connected, Serial2
C        192.168.1.16 is directly connected, Serial0
D     192.168.101.0/24 [90/40640000] via 192.168.1.18, 00:03:57, Serial0
                       [90/40640000] via 192.168.1.34, 00:03:57, Serial1
p1r1#
```

**Step 4**   Configure IP policy-based routing at p*x*r1 as follows:

All IP traffic sourced from 172.26.*x*.17 should be forwarded out on the p*x*r1 S0 interface. Which commands should you type to create this policy?

```
p1r1(config)#int s2
p1r1(config-if)#ip policy route-map test
p1r1(config-if)#exit
p1r1(config)#route-map test permit 10
p1r1(config-route-map)#match ip address 1
p1r1(config-route-map)#set int s0
p1r1(config-route-map)#exit
p1r1(config)#access-list 1 permit 172.26.1.17
```

All IP traffic sourced from 172.26.*x*.33 should be forwarded out on the p*x*r1 S1 interface. Which commands should you type to create this policy?

```
p1r1(config)#route-map test permit 20
p1r1(config-route-map)#match ip address 2
p1r1(config-route-map)#set int s1
p1r1(config-route-map)#exit
p1r1(config)#access-list 2 permit 172.26.1.33
```

All other traffic should not be policy-routed.

Issue the **show ip policy** command at p*x*r1 to verify that the route map is associated with the correct interface.

```
p1r1#show ip policy
Interface       Route map
Serial2         test
```

What command could you issue at p*x*r1 to verify that the route map is configured correctly?

```
p1r1#show route-map
route-map test, permit, sequence 10
  Match clauses:
    ip address (access-lists): 1
  Set clauses:
    interface Serial0
  Policy routing matches: 0 packets, 0 bytes
route-map test, permit, sequence 20
  Match clauses:
```

```
    ip address (access-lists): 2
Set clauses:
  interface Serial1
Policy routing matches: 0 packets, 0 bytes
```

What command could you issue at p*x*r1 to confirm that your access lists are configured correctly?

```
p1r1#show access-list
Standard IP access list 1
    permit 172.26.1.17
Standard IP access list 2
    permit 172.26.1.33
```

**Step 5**   Clear all logging on p*x*r1. Enable debugging of IP policy-based routing at p*x*r1. What commands would you type to achieve this?

```
p1r1#clear logging
Clear logging buffer [confirm]
p1r1#debug ip policy
```

From p*x*r3, use the extended **trace** command to perform a trace to 192.168.10*x*.10*x*, using a source address of 172.26.*x*.17 (loopback address of p*x*r3).

```
p1r3#trace
Protocol [ip]:
Target IP address: 192.168.101.101
Source address: 172.26.1.17
Numeric display [n]:
Timeout in seconds [3]:
Probe count [3]:
Minimum Time to Live [1]:
Maximum Time to Live [30]:
Port Number [33434]:
Loose, Strict, Record, Timestamp, Verbose[none]:
Type escape sequence to abort.
Tracing the route to 192.168.101.101

  1 p1r1 (192.168.1.49) 16 msec 20 msec 16 msec
  2 p1r2 (192.168.1.18) 44 msec *  44 msec
p1r3#
```

Which command would show you the buffered debug output on p*x*r1?

```
p1r1#show logging
Syslog logging: enabled (0 messages dropped, 0 flushes, 0 overruns)
    Console logging: level debugging, 55 messages logged
    Monitor logging: level debugging, 0 messages logged
    Buffer logging: level debugging, 55 messages logged
    Trap logging: level informational, 29 message lines logged

Log Buffer (4096 bytes):

00:35:34: IP: s=172.26.1.17 (Serial2), d=192.168.101.101, len 28, policy match
00:35:34: IP: route map test, item 10, permit
```

```
00:35:34: IP: s=172.26.1.17 (Serial2), d=192.168.101.101 (Serial0), len 28,
policy routed
00:35:34: IP: Serial2 to Serial0 192.168.1.18
00:35:34: IP: s=172.26.1.17 (Serial2), d=192.168.101.101, len 28, policy match
00:35:34: IP: route map test, item 10, permit
00:35:34: IP: s=172.26.1.17 (Serial2), d=192.168.101.101 (Serial0), len 28,
policy routed
00:35:34: IP: Serial2 to Serial0 192.168.1.18
00:35:37: IP: s=172.26.1.17 (Serial2), d=192.168.101.101, len 28, policy match
00:35:37: IP: route map test, item 10, permit
00:35:37: IP: s=172.26.1.17 (Serial2), d=192.168.101.101 (Serial0), len 28,
policy routed
00:35:37: IP: Serial2 to Serial0 192.168.1.18
```

Which path did the packets use at pxr1, S0 or S1?

**If your policy is working at pxr1, the packets should have used the S0 path.**

What command could you use to see the matches on the route map that you created?

```
p1r1#show route-map
route-map test, permit, sequence 10
  Match clauses:
    ip address (access-lists): 1
  Set clauses:
    interface Serial0
  Policy routing matches: 3 packets, 96 bytes
route-map test, permit, sequence 20
  Match clauses:
    ip address (access-lists): 2
  Set clauses:
    interface Serial1
  Policy routing matches: 0 packets, 0 bytes
p1r1#
```

**Step 6**   Clear the logging on pxr1. From pxr3, use the extended **trace** command to perform a trace to 192.168.10x.10x, using a source address of 172.26.x.33.

```
p1r1#clear logging
Clear logging buffer [confirm]
p1r1#

p1r3#trace
Protocol [ip]:
Target IP address: 192.168.101.101
Source address: 172.26.1.33
Numeric display [n]:
Timeout in seconds [3]:
Probe count [3]:
Minimum Time to Live [1]:
Maximum Time to Live [30]:
```

```
Port Number [33434]:
Loose, Strict, Record, Timestamp, Verbose[none]:
Type escape sequence to abort.
Tracing the route to 192.168.101.101

  1 p1r1 (192.168.1.49) 20 msec 20 msec 16 msec
  2 p1r2 (192.168.1.34) 44 msec *  44 msec
p1r3#
```

On p*xr*1, what command will you type to show the buffered debug output?

```
p1r1#show logging
Syslog logging: enabled (0 messages dropped, 0 flushes, 0 overruns)
    Console logging: level debugging, 76 messages logged
    Monitor logging: level debugging, 0 messages logged
    Buffer logging: level debugging, 76 messages logged
    Trap logging: level informational, 29 message lines logged

Log Buffer (4096 bytes):

00:42:20: IP: s=172.26.1.33 (Serial2), d=192.168.101.101, len 28, policy match
00:42:20: IP: route map test, item 20, permit
00:42:20: IP: s=172.26.1.33 (Serial2), d=192.168.101.101 (Serial1), len 28,
policy routed
00:42:20: IP: Serial2 to Serial1 192.168.1.34
00:42:20: IP: s=172.26.1.33 (Serial2), d=192.168.101.101, len 28, policy match
00:42:20: IP: route map test, item 20, permit
00:42:20: IP: s=172.26.1.33 (Serial2), d=192.168.101.101 (Serial1), len 28,
policy routed
00:42:20: IP: Serial2 to Serial1 192.168.1.34
00:42:23: IP: s=172.26.1.33 (Serial2), d=192.168.101.101, len 28, policy match
00:42:23: IP: route map test, item 20, permit
00:42:23: IP: s=172.26.1.33 (Serial2), d=192.168.101.101 (Serial1), len 28,
 policy routed
00:42:23: IP: Serial2 to Serial1 192.168.1.34
```

Which path did the packets use at p*xr*1, S0 or S1?

**If your policy is working at p*xr*1, the packets should have used the S1 path.**

What command could you use to see the matches on the route map that you created?

```
p1r1#show route-map
route-map test, permit, sequence 10
  Match clauses:
    ip address (access-lists): 1
  Set clauses:
    interface Serial0
  Policy routing matches: 3 packets, 96 bytes
route-map test, permit, sequence 20
  Match clauses:
    ip address (access-lists): 2
  Set clauses:
```

```
      interface Serial1
      Policy routing matches: 3 packets, 96 bytes
    p1r1#
```

**Step 7**   Enter the **clear logging** command on p*x*r1. From p*x*r3, use the extended
**trace** command to perform a trace to 192.168.10*x*.10*x*, using a source
address of 172.26.*x*.49.

```
p1r1#clear logging
Clear logging buffer [confirm]
p1r1#

p1r3#trace
Protocol [ip]:
Target IP address: 192.168.101.101
Source address: 172.26.1.49
Numeric display [n]:
Timeout in seconds [3]:
Probe count [3]:
Minimum Time to Live [1]:
Maximum Time to Live [30]:
Port Number [33434]:
Loose, Strict, Record, Timestamp, Verbose[none]:
Type escape sequence to abort.
Tracing the route to 192.168.101.101

  1 p1r1 (192.168.1.49) 16 msec 16 msec 20 msec
  2 p1r2 (192.168.1.18) 36 msec
    p1r2 (192.168.1.34) 36 msec *
p1r3#
```

On p*x*r1, show the buffered debug output with the **show logging**
command.

```
p1r1#show logging
Syslog logging: enabled (0 messages dropped, 0 flushes, 0 overruns)
    Console logging: level debugging, 85 messages logged
    Monitor logging: level debugging, 0 messages logged
    Buffer logging: level debugging, 85 messages logged
    Trap logging: level informational, 29 message lines logged

Log Buffer (4096 bytes):

00:43:51: IP: s=172.26.1.49 (Serial2), d=192.168.101.101 (Serial0), len 28,
 policy rejected -- normal forwarding
00:43:51: IP: s=172.26.1.49 (Serial2), d=192.168.101.101 (Serial1), len 28,
policy rejected -- normal forwarding
00:43:51: IP: s=172.26.1.49 (Serial2), d=192.168.101.101 (Serial0), len 28,
policy rejected -- normal forwarding
```

Which path did the packets use at p*x*r1, S0 or S1?

**If your policy is working at p*x*r1, packets from 172.26.*x*.49 should
not be policy-routed; the packets will be forwarded normally.**

Which command could you type to see a summary of the policy matches for policy routing?

```
p1r1#show route-map
route-map test, permit, sequence 10
  Match clauses:
    ip address (access-lists): 1
  Set clauses:
    interface Serial0
  Policy routing matches: 3 packets, 96 bytes
route-map test, permit, sequence 20
  Match clauses:
    ip address (access-lists): 2
  Set clauses:
    interface Serial1
  Policy routing matches: 3 packets, 96 bytes
p1r1#
```

**Step 8**    From p*x*r3, use the extended **ping** command to perform a ping to 192.168.10*x*.10*x*, using a source address of 172.26.*x*.17 with a count of 100.

```
p1r3#ping
Protocol [ip]:
Target IP address: 192.168.101.101
Repeat count [5]: 100
Datagram size [100]:
Timeout in seconds [2]:
Extended commands [n]: y
Source address or interface: 172.26.1.17
Type of service [0]:
Set DF bit in IP header? [no]:
Validate reply data? [no]:
Data pattern [0xABCD]:
Loose, Strict, Record, Timestamp, Verbose[none]:
Sweep range of sizes [n]:
Type escape sequence to abort.
Sending 100, 100-byte ICMP Echos to 192.168.101.101, timeout is 2 seconds:
!!!!!!!!!!!!!!!!
```

At p*x*r1, look at the debug output.

```
00:46:10: IP: Serial2 to Serial0 192.168.1.18
00:46:10: IP: s=172.26.1.17 (Serial2), d=192.168.101.101, len 100, policy match
00:46:10: IP: route map test, item 10, permit
00:46:10: IP: s=172.26.1.17 (Serial2), d=192.168.101.101 (Serial0), len 100,
policy routed
00:46:10: IP: Serial2 to Serial0 192.168.1.18
00:46:10: IP: s=172.26.1.17 (Serial2), d=192.168.101.101, len 100, policy match
00:46:10: IP: route map test, item 10, permit
00:46:10: IP: s=172.26.1.17 (Serial2), d=192.168.101.101 (Serial0), len 100,
policy routed
00:46:10: IP: Serial2 to Serial0 192.168.1.18
00:46:10: IP: s=172.26.1.17 (Serial2), d=192.168.101.101, len 100, policy match
00:46:10: IP: route map test, item 10, permit
00:46:10: IP: s=172.26.1.17 (Serial2), d=192.168.101.101 (Serial0), len 100,
policy routed
p1r1#
```

Is the ping packet from 172.26.*x*.17 being policy-routed correctly?

**Yes**

**Step 9** From p*x*r3, use the extended **ping** command to perform a ping to 192.168.10*x*.10*x*, using a source address of 172.26.*x*.33 with a count of 100.

```
p1r3#ping
Protocol [ip]:
Target IP address: 192.168.101.101
Repeat count [5]: 100
Datagram size [100]:
Timeout in seconds [2]:
Extended commands [n]: y
Source address or interface: 172.26.1.33
Type of service [0]:
Set DF bit in IP header? [no]:
Validate reply data? [no]:
Data pattern [0xABCD]:
Loose, Strict, Record, Timestamp, Verbose[none]:
Sweep range of sizes [n]:
Type escape sequence to abort.
Sending 100, 100-byte ICMP Echos to 192.168.101.101, timeout is 2 seconds:
!!!!!!!!!!!!!!!!!!!!!!
```

At p*x*r1, look at the debug output.

```
On p1r1:
00:48:05: IP: Serial2 to Serial1 192.168.1.34
00:48:05: IP: s=172.26.1.33 (Serial2), d=192.168.101.101, len 100, policy match
00:48:05: IP: route map test, item 20, permit
00:48:05: IP: s=172.26.1.33 (Serial2), d=192.168.101.101 (Serial1),
len 100, policy routed
00:48:05: IP: Serial2 to Serial1 192.168.1.34
00:48:05: IP: s=172.26.1.33 (Serial2), d=192.168.101.101, len 100,
policy match
00:48:05: IP: route map test, item 20, permit
00:48:05: IP: s=172.26.1.33 (Serial2), d=192.168.101.101 (Serial1),
len 100, policy routed
00:48:05: IP: Serial2 to Serial1 192.168.1.34
00:48:05: IP: s=172.26.1.33 (Serial2), d=192.168.101.101, len 100, policy match
00:48:05: IP: route map test, item 20, permit
00:48:05: IP: s=172.26.1.33 (Serial2), d=192.168.101.101 (Serial1),
len 100, policy routed
p1r1#
```

Is the ping packet from 172.26.*x*.33 being policy-routed correctly?

**Yes**

**Step 10**  From p*x*r3, use the extended **ping** command to perform a ping to 192.168.10*x*.10*x*, using a source address of 172.26.*x*.49 with a count of 100.

```
p1r3#ping
Protocol [ip]:
Target IP address: 192.168.101.101
Repeat count [5]: 100
Datagram size [100]:
Timeout in seconds [2]:
Extended commands [n]: y
Source address or interface: 172.26.1.49
Type of service [0]:
Set DF bit in IP header? [no]:
Validate reply data? [no]:
Data pattern [0xABCD]:
Loose, Strict, Record, Timestamp, Verbose[none]:
Sweep range of sizes [n]:
Type escape sequence to abort.
Sending 100, 100-byte ICMP Echos to 192.168.101.101, timeout is 2 seconds:
!!!!!!!!!!!!!!!!!!!!!!!!!!!!!!!!!!!!!!!!!
```

At p*x*r1, look at the debug output.

```
On p1r1:
00:49:32: IP: s=172.26.1.49 (Serial2), d=192.168.101.101 (Serial0),
len 100, policy rejected -- normal forwarding
00:49:32: IP: s=172.26.1.49 (Serial2), d=192.168.101.101 (Serial1),
len 100, policy rejected -- normal forwarding
00:49:33: IP: s=172.26.1.49 (Serial2), d=192.168.101.101 (Serial0),
len 100, policy rejected -- normal forwarding
00:49:33: IP: s=172.26.1.49 (Serial2), d=192.168.101.101 (Serial1),
len 100, policy rejected -- normal forwarding
00:49:33: IP: s=172.26.1.49 (Serial2), d=192.168.101.101 (Serial0),
len 100, policy rejected -- normal forwarding
p1r1#
```

Is the ping packet from 172.26.*x*.49 being policy-routed?

**No, it is rejected.**

**Step 11**  Type in the command to save the current configurations of all the routers within your pod to NVRAM.

```
p1r1#copy run start
Destination filename [startup-config]?
Building configuration...


p1r2#copy run start
Destination filename [startup-config]?
Building configuration...


p1r3#copy run start
Destination filename [startup-config]?
Building configuration...
```

# Configuration Exercise #2 Answers: Configuring Route Redistribution Between OSPF and EIGRP

This section provides the answers to the questions in Configuration Exercise #2. The answers are in **bold**.

## Answers to Setup

Perform these steps:

**Step 1**    At p*x*r1, disable EIGRP.

```
p1r1#conf t
Enter configuration commands, one per line.  End with CNTL/Z.
p1r1(config)#no router eigrp 200
p1r1(config)#^Z
p1r1#
00:52:33: %SYS-5-CONFIG_I: Configured from console by console
p1r1#
```

**Step 2**    At p*x*r2, disable EIGRP.

```
p1r2#conf t
Enter configuration commands, one per line.  End with CNTL/Z.
p1r2(config)#no router eigrp 200
p1r2(config)#^Z
p1r2#
00:52:39: %SYS-5-CONFIG_I: Configured from console by console
p1r2#
```

## Answers to Task 1: Enable OSPF Between p*x*r1 (S0 and S1) and p*x*r2 (S0 and S1)

Complete the following steps:

**Step 1**    What commands would you use to enable OSPF process ID 200 (area 0) between the S0 and S1 interfaces of p*x*r1 and p*x*r2?

```
p1r1(config)#router ospf 200
p1r1(config-router)#network 192.168.1.17 0.0.0.0 area 0
p1r1(config-router)#network 192.168.1.33 0.0.0.0 area 0

p1r2(config)#router ospf 200
p1r2(config-router)#network 192.168.1.18 0.0.0.0 area 0
p1r2(config-router)#network 192.168.1.34 0.0.0.0 area 0
```

**Step 2**    What command would you type to place your loopback interface (192.168.10*x*.10*x*/28) of p*x*r2 into OSPF area 0?

```
p1r2(config)#router ospf 200
p1r2(config-router)#network 192.168.101.101 0.0.0.0 area 0
```

**Step 3**    From pxr1, ping the pxr2 loopback interface to verify OSPF connectivity.

```
p1r1#ping 192.168.101.101

Type escape sequence to abort.
Sending 5, 100-byte ICMP Echos to 192.168.101.101, timeout is 2 seconds:
!!!!!
Success rate is 100 percent (5/5), round-trip min/avg/max = 28/30/32 ms
```

# Answers to Task 2: Enable EIGRP Between pxr1 (S2) and pxr3 (S0)

Complete the following steps:

**Step 1**    What commands would you use to enable EIGRP AS 200 between the S2 interface of pxr1 and the S0 interface of pxr3? (Ensure that EIGRP is running only between pxr1 and pxr3.)

```
p1r1(config)#router eigrp 200
p1r1(config-router)#network 192.168.1.0
p1r1(config-router)#passive-interface s0
p1r1(config-router)#passive-interface s1


p1r3(config)#router eigrp 200
p1r3(config-router)#network 192.168.1.0
```

**Step 2**    On pxr3, which command could you type to verify that EIGRP is enabled on your loopback interfaces (172.26.x.17/28, 172.26.x.33/28, and 172.26.x.49/28)?

```
p1r3#show ip protocols
Routing Protocol is "eigrp 200"
  Outgoing update filter list for all interfaces is
  Incoming update filter list for all interfaces is
  Default networks flagged in outgoing updates
  Default networks accepted from incoming updates
  EIGRP metric weight K1=1, K2=0, K3=1, K4=0, K5=0
  EIGRP maximum hopcount 100
  EIGRP maximum metric variance 1
  Redistributing: eigrp 200
  Automatic network summarization is in effect
  Automatic address summarization:
    172.26.0.0/16 for Ethernet0, Serial0
      Summarizing with metric 128256
    192.168.1.0/24 for Loopback11, Loopback12, Loopback13
      Summarizing with metric 40512000
  Routing for Networks:
    172.26.0.0
    192.168.1.0
  Routing Information Sources:
    Gateway         Distance      Last Update
```

```
       (this router)          5      00:34:49
       192.168.1.49          90      00:00:58
     Distance: internal 90 external 170
```

**Step 3** From p*x*r1, ping the p*x*r3 loopback interfaces to verify EIGRP connectivity.

```
p1r1#ping 172.26.1.17

Type escape sequence to abort.
Sending 5, 100-byte ICMP Echos to 172.26.1.17, timeout is 2 seconds:
!!!!!
Success rate is 100 percent (5/5), round-trip min/avg/max = 32/32/32 ms
p1r1#ping 172.26.1.33

Type escape sequence to abort.
Sending 5, 100-byte ICMP Echos to 172.26.1.33, timeout is 2 seconds:
!!!!!
Success rate is 100 percent (5/5), round-trip min/avg/max = 28/34/48 ms
p1r1#ping 172.26.1.49

Type escape sequence to abort.
Sending 5, 100-byte ICMP Echos to 172.26.1.49, timeout is 2 seconds:
!!!!!
Success rate is 100 percent (5/5), round-trip min/avg/max = 32/32/32 ms
```

**Step 4** From p*x*r3, would a ping to the loopback interface on p*x*r2 be successful?

**No**

```
p1r3#ping 192.168.101.101

Type escape sequence to abort.
Sending 5, 100-byte ICMP Echos to 192.168.101.101, timeout is 2 seconds:
.....
Success rate is 0 percent (0/5)
```

Why or why not?

**Because p*x*r3 does not have a route to make it to p*x*r2's loopback interface (a route to 192.168.101.*x*)**

```
p1r3#show ip route
Codes: C - connected, S - static, I - IGRP, R - RIP, M - mobile, B - BGP
       D - EIGRP, EX - EIGRP external, O - OSPF, IA - OSPF inter area
       N1 - OSPF NSSA external type 1, N2 - OSPF NSSA external type 2
       E1 - OSPF external type 1, E2 - OSPF external type 2, E - EGP
       i - IS-IS, L1 - IS-IS level-1, L2 - IS-IS level-2, * - candidate default
       U - per-user static route, o - ODR
       T - traffic engineered route

Gateway of last resort is not set

     172.26.0.0/16 is variably subnetted, 4 subnets, 2 masks
C       172.26.1.48/28 is directly connected, Loopback13
C       172.26.1.32/28 is directly connected, Loopback12
C       172.26.1.16/28 is directly connected, Loopback11
D       172.26.0.0/16 is a summary, 00:36:00, Null0
     192.168.1.0/24 is variably subnetted, 4 subnets, 2 masks
```

```
D       192.168.1.32/28 [90/41024000] via 192.168.1.49, 00:02:10, Serial0
C       192.168.1.48/28 is directly connected, Serial0
D       192.168.1.0/24 is a summary, 00:36:00, Null0
D       192.168.1.16/28 [90/41024000] via 192.168.1.49, 00:02:10, Serial0
p1r3#
```

**Step 5**   What command would you type to save the current configurations of all the routers within your pod to NVRAM?

```
p1r1#copy running-config startup-config
Destination filename [startup-config]?
Building configuration...

p1r1#

p1r2# copy running-config startup-config
Destination filename [startup-config]?
Building configuration...

p1r2#

p1r3# copy running-config startup-config
Destination filename [startup-config]?
Building configuration...

p1r3#
```

# Answers to Task 3: Enable Route Redistribution Between OSPF and EIGRP

Complete the following steps:

**Step 1**   Which router within your pod is the ASBR?

**p1r1**

**Step 2**   At your ASBR, what command would you type to redistribute from OSPF into EIGRP?

```
p1r1(config)#router eigrp 200
p1r1(config-router)#redistribute ospf 200 metric 64 2000 255 1 1500
```

**Step 3**   At your ASBR, what command would you type to redistribute from EIGRP into OSPF?

```
p1r1(config)#router ospf 200
p1r1(config-router)#redistribute eigrp 200 subnets
```

**Step 4** What command would you type to examine the routing tables of pxr2 and pxr3?

```
p1r2#show ip route
Codes: C - connected, S - static, I - IGRP, R - RIP, M - mobile, B - BGP
       D - EIGRP, EX - EIGRP external, O - OSPF, IA - OSPF inter area
       N1 - OSPF NSSA external type 1, N2 - OSPF NSSA external type 2
       E1 - OSPF external type 1, E2 - OSPF external type 2, E - EGP
       i - IS-IS, L1 - IS-IS level-1, L2 - IS-IS level-2, * - candidate default
       U - per-user static route, o - ODR
       T - traffic engineered route

Gateway of last resort is not set

O E2 172.26.0.0/16 [110/20] via 192.168.1.33, 00:00:39, Serial1
                   [110/20] via 192.168.1.17, 00:00:40, Serial0
     192.168.1.0/28 is subnetted, 3 subnets
C       192.168.1.32 is directly connected, Serial1
O E2    192.168.1.48 [110/20] via 192.168.1.33, 00:00:40, Serial1
                     [110/20] via 192.168.1.17, 00:00:40, Serial0
C       192.168.1.16 is directly connected, Serial0
C    192.168.101.0/24 is directly connected, Loopback10
p1r2#

p1r3#show ip route
Codes: C - connected, S - static, I - IGRP, R - RIP, M - mobile, B - BGP
       D - EIGRP, EX - EIGRP external, O - OSPF, IA - OSPF inter area
       N1 - OSPF NSSA external type 1, N2 - OSPF NSSA external type 2
       E1 - OSPF external type 1, E2 - OSPF external type 2, E - EGP
       i - IS-IS, L1 - IS-IS level-1, L2 - IS-IS level-2, * - candidate default
       U - per-user static route, o - ODR
       T - traffic engineered route

Gateway of last resort is not set

     172.26.0.0/16 is variably subnetted, 4 subnets, 2 masks
C       172.26.1.48/28 is directly connected, Loopback13
C       172.26.1.32/28 is directly connected, Loopback12
C       172.26.1.16/28 is directly connected, Loopback11
D       172.26.0.0/16 is a summary, 00:40:08, Null0
     192.168.1.0/24 is variably subnetted, 4 subnets, 2 masks
D       192.168.1.32/28 [90/41024000] via 192.168.1.49, 00:06:18, Serial0
C       192.168.1.48/28 is directly connected, Serial0
D       192.168.1.0/24 is a summary, 00:40:08, Null0
D       192.168.1.16/28 [90/41024000] via 192.168.1.49, 00:06:18, Serial0
     192.168.101.0/32 is subnetted, 1 subnets
D EX    192.168.101.101 [170/41024000] via 192.168.1.49, 00:01:56, Serial0
p1r3#
```

Do you see the external EIGRP route at the pxr3 router?

**Yes**

Do you see the external OSPF route at the p*x*r2 router? What is the metric type?

**Yes, the metric is 20, and the metric type is OE2 (OSPF, external type 2). (Note that 20 is the default metric for OSPF only.)**

**Step 5**    From p*x*r2, ping the loopback interfaces on p*x*r3.

```
p1r2#ping 172.26.1.17

Type escape sequence to abort.
Sending 5, 100-byte ICMP Echos to 172.26.1.17, timeout is 2 seconds:
!!!!!
Success rate is 100 percent (5/5), round-trip min/avg/max = 72/73/76 ms

p1r2#ping 172.26.1.33

Type escape sequence to abort.
Sending 5, 100-byte ICMP Echos to 172.26.1.33, timeout is 2 seconds:
!!!!!
Success rate is 100 percent (5/5), round-trip min/avg/max = 72/73/76 ms

p1r2#ping 172.26.1.49

Type escape sequence to abort.
Sending 5, 100-byte ICMP Echos to 172.26.1.49, timeout is 2 seconds:
!!!!!
Success rate is 100 percent (5/5), round-trip min/avg/max = 64/69/84 ms
p1r2#
```

From p*x*r3, ping the loopback interface on p*x*r2.

```
p1r3#ping 192.168.101.101

Type escape sequence to abort.
Sending 5, 100-byte ICMP Echos to 192.168.101.101, timeout is 2 seconds:
!!!!!
Success rate is 100 percent (5/5), round-trip min/avg/max = 64/69/80 ms
p1r3#
```

Were the pings successful?

**Yes**

**Step 6**    Why is your p*x*r2 router seeing only the 172.26.0.0 summarized route and not the 172.26.*x*.16/28, 172.26.*x*.32/28, and 172.26.*x*.48/32 subnets in its routing table?

```
p1r2#show ip route
Codes: C - connected, S - static, I - IGRP, R - RIP, M - mobile, B - BGP
       D - EIGRP, EX - EIGRP external, O - OSPF, IA - OSPF inter area
       N1 - OSPF NSSA external type 1, N2 - OSPF NSSA external type 2
       E1 - OSPF external type 1, E2 - OSPF external type 2, E - EGP
       i - IS-IS, L1 - IS-IS level-1, L2 - IS-IS level-2, * - candidate default
```

```
            U - per-user static route, o - ODR
            T - traffic engineered route

Gateway of last resort is not set

O E2 172.26.0.0/16 [110/20] via 192.168.1.33, 00:02:42, Serial1
                   [110/20] via 192.168.1.17, 00:02:43, Serial0
       192.168.1.0/28 is subnetted, 3 subnets
C         192.168.1.32 is directly connected, Serial1
O E2      192.168.1.48 [110/20] via 192.168.1.33, 00:02:43, Serial1
                       [110/20] via 192.168.1.17, 00:02:43, Serial0
C         192.168.1.16 is directly connected, Serial0
C      192.168.101.0/24 is directly connected, Loopback10
p1r2#
```

### Because EIGRP performs an autosummarization

**Step 7**   At your p*x*r3 router, what command would you enter to disable EIGRP autosummarization?

```
p1r3(config)#router eigrp 200
p1r3(config-router)#no auto-summary
```

**Step 8**   Reexamine the p*x*r2 routing table; do you see the 172.26.*x*.16/28, 172.26.*x*.32/28, and 172.26.*x*.48/28 subnets now?

```
p1r2#show ip route
Codes: C - connected, S - static, I - IGRP, R - RIP, M - mobile, B - BGP
       D - EIGRP, EX - EIGRP external, O - OSPF, IA - OSPF inter area
       N1 - OSPF NSSA external type 1, N2 - OSPF NSSA external type 2
       E1 - OSPF external type 1, E2 - OSPF external type 2, E - EGP
       i - IS-IS, L1 - IS-IS level-1, L2 - IS-IS level-2, * - candidate default
       U - per-user static route, o - ODR
       T - traffic engineered route

Gateway of last resort is not set

       172.26.0.0/28 is subnetted, 3 subnets
O E2      172.26.1.48 [110/20] via 192.168.1.33, 00:00:31, Serial1
                      [110/20] via 192.168.1.17, 00:00:31, Serial0
O E2      172.26.1.32 [110/20] via 192.168.1.33, 00:00:31, Serial1
                      [110/20] via 192.168.1.17, 00:00:31, Serial0
O E2      172.26.1.16 [110/20] via 192.168.1.33, 00:00:31, Serial1
                      [110/20] via 192.168.1.17, 00:00:31, Serial0
       192.168.1.0/28 is subnetted, 3 subnets
C         192.168.1.32 is directly connected, Serial1
O E2      192.168.1.48 [110/20] via 192.168.1.33, 00:03:52, Serial1
                       [110/20] via 192.168.1.17, 00:03:52, Serial0
C         192.168.1.16 is directly connected, Serial0
C      192.168.101.0/24 is directly connected, Loopback10
p1r2#
```

Do not proceed to the next task if you don't see these subnets in your p*x*r2 routing table. If you don't see the subnets, confirm that the **no auto-summary** command is configured, and be patient because the change will not be instantaneous.

**Step 9**    Save the current configurations of all the routers within your pod to NVRAM.

```
p1r1# copy running-config startup-config
Destination filename [startup-config]?
Building configuration...

p1r2# copy running-config startup-config
Destination filename [startup-config]?
Building configuration...

p1r3# copy running-config startup-config
Destination filename [startup-config]?
Building configuration...
```

# Answers to Task 4: Enable Route Redistribution from EIGRP to OSPF with Filtering

Complete the following steps:

**Step 1**    Reconfigure your redistribution from EIGRP into OSPF to allow only the 172.26.*x*.16/28 and the 192.168.*x*.48/28 subnets to be redistributed from EIGRP into OSPF. Using the **distribute-list** command to perform this task, list all the commands used.

```
p1r1(config)#access-list 10 permit 172.26.1.16
p1r1(config)#access-list 10 permit 192.168.1.48
p1r1(config)#router ospf 200
p1r1(config-router)#distribute-list 10 out eigrp 200
```

What command would you use on p*x*r1 to clear the routing table?

```
p1r1#clear ip route *
p1r1#
```

**Step 2**    Examine the p*x*r2 routing table. Are the 172.26.*x*.32/28 and 172.26.*x*.48/28 external routes filtered out?

**Yes**

```
p1r2#show ip route
Codes: C - connected, S - static, I - IGRP, R - RIP, M - mobile, B - BGP
       D - EIGRP, EX - EIGRP external, O - OSPF, IA - OSPF inter area
       N1 - OSPF NSSA external type 1, N2 - OSPF NSSA external type 2
       E1 - OSPF external type 1, E2 - OSPF external type 2, E - EGP
       i - IS-IS, L1 - IS-IS level-1, L2 - IS-IS level-2, * - candidate default
```

```
        U - per-user static route, o - ODR
        T - traffic engineered route

Gateway of last resort is not set

     172.26.0.0/28 is subnetted, 1 subnets
O E2    172.26.1.16 [110/20] via 192.168.1.33, 00:03:18, Serial1
                    [110/20] via 192.168.1.17, 00:03:18, Serial0
     192.168.1.0/28 is subnetted, 3 subnets
C        192.168.1.32 is directly connected, Serial1
O E2    192.168.1.48 [110/20] via 192.168.1.33, 00:06:39, Serial1
                    [110/20] via 192.168.1.17, 00:06:39, Serial0
C        192.168.1.16 is directly connected, Serial0
C    192.168.101.0/24 is directly connected, Loopback10
p1r2#
```

Bonus question: What will happen if we allow only the 172.26.*x*.16/28 subnet and not the 192.168.*x*.48/28 subnet? Will the ping from p*x*r3 to p*x*r2 fail? Why or why not?

**The ping would fail because p*x*r2 would not know how to get back to p*x*r3 s0.**

**Step 3**  Type the command to remove the distribute list filtering after it is working correctly. Clear the IP routing table on p*x*r1 and then look at the p*x*r2 routing table once more. Which commands would accomplish all this?

```
p1r1(config)#router ospf 200
p1r1(config-router)#no distribute-list 10 out eigrp 200
p1r1(config-router)#exit
p1r1(config)#no access-list 10
p1r1#clear ip route
p1r2#show ip route
Codes: C - connected, S - static, I - IGRP, R - RIP, M - mobile, B - BGP
       D - EIGRP, EX - EIGRP external, O - OSPF, IA - OSPF inter area
       N1 - OSPF NSSA external type 1, N2 - OSPF NSSA external type 2
       E1 - OSPF external type 1, E2 - OSPF external type 2, E - EGP
       i - IS-IS, L1 - IS-IS level-1, L2 - IS-IS level-2, * - candidate default
       U - per-user static route, o - ODR
       T - traffic engineered route

Gateway of last resort is not set

     172.26.0.0/28 is subnetted, 3 subnets
O E2    172.26.1.48 [110/20] via 192.168.1.33, 00:00:28, Serial1
                    [110/20] via 192.168.1.17, 00:00:28, Serial0
O E2    172.26.1.32 [110/20] via 192.168.1.33, 00:00:28, Serial1
                    [110/20] via 192.168.1.17, 00:00:28, Serial0
O E2    172.26.1.16 [110/20] via 192.168.1.33, 00:05:04, Serial1
                    [110/20] via 192.168.1.17, 00:05:04, Serial0
     192.168.1.0/28 is subnetted, 3 subnets
```

```
C        192.168.1.32 is directly connected, Serial1
O E2     192.168.1.48 [110/20] via 192.168.1.33, 00:08:25, Serial1
                       [110/20] via 192.168.1.17, 00:08:25, Serial0
C        192.168.1.16 is directly connected, Serial0
C     192.168.101.0/24 is directly connected, Loopback10
p1r2#
```

**Step 4**   Save the current configurations of all the routers within your pod to
NVRAM.

```
p1r1#copy running-config startup-config
Destination filename [startup-config]?
Building configuration...

p1r2#copy running-config startup-config
Destination filename [startup-config]?
Building configuration...

p1r3#copy running-config startup-config t
Destination filename [startup-config]?
Building configuration...
```

# Answers to Bonus Task

Complete the following steps:

**Step 1**   Which commands would you use to repeat Task 4 using a route map
instead of a distribute list?

```
p1r1(config)#router ospf 200
p1r1(config-router)#redistribute eigrp 200 subnets route-map twoonly
p1r1(config-router)#exit
p1r1(config)#route-map twoonly permit 10
p1r1(config-route-map)#match ip address 10
p1r1(config-route-map)#exit
p1r1(config)#access-list 10 permit 172.26.1.16
p1r1(config)#access-list 10 permit 192.168.1.48

p1r1#clear ip route *

p1r2#show ip route
Codes: C - connected, S - static, I - IGRP, R - RIP, M - mobile, B - BGP
       D - EIGRP, EX - EIGRP external, O - OSPF, IA - OSPF inter area
       N1 - OSPF NSSA external type 1, N2 - OSPF NSSA external type 2
       E1 - OSPF external type 1, E2 - OSPF external type 2, E - EGP
       i - IS-IS, L1 - IS-IS level-1, L2 - IS-IS level-2, * - candidate default
       U - per-user static route, o - ODR
       T - traffic engineered route

Gateway of last resort is not set

     172.26.0.0/28 is subnetted, 1 subnets
O E2    172.26.1.16 [110/20] via 192.168.1.33, 00:00:37, Serial1
                    [110/20] via 192.168.1.17, 00:00:37, Serial0
```

```
        192.168.1.0/28 is subnetted, 3 subnets
C          192.168.1.32 is directly connected, Serial1
O E2    192.168.1.48 [110/20] via 192.168.1.33, 00:00:37, Serial1
                      [110/20] via 192.168.1.17, 00:00:37, Serial0
C          192.168.1.16 is directly connected, Serial0
C       192.168.101.0/24 is directly connected, Loopback10
p1r2#
```

**Step 2**    Remove the route map filtering and clear the IP routing table on p.xr1.

```
p1r1(config)#router ospf 200
p1r1(config-router)#no redistribute eigrp 200 subnets route-map twoonly
p1r1(config-router)#redistribute eigrp 200 subnets
p1r1(config-router)#exit
p1r1(config)#no route-map twoonly permit 10
p1r1(config)#no access-list 10
p1r1# clear ip route*
```

# Review Questions

Answer the following questions, and then refer to Appendix G, "Answers to the Review Questions," for the answers.

1  List three reasons why you might use multiple routing protocols in a network.

2  What two parameters are used by routers to select the best path when they learn two or more routes to the same destination from different routing protocols?

3  What are the components of the EIGRP routing metric?

4  Consider that you have a dialup WAN connection between site A and site B. What can you do to prevent excess routing update traffic from crossing the link, but still have the boundary routers know the networks that are at the remote sites?

5  What command is used to cause RIP to source a default route?

6  If no filter is associated with an interface, what happens to packets destined for that interface?

7  What command can be used to discover the path that a packet takes through a network?

8  How can a routing loop result in a network that has redundant paths between two routing processes?

9  What is redistribution?

10  What is the default administrative distance for IGRP? For RIP? For OSPF?

11  When configuring a default metric for redistributed routes, should the metric be set to a value *larger or smaller* than the largest metric within the AS?

**12** What command is used for policy-based routing to establish criteria based on the packet length?

**13** What command is used to configure filtering of the routing update traffic from an interface? What command mode is this command entered in?

**14** What does the following command do?

```
distance 150 0.0.0.0 255.255.255.255 3
```

**15** What are the benefits of policy-based routing?

**16** Policy-based routing is applied to *what* packets?

This chapter is a review of the contents in the rest of the book. It culminates with a large Configuration Exercise that allows you to configure many of the features discussed. This chapter includes the following sections:

- Routing Principles
- Extending IP Addressing Space
- Connecting to ISPs
- Controlling Routing Updates and Policies
- Route Redistribution
- Case Study: Summary
- Summary
- Configuration Exercise: Super Lab, Part I
- Configuration Exercise: Super Lab, Part II
- Answers to Configuration Exercise: Super Lab, Part I
- Answers to Configuration Exercise: Super Lab, Part II
- Review Questions

# CHAPTER 9

# Implementing Scalability Features in Your Internetwork

At the end of this chapter, when given a set of network requirements, you will be able to configure many of the features discussed in this book and verify proper operation (within described guidelines) of your routers.

## Routing Principles

This section reviews the principles of routing. The following subjects are covered:

- Routing defined
- Classful routing
- Classless routing

## Routing Defined

Routing is a relay process in which items are forwarded from one location to another. Each device in the network has a logical address so that it can be reached individually; in some cases, devices can also be reached as part of a larger group of devices.

For a router to act as an effective relay device, it must have knowledge of the logical topology of the network and must be capable of communicating with its neighboring devices. A router can be configured to recognize several different logical addressing schemes and to regularly exchange topology information with other devices in the network. The mechanism of learning and maintaining awareness of the network topology is considered to be the *routing* function. The actual movement of transient traffic through the router, from an inbound interface to an outbound interface, is a separate function and is considered to be the *switching* function. A routing device must perform both the routing and the switching function to be an effective relay device.

## Classful Routing

One way that Internet Protocol (IP) routing protocols can be classified is whether they are classful or classless.

Classful routing is the result of subnet masks not being included in the routing advertisements generated by most distance vector routing protocols.

When using a classful routing protocol, all subnets of the same major (Class A, B, or C) network number must use the same subnet mask. Upon receiving a routing update packet, a router running a classful routing protocol does one of the following to determine the network portion of the route:

- If the routing update information is about the same major network number as configured on the receiving interface, the router applies the subnet mask that is configured on the receiving interface.

- If the routing update information is about a different major network as configured on the receiving interface, the router will apply the default (by address class) subnet mask.

Classful routing protocols, such as the Routing Information Protocol version 1 (RIPv1) and the Interior Gateway Routing Protocol (IGRP), exchange routes to all subnetworks within the same classful network. This is possible because all the subnetworks in the major network should have the same subnet mask.

When routes are exchanged with foreign networks (in other words, with different major network numbers), receiving routers will not know the subnet mask in use because subnet masks are not included in the routing updates. As a result, the subnetwork information from each major network must be summarized to a classful boundary, using the default classful mask, before they are included in the routing update. Thus, only routers configured to participate in the major network to which the subnets belong exchange subnet routes; routers that participate in different major networks exchange classful summary routes. The creation of a classful summary route at major network boundaries is handled automatically by classful routing protocols. Summarization at other bit positions within the major network address is *not* allowed by classful routing protocols.

## Classless Routing

Classless routing protocols can be considered second-generation protocols because they are designed to deal with some of the limitations of the earlier classful protocols. Classless routing protocols include Open Shortest Path First (OSPF), Enhanced Interior Gateway Routing Protocol (EIGRP), RIP version 2 (RIPv2), Intermediate System-to-Intermediate System (IS-IS), and the Border Gateway Protocol version 4 (BGP-4).

One of the most serious limitations in a classful network environment is that the subnet mask is not exchanged during the routing update process. This approach requires the same mask to be used on all subnetworks of a major network. The classless approach advertises the subnet mask for each route, so a more precise lookup can be performed in the routing table.

Classless routing protocols also address another limitation of classful routing protocols: the automatic summarization to a classful network with a default classful subnet mask at major network boundaries. In the classless environment, the summarization process is manually controlled and can usually be invoked at any bit position within the network. Because subnet routes are propagated throughout the routing domain, summarization is often required to keep the size of the routing tables at a manageable size.

# Extending IP Addressing Space

This section reviews some of the features available to extend the IP addressing space. The following subjects are covered:

- IP addressing solutions
- VLSM overview
- Route summarization overview
- CIDR overview

## IP Addressing Solutions

Since the 1980s, solutions have been developed to slow the depletion of IP addresses and to reduce the number of Internet route table entries by enabling a hierarchy in an IP address. These solutions include the following:

- **Subnet masking**—Covered by RFCs 950 (1985) and 1812 (1995). Developed to add another level of hierarchy to an IP address. This additional level allows for extending the number of network addresses derived from a single IP address.

- **Address allocation for private internets**—Covered by RFC 1918 (1996). Developed for organizations that do not need much access to the Internet. The only reason to have an IP address assigned by the Network Information Center (NIC) is to interconnect to the Internet. Any and all companies can use the privately assigned IP addresses within their organization rather than using a NIC-assigned IP address unnecessarily.

- **Network address translation (NAT)**—Covered by RFC 1631 (1994). Developed for those companies that use private addressing or use IP addresses not assigned by NIC. This strategy enables an organization to access the Internet with a NIC-assigned address without having to reassign the private addresses (sometimes called *illegal* addresses) that are already in place.

- **Hierarchical addressing**—The process of applying a structure to addressing so that multiple addresses share the same left-most bits.

- **Variable-length subnet masks (VLSMs)**—Covered by RFC 1812 (1995). Developed to allow multiple levels of subnetworked IP addresses within a single network. This strategy can be used only when it is supported by the routing protocol in use, such as the classless routing protocols OSPF protocol and EIGRP.

- **Route summarization**—Covered by RFC 1518 (1993). A way of having a single IP address represent a collection of IP addresses when you employ a hierarchical addressing plan.

- **Classless interdomain routing (CIDR)**—Covered by RFCs 1518 (1993), 1519 (1993), and 2050 (1996). Developed for Internet service providers (ISPs). This strategy suggests that the remaining IP addresses be allocated to ISPs in contiguous blocks, with geography being a consideration. CIDR allows ISPs to represent a block of Class C addresses by a single supernet or summarized route.

## VLSM Overview

VLSMs provide the capability to include more than one subnet mask within a major network and the capability to subnet an already subnetted network address. The benefits of VLSMs include these:

- **Even more efficient use of IP addresses**—Without the use of VLSMs, companies are locked into implementing a single subnet mask within an entire Class A, B, or C network number.

  For example, consider the 172.16.0.0/16 network address divided into subnets using /24 masking, and one of the subnetworks in this range, 172.16.14.0/24, further divided into smaller subnets with the /27 masking, as shown in Figure 9-1. These smaller subnets range from 172.16.14.0/27 to 172.16.14.224/27. In Figure 9-1, one of these smaller subnets, 172.16.14.128, is further divided with the /30 prefix, creating subnets with only two hosts, to be used on the WAN links.

- **Greater capability to use route summarization**—VLSMs allow for more hierarchical levels within your addressing plan, and thus allow for better route summarization within routing tables. For example, in Figure 9-1, address 172.16.14.0/24 could summarize all the subnets that are further subnets of 172.16.14.0, including those from subnets 172.16.14.0/27 and 172.16.14.128/30.

**Figure 9-1**    *VLSMs Allow More Than One Subnet Mask Within a Major Network*

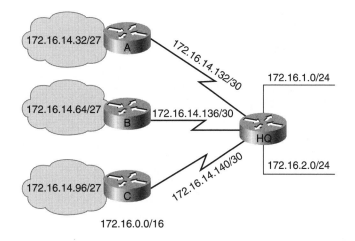

## Route Summarization Overview

In large internetworks, hundreds or even thousands of networks can exist. In these environments, it is often not desirable for routers to maintain all these routes in their routing table. Route summarization (also called *route aggregation* or *supernetting*) can reduce the number of routes that a router must maintain because it is a method of representing a series of network numbers in a single summary address. For example, in Figure 9-2, Router A either can send three routing update entries or can summarize the three addresses into a single network number.

---

**NOTE**    Router A in Figure 9-2 is advertising that it can route to the network 172.16.0.0/16, including all subnets of that network. However, if there were other subnets of 172.16.0.0 elsewhere in the network (for example, if 172.16.0.0 were discontiguous), summarizing in this way might not be valid.

---

**Figure 9-2** *Routers Can Summarize to Reduce the Number of Routes*

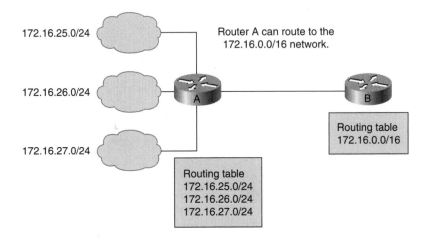

## CIDR Overview

CIDR is a mechanism developed to help alleviate the problem of exhaustion of IP addresses and growth of routing tables. The idea behind CIDR is that blocks of multiple Class C addresses can be combined, or aggregated, to create a larger classless set of IP addresses (that is, with more hosts allowed). Blocks of Class C network numbers are allocated to each network service provider. Organizations using the network service provider for Internet connectivity are allocated subsets of the service provider's address space as required.

These multiple Class C addresses can then be summarized in routing tables, resulting in fewer route advertisements.

CIDR is described further in RFCs 1518 and 1519. RFC 2050, "Internet Registry IP Allocation Guidelines," specifies guidelines for the allocation of IP addresses.

Figure 9-3 shows an example of CIDR and route summarization. The Class C network addresses 192.168.8.0/24 through 192.168.15.0/24 are being used and are being advertised to the ISP router. When the ISP router advertises the networks available, it can summarize them into one route instead of separately advertising the eight Class C networks. By advertising 192.168.8.0/21, the ISP router is indicating that it can get to all destination addresses that have the first 21 bits the same as the first 21 bits of the address 192.168.8.0.

**Figure 9-3**  *CIDR Allows a Router to Summarize Multiple Class C Addresses*

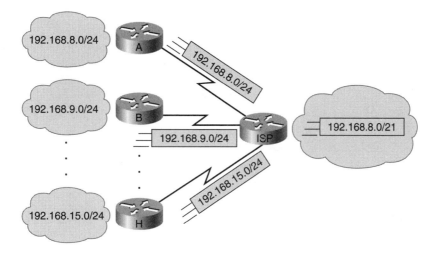

# Connecting to ISPs

This section reviews autonomous systems and the Border Gateway Protocol (BGP) as they relate to connecting to Internet service providers. The following subjects are covered:

- Autonomous systems
- BGP characteristics
- BGP route selection decision process
- BGP multihoming

## Autonomous Systems

One way to categorize routing protocols is by whether they are interior or exterior. Two types of routing protocols are as follows:

- **Interior Gateway Protocol (IGP)**—A routing protocol used to exchange routing information *within* an autonomous system. RIP, IGRP, OSPF, and EIGRP are examples of IGPs.

- **Exterior Gateway Protocol (EGP)**—A routing protocol used to connect *between* autonomous systems. BGP is an example of an EGP.

This concept is illustrated in Figure 9-4.

**Figure 9-4**    *IGPs Operate Within an Autonomous System, and EGPs Operate Between Autonomous Systems*

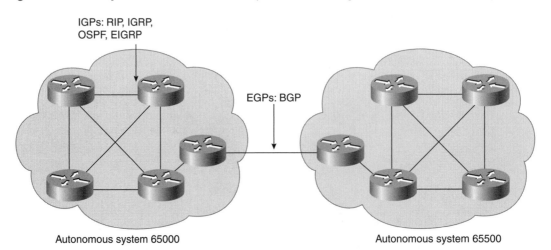

BGP version 4 (BGP-4) is the latest version of BGP and is defined in RFC 1771. As noted in this RFC, the classic definition of an *autonomous system* is "a set of routers under a single technical administration, using an Interior Gateway Protocol and common metrics to route packets within the AS, and using an Exterior Gateway Protocol to route packets to other" autonomous systems.

Today, autonomous systems may use more than one IGP, with potentially several sets of metrics. The important characteristic of an AS from the BGP point of view is that the AS appears to other autonomous systems to have a single, coherent interior routing plan and presents a consistent picture of what destinations are reachable through it. All parts of the AS must be connected to each other.

## BGP Characteristics

BGP is a distance vector protocol, though it has many differences from the likes of RIP.

BGP uses the transmission control protocol (TCP) as its transport protocol, which provides connection-oriented reliable delivery. In this way, BGP assumes that its communication is reliable; therefore, it doesn't have to implement any retransmission or error-recovery mechanisms. BGP uses TCP port 179. Two routers speaking BGP form a TCP connection with one another and exchange messages to open and confirm the connection parameters. These two routers are called peer routers or neighbors.

After the connection is made, full routing tables are exchanged. However, because the connection is reliable, BGP routers need send only changes (incremental updates) after that. Periodic routing updates are also not required on a reliable link, so triggered updates are used. BGP sends keepalive messages, similar to the hello messages sent by OSPF and EIGRP.

BGP routers exchange network reachability information, called path vectors, made up of path attributes, including a list of the full path (of BGP AS numbers) that a route should take to reach a destination network. This path information is used in constructing a graph of autonomous systems that is loop-free. The path is loop-free because a router running BGP will not accept a routing update that already includes its AS number in the path list—this would mean that the update has already passed through its AS, and accepting it again would result in a routing loop. Routing policies can also be applied to the path of BGP AS numbers to enforce some restrictions on the routing behavior.

## BGP Route Selection Decision Process

After BGP receives updates about different destinations from different autonomous systems, the protocol decides which path to choose to reach a specific destination. BGP chooses only a single path to reach a specific destination.

The decision process is based on the BGP attributes. When faced with multiple routes to the same destination, BGP chooses the best route for routing traffic toward the destination. The following process summarizes how BGP on a Cisco router chooses the best route:

**Step 1**  If the path is internal, synchronization is on, and the route is not synchronized (in other words, the route is not in the IGP routing table), do not consider it.

**Step 2**  If the next-hop address of a route is not reachable, do not consider it.

**Step 3**  Prefer the route with the highest weight. (Recall that the weight is Cisco proprietary and is local to the router only.)

**Step 4**  If multiple routes have the same weight, prefer the route with the highest local preference. (Recall that the local preference is used within an AS.)

**Step 5**  If multiple routes have the same local preference, prefer the route that was originated by the local router.

**Step 6**  If multiple routes have the same local preference, or if no route was originated by the local router, prefer the route with the shortest AS path.

**Step 7**  If the AS path length is the same, prefer the lowest origin code (IGP < EGP < incomplete).

**Step 8**  If all origin codes are the same, prefer the path with the lowest MED. (Recall that the MED is sent from other autonomous systems.)

The MED comparison is done only if the neighboring autonomous system is the same for all routes considered, unless the **bgp always-compare-med** command is enabled.

---

**NOTE**    The most recent Internet Engineering Task Force (IETF) decision regarding BGP MED assigns a value of infinity to the missing MED, making the route lacking the MED variable as the least preferred. The default behavior of BGP routers running Cisco IOS software is to treat routes without the MED attribute as having a MED of 0, making the route lacking the MED variable the most preferred. To configure the router to conform to the IETF standard, use the **bgp bestpath missing-as-worst** command.

---

**Step 9**    If the routes have the same MED, prefer external paths (EBGP) over internal paths (IBGP).

**Step 10**   If synchronization is disabled and only internal paths remain, prefer the path through the closest IGP neighbor. This means that the router will prefer the shortest internal path within the AS to reach the destination (the shortest path to the BGP next hop).

**Step 11**   For EBGP paths, select the oldest route, to minimize the effect of routes going up and down (flapping).

**Step 12**   Prefer the route with the lowest neighbor BGP router ID value.

**Step 13**   Prefer the route with the lowest neighbor IP address.

---

**NOTE**    Remember that for some attributes, the highest value is preferred (for example, the weight attribute); for others, the lowest value is preferred (for example, the MED attribute).

---

The path is put in the routing table and is propagated to the router's BGP neighbors.

## BGP Multihoming

In the example shown in Figure 9-5, AS 64520 is connected to two ISPs, AS 65000 and AS 65250, using BGP. AS 64520 is said to have a multihomed connection to the Internet and will choose the path that it takes to various destinations as detailed in the decision process in the previous section, "BGP Route Selection Decision Process."

**Figure 9-5** *AS 64520 Is Multihomed*

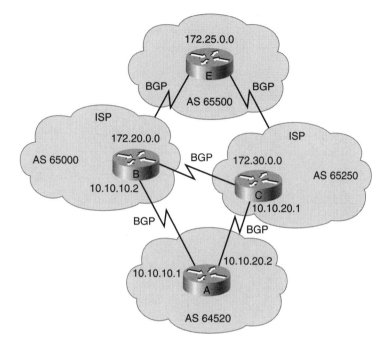

# Controlling Routing Updates and Policies

This section reviews some of the features available to control routing updates and policies. The following subjects are covered:

- Route filters with distribute lists
- Route maps
- Policy-based routing
- BGP policy control

## Route Filters with Distribute Lists

The Cisco IOS software can filter incoming and outgoing routing updates by using distribute lists that use access lists. In general, the process the router uses is as follows:

**Step 1** The router receives a routing update or is getting ready to send an update about one or more networks.

**Step 2** The router looks at the interface involved with the action.

For example, if it is an incoming update, then the interface on which it arrived is checked. If it is an update that must be advertised, the interface out of which it should be advertised is checked.

**Step 3** The router determines whether a filter is associated with the interface.

**Step 4** If a filter is associated with the interface, the router views the access list to learn if there is a match for the given routing update.

If a filter is not associated with the interface, the packet is processed as normal.

**Step 5** If there is a match, the route entry is processed as configured.

If no match is found in the access list, the implicit deny any at the end of the access list will cause the update to be dropped.

This process is illustrated in Figure 9-6.

**Figure 9-6** *Incoming and Outgoing Routing Updates Can Be Filtered Using Distribute Lists*

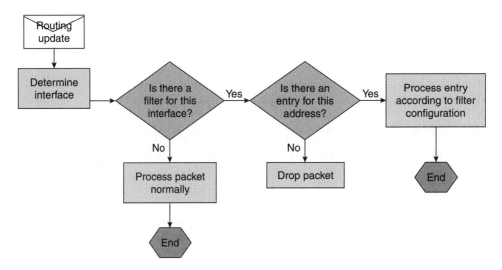

## Route Maps

A route map is a method used to control and modify routing information. This is done by defining conditions for redistributing routes from one routing protocol to another, or by controlling routing information when injected in and out of BGP.

Route maps are complex access lists that allow some conditions to be tested against the route in question. If the conditions **match**, some actions can be taken to modify the route. These actions are specified by **set** commands.

## Policy-Based Routing

In today's high-performance internetworks, organizations need the freedom to implement packet forwarding and routing according to their own defined policies in a way that goes beyond traditional routing protocol concerns. By using policy-based routing, introduced in Cisco IOS Release 11.0, policies that selectively cause packets to take different paths can be implemented.

Policy-based routing also provides a mechanism to mark packets with different types of service (ToS). This feature can be used in conjunction with Cisco IOS queuing techniques so that certain kinds of traffic can receive preferential service.

Policy-based routing is applied to *incoming* packets. All packets received on an interface with policy-based routing enabled are considered for policy-based routing. The router passes the packets through a route map. Based on the criteria defined in a route map, packets are forwarded to the appropriate next hop.

## BGP Policy Control

BGP has additional features for controlling update traffic. If you want to restrict the BGP routing information that the Cisco IOS software learns or advertises, you can filter BGP routing updates to and from particular neighbors. To do this, you can define either an access list or a prefix list, and apply it to the updates. Distribute lists use access lists to specify what routing information is to be filtered. Distribute lists for BGP have been obsoleted by prefix lists in the Cisco IOS; prefix lists are available only in Cisco IOS Release 12.0 and later.

# Route Redistribution

This section reviews route redistribution. The following subjects are covered:

- When to use multiple routing protocols
- Redistribution overview
- Redistribution implementation guidelines

## When to Use Multiple Routing Protocols

Sometimes you may need to use multiple routing protocols. Some reasons you may need multiple routing protocols are as follows:

- When you are migrating from an older IGP to a new IGP, multiple redistribution boundaries may exist until the new protocol has displaced the old protocol completely. Dual existence of protocols during migration is effectively the same as long-term coexistence of the protocols.

- You want to use another protocol but need to keep the old protocol due to the needs of host systems.

- Different departments might not want to upgrade their routers, or they might not implement a sufficiently strict filtering policy. In these cases, you can protect yourself by terminating the other routing protocol on one of your routers.

- If you have a mixed-router vendor environment, you can use a Cisco-specific protocol in the Cisco portion of the network, and then use a common protocol to communicate with non-Cisco devices.

## Redistribution Overview

When any of the situations mentioned in the previous section arises, Cisco routers allow internetworks using different routing protocols (referred to as autonomous systems) to exchange routing information through a feature called route *redistribution*. Redistribution is defined as the capability of boundary routers connecting different autonomous systems to exchange and advertise routing information received from one autonomous system to the other autonomous system.

---

**NOTE**     The term *autonomous system* as used here denotes internetworks using different routing protocols. These routing protocols may be IGPs and/or EGPs. This is a different use of the term *autonomous system* than used when discussing BGP.

---

Within each autonomous system, the internal routers have complete knowledge about their network. The router interconnecting autonomous systems is called a boundary router.

In the example shown in Figure 9-7, AS 200 is running IGRP and AS 300 is running EIGRP. The internal routers within each autonomous system have complete knowledge about their networks. Router A is the boundary router; it has both IGRP and EIGRP processes active and is responsible for advertising routes learned from one autonomous system into the other autonomous system.

**Figure 9-7** *Router A Is Redistributing Between IGRP 200 and EIGRP 300*

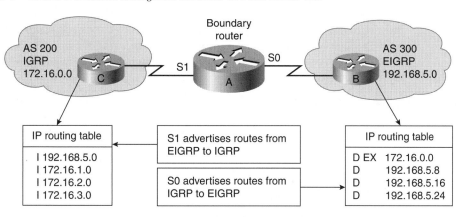

In this example, Router A learns about network 192.168.5.0 from Router B via the EIGRP protocol running on its S0 interface. It passes that information to Router C on its S1 interface via IGRP. Routing information is also passed the other way, from IGRP into EIGRP.

Router B's routing table shows that it has learned about network 172.16.0.0 via EIGRP (as indicated by the "D" in the routing table), and that the route is external to this autonomous system (as indicated by the "EX" in the routing table). Router C's routing table shows that it has learned about network 192.168.5.0 via IGRP (as indicated by the "I" in the routing table). Note that there is no indication in IGRP of whether the route is external to the autonomous system.

## Redistribution Implementation Guidelines

At a high level, Cisco recommends that you consider employing the following guidelines when using redistribution, as illustrated in Figure 9-8:

- **Be familiar with your network and your network traffic**—This is the overriding recommendation. There are many ways to implement redistribution, so knowing your network will enable you to make the best decision.

- **Do not overlap routing protocols**—Do not run two different protocols in the same internetwork. Instead, have distinct boundaries between networks that use different protocols.

- **One-way redistribution**—To avoid routing loops and problems with varying convergence time, allow routes to be exchanged in only one direction, not both directions. In the other direction, you should consider using a default or static route.

- **Two-way redistribution**—If you must allow two-way redistribution, enable a mechanism to reduce the chances of routing loops. Examples of mechanisms are default routes, route filters, modification of the metrics advertised, and modification of the administrative distance of one of the protocols. With these types of mechanisms, you can reduce the chances of routes imported from one autonomous system being reinjected into the same autonomous system as new route information.

**Figure 9-8**    *Guidelines for Redistributing Between Autonomous Systems*

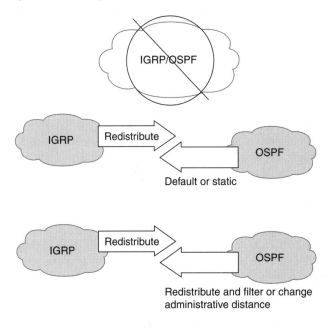

## Case Study: Summary

Refer to Chapter 1, "Routing Principles," for introductory information on the JKL case study.

This case study acts as a summary of all the topics covered in earlier chapters. It reinforces the quantity of the information that has been discussed earlier.

Throughout this book, we have been using a case study of JKL Corporation, as illustrated in Figure 9-9, to discuss various aspects of scalable routing. The case study was used to review key concepts, discuss critical issues surrounding network operation, and provide a focus for the configuration exercises.

**Figure 9-9**   *JKL Corporation Used in Case Study Sections Throughout the Book*

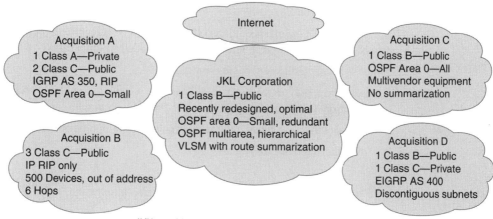

JKL's problem: How to integrate acquisitions A–D?

JKL is an enterprise that is making four acquisitions: A, B, C, and D. JKL's ultimate goal is to integrate the acquired networks with its own network.

You have seen the multiarea OSPF design used within JKL, including VLSM and route summarization. JKL has a Class B public address. Recall that JKL has two ISP connections.

You have seen that Acquisition A is using a mixture of routing protocols: RIP, IGRP, and OSPF. It has two Class C public addresses and uses a Class A private address. We have discussed how Acquisition A will redistribute routing information between the three routing domains.

You have seen that Acquisition B is using three Class C public addresses and is using only IP RIP as its routing protocol. It has run out of IP addresses.

Recall that Acquisition C has a multivendor environment and is using OSPF and one Class B public address. It is not using summarization.

You have also seen that Acquisition D is using EIGRP, has one Class B public and one Class C private address, and has discontiguous subnets.

In this last case study, you will look at what would be the most appropriate way for JKL to integrate these acquisitions into its own network. Analyze the following topics with respect to Figure 9-9:

- Routing domains, including scaling issues:
    - Are there any parts of the acquisition's networks that do not scale? How should these be incorporated into JKL's network?

—  Should the routing protocols in any of the acquisitions be changed to another protocol? What issues would be involved in selecting those that should be changed?

—  Where in JKL's network should the other networks be integrated? Should they be part of Area 0, or should new areas be added in some cases?

- Redistribution between different routing protocols:

    —  If the resulting JKL network has more than one routing protocol, how will redistribution be handled?

    —  What issues may arise when configuring redistribution in this network?

    —  Will any filtering be necessary?

- Addressing:

    —  How will all the current addresses be incorporated into the integrated network?

    —  If private addresses are kept, what will be required to access the Internet?

- Internet access:

    —  In the integrated network, where will access to the Internet be implemented?

    —  Will BGP be used for the Internet connections?

## Case Study Solution

The answers to this chapter's case study questions are as follows.

Routing domains, including scaling issues:

- Are there any parts of the acquisition's networks that do not scale?

    **Yes, Acquisition B is out of addresses. Acquisition C could grow to a degree that it could have more than 50 routers, and it would then be advisable to create separate areas for that network.**

- How should these be incorporated into JKL's network?

    **Allocate one or more Class C private addresses for Acquisition B, and use NAT to translate the private addresses to one of its public address spaces. Acquisition C should join the JKL OSPF backbone as a separate area and be reorganized to control its growth.**

- Should the routing protocols in any of the acquisitions be changed to another protocol? What issues would be involved in selecting those that should be changed?

**Acquisition B is the only candidate, although this is not a requirement. One possibility is to convert part of the network to OSPF and redistribute the RIP networks into it. If this step is accomplished, Acquisition B could join the JKL OSPF backbone as another area.**

**Some issues to be considered include these:**

— **The ease of converting a portion of the network**

— **The effect that the new routing protocol would have on any current network problems**

— **The effect that the conversion would have on the size of the routing table**

- Where in JKL's network should the other networks be integrated? Should they be part of Area 0, or should new areas be added in some cases?

**Acquisition A—Convert its Area 0 number to another number, and add it to JKL as another area attached to the backbone.**

**Acquisition B—Inject the three Class C addresses into JKL via an ASBR in Area 0. Alternately, if part of the Acquisition B network is converted to OSPF, that area could be attached to the JKL backbone and the three Class C addresses would be routed normally.**

**Acquisition C—The Acquisition C Area 0 should be converted to another area number (or separated into multiple areas), and that area could be attached to the JKL backbone and the Class B address would be routed normally.**

**Acquisition D—Inject the Class B address into JKL via an ASBR in Area 0.**

Redistribution between different routing protocols:

- If the resulting JKL network has more than one routing protocol, how will redistribution be handled?

**Acquisition A is already handling redistribution into its local area; this would not change if it joined JKL's backbone.**

**Acquisitions B and D would be separate autonomous systems to JKL, and redistribution would be handled at the ASBR in the backbone. Alternately, if part of the Acquisition B network is converted to OSPF, redistribution will take place local to Acquisition B.**

- What issues may arise when configuring redistribution in this network?

**Very few issues would be anticipated, but Acquisition D could be a problem due to the lower administrative distance of its EIGRP protocol versus OSPF.**

- Will any filtering be necessary?

**Route feedback filters should already be present in Acquisition A, but no additional filters should be required. If part of the Acquisition B network is converted to OSPF, then filtering may be necessary for the redistribution within Acquisition B.**

Addressing:

- How will all the current addresses be incorporated into the integrated network?

  **The acquisitions all had some registered public addresses before the planned integration began; as such, those addresses will be retained. For acquisitions B and D, the addresses will be automatically summarized to the classful boundary before entering the JKL backbone (unless Acquisition B is also converted to OSPF). Acquisitions A and C (and possibly B) will require manual summarization at the ABR because their addresses are sourced by OSPF.**

- If private addresses are kept, what will be required to access the Internet?

  **NAT will be required at key locations within the acquisitions to simplify the integration into the JKL network. NAT was already in place within Acquisition A because there was an existing Internet connection via the OSPF Class C public network. In addition, NAT is already in place within Acquisition D because of the remote office usage of a private Class C address space.**

Internet access:

- In the integrated network, where will access to the Internet be implemented?

  **Existing connections from the acquisitions to ISPs will be terminated. For the new integrated network, Internet access will be through the JKL backbone.**

- Will BGP be used for the Internet connections?

  **Yes, the only change will be the addition of the seven networks (the public networks owned by the acquisitions) that JKL will advertise to its ISPs.**

# Summary

This chapter reviewed a lot of the material that you learned in previous chapters.

You learned that routers perform two major functions: routing and switching.

There are many ways to categorize routing protocols; one way is whether they are classful or classless. Classful routing protocols do not carry subnet masks and automatically summarize routes at major network boundaries. Classless routing protocols do carry subnet masks and can usually summarize routes at any bit boundary.

VLSMs provide the capability to include more than one subnet mask within a network, and the capability to subnet an already subnetted network address.

Route summarization is a method of representing a series of network numbers in a single summary address.

With CIDR, blocks of multiple Class C addresses can be combined, or aggregated, to create a larger classless set of IP addresses.

An autonomous system is a collection of networks under a single technical administration. BGP is used between autonomous systems. BGP uses TCP port 179 and has a complex decision process to determine the best path.

Route maps are complex access lists. Some conditions are tested against the route in question; if the conditions match, some actions can be taken to modify the route. These actions are specified by **set** commands.

Policy-based routing is applied to *incoming* packets.

BGP policy control can be done with distribute lists (using access lists) or with prefix lists. Prefix lists are available only in Cisco IOS Release 12.0 and later.

Route redistribution allows routes discovered by one routing process to be advertised in the updates of another process.

# Configuration Exercise: Super Lab, Part I

### Configuration Exercises

In this book, Configuration Exercises are used to provide practice in configuring routers with the commands presented. If you have access to real hardware, you can try these exercises on your routers; refer to Appendix H, "Configuration Exercise Equipment Requirements and Backbone Configurations," for a list of recommended equipment and configuration commands for the backbone routers. However, even if you don't have access to any routers, you can go through the exercises and keep a log of your own "running configurations" on separate sheets of paper. Commands used and answers to the Configuration Exercises are provided at the end of the exercise.

In these exercises, you are in control of a pod of three routers; there are assumed to be 12 pods in the network. The pods are interconnected to a backbone. In most of the exercises, there is only one router in the backbone; in some cases, another router is added to the backbone. Each of the Configuration Exercises in this book assumes that you have completed the previous chapter's exercises on your pod.

This is the first of two parts of a summary Configuration Exercise.

## Objectives

In this Configuration Exercise, you will configure EIGRP within your pod, OSPF to the backbone_r1 router, and redistribution between the two routing protocols. You will also perform route filtering and route summarization, and verify that your configuration works.

## Visual Objective

Figure 9-10 illustrates the visual objective of this configuration exercise.

**Figure 9-10** *Super Lab, Part I, Configuration Exercise Topology*

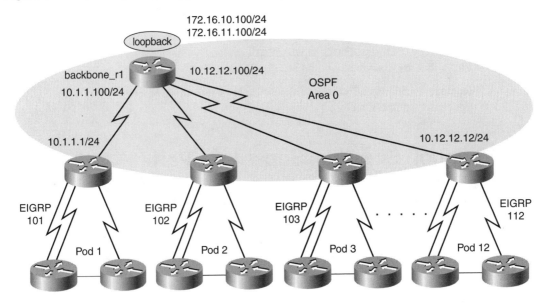

## Command List

You must determine which commands are necessary to complete this Configuration Exercise.

## Setup

Do an **erase start** and **reload** on the p*x*r1, p*x*r2, and p*x*r3 routers within your pod.

## Task: Super Lab, Part I, Configuration

Determine the necessary tasks to perform to complete the following steps:

**Step 1**   Use a clock rate of 64000 on your serial interfaces. Set the bandwidth of your serial interfaces to 64 Kbps. Set the passwords on all routers to the following:

Secret: cisco

Enable: sanfran

Vty: cisco

**Step 2**   Use the same IP address scheme as in the previous Configuration Exercises to configure your pod. The addresses are provided in the following table.

| Router | Interface | IP Address | Subnet Mask |
|--------|-----------|------------|-------------|
| p*x*r1 | S0 | 192.168.*x*.17 | 255.255.255.240 |
| p*x*r1 | S1 | 192.168.*x*.33 | 255.255.255.240 |
| p*x*r1 | S2 | 192.168.*x*.49 | 255.255.255.240 |
| p*x*r1 | S3 | 10.*x.x.x* | 255.255.255.0 |
| p*x*r2 | S0 | 192.168.*x*.18 | 255.255.255.240 |
| p*x*r2 | S1 | 192.168.*x*.34 | 255.255.255.240 |
| p*x*r2 | E0 | 192.168.*x*.65 | 255.255.255.240 |
| p*x*r3 | S0 | 192.168.*x*.50 | 255.255.255.240 |
| p*x*r3 | E0 | 192.168.*x*.66 | 255.255.255.240 |

**Step 3**   Configure EIGRP within your pod (use AS number 10*x*, where *x* is your pod number).

**Step 4**   Configure OSPF connectivity from your p*x*r1 router to the backbone_r1 router.

**Step 5**   Perform the route redistribution between OSPF and EIGRP at your p*x*r1 router.

**Step 6**   Perform route filtering to only block the 172.16.11.0/24 network from being redistributed from OSPF into EIGRP.

**Step 7**   At your p*x*r1 router, enable OSPF to announce only a summarized route of 192.168.*x*.0/24 to the other pods (where *x* is your pod number).

**Step 8**    Verify connectivity. Your p*x*r2 and p*x*r3 routers should have the capability to **ping** the 172.16.10.100 loopback interface, but not the 172.16.11.100 loopback interface, of the backbone_r1 router. You may also **ping** the interfaces on the routers of other pods, if other pods are configured. Your p*x*r2 and p*x*r3 routers should have the capability to **ping** the 10.*x.x*.0 network.

## Completion Criteria

You have completed Part I of the Super Lab Configuration Exercise if all the routers within your pod can **ping** the 172.16.10.100 loopback interface, but not the 172.16.11.100 loopback interface, of the backbone_r1 router. Your p*x*r2 and p*x*r3 routers should also be able to ping 10.*x.x*.100 on the backbone_r1 router.

# Configuration Exercise: Super Lab, Part II

This is the second of two parts of a summary Configuration Exercise.

## Objectives

In this Configuration Exercise, you will establish EBGP connectivity from your p*x*r3 router to the backbone_r2 router.

## Visual Objective

Figure 9-11 illustrates the visual objective of this Configuration Exercise.

**Figure 9-11**   *Super Lab, Part II, Configuration Exercise Topology*

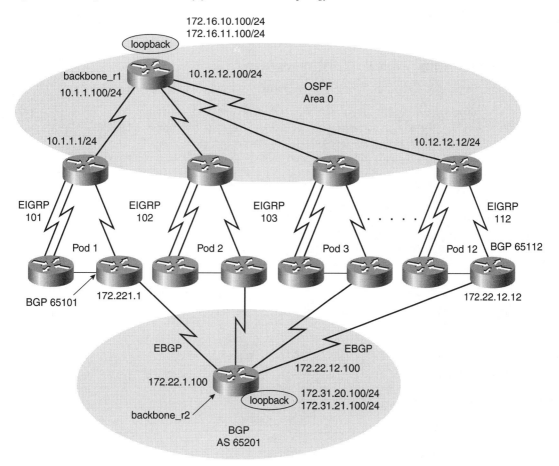

## Command List

You must determine which commands are necessary to complete this Configuration Exercise.

## Setup

Ensure that Part I of the Super Lab is working properly before proceeding with this part.

## Task: Super Lab, Part II, Configuration

Determine the necessary tasks to perform to complete the following steps:

**Step 1**    Enable EBGP connectivity between your pxr3 router and the
backbone_r2 router (in AS 65201) using the IP addresses and AS
numbers shown in the following table.

| Pod | AS Number | Your pxr3 S1 IP Address | Corresponding Backbone_r2 Serial Interface IP Address |
|-----|-----------|-------------------------|-------------------------------------------------------|
| 1   | 65101     | 172.22.1.1/24           | 172.22.1.100/24                                       |
| 2   | 65102     | 172.22.2.2/24           | 172.22.2.100/24                                       |
| 3   | 65103     | 172.22.3.3/24           | 172.22.3.100/24                                       |
| 4   | 65104     | 172.22.4.4/24           | 172.22.4.100/24                                       |
| 5   | 65105     | 172.22.5.5/24           | 172.22.5.100/24                                       |
| 6   | 65106     | 172.22.6.6/24           | 172.22.6.100/24                                       |
| 7   | 65107     | 172.22.7.7/24           | 172.22.7.100/24                                       |
| 8   | 65108     | 172.22.8.8/24           | 172.22.8.100/24                                       |
| 9   | 65109     | 172.22.9.9/24           | 172.22.9.100/24                                       |
| 10  | 65110     | 172.22.10.10/24         | 172.22.10.100/24                                      |
| 11  | 65111     | 172.22.11.11/24         | 172.22.11.100/24                                      |
| 12  | 65112     | 172.22.12.12/24         | 172.22.12.100/24                                      |

**Step 2**    Only advertise your 192.168.*x*.0/24 and your 10.*x.x*.0/24 networks, and
the 172.16.0.0/16 network, to the backbone_r2 router via your EBGP
connection.

**NOTE**    Do not redistribute BGP into EIGRP.

**Step 3**    Your pxr2 and pxr1 routers within your pod should use a default route to
access the loopback interfaces of the backbone_r2 router. Configure your
pxr3 router so that it will advertise a default route to your pxr1 and pxr2
routers. The default route should point toward the backbone_r2 router.

(Hint: Use the **ip route 0.0.0.0 0.0.0.0 S1** command and don't forget to add a **network 0.0.0.0** statement under EIGRP to allow advertisement of the default route.)

**Step 4**    You should be able to **ping** from any router within your pod to 172.31.20.100 (one of the loopback addresses on the backbone_r2 router).

**NOTE**    You will not be able to **ping** from the backbone_r1 router to 172.31.20.100 because the backbone_r1 router has no route to network 172.31.20.0/24. Perform the bonus step in this section to enable connectivity from the backbone_r1 router to the backbone_r2 router.

**Step 5**    **Bonus step** (This step should only be performed on one pod at one time.)

Telnet to the backbone_r1 router. Add a default route in the backbone_r1 router, pointing the default route to your pxr1 router. (The backbone_r1 router will use the default route to reach 172.31.20.100.)

You should now be able to **ping** from the backbone_r1 router to 172.31.20.100.

Trace from the backbone_r1 router to 172.31.20.100. Ensure that the path taken is through your pod.

Telnet to the backbone_r2 router, and display the routing table of the backbone_r2 router. Which is the preferred path from the backbone_r2 router to network 172.16.0.0/16 (the loopback address on the backbone_r1 router)? At the backbone_r2 router, set the weight attribute in the BGP **neighbor** statement to your pxr3 router so that the backbone_r2 router will prefer your pxr3 route to the others.

Clear all the BGP sessions from the backbone_r2 router.

You should be able to **ping** from the backbone_r2 router to 172.16.10.100.

Trace from the backbone_r2 router to 172.16.10.100. Ensure that the path taken is through your pod.

Remove your default route from the backbone_r1 router and the weight configuration at the backbone_r2 router when you are done.

## Completion Criteria

You have completed Part II of the Super Lab Configuration Exercise if all your routers within your pod can **ping** the loopback interface of the backbone_r2 router. If you performed the bonus step, the backbone_r1 router should also have the capability to **ping** the loopback interface of the backbone_r2 router.

# Answers to Configuration Exercise: Super Lab, Part I

This section provides the answers to the questions in the first Super Lab Configuration Exercise. The answers are in **bold**.

## Answers to Setup

**The following example shows how to erase and reload the p1r1 router.**

```
p1r1#erase start
Erasing the nvram filesystem will remove all files! Continue? [confirm]
[OK]
Erase of nvram: complete
p1r1#reload
Proceed with reload? [confirm]

System Bootstrap, Version 11.0(10c), SOFTWARE
Copyright  1986-1996 by cisco Systems
```

## Answers to Task: Super Lab, Part I, Configuration

**The answers are provided for the routers in pod 1. Pod 2 is also configured to allow some interesting aspects of the Configuration Exercise to be viewed.**

---

**NOTE**    In some cases, the answers for multiple steps are combined; the answers appear after the steps to be answered are shown.

---

**Step 1**    Use a clock rate of 64000 on your serial interfaces. Set the bandwidth of your serial interfaces to 64 Kbps. Set the passwords on all routers to the following:

- Secret:    cisco
- Enable:    sanfran
- Vty:        cisco

**Step 2**    Use the same IP address scheme as in the previous Configuration
Exercises to configure your pod. The addresses are provided in the
following table.

| Router | Interface | IP Address | Subnet Mask |
|--------|-----------|-----------|-------------|
| p.xr1 | S0 | 192.168.x.17 | 255.255.255.240 |
| p.xr1 | S1 | 192.168.x.33 | 255.255.255.240 |
| p.xr1 | S2 | 192.168.x.49 | 255.255.255.240 |
| p.xr1 | S3 | 10.x.x.x | 255.255.255.0 |
| p.xr2 | S0 | 192.168.x.18 | 255.255.255.240 |
| p.xr2 | S1 | 192.168.x.34 | 255.255.255.240 |
| p.xr2 | E0 | 192.168.x.65 | 255.255.255.240 |
| p.xr3 | S0 | 192.168.x.50 | 255.255.255.240 |
| p.xr3 | E0 | 192.168.x.66 | 255.255.255.240 |

**In this example, setup mode is used to configure the p1r1 router to do a basic
configuration of the router. Alternatively, the router could have been
configured from configuration mode; see the Configuration Exercise in
Chapter 1 for an example of how a basic configuration is done from
configuration mode.**

```
Would you like to enter the initial configuration dialog? [yes/no]: y

At any point you may enter a question mark '?' for help.
Use ctrl-c to abort configuration dialog at any prompt.
Default settings are in square brackets '[]'.

Basic management setup configures only enough connectivity
for management of the system, extended setup will ask you
to configure each interface on the system

Would you like to enter basic management setup? [yes/no]: n

First, would you like to see the current interface summary? [yes]: n

Configuring global parameters:

  Enter host name [Router]: p1r1

  The enable secret is a password used to protect access to
  privileged EXEC and configuration modes. This password, after
  entered, becomes encrypted in the configuration.
  Enter enable secret: cisco

  The enable password is used when you do not specify an
  enable secret password, with some older software versions, and
  some boot images.
  Enter enable password: sanfran

  The virtual terminal password is used to protect
  access to the router over a network interface.
```

```
Enter virtual terminal password: cisco
Configure SNMP Network Management? [yes]: n
Configure LAT? [yes]: n
Configure AppleTalk? [no]:
Configure DECnet? [no]:
Configure IP? [yes]:
  Configure IGRP routing? [yes]: n
  Configure RIP routing? [no]:
Configure CLNS? [no]:
Configure IPX? [no]:
Configure Vines? [no]:
Configure XNS? [no]:
Configure Apollo? [no]:

BRI interface needs isdn switch-type to be configured
Valid switch types are :
            [0]  none..........Only if you don't want to configure BRI.
            [1]  basic-1tr6....1TR6 switch type for Germany
            [2]  basic-5ess....AT&T 5ESS switch type for the US/Canada
            [3]  basic-dms100..Northern DMS-100 switch type for US/Canada
            [4]  basic-net3....NET3 switch type for UK and Europe
            [5]  basic-ni......National ISDN switch type
            [6]  basic-ts013...TS013 switch type for Australia
            [7]  ntt..........NTT switch type for Japan
            [8]  vn3..........VN3 and VN4 switch types for France
    Choose ISDN BRI Switch Type [2]:

Configuring interface parameters:

Do you want to configure BRI0 (BRI d-channel) interface? [yes]: n

Do you want to configure Ethernet0  interface? [yes]: n

Do you want to configure Serial0  interface? [yes]:
  Configure IP on this interface? [yes]:
    IP address for this interface: 192.168.1.17
    Subnet mask for this interface [255.255.255.0] : 255.255.255.240
    Class C network is 192.168.1.0, 28 subnet bits; mask is /28

Do you want to configure Serial1  interface? [yes]:
  Configure IP on this interface? [yes]:
  Configure IP unnumbered on this interface? [no]:
    IP address for this interface: 192.168.1.33
    Subnet mask for this interface [255.255.255.0] : 255.255.255.240
    Class C network is 192.168.1.0, 28 subnet bits; mask is /28

Do you want to configure Serial2  interface? [yes]:
  Configure IP on this interface? [yes]:
  Configure IP unnumbered on this interface? [no]:
    IP address for this interface: 192.168.1.49
    Subnet mask for this interface [255.255.255.0] : 255.255.255.240
    Class C network is 192.168.1.0, 28 subnet bits; mask is /28

Do you want to configure Serial3  interface? [yes]:
  Configure IP on this interface? [yes]:
  Configure IP unnumbered on this interface? [no]:
    IP address for this interface: 10.1.1.1
    Subnet mask for this interface [255.0.0.0] : 255.255.255.0
    Class A network is 10.0.0.0, 24 subnet bits; mask is /24
```

```
The following configuration command script was created:
hostname p1r1
enable secret 5 $1$WDFf$vYqhAY6RstXPupfVVxyj8/
enable password sanfran
line vty 0 4
password cisco
no snmp-server
!
no appletalk routing
no decnet routing
ip routing
no clns routing
no ipx routing
no vines routing
no xns routing
no apollo routing
isdn switch-type  basic-5ess
!
interface BRI0
shutdown
no ip address
!
interface Ethernet0
shutdown
no ip address
!
interface Serial0
ip address 192.168.1.17 255.255.255.240
no mop enabled
!
interface Serial1
ip address 192.168.1.33 255.255.255.240
no mop enabled
!
interface Serial2
ip address 192.168.1.49 255.255.255.240
no mop enabled
!
interface Serial3
ip address 10.1.1.1 255.255.255.0
no mop enabled
dialer-list 1 protocol ip permit
dialer-list 1 protocol ipx permit
!
end


[0] Go to the IOS command prompt without saving this config.
[1] Return back to the setup without saving this config.
[2] Save this configuration to nvram and exit.

Enter your selection [2]:
Building configuration...
Use the enabled mode 'configure' command to modify this configuration.
```

The following example shows how to set clock rate and bandwidth on the interfaces of the p1r1 router; the output from the router is also shown. Note that the p1r1 router was the first one in the pod to be configured. Recall that the Serial 0, Serial 1, and Serial 2 interfaces of the p*x*r1 routers have DCE cables attached (and, therefore, require the clock rate command); the Serial 3 interface of the p*x*r1 routers has a DTE cable attached.

```
p1r1#conf t
Enter configuration commands, one per line.  End with CNTL/Z.
p1r1(config)#int s0
p1r1(config-if)#clock rate 64000
p1r1(config-if)#bandwidth 64
p1r1(config-if)#int s1
p1r1(config-if)#clock rate 64000
p1r1(config-if)#bandwidth 64
p1r1(config-if)#
00:21:34: %LINK-3-UPDOWN: Interface Serial1, changed state to up
00:21:34: %LINEPROTO-5-UPDOWN: Line protocol on Interface Serial0, changed state to
up
00:21:35: %LINEPROTO-5-UPDOWN: Line protocol on Interface Serial1, changed state to
up
p1r1(config-if)#int s2
p1r1(config-if)#clock rate 64000
p1r1(config-if)#bandwidth 64
p1r1(config-if)#int s3
p1r1(config-if)#bandwidth 64
```

Other commands may also be added to the console port configuration to make configuring the router easier. The following example shows how to configure the console line on the p1r1 router. (Recall that the exec-timeout 0 0 command ensures that your console session will not time out. When you are typing on the console, the logging synchronous command ensures that any router output will not interfere with your command input. The no ip domain-lookup command disables the IP Domain Naming System [DNS]-based host name-to-address translation.)

```
p1r1(config)#line con 0
p1r1(config-line)#exec-timeout 0 0
p1r1(config-line)#logging synchronous
p1r1(config-line)#exit
p1r1(config)#no ip domain-lookup
```

**Step 3**    Configure EIGRP within your pod (use AS number 10*x*, where *x* is your pod number).

**Step 4**    Configure OSPF connectivity from your p*x*r1 router to the backbone_r1 router.

The following example shows how to enable EIGRP and OSPF on the p1r1 router.

```
p1r1(config)#router eigrp 101
p1r1(config-router)#network 192.168.1.0
p1r1(config-router)#exit
p1r1(config)#router ospf 101
p1r1(config-router)#network 10.0.0.0 0.255.255.255 area 0
```

**Step 5**  Perform the route redistribution between OSPF and EIGRP at your p*x*r1 router.

**The following example shows how to configure redistribution on the p1r1 router.**

```
p1r1(config)#router eigrp 101
p1r1(config-router)#redistribute ospf 101 metric 64 2000 255 1 1500
p1r1(config-router)#exit
p1r1(config)#router ospf 101
p1r1(config-router)#redistribute eigrp 101 subnets
```

**To verify that redistribution is working correctly, view the routing table of one of the other routers in your pod. The following example shows the routing table of the p1r2 router. (Note that both pods 1 and 2 are configured, so you will see routes from pod 2 in the routing table.) The routing table shows that many routes have been learned from external EIGRP (as indicated by the "D EX" code in the routing table); these are the redistributed routes. (Note also that p1r2 can see both 172.16.10.0 and 172.16.11.0; the latter will be filtered out in the next step.)**

```
p1r2#show ip route
<output omitted>
Gateway of last resort is not set

     172.16.0.0/24 is subnetted, 2 subnets
D EX    172.16.10.0 [170/41024000] via 192.168.1.17, 00:18:06, Serial0
                    [170/41024000] via 192.168.1.33, 00:18:06, Serial1
D EX    172.16.11.0 [170/41024000] via 192.168.1.17, 00:18:06, Serial0
                    [170/41024000] via 192.168.1.33, 00:18:06, Serial1
     10.0.0.0/24 is subnetted, 2 subnets
D EX    10.2.2.0 [170/41024000] via 192.168.1.17, 00:04:25, Serial0
                 [170/41024000] via 192.168.1.33, 00:04:25, Serial1
D EX    10.1.1.0 [170/41024000] via 192.168.1.33, 00:18:22, Serial1
                 [170/41024000] via 192.168.1.17, 00:18:22, Serial0
     192.168.1.0/28 is subnetted, 4 subnets
C       192.168.1.64 is directly connected, Ethernet0
C       192.168.1.32 is directly connected, Serial1
D       192.168.1.48 [90/40537600] via 192.168.1.66, 00:24:34, Ethernet0
C       192.168.1.16 is directly connected, Serial0
     192.168.2.0/28 is subnetted, 4 subnets
D EX    192.168.2.64 [170/41024000] via 192.168.1.33, 00:02:11, Serial1
                     [170/41024000] via 192.168.1.17, 00:02:11, Serial0
D EX    192.168.2.32 [170/41024000] via 192.168.1.17, 00:02:13, Serial0
                     [170/41024000] via 192.168.1.33, 00:02:13, Serial1
D EX    192.168.2.48 [170/41024000] via 192.168.1.17, 00:01:37, Serial0
                     [170/41024000] via 192.168.1.33, 00:01:37, Serial1
D EX    192.168.2.16 [170/41024000] via 192.168.1.33, 00:02:15, Serial1
                     [170/41024000] via 192.168.1.17, 00:02:15, Serial0
p1r2#
```

**Step 6**  Perform route filtering to only block the 172.16.11.0/24 network from being redistributed from OSPF into EIGRP.

**Step 7**   At your pxr1 router, enable OSPF to announce only a summarized route of 192.168.x.0/24 to the other pods (where x is your pod number).

**The following example shows how to configure route filtering and summarization on the p1r1 router.**

```
p1r1(config)#router eigrp 101
p1r1(config-router)#distribute-list 10 out ospf 101
p1r1(config-router)#exit
p1r1(config)#access-list 10 deny 172.16.11.0
p1r1(config)#access-list 10 permit any
p1r1(config)#router ospf 101
p1r1(config-router)#summary-address 192.168.1.0 255.255.255.0
```

**To verify that route filtering is working correctly, view the routing table of one of the other routers in your pod. The following example shows the routing table of the p1r2 router. You can see that only 172.16.10.0 is learned from the backbone; 172.16.11.0 is being filtered correctly. This example also shows that the summarization on p2r1 (configured similarly to p1r1) is working correctly; only 192.168.2.0 is learned from pod 2.**

```
p1r2#show ip route

<output omitted>
Gateway of last resort is not set

     172.16.0.0/24 is subnetted, 1 subnets
D EX    172.16.10.0 [170/41024000] via 192.168.1.17, 00:00:00, Serial0
                     [170/41024000] via 192.168.1.33, 00:00:00, Serial1
     10.0.0.0/24 is subnetted, 2 subnets
D EX    10.2.2.0 [170/41024000] via 192.168.1.17, 00:00:00, Serial0
                 [170/41024000] via 192.168.1.33, 00:00:00, Serial1
D EX    10.1.1.0 [170/41024000] via 192.168.1.17, 00:00:00, Serial0
                 [170/41024000] via 192.168.1.33, 00:00:00, Serial1
     192.168.1.0/24 is variably subnetted, 5 subnets, 2 masks
C       192.168.1.64/28 is directly connected, Ethernet0
C       192.168.1.32/28 is directly connected, Serial1
D       192.168.1.48/28 [90/40537600] via 192.168.1.66, 00:00:00, Ethernet0
D EX    192.168.1.0/24 [170/41024000] via 192.168.1.17, 00:00:00, Serial0
                       [170/41024000] via 192.168.1.33, 00:00:00, Serial1
C       192.168.1.16/28 is directly connected, Serial0
D EX 192.168.2.0/24 [170/41024000] via 192.168.1.17, 00:00:02, Serial0
                    [170/41024000] via 192.168.1.33, 00:00:02, Serial1
p1r2#
```

**Step 8**   Verify connectivity. Your pxr2 and pxr3 routers should have the capability to **ping** the 172.16.10.100 loopback interface, but not the 172.16.11.100 loopback interface, of the backbone_r1 router. You may also **ping** the interfaces on the routers of other pods, if other pods are configured. Your pxr2 and pxr3 routers should have the capability to **ping** the 10.x.x.0 network.

To verify that all steps of the Configuration Exercises are working correctly, try to ping from one of the other routers in your pod. The following example shows the results of some pings from the p1r2 router; the results confirm that the Configuration Exercise is working correctly.

```
p1r2#ping 172.16.10.100

Type escape sequence to abort.
Sending 5, 100-byte ICMP Echos to 172.16.10.100, timeout is 2 seconds:
!!!!!
Success rate is 100 percent (5/5), round-trip min/avg/max = 56/59/64 ms
p1r2#ping 172.16.11.100

Type escape sequence to abort.
Sending 5, 100-byte ICMP Echos to 172.16.11.100, timeout is 2 seconds:
.....
Success rate is 0 percent (0/5)
p1r2#ping 10.1.1.1

Type escape sequence to abort.
Sending 5, 100-byte ICMP Echos to 10.1.1.1, timeout is 2 seconds:
!!!!!
Success rate is 100 percent (5/5), round-trip min/avg/max = 28/31/32 ms
p1r2#ping 192.168.2.66

Type escape sequence to abort.
Sending 5, 100-byte ICMP Echos to 192.168.2.66, timeout is 2 seconds:
!!!!!
Success rate is 100 percent (5/5), round-trip min/avg/max = 116/118/128 ms
p1r2#
```

# Answers to Configuration Exercise: Super Lab, Part II

This section provides the answers to the questions in the second Super Lab Configuration Exercise. The answers are in **bold**.

## Answers to Task: Super Lab, Part II, Configuration

The answers are provided for the routers in pod 1. Pod 2 is also configured to allow some interesting aspects of the Configuration Exercise to be viewed.

---

**NOTE**    In some cases, the answers for multiple steps are combined; the answers appear after the steps to be answered are shown.

---

**Step 1**  Enable EBGP connectivity between your p*x*r3 router and the backbone_r2 router (in AS 65201) using the IP addresses and AS numbers shown in the following table.

| Pod | AS Number | Your pxr3 S1 IP Address | Corresponding Backbone_r2 Serial Interface IP Address |
|-----|-----------|-------------------------|-------------------------------------------------------|
| 1   | 65101     | 172.22.1.1/24           | 172.22.1.100/24                                       |
| 2   | 65102     | 172.22.2.2/24           | 172.22.2.100/24                                       |
| 3   | 65103     | 172.22.3.3/24           | 172.22.3.100/24                                       |
| 4   | 65104     | 172.22.4.4/24           | 172.22.4.100/24                                       |
| 5   | 65105     | 172.22.5.5/24           | 172.22.5.100/24                                       |
| 6   | 65106     | 172.22.6.6/24           | 172.22.6.100/24                                       |
| 7   | 65107     | 172.22.7.7/24           | 172.22.7.100/24                                       |
| 8   | 65108     | 172.22.8.8/24           | 172.22.8.100/24                                       |
| 9   | 65109     | 172.22.9.9/24           | 172.22.9.100/24                                       |
| 10  | 65110     | 172.22.10.10/24         | 172.22.10.100/24                                      |
| 11  | 65111     | 172.22.11.11/24         | 172.22.11.100/24                                      |
| 12  | 65112     | 172.22.12.12/24         | 172.22.12.100/24                                      |

**Step 2**  Only advertise your 192.168.*x*.0/24 and your 10.*x.x*.0/24 networks, and the 172.16.0.0/16 network, to the backbone_r2 router via your EBGP connection.

**NOTE**  Do not redistribute BGP into EIGRP.

**The following example shows how to configure EBGP on p1r3 to advertise the specified networks, and how to enable the p1r3 serial 1 interface.**

```
p1r3#conf t
Enter configuration commands, one per line.  End with CNTL/Z.
p1r3(config)#router bgp 65101
p1r3(config-router)#neighbor 172.22.1.100 remote-as 65201
p1r3(config-router)#network 192.168.1.0 mask 255.255.255.0
p1r3(config-router)#network 10.1.1.0 mask 255.255.255.0
p1r3(config-router)#network 172.16.0.0 mask 255.255.0.0
p1r3(config-router)#exit
p1r3(config)#int s1
p1r3(config-if)#ip address 172.22.1.1 255.255.255.0
p1r3(config-if)#no shutdown
```

**Step 3**    Your p*x*r2 and p*x*r1 routers within your pod should use a default route to access the loopback interfaces of the backbone_r2 router. Configure your p*x*r3 router so that it will advertise a default route to your p*x*r1 and p*x*r2 routers. The default route should point toward the backbone_r2 router. (Hint: Use the **ip route 0.0.0.0 0.0.0.0 S1** command, and don't forget to add a **network 0.0.0.0** statement under EIGRP to allow advertisement of the default route.)

**The following example shows how to configure the default route on p1r3.**

```
p1r3(config)#ip route 0.0.0.0 0.0.0.0 s1
p1r3(config)#router eigrp 101
p1r3(config-router)#network 0.0.0.0
```

**To verify that the static route is configured properly, display the routing table of the p1r3 router and of another router in your pod.**

**The following example shows the p1r3 routing table (note that pod 2 is also configured for BGP, so you will see a route to its network), with the static route configured.**

```
p1r3#show ip route
<output omitted>

Gateway of last resort is 0.0.0.0 to network 0.0.0.0

     172.16.0.0/24 is subnetted, 1 subnets
D EX    172.16.10.0 [170/41024000] via 192.168.1.49, 00:18:37, Serial0
     172.22.0.0/24 is subnetted, 1 subnets
C       172.22.1.0 is directly connected, Serial1
     172.31.0.0/24 is subnetted, 2 subnets
B       172.31.21.0 [20/0] via 172.22.1.100, 00:09:15
B       172.31.20.0 [20/0] via 172.22.1.100, 00:09:15
     10.0.0.0/24 is subnetted, 2 subnets
B       10.2.2.0 [20/0] via 172.22.1.100, 00:00:01
D EX    10.1.1.0 [170/41024000] via 192.168.1.49, 00:18:38, Serial0
     192.168.1.0/24 is variably subnetted, 5 subnets, 2 masks
C       192.168.1.64/28 is directly connected, Ethernet0
D       192.168.1.32/28 [90/40537600] via 192.168.1.65, 00:18:38, Ethernet0
C       192.168.1.48/28 is directly connected, Serial0
D EX    192.168.1.0/24 [170/41024000] via 192.168.1.49, 00:18:39, Serial0
D       192.168.1.16/28 [90/40537600] via 192.168.1.65, 00:18:39, Ethernet0
B    192.168.2.0/24 [20/0] via 172.22.1.100, 00:00:31
S*   0.0.0.0/0 is directly connected, Serial1
p1r3#
```

The following example shows the p1r1 routing table, with the static route
learned from p1r3.

```
p1r1#show ip route
<output omitted>
Gateway of last resort is 192.168.1.50 to network 0.0.0.0

     172.16.0.0/24 is subnetted, 2 subnets
O E2    172.16.10.0 [110/20] via 10.1.1.100, 00:18:09, Serial3
O E2    172.16.11.0 [110/20] via 10.1.1.100, 00:18:09, Serial3
     10.0.0.0/24 is subnetted, 2 subnets
O        10.2.2.0 [110/3124] via 10.1.1.100, 00:18:10, Serial3
C        10.1.1.0 is directly connected, Serial3
     192.168.1.0/24 is variably subnetted, 5 subnets, 2 masks
D        192.168.1.64/28 [90/40537600] via 192.168.1.34, 00:17:58, Serial1
                         [90/40537600] via 192.168.1.18, 00:17:58, Serial0
                         [90/40537600] via 192.168.1.50, 00:17:58, Serial2
C        192.168.1.32/28 is directly connected, Serial1
C        192.168.1.48/28 is directly connected, Serial2
O        192.168.1.0/24 is a summary, 00:17:54, Null0
C        192.168.1.16/28 is directly connected, Serial0
O E2 192.168.2.0/24 [110/20] via 10.1.1.100, 00:16:21, Serial3
D*   0.0.0.0/0 [90/41024000] via 192.168.1.50, 00:06:09, Serial2
p1r1#
```

**Step 4**   You should be able to **ping** from any router within your pod to
172.31.20.100 (one of the loopback addresses on the backbone_r2
router).

---

**NOTE**   You will not be able to **ping** from the backbone_r1 router to 172.31.20.100 because the
backbone_r1 router has no route to network 172.31.20.0/24. Perform the bonus step in this
section to enable connectivity from the backbone_r1 router to the backbone_r2 router.

---

The following example shows the results of a ping to 172.31.20.100 from the
p1r1 router.

```
p1r1#ping 172.31.20.100

Type escape sequence to abort.
Sending 5, 100-byte ICMP Echos to 172.31.20.100, timeout is 2 seconds:
!!!!!
Success rate is 100 percent (5/5), round-trip min/avg/max = 56/59/64 ms
```

Verify that you cannot ping from backbone_r1 to 172.31.20.100.

```
backbone_r1>ping 172.31.20.100

Type escape sequence to abort.
Sending 5, 100-byte ICMP Echos to 172.31.20.100, timeout is 2 seconds:
```

```
.....
Success rate is 0 percent (0/5)
backbone_r1>
```

**Step 5**   **Bonus step** (This step should be performed on only one pod at one time.)

Telnet to the backbone_r1 router. Add a default route in the backbone_r1 router, pointing the default route to your p*x*r1 router. (The backbone_r1 router will use the default route to reach 172.31.20.100.)

**The following example shows how to put a default route on the backbone_r1 router, pointing to p1r1.**

```
backbone_r1(config)#ip route 0.0.0.0 0.0.0.0 s1/0
```

You should now be able to **ping** from the backbone_r1 router to 172.31.20.100.

**The following example verifies that the default route on the backbone_r1 router is working by the results of a ping to the backbone_r2 loopback interface.**

```
backbone_r1#ping 172.31.20.100

Type escape sequence to abort.
Sending 5, 100-byte ICMP Echos to 172.31.20.100, timeout is 2 seconds:
!!!!!
Success rate is 100 percent (5/5), round-trip min/avg/max = 92/97/120 ms
backbone_r1#
```

Trace from the backbone_r1 router to 172.31.20.100. Ensure that the path taken is through your pod.

**The following example shows a trace from the backbone_r1 router to the backbone_r2 loopback interface, to ensure that the path taken is through pod 1. The output indicates that the trace goes via pod 1.**

```
backbone_r1#trace 172.31.20.100

Type escape sequence to abort.
Tracing the route to 172.31.20.100

  1 p1r1 (10.1.1.1) 32 msec 24 msec 20 msec
  2 p1r3 (192.168.1.50) 28 msec 36 msec 36 msec
  3 172.22.1.100 48 msec *  52 msec
backbone_r1#
```

Telnet to the backbone_r2 router, and display the routing table of the backbone_r2 router. Which is the preferred path from the backbone_r2 router to network 172.16.0.0/16 (the loopback address on the backbone_r1 router)? At the backbone_r2 router, set the weight attribute in the BGP **neighbor** statement to your p*x*r3 router so that the backbone_r2 router will prefer your p*x*r3 route to the others.

The following example shows the backbone_r2 router's routing table. The preferred path to the 172.16.0.0 network is through pod 1.

```
backbone_r2>show ip route
<output omitted>

Gateway of last resort is not set

     10.0.0.0/24 is subnetted, 2 subnets
B       10.2.2.0 [20/41024000] via 172.22.2.2, 00:04:41
B       10.1.1.0 [20/41024000] via 172.22.1.1, 00:13:26
B    192.168.1.0/24 [20/41024000] via 172.22.1.1, 00:13:27
B    192.168.2.0/24 [20/41024000] via 172.22.2.2, 00:04:42
     172.31.0.0/24 is subnetted, 2 subnets
C       172.31.21.0 is directly connected, Loopback101
C       172.31.20.0 is directly connected, Loopback100
     172.22.0.0/24 is subnetted, 2 subnets
C       172.22.2.0 is directly connected, Serial0/1
C       172.22.1.0 is directly connected, Serial0/0
B    172.16.0.0/16 [20/0] via 172.22.1.1, 00:13:26
```

From the backbone_r2 BGP table, as shown in the following example, you can see that the router knows two ways to network 172.16.0.0 and has selected the pod 1 path as the best way. This is because pod 1 was configured first, so the path through pod 1 is the oldest route.

```
backbone_r2>show ip bgp
BGP table version is 46, local router ID is 172.31.21.100
Status codes: s suppressed, d damped, h history, * valid, > best, i - internal
Origin codes: i - IGP, e - EGP, ? - incomplete

   Network          Next Hop         Metric LocPrf Weight Path
*> 10.1.1.0/24      172.22.1.1       41024000          0 65101 i
*> 10.2.2.0/24      172.22.2.2       41024000          0 65102 i
*  172.16.0.0       172.22.2.2              0          0 65102 i
*>                  172.22.1.1              0          0 65101 i
*> 172.31.20.0/24   0.0.0.0                 0      32768 i
*> 172.31.21.0/24   0.0.0.0                 0      32768 i
*> 192.168.1.0      172.22.1.1       41024000          0 65101 i
*> 192.168.2.0      172.22.2.2       41024000          0 65102 i
backbone_r2>
```

Because the backbone_r2 router already prefers pod 1, the following example shows how to change the weight attribute of the pod 2 connection to 200 so that the backbone_r2 router will prefer the path through pod 2 for the 172.16.0.0 network. (Recall that higher weight values are preferred.)

```
backbone_r2(config)#router bgp 65201
backbone_r2(config-router)#neighbor 172.22.2.2 weight 200
```

Clear all the BGP sessions from the backbone_r2 router.

**The following example shows how to clear all the BGP sessions from the backbone_r2 router.**

```
backbone_r2#clear ip bgp *
backbone_r2#
```

You should be able to **ping** from the backbone_r2 router to 172.16.10.100.

**From the backbone_r2 BGP table, as shown in the following example, you can see that the router still knows two ways to network 172.16.0.0, but it has now selected the pod 2 path as the best way.**

```
backbone_r2#show ip bgp
BGP table version is 8, local router ID is 172.31.21.100
Status codes: s suppressed, d damped, h history, * valid, > best, i - internal
Origin codes: i - IGP, e - EGP, ? - incomplete

   Network          Next Hop          Metric LocPrf Weight Path
*> 10.1.1.0/24      172.22.1.1        41024000          0 65101 i
*> 10.2.2.0/24      172.22.2.2        41024000        200 65102 i
*  172.16.0.0       172.22.1.1               0          0 65101 i
*>                  172.22.2.2               0        200 65102 i
*> 172.31.20.0/24   0.0.0.0                  0      32768 i
*> 172.31.21.0/24   0.0.0.0                  0      32768 i
*> 192.168.1.0      172.22.1.1        41024000          0 65101 i
*> 192.168.2.0      172.22.2.2        41024000        200 65102 i
```

**From the backbone_r2 routing table, as shown in the following example, you can also see that the router has now selected the pod 2 path as the best way to network 172.16.0.0.**

```
backbone_r2#show ip route
<output omitted>

Gateway of last resort is not set
     10.0.0.0/24 is subnetted, 2 subnets
B       10.1.1.0 [20/41024000] via 172.22.1.1, 00:00:30
B       10.2.2.0 [20/41024000] via 172.22.2.2, 00:00:40
B    192.168.1.0/24 [20/41024000] via 172.22.1.1, 00:00:30
B    192.168.2.0/24 [20/41024000] via 172.22.2.2, 00:00:40
     172.31.0.0/24 is subnetted, 2 subnets
C       172.31.21.0 is directly connected, Loopback101
C       172.31.20.0 is directly connected, Loopback100
     172.22.0.0/24 is subnetted, 2 subnets
C       172.22.2.0 is directly connected, Serial0/1
C       172.22.1.0 is directly connected, Serial0/0
B    172.16.0.0/16 [20/0] via 172.22.2.2, 00:00:40
```

The following example verifies that the backbone_r2 router can ping 172.16.10.100.

```
backbone_r2#ping 172.16.10.100

Type escape sequence to abort.
Sending 5, 100-byte ICMP Echos to 172.16.10.100, timeout is 2 seconds:
!!!!!
Success rate is 100 percent (5/5), round-trip min/avg/max = 84/86/92 ms
```

Trace from the backbone_r2 router to 172.16.10.100. Ensure that the path taken is through your pod.

**The following example verifies that the backbone_r2 router takes the path through pod 2 to get to 172.16.10.100.**

```
backbone_r2#trace 172.16.10.100

Type escape sequence to abort.
Tracing the route to 172.16.10.100

  1 172.22.2.2 12 msec 16 msec 16 msec
  2 p2r1 (192.168.2.49) [AS 65102] 32 msec 28 msec 28 msec
  3 10.2.2.100 [AS 65102] 44 msec *  40 msec
backbone_r2#
```

Remove your default route from the backbone_r1 router and the weight configuration at the backbone_r2 router when you are done.

**The following example shows how to remove the default route for the p2r1 router from the backbone_r1 router (configured similarly to the default route for the p1r1 router).**

```
backbone_r1(config)#no ip route 0.0.0.0 0.0.0.0 s1/1
```

**The following example shows how to remove the weight configuration from the backbone_r2 router.**

```
backbone_r2(config)#router bgp 65201
backbone_r2(config-router)#no neighbor 172.22.2.2 weight 200
```

# Review Questions

Answer the following questions, and then refer to Appendix G, "Answers to the Review Questions," for the answers.

**1** Name the two major functions performed by routers.

**2** What are the benefits of VLSMs?

**3** If the subnet 172.17.2.32/28 was further subnetted with a /30 prefix, how many more subnets would be created? How many hosts would be available on each of these new subnets?

**4** Define the following terms:

— IGP

— EGP

— Autonomous system

— Redistribution

**5** Describe some of the characteristics of BGP.

**6** Policy-based routing is applied to packets going in which direction on an interface?

**7** What distinguishes classful routing protocols from classless routing protocols?

**8** A router has networks 192.168.160.0/24 through 192.168.175.0/24 in its routing table. How could it summarize these networks into one route?

**9** In the BGP selection process, which attribute is checked first, AS path, weight, or local preference?

# PART IV

# Appendixes

This appendix contains job aids and supplements for the following topics:

- Extending IP Addressing Job Aids
- Supplement 1: Addressing Review
- Supplement 2: IP Access Lists
- Supplement 3: OSPF
- Supplement 4: EIGRP
- Supplement 5: BGP
- Supplement 6: Route Optimization

# APPENDIX A

# Job Aids and Supplements

The job aids and supplements in this appendix are provided to give you some background information and additional examples of the concepts covered in this book.

The IP addressing job aids are intended for your use when working with IP addresses. The information in Supplement 1, "Addressing Review," and Supplement 2, "IP Access Lists," should be a review of the fundamentals of IP addressing and of the concepts and configuration of access lists, respectively. The other supplements contain examples and additional material on the OSPF, EIGRP, and BGP routing protocols, and on route optimization.

## Extending IP Addressing Job Aids

This section includes the following job aids that you may find useful when working with IP addressing:

- IP addresses and subnetting
- Decimal-to-binary conversion chart

### IP Addresses and Subnetting

Figure A-1 is a job aid to help you with various aspects of IP addressing, including how to distinguish address classes, the number of subnets and hosts available with various subnet masks, and how to interpret IP addresses.

**Figure A-1**   *IP Addresses and Subnetting Job Aid*

| Class | Net host | First octet | Standard mask binary |
|-------|----------|-------------|----------------------|
| A | N.H.H.H | 1–126 | 1111 1111 0000 0000 0000 0000 0000 0000 |
| B | N.N.H.H | 128–191 | 1111 1111 1111 1111 0000 0000 0000 0000 |
| C | N.N.N.H | 192–223 | 1111 1111 1111 1111 1111 1111 0000 0000 |

| Subnet bits | Subnet mask | Number of subnets | Number of hosts |
|-------------|-------------|-------------------|-----------------|
| **Class B** | | | |
| 2 | 255.255.192.0 | 4 | 16382 |
| 3 | 255.255.224.0 | 8 | 8190 |
| 4 | 255.255.240.0 | 16 | 4094 |
| 5 | 255.255.248.0 | 32 | 2046 |
| 6 | 255.255.252.0 | 64 | 1022 |
| 7 | 255.255.254.0 | 128 | 510 |
| 8 | 255.255.255.0 | 256 | 254 |
| 9 | 255.255.255.128 | 512 | 126 |
| 10 | 255.255.255.192 | 1024 | 62 |
| 11 | 255.255.255.224 | 2048 | 30 |
| 12 | 255.255.255.240 | 4096 | 14 |
| 13 | 255.255.255.248 | 8192 | 6 |
| 14 | 255.255.255.252 | 16384 | 2 |
| **Class C** | | | |
| 2 | 255.255.255.192 | 4 | 62 |
| 3 | 255.255.255.224 | 8 | 30 |
| 4 | 255.255.255.240 | 16 | 14 |
| 5 | 255.255.255.248 | 32 | 6 |
| 6 | 255.255.255.252 | 64 | 2 |

| | Address | 172.16.5.72 | 1000 0011 0001 0000 0000 0101 0100 1000 |
|---|---------|-------------|------------------------------------------|
| | Subnet mask | 255.255.255.192 | 1111 1111 1111 1111 1111 1111 1100 0000 |

Subnetting

First octet (172 - Class B) defines network portion.

1010 1100 0001 0000 | 0000 0101 0100 1000

1111 1111 1111 1111 | 1111 1111 1100 0000

Network

Of the part that remains, the subnet mask bits define the subnet portion.

0000 0101 0100 1000

1111 1111 1100 0000

Subnet

Whatever bits remain define the host portion.

00 1000

00 0000

Host

# Decimal-to-Binary Conversion Chart

The following can be used to convert from decimal to binary, and from binary to decimal:

| Decimal | Binary | Decimal | Binary | Decimal | Binary | Decimal | Binary |
|---------|--------|---------|--------|---------|--------|---------|--------|
| 0 | 00000000 | 64 | 01000000 | 128 | 10000000 | 192 | 11000000 |
| 1 | 00000001 | 65 | 01000001 | 129 | 10000001 | 193 | 11000001 |
| 2 | 00000010 | 66 | 01000010 | 130 | 10000010 | 194 | 11000010 |
| 3 | 00000011 | 67 | 01000011 | 131 | 10000011 | 195 | 11000011 |
| 4 | 00000100 | 68 | 01000100 | 132 | 10000100 | 196 | 11000100 |
| 5 | 00000101 | 69 | 01000101 | 133 | 10000101 | 197 | 11000101 |
| 6 | 00000110 | 70 | 01000110 | 134 | 10000110 | 198 | 11000110 |
| 7 | 00000111 | 71 | 01000111 | 135 | 10000111 | 199 | 11000111 |
| 8 | 00001000 | 72 | 01001000 | 136 | 10001000 | 200 | 11001000 |
| 9 | 00001001 | 73 | 01001001 | 137 | 10001001 | 201 | 11001001 |
| 10 | 00001010 | 74 | 01001010 | 138 | 10001010 | 202 | 11001010 |
| 11 | 00001011 | 75 | 01001011 | 139 | 10001011 | 203 | 11001011 |
| 12 | 00001100 | 76 | 01001100 | 140 | 10001100 | 204 | 11001100 |
| 13 | 00001101 | 77 | 01001101 | 141 | 10001101 | 205 | 11001101 |

*(Continued)*

| Decimal | Binary | Decimal | Binary | Decimal | Binary | Decimal | Binary |
|---------|--------|---------|--------|---------|--------|---------|--------|
| 14 | 00001110 | 78 | 01001110 | 142 | 10001110 | 206 | 11001110 |
| 15 | 00001111 | 79 | 01001111 | 143 | 10001111 | 207 | 11001111 |
| 16 | 00010000 | 80 | 01010000 | 144 | 10010000 | 208 | 11010000 |
| 17 | 00010001 | 81 | 01010001 | 145 | 10010001 | 209 | 11010001 |
| 18 | 00010010 | 82 | 01010010 | 146 | 10010010 | 210 | 11010010 |
| 19 | 00010011 | 83 | 01010011 | 147 | 10010011 | 211 | 11010011 |
| 20 | 00010100 | 84 | 01010100 | 148 | 10010100 | 212 | 11010100 |
| 21 | 00010101 | 85 | 01010101 | 149 | 10010101 | 213 | 11010101 |
| 22 | 00010110 | 86 | 01010110 | 150 | 10010110 | 214 | 11010110 |
| 23 | 00010111 | 87 | 01010111 | 151 | 10010111 | 215 | 11010111 |
| 24 | 00011000 | 88 | 01011000 | 152 | 10011000 | 216 | 11011000 |
| 25 | 00011001 | 89 | 01011001 | 153 | 10011001 | 217 | 11011001 |
| 26 | 00011010 | 90 | 01011010 | 154 | 10011010 | 218 | 11011010 |
| 27 | 00011011 | 91 | 01011011 | 155 | 10011011 | 219 | 11011011 |
| 28 | 00011100 | 92 | 01011100 | 156 | 10011100 | 220 | 11011100 |
| 29 | 00011101 | 93 | 01011101 | 157 | 10011101 | 221 | 11011101 |
| 30 | 00011110 | 94 | 01011110 | 158 | 10011110 | 222 | 11011110 |
| 31 | 00011111 | 95 | 01011111 | 159 | 10011111 | 223 | 11011111 |
| 32 | 00100000 | 96 | 01100000 | 160 | 10100000 | 224 | 11100000 |
| 33 | 00100001 | 97 | 01100001 | 161 | 10100001 | 225 | 11100001 |
| 34 | 00100010 | 98 | 01100010 | 162 | 10100010 | 226 | 11100010 |
| 35 | 00100011 | 99 | 01100011 | 163 | 10100011 | 227 | 11100011 |
| 36 | 00100100 | 100 | 01100100 | 164 | 10100100 | 228 | 11100100 |
| 37 | 00100101 | 101 | 01100101 | 165 | 10100101 | 229 | 11100101 |
| 38 | 00100110 | 102 | 01100110 | 166 | 10100110 | 230 | 11100110 |
| 39 | 00100111 | 103 | 01100111 | 167 | 10100111 | 231 | 11100111 |
| 40 | 00101000 | 104 | 01101000 | 168 | 10101000 | 232 | 11101000 |
| 41 | 00101001 | 105 | 01101001 | 169 | 10101001 | 233 | 11101001 |
| 42 | 00101010 | 106 | 01101010 | 170 | 10101010 | 234 | 11101010 |
| 43 | 00101011 | 107 | 01101011 | 171 | 10101011 | 235 | 11101011 |

*continues*

*(Continued)*

| Decimal | Binary | Decimal | Binary | Decimal | Binary | Decimal | Binary |
|---------|--------|---------|--------|---------|--------|---------|--------|
| 44 | 00101100 | 108 | 01101100 | 172 | 10101100 | 236 | 11101100 |
| 45 | 00101101 | 109 | 01101101 | 173 | 10101101 | 237 | 11101101 |
| 46 | 00101110 | 110 | 01101110 | 174 | 10101110 | 238 | 11101110 |
| 47 | 00101111 | 111 | 01101111 | 175 | 10101111 | 239 | 11101111 |
| 48 | 00110000 | 112 | 01110000 | 176 | 10110000 | 240 | 11110000 |
| 49 | 00110001 | 113 | 01110001 | 177 | 10110001 | 241 | 11110001 |
| 50 | 00110010 | 114 | 01110010 | 178 | 10110010 | 242 | 11110010 |
| 51 | 00110011 | 115 | 01110011 | 179 | 10110011 | 243 | 11110011 |
| 52 | 00110100 | 116 | 01110100 | 180 | 10110100 | 244 | 11110100 |
| 53 | 00110101 | 117 | 01110101 | 181 | 10110101 | 245 | 11110101 |
| 54 | 00110110 | 118 | 01110110 | 182 | 10110110 | 246 | 11110110 |
| 55 | 00110111 | 119 | 01110111 | 183 | 10110111 | 247 | 11110111 |
| 56 | 00111000 | 120 | 01111000 | 184 | 10111000 | 248 | 11111000 |
| 57 | 00111001 | 121 | 01111001 | 185 | 10111001 | 249 | 11111001 |
| 58 | 00111010 | 122 | 01111010 | 186 | 10111010 | 250 | 11111010 |
| 59 | 00111011 | 123 | 01111011 | 187 | 10111011 | 251 | 11111011 |
| 60 | 00111100 | 124 | 01111100 | 188 | 10111100 | 252 | 11111100 |
| 61 | 00111101 | 125 | 01111101 | 189 | 10111101 | 253 | 11111101 |
| 62 | 00111110 | 126 | 01111110 | 190 | 10111110 | 254 | 11111110 |
| 63 | 00111111 | 127 | 01111111 | 191 | 10111111 | 255 | 11111111 |

# Supplement 1: Addressing Review

This supplement reviews the basics of IP addresses, including the following:

- Converting IP addresses between decimal and binary
- Determining an IP address class
- Extending an IP classful address using subnet masks
- Calculating a subnet mask
- Calculating the networks for a subnet mask
- Using prefixes to represent a subnet mask
- Review questions

# Converting IP Addresses Between Decimal and Binary

An IP address is a 32-bit, two-level hierarchical number. It is hierarchical because the first portion of the address represents the network, and the second portion of the address represents the node (host).

The 32 bits are grouped into four octets, with 8 bits per octet. The value of each octet ranges from 0 to 255 decimal, or 00000000 to 11111111 binary. IP addresses are usually written in dotted-decimal notation—each of the four octets is written in decimal notation, and dots are put between the octets. Figure A-2 illustrates how you convert an octet of an IP address in binary to decimal notation.

**Figure A-2**   *Converting an Octet of an IP Address from Binary to Decimal*

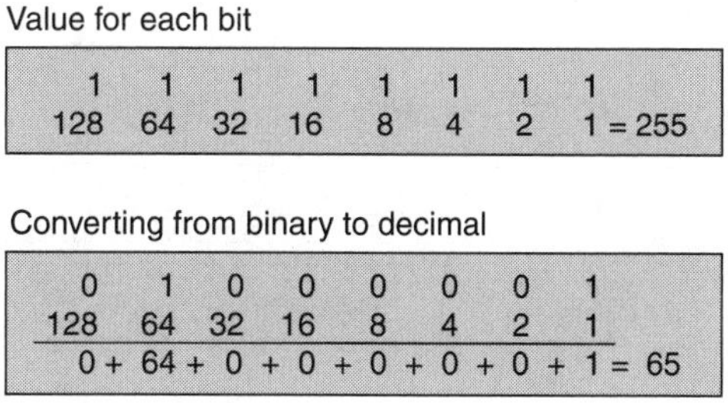

Value for each bit

| 1 | 1 | 1 | 1 | 1 | 1 | 1 | 1 |
|---|---|---|---|---|---|---|---|
| 128 | 64 | 32 | 16 | 8 | 4 | 2 | 1 = 255 |

Converting from binary to decimal

| 0 | 1 | 0 | 0 | 0 | 0 | 0 | 1 |
|---|---|---|---|---|---|---|---|
| 128 | 64 | 32 | 16 | 8 | 4 | 2 | 1 |

0 + 64 + 0 + 0 + 0 + 0 + 0 + 1 = 65

It is important that you understand how this conversion is done because it is used when calculating subnet masks, as discussed later in this section.

Figure A-3 shows three examples of converting IP addresses between binary and decimal.

**Figure A-3**   *Examples of Converting IP Addresses Between Binary and Decimal*

Binary
address:   00001010.00000001.00010111.0001001

Decimal
address:   10 . 1 . 23 . 19

Binary
address:   10101100.00010010.01000001.10101010

Decimal
address:   172 . 18 . 65 . 170

Binary
address:   11000000.10101000.00001110.00000110

Decimal
address:   192 . 168 . 14 . 6

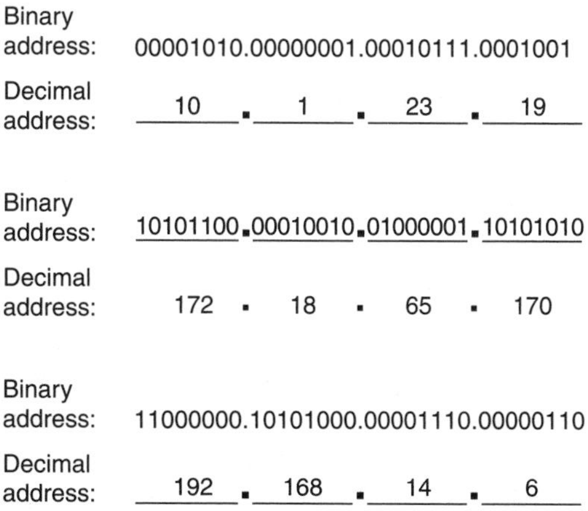

## Determining an IP Address Class

To accommodate large and small networks, the Network Information Center (NIC) segregated the 32-bit IP address into Classes A through E. The first few bits of the first octet determine the class of an address; this then determines how many network bits and host bits are in the address. This is illustrated for Class A, B, and C addresses in Figure A-4. Each address class therefore allows for a certain number of network addresses and a certain number of host addresses within a network. Table A-1 shows the address range, number of networks, and number of hosts for each of the classes. (Note that Class D and E addresses are used for other purposes, not for addressing hosts.)

**Figure A-4**    *Determining an IP Address Class from the First Few Bits of an Address*

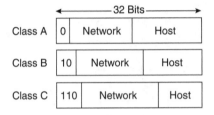

**Table A-1**    *IP Address Classes*

| Class | Address Range | Number of Networks | Number of Hosts |
|-------|---------------|--------------------|--------------------|
| Class A | 1.0.0.0 to 126.0.0.0 | 128 ($2^7$ ) | 16,777,214 |
| Class B | 128.0.0.0 to 191.255.0.0 | 16,386 ($2^{14}$) | 65,532 |
| Class C | 192.0.0.0 to 223.255.255.0 | Approximately 2 million ($2^{21}$) | 254 |
| Class D | 224.0.0.0 to 239.255.255.254 | Reserved for multicast addresses | — |
| Class E | 240.0.0.0 to 254.255.255.255 | Reserved for research | — |

**NOTE**    The network 127.0.0.0 is reserved for loopback.

Using classes to denote which portion of the address represents the network number and which portion is the node or host address is referred to as classful addressing. Several issues must be addressed with classful addressing, however. The number of available Class A, B, and C addresses is finite. Another problem is that not all classes are useful for a midsize organization, as illustrated in Table A-1. As can be expected, the Class B range is the most accommodating to a majority of today's organizational network topologies. To maximize the use of the IP addresses received by an organization regardless of the class, *subnet masks* were introduced.

## Extending an IP Classful Address Using Subnet Masks

RFC 950 was written to address the problem of IP address shortage. It proposed a procedure, called *subnet masking*, for dividing Class A, B, and C addresses into smaller pieces, thus increasing the number of possible networks. A subnet mask is a 32-bit value that identifies which bits in an address represent network bits and which represent host bits. In other words, the router doesn't determine the network portion of the address by looking at the value of the first octet; it looks at the subnet mask associated with the address. In this way, subnet masks enable you to extend the usage of an IP address. This is a way of making an IP address a three-level hierarchy, as shown in Figure A-5.

**Figure A-5**    *A Subnet Mask Determines How an IP Address Is Interpreted*

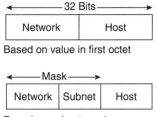

To create a subnet mask for an address, use a 1 for each bit that you want to represent the network or subnet portion of the address, and use a 0 for each bit that you want to represent the node portion of the address. Note that the 1s in the mask are contiguous. The default subnet masks for Class A, B, and C addresses are as shown Table A-2.

**Table A-2**    *IP Address Default Subnet Masks*

| Class | Default Mask in Binary | Default Mask in Decimal |
|-------|------------------------|-------------------------|
| Class A | 11111111.00000000.00000000.00000000 | 255.0.0.0 |
| Class B | 11111111.11111111.00000000.00000000 | 255.255.0.0 |
| Class C | 11111111.11111111.11111111.00000000 | 255.255.255.0 |

## Calculating a Subnet Mask

Because subnet masks extend the number of network addresses that you can use by using bits from the host portion, you do not want to randomly decide how many additional bits to use for the network portion. Instead, you want to do some research to determine how many network addresses you need to derive from your NIC-given IP address. For example, consider that you have IP address 172.16.0.0 and want to configure the network shown in Figure A-6. To establish your subnet mask, you would do the following:

**Step 1**  Determine the number of networks (subnets) needed. In Figure A-6, for example, there are five networks.

**Step 2**  Determine how many nodes per subnet must be defined. This example has five nodes (two routers and three workstations) on each subnet.

**Step 3**  Determine future network and node requirements. For example, assume 100 percent growth.

**Step 4**  Given the information gathered from Steps 1 through 3, determine the total number of subnets required. For this example, 10 subnets are required. Refer to the "Job Aid: IP Addressing and Subnetting" section, earlier in this appendix, and select the appropriate subnet mask value that can accommodate 10 networks.

**Figure A-6**  *Network Used in Subnet Mask Example*

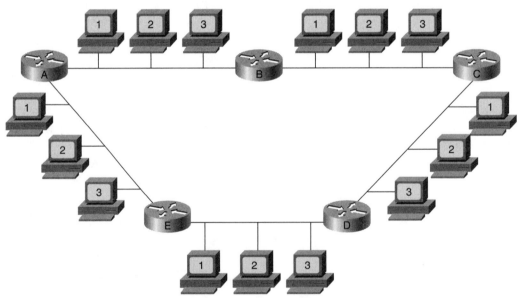

No mask exactly accommodates 10 subnets. Depending on your network growth trends, you may select 4 subnet bits, resulting in a subnet mask of 255.255.240.0. The binary representation of this subnet mask is as follows:

11111111.11111111.11110000.00000000

The number of additional subnets given by $n$ additional bits is $2^n$. For example, the additional 4 subnet bits would give you 16 subnets.

## Calculating the Networks for a Subnet Mask

For the example in Figure A-6, after you identify your subnet mask, you must calculate the 10 subnetted network addresses to use with 172.16.0.0 255.255.240.0. One way to do this is as follows:

**Step 1**   Write the subnetted address in binary format, as shown at the top of Figure A-7. Use the job aid "Decimal-to-Binary Conversion Chart," provided earlier in this appendix, if necessary.

**Step 2**   On the binary address, draw a line between the 16th and 17th bits, as shown in Figure A-7. Then draw a line between the 20th and 21st bits. Now you can focus on the target subnet bits.

**Step 3**   Historically, it was recommended that you begin choosing subnets from highest (from the left-most bit) to lowest so that you could have available network addresses. However, this strategy does not allow you to adequately summarize subnet addresses, so the present recommendation is to choose subnets from lowest to highest (right to left).

When calculating the subnet address, all the host bits are set to zero. To convert back to decimal, it is important to note that you must always convert an entire octet, 8 bits. For the first subnet, your subnet bits are 0000, and the rest of the octet (all host bits) is 0000.

Use the job aid "Decimal-to-Binary Conversion Chart," provided earlier in this appendix, if necessary, and locate this first subnet number. The first subnet number would be 00000000, or decimal 0.

**Step 4**   (Optional) It is recommended that you list each subnet in binary form to reduce the number of errors. In this way, you will not forget where you left off in your subnet address selection.

**Step 5**   Locate the second-lowest subnet number. In this case, it would be 0001. When combined with the next 4 bits (the host bits) of 0000, this is subnet binary 00010000, or decimal 16.

**Step 6**   Continue locating subnet numbers until you have as many as you need—in this case, 10 subnets, as shown in Figure A-7.

**Figure A-7**   *Calculating the Subnets for the Example in Figure A-6*

Assigned address: 172.16.0.0/16
In binary 10101100.00010000.00000000.00000000

Subnetted address: 172.16.0.0/20
In binary 10101100.00010000.xxxx 0000.00000000

| 1st subnet: | 10101100 . 00010000 | .0000 | 0000.00000000 | = 172.16.0.0 |
| 2nd subnet: | 172 . 16 | .0001 | 0000.00000000 | = 172.16.16.0 |
| 3rd subnet: | 172 . 16 | .0010 | 0000.00000000 | = 172.16.32.0 |
| 4th subnet: | 172 . 16 | .0011 | 0000.00000000 | = 172.16.48.0 |
| . | | | | |
| . | | | | |
| 10th subnet: | 172 . 16 | .1001 | 0000.00000000 | = 172.16.144.0 |

Network          Subnet          Host

# Using Prefixes to Represent a Subnet Mask

As already discussed, subnet masks are used to identify the number of bits in an address that represent the network, subnet, and host portions of the address. Another way of indicating this is to use a *prefix*. A prefix is a slash (/) and a numerical value that is the sum of the bits that represent the network and subnet portion of the address. For example, if you were using a subnet mask of 255.255.255.0, the prefix would be /24 for 24 bits.

Table A-3 shows some examples of the different ways that you can represent a prefix and subnet mask.

**Table A-3**   *Representing Subnet Masks*

| IP Address/Prefix | Subnet Mask in Decimal | Subnet Mask in Binary |
|---|---|---|
| 192.168.112.0/21 | 255.255.248.0 | 11111111.11111111.11111000.00000000 |
| 172.16.0.0/16 | 255.255.0.0 | 11111111.11111111.00000000.00000000 |
| 10.1.1.0/27 | 255.255.255.224 | 11111111.11111111.11111111.11100000 |

It is important to know how to write subnet masks and prefixes because Cisco routers use both, as shown in Example A-1. You will typically be asked to input a subnet mask when configuring an IP address, but the output generated using **show** commands typically shows an IP address with a prefix.

**Example A-1**  *Examples of Subnet Mask and Prefix Use on Cisco Routers*

```
p1r3#show run
<Output Omitted>
interface Ethernet0
 ip address 10.64.4.1 255.255.255.0
!
interface Serial0
 ip address 10.1.3.2 255.255.255.0
<Output Omitted>

p1r3#show interface ethernet0
Ethernet0 is administratively down, line protocol is down
  Hardware is Lance, address is 00e0.b05a.d504 (bia 00e0.b05a.d504)
  Internet address is 10.64.4.1/24
<Output Omitted>

p1r3#show interface serial0
Serial0 is down, line protocol is down
  Hardware is HD64570
  Internet address is 10.1.3.2/24
<Output Omitted>
```

# Supplement 1 Review Questions

Answer the following questions, and then refer to Appendix G, "Answers to the Review Questions," for the answers.

1  You need to design an IP network for your organization. Your organization's IP address is 172.16.0.0. Your assessment indicates that the organization needs at least 130 networks of no more than 100 nodes in each network.

   As a result, you have decided to use a classful subnetting scheme based on the 172.16.0.0/24 scheme. In the space that follows, write any four IP addresses that are part of the range of subnetwork numbers. Also, write the subnet address and subnet mask for these addresses. One address is provided as an example.

| IP Address | Subnet Address and Mask |
| --- | --- |
| 172.16.1.0/24 | 172.16.1.0 255.255.255.0 |
| | |
| | |
| | |
| | |

2  Your network has the address 172.16.168.0/21. Write eight IP addresses in this network.

**3** Write the four IP addresses in the range described by the 192.168.99.16/30 address.

**4** Of the four addresses in question 3, which two could you use as host addresses in a point-to-point connection?

# Supplement 2: IP Access Lists

This supplement covers the following topics:

- IP access list overview
- IP standard access lists
- IP extended access lists
- Restricting virtual terminal access
- Verifying access list configuration
- Review questions

## IP Access List Overview

Packet filtering helps control packet movement through the network, as illustrated in Figure A-8. Such control can help limit network traffic and restrict network use by certain users or devices. To permit or deny packets from crossing specified router interfaces, Cisco provides access lists. An IP access list is a sequential collection of permit and deny conditions that apply to IP addresses or upper-layer IP protocols.

**Figure A-8** *Access Lists Control Packet Movement Through a Network*

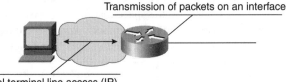

Transmission of packets on an interface

Virtual terminal line access (IP)

Table A-4 shows some of the available types of access lists on a Cisco router and their access list numbers.

**Table A-4** *Access List Numbers*

| Type of Access List | Range of Access List Numbers |
| --- | --- |
| IP standard | 1 to 99 |
| IP extended | 100 to 199 |

**Table A-4**    *Access List Numbers (Continued)*

| Type of Access List | Range of Access List Numbers |
| --- | --- |
| Bridge type-code | 200 to 299 |
| IPX standard | 800 to 899 |
| IPX extended | 900 to 999 |
| IPX SAP | 1000 to 1099 |

This supplement covers IP standard and extended access lists. For information on other types of access lists, refer to the technical documentation on Cisco's web site at www.cisco.com.

**WARNING**    The Cisco IOS Release 10.3 introduced substantial additions to IP access lists. These extensions are backward compatible. Migrating from existing releases to the Cisco IOS Release 10.3 or later image will convert your access lists automatically. However, previous releases are not upwardly compatible with these changes. Thus, if you save an access list with the Cisco IOS Release 10.3 or later image and then use older software, the resulting access list will not be interpreted correctly. This incompatibility can cause security problems. Save your old configuration file before booting Cisco IOS Release 10.3 (or later) images in case you need to revert to an earlier version.

# IP Standard Access Lists

This section discusses IP standard access list operation and implementation.

Standard access lists permit or deny packets based only on the source IP address of the packet, as shown in Figure A-9. The access list number range for standard IP access lists is 1 to 99. Standard access lists are easier to configure than their more robust counterparts, extended access lists.

**Figure A-9**    *Standard IP Access Lists Filter Based Only on the Source Address*

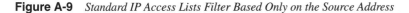

Source address

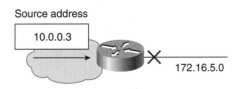

10.0.0.3

172.16.5.0

A standard access list is a sequential collection of permit and deny conditions that apply to source IP addresses. The router tests addresses against the conditions in an access list one by one. The first match determines whether the router accepts or rejects the packet. Because the router stops testing conditions after the first match, the order of the conditions is critical. If no conditions match, the router rejects the packet.

The processing of inbound standard access lists is illustrated in Figure A-10. After receiving a packet, the router checks the source address of the packet against the access list. If the access list permits the address, the router exits the access list and continues to process the packet. If the access list rejects the address, the router discards the packet and returns an Internet Control Message Protocol (ICMP) administratively prohibited message.

**Figure A-10**   *Inbound Standard IP Access List Processing*

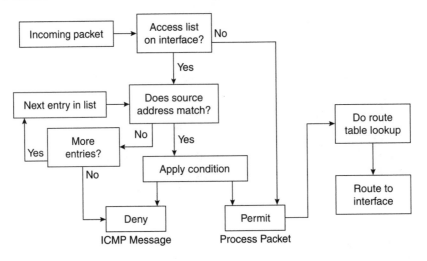

Note that the action taken if no more entries are found in the access list is to deny the packet; this illustrates an important concept to remember when creating access lists. The last entry in an access list is what is known as an implicit deny any. All traffic not explicitly permitted will be implicitly denied.

---

**NOTE**   When configuring access lists, order is important. Make sure that you list the entries in order from specific to general. For example, if you want to deny a specific host address and permit all other addresses, make sure that your entry about the specific host appears first.

---

The processing of outbound standard IP access lists is illustrated in Figure A-11. After receiving and routing a packet to a controlled interface, the router checks the source address of the packet against the access list. If the access list permits the address, the router transmits the packet. If the access list denies the address, the router discards the packet and returns an ICMP administratively prohibited message.

**Figure A-11** *Outbound Standard IP Access List Processing*

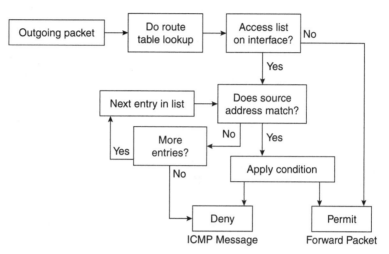

Both standard and extended IP access lists use a wildcard mask. Like an IP address, a wildcard mask is a 32-bit quantity written in dotted-decimal format. The wildcard mask tells the router which bits of the address to use in comparisons. Address bits corresponding to wildcard mask bits set to 1 are ignored in comparisons; address bits corresponding to wildcard mask bits set to 0 are used in comparisons.

An alternative way to think of the wildcard mask is as follows. If a 0 bit appears in the wildcard mask, then the corresponding bit location in the access list address and the same bit location in the packet address must match (either both must be 0 or both must be 1). If a 1 bit appears in the wildcard mask, then the corresponding bit location in the packet will match (whether it is 0 or 1), and that bit location in the access list address is ignored. For this reason, bits set to 1 in the wildcard mask are sometimes called "don't care" bits.

Remember that the order of the access list statements is important because the access list is not processed further after a match has been found.

---

### Wildcard Masks

The concept of a wildcard mask is similar to the wildcard character used in DOS-based computers. For example, to delete all files on your computer that begin with the letter "f," you would type:

**delete f*.***

The * character is the wildcard; any files that start with "f," followed by any other characters, then a dot, and then any other characters, will be deleted.

Instead of using wildcard characters, routers use wildcard masks to implement this concept.

Examples of addresses and wildcard masks, and what they match, are shown in Table A-5.

**Table A-5**    *Access List Wildcard Mask Examples*

| Address | Wildcard Mask | Matches |
| --- | --- | --- |
| 0.0.0.0 | 255.255.255.255 | Any address |
| 172.16.0.0/16 | 0.0.255.255 | Any host on network 172.16.0.0 |
| 172.16.7.11/16 | 0.0.0.0 | Host address 172.16.7.11 |
| 255.255.255.255 | 0.0.0.0 | Local broadcast address 255.255.255.255 |
| 172.16.8.0/21 | 0.0.7.255 | Any host on subnet 172.16.8.0/21 |

Whether you are creating a standard or extended access list, you will need to complete the following two tasks:

**Step 1**    Create an access list in global configuration mode by specifying an access list number and access conditions.

Define a standard IP access list using a source address and wildcard, as shown later in this section.

Define an extended access list using source and destination addresses, as well as optional protocol-type information for finer granularity of control, as shown in the "IP Extended Access Lists" section, later in this supplement.

**Step 2**    Apply the access list in interface configuration mode to interfaces or terminal lines.

After an access list is created, you can apply it to one or more interfaces. Access lists can be applied on either outbound or inbound interfaces.

## IP Standard Access List Configuration

Use the **access-list** *access-list-number* {**permit** | **deny**} {*source source-wildcard* | **any**} [**log**] global configuration command to create an entry in a standard traffic filter list, as detailed in Table A-6.

**Table A-6**    *Standard IP **access-list** Command Description*

| access-list Command | Description |
|---|---|
| *access-list-number* | Identifies the list to which the entry belongs, a number from 1 to 99. |
| **permit | deny** | Indicates whether this entry allows or blocks traffic from the specified address. |
| *source* | Identifies the source IP address. |
| *source-wildcard* | (Optional) Identifies which bits in the address field must match. A 1 in a bit position indicates "don't care" bits, and a 0 in any bit position indicates that bit must strictly match. If this field is omitted, the wildcard mask 0.0.0.0 is assumed. |
| **any** | Use this keyword as an abbreviation for a source and source-wildcard of 0.0.0.0 255.255.255.255. |
| **log** | (Optional) Causes an informational logging message about the packet that matches the entry to be sent to the console. Exercise caution when using this keyword because it consumes CPU cycles. |

When a packet does not match any of the configured lines in an access list, the packet is denied by default because there is an invisible line at the end of the access list that is equivalent to **deny any**. (**deny any** is the same as denying an address of 0.0.0.0 with a wildcard mask of 255.255.255.255.)

The keyword **host** can also be used in an access list; it causes the address that immediately follows it to be treated as if it were specified with a mask of 0.0.0.0. For example, configuring **host 10.1.1.1** in an access list is equivalent to configuring **10.1.1.1 0.0.0.0**.

Use the **ip access-group** *access-list-number* {**in | out**} interface configuration command to link an existing access list to an interface, as shown in Table A-7. Each interface may have both an inbound and an outbound IP access list.

**Table A-7**    ***ip access-group** Command Description*

| ip access-group Command | Description |
|---|---|
| *access-list-number* | Indicates the number of the access list to be linked to this interface. |
| **in | out** | Processes packets arriving on or leaving from this interface. **Out** is the default. |

Eliminate the entire list by typing the **no access-list** *access-list-number* global configuration command. De-apply the access list with the **no ip access-group** *access-list-number* {**in** | **out**} interface configuration command.

## Implicit Wildcard Masks

Implicit, or default, wildcard masks reduce typing and simplify configuration, but care must be taken when relying on the default mask.

The access list line shown in Example A-2 is an example of a specific host configuration. For standard access lists, if no wildcard mask is specified, the wildcard mask is assumed to be 0.0.0.0. The implicit mask makes it easier to enter a large number of individual addresses.

**Example A-2**  *Standard Access List Using the Default Wildcard Mask*

```
access-list 1 permit 172.16.5.17
```

Common errors found in access list lines are illustrated in Example A-3.

**Example A-3**  *Standard Access List Using the Default Wildcard Mask*

```
access-list 1 permit 0.0.0.0
access-list 2 permit 172.16.0.0
access-list 3 deny any
access-list 3 deny 0.0.0.0 255.255.255.255
```

The first list in Example A-3—**permit 0.0.0.0**—would exactly match the address 0.0.0.0 and then permit it. In most cases, this address is illegal, so this list would prevent all traffic from getting through (because of the implicit **deny any** at the end of the list).

The second list in Example A-3—**permit 172.16.0.0**—is probably a configuration error. The intention is probably 172.16.0.0 0.0.255.255. The exact address 172.16.0.0 refers to the network and would never be assigned to a host. As a result, nothing would get through with this list, again because of the implicit **deny any** at the end of the list. To filter networks or subnets, use an explicit wildcard mask.

The next two lines in Example A-3—**deny any** and **deny 0.0.0.0 255.255.255.255**—are unnecessary to configure because they duplicate the function of the implicit deny that occurs when a packet fails to match all the configured lines in an access list. Although not necessary, you may want to add one of these entries for record-keeping purposes.

## Configuration Principles

Following these general principles helps ensure that the access lists you create have the intended results:

- Top-down processing

  — Organize your access list so that more specific references in a network or subnet appear before more general ones.

  — Place more frequently occurring conditions before less frequent conditions.

- Implicit **deny any**

  — Unless you end your access list with an explicit **permit any**, it will deny by default all traffic that fails to match any of the access list lines.

- New lines added to the end

  — Subsequent additions are always added to the end of the access list.

  — You cannot selectively add or remove lines when using numbered access lists, but you can when using IP named access lists (a feature available in Cisco IOS Release 11.2 and later).

- Undefined access list = **permit any**

  — If you apply an access list with the **ip access-group** command to an interface before any access list lines have been created, the result will be **permit any**. The list is live, so if you enter only one line, it goes from a **permit any** to a **deny most** (because of the implicit **deny any**) as soon as you press Return. For this reason, you should create your access list before you apply it to an interface.

## Standard Access List Example

An example network is shown in Figure A-12, and the configuration on Router X in that figure is shown in Example A-4.

**Figure A-12** *Network Used for Standard IP Access List Example*

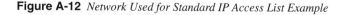

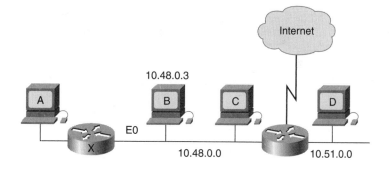

Consider which devices can communicate with Host A in this example:

**Example A-4** *Standard Access List Configuration of Router X in Figure A-12*

```
Router(config)#access-list 2 permit 10.48.0.3
Router(config)#access-list 2 deny 10.48.0.0 0.0.255.255
Router(config)#access-list 2 permit 10.0.0.0 0.255.255.255
Router(config)#!(Note: all other access implicitly denied)
Router(config)#interface ethernet 0
Router(config-if)#ip access-group 2 in
```

- Host B can communicate with Host A. It is permitted by the first line of the access list, which uses an implicit host mask.

- Host C cannot communicate with Host A. Host C is in the subnet denied by the second line in the access list.

- Host D can communicate with Host A. Host D is on a subnet that is explicitly permitted by the third line of the access list.

- Users on the Internet cannot communicate with Host A. Users outside of this network are not explicitly permitted, so they are denied by default with the implicit **deny any** at the end of the access list.

## Location of Standard Access Lists

Access list location can be more of an art than a science, but some general guidelines can be discovered by looking at the simple example illustrated in Figure A-13. An access list configuration for this network is shown in Example A-5. If the policy goal is to deny Host Z access to Host V on another network, and not to change any other access policy, determine on which interface of which router this access list should be configured.

**Figure A-13** *Location of Standard IP Access List Example*

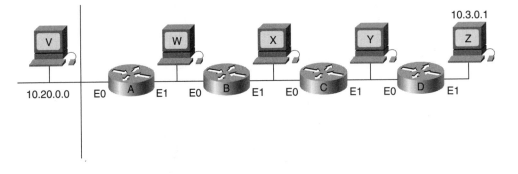

**Example A-5** *Standard Access List to Be Configured on a Router in Figure A-13*

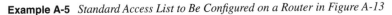

```
access-list 3 deny 10.3.0.1
access-list 3 permit any
```

The access list should be placed on Router A. The reason is that a standard access list can specify only a source address. No hosts beyond the point in the path that the traffic is denied can connect.

The access list could be configured as an outbound list on E0 of Router A, but it would most likely be configured as an inbound list on E1 so that packets to be denied would not have to be routed through Router A first.

Consider the effect of placing the access list on other routers:

- **Router B**—Host Z could not connect with Host W (and Host V).
- **Router C**—Host Z could not connect with hosts W and X (and Host V).
- **Router D**—Host Z could not connect with hosts W, X, and Y (and Host V).

Thus, for standard access lists, the rule is to place them as close to the *destination* router as possible to exercise the most control. Note, however, that this means that traffic is routed through the network, only to be denied close to its destination.

# IP Extended Access Lists

This section discusses extended access list operation and implementation.

Standard access lists offer quick configuration and low overhead in limiting traffic based on source address within a network. Extended access lists provide a higher degree of control by enabling filtering based on the source and destination addresses, transport layer protocol, and application port number. These features make it possible to limit traffic based on the uses of the network.

## Extended Access List Processing

As shown in Figure A-14, every condition tested in a line of an extended access list must match for the line of the access list to match and for the permit or deny condition to be applied. As soon as one parameter or condition fails, the next line in the access list is compared.

**Figure A-14** *Extended IP Access List Processing Flow*

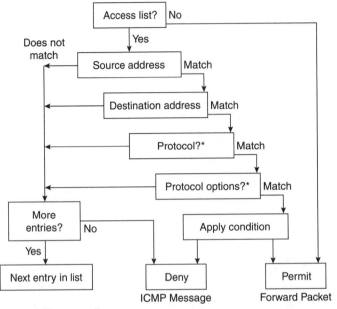

* If present in access list

The extended access list checks source address, destination address, and protocol. Depending on the protocol configured, there may be more protocol-dependent options tested. For example, a TCP port may be checked, which allows routers to filter at the application layer.

## Extended IP Access List Configuration

Use the **access-list** *access-list-number* {**permit** | **deny**} {*protocol* | *protocol-keyword*} {*source source-wildcard* | **any**} {*destination destination-wildcard* | **any**} [*protocol-specific options*] [**log**] global configuration command to create an entry in an extended traffic filter list, as described in Table A-8.

**Table A-8** *Extended IP access-list Command Description*

| access-list Command | Description |
|---|---|
| *access-list-number* | Identifies the list to which the entry belongs, a number from 100 to 199. |
| **permit** | **deny** | Indicates whether this entry allows or blocks traffic. |

**Table A-8**    *Extended IP **access-list** Command Description (Continued)*

| access-list Command | Description |
|---|---|
| *protocol* | **ip**, **tcp**, **udp**, **icmp**, **igmp**, **gre**, **igrp**, **eigrp**, **ospf**, **nos**, or a number in the range of 0 through 255. To match any Internet protocol, use the keyword **ip**. Some protocols have more options that are supported by an alternate syntax for this command, as shown later in this section. |
| *source* and *destination* | Identifies the source and destination IP addresses. |
| *source-wildcard* and *destination-wildcard* | Identifies which bits in the address field must match. A 1 in a bit position indicates "don't care" bits, and a 0 in any bit position indicates that the bit must strictly match. |
| **any** | Use this keyword as an abbreviation for a source and source-wildcard, or a destination and destination-wildcard of 0.0.0.0 255.255.255.255. |
| **log** | (Optional) Causes informational logging messages about a packet that matches the entry to be sent to the console. Exercise caution when using this keyword because it consumes CPU cycles. |

The wildcard masks in an extended access list operate the same way as they do in standard access lists. The keyword **any** in either the source or the destination position matches any address and is equivalent to configuring an address of 0.0.0.0 with a wildcard mask of 255.255.255.255. An example of an extended access list is shown in Example A-6.

**Example A-6**    *Use of the Keyword **any***

```
access-list 101 permit ip  0.0.0.0  255.255.255.255  0.0.0.0  255.255.255.255
! (alternate configuration)
access-list 101 permit ip any any
```

The keyword **host** can be used in either the source or the destination position; it causes the address that immediately follows it to be treated as if it were specified with a mask of 0.0.0.0. An example is shown in Example A-7.

**Example A-7**    *Use of the Keyword **host***

```
access-list 101 permit ip  0.0.0.0  255.255.255.255  172.16.5.17  0.0.0.0
! (alternate configuration)
access-list 101 permit ip any host 172.16.5.17
```

Use the **access-list** *access-list-number* {**permit** | **deny**} **icmp** {*source source-wildcard* | **any**} {*destination destination-wildcard* | **any**} [*icmp-type* [*icmp-code*] | *icmp-message*] global configuration command to filter ICMP traffic. The protocol keyword **icmp** indicates that an alternate syntax is being used for this command and that protocol-specific options are available, as described in Table A-9.

**Table A-9**  *Extended IP **access-list icmp** Command Description*

| access-list icmp Command | Description |
|---|---|
| *access-list-number* | Identifies the list to which the entry belongs, a number from 100 to 199. |
| **permit \| deny** | Indicates whether this entry allows or blocks traffic. |
| *source* and *destination* | Identifies the source and destination IP addresses. |
| *source-wildcard* and *destination-wildcard* | Identifies which bits in the address field must match. A 1 in a bit position indicates "don't care" bits, and a 0 in any bit position indicates that the bit must strictly match. |
| **any** | Use this keyword as an abbreviation for a source and source-wildcard, or a destination and destination-wildcard of 0.0.0.0 255.255.255.255. |
| *icmp-type* | (Optional) Packets can be filtered by ICMP message type. The type is a number from 0 to 255. |
| *icmp-code* | (Optional) Packets that have been filtered by ICMP message type can also be filtered by ICMP message code. The code is a number from 0 to 255. |
| *icmp-message* | (Optional) Packets can be filtered by a symbolic name representing an ICMP message type or a combination of ICMP message type and ICMP message code. A list of these names is provided in Table A-10. |

Cisco IOS Release 10.3 and later versions provide symbolic names that make configuration and reading of complex access lists easier. With symbolic names, it is no longer critical to understand the meaning of the ICMP message type and code (for example, message 8 and message 0 can be used to filter the **ping** command). Instead, the configuration can use symbolic names (for example, the **echo** and **echo-reply** symbolic names can be used to filter the **ping** command), as shown in Table A-10. (You can use the Cisco IOS context-sensitive help feature by entering **?** when entering the access-list command, to verify the available names and proper command syntax.)

**Table A-10**  *ICMP Message and Type Names*

| | | |
|---|---|---|
| Administratively-prohibited | Information-reply | Precedence-unreachable |
| Alternate-address | Information-request | Protocol-unreachable |
| Conversion-error | Mask-reply | Reassembly-timeout |
| Dod-host-prohibited | Mask-request | Redirect |

**Table A-10**  *ICMP Message and Type Names (Continued)*

| | | |
|---|---|---|
| Dod-net-prohibited | Mobile-redirect | Router-advertisement |
| Echo | Net-redirect | Router-solicitation |
| Echo-reply | Net-tos-redirect | Source-quench |
| General-parameter-problem | Net-tos-unreachable | Source-route-failed |
| Host-isolated | Net-unreachable | Time-exceeded |
| Host-precedence-unreachable | Network-unknown | Timestamp-reply |
| Host-redirect | No-room-for-option | Timestamp-request |
| Host-tos-redirect | Option-missing | Traceroute |
| Host-tos-unreachable | Packet-too-big | Ttl-exceeded |
| Host-unknown | Parameter-problem | Unreachable |
| Host-unreachable | Port-unreachable | |

Use the **access-list** *access-list-number* {**permit** I **deny**} **tcp** {*source source-wildcard* I **any**} [*operator source-port* I *source-port*] {*destination destination-wildcard* I **any**} [*operator destination-port* I *destination-port*] [**established**] global configuration command to filter TCP traffic. The protocol keyword **tcp** indicates that an alternate syntax is being used for this command and that protocol-specific options are available, as described in Table A-11.

**Table A-11**  *Extended IP **access-list tcp** Command Description*

| access-list tcp Command | Description |
|---|---|
| *access-list-number* | Identifies the list to which the entry belongs, a number from 100 to 199. |
| **permit** I **deny** | Indicates whether this entry allows or blocks traffic. |
| *source* and *destination* | Identifies the source and destination IP addresses. |
| *source-wildcard* and *destination-wildcard* | Identifies which bits in the address field must match. A 1 in a bit position indicates "don't care" bits, and a 0 in any bit position indicates that the bit must strictly match. |
| **any** | Use this keyword as an abbreviation for a source and source-wildcard, or a destination and destination-wildcard of 0.0.0.0 255.255.255.255. |
| *operator* | (Optional) A qualifying condition. Can be: **lt**, **gt**, **eq**, **neq**. |
| *source-port* and *destination-port* | (Optional) A decimal number from 0 to 65535 or a name that represents a TCP port number. |
| **established** | (Optional) A match occurs if the TCP segment has the ACK or RST bits set. Use this if you want a Telnet or another activity to be established in one direction only. |

## established Keyword in Extended Access Lists

When a TCP session is started between two devices, the first segment sent has the SYN (synchronize) code bit set but does not have the ACK (acknowledge) code bit set in the segment header because it is not acknowledging any other segments. All subsequent segments sent do have the ACK code bit set because they are acknowledging previous segments sent by the other device. This is how a router can distinguish between a segment from a device that is attempting to *start* a TCP session and a segment of an ongoing already *established* session. The RST (reset) code bit is set when an established session is being terminated.

When you configure the **established** keyword in a TCP extended access list, it indicates that that access list statement should match only TCP segments in which the ACK or RST code bit is set. In other words, only segments that are part of an already established session will be matched; segments that are attempting to start a session will not match the access list statement.

Table A-12 is a list of TCP port names that can be used instead of port numbers. Port numbers corresponding to these protocols can be found by typing a **?** in the place of a port number, or by looking at RFC 1700, "Assigned Numbers." (This RFC is available at URL www.cis.ohio-state.edu/htbin/rfc/rfc1700.html.)

**Table A-12**  *TCP Port Names*

| Bgp | Hostname | Syslog |
|---|---|---|
| Chargen | Irc | Tacacs-ds |
| Daytime | Klogin | Talk |
| Discard | Kshell | telnet |
| Domain | Lpd | Time |
| Echo | nntp | Uucp |
| Finger | Pop2 | Whois |
| ftp control | Pop3 | www |
| ftp-data | Smtp | |
| Gopher | Sunrpc | |

Other port numbers can also be found in RFC 1700, "Assigned Numbers." A partial list of the assigned TCP port numbers is shown in Table A-13.

**Table A-13**  *Some Reserved TCP Port Numbers*

| Decimal | Keyword | Description |
|---------|---------|-------------|
| 7 | ECHO | Echo |
| 9 | DISCARD | Discard |
| 13 | DAYTIME | Daytime |
| 19 | CHARGEN | Character generator |
| 20 | FTP-DATA | File Transfer Protocol (data) |
| 21 | FTP-CONTROL | File Transfer Protocol |
| 23 | TELNET | Terminal connection |
| 25 | SMTP | Simple Mail Transfer Protocol |
| 37 | TIME | Time of day |
| 43 | WHOIS | Who is |
| 53 | DOMAIN | Domain name server |
| 79 | FINGER | Finger |
| 80 | WWW | World Wide Web HTTP |
| 101 | HOSTNAME | NIC host name server |

Use the **access-list** *access-list-number* {**permit** | **deny**} **udp** {*source source-wildcard* | **any**} [*operator source-port* | *source-port*] {*destination destination-wildcard* | **any**} [*operator destination-port* | *destination-port*] global configuration command to filter UDP traffic. The protocol keyword **udp** indicates that an alternate syntax is being used for this command and that protocol-specific options are available, as described in Table A-14.

**Table A-14**  *Extended IP access-list udp Command Description*

| access-list udp Command | Description |
|-------------------------|-------------|
| *access-list-number* | Identifies the list to which the entry belongs, a number from 100 to 199. |
| **permit** | **deny** | Indicates whether this entry allows or blocks traffic. |
| *source* and *destination* | Identifies the source and destination IP addresses. |
| *source-wildcard* and *destination-wildcard* | Identifies which bits in the address field must match. A 1 in a bit position indicates "don't care" bits, and a 0 in any bit position indicates that bit must strictly match. |
| **any** | Use this keyword as an abbreviation for a source and source-wildcard, or a destination and destination-wildcard of 0.0.0.0 255.255.255.255. |

*continues*

**Table A-14** *Extended IP **access-list udp** Command Description (Continued)*

| access-list udp Command | Description |
|---|---|
| *operator* | (Optional) A qualifying condition. Can be: **lt, gt, eq, neq**. |
| *source-port* and *destination-port* | (Optional) A decimal number from 0 to 65535 or a name that represents a UDP port number. |

Table A-15 is a list of UDP port names that can be used instead of port numbers. Port numbers corresponding to these protocols can be found by typing a **?** in the place of a port number, or by looking at RFC 1700, "Assigned Numbers."

**Table A-15** *UDP Port Names*

| | | |
|---|---|---|
| Biff | Nameserver | Syslog |
| Bootpc | NetBios-dgm | Tacasds-ds |
| Bootps | NetBios-ns | Talk |
| Discard | Ntp | Tftp |
| Dns | Rip | Time |
| Dnsix | Snmp | Whois |
| Echo | Snmptrap | Xdmcp |
| Mobile-ip | Sunrpc | |

Other port numbers can also be found in RFC 1700, "Assigned Numbers." A partial list of the assigned UDP port numbers is shown in Table A-16.

**Table A-16** *Some Reserved UDP Port Numbers*

| Decimal | Keyword | Description |
|---|---|---|
| 7 | ECHO | Echo |
| 9 | DISCARD | Discard |
| 37 | TIME | Time of day |
| 42 | NAMESERVER | Host name server |
| 43 | WHOIS | Who is |
| 53 | DNS | Domain name server |
| 67 | BOOTPS | Bootstrap protocol server |
| 68 | BOOTPC | Bootstrap protocol client |
| 69 | TFTP | Trivial File Transfer Protocol |
| 123 | NTP | Network Time Protocol |
| 137 | NetBios-ns | NetBios Name Service |

**Table A-16**  *Some Reserved UDP Port Numbers (Continued)*

| Decimal | Keyword | Description |
|---------|---------|-------------|
| 138 | NetBios-dgm | NetBios Datagram Service |
| 161 | SNMP | SNMP |
| 162 | SNMPTrap | SNMP Traps |
| 520 | RIP | RIP |

## Extended Access List Examples

In the example shown in Figure A-15, Router A's interface Ethernet 1 is part of a Class B subnet with the address 172.22.3.0, Router A's interface Serial 0 is connected to the Internet, and the e-mail server's address is 172.22.1.2. The access list configuration applied to Router A is shown in Example A-8.

**Figure A-15**  *Network Used for Extended IP Access List Example*

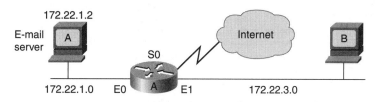

**Example A-8**  *Configuration on Router A in Figure A-15*

```
access-list 104 permit tcp any 172.22.0.0 0.0.255.255 established
access-list 104 permit tcp any host 172.22.1.2 eq smtp
access-list 104 permit udp any any eq dns
access-list 104 permit icmp any any echo
access-list 104 permit icmp any any echo-reply
!
interface serial 0
  ip access-group 104 in
```

In Example A-8, access list 104 is applied inbound on Router A's Serial 0 interface. The keyword **established** is used only for the TCP protocol to indicate an established connection. A match occurs if the TCP segment has the ACK or RST bits set, which indicate that the packet belongs to an existing connection. If the session is not already established (the ACK bit is not set and the SYN bit is set), it means that someone on the Internet is attempting to initialize a session, in which case the packet is denied. This configuration also permits SMTP traffic from any address to the e-mail server. UDP domain name server packets and ICMP echo and echo-reply packets are also permitted, from any address to any other address.

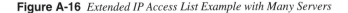

Another example is shown in Figure A-16. The access list configuration applied to Router A is shown in Example A-9.

**Figure A-16** *Extended IP Access List Example with Many Servers*

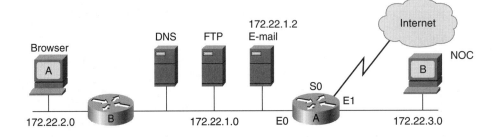

**Example A-9** *Configuration on Router A in Figure A-16*

```
access-list 118 permit tcp any 172.22.0.0  0.0.255.255 eq www established
access-list 118 permit tcp any host 172.22.1.2 eq smtp
access-list 118 permit udp any any eq dns
access-list 118 permit udp 172.22.3.0  0.0.0.255 172.22.1.0 0.0.0.255 eq snmp
access-list 118 deny icmp any 172.22.0.0  0.0.255.255 echo
access-list 118 permit icmp any any echo-reply
!
interface ethernet 0
  ip access-group 118 out
```

In Example A-9, access list 118 is applied outbound on Router A's Ethernet 0 interface. With the configuration shown in Example A-9, *replies* to queries from the Client A browser to the Internet will be allowed back into the corporate network (because they are established sessions). Browser queries *from* external sources are not explicitly allowed and will be discarded by the implicit **deny any** at the end of the access list.

The access list in Example A-9 also allows e-mail (SMTP) to be delivered exclusively to the mail server. The name server is permitted to resolve DNS requests. The 172.22.1.0 subnet is controlled by the network management group located at the NOC server (Client B), so network-management queries (Simple Network Management Protocol [SNMP]) will be allowed to reach these devices in the server farm. Attempts to ping the corporate network from outside or from subnet 172.22.3.0 will fail because the access list blocks the echo requests. However, the replies to echo requests generated from within the corporate network will be allowed to re-enter the network.

## Location of Extended Access Lists

Because extended access lists can filter on more than source address, location is no longer a constraint as it was when considering the location of a standard access list. Frequently, policy decisions and goals are the driving forces behind extended access list placement.

If your goal is to minimize traffic congestion and maximize performance, you might want to push the access lists close to the source to minimize cross-traffic and administratively prohibited ICMP messages. If your goal is to maintain tight control over access lists as part of your network security strategy, you might want to have them more centrally located. Notice how changing network goals will affect access list configuration.

Some things to consider when placing extended access lists include the following:

- Minimize distance traveled by traffic that will be denied (and ICMP unreachable messages).
- Keep denied traffic off the backbone.
- Select the router to receive CPU overhead from access lists.
- Consider the number of interfaces affected.
- Consider access list management and security.
- Consider network growth impacts on access list maintenance.

# Restricting Virtual Terminal Access

This section discusses how standard access lists can be used to limit virtual terminal access.

Standard and extended access lists will block packets from going *through* the router. They are not designed to block packets that originate within the router. An outbound Telnet extended access list does not prevent router-initiated Telnet sessions, by default.

For security purposes, users can be denied virtual terminal (vty) access to the router, or users can be permitted vty access to the router but denied access to destinations from that router. Restricting virtual terminal access is less a traffic control mechanism than one technique for increasing network security.

Because vty access is accomplished using the Telnet protocol, there is only one type of vty access list.

## How to Control vty Access

Just as a router has physical ports or interfaces such as Ethernet 0 and Ethernet 1, it also has virtual ports. These virtual ports are called virtual terminal lines. By default, there are five such virtual terminal lines, numbered vty 0 through 4, as shown in Figure A-17.

**Figure A-17**  *A Router Has Five Virtual Terminal Lines (Virtual Ports) by Default*

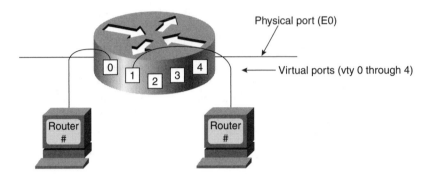

You should set identical restrictions on all virtual terminal lines because you cannot control on which virtual terminal line a user will connect.

---

**NOTE**   Some experts recommend that you configure one of the vty terminal lines differently than the others. This way you will have a "back door" into the router.

---

## Virtual Terminal Line Access Configuration

Use the **line vty** {*vty-number* | *vty-range*} global configuration command to place the router in line configuration mode, as described in Table A-17.

**Table A-17**   *line vty Command Description*

| line vty Command | Description |
|---|---|
| *vty-number* | Indicates the number of the vty line to be configured. |
| *vty-range* | Indicates the range of vty lines to which the configuration will apply. |

Use the **access-class** *access-list-number* {**in** | **out**} line configuration command to link an existing access list to a terminal line or range of lines, as described in Table A-18.

**Table A-18**   *access-class Command Description*

| access-class Command | Description |
|---|---|
| *access-list-number* | Indicates the number of the standard access list to be linked to a terminal line. This is a decimal number from 1 to 99. |
| **in** | Prevents the router from receiving incoming connections *from* the addresses in the access list. |
| **out** | Prevents someone from initiating a Telnet *to* addresses defined in the access list. |

| NOTE | When using the **out** keyword in the access-class command, the addresses in the specified standard access list are treated as *destination* addresses rather than source addresses. |
|---|---|

In the example configuration in Example A-10, any device on network 192.168.55.0 is permitted to establish a virtual terminal (Telnet) session with the router. Of course, the user must know the appropriate passwords to enter user mode and privileged mode.

**Example A-10** *Configuration to Restrict Telnet Access to a Router*

```
access-list 12 permit 192.168.55.0 0.0.0.255
!
line vty 0 4
  access-class 12 in
```

Notice that in this example, identical restrictions have been set on all virtual terminal lines (0 to 4) because you cannot control on which virtual terminal line a user will connect. (Note that the implicit **deny any** still applies to this alternate application of access lists.)

## Verifying Access List Configuration

This section describes how to verify access list configuration.

Use the **show access-lists** [*access-list-number* | *name*] privileged EXEC command to display access lists from all protocols, as described in Table A-19. If no parameters are specified, all access lists will be displayed.

**Table A-19**    *show access-list Command Description*

| show access-lists Command | Description |
|---|---|
| *access-list-number* | (Optional) Number of the access list to display |
| *name* | (Optional) Name of the access list to display |

The system counts how many packets match each line of an extended access list; the counters are displayed by the **show access-lists** command.

Example A-11 illustrates an example output from the **show access-lists** command. In this example, the first line of the access list has been matched three times, and the last line has been matched 629 times. The second line has not been matched.

**Example A-11** *Output of the **show access-lists** Command*

```
p1r1#show access-lists
Extended IP access list 100
    deny tcp host 10.1.1.2 host 10.1.1.1 eq telnet (3 matches)
    deny tcp host 10.1.2.2 host 10.1.2.1 eq telnet
    permit ip any any (629 matches)
```

Use the **show ip access-list** [*access-list-number* | *name*] EXEC command to display IP access lists, as described in Table A-20. If no parameters are specified, all IP access lists will be displayed.

**Table A-20** *show ip access-list Command Description*

| show ip access-list Command | Description |
| --- | --- |
| *access-list-number* | (Optional) Number of the IP access list to display |
| *name* | (Optional) Name of the IP access list to display |

Use the **clear access-list counters** [*access-list-number* | *name*] EXEC command to clear the counters for the number of matches in an extended access list, as described in Table A-21. If no parameters are specified, the counters will be cleared for all access lists.

**Table A-21** *clear access-list counters Command Description*

| clear access-list counters Command | Description |
| --- | --- |
| *access-list-number* | (Optional) Number of the access list for which to clear the counters |
| *name* | (Optional) Name of the access list for which to clear the counters |

Use the **show line** [*line-number*] EXEC command to display information about terminal lines. The *line-number* is optional and indicates the absolute line number of the line for which you want to list parameters. If a line number is not specified, all lines are displayed.

## Supplement 2 Review Questions

Answer the following questions, and then refer to Appendix G for the answers.

1 Figure A-18 shows the network for this question.

Create an access list and place it in the proper location to satisfy the following requirements:

— Prevent all hosts on subnet 172.16.1.0/24, except host 172.16.1.3, from accessing the web server on subnet 172.16.4.0. Allow all other hosts, including from the outside world, to access the web server.

**Figure A-18** *Network for Review Question 1*

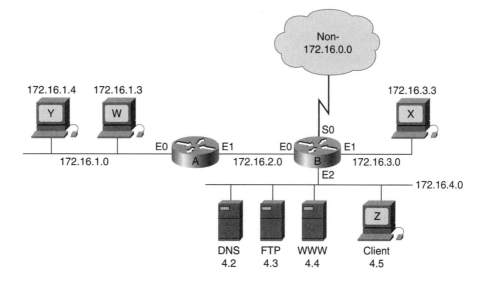

— Prevent the outside world from pinging subnet 172.16.4.0.

— Allow all hosts on all subnets of network 172.16.0.0 (using subnet mask 255.255.255.0) to send queries to the DNS server on subnet 172.16.4.0. The outside world is not allowed to access the DNS server.

— Prevent host 172.16.3.3 from accessing subnet 172.16.4.0 for any reason.

— Prevent all other access to the 172.16.4.0 subnet.

Write your configuration in the spaces that follow. Be sure to include the router name (A or B), interface name (E0, E1, or E2), and access list direction (in or out).

**Global commands:**

_____

_____

_____

_____

_____

**Interface commands:**

_____

_____

_____

   **2**  What do bits set to 1 in a wildcard mask indicate when matching an address?

   **3**  By default, what happens to all traffic in an access list?

   **4**  Where should an extended access list be placed to save network resources?

   **5**  Using the keyword **host** in an access list is a substitute for using what value of a wildcard mask?

# Supplement 3: OSPF

This supplement covers the following OSPF-related topics:

- Not-so-stubby areas
- OSPF single-area configuration example
- OSPF multiarea configuration example

## OSPF Not-So-Stubby Areas

Not-so-stubby areas (NSSAs) were first introduced in Cisco IOS Release 11.2. NSSAs are based on RFC 1587, "The OSPF NSSA Option." NSSAs enable you to make a hybrid stub area that can accept some autonomous system external routes, referred to as type 7 LSAs. Type 7 LSAs may be originated by and advertised throughout an NSSA. Type 7 LSAs are advertised only within a single NSSA; they are not flooded into the backbone area or any other area by border routers, although the information that they contain can be propagated into the backbone area by being translated into type 5 LSAs by the ABR. As with stub areas, NSSAs do not receive or originate type 5 LSAs.

Use an NSSA if you are an Internet service provider (ISP) or a network administrator that must connect a central site using Open Shortest Path First (OSPF) to a remote site using a different protocol, such as the Routing Information Protocol (RIP) or Enhanced Interior Gateway Routing Protocol (EIGRP), as shown in Figure A-19. You can use NSSA to simplify the administration of this kind of topology.

Prior to NSSA, the limitation that a stub area cannot import external routes meant that the connection between Router A and Router B in Figure A-19 could not be a stub area. Therefore, if the connection ran OSPF, it would be a standard area and would import the routes learned from RIP or EIGRP as type 5 LSAs. Because it is likely not desirable for the branch office to get all the type 5 routes from the central site, Router B would be forced to run OSPF and RIP or EIGRP.

Now, with NSSA you can extend OSPF to cover the remote connection by defining the area between the corporate router and the remote router as an NSSA, as shown in Figure A-19.

**Figure A-19**  *Example of a Topology Where an NSSA Is Used*

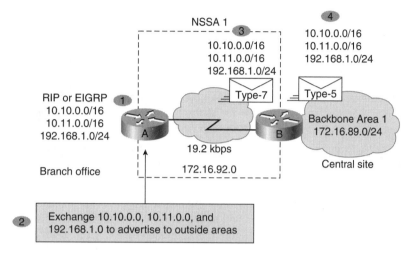

In Figure A-19, Router A is defined as an autonomous system boundary router (ASBR). It is configured to exchange any routes within the RIP/EIGRP domain to the NSSA. The following is what happens when using an NSSA:

1  Router A receives RIP or EGRP routes for networks 10.10.0.0/16, 10.11.0.0/16, and 192.168.1.0/24.

2  Router A, connected to the NSSA, imports the non-OSPF routes as type 7 LSAs into the NSSA.

3  Router B, an ABR between the NSSA and the backbone area 0, receives the type 7 LSAs.

4  After the SPF calculation on the forwarding database, Router B translates the type 7 LSAs into type 5 LSAs and then floods them throughout backbone area 0.

At this point Router B could have summarized routes 10.10.0.0/16 and 10.11.0.0/16 as 10.0.0.0/8, or could have filtered one or more of the routes.

## Configuring NSSA

The steps used to configure OSPF NSSA are as follows:

**Step 1**  On the ABR connected to the NSSA, configure OSPF, as described in Chapter 3, "Configuring OSPF in a Single Area," and Chapter 4, "Interconnecting Multiple OSPF Areas."

**Step 2**  Configure an area as NSSA using the following command, explained in Table A-22:

```
router(config-router)#area area-id nssa [no-redistribution]
[default-information-originate]
```

**Table A-22** *area nssa Command*

| Command | Description |
| --- | --- |
| *area-id* | Identifier of the area that is to be an NSSA. The identifier can be specified as either a decimal value or an IP address. |
| **no-redistribution** | (Optional) Used when the router is an NSSA ABR and you want the **redistribute** command to import routes only into the normal areas, but not into the NSSA area. |
| **default-information-originate** | (Optional) Used to generate a type 7 default into the NSSA area. This argument takes effect only on the NSSA ABR. |

**Step 3** Every router within the same area must agree that the area is NSSA; otherwise, the routers will not be capable of communicating with each other. Therefore, configure this command on every router in the NSSA area.

**Step 4** (Optional) Control the summarization or filtering during the translation, using the following command explained in Table A-23:

```
router(config-router)#summary-address address mask [prefix mask] [not-advertise]
[tag tag]
```

**Table A-23** *summary-address Command*

| Command | Description |
| --- | --- |
| *address* | Summary address designated for a range of addresses |
| *prefix* | (Optional) IP route prefix for the destination |
| *mask* | (Optional) IP subnet mask used for the summary route |
| **not-advertise** | (Optional) Used to suppress routes that match the prefix/mask pair |
| *tag* | (Optional) Tag value that can be used as a match value for controlling redistribution via route maps |

Figure A-20 and Example A-12 provide an example of NSSA configuration.

**Figure A-20** *Example of NSSA Topology*

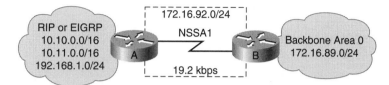

**Example A-12** *Configuring NSSA on the Routers in Figure A-20*

```
Router A Configuration:
router ospf 1
  redistribute rip subnets
  network 172.16.92.0.0.0.255 area 1
  area 1 nssa

Router B Configuration:
router ospf 1
  summary-address 10.0.0.0.255.0.0.0
  network 172.16.89.0.0.0.255 area 0
  network 172.16.92.0.0.0.255 area 1
  area 1 nssa
```

**NOTE**    The **redistribute** command shown in Example A-12 instructs the router to import RIP packets into the OSPF network. Redistribution is discussed in detail in Chapter 8, "Optimizing Routing Update Operation."

## OSPF Single-Area Configuration Example

This section includes configuration and **show** command output examples that result from configuring the network shown in Figure A-21.

**Figure A-21** *OSPF Single-Area Topology*

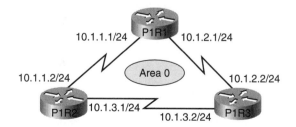

Example A-13 shows a typical configuration for single-area OSPF, for P1R3.

**Example A-13** *P1R3 in Figure A-21 Configuration*

```
P1R3#show run
Building configuration...

Current configuration:
!
version 11.2
no service password-encryption
no service udp-small-servers
no service tcp-small-servers
!
hostname P1R3
!
interface Ethernet0
 no ip address
 shutdown
!
interface Ethernet1
 no ip address
 shutdown
!
interface Serial0
 ip address 10.1.3.2 255.255.255.0
 no fair-queue
 clockrate 64000
!
interface Serial1
 ip address 10.1.2.2 255.255.255.0
!

router ospf 1
 network 10.1.2.0 0.0.0.255 area 0
 network 10.1.3.0 0.0.0.255 area 0
!
no ip classless
!
!
line con 0
 exec-timeout 0 0
line aux 0
line vty 0 4
 login
!
end
```

As shown in Example A-13, OSPF is activated on both Serial 0 and Serial 1 interfaces.

Example A-14 provides output of some **show commands** on P1R3. From the **show ip route** output, you can confirm that OSPF is receiving OSPF routing information. From the **show ip ospf neighbor detail** output, you can confirm that P1R3 has reached the full state with its two neighbors. From the **show ip ospf database** output, you can confirm that P1R3 is receiving only type 1 LSAs—router link states LSA. No type 2 LSAs are received because all the connections are point-to-point and, therefore, no designated router (DR) was elected.

**Example A-14** *P1R3 in Figure A-21 Output for* **show ip route, show ip ospf neighbor detail,** *and* **show ip ospf database** *Commands*

```
P1R3#show ip route
Codes: C - connected, S - static, I - IGRP, R - RIP, M - mobile, B - BGP
       D - EIGRP, EX - EIGRP external, O - OSPF, IA - OSPF inter area
       N1 - OSPF NSSA external type 1, N2 - OSPF NSSA external type 2
       E1 - OSPF external type 1, E2 - OSPF external type 2, E - EGP
       i - IS-IS, L1 - IS-IS level-1, L2 - IS-IS level-2, * - candidate default
       U - per-user static route, o - ODR

Gateway of last resort is not set

     10.0.0.0/24 is subnetted, 3 subnets
C        10.1.3.0 is directly connected, Serial0
C        10.1.2.0 is directly connected, Serial1
O        10.1.1.0 [110/128] via 10.1.3.1, 00:01:56, Serial0
                  [110/128] via 10.1.2.1, 00:01:56, Serial1

P1R3#show ip ospf neighbor detail
 Neighbor 10.1.3.1, interface address 10.1.3.1
    In the area 0 via interface Serial0
    Neighbor priority is 1, State is FULL
    Options 2
    Dead timer due in 00:00:34
 Neighbor 10.1.2.1, interface address 10.1.2.1
    In the area 0 via interface Serial1
    Neighbor priority is 1, State is FULL
    Options 2
    Dead timer due in 00:00:36

P1R3#show ip ospf database
        OSPF Router with ID (10.1.3.2) (Process ID 1)
                Router Link States (Area 0)

Link ID         ADV Router      Age         Seq#       Checksum Link count
10.1.2.1        10.1.2.1        301         0x80000004 0x4A49   4
10.1.3.1        10.1.3.1        292         0x80000004 0x1778   4
10.1.3.2        10.1.3.2        288         0x80000004 0x5D2E   4
P1R3#
```

# OSPF Multiarea Configuration Example

This section includes configuration and **show** command output examples that result from configuring the network shown in Figure A-22.

**Figure A-22** *OSPF Multiarea Topology*

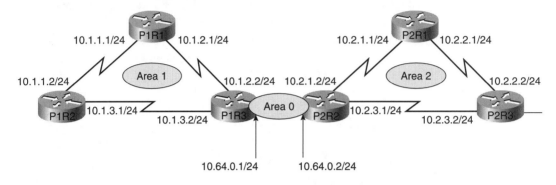

Example A-15 provides output for P1R3 before any areas are configured for stub and route summarization. You can observe that the OSPF database is quite large and has multiple entries from type 1 (Router Link States), type 2 (Net Link States), and type 3 (Summary Net Link States) LSAs.

**Example A-15** *P1R3 in Figure A-22 Output Prior to Stub and Route Summarization*

```
P1R3#show ip ospf database

        OSPF Router with ID (10.64.0.1) (Process ID 1)

             Router Link States (Area 0)

Link ID         ADV Router      Age       Seq#        Checksum Link count
10.64.0.1       10.64.0.1       84        0x80000009 0x6B87    1
10.64.0.2       10.64.0.2       85        0x8000000C 0x6389    1

             Net Link States (Area 0)

Link ID         ADV Router      Age       Seq#        Checksum
10.64.0.2       10.64.0.2       85        0x80000001 0x7990

             Summary Net Link States (Area 0)

Link ID         ADV Router      Age       Seq#        Checksum
10.1.1.0        10.64.0.1       128       0x80000001 0x92D2
10.1.2.0        10.64.0.1       129       0x80000001 0x59F
10.1.3.0        10.64.0.1       129       0x80000001 0xF9A9
10.2.1.2        10.64.0.2       71        0x80000001 0x716F
10.2.2.1        10.64.0.2       41        0x80000001 0x7070
10.2.3.1        10.64.0.2       51        0x80000001 0x657A

             Router Link States (Area 1)

Link ID         ADV Router      Age       Seq#        Checksum Link count
10.1.2.1        10.1.2.1        859       0x80000004 0xD681    4
```

**Example A-15** *P1R3 in Figure A-22 Output Prior to Stub and Route Summarization (Continued)*

```
10.1.3.1        10.1.3.1        868     0x80000004 0xEB68   4
10.64.0.1       10.64.0.1       133     0x80000007 0xAF61   4

                Summary Net Link States (Area 1)

Link ID         ADV Router      Age     Seq#        Checksum
10.2.1.2        10.64.0.1       74      0x80000001 0xDBFB
10.2.2.1        10.64.0.1       45      0x80000001 0xDAFC
10.2.3.1        10.64.0.1       55      0x80000001 0xCF07
10.64.0.0       10.64.0.1       80      0x80000003 0x299
P1R3#
```

Example A-16 shows the configuration output for P1R3, a router that is an ABR for a stub area and that is doing route summarization.

**Example A-16** *P1R3 in Figure A-22 Configuration*

```
P1R3#show run
Building configuration...

Current configuration:
!
version 11.2
no service password-encryption
no service udp-small-servers
no service tcp-small-servers
!
hostname P1R3
!
interface Ethernet0
 ip address 10.64.0.1 255.255.255.0
!
interface Ethernet1
 no ip address
 shutdown
!
interface Serial0
 ip address 10.1.3.2 255.255.255.0
 no fair-queue
 clockrate 64000
!
interface Serial1
 ip address 10.1.2.2 255.255.255.0
!
router ospf 1
 network 10.64.0.0 0.0.0.255 area 0
 network 10.1.2.0 0.0.0.255 area 1
 network 10.1.3.0 0.0.0.255 area 1
 area 1 stub no-summary
 area 1 range 10.1.0.0 255.255.0.0
```

*continues*

**Example A-16** *P1R3 in Figure A-22 Configuration (Continued)*

```
!
no ip classless
!
!
line con 0
 exec-timeout 0 0
line aux 0
line vty 0 4
 login
!
end
```

Example A-17 provides output from P1R3, after the network is configured with stub areas and route summarization. The number of entries in the OSPF topology database is reduced.

**Example A-17** *P1R3 in Figure A-22* **show ip ospf database** *Output After Stub and Route Summarization Were Configured*

```
P1R3#show ip ospf database

        OSPF Router with ID (10.64.0.1) (Process ID 1)

                Router Link States (Area 0)

Link ID          ADV Router       Age        Seq#         Checksum Link count
10.64.0.1        10.64.0.1        245        0x80000009 0x6B87   1
10.64.0.2        10.64.0.2        246        0x8000000C 0x6389   1

                Net Link States (Area 0)

Link ID          ADV Router       Age        Seq#         Checksum
10.64.0.2        10.64.0.2        246        0x80000001 0x7990

                Summary Net Link States (Area 0)

Link ID          ADV Router       Age        Seq#         Checksum
10.1.0.0         10.64.0.1        54         0x80000001 0x1B8B
10.2.0.0         10.64.0.2        25         0x80000001 0x9053

                Router Link States (Area 1)

Link ID          ADV Router       Age        Seq#         Checksum Link count
10.1.2.1         10.1.2.1         1016       0x80000004 0xD681   4
10.1.3.1         10.1.3.1         1026       0x80000004 0xEB68   4
10.64.0.1        10.64.0.1        71         0x80000009 0xE9FF   2

                Summary Net Link States (Area 1)

Link ID          ADV Router       Age        Seq#         Checksum
0.0.0.0          10.64.0.1        76         0x80000001 0x4FA3
P1R3#
```

# Supplement 4: EIGRP

This supplement covers the following EIGRP-related topics:

- IPX and EIGRP
- AppleTalk and EIGRP
- EIGRP configuration examples

## IPX and EIGRP

The following section provides information on EIGRP for Novell IPX networks.

EIGRP for a Novell IPX network has the same fast routing and partial update capabilities as EIGRP for IP. In addition, EIGRP has several capabilities that are designed to facilitate the building of large, robust Novell IPX networks.

The first capability is support for incremental SAP updates. Novell IPX RIP routers send out large RIP and SAP updates every 60 seconds. This can consume substantial amounts of bandwidth. EIGRP for IPX sends out SAP updates only when changes occur and sends only changed information.

The second capability that EIGRP adds to IPX networks is the capability to build large networks. IPX RIP networks have a diameter limit of 15 hops. EIGRP networks can have a diameter of 224 hops.

The third capability that EIGRP for Novell IPX provides is optimal path selection. The RIP metric for route determination is based on ticks, with hop count used as a tie-breaker. If more than one route has the same value for the tick metric, the route with the least number of hops is preferred. Instead of ticks and hop count, IPX EIGRP uses a combination of these metrics: delay, bandwidth, reliability, and load.

To add EIGRP to a Novell RIP and SAP network, configure EIGRP on the Cisco router interfaces that connect to other Cisco routers also running EIGRP. Configure RIP and SAP on the interfaces that connect to Novell hosts and or Novell routers that do not support EIGRP. With EIGRP configured, periodic SAP updates are replaced with EIGRP incremental updates when an EIGRP peer is found. However, note that unless RIP is explicitly disabled for an IPX network number, both RIP and EIGRP will be active on the interface associated with that network number.

### Route Selection

IPX EIGRP routes are automatically preferred over RIP routes regardless of metrics unless a RIP route has a hop count less than the external hop count carried in the EIGRP update—for example, a server advertising its own internal network.

## Redistribution and Metric Handling

Redistribution is automatic between RIP and EIGRP, and vice versa. Automatic redistribution can be turned off using the **no redistribute** command. Redistribution is not automatic between different EIGRP autonomous systems.

## Reducing SAP Traffic

Novell IPX RIP routers send out large RIP and SAP updates every 60 seconds regardless of whether a change has occurred. These updates can consume a substantial amount of bandwidth. You can reduce SAP update traffic by configuring EIGRP to do incremental SAP updates. When EIGRP is configured for incremental SAP updates, the updates consist only of information that has changed, and the updates are sent out only when a change occurs, thus saving bandwidth.

When you configure EIGRP for incremental SAP updates, you can do the following:

- Retain RIP, in which case only the reliable transport of EIGRP is used for sending incremental SAP updates. (This is the preferred configuration over bandwidth-sensitive connections.)
- Turn off RIP, in which case EIGRP replaces RIP as the routing protocol.

# AppleTalk and EIGRP

The following section provides information on EIGRP for AppleTalk network.

Cisco routers support AppleTalk Phase 1 and AppleTalk Phase 2. For AppleTalk Phase 2, Cisco routers support both extended and nonextended networks.

To add EIGRP to an AppleTalk network, configure EIGRP on the Cisco router interfaces that connect to other Cisco routers also running EIGRP. Do not disable Routing Table Maintenance Protocol (RTMP) on the interfaces that connect to AppleTalk hosts or that connect to AppleTalk routers that do not support EIGRP. RTMP is enabled by default when AppleTalk routing is enabled and when an interface is assigned an AppleTalk cable range.

## Route Selection

AppleTalk EIGRP routes are automatically preferred over RTMP routes. Whereas the AppleTalk metric for route determination is based on hop count only, AppleTalk EIGRP uses a combination of these configurable metrics: delay, bandwidth, reliability, and load.

## Metric Handling

The formula for converting RTMP metrics to AppleTalk EIGRP metrics is hop count multiplied by 252,524,800. This is a constant based on the bandwidth for a 9.6-kbps serial line and includes an RTMP factor. An RTMP hop distributed into EIGRP appears as a slightly worse path than an EIGRP-native, 9.6-kbps serial link. The formula for converting EIGRP to RTMP is the value of the EIGRP external metric plus 1.

## Redistribution

Redistribution between AppleTalk and EIGRP, and vice versa, is automatic by default. Redistribution involves converting the EIGRP metric back into an RTMP hop count metric. In reality, there is no conversion of an EIGRP composite metric into an RTMP metric. Because a hop count is carried in an EIGRP metric tuple as the EIGRP route spreads through the network, 1 is added to the hop count carried in the EIGRP metric blocks through the network and put into any RTMP routing tuple generated.

There is no conversion of an EIGRP metric back into an RTMP metric because, in reality, what RTMP uses as a metric (the hop count) is carried along the EIGRP metric all the way through the network. This is true of EIGRP-derived routes and routes propagated through the network that were originally derived from an RTMP route.

# EIGRP Configuration Examples

This section includes configuration and **show** command output examples that result from configuring the network shown in Figure A-23.

**Figure A-23**  *Topology for the EIGRP Configuration Examples*

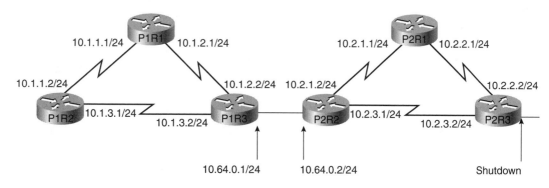

Example A-18 provides the configuration output for router P1R3 while running EIGRP.

**Example A-18** *P1R3 in Figure A-23 Configured for EIGRP*

```
P1R3#show run
Building configuration...

Current configuration:
!
version 11.2
no service password-encryption
no service udp-small-servers
no service tcp-small-servers
!
hostname P1R3
!
enable password san-fran
!
no ip domain-lookup
ipx routing 0000.0c01.3333
ipx maximum-paths 2
!
interface Loopback0
no ip address
ipx network 1013
!
interface Ethernet0
ip address 10.64.0.1 255.255.255.0
!
interface Serial0
 ip address 10.1.3.2 255.255.255.0
 ipx input-sap-filter 1000
 ipx network 1003
!
interface Serial1
 ip address 10.1.2.2 255.255.255.0
 ipx input-sap-filter 1000
 ipx network 1002
 clockrate 56000
!
<Output Omitted>
!
router eigrp 200
 network 10.0.0.0
!
no ip classless
!
!
line con 0
 exec-timeout 0 0
line aux 0
line vty 0 4
 login
!
end
```

Example A-19 shows the topology database of P1R3 running EIGRP before modifying the bandwidth—in other words, all links are equal bandwidth. You can see that in the case of equal-cost paths to the same network (10.1.1.0), both routes appear in the topology table as successors.

**Example A-19** *P1R3 in Figure A-23 EIGRP Topology Database Prior to Changing the **bandwidth** Value*

```
P1R3#show ip eigrp topology
IP-EIGRP Topology Table for process 200
Codes: P - Passive, A - Active, U - Update, Q - Query, R - Reply,
       r - Reply status
   P 10.1.3.0/24, 1 successors, FD is 2169856
          via Connected, Serial0
   P 10.1.2.0/24, 1 successors, FD is 2169856
          via Connected, Serial1
   P 10.1.1.0/24, 2 successors, FD is 2681856
          via 10.1.3.1 (2681856/2169856), Serial0
          via 10.1.2.1 (2681856/2169856), Serial1
```

Example A-20 shows the configuration output for P1R3 running EIGRP with **bandwidth** and **ip summary-address** commands configured. The bandwidth on Serial 0 is changed from its default of 1.544 Mbps to 64 kbps.

**Example A-20** *P1R3 in Figure A-23 Configuration for EIGRP with **bandwidth** and **ip summary-address** Commands*

```
P1R3#show run
Building configuration...

Current configuration:
!
version 11.2
no service password-encryption
no service udp-small-servers
no service tcp-small-servers
!
hostname P1R3
!
enable password san-fran
!
no ip domain-lookup
ipx routing 0000.0c01.3333
ipx maximum-paths 2
!
interface Loopback0
no ip address
ipx network 1013
!
interface Ethernet0
 ip address 10.64.0.1 255.255.255.0
 ip summary-address eigrp 200 10.1.0.0 255.255.0.0
!
```

*continues*

**Example A-20** *P1R3 in Figure A-23 Configuration for EIGRP with **bandwidth** and **ip summary-address***
*Commands (Continued)*

```
interface Serial0
 ip address 10.1.3.2 255.255.255.0
 ipx input-sap-filter 1000
 ipx network 1003
 bandwidth 64
!
interface Serial1
 ip address 10.1.2.2 255.255.255.0
 ipx input-sap-filter 1000
 ipx network 1002
 clockrate 56000
!
<Output Omitted>
!
router eigrp 200
 network 10.0.0.0
!
no ip classless
!
!
line con 0
 exec-timeout 0 0
line aux 0
line vty 0 4
 login
!
end
```

Example A-21 shows the topology database of P1R3 running EIGRP, after modifying the
bandwidth on interface Serial 0 and summarizing addresses.  You will notice that for
network 10.1.1.0, only one route appears as a successor.

**Example A-21** *P1R3 in Figure A-23 EIGRP Topology Database After Applying the **bandwidth** and **ip summary-***
*address** Commands*

```
P1R3#show ip eigrp topology
IP-EIGRP Topology Table for process 200
Codes: P - Passive, A - Active, U - Update, Q - Query, R - Reply, r - Reply status
  P 10.1.3.0/24, 1 successors, FD is 40512000
          via Connected, Serial0
          via 10.1.2.1 (3193856/2681856), Serial1
  P 10.1.2.0/24, 1 successors, FD is 2169856
          via Connected, Serial1
  P 10.1.1.0/24, 1 successors, FD is 2681856
          via 10.1.2.1 (2681856/2169856), Serial1
```

# Supplement 5: BGP

This supplement covers the following BGP-related topics:

- BGP configuration output examples
- Distribute lists
- Route maps
- Communities
- Peer groups

## BGP Configuration Output Examples

This section includes configuration and **show** command output examples that result from configuring the network shown in Figure A-24. RIP is configured as the internal routing protocol within the autonomous systems, and BGP is the external protocol between the autonomous systems. BGP routes are redistributed into RIP.

**Figure A-24** *Example BGP/RIP Network*

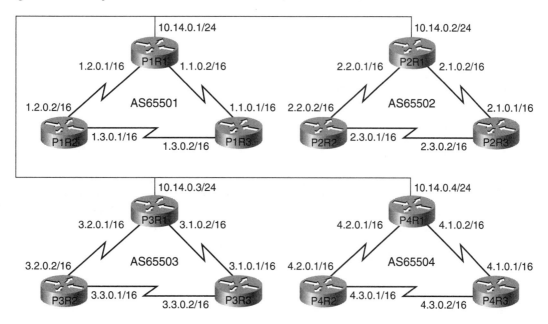

## Example of BGP/RIP Configuration for P1R1

Example A-22 shows part of the configuration for P1R1 in Figure A-24, running both RIP and BGP.

**Example A-22** *Configuration of P1R1 in Figure A-24*

```
P1R1#show run
<output omitted>
!
interface Ethernet0
 ip address 10.14.0.1 255.255.255.0
!
interface Serial0
 ip address 1.1.0.2 255.255.0.0
!

interface Serial1
 ip address 1.2.0.1 255.255.0.0
!
router rip
 network 10.0.0.0
 network 1.0.0.0
 passive-interface e0
 redistribute bgp 65501 metric 3
!
router bgp 65501
 network 1.0.0.0
 neighbor 10.14.0.2 remote-as 65502
 neighbor 10.14.0.3 remote-as 65503
 neighbor 10.14.0.4 remote-as 65504
!
no ip classless
!
<output omitted>
```

In Example A-22, the **network 10.0.0.0** command advertises network 10.0.0.0 in RIP so that internal routers can see network 10.0.0.0. The **passive-interface e0** command does not allow RIP to advertise any routes on the backbone. The **redistribute bgp 65501 metric 3** command redistributes BGP information into RIP, with a hop count of 3. The **network 1.0.0.0** command under the BGP configuration advertises network 1.0.0.0 to each of Router P1R1's three BGP neighbors.

## Example of RIP Configuration for P1R2

Example A-23 shows part of the configuration for P1R2 in Figure A-24, one of the routers running only RIP.

**Example A-23** *Configuration of P1R2 in Figure A-24*

```
P1R2#show run
<output omitted>
!
interface Ethernet0
 shutdown
!
interface Serial0
 ip address 1.2.0.2 255.255.0.0
!
interface Serial1
 ip address 1.3.0.1 255.255.0.0

!
router rip
 network 1.0.0.0
!
no ip classless
!
<output omitted>
```

In Example A-23, the **network 1.0.0.0** command starts up RIP on all interfaces that P1R2 has in network 1.0.0.0 and allows the router to advertise network 1.0.0.0.

## Example Output of **show ip route** for P1R1

Example A-24 displays the output of the **show ip route** command on P1R1 in Figure A-24.

**Example A-24** *show ip route Command Output on P1R1 in Figure A-24*

```
P1R1#show ip route

<output omitted>

     1.0.0.0/16 is subnetted, 3 subnets
C       1.1.0.0 is directly connected, Serial0
R       1.3.0.0 [120/1] via 1.2.0.2, 00:00:25, Serial1
               [120/1] via 1.1.0.1, 00:00:22, Serial0
C       1.2.0.0 is directly connected, Serial1

B    2.0.0.0/8 [20/0] via 10.14.0.2, 00:03:26
B    3.0.0.0/8 [20/0] via 10.14.0.3, 00:03:26
B    4.0.0.0/8 [20/0] via 10.14.0.4, 00:03:26
     10.0.0.0/24 is subnetted, 1 subnets
C       10.14.0.0 is directly connected, Ethernet0
P1R1#
```

The shaded lines in Example A-24 indicate the routes that P1R1 has learned from its BGP neighbors.

## Example Output of **show ip route** for P1R2

Example A-25 displays the output of the **show ip route** command on P1R2 in Figure A-24.

**Example A-25** *show ip route Command Output on P1R2 in Figure A-24*

```
P1R2#show ip route
<output omitted>

     1.0.0.0/16 is subnetted, 3 subnets
R       1.1.0.0 [120/1] via 1.2.0.1, 00:00:17, Serial0
                [120/1] via 1.3.0.2, 00:00:26, Serial1
C       1.3.0.0 is directly connected, Serial1

C       1.2.0.0 is directly connected, Serial0
R    2.0.0.0/8 [120/3] via 1.2.0.1, 00:00:17, Serial0
R    3.0.0.0/8 [120/3] via 1.2.0.1, 00:00:17, Serial0
R    4.0.0.0/8 [120/3] via 1.2.0.1, 00:00:17, Serial0
R   10.0.0.0/8 [120/1] via 1.2.0.1, 00:00:17, Serial0
P1R2#
```

The shaded lines in Example A-25 indicate the routes that P1R2 has learned from P1R1, by P1R1 redistributing them into RIP from BGP.

# Distribute Lists

This section details the configuration of distribute lists for filtering BGP information.

The **neighbor distribute-list** {*ip-address* | *peer-group-name*} **distribute-list** *access-list-number* **in** | **out** router configuration command is used to distribute BGP neighbor information as specified in an access list. The parameters for this command are detailed in Table A-24.

**Table A-24** *neighbor distribute-list Command Description*

| neighbor distribute-list Command | Description |
| --- | --- |
| *ip address* | Gives the IP address of the BGP neighbor for which routes will be filtered. |
| *peer-group-name* | Gives the name of a BGP peer group. (Peer groups are detailed in the "Peer Groups" section later in this supplement.) |

**Table A-24**  *neighbor distribute-list Command Description (Continued)*

| neighbor distribute-list Command | Description |
| --- | --- |
| *access-list-number* | Gives the number of a standard or extended access list. It can be an integer from 1 to 199. (A named access list can also be referenced.) |
| **in** | Indicates that the access list is applied to incoming advertisements from the neighbor. |
| **out** | Indicates that the access list is applied to outgoing advertisements to the neighbor. |

Example A-26 provides a configuration for Router A in Figure A-25.

**Figure A-25**  *Network for BGP Distribute List Example*

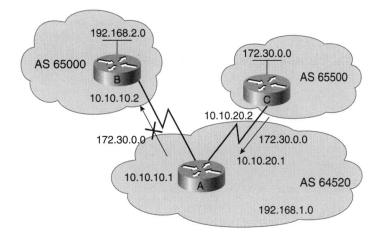

**Example A-26** *Configuration of Router A in Figure A-25*

```
RtrA(config)#router bgp 64520
RtrA(config-router)# network 192.168.1.0
RtrA(config-router)# neighbor 10.10.10.2 remote-as 65000
RtrA(config-router)# neighbor 10.10.20.2 remote-as 65500
RtrA(config-router)# neighbor 10.10.10.2 distribute-list 1 out
RtrA(config-router)# exit
RtrA(config)# access-list 1 deny 172.30.0.0 0.0.255.255
RtrA(config)# access-list 1 permit 0.0.0.0 255.255.255.255
```

In this example, Router A has two neighbors, Router B (10.10.10.2 in AS 65000) and Router C (10.10.20.2 in AS 65500). When Router A sends updates to neighbor Router B, the **neighbor distribute-list** statement specifies that it will use the **access-list 1** to determine which updates are to be sent.

Access list 1 specifies that any route starting with 172.30—in this case, the route to 172.30.0.0—should not be sent (it is denied in the access list). All other routes will be sent to Router B. (Recall that because access lists have an implicit deny any at the end, the permit statement is required in the access list for the other routes to be sent.)

As shown in Example A-26, a standard IP access list can be used to control the sending of updates about a specific network number. However, if you need to control updates about subnets and supernets of a network with a distribute list, extended access lists would be required.

## Extended Access List Use in a Distribute List

When an IP extended access list is used with a distribute list, the parameters have different meanings than when the extended access list is used in other ways. The syntax of the IP extended access list is the same as usual, with a source address and wildcard, and a destination address and wildcard. However, the meanings of these parameters are different.

The *source* parameters of the extended access list are used to indicate the *address of the network* whose updates are to be permitted or denied. The *destination* parameters of the extended access list are used to indicate the *subnet mask of that network*.

The *wildcard* parameters indicate, for the network and subnet mask, which bits are relevant. Network and subnet mask bits corresponding to wildcard bits set to 1 are ignored during comparisons, and network and subnet mask bits corresponding to wildcard bits set to 0 are used in comparisons.

The following example shows an extended access list:

```
access-list 101 ip permit 172.0.0.0 0.255.255.255 255.0.0.0 0.0.0.0
```

The interpretation of the previous **access-list** when used with a **neighbor distribute-list** command is to permit only a route to network 172.0.0.0 255.0.0.0. Therefore, the list would allow only the supernet 172.0.0.0/8 to be advertised. For example, assume that Router A had routes to networks 172.20.0.0/16 and 172.30.0.0/16, and also had an aggregated route to 172.0.0.0/8. The use of this **access-list** would allow only the supernet 172.0.0.0/8 to be advertised; networks 172.20.0.0/16 and 172.30.0.0/16 would not be advertised.

# Route Maps

Route maps were introduced in Chapter 8. They are reviewed here in the context of BGP and for use in communities, discussed in the next section.

A route map is a method used to control and modify routing information. This is done by defining conditions for redistributing routes from one routing protocol to another or controlling routing information when injected into and out of BGP.

Route maps are complex access lists that allow some conditions to be tested against the route in question using **match** commands. If the conditions match, some actions can be taken to modify the route. These actions are specified by **set** commands.

If the **match** criteria are met and the route map specifies **permit**, then the routes will be controlled as specified by the **set** actions, and the rest of the route map list will be ignored.

If the **match** criteria are met and the route map specifies **deny**, then the routes will not be controlled and the rest of the route-map list will be ignored.

If all sequences in the list are checked without a match, then the route will not be accepted nor forwarded (this is the implicit **deny any** at the end of the route map).

**match** commands include the following:

- **match as-path**
- **match community**
- **match clns**
- **match interface**
- **match ip address**
- **match ip next-hop**
- **match ip route-source**
- **match metric**
- **match route-type**
- **match tag**

**set** commands include the following:

- **set as-path**
- **set clns**
- **set automatic-tag**
- **set community**
- **set interface**
- **set default interface**
- **set ip default next-hop**
- **set level**
- **set local-preference**
- **set metric**
- **set metric-type**
- **set next-hop**

- **set origin**
- **set tag**
- **set weight**

For example, the **set local-preference** *value* route map command is used to specify a preference value for the autonomous system path. The *value* is the local preference value from 0 to 4,294,967,295; a higher value is more preferred.

---

**NOTE**    A prefix list can be used as an alternative to an access list in the **match {ip address | next-hop | route-source}** *access-list* command of a route map. The configuration of prefix lists and access lists are mutually exclusive within the same sequence of a route map.

---

## Configuring Route Maps for BGP Updates

The **neighbor** {*ip-address* | *peer-group-name*} **route-map** *map-name* {**in** | **out**} router configuration command is used to apply a route map to incoming or outgoing BGP routes, as detailed in Table A-25.

**Table A-25**    *neighbor route-map Command Description*

| neighbor route-map Command | Description |
|---|---|
| *ip-address* | Gives the IP address of the BGP neighbor for which routes will be filtered. |
| *peer-group-name* | Gives the name of a BGP peer group. (Peer groups are detailed in the "Peer Groups" section, later in this supplement.) |
| *map-name* | Gives the name of the route map to apply. |
| **in** | Apply route map to incoming routes from the neighbor. |
| **out** | Apply route map to outgoing routes to the neighbor. |

---

**NOTE**    When used for filtering BGP updates, route maps *cannot* be used to filter inbound updates when using a match on the IP address. Filtering outbound updates is permitted.

---

Example A-27 shows BGP running on a router. A route map named changemetric is being used when routes are sent out to neighbor 172.20.1.1.

**Example A-27** *Configuration Filtering BGP Updates Using a Route Map*

```
RtrA(config)# router bgp 64520
RtrA(config-router)# neighbor 172.20.1.1 route-map changemetric out
RtrA(config)# route-map changemetric permit 10
RtrA(config-route-map)# match ip address 1
RtrA(config-route-map)# set metric 2
RtrA(config-route-map)# exit
RtrA(config)# route-map changemetric permit 20
RtrA(config-route-map)# set metric 5
RtrA(config-route-map)# exit
RtrA(config)# access-list 1 permit 172.16.0.0 0.0.255.255
```

**NOTE**    Other **router bgp** configuration commands have been omitted from the commands in Example A-27.

In this example, two instances of changemetric have been defined. Sequence number 10 will be checked first. If a route's IP address matches access list 1—in other words, if the IP address starts with 172.16—the route will have its metric (MED) set to 2, and the rest of the list will be ignored. If there is no match, then sequence number 20 will be checked. Because there is no match statement in this instance, the metric (MED) on all other routes will be set to 5.

**NOTE**    It is always very important to plan what will happen to routes that do not match any of the route map instances because they will be dropped by default.

# Communities

This section discusses BGP communities and how to configure them.

As discussed in Chapter 6, "Configuring Basic Border Gateway Protocol," BGP communities are another way to filter incoming or outgoing BGP routes. Distribute lists and prefix lists (discussed in the previous section in this supplement, "Distribute Lists," and in Chapter 7, "Implementing BGP in Scalable Networks," respectively) would be cumbersome to configure for a large network with a complex routing policy. For example, individual neighbor statements and access lists or prefix lists would need to be configured for each neighbor on each router that was involved in the policy.

The BGP communities function allows routers to tag routes with an indicator (the *community*) and allows other routers to make decisions (filter) based upon that tag. BGP communities are used for destinations (routes) that share some common properties and that therefore share common policies; routers, therefore, act on the community rather than on individual routes. Communities are not restricted to one network or one autonomous system (AS), and they have no physical boundaries.

If a router does not understand the concept of communities, it will pass it on to the next router. However, if the router does understand the concept, it must be configured to propagate the community; otherwise, communities are dropped by default.

## Community Attribute

The community attribute is an optional transitive attribute that can have a value in the range 0 to 4,294,967,200. Each network can be a member of more than one community.

The community attribute is a 32-bit number, with the upper 16 bits indicating the AS number of the AS that defined the community. The lower 16 bits are the community number and have local significance. The community value can be entered as one decimal number or in the format *AS:nn* (where *AS* is the AS number and *nn* is the lower 16-bit local number). The community value is displayed as one decimal number by default.

## Setting and Sending Communities Configuration

Route maps can be used to set the community attributes.

The **set community** {*community-number* [**additive**]} | **none** route map configuration command is used within a route map to set the BGP communities attribute, as described in Table A-26.

**Table A-26** *set community Command Description*

| set community Command | Description |
| --- | --- |
| *community-number* | Is the community number; values are 1 to 4,294,967,200. |
| **additive** | (Optional) Specifies that the community is to be added to the already existing communities. |
| **none** | Removes the community attribute from the prefixes that pass the route map. |

Predefined well-known community numbers that can be used in the **set community** command are as follows:

- **no-export**—Do not advertise to EBGP peers.
- **no-advertise**—Do not advertise this route to any peer.
- **local-AS**—Do not send outside local AS.

| NOTE | The **set community** command is used along with the **neighbor route-map** command to apply the route map to updates. |
|---|---|

The **neighbor** {*ip-address* | *peer-group-name*} **send-community** router configuration command is used to specify that the BGP communities attribute should be sent to a BGP neighbor. This command is detailed in Table A-27.

**Table A-27**  *neighbor send-community Command Description*

| neighbor send-community Command | Description |
|---|---|
| *ip address* | IP address of the BGP neighbor to which the communities attribute will be sent. |
| *peer-group-name* | Name of a BGP peer group. (Peer groups are detailed in the "Peer Groups" section, later in this supplement.) |

By default, the communities attribute is not sent to any neighbor (communities are stripped in outgoing BGP updates).

In the example shown in Figure A-26, Router C is sending BGP updates to Router A, but it does not want Router A to propagate these routes to Router B.

**Figure A-26**  *Network for BGP Communities Example*

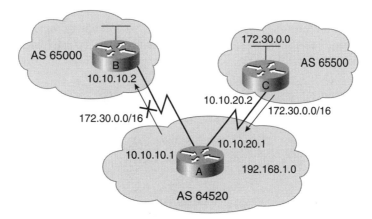

The configuration for Router C in this example is provided in Example A-28. Router C sets the community attribute in the BGP routes that it is advertising to Router A. The **no-export**

community attribute is used to indicate that Router A should not send the routes to its external BGP peers.

**Example A-28** *Configuration of Router C in Figure A-26*

```
router bgp 65500
  network 172.30.0.0
  neighbor 10.10.20.1 remote-as 64520
  neighbor 10.10.20.1 send-community
  neighbor 10.10.20.1 route-map SETCOMM out
!
route-map SETCOMM permit 10
  match ip address 1
  set community no-export
!
access-list 1 permit 0.0.0.0 255.255.255.255
```

In this example, Router C has one neighbor, 10.10.20.1 (Router A). When communicating with Router A, the community attribute is sent, as specified by the **neighbor send-community** command. The route map SETCOMM is used when sending routes to Router A, to set the community attribute. Any route that matches **access-list 1** will have the community attribute set to **no-export**. Access list 1 permits any routes; therefore, all routes will have the community attribute set to **no-export**.

In this example, Router A will receive all of Router C's routes but will not pass them on to Router B.

## Using Communities Configuration

The **ip community-list** *community-list-number* **permit | deny** *community-number* global configuration command is used to create a community list for BGP and to control access to it, as described in Table A-28.

**Table A-28** *ip community-list Command Description*

| ip community-list Command | Description |
| --- | --- |
| *community-list-number* | Community list number, in the range 1 to 99 |
| *community-number* | Community number, configured by a **set community** command |

Some predefined well-known community numbers that can be used with the **ip community-list** command are as follows:

- **no-export**—Do not advertise to EBGP peers.
- **no-advertise**—Do not advertise this route to any peer.

- **local-AS**—Do not send outside local AS.

- **internet**—Advertise this route to the Internet community and any router that belongs to it.

The **match community** *community-list-number* [**exact**] route map configuration command is used to match a BGP community attribute to a value in a community list, as described in Table A-29.

**Table A-29**   *match community Command Description*

| match community Command | Description |
|---|---|
| *community-list-number* | Community list number, in the range 1 to 99, that will be used to compare the community attribute. |
| **exact** | (Optional) Indicates that an exact match is required. All the communities and only those communities in the community list must be present in the community attribute. |

**NOTE**   The **match community** command appears in the documentation as the **match community-list** command; however, only **match community** actually works on the routers.

In the example shown in Figure A-27, Router C is sending BGP updates to Router A. Router A will set the weight of these routes based on the community value set by Router C.

**Figure A-27** *Network for BGP Communities Example Using Weight*

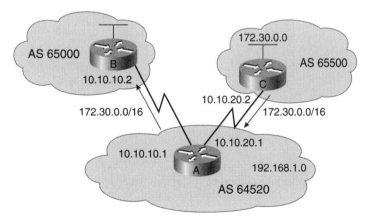

The configuration for Router C in Figure A-27 is shown in Example A-29. Router C has one neighbor, 10.10.20.1 (Router A).

**Example A-29** *Configuration of Router C in Figure A-27*

```
router bgp 65500
  network 172.30.0.0
  neighbor 10.10.20.1 remote-as 64520
  neighbor 10.10.20.1 send-community
  neighbor 10.10.20.1 route-map SETCOMM out
!
route-map SETCOMM permit 10
  match ip address 1
  set community 100 additive
!
access-list 1 permit 0.0.0.0 255.255.255.255
```

In this example, the community attribute will be sent to Router A, as specified by the **neighbor send-community** command. The route map SETCOMM is used when sending routes to Router A to set the community attribute. Any route that matches access-list 1 will have community 100 added to the existing communities in the community attribute of the route. In this example, access list 1 permits any routes; therefore, all routes will have 100 added to the list of communities. If the **additive** keyword in the **set community** command was not set, 100 will replace any old community that already exits; because the keyword **additive** is used, the 100 will be added to the list of communities that the route is part of.

The configuration for Router A in Figure A-27 is shown in Example A-30.

**Example A-30** *Configuration of Router A in Figure A-27*

```
router bgp 64520
  neighbor 10.10.20.2 remote-as 65500
  neighbor 10.10.20.2 route-map CHKCOMM in
!
route-map CHKCOMM permit 10
  match community 1
  set weight 20
route-map CHKCOMM permit 20
  match community 2
!
ip community-list 1 permit 100
ip community-list 2 permit internet
```

**NOTE**   Other **router bgp** configuration commands for Router A are not shown in Example A-30.

In this example, Router A has a neighbor, 10.10.20.2 (Router C). The route map CHKCOMM is used when receiving routes from Router C to check the community attribute. Any route whose community attribute matches community list 1 will have its weight attribute set to 20. Community list 1 permits routes with a community attribute of 100; therefore, all routes from Router C (which all have 100 in their list of communities) will have their weight set to 20.

In this example, any route that did not match community list 1 would be checked against community list 2. Any route matching community list 2 would be permitted but would not have any of its attributes changed. Community list 2 specifies the **internet** keyword, which means all routes.

The example output shown in Example A-31 is from Router A in Figure A-27. The output shows the details about the route 172.30.0.0 from Router C, including that its community attribute is 100 and its weight attribute is now 20.

**Example A-31** *Output from Router A in Figure A-27*

```
RtrA #show ip bgp 172.30.0.0/16
BGP routing table entry for 172.30.0.0/16, version 2
Paths: (1 available, best #1)
  Advertised to non peer-group peers:
    10.10.10.2
  65500
    10.10.20.2 from 10.10.20.2 (172.30.0.1)
      Origin IGP, metric 0, localpref 100, weight 20, valid, external, best, ref 2
      Community: 100
```

## Peer Groups

This section discusses peer groups and how to configure them.

In BGP, many neighbors often are configured with the same update policies (that is, the same outbound route maps, distribute lists, filter lists, update source, and so on). On Cisco routers, neighbors with the same update policies can be grouped into peer groups to simplify configuration and, more importantly, to make updating more efficient. When you have many peers, this approach is highly recommended.

A BGP peer group is a group of BGP neighbors with the same update policies. Instead of separately defining the same policies for each neighbor, a peer group can be defined with these policies assigned to the peer group. Individual neighbors are then made members of the peer group.

Members of the peer group inherit all the configuration options of the peer group. Members can also be configured to override these options if these options do not affect outbound updates; in other words, only options that affect the inbound updates can be overridden.

Peer groups are useful to simplify configurations when many neighbors have the same policy. They are also more efficient because updates are generated only once per peer group rather than once for each neighbor.

The peer group name is local only to the router it is configured on; it is not passed to any other router.

## Peer Group Configuration

The **neighbor** *peer-group-name* **peer-group** router configuration command is used to create a BGP peer group. The *peer-group-name* is the name of the BGP peer group to be created.

Another syntax of the **neighbor peer-group** command is used to assign neighbors as part of the group; use the **neighbor** *ip-address* **peer-group** *peer-group-name* router configuration command. The details of this command are shown in Table A-30.

**Table A-30** *neighbor peer-group Command Description*

| neighbor peer-group Command | Description |
| --- | --- |
| *ip-address* | IP address of the neighbor that is to be assigned as a member of the peer group |
| *peer-group-name* | Name of the BGP peer group |

The **clear ip bgp peer-group** *peer-group-name* EXEC command is used to clear the BGP connections for all members of a BGP peer group. The *peer-group-name* is the name of the BGP peer group for which connections are to be cleared.

**NOTE** The Cisco documentation says that the **clear ip bgp peer-group** command is used to *remove* all the members of a BGP peer group; however, it actually clears the connections.

## Peer Group Example

In the example shown in Figure A-28, Router A has two internal neighbors, routers D and E, and two external neighbors, routers B and C. The routing policies for routers D and E are the same, and the routing policies for routers B and C are the same.

**Figure A-28** *Network for BGP Peer Group Example*

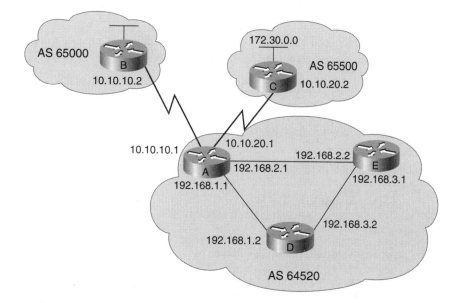

Router A is configured with two peer groups, one for internal neighbors and one for external neighbors, rather than individual neighbor configurations. Example A-32 shows part of the configuration for Router A, for the internal neighbors.

**Example A-32** *Router A in Figure A-28 Configuration for Internal Neighbors*

```
router bgp 64520
  neighbor INTERNALMAP peer-group
  neighbor INTERNALMAP remote-as 64520
  neighbor INTERNALMAP prefix-list PREINTIN in
  neighbor INTERNALMAP prefix-list PREINTOUT out
  neighbor INTERNALMAP route-map SETINTERNAL out
  neighbor 192.168.2.2 peer-group INTERNALMAP
  neighbor 192.168.1.2 peer-group INTERNALMAP
  neighbor 192.168.2.2 prefix-list JUST2 in
```

This configuration creates a peer group called INTERNALMAP. All members of this peer group are in AS 64520. A prefix list called PREINTIN will be applied to all routes from members of this peer group, and a prefix list called PREINTOUT will be applied to all routes going to members of this peer group. A route map called SETINTERNAL will be applied to all routes going to members of this peer group.

Router E (192.168.2.2) and Router D (192.168.1.2) are members of the peer group INTERNALMAP.

A prefix list called JUST2 will be applied to all routes from Router E (192.168.2.2). Recall that you can override only peer group options that affect inbound updates.

Example A-33 shows part of the configuration for Router A in Figure A-28, for the external neighbors.

**Example A-33** *Router A in Figure A-28 Configuration for External Neighbors*

```
router bgp 64520
  neighbor EXTERNALMAP peer-group
  neighbor EXTERNALMAP prefix-list PREEXTIN in
  neighbor EXTERNALMAP prefix-list PREEXTOUT out
  neighbor EXTERNALMAP route-map SETEXTERNAL out
  neighbor 10.10.10.2 remote-as 65000
  neighbor 10.10.10.2 peer-group EXTERNALMAP
  neighbor 10.10.10.2 prefix-list JUSTEXT2 in
  neighbor 10.10.20.2 remote-as 65500
  neighbor 10.10.20.2 peer-group EXTERNALMAP
```

This configuration creates a peer group called EXTERNALMAP. A prefix list called PREEXTIN will be applied to all routes from members of this peer group, and a prefix list called PREEXTOUT will be applied to all routes going to members of this peer group. A route map called SETEXTERNAL will be applied to all routes going to members of this peer group.

Router B (10.10.10.2) is in AS 65000 and is a member of the peer group EXTERNALMAP. Router C (10.10.20.2) is in AS 65500 and is a member of the peer group EXTERNALMAP.

A prefix list called JUSTEXT2 will be applied to all routes from Router B (10.10.10.2). Recall that you can override only peer group options that affect inbound updates.

# Supplement 6: Route Optimization

This supplement reviews the following topics:

*   Examples of redistribution in a nonredundant configuration
*   Miscellaneous redistribution configuration examples

## Examples of Redistribution in a Nonredundant Configuration

This section includes configuration and **show** command output examples that result from configuring the network shown in Figure A-29. The addresses for this configuration are also shown in Figure A-29; protocols for the example are shown in Figure A-30.

**Figure A-29** *Addressing for Redistribution Configuration Example*

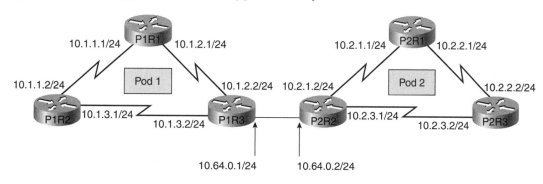

**Figure A-30** *Example Nonredundant Redistribution Configuration*

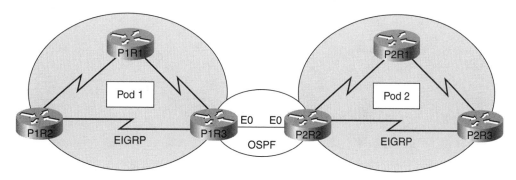

## Example of Redistribution Between EIGRP and OSPF

Example A-34 shows the configuration output for P1R3, an ASBR supporting EIGRP and OSPF.

**Example A-34** *ASBR in Figures A-29 and A-30, Redistributing Between EIGRP and OSPF*

```
P1R3#show run
Building configuration...
Current configuration:
!
version 11.2
hostname P1R3
!
enable password san-fran
!
no ip domain-lookup
ipx routing 0000.0c01.3333
ipx maximum-paths 2
!
interface Loopback0
 no ip address
 ipx network 1013
!
interface Ethernet0
ip address 10.64.0.1 255.255.255.0
!
interface Serial0
ip address 10.1.3.2 255.255.255.0
bandwidth 64
ipx input-sap-filter 1000
ipx network 1003
!
interface Serial1
ip address 10.1.2.2 255.255.255.0
ipx input-sap-filter 1000
ipx network 1002
clockrate 56000
<Output Omitted>
!
router eigrp 200

redistribute ospf 300 metric 10000 100 255 1 1500
passive-interface Ethernet0
network 10.0.0.0
!
router ospf 300

redistribute eigrp 200 subnets
network 10.64.0.0 0.0.255.255 area 0
!
no ip classless
```

**Example A-34** *ASBR in Figures A-29 and A-30, Redistributing Between EIGRP and OSPF (Continued)*

```
line con 0
exec-timeout 20 0
password cisco
!
line aux 0
line vty 0 4
password cisco
!
end
```

In Example A-34, EIGRP in AS 200 is configured for all interfaces in network 10.0.0.0. The **passive-interface** command is used to disable EIGRP on the ethernet (because OSPF will be running there). Routes from OSPF are redistributed into EIGRP with the **redistribute** command, using the defined metrics. OSPF is configured to run on the ethernet 0 interface, in area 0. Routes from EIGRP are redistributed into EIGRP; the **subnets** keyword is included so that subnetted routes (in this case, subnets of network 10.0.0.0) will be redistributed. If this keyword were omitted, no routes would be redistributed from OSPF to EIGRP in this example.

Example A-35 shows outputs verifying that external routes are learned by OSPF and EIGRP, respectively, on an ASBR.

**Example A-35** *OSPF and EIGRP Topology Databases of P1R3 in Figures A-29 and A-30*

```
P1R3#show ip ospf database

        OSPF Router with ID (10.64.0.1) (Process ID 300)

                Router Link States (Area 0)

Link ID        ADV Router      Age       Seq#        Checksum Link count
10.64.0.1      10.64.0.1       280       0x80000005 0x767F    1
10.64.0.2      10.64.0.2       274       0x80000004 0x767D    1

                Net Link States (Area 0)

Link ID        ADV Router      Age       Seq#        Checksum

10.64.0.2      10.64.0.2       274       0x80000002 0x7791

                Type-5 AS External Link States

Link ID        ADV Router      Age       Seq#        Checksum Tag
10.1.1.0       10.64.0.1       202       0x80000002 0xE95E    0
10.1.2.0       10.64.0.1       202       0x80000002 0xDE68    0
10.1.3.0       10.64.0.1       202       0x80000002 0xD372    0
10.2.1.0       10.64.0.2       1686      0x80000001 0xD96D    0
10.2.2.0       10.64.0.2       1686      0x80000001 0xCE77    0
```

*continues*

**Example A-35** *OSPF and EIGRP Topology Databases of P1R3 in Figures A-29 and A-30 (Continued)*

```
10.2.3.0        10.64.0.2       1686       0x80000001 0xC381    0
10.64.0.0       10.64.0.1       204        0x80000002 0xFD0C    0
10.64.0.0       10.64.0.2       1688       0x80000001 0xF910    0
P1R3#


P1R3#show ip eigrp topology
IP-EIGRP Topology Table for process 200
Codes: P - Passive, A - Active, U - Update, Q - Query, R - Reply,
       r - Reply status
P 10.1.3.0/24, 1 successors, FD is 40512000
          via Connected, Serial0
          via 10.1.2.1 (3193856/2681856), Serial1
P 10.2.1.0/24, 1 successors, FD is 281600
          via Redistributed (281600/0)
P 10.1.2.0/24, 1 successors, FD is 2169856
          via Connected, Serial
P 10.2.2.0/24, 1 successors, FD is 281600
          via Redistributed (281600/0)
P 10.1.1.0/24, 1 successors, FD is 2681856
          via 10.1.2.1 (2681856/2169856), Serial1
P 10.2.3.0/24, 1 successors, FD is 281600
          via Redistributed (281600/0)
P 10.64.0.0/24, 1 successors, FD is 281600
          via Connected, Ethernet0
```

In Example A-35, you can see from the **show ip ospf database** command output that P1R3 learns external routes (type 5 LSAs) in OSPF. Note that subnetted networks are included. EIGRP also learns external routes, shown as redistributed routes in the **show ip eigrp topology** command output.

# Miscellaneous Redistribution Configuration Examples

This section presents examples of one-way redistribution.

## IGRP Redistribution Example

Cisco IOS software supports multiple IGRP autonomous systems. Each autonomous system maintains its own routing database. You can redistribute routing information among these routing databases. Table A-31 describes some of the commands seen in Example A-36. Refer to Figure A-31 for the topology used in Example A-36.

**Figure A-31**  *Figure A-31 IGRP Redistribution Configuration Example*

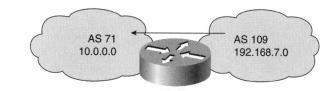

**Example A-36** *Routes Redistributed from AS 109 into AS 71 in Figure A-31*

```
router igrp 71
  redistribute igrp 109
  distribute-list 3 out igrp 109
access-list 3 permit 192.168.7.0 0.0.0.255
```

**Table A-31**    *Redistribution Commands in Example A-36*

| Command | Description |
|---|---|
| **redistribute igrp 109** | Redistributes routes from IGRP 109 into IGRP 71. |
| **distribute list 3 out igrp 109** | Uses access list 3 to define which routes will be redistributed from IGRP 109 into IGRP 71. |
| **3** | Redistributes per access list 3. |
| **out** | Applies the access list to outgoing routing updates. |
| **igrp 109** | Identifies the IGRP routing process to filter. |
| **access-list 3 permit 192.168.7.0 0.0.0.255** | Permits routes from only network 192.168.7.0. |

In Example A-36, only routing updates from the 192.168.7.0 network are redistributed into autonomous system 71. Updates from other networks are denied.

## RIP/OSPF Redistribution Example

In Example A-37 and Figure A-32, there is an additional path connecting the RIP clouds. These paths, or "back doors," frequently exist, allowing the potential for feedback loops. You can use access lists to determine the routes that are advertised and accepted by each router.

**Figure A-32** *Blocking Paths to Avoid Looping*

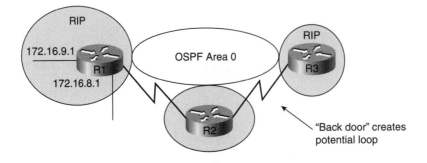

**Example A-37** *Avoiding Loops While Redistributing on Router R1 in Figure A-32*

```
hostname R1
!
router ospf 109
  network 172.16.62.0 0.0.0.255 area 0
  network 172.16.63.0 0.0.0.255 area 0
  redistribute rip subnets metric-type 1 metric 20
  distribute-list 11 out rip

access-list 11 permit 172.16.8.0 0.0.7.255
```

For example, access list 11 in the configuration file for Router R1 allows OSPF to redistribute information learned from RIP only for networks 172.16.8.0 through 172.16.15.0. These commands prevent Router R1 from advertising networks in other RIP domains onto the OSPF backbone, thereby preventing other boundary routers from using false information and forming a loop. You would configure similar access lists on R2 and R3.

## Redistribution Example Using Default Metric

In Figure A-33 and Example A-38, the router is redistributing IP RIP and EIGRP routes. The 192.168.5.0 network is redistributed to the IP RIP network with a metric of three hops. EIGRP in autonomous system 300 learns routes from IP RIP.

**Figure A-33** *Redistributing RIP and EIGRP*

**Example A-38** *Redistribution Using Default Metric in Figure A-33*

```
router rip
    network 172.16.0.0
    redistribute eigrp 300
    default-metric 3
router eigrp 300
    network 192.168.5.0
    redistribute rip
    default-metric 56 2000 255 1 1500
```

Table A-32 describes some of the commands seen in Example A-38.

**Table A-32** *Redistribution Commands in Example A-38*

| Command | Description |
|---|---|
| **redistribute eigrp 300** | Enables redistribution of routes learned from EIGRP autonomous system 300 into the IP RIP network. |
| **default-metric 3** | Specifies that EIGRP-learned routes are three hops away. |
| **redistribute rip** | Enables redistribution of routes learned from the IP RIP network into EIGRP autonomous system 300. |
| **default-metric 56 2000 255 1 1500** | Indicates that the RIP-derived network is being redistributed with the following EIGRP metric values: |
| **56** | Bandwidth is 56 kbps. |
| **2000** | Delay is 2000 tens of microseconds. |
| **255** | Reliability is 100 percent (255 of 255). |
| **1** | Loading is less than 1 percent (1 of 255). |
| **1500** | MTU is 1500 bytes. |

## Redistribution Example Using Filtering

Figure A-34 and Example A-39 provide an example of a redistribution filtering.

**Figure A-34** *Redistribution Using Filtering and Default Metric*

**Example A-39** *R1 in Figure A-34 Hides Network 10.0.0.0 Using Redistribution Filtering*

```
hostname R1
!
router rip
  network 192.168.5.0
  redistribute eigrp 1
  default-metric 3
  distribute-list 7 out eigrp 1
!
router eigrp 1
  network 172.16.0.0
  redistribute rip
  default-metric 56 2000 255 1 1500
!
access-list 7 deny 10.0.0.0 0.255.255.255
access-list 7 permit  0.0.0.0 255.255.255.255
```

Table A-33 describes some of the commands seen in Example A-39.

**Table A-33** *R6 Redistribution Filtering Commands in Example A-39*

| Command | Description |
| --- | --- |
| **redistribute eigrp 1** | Enables routes learned from EIGRP autonomous system 1 to be redistributed into IP RIP. |
| **default-metric 3** | Specifies that all routes learned from EIGRP will be advertised by RIP as reachable in three hops. |
| **distribute-list 7 out eigrp 1** | Defines that routes defined by access-list 7 leaving the EIGRP process will be filtered before being given to the RIP process. |

## Redistribution Example Using Filtering and Default Metric

Figure A-35 and Example A-40 provide an example of a redistribution filtering and default metric.

**Figure A-35** *Figure A-35 Redistribution Filtering and Default Metric*

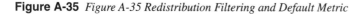
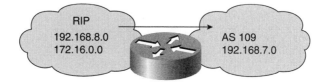

**Example A-40** *Redistributing RIP and IGRP*

```
router rip
  network 192.168.8.0
  network 172.16.0.0
  redistribute igrp 109
  default-metric 4
  distribute-list 11 out igrp 109
!
router igrp 109
  network 192.168.7.0
  redistribute rip
  default-metric 10000 100 255 1 1500
  distribute-list 10 out rip

access-list 10 permit 172.16.0.0 0.0.255.255
access-list 11 permit 192.168.7.0 0.0.0.255
```

Table A-34 describes some of the commands seen in Example A-40.

**Table A-34** *Redistribution and Route Filtering Commands in Example A-40*

| Command | Description |
|---|---|
| **redistribute igrp 109** | Redistributes IGRP routes into RIP. |
| **default-metric 4** | Sets the metric for IGRP-derived routes to four hops. |
| **redistribute rip** | Redistributes RIP routes into IGRP. |
| **default-metric** | Sets the metric for IGRP for all redistributed routes. |
| **10000** | Sets the minimum bandwidth of the route to 10,000 kbps. |
| **100** | Sets the delay to 100 tens of microseconds. |
| **255** | Sets the reliability, in this case, to the maximum. |
| **1** | Sets the loading to 1. |
| **1500** | Sets the MTU to 1500 bytes. |
| **distribute list 10 out rip** | Uses access list 10 to limit updates going out of RIP into IGRP. |

# APPENDIX B

# Router Password Recovery Procedure

This appendix contains the procedure for password recovery on Cisco routers.

**NOTE**     Two different types of commands are used to perform password recovery, depending on the type of router. For example, the 2500 series routers use the more cryptic commands shown in this appendix, while the 1600 series routers use the **confreg** utility. The following lists categorize routers by password recovery. Current listings can be found on CCO at www.cisco.com/warp/customer/474/index.shtml.

According to the Cisco documentation (reference: www.cisco.com/warp/customer/474/index.shtml) the following Cisco products use the more cryptic commands:

Cisco 2000
Cisco 2500
Cisco 3000
Cisco 4000
Cisco AccessPro
Cisco 7000 (RP)
Cisco AGS
Cisco IGS
Cisco STS-10x

The following Cisco products use the **confreg** utility:

| | |
|---|---|
| Cisco 1003 | Cisco 7200 |
| Cisco 1004 | Cisco uBR7200 |
| Cisco 1005 | Cisco 7500 |
| Cisco 1600 | Cisco 12000 |
| Cisco 1700 | Cisco LS1010 |
| Cisco 2600 | Catalyst 5500 (RSM) |
| Cisco 3600 | Catalyst 8510-CSR |
| Cisco 4500 | Catalyst 8510-MSR |
| Cisco 4700 | Catalyst 8540-CSR |
| Cisco AS5x00 | Catalyst 8540-MSR |
| Cisco 6x00 | Cisco VG200 Analog Gateway |
| Cisco 7000 (RSP7000) | Cisco MC3810 |
| Cisco 7100 | |

Follow these steps to recover passwords on Cisco routers:

**Step 1**   To enter ROM Monitor mode, power cycle the router; within 60 seconds after the router comes up, press the Break key. (On a PC, the Break key is probably a combination: <Ctrl>+<Break>.)

**Step 2**   Enter the letter **o** or the **e/s 2000002** command to read the original value of the configuration register. (The configuration register default value is 0x2102.) When the configuration register value is displayed, press the Esc key to return to the prompt.

On some routers (see previous listings), you must use the confreg utility to read the configuration register settings. When you use this utility, you won't actually see the value of the configuration register, but you will see what settings are enabled; note what they are.

Set bit 6 in the configuration register (along with the original bit settings) to ignore NVRAM on boot up, using the **o/r** command. (Refer to the "Configuration Register Bits" sidebar later in this appendix for a description of configuration register bits.)

For example, if the original configuration register value was 0x2102, then setting bit 6 means setting a value of 0x2142 for the configuration register. In this example, to set the configuration register, use the following command:

```
>o/r 0x2142
```

On some routers, you must use the confreg utility to set the configuration register. In the utility, enter **y** when asked if you want to enable the system to ignore system configuration information. Keep all other settings the same as you noted in Step 2.

**Step 3**   Initialize and reboot the router, using the **i** command. On some routers, you must use the **boot** command to initialize and reboot the router.

**Step 4**   When the router boots, it will go into setup mode. Answer **no** to all questions.

**Step 5**   When you are back at the Router prompt, enter privileged mode using the following command:

```
Router>enable
```

**Step 6**    Load the configuration that is in NVRAM into active memory using the following command:

```
Router#copy startup-config running-config
```

On releases of the Cisco IOS prior to release 10.3, use the following command:

```
Router#config memory
```

Remember that this operation is a merge, so all interfaces will be shut down at this point because they were shut down when the router loaded without a configuration.

**Step 7**    Enable all interfaces that should be enabled using the following commands (where *x/y* represents the appropriate interface name):

```
hostname#config term
hostname(config)#interface x/y
hostname(config-if)#no shutdown
```

For example, to enable the Ethernet 0 interface, use the following commands:

```
hostname#config term
hostname(config)#interface e0
hostname(config-if)#no shutdown
```

**Step 8**    Restore the original configuration register value as follows, where *0xvalue* is the original configuration value:

```
hostname#config term
hostname(config)#config-register 0xvalue
```

For example, to restore the configuration value to 0x2102, use the following commands:

```
hostname#config term
hostname(config)#config-register 0x2102
```

**Step 9**    To recover or record lost passwords, display the running configuration in RAM using the following command:

```
hostname#show running-config
```

On releases of the Cisco IOS prior to release 10.3, use the following command:

```
hostname#write term
```

To change passwords, use the following commands, inserting the appropriate new passwords (you must use this method if passwords are encrypted):

```
hostname#config term
hostname(config)#enable secret newpassword
hostname(config)#enable password newpassword
hostname(config)#line con 0
hostname(config-line)#login
hostname(config-line)#password newpassword
```

**Step 10** Save your new configuration into NVRAM using the following command:

```
hostname#copy running-config startup-config
```

On releases of the Cisco IOS prior to release 10.3, use the following command:

```
hostname#write memory
```

### Configuration Register Bits

The configuration register is a 16-bit register. Table B-1 describes the meaning of these bits (source: Cisco Installation and Maintenance of Cisco Routers [IMCR] course student material).

**Table B-1**  *Configuration Register Bit Meanings*

| Bit Number(s) | Hex Value | Meaning |
| --- | --- | --- |
| 0 to 3 | 0x0000 to 0x000f | Boot field |
| 4 | 0x0010 | Fast Boot, 1 = bypass bootstrap image load, boot IOS indicated by boot system |
| 5 | 0x0020 | On 3600, set baud rate up to 115,200 bps |
| 6 | 0x0040 | 1 = ignore startup configuration file |
| 7 | 0x0080 | OEM bit, 1 = disable display of Cisco banner on startup |
| 8 | 0x0100 | 1 = break key disabled after first 60 seconds |

**Table B-1**    *Configuration Register Bit Meanings (Continued)*

| Bit Number(s) | Hex Value | Meaning |
| --- | --- | --- |
| 9 | 0x0200 | Controls the secondary bootstrap program function used for system debugging |
| 10 | 0x0400 | Netboot broadcast format, 1 = use all 0s broadcast address |
| 11 and 12 | 0x0800 to 0x1000 | Console baud rate, 00 = 9600 bps |
| 13 | 0x2000 | Response to netboot failure, 1 = boot from ROM after five failures |
| 14 | 0x4000 | Netboot subnet broadcast, 1 = use subnet broadcast address |
| 15 | 0x8000 | Enable diagnostic messages, 1 = enabled and use test-system configuration |

This appendix is organized in the following sections:

- General Commands
- Comparison of Configuration File Commands
- General Configuration Commands
- General Interface Configuration Commands
- General IP Commands
- IP Configuration Commands
- General IPX Commands
- IPX Configuration Commands
- General AppleTalk Commands
- AppleTalk Configuration Commands
- General WAN Commands
- WAN Configuration Commands

# Summary of ICND Router Commands

This appendix contains a listing of some of the Cisco router IOS commands you might find in the Cisco Press *Interconnecting Cisco Network Devices* (ICND) coursebook, organized in various categories.

| | |
|---|---|
| **NOTE** | Only the commands are listed here; parameters are not included. |

For details on the parameters and how each command works, please see the *Command Reference Manuals* on the Cisco documentation CD-ROM or on Cisco's web site at www.cisco.com. This information was adapted from the "ICND Annexes" document from Global Knowledge Network (Canada), Inc.

| | |
|---|---|
| **NOTE** | In the tables in this appendix, words within angled brackets, < >, are single keys that should be typed, not command words that should be typed out in full. A plus sign (+) between keys indicates that the keys should be typed simultaneously. For example, **<Ctrl>+<a>** indicates that the "Ctrl" key and the "a" key should be typed at the same time. |

## General Commands

Table C-1 contains some Cisco router EXEC IOS commands.

**Table C-1**   *General Commands*

| Command | Meaning |
|---|---|
| ? | Help. |
| **<Ctrl>+<a>** | Moves to the beginning of the command line. |
| **<Ctrl>+<b>** | Moves backward one character. |
| **<Ctrl>+<c>** | Aborts from setup mode. |

*continues*

**Table C-1**   *General Commands (Continued)*

| Command | Meaning |
|---|---|
| **\<Ctrl\>+\<e\>** | Moves to the end of the command line. |
| **\<Ctrl\>+\<f\>** | Moves forward one character. |
| **\<Ctrl\>+\<n\>** or **\<Down arrow\>** | Returns to more recent commands in the history buffer after recalling commands with **\<Ctrl\>+\<p\>** or **\<Up arrow\>**. Repeat the key sequence to recall successively more recent commands. |
| **\<Ctrl\>+\<p\>** or **\<Up arrow\>** | Recalls commands in the history buffer, beginning with the most recent command. Repeat the key sequence to recall successively older commands. |
| **\<Ctrl\>+\<Shift\>+\<6\> \<x\>** | The *escape sequence*, used to suspend a session. |
| **\<Ctrl\>+\<r\>** | Redisplays a line. |
| **\<Ctrl\>+\<u\>** | Erases a line from the beginning of the line. |
| **\<Ctrl\>+\<w\>** | Erases a word. |
| **\<Ctrl\>+\<z\>** | Exits from configuration mode back to privileged EXEC mode. |
| **\<Esc\>+\<b\>** | Moves to the beginning of the previous word. |
| **\<Esc\>+\<f\>** | Moves forward one word. |
| **\<Backspace\>** | Removes one character to the left of the cursor. |
| **\<Enter\>** or **\<Return\>** | Resumes the last suspended Telnet session. |
| **\<Tab\>** | Completes the keyword. |
| **clear counters** | Resets the **show interface** counters to zero. |
| **clear line** | Disconnects a Telnet session from a foreign host. |
| **clock set** | Sets the router's clock. |
| **configure terminal** | Enters configuration mode. |
| **connect** | Logs on to a host that supports Telnet, rlogin, or LAT. |
| **copy flash tftp** | Copies a file from Flash memory to a TFTP server. |

**Table C-1**    *General Commands (Continued)*

| Command | Meaning |
| --- | --- |
| **copy running-config startup-config** | Copies configuration from RAM to NVRAM (overwrites). |
| **copy running-config tftp** | Copies configuration from RAM to TFTP server (overwrites). |
| **copy startup-config running-config** | Executes configuration from NVRAM into RAM (executes line by line, merges, does not overwrite). |
| **copy startup-config tftp** | Copies configuration from NVRAM to TFTP server (overwrites). |
| **copy tftp flash** | Copies a file from a TFTP server to Flash memory. |
| **copy tftp running-config** | Executes configuration from TFTP server into RAM (executes line by line, merges, does not overwrite). |
| **copy tftp startup-config** | Copies configuration from TFTP server to NVRAM (overwrites). |
| **debug** | Starts the console display of the events on the router. |
| **disable** | Exits privileged EXEC mode. |
| **disconnect** | Disconnects a Telnet session. |
| **enable** | Enters privileged mode. |
| **erase startup-config** | Erases the configuration in NVRAM. |
| **exit** | Closes an active terminal session and terminates the EXEC. (Also used to exit any level in configuration mode.) |
| **logout** | Closes an active terminal session and terminates the EXEC. |
| **ping** | Sends an echo and expects an echo reply (**extend ping** also allows ping for protocols other than IP). |
| **reload** | Reloads the operating system. |
| **resume** | Resumes a suspended Telnet session. |
| **setup** | Enters prompted dialog to establish an initial configuration. |
| **show access-lists** | Displays the contents of all access lists configured. |

*continues*

**Table C-1**  *General Commands (Continued)*

| Command | Meaning |
| --- | --- |
| **show cdp entry** | Displays a single cached CDP entry; use **show cdp entry** * to display cached information on all neighbors. |
| **show cdp interface** | Displays values of CDP timers and CDP interface status. |
| **show cdp neighbors** | Displays a summary of CDP information received from neighbors. |
| **show cdp neighbors detail** | Displays detailed CDP information received from neighbors. |
| **show cdp traffic** | Displays information about interface CDP traffic. |
| **show controller** | Displays the Layer 1 information about an interface (including cable type and DCE/DTE status for serial interfaces). |
| **show flash** | Displays information about Flash memory. |
| **show history** | Displays the list of recorded command lines during the current terminal session. |
| **show interfaces** | Displays information about interfaces or an interface, including the state of the interface. |
| **show running-config** | Displays the active configuration (in RAM). |
| **show sessions** | Displays a list of hosts to which you have established Telnet connectivity. |
| **show startup-config** | Displays the backup configuration (in NVRAM). |
| **show user** | Displays a list of all active users on the router. |
| **show version** | Displays configuration of system hardware, software version, and configuration register value. |
| **telnet** | Connects to a host. |
| **terminal editing** | Reenables advanced editing (use **no terminal editing** to disable advanced editing features). By default, advanced editing is enabled. |
| **terminal history size** | Changes the number of command lines the system will record during the current terminal session. |

**Table C-1**    *General Commands (Continued)*

| Command | Meaning |
|---|---|
| **terminal monitor** | Forwards debug and error output to your Telnet session (use **terminal no monitor** to turn this off). |
| **traceroute** | Traces the route that packets are taking through the network. |
| **undebug** | Turns off debugging (also use **no debug**). |

# Comparison of Configuration File Commands

With Cisco IOS Release 12.0, commands used to copy and transfer configuration and system files have changed to conform to IOS File System (IFS) specifications. The old commands continue to perform their normal functions in the current release, but support for these commands will cease in a future release. Table C-2 contains the old and new commands used for configuration file movement and management.

**Table C-2**    *Comparison of Configuration File Commands*

| Old Commands | New Commands |
|---|---|
| **configure network** (pre-IOS release 10.3) | **copy ftp: system:running-config** |
| **copy rcp running-config** | **copy rcp: system:running-config** |
| **copy tftp running-config** | **copy tftp: system:running-config** |
| **configure overwrite-network** (pre-IOS release 10.3) | **copy ftp: nvram:startup-config** |
| | **copy rcp: nvram:startup-config** |
| **copy rcp startup-config** | **copy tftp: nvram:startup-config** |
| **copy tftp startup-config** | |
| **show configuration** (pre-IOS release 10.3) | **more nvram:startup-config** |
| **show startup-config** | |
| **write erase** (pre-IOS release 10.3) | **erase nvram:** |
| **erase startup-config** | |
| **write memory** (pre-IOS release 10.3) | **copy system:running-config nvram:startup-config** |
| **copy running-config startup-config** | |
| **write network** (pre-IOS release 10.3) | **copy system:running-config ftp:** |
| **copy running-config rcp** | **copy system:running-config rcp:** |
| **copy running-config tftp** | **copy system:running-config tftp:** |
| **write terminal** (pre-IOS release 10.3) | **more system:running-config** |
| **show running-config** | |

# General Configuration Commands

Table C-3 contains some Cisco IOS configuration commands.

**Table C-3**  *General Configuration Commands*

| Command | Meaning |
|---------|---------|
| <Ctrl>+<z> | Exits from configuration mode back to privileged EXEC mode. |
| banner | Specifies a banner for the router (can be **motd**, **idle**, or **exec** banner). |
| boot system | Specifies the source of IOS images. |
| cdp run | Enables CDP on a router. (CDP is enabled by default; use **no cdp run** to disable it.) |
| config-register | Sets the 16-bit configuration register. |
| enable password | Specifies the enable password for the router. |
| enable secret | Specifies the enable secret password for the router. |
| end | Exits from configuration mode. |
| exec-timeout 0 0 | Sets the timeout for a line EXEC session to zero, preventing the session from timing out and disconnecting. |
| exit | Exits any level in configuration mode. |
| history size | Specifies the number of command lines the system will record on a line. |
| hostname | Specifies the router's name. |
| interface | Enters interface configuration mode (**ethernet**, **serial**, **loopback**, and so on); also used to enter subinterface configuration mode. For virtual interfaces (**loopback**, **tunnel**, **dialer**, and so on), the first time that this command is used for a specific virtual interface, it creates that virtual interface. |
| line | Enters line configuration mode (**console**, **aux**, **vty**). |
| login | Enables password checking on a line. |
| logging synchronous | Used on a line (**console**, **aux**, **vty**), causes input to be redisplayed on a single display line, at the end of each console message that interrupts the input. |

**Table C-3**  *General Configuration Commands (Continued)*

| Command | Meaning |
|---|---|
| **password** | Specifies the password for a line. |
| **service password-encryption** | Specifies that any passwords set subsequent to this command will be encrypted. Use **no service password-encryption** after all such passwords have been set. |

# General Interface Configuration Commands

Table C-4 contains some Cisco IOS interface configuration commands.

**Table C-4**  *General Interface Configuration Commands*

| Command | Meaning |
|---|---|
| **bandwidth** | Sets bandwidth of interface (used by some routing protocols, including OSPF, EIGRP, IGRP; also used for load calculations). |
| **cdp enable** | Enables CDP on an interface. (CDP is enabled by default; use **no cdp enable** to disable it.) |
| **clock rate** | Sets clock rate in bits per second (used if interface is DCE); note that **clockrate** also works. |
| **description** | Adds a text description to the interface. |
| **encapsulation isl** | Defines the data-link encapsulation and VLAN number for a subinterface; is used for inter-VLAN routing on a Fast Ethernet subinterface. |
| **interface** | Enters interface configuration mode (or subinterface mode, if already in interface mode). |
| **media-type** | On Cisco routers with more than one connector for an Ethernet interface, selects the media-type connector for the Ethernet interface (for example, use **10baset** for RJ-45 connectors). |
| **shutdown** | Administratively shuts down an interface. (Use **no shutdown** to bring up the interface.) |

# General IP Commands

Table C-5 contains some Cisco IOS EXEC commands related to IP.

**Table C-5** *General IP Commands*

| Command | Meaning |
|---|---|
| **debug ip igrp** | Starts the console display of the IP IGRP-related transactions or events on the router. |
| **debug ip rip** | Starts the console display of the IP RIP-related events on the router. |
| **show hosts** | Displays the cached list of host names and addresses (both static and obtained from a DNS server). |
| **show ip access-list** | Displays the IP access lists configured. |
| **show ip interface** | Displays IP-specific information about an interface, including whether access lists are applied. |
| **show ip protocols** | Displays the IP routing protocols that are running. |
| **show ip route** | Displays the IP routing table; use other keywords to display specific parts of the routing table. |
| **term ip netmask-format** | Specifies the format of how network masks will be shown for the current session (bit count, decimal, or hexadecimal). |

# IP Configuration Commands

Table C-6 contains some Cisco IOS configuration commands related to IP.

**Table C-6** *IP Configuration Commands*

| Command | Meaning |
|---|---|
| **access-class** | Activates an access list on a line (**console**, **aux**, **vty**) to restrict incoming and outgoing connections. |
| **access-list** | Defines access lists: IP standard = numbers 1 to 99; IP extended = numbers 100 to 199. |
| **ip access-group** | Activates an access list on an interface. |
| **ip access-list** | Defines a named access list, in Cisco IOS 11.2 or later. |

**Table C-6**   *IP Configuration Commands (Continued)*

| Command | Meaning |
| --- | --- |
| **ip address** | Assigns an IP address and subnet mask to an interface. |
| **ip classless** | Specifies that if a packet is received with a destination address within an unknown subnet of a directly attached network, the router will match it to the default route and forward it to the next hop specified by the default route. |
| **ip domain-lookup** | Turns on name service (DNS) lookups. (Use **no ip domain-lookup** to turn off DNS lookup.) |
| **ip host** | Defines a static host name to IP address mapping. |
| **ip name-server** | Defines one or more (up to six) hosts that supply host name information (DNS). |
| **ip netmask-format** | Specifies the format of how network masks will be shown (bit count, decimal, or hexadecimal) for a specific line (con, aux, vty). |
| **ip route** | Defines a static route to an IP destination. |
| **network** | Defines the networks that the routing protocol will run on (for RIP, IGRP, and EIGRP). Starts up the routing protocol on all interfaces that are in that network and allows the router to advertise that network. |
| **router igrp** | Defines IGRP as an IP routing protocol and enters configuration mode for that protocol. |
| **router rip** | Defines RIP as an IP routing protocol and enters configuration mode for that protocol. |
| **traffic-share** | Defines how traffic is distributed among multiple unequal cost routes for the same destination network (for IGRP and EIGRP). |
| **variance** | Defines unequal cost load balancing when using IGRP or EIGRP. |

# General IPX Commands

Table C-7 contains some Cisco IOS EXEC commands related to IPX.

**Table C-7**   *General IPX Commands*

| Command | Meaning |
|---|---|
| **debug ipx routing activity** | Starts the console display of the IPX routing-related events on the router. |
| **debug ipx sap activity** | Starts the console display of the IPX SAP-related events on the router. |
| **ping ipx** | Sends an echo and expects an echo reply. |
| **show ipx access-list** | Displays the IPX access lists configured. |
| **show ipx interface** | Displays IPX-specific information about an interface, including whether access lists are applied. |
| **show ipx route** | Displays the IPX routing table. |
| **show ipx servers** | Displays the IPX server list. |
| **show ipx traffic** | Displays statistics on IPX traffic. |

# IPX Configuration Commands

Table C-8 contains some Cisco IOS configuration commands related to IPX.

**Table C-8**   *IPX Configuration Commands*

| Command | Meaning |
|---|---|
| **access-list** | Defines access lists: IPX standard = numbers 800 to 899; IPX extended = numbers 900 to 999; IPX SAP = numbers 1000 to 1099. |
| **ipx access-group** | Activates an IPX standard or extended access list on an interface. |
| **ipx delay** | Defines the delay tick metric to associate with an interface. |
| **ipx input-sap-filter** | Activates an IPX SAP access list input on an interface. |
| **ipx maximum-paths** | Enables round-robin load sharing over multiple equal metric paths. |

**Table C-8**   *IPX Configuration Commands (Continued)*

| Command | Meaning |
|---|---|
| **ipx network** | Assigns IPX network number and encapsulation type to an interface or subinterface. |
| **ipx output-sap-filter** | Activates an IPX SAP access list output on an interface. |
| **ipx routing** | Enables IPX routing on the router. |

# General AppleTalk Commands

Table C-9 contains some Cisco IOS EXEC commands related to AppleTalk.

**Table C-9**   *General AppleTalk Commands*

| Command | Meaning |
|---|---|
| **debug appletalk routing** | Starts the console display of the AppleTalk routing-related events on the router. |
| **show appletalk globals** | Displays information and settings about the router's global AppleTalk configuration parameters. |
| **show appletalk interface** | Displays AppleTalk-specific information about an interface, including whether access lists are applied. |
| **show appletalk route** | Displays the AppleTalk routing table. |
| **show appletalk zone** | Displays the AppleTalk zone information table. |

# AppleTalk Configuration Commands

Table C-10 contains some Cisco IOS configuration commands related to AppleTalk.

**Table C-10**   *AppleTalk Configuration Commands*

| Command | Meaning |
|---|---|
| **appletalk cable-range** | Assigns an AppleTalk cable-range to an interface (for phase 2 or extended addressing). |
| **appletalk discovery** | Enables an interface to learn a cable-range and zone name (or use **appletalk cable-range 0-0**). |
| **appletalk protocol** | Selects an AppleTalk routing protocol (RTMP, EIGRP, or AURP). |

*continues*

**Table C-10**    *AppleTalk Configuration Commands (Continued)*

| Command | Meaning |
| --- | --- |
| **appletalk routing** | Enables AppleTalk routing on the router. |
| **appletalk zone** | Assigns an AppleTalk zone name to an interface. |

# General WAN Commands

Table C-11 contains some Cisco IOS EXEC commands related to WAN interfaces.

**Table C-11**    *General WAN Commands*

| Command | Meaning |
| --- | --- |
| **clear frame-relay-inarp** | Clears dynamically created Frame Relay maps, which are created by the use of Inverse Address Resolution Protocol (ARP). |
| **debug dialer** | Starts the console display of dialer events, including the number that the interface is dialing. |
| **debug frame-relay lmi** | Starts the console display of LMI packets between the router and the Frame Relay switch. |
| **debug isdn q921** | Starts the console display of data link layer (Layer 2) access procedures that are taking place at the router on the D channel (LAPD) of its ISDN interface. |
| **debug isdn q931** | Starts the console display of call setup and teardown of ISDN network connections (Layer 3). |
| **debug ppp authentication** | Starts the console display of the PPP authentication–related events on the router. |
| **show frame-relay lmi** | Displays the LMI traffic statistics. |
| **show frame-relay map** | Displays the route maps (between network layer addresses and DLCIs), both static and dynamic. |
| **show frame-relay pvc** | Displays the status of each configured PVC as well as traffic statistics (including the number of BECN and FECN). |
| **show dialer** | Displays the current status of a dialer link, including the amount of time the link has been connected. |

**Table C-11**   *General WAN Commands (Continued)*

| Command | Meaning |
|---|---|
| **show isdn active** | Displays the current call information, including the called number and the time until the call is disconnected. |
| **show isdn status** | Displays the status of an ISDN interface. |

# WAN Configuration Commands

Table C-12 contains some Cisco IOS configuration commands related to WAN interfaces.

**Table C-12**   *WAN Configuration Commands*

| Command | Meaning |
|---|---|
| **bandwidth** | Defines the bandwidth (in kilobits per second) of the interface (used in routing protocol calculations and load calculations). |
| **dialer idle-timeout** | Defines the number of seconds of idle (no *interesting data*) time before circuit is disconnected. |
| **dialer load-threshold** | Enables the router to place another call (if channels are available) to the same destination, based on the load on the line. |
| **dialer map** | Defines how to reach a destination, maps protocol addresses to the phone number of the destination, and defines options, including broadcast, speed, and name of remote device. |
| **dialer-group** | Assigns a dialer list to an interface to determine when to trigger a call. |
| **dialer-list list** | Defines a dialer list to trigger a call based on an access list. (Used only for IP or IPX.) |
| **dialer-list protocol** | Defines a dialer list to trigger a call based on a protocol type or an access list. |
| **encapsulation** | Defines the data-link encapsulation for an interface (ppp, hldc, x25 [dte is the default, can use dce], **frame-relay**, **smds**, and so on). |
| **frame-relay interface-dlci** | Assigns a DLCI to the subinterface. (Used only on subinterfaces, which are defined by the **interface** <*type*>.<*subinterface number*> {**point-to-point** \| **multipoint**} command.) |

*continues*

**Table C-12** *WAN Configuration Commands (Continued)*

| Command | Meaning |
|---|---|
| **frame-relay inverse-arp** | Enables Inverse ARP on an interface. (Needed only if it was disabled at some point; default is enabled.) |
| **frame-relay lmi-type** | Defines the Local Management Interface (LMI) format (to match the Frame Relay switch). |
| **frame-relay map** | Defines how an interface will reach a destination, maps protocol addresses to the DLCI to the destination, and defines options including broadcast. |
| **isdn spid1** | Sets a B-channel SPID (required by many service providers/ISDN switches). |
| **isdn spid2** | Sets a B-channel SPID for the second B channel (required by many service providers/ ISDN switches). |
| **isdn switch-type** | Specifies the ISDN switch that the router is connected to; can be done as a global or interface command from Cisco IOS 11.3 onward. |
| **ppp authentication** | Sets password authentication on an interface (using CHAP or PAP). |
| **username** | Defines a host name and password for verification (used in PAP or CHAP). |

This appendix is organized in the following sections:

- General Commands
- Comparison of Configuration File Commands
- General Configuration Commands
- General Interface Configuration Commands
- General IP Commands
- IP Configuration Commands
- General WAN Commands
- WAN Configuration Commands

# Summary of BSCN Router Commands

This appendix contains a listing of some of the Cisco router IOS commands you may find in this *Building Scalable Cisco Networks* (BSCN) coursebook, organized in various categories.

---

NOTE | Only the command is listed here; parameters are not included.

---

For details on the parameters and how the command works, see the *Command Reference Manuals* on the Cisco Documentation CD-ROM or on Cisco's web site at www.cisco.com. This information was adapted from the "BSCN Annexes" document from Global Knowledge Network (Canada), Inc.

## General Commands

Table D-1 contains some Cisco router EXEC IOS commands.

**Table D-1** *General Commands*

| Command | Meaning |
| --- | --- |
| **clear access-list counters** | Clears packet counters in extended access lists. |
| **clear logging** | Clears the logging buffer. |
| **configure terminal** | Enters configuration mode. |
| **copy running-config startup-config** | Copies configuration from RAM to NVRAM (overwrites). |
| **debug** | Starts the console display of the events on the router. |
| **debug eigrp neighbors** | Starts the console display of the EIGRP neighbor interaction. |
| **debug eigrp packets** | Starts the console display of EIGRP packets, both sent and received. |

*continues*

**Table D-1**   *General Commands (Continued)*

| Command | Meaning |
|---|---|
| **erase startup-config** | Erases the configuration in NVRAM. |
| **ping** | Sends an echo and expects an echo reply. Extended **ping** allows specification of the source address and allows **ping** for protocols other than IP. |
| **reload** | Reloads the operating system. |
| **setup** | Enters prompted dialog to establish an initial configuration. |
| **show access-lists** | Displays the contents of all access lists configured. |
| **show CDP neighbors** | Displays a summary of CDP information received from neighbors. |
| **show CDP neighbors detail** | Displays detailed CDP information received from neighbors. |
| **show controller** | Displays the Layer 1 information about an interface (including cable type and DCE/DTE status for serial interfaces). |
| **show interfaces** | Displays information about interfaces or an interface, including the state of the interface and queuing information. |
| **show line** | Displays information about line (**console**, **aux**, **vty**) configuration. |
| **show logging** | Displays the logging buffer, including logged output of debug commands. |
| **show route-map** | Displays configured route maps; includes number of matches. |
| **show running-config** | Displays the active configuration (in RAM). |
| **show startup-config** | Displays the backup configuration (in NVRAM). |
| **show version** | Displays configuration of system hardware, software version, and configuration register value. |
| **telnet** | Connects to a host. |
| **traceroute** | Traces the route that packets are taking through the network; extended **traceroute** allows specification of the source address. |

# Comparison of Configuration File Commands

With Cisco IOS Release 12.0, commands used to copy and transfer configuration and system files have changed to conform to IOS File System (IFS) specifications. The old commands continue to perform their normal functions in the current release, but support for these commands will cease in a future release. Table D-2 contains the old and new commands used for configuration file movement and management.

**Table D-2**     *Comparison of Configuration File Commands*

| Old Commands | New Commands |
| --- | --- |
| **configure network** (pre-IOS release 10.3) | **copy ftp: system:running-config** |
| **copy rcp running-config** | **copy rcp: system:running-config** |
| **copy tftp running-config** | **copy tftp: system:running-config** |
| **configure overwrite-network** (pre-IOS release 10.3) | **copy ftp: nvram:startup-config** |
| | **copy rcp: nvram:startup-config** |
| **copy rcp startup-config** | **copy tftp: nvram:startup-config** |
| **copy tftp startup-config** | |
| **show configuration** (pre-IOS release 10.3) | **more nvram:startup-config** |
| **show startup-config** | |
| **write erase** (pre-IOS release 10.3) | **erase nvram:** |
| **erase startup-config** | |
| **write memory** (pre-IOS release 10.3) | **copy system:running-config nvram: startup-config** |
| **copy running-config startup-config** | |
| **write network** (pre-IOS release 10.3) | **copy system:running-config ftp:** |
| **copy running-config rcp** | **copy system:running-config rcp:** |
| **copy running-config tftp** | **copy system:running-config tftp:** |
| **write terminal** (pre-IOS release 10.3) | **more system:running-config** |
| **show running-config** | |

# General Configuration Commands

Table D-3 contains some Cisco IOS configuration commands.

**Table D-3** *General Configuration Commands*

| Command | Meaning |
| --- | --- |
| **config-register** | Changes the value of the configuration register. |
| **enable password** | Specifies the enable password for the router. |
| **enable secret** | Specifies the enable secret password for the router. |
| **exec-timeout 0 0** | Sets the timeout for a line EXEC session to zero, preventing the session from timing out and disconnecting. |
| **hostname** | Specifies the router's name. |
| **interface** | Enters interface configuration mode (**ethernet**, **serial**, **loopback**, and so on). Also used to enter subinterface configuration mode. For virtual interfaces (**loopback**, **tunnel**, **dialer**, and so on), the first time that this command is used for a specific virtual interface, it creates that virtual interface. |
| **line** | Enters line configuration mode (**console**, **aux**, **vty**). |
| **logging synchronous** | When used on a line (**console**, **aux**, **vty**), causes input to be redisplayed on a single display line, at the end of each console message that interrupts the input. |
| **login** | Enables password checking on a line. |
| **password** | Specifies the password for a line. |
| **route-map** | Defines a route map and enters configuration mode for the route map. |

# General Interface Configuration Commands

Table D-4 contains some Cisco IOS interface configuration commands.

**Table D-4**    *General Interface Configuration Commands*

| Command | Meaning |
|---|---|
| **bandwidth** | Sets bandwidth of interface (used by some routing protocols, including OSPF, EIGRP, IGRP; also used for load calculations). |
| **clock rate** | Sets clock rate in bits per second (used if interface is DCE). Note that the **clockrate** command also works. |
| **interface** | Enters interface configuration mode (or subinterface mode, if already in interface mode). |
| **interface serial multipoint | point-to-point** | Enters subinterface configuration mode for a serial interface, and defines whether it is a point-to-multipoint or point-to-point subinterface. |
| **shutdown** | Administratively shuts down an interface (use **no shutdown** to bring up the interface). |

# General IP Commands

Table D-5 contains some Cisco IOS EXEC commands related to IP.

**Table D-5**    *General IP Commands*

| Command | Meaning |
|---|---|
| **clear ip bgp** | Clears entries from the BGP routing table and resets BGP sessions; use the * option to delete all entries. |
| **clear ip bgp peer-group** | Clears the BGP connections for all members of a BGP peer group. |
| **clear ip prefix-list** | Resets the hit count shown on IP prefix list entries. |
| **clear ip route** | Clears the IP routing table; use the * option to delete all routes. |
| **debug ip bgp** | Starts the console display of BGP-related events on the router, according to the option specified (**dampening**, **events**, **keepalives**, **updates**). |

*continues*

**Table D-5** *General IP Commands (Continued)*

| Command | Meaning |
| --- | --- |
| **debug ip bgp updates** | Starts the console display of BGP updates. |
| **debug ip eigrp** | Starts the console display of the IP EIGRP advertisements and changes to the IP routing table. |
| **debug ip eigrp neighbors** | Starts the console display of the neighbors discovered by IP EIGRP and the contents of the hello packets. |
| **debug ip eigrp notification** | Starts the console display of notification of IP EIGRP events. |
| **debug ip eigrp summary** | Starts the console display of a brief report of IP EIGRP routing activity. |
| **debug ip igrp** | Starts the console display of the IGRP-related transactions or events on the router. |
| **debug ip ospf** | Starts the console display of the OSPF-related events on the router. |
| **debug ip ospf adj** | Starts the console display of OSPF adjacency-related events on the router. |
| **debug ip ospf events** | Starts the console display of OSPF-related events, such as adjacencies, flooding information, designated router selection, and SPF calculation on the router. |
| **debug ip ospf lsa-generation** | Starts the console display of OSFP LSA generation-related events on the router. |
| **debug ip ospf packet** | Starts the console display about each OSPF packet received. |
| **debug ip ospf spf** | Starts the console display of SPF calculation-related events on the router. |
| **debug ip policy** | Starts the console display of IP policy routing events. |
| **debug ip rip** | Starts the console display of IP RIP-related events on the router. |
| **debug ip routing** | Starts the console display of IP routing-related events on the router. |
| **show eigrp traffic** | Displays the types of EIGRP packets sent and received. This command displays statistics on route compilation. |
| **show ip access-list** | Displays the IP access lists configured. |

**Table D-5**   *General IP Commands (Continued)*

| Command | Meaning |
| --- | --- |
| **show ip bgp** | Displays the BGP routing table; specify a network number to get more specific information about a particular network. |
| **show ip bgp neighbors** | Displays information about the TCP and BGP connections to neighbors. |
| **show ip bgp summary** | Displays the status of all BGP connections. |
| **show ip eigrp neighbors** | Displays the neighbors discovered by IP EIGRP. |
| **show ip eigrp topology** | Displays the IP EIGRP topology table; use the **all** keyword to display all of the topology table, including those routes that are not feasible successors. |
| **show ip eigrp traffic** | Displays the number of IP EIGRP packets sent and received. |
| **show ip interface** | Displays IP-specific information about an interface, including whether access lists are applied. |
| **show ip ospf** | Displays OSPF-specific parameters on the router, including the router ID, information about each area to which the router is connected, and the number of times the SPF algorithm has been executed. |
| **show ip ospf border-routers** | Displays the internal OSPF routing table entries to ABRs and ASBRs. |
| **show ip ospf database** | Displays the contents of the OSPF topological database maintained by the router. This command also shows the router ID and OSPF process ID. Use additional keywords to view detailed information in each part of the database. |
| **show ip ospf interface** | Displays details of the OSPF protocol on the interfaces, including the area, state, timers, neighbors, router ID, and network type. |
| **show ip ospf neighbor** | Displays the list of OSPF neighbors; use the **detail** keyword to display more details of each neighbor (including priority and state). |
| **show ip ospf virtual-links** | Displays the OSPF virtual links. |

*continues*

**Table D-5**   *General IP Commands (Continued)*

| Command | Meaning |
| --- | --- |
| **show ip policy** | Displays route maps configured on the routers interfaces for policy routing. |
| **show ip prefix-list** | Displays information on all prefix lists; use the **detail** keyword to include the description and hit count. Other parameters can be used to display other details or specific parts of the prefix lists. |
| **show ip protocols** | Displays the IP routing protocols that are running. |
| **show ip route** | Displays the IP routing table; use other keywords to display specific parts of the routing table. |
| **show ip route eigrp** | Displays the current EIGRP entries in the IP routing table. |

# IP Configuration Commands

Table D-6 contains some Cisco IOS configuration commands related to IP.

**Table D-6**   *IP Configuration Commands*

| Command | Meaning |
| --- | --- |
| **access-class** | Activates an access list on a line (**console**, **aux**, **vty**) to restrict incoming and outgoing connections. |
| **access-list** | Defines access lists: IP standard = numbers 1 to 99; IP extended = numbers 100 to –199. |
| **aggregate-address** | Creates an aggregate, or summary, entry in the BGP table. |
| **area default-cost** | Defines the cost of the default route sent into an OSPF stub area; default is 1. |
| **area nssa** | Defines the OSPF area as a not-so-stubby area. |
| **area range** | Defines route summarization of intra-area routes on an OSPF ABR. |
| **area stub** | Defines the OSPF area as a stub area; use the **no-summary** keyword on the ABR to define a totally stubby area. |

**Table D-6**    *IP Configuration Commands (Continued)*

| Command | Meaning |
|---|---|
| **area virtual-link** | Defines an OSPF virtual link across an area to another OSPF router. |
| **auto-cost reference-bandwidth** | Defines the numerator of the OSPF cost formula (numerator/bandwidth), in megabits per second. The default is 100. |
| **bgp always-compare-med** | Forces the comparison of the BGP MED attribute to be done, even if the neighboring AS is not the same for all the routes considered. |
| **bgp bestpath missing-as-worst** | Forces BGP routes without the MED attribute to have a MED value of infinity, making the route the least preferred. |
| **bgp cluster-id** | Configures the cluster ID; used if a BGP cluster has more than one route reflector. |
| **bgp default local-preference** | Defines the default BGP local-preference attribute value. |
| **default-information originate always** | Propagates a default route into the OSPF routing domain, whether or not the router has a default route. |
| **default-metric** | Defines the seed metric that this routing protocol uses before redistributing a route. |
| **distance** | Defines the administrative distance that will be used for this routing protocol (for all routing protocols except BGP and EIGRP). |
| **distance bgp** | Defines the administrative distance that will be used for BGP. |
| **distance eigrp** | Defines the administrative distance that will be used for EIGRP. |
| **distribute-list** | Activates an access list to be used to filter outbound or inbound routing updates for a routing protocol. |
| **eigrp log-neighbor-changes** | Enables the logging of changes in EIGRP neighbor adjacencies. |
| **ip access-group** | Activates an access list on an interface. |
| **ip address** | Assigns an IP address and subnet mask to an interface. |

*continues*

**Table D-6** *IP Configuration Commands (Continued)*

| Command | Meaning |
|---|---|
| **ip bandwidth-percent eigrp** | Defines the maximum percentage of bandwidth that EIGRP packets will be capable of utilizing on an interface. |
| **ip classless** | Specifies that if a packet is received with a destination address within an unknown subnet of a directly attached network, the router will match it to the default route and forward it to the next hop specified by the default route. |
| **ip community-list** | Creates a community list for BGP and controls access to the list. |
| **ip default-gateway** | Defines a default gateway (router); used on routers or communication servers that have IP routing turned off. The router or communication server acts just like a host on the network. |
| **ip default-network** | Defines a default route. |
| **ip domain-lookup** | Turns on name service (DNS) lookups; use **no ip domain-lookup** to turn off DNS lookup. |
| **ip eigrp hello-interval** | Defines the interval at which EIGRP hello packets are sent. |
| **ip eigrp hold-time** | Defines the time that a router will consider an EIGRP neighbor up without receiving a hello (or some other packet). |
| **ip forward-protocol** | Defines the protocols that will be forwarded with the **ip helper-address** command. |
| **ip helper-address** | Defines an address to which the router will forward certain broadcasts (this is usually a server address) that are sent to this interface. |
| **ip host** | Defines a static host name to IP address mapping. |
| **ip ospf cost** | Defines the outgoing OSPF cost of an interface. |
| **ip ospf network** | Defines the OSPF network mode configuration (**non-broadcast**, **point-to-multipoint [non-broadcast]**, **broadcast**, or **point-to-point**). |
| **ip ospf priority** | Defines the OSPF priority on an interface (the default is 1); used to determine which router will be the DR on a multiaccess network. |

**Table D-6** *IP Configuration Commands (Continued)*

| Command | Meaning |
| --- | --- |
| **ip policy route-map** | Defines a route map to use for policy routing on an interface. |
| **ip prefix-list** | Defines a prefix list. |
| **ip prefix-list description** | Defines a description for a prefix list. |
| **ip prefix-list sequence-number** | Re-enables the automatic generation of sequence numbers for a prefix list (automatic generation is the default); use the no form of this command to disable the automatic generation of sequence numbers. |
| **ip route** | Defines a static route to an IP destination. |
| **ip route-cache policy** | Enables fast switching of IP policy routing on an interface. |
| **ip subnet-zero** | Allows use of subnets with all subnet bits equal to zero. |
| **ip summary-address eigrp** | Defines route summarization on an interface for the EIGRP routing protocol. |
| **ip unnumbered** | Enables IP processing on a serial interface without assigning an explicit address to the interface. |
| **match** | Defines conditions to be checked within a route map. |
| **match community** | Matches a BGP community attribute to a value in a community list in a route map. |
| **match ip address** | Defines IP addresses to be matched in a route map, using IP standard or extended access lists. |
| **match ip next-hop** | Defines routes to be matched in a route map as those that have a next-hop router address passed by one of the access lists specified, using IP standard or extended access lists. |
| **match ip route-source** | Defines routes to be matched in a route map as those that have been advertised by routers and access servers at an address passed by one of the access lists specified, using IP standard or extended access lists. |
| **match length** | Defines minimum and maximum packet length values to be matched in a route map. |

*continues*

**Table D-6** *IP Configuration Commands (Continued)*

| Command | Meaning |
| --- | --- |
| **maximum-paths** | Controls the maximum number of parallel routes that an IP routing protocol can support. |
| **metric weights** | Allows tuning of the IGRP or EIGRP metric calculations. |
| **neighbor** (OSPF) | Identifies a peer router with which this OSPF router interconnects over a nonbroadcast network. |
| **neighbor distribute-list** | Distributes BGP neighbor information, as specified in an access list. |
| **neighbor ebgp-multihop** | Allows the router to accept and attempt BGP connections to external peers residing on networks that are not directly connected. |
| **neighbor next-hop-self** | Forces all BGP updates for this neighbor to be advertised with this router as the next-hop address. |
| **neighbor peer-group** | Creates a BGP peer group; assigns neighbors as part of a peer group. |
| **neighbor prefix-list** | Identifies a prefix list to be used to filter BGP routes from or to a peer router. |
| **neighbor remote-as** | Identifies a peer router with which this router will establish a BGP session. |
| **neighbor route-map** | Applies a route map to incoming or outgoing BGP routes. |
| **neighbor route-reflector-client** | Defines the router as a BGP route reflector and identifies the specified neighbor as its route reflector client. |
| **neighbor send-community** | Specifies that the BGP communities attribute should be sent to a BGP neighbor. |
| **neighbor shutdown** | Disables an existing BGP neighbor or neighbor peer group. |
| **neighbor soft-reconfiguration** | Forces the router to store all received BGP updates without modification so that they can be used to do an inbound soft reconfiguration. |
| **neighbor update-source loopback** | Allows internal BGP sessions to use the specified operational loopback interface for TCP connections. |

**Table D-6**    *IP Configuration Commands (Continued)*

| Command | Meaning |
| --- | --- |
| **neighbor weight** | Defines the BGP weight attribute to a neighbor connection. |
| **network** | For RIP, IGRP, EIGRP, and OSPF, defines the networks on which the routing protocol will run. Starts up the routing protocol on all interfaces that are in that network and allows the router to advertise that network. |
| | For OSPF, this command also defines the area that the interface will be in. |
| | For BGP, this command allows BGP to advertise a route if it is already in the routing table (use the **neighbor** command to start up BGP) and can define the subnet mask of the route. |
| **no auto-summary** | Disables automatic route summarization for the EIGRP routing protocol. |
| **no ip prefix-list sequence-number** | Disables the automatic generation of sequence numbers for a prefix list. |
| **no synchronization** | Disables BGP synchronization. |
| **passive-interface** | Prevents routing updates from this routing protocol from being generated on an interface. |
| **redistribute** | Defines the protocol that will be redistributed into this routing protocol; the protocol can include static and connected routes. |
| **router bgp** | Defines BGP as an IP routing protocol and enters configuration mode for that protocol. |
| **router eigrp** | Defines EIGRP as an IP routing protocol and enters configuration mode for that protocol. |
| **router igrp** | Defines IGRP as an IP routing protocol and enters configuration mode for that protocol. |
| **router ospf** | Defines OSPF as an IP routing protocol and enters configuration mode for that protocol. |
| **router rip** | Defines RIP as an IP routing protocol and enters configuration mode for that protocol. |
| **set** | Defines actions to be followed if there is a match within a route map. |

*continues*

**Table D-6**  *IP Configuration Commands (Continued)*

| Command | Meaning |
|---|---|
| set community | Sets the BGP communities attribute within a route map. |
| set default interface | Defines the default interface to which packets that have no explicit route to the destination should be forwarded from a route map. |
| set interface | Defines the interface to which packets should be forwarded from a route map. |
| set ip default next-hop | Defines the default next-hop address to which packets that have no explicit route to the destination should be forwarded from a route map. |
| set ip next-hop | Defines the next-hop address to which packets should be forwarded from a route map. |
| set ip precedence | Sets the IP precedence in the IP packets from a route map. |
| set ip tos | Sets the IP TOS value in the IP packets from a route map. |
| set local-preference | Specifies a BGP local preference value for the autonomous system path from a route map. |
| set metric | Sets the BGP metric (MED) value from a route map. |
| summary-address | Defines route summarization of external routes on an OSPF ASBR. |
| timers spf | Defines the time that an OSPF router waits before recalculating its routing table and the minimum time between two consecutive SPF calculations. |
| traffic-share | Defines how traffic is distributed among multiple unequal cost routes for the same destination network (for IGRP and EIGRP). |
| variance | Defines unequal cost load balancing when using IGRP or EIGRP. |

# General WAN Commands

Table D-7 contains a Cisco IOS EXEC command related to WAN interfaces.

**Table D-7**    *General WAN Commands*

| Command | Meaning |
| --- | --- |
| **show frame-relay map** | Displays the mapping between network layer addresses and DLCIs, both static and dynamic mappings. |

# WAN Configuration Commands

Table D-8 contains some Cisco IOS configuration commands related to WAN interfaces.

**Table D-8**    *WAN Configuration Commands*

| Command | Meaning |
| --- | --- |
| **async default routing** | Enables the router to pass routing updates to other routers over an asynchronous interface. |
| **dialer map** | Configures a serial or ISDN interface to call one or multiple sites, or to receive calls from multiple sites. |
| **dialer string** | Specifies the destination string (telephone number) to be called for interfaces calling a single site. |
| **encapsulation** | Defines the data-link encapsulation for an interface (**ppp**, **hdlc**, **x25** [**dte** is the default, can use **dce**], **frame-relay**, **smds**, and so on). |
| **frame-relay interface-dlci** | Defines the Frame Relay DLCI number on a subinterface. |
| **frame-relay intf-type dce** | Defines an interface as a Frame Relay DCE device. |
| **frame-relay switching** | Enables Frame Relay switching on the router. |
| **frame-relay route** | Defines a static entry in the Frame Relay switching table. |

# Open Systems Interconnection (OSI) Reference Model

The OSI reference model describes how information from a software application in one computer moves through a network medium to a software application in another computer. The OSI reference model is a conceptual model composed of seven layers, each specifying particular network functions. The model was developed by the International Organization for Standardization (ISO) in 1984, and it is now considered the primary architectural model for intercomputer communications. The OSI model divides the tasks involved with moving information between networked computers into seven smaller, more manageable task groups. A task or group of tasks is then assigned to each of the seven OSI layers. Each layer is reasonably self-contained so that the tasks assigned to each layer can be implemented independently. This enables the solutions offered by one layer to be updated without adversely affecting the other layers. The following list details the seven layers of the Open Systems Interconnection (OSI) reference model:

- Layer 7—Application layer
- Layer 6—Presentation layer
- Layer 5—Session layer
- Layer 4—Transport layer
- Layer 3—Network layer
- Layer 2—Data link layer
- Layer 1—Physical layer

Figure E-1 illustrates the seven-layer OSI reference model.

**Figure E-1**    *The OSI Reference Model Contains Seven Independent Layers*

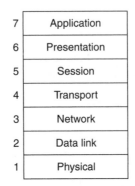

# Characteristics of the OSI Layers

The seven layers of the OSI reference model can be divided into two categories: upper layers and lower layers.

The *upper layers* of the OSI model deal with application issues and generally are implemented only in software. The highest layer, the application layer, is closest to the end user. Both users and application layer processes interact with software applications that contain a communications component. The term *upper layer* is sometimes used to refer to any layer above another layer in the OSI model.

---

### Terminology: Upper Layers

Generally speaking, the term *upper layers* is often used to refer to Layers 5, 6, and 7, although this terminology is relative.

---

The *lower layers* of the OSI model handle data transport issues. The physical layer and the data link layer are implemented in hardware and software. The other lower layers generally are implemented only in software. The lowest layer, the physical layer, is closest to the physical network medium (the network cabling, for example) and is responsible for actually placing information on the medium.

---

**Terminology: Lower Layers**

Generally speaking, the term *lower layers* is often used to refer to Layers 1 and 2, although this terminology is relative.

---

Figure E-2 illustrates the division between the upper and lower OSI layers.

**Figure E-2**   *Two Sets of Layers Make Up the OSI Layers*

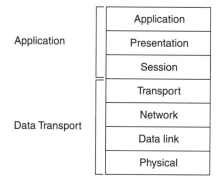

# Protocols

The OSI model provides a conceptual framework for communication between computers, but the model itself is not a method of communication. Actual communication is made possible by using communication protocols. In the context of data networking, a *protocol* is a formal set of rules and conventions that governs how computers exchange information over a network medium. A protocol implements the functions of one or more of the OSI layers. A wide variety of communication protocols exist, but all tend to fall into one of the following groups: LAN protocols, WAN protocols, network protocols, and routing protocols. *LAN protocols* operate at the physical and data link layers of the OSI model and define communication over the various LAN media. *WAN protocols* operate at the lowest three layers of the OSI model and define communication over the various wide-area media. *Routing protocols* are network layer protocols that are responsible for path determination and traffic switching. Finally, *network protocols* are the various upper-layer protocols that exist in a given protocol suite.

# OSI Model and Communication Between Systems

Information being transferred from a software application in one computer system to a software application in another must pass through each of the OSI layers. For example, if a software application in System A has information to transmit to a software application in System B, the application program in System A will pass its information to the application layer (Layer 7) of System A. The application layer then passes the information to the presentation layer (Layer 6), which relays the data to the session layer (Layer 5), and so on, down to the physical layer (Layer 1). At the physical layer, the information is placed on the physical network medium and is sent across the medium to System B. The physical layer of System B removes the information from the physical medium, and then its physical layer passes the information up to the data link layer (Layer 2), which passes it to the network layer (Layer 3), and so on, until it reaches the application layer (Layer 7) of System B. Finally, the application layer of System B passes the information to the recipient application program to complete the communication process.

## Interaction Between OSI Model Layers

A given layer in the OSI layers generally communicates with three other OSI layers: the layer directly above it, the layer directly below it, and its peer layer in other networked computer systems. The data link layer in System A, for example, communicates with the network layer of System A, the physical layer of System A, and the data link layer in System B. Figure E-3 illustrates this example.

**Figure E-3**   *OSI Model Layers Communicate with Other Layers*

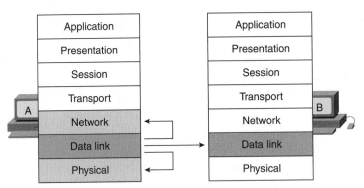

## OSI Layer Services

One OSI layer communicates with another layer to make use of the services provided by the second layer. The services provided by adjacent layers help a given OSI layer communicate with its peer layer in other computer systems. Three basic elements are involved in layer services: the service user, the service provider, and the service access point (SAP).

In this context, the service *user* is the OSI layer that requests services from an adjacent OSI layer. The service *provider* is the OSI layer that provides services to service users. OSI layers can provide services to multiple service users. The *SAP* is a conceptual location at which one OSI layer can request the services of another OSI layer.

Figure E-4 illustrates how these three elements interact at the network and data link layers.

**Figure E-4**    *Service Users, Providers, and SAPs Interact at the Network and Data Link Layers*

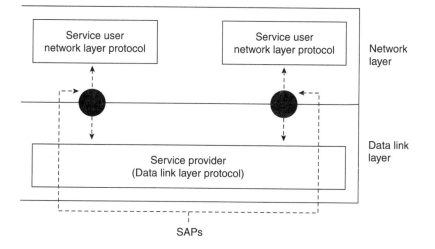

## OSI Model Layers and Information Exchange

The seven OSI layers use various forms of control information to communicate with their peer layers in other computer systems. This *control information* consists of specific requests and instructions that are exchanged between peer OSI layers.

Control information typically takes one of two forms: headers and trailers. Headers are prepended to data that has been passed down from upper layers. Trailers are appended to data that has been passed down from upper layers. An OSI layer is not required to attach a header or a trailer to data from upper layers.

Headers, trailers, and data are relative concepts, depending on the layer that analyzes the information unit. At the network layer, an information unit, for example, consists of a Layer 3 header and data. At the data link layer, however, all the information passed down by the network layer (the Layer 3 header and the data) is treated as data.

In other words, the data portion of an information unit at a given OSI layer potentially can contain headers, trailers, and data from all the higher layers. This is known as *encapsulation*. Figure E-5 shows how the header and data from one layer are encapsulated into the header of the next lowest layer.

**Figure E-5**    *Headers and Data Can Be Encapsulated During Information Exchange*

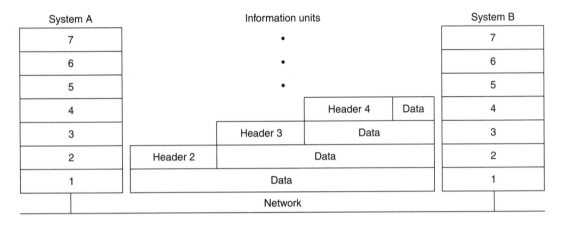

## Information Exchange Process

The information exchange process occurs between peer OSI layers. Each layer in the source system adds control information to data, and each layer in the destination system analyzes and removes the control information from that data.

If System A has data from a software application to send to System B, the data is passed to the application layer. The application layer in System A then communicates any control information required by the application layer in System B by prepending a header to the data. The resulting information unit (a header and the data) is passed to the presentation layer, which prepends its own header containing control information intended for the presentation layer in System B.

The information unit grows in size as each layer prepends its own header (and, in some cases, a trailer) that contains control information to be used by its peer layer in System B. At the physical layer, the entire information unit is placed onto the network medium.

The physical layer in System B receives the information unit and passes it to the data link layer. The data link layer in System B then reads the control information contained in the header prepended by the data link layer in System A. The header is then removed, and the remainder of the information unit is passed to the network layer. Each layer performs the same actions: The layer reads the header from its peer layer, strips it off, and passes the remaining information unit to the next highest layer. After the application layer performs these actions, the data is passed to the recipient software application in System B, in exactly the form in which it was transmitted by the application in System A.

# OSI Model Physical Layer

The physical layer defines the electrical, mechanical, procedural, and functional specifications for activating, maintaining, and deactivating the physical link between communicating network systems. Physical layer specifications define characteristics such as voltage levels, timing of voltage changes, physical data rates, maximum transmission distances, and physical connectors. Physical layer implementations can be categorized as either LAN or WAN specifications. Figure E-6 illustrates some common LAN and WAN physical layer implementations.

**Figure E-6**    *Physical Layer Implementations Can Be LAN or WAN Specifications*

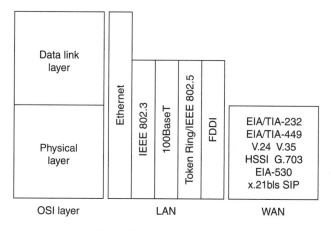

Physical layer implementations

# OSI Model Data Link Layer

The data link layer provides reliable transit of data across a physical network link. Different data link layer specifications define different network and protocol characteristics, including physical addressing, network topology, error notification, sequencing of frames, and flow control. Physical addressing (as opposed to network addressing) defines how devices are addressed at the data link layer. Network topology consists of the data link layer specifications that often define how devices are to be physically connected, such as in a bus or a ring topology. Error notification alerts upper-layer protocols that a transmission error has occurred, and the sequencing of data frames reorders frames that are transmitted out of sequence. Finally, flow control moderates the transmission of data so that the receiving device is not overwhelmed with more traffic than it can handle at one time.

The Institute of Electrical and Electronics Engineers (IEEE) has subdivided the data link layer into two sublayers: Logical Link Control (LLC) and Media Access Control (MAC). Figure E-7 illustrates the IEEE sublayers of the data link layer.

**Figure E-7**   *The Data Link Layer Contains Two Sublayers*

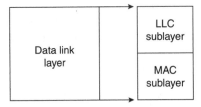

The Logical Link Control (LLC) sublayer of the data link layer manages communications between devices over a single link of a network. LLC is defined in the IEEE 802.2 specification and supports both connectionless and connection-oriented services used by higher-layer protocols. IEEE 802.2 defines a number of fields in data link layer frames that enable multiple higher-layer protocols to share a single physical data link. The Media Access Control (MAC) sublayer of the data link layer manages protocol access to the physical network medium. The IEEE MAC specification defines MAC addresses, which enable multiple devices to uniquely identify one another at the data link layer.

# OSI Model Network Layer

The network layer provides routing and related functions that enable multiple data links to be combined into an internetwork. This is accomplished by the logical addressing (as opposed to the physical addressing) of devices. The network layer supports both connection-oriented and connectionless service from higher-layer protocols. Network layer protocols typically are routing protocols, but other types of protocols are implemented at the network layer as well. Some common routing protocols include Border Gateway Protocol (BGP), an Internet interdomain routing protocol; Open Shortest Path First (OSPF), a link-state, interior gateway protocol developed for use in TCP/IP networks; and Routing Information Protocol (RIP), an Internet routing protocol that uses hop count as its metric.

# OSI Model Transport Layer

The transport layer implements optional reliable internetwork data transport services that are transparent to upper layers. Transport layer functions can include flow control, multiplexing, virtual circuit management, and error checking and recovery.

Flow control manages data transmission between devices so that the transmitting device does not send more data than the receiving device can process. Multiplexing enables data from several applications to be transmitted onto a single physical link. Virtual circuits are established, maintained, and terminated by the transport layer. Error checking involves creating various mechanisms for detecting transmission errors, while error recovery involves taking an action, such as requesting that data be retransmitted, to resolve any errors that occur.

Some transport layer implementations include Transmission Control Protocol, Name Binding Protocol, and OSI transport protocols. Transmission Control Protocol (TCP) is the protocol in the TCP/IP suite that provides reliable transmission of data. Name Binding Protocol (NBP) is the protocol that associates AppleTalk names with addresses. OSI transport protocols are a series of transport protocols in the OSI protocol suite.

# OSI Model Session Layer

The session layer establishes, manages, and terminates communication sessions between presentation layer entities. Communication sessions consist of service requests and service responses that occur between applications located in different network devices. These requests and responses are coordinated by protocols implemented at the session layer. Some examples of session layer implementations include Zone Information Protocol (ZIP), the AppleTalk protocol that coordinates the name binding process; and Session Control Protocol (SCP), the DECnet Phase IV session layer protocol.

# OSI Model Presentation Layer

The presentation layer provides a variety of coding and conversion functions that are applied to application layer data. These functions ensure that information sent from the application layer of one system will be readable by the application layer of another system. Some examples of presentation layer coding and conversion schemes include common data representation formats, conversion of character representation formats, common data compression schemes, and common data encryption schemes.

Common data representation formats, or the use of standard image, sound, and video formats, enable the interchange of application data between different types of computer systems. Conversion schemes are used to exchange information with systems by using different text and data representations, such as EBCDIC and ASCII. Standard data compression schemes enable data that is compressed at the source device to be properly decompressed at the destination. Standard data-encryption schemes enable data encrypted at the source device to be properly deciphered at the destination.

Presentation layer implementations are not typically associated with a particular protocol stack. Some well-known standards for video include QuickTime and Motion Picture Experts Group (MPEG). QuickTime is an Apple Computer specification for video and audio, and MPEG is a standard for video compression and coding.

Among the well-known graphic image formats are Graphics Interchange Format (GIF), Joint Photographic Experts Group (JPEG), and Tagged Image File Format (TIFF). GIF is a standard for compressing and coding graphic images. JPEG is another compression and coding standard for graphic images, and TIFF is a standard coding format for graphic images.

# OSI Model Application Layer

The application layer is the OSI layer closest to the end user, which means that both the OSI application layer and the user interact directly with the software application.

This layer interacts with software applications that implement a communicating component. Such application programs fall outside the scope of the OSI model. Application layer functions typically include identifying communication partners, determining resource availability, and synchronizing communication.

When identifying communication partners, the application layer determines the identity and availability of communication partners for an application with data to transmit. When determining resource availability, the application layer must decide whether sufficient network resources for the requested communication exist. In synchronizing communication, all communication between applications requires cooperation that is managed by the application layer.

Two key types of application layer implementations are TCP/IP applications and OSI applications. TCP/IP applications are protocols, such as Telnet, File Transfer Protocol (FTP), and Simple Mail Transfer Protocol (SMTP), that exist in the Internet Protocol suite. OSI applications are protocols, such as File Transfer, Access, and Management (FTAM), Virtual Terminal Protocol (VTP), and Common Management Information Protocol (CMIP), that exist in the OSI suite.

# Information Formats

The data and control information that is transmitted through internetworks takes a wide variety of forms. The terms used to refer to these information formats are not used consistently in the internetworking industry but sometimes are used interchangeably.

Common information formats include frames, packets, datagrams, segments, messages, cells, and data units.

A frame is an information unit whose source and destination are data link layer entities. A frame is composed of the data link layer header (and possibly a trailer) and upper-layer data. The header and trailer contain control information intended for the data link layer entity in the destination system. Data from upper-layer entities is encapsulated in the data link layer header and trailer. Figure E-8 illustrates the basic components of a data link layer frame.

**Figure E-8**    *Data from Upper-Layer Entities Makes Up the Data Link Layer Frame*

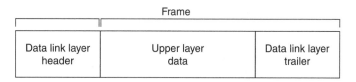

A packet is an information unit whose source and destination are network layer entities. A packet is composed of the network layer header (and possibly a trailer) and upper-layer data. The header and trailer contain control information intended for the network layer entity in the destination system. Data from upper-layer entities is encapsulated in the network layer header and trailer. Figure E-9 illustrates the basic components of a network layer packet.

**Figure E-9**    *Three Basic Components Make Up a Network Layer Packet*

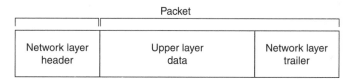

The term *datagram* usually refers to an information unit whose source and destination are network layer entities that use connectionless network service.

The term *segment* usually refers to an information unit whose source and destination are transport layer entities.

A *message* is an information unit whose source and destination entities exist above the network layer (often the application layer).

A *cell* is an information unit of a fixed size whose source and destination are data link layer entities. Cells are used in switched environments, such as Asynchronous Transfer Mode (ATM) and Switched Multimegabit Data Service (SMDS) networks. A cell is composed of the header and payload. The header contains control information intended for the destination data link layer entity and is typically 5 bytes long. The payload contains upper-layer data that is encapsulated in the cell header and is typically 48 bytes long.

The length of the header and the payload fields always are exactly the same for each cell. Figure E-10 depicts the components of a typical cell.

**Figure E-10**  *Two Components Make Up a Typical Cell*

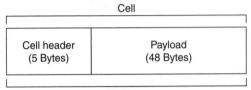

*Data unit* is a generic term that refers to a variety of information units. Some common data units are service data units (SDUs), protocol data units (PDUs), and bridge protocol data units (BPDUs). SDUs are information units from upper-layer protocols that define a service request to a lower-layer protocol. PDU is OSI terminology for describing the data unit at a given layer. For example, the Layer 3 PDU is also known as a packet; the Layer 4 PDU is also known as a segment. BPDUs are used by the spanning-tree algorithm as hello messages.

# Common Requests For Comments

The Internet Requests For Comments (RFCs) documents are the written definitions of the protocols and policies of the Internet.

## Requests For Comments Information

The following information about RFCs was adapted from RFC 1594, "FYI Q/A—For New Internet Users":

The Internet Architecture Board (IAB) is concerned with technical and policy issues involving the evolution of the Internet architecture. All decisions of the IAB are made public. The principal vehicle by which IAB decisions are propagated to the parties interested in the Internet and its TCP/IP protocol suite is the Request For Comments (RFC) note series and the Internet Monthly Report.

RFCs are the working notes of the Internet research and development community. A document in this series may be on essentially any topic related to computer communication, and may be anything from a meeting report to the specification of a standard. Submissions for Requests For Comments may be sent to the RFC Editor (RFC-EDITOR@ISI.EDU).

Most RFCs are the descriptions of network protocols or services, often giving detailed procedures and formats for their implementation. Other RFCs report on the results of policy studies or summarize the work of technical committees or workshops. All RFCs are considered public domain unless explicitly marked otherwise.

While RFCs are not refereed publications, they do receive technical review from either the task forces, individual technical experts, or the RFC Editor, as appropriate. Currently, most standards are published as RFCs, but not all RFCs specify standards.

Anyone can submit a document for publication as an RFC. Submissions must be made via electronic mail to the RFC Editor. Please consult RFC 1543, "Instructions to RFC Authors," for further information.

Once a document is assigned an RFC number and published, that RFC is never revised or reissued with the same number. There is never a question of having the most recent version of a particular RFC. However, a protocol (such as File Transfer Protocol [FTP]) may be improved and redocumented many times in several different RFCs. It is important to verify that you have the most recent RFC on a particular protocol. The "Internet Official Protocol

Standards" memo is the reference for determining the correct RFC to refer to for the current specification of each protocol.

RFCs are available online at several repositories around the world.

Table F-1 lists some common Requests For Comments (RFCs). A complete list and the documents can be found at www.cis.ohio-state.edu/htbin/rfc/rfc-index.html. info.internet.isi.edu/in-notes/rfc/ also provides RFCs.

**Table F-1**  *Common Requests For Comments*

| RFC | Title |
|-----|-------|
| 2439 | BGP Route Flap Damping |
| 2385 | Protection of BGP Sessions via TCP MD5 Signature Option |
| 2370 | The OSPF Opaque LSA Option |
| 2329 | OSPF Standardization Report |
| 2328 | OSPF Version 2 |
| 2283 | Multiprotocol Extensions for BGP-4 |
| 2236 | Internet Group Message Protocol (IGMP), Version 2 |
| 2226 | IP Broadcast over ATM Networks |
| 2200 | Internet Official Protocol Standards (obsoletes RFC 2000, RFC 1920, RFC 1880, RFC 1800, RFC 1780, RFC 1720, RFC 1610, RFC 1600, RFC 1540, RFC 1500, RFC 1410, RFC 1360, RFC 1280, RFC 1250, RFC 1200, RFC 1140, RFC 1130, RFC 1100, and RFC 1083) |
| 2185 | Routing Aspects of IPv6 Transition |
| 2178 | OSPF Version 2 (Obsoleted by RFC 2328) |
| 2131 | Dynamic Host Configuration Protocol (DHCP) |
| 2105 | Cisco Systems' Tag Switching Architecture Overview |
| 2050 | Internet Registry IP Allocation Guidelines |
| 2042 | Registering New BGP Attribute Types |
| 1998 | Application of the BGP Community Attribute in Multi-Home Routing |
| 1997 | BGP Communities Attribute |
| 1994 | PPP Challenge Handshake Authentication Protocol (CHAP) |
| 1990 | The PPP Multilink Protocol (MP) |
| 1983 | Internet Users' Glossary |
| 1966 | BGP Route Reflection—An Alternative to Full-Mesh IBGP |

**Table F-1**    *Common Requests For Comments (Continued)*

| RFC | Title |
| --- | --- |
| 1965 | AS Confederations for BGP |
| 1932 | IP over ATM: A Framework Document |
| 1930 | Guidelines for Creation, Selection, and Registration of an Autonomous System (AS) |
| 1918 | Address Allocation for Private Internets |
| 1863 | A BGP/IDRP Route Server Alternative to a Full-Mesh Routing |
| 1850 | OSPF Version 2 Management Information Base |
| 1817 | CIDR and Classful Routing |
| 1812 | Requirements for IP Version 4 Routers |
| 1793 | Extending OSPF to Support Demand Circuits |
| 1774 | BGP-4 Protocol Analysis |
| 1773 | Experience with the BGP-4 Protocol |
| 1772 | An Application of BGP in the Internet |
| 1771 | A Border Gateway Protocol 4 (BGP-4) |
| 1765 | OSPF Database Overflow |
| 1700 | Assigned Numbers |
| 1663 | PPP Reliable Transmission |
| 1661 | The Point-to-Point Protocol (PPP) |
| 1631 | The IP Network Address Translator (NAT) |
| 1613 | Cisco Systems X.25 over TCP (XOT) |
| 1587 | OSPF NSSA Option |
| 1586 | Guidelines for Running OSPF over Frame Relay Networks |
| 1583 | OSPF Version 2 (obsoleted by RFC 2178) |
| 1570 | PPP LCP Extensions |
| 1548 | The Point-to-Point Protocol (PPP) |
| 1519 | Classless Interdomain Routing (CIDR): An Address Assignment and Aggregation Strategy |
| 1518 | An Architecture for IP Address Allocation with CIDR |
| 1490 | Multiprotocol Interconnect over Frame Relay |
| 1467 | Status of CIDR Deployment in the Internet |
| 1350 | The TFTP Protocol (Revision 2) |

*continues*

**Table F-1**    *Common Requests For Comments (Continued)*

| RFC | Title |
|-----|-------|
| 1305 | Network Time Protocol (Version 3) Specification, Implementation |
| 1247 | OSPF Version 2 (obsoleted by RFC 1583) |
| 1246 | Experience with the OSPF Protocol |
| 1245 | OSPF Protocol Analysis |
| 1219 | On the Assignment of Subnet Numbers |
| 1144 | Compressing TCP/IP Headers for Low-Speed Serial Links |
| 1058 | Routing Information Protocol |
| 1042 | Standard for the Transmission of IP Datagrams over IEEE 802 Networks |
| 1020 | Internet Numbers |
| 951 | Bootstrap Protocol |
| 950 | Internet Standard Subnetting Procedure |
| 903 | Reverse Address Resolution Protocol |
| 821 | Simple Mail Transfer Protocol |
| 793 | Transmission Control Protocol |
| 792 | Internet Control Message Protocol |
| 791 | Internet Protocol |

# Answers to the Review Questions

This appendix contains the answers to each chapter's review questions. The correct answers are in bold.

## Chapter 1

1 What characteristic defines the difference between classful and classless protocols?

 **Classless routing protocols send a subnet mask with each route advertisement.**

2 What characteristic of distance vector protocols is responsible for their slower convergence?

 **Distance vector protocols will not accept any updated information about a route when the route is marked as being in holddown (unless the new routing information has a better metric). A route remains in holddown based upon the holddown timer setting for that protocol. RIP and IGRP have a default holddown time of 180 and 280 seconds, respectively.**

3 Which field in a routing table entry measures the reachability of the destination network?

 **The reachability of a destination network is specified by the metric assigned to the route.**

4 Complete the following table by indicating which protocols demonstrate the characteristic shown in the right column. Indicate your choices in the left column by entering one or more of the following routing protocols: **RIPv1, RIPv2, IGRP, EIGRP, or OSPF.**

| Protocol | Characteristic |
| --- | --- |
| **EIGRP** | Maintains a topology table to assist in rapid convergence |
| **RIPv1, IGRP** | Uses broadcast packets to propagate topology updates |
| **OSPF** | Has an administrative distance of 110 |
| **OSPF** | Supports flooding of updates to avoid routing loops |

*continues*

| Protocol | Characteristic |
|---|---|
| OSPF | Requires a hierarchical design to operate correctly |
| EIGRP | Allows manual route summarization at any location |
| IGRP, EIGRP, OSFP | Can select preferred path based upon bandwidth consideration |
| RIPv2, EIGRP, OSPF | Supports variable-length subnet masks |
| OSPF | Is a link-state protocol supported by all vendors of routing equipment |

**5** For distance vector protocols, what did Cisco implement as a way to enable routers to become aware of topology changes more quickly?

**Cisco implemented flash updates to enable routers that are running distance vector protocols to become aware of topology changes more quickly.**

**6** Which characteristic of OSPF ensures that convergence time will always be greater than 5 seconds?

**OSPF allows a 5-second (by default) window to gather all the LSA input about the topology change before executing the SPF algorithm.**

---

NOTE    **Also note that after the SPF algorithm has rebuilt the topology database and created a new routing table, the algorithm cannot be executed for another 10 seconds (by default). This delay helps prevent a thrashing condition from occurring in the network. A thrashing condition represents an almost continuous execution of the algorithm (due to link flapping) that prevents traffic forwarding due to traffic suspension during a route calculation phase.**

---

**7** What function does the **clear ip route 172.16.3.0** command perform?

**The clear ip route 172.16.3.0 command results in requests for updated route information being sent to all neighboring routers in an attempt to update the routing table contents for the 172.16.3.0 entry.**

# Chapter 2

**1**  You are in charge of the network in the following figure. It consists of 5 LANs with 25 users on each LAN, and 5 serial links. You have been assigned the IP address 192.168.49.0/24 to allocate addressing for all links.

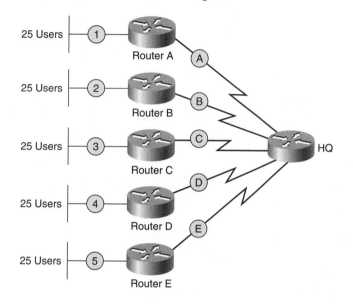

Write the addresses that you would assign to each of the LANs and the serial links in the following spaces.

**For 5 LANs with 25 users each, 3 subnet bits and 5 host bits will be needed, yielding a maximum of 8 subnets with 30 hosts each. A prefix of /27 will therefore be used. The available subnets are these:**

— **192.168.49.0/27**

— **192.168.49.32/27**

— **192.168.49.64/27**

— **192.168.49.96/27**

— **192.168.49.128/27**

— **192.168.49.160/27**

— **192.168.49.192/27**

— **192.168.49.224/27**

For the WAN addresses, one of the previous subnets that is not used on the LANs would be further subnetted. A prefix of /30 would be used to allow for two host addresses on each WAN. This would leave 3 bits for additional subnetting, giving eight subnets for the WANs. For example, if 192.168.49.160/27 is further subnetted, the available subnets for the WANs are these:

— **192.168.49.160/30**

— **192.168.49.164/30**

— **192.168.49.168/30**

— **192.168.49.172/30**

— **192.168.49.176/30**

— **192.168.49.180/30**

— **192.168.49.184/30**

— **192.168.49.188/30**

**One possible allocation of the addresses is as follows:**

| | |
|---|---|
| LAN 1 | **192.168.49.0/27** |
| LAN 2 | **192.168.49.32/27** |
| LAN 3 | **192.168.49.64/27** |
| LAN 4 | **192.168.49.96/27** |
| LAN 5 | **192.168.49.128/27** |
| WAN A | **192.168.49.160/30** |
| WAN B | **192.168.49.164/30** |
| WAN C | **192.168.49.168/30** |
| WAN D | **192.168.49.172/30** |
| WAN E | **192.168.49.176/30** |

**2** The following figure shows a network with subnets of the 172.16.0.0 network configured. Indicate where route summarization can occur in this network and what the summarized addresses would be in the spaces that follow.

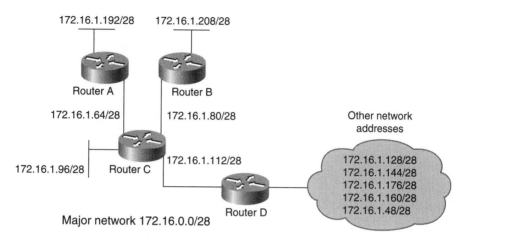

| Router C Routing Table Entries | Summarized Routes That Can Be Advertised to Router D from Router C |
|---|---|
| **172.16.1.192/28** | **172.16.1.192/27** |
| | **Summarizes: 172.16.1.192/28, 172.16.1.208/28** |
| **172.16.1.208/28** | |
| **172.16.1.64/28** | **172.16.1.64/26** |
| | **Summarizes: 172.16.1.64/28, 172.16.1.80/28, 172.16.1.96/28, 172.16.1.112/28** |
| **172.16.1.80/28** | |
| **172.16.1.96/28** | |
| **172.16.1.112/28** | |

**3** The following figure shows a network with subnets of the 172.16.0.0 network configured. Indicate where route summarization can occur in this network and what the summarized address would be in the spaces that follow.

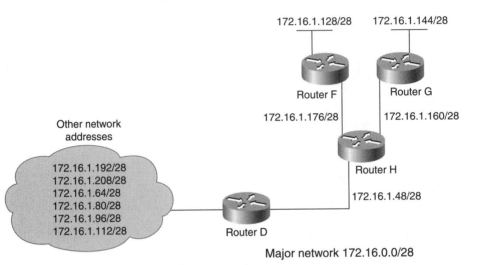

172.16.1.128/28          172.16.1.144/28

Router F          Router G

172.16.1.176/28          172.16.1.160/28

Other network addresses

172.16.1.192/28
172.16.1.208/28
172.16.1.64/28
172.16.1.80/28
172.16.1.96/28
172.16.1.112/28

Router H

172.16.1.48/28

Router D

Major network 172.16.0.0/28

| Router H Routing Table Entries | Summarized Routes That Can Be Advertised to Router D from Router H |
|---|---|
| 172.16.1.48/28 | 172.16.1.48/28 |
| 172.16.1.128/28 | 172.16.1.128/26 |
| | **Summarizes:** |
| | 172.16.1.128/28, 172.16.1.144/28, 172.16.1.160/28, 172.16.1.176/28 |
| 172.16.1.144/28 | |
| 172.16.1.160/28 | |
| 172.16.1.176/28 | |

**4** What are some of the advantages of using a hierarchical IP addressing model?

**Some of the advantages of using a hierarchical IP addressing model include a reduced number of routing table entries and efficient allocation of addresses.**

**5** Given an address with a prefix of /20, how many additional subnets are gained when subnetting with a prefix of /28?

$2^8 = 256$ **additional subnets are gained.**

**6** When selecting a route, which prefix match is used?

**When selecting a route, the longest prefix match is used.**

# Chapter 3

**1** List three reasons why OSPF operates better than RIP in a large internetwork.

**The reasons include:**

— **OSPF has faster convergence.**

— **OSPF supports VLSMs.**

— **OSPF has virtually no network reachability limitations.**

— **OSPF uses bandwidth more efficiently.**

— **OSPF path selection is based on cost rather than on hops.**

**2** What does a router do when it receives an LSU?

**When a router receives an LSU, it does the following:**

— **If the entry does not already exist, it adds the entry to its link-state database, sends an LSAck to the DR, floods the information to other routers, and updates its routing table.**

— **If the entry already exists and the received LSU has the same information, it ignores the LSA entry.**

— **If the entry already exists but the LSU includes new information, it adds the entry to its link-state database, sends an LSAck to the DR, floods the information to other routers, and updates its routing table.**

— **If the entry already exists but the LSU includes older information, it sends an LSU to the sender with its newer information.**

**3** Identify when the exchange protocol and the flooding process are used, and describe how each operates.

**The exchange protocol is used to get neighboring routers into a full state. The first step in this protocol is for the DR and the BDR to establish adjacencies with each of the other routers. During this process, a master-slave relationship is created between each router and its adjacent DR and BDR. The master and slave routers exchange DBDs to synchronize their databases. When adjacent routers are in a full state, they do not redo the exchange protocol unless the full state is changed to a different state.**

**The flooding process is used anytime there is a change in a link-state, such as when a link goes down or a new link is added to the network. In this process, all link-state changes are sent in LSU packets to the DR and the BDR. The DR is then responsible for forwarding the LSUs to all other routers on the network. If a router is connected to other networks, it floods the LSU to those other networks.**

**4**  Write a brief description of the following:

— Internal router—**A router that resides within an area and routes traffic.**

— LSU—**A link-state update packet. This packet includes link-state advertisements.**

— DBD—**A database description packet (also DDP). This packet is used during the exchange protocol and includes summary information about link-state entries.**

— Hello packet—**Used during the Hello protocol. This packet includes information that enables routers to establish themselves as neighbors.**

**5**  Match the term in the table with the statement most closely describing it:

A. Indicates the router responsible for route synchronization

B. Indicates routers that can route information

C. Indicates that routers can discover link-state information

D. A collection of routers and networks

| Term | Answer |
|------|--------|
| Area | **D** |
| Full state | **B** |
| DR | **A** |
| Exchange state | **C** |

**6**  Name the two RFC-compliant modes for OSPF over nonbroadcast multiaccess networks. Name the additional Cisco modes for OSPF over NBMA.

**RFC-compliant modes for OSPF over NBMA:**

— **Nonbroadcast multiaccess (NBMA)**

— **Point-to-multipoint**

**Cisco modes for OSPF over NBMA:**

— **Point-to-multipoint nonbroadcast**

— **Broadcast**

— **Point-to-point**

**7** How many subnets are there when OSPF is used in an NBMA environment with nonbroadcast multiaccess mode?

**One**

**8** What command should be used to run OSPF on all interfaces on a router?

**network 0.0.0.0 255.255.255.255 area 0**

**9** What command is used to configure OSPF in broadcast mode?

**ip ospf network broadcast**

**10** How do you configure OSPF point-to-point mode on a point-to-point subinterface?

**Point-to-point mode is the default OSPF mode for point-to-point subinterfaces, so no configuration is required.**

# Chapter 4

**1** Define hierarchical routing and explain what internetwork problems it solves.

**OSPF's capability to separate a large internetwork into multiple areas is also referred to as hierarchical routing. Hierarchical routing enables you to separate your large internetwork (autonomous system) into smaller internetworks that are called areas. The advantages include smaller routing tables, reduced frequency of SPF calculations, and reduced LSU overhead.**

**2** An internal router will receive type 5 LSAs if it is what type of area?

**If it is an area that is not configured as stub, totally stubby, or not-so-stubby**

**3** What area types are connected to the backbone area?

**All area types are connected to the backbone.**

**4** The backbone must be configured as what area?

**The backbone area must always be Area 0.**

**5** Write a brief description of the following LSA types:

Type 1: Router link entry (record)

Type 2: Network link entry

Type 3 or 4: Summary link entry

Type 5: Autonomous system external link entry

| LSA Type | Name | Description |
|---|---|---|
| 1 | Router link entry (record) (O—OSPF) (Router link states) | Generated by each router for each area it belongs to. It describes the states of the router's link to the area. These are flooded only within a particular area. The link status and cost are two of the descriptors provided. |
| 2 | Network link entry (O—OSPF) (Net link states) | Generated by DRs in multiaccess networks. They describe the set of routers attached to a particular network. Flooded within the area that contains the network only. |
| 3 or 4 | Summary link entry (IA—OSPF Interarea) (Summary net link states and summary ASB link states) | Originated by ABRs. Describes the links between the ABR and the internal routers of a local area. These entries are flooded throughout the backbone area to the other ABRs. Type 3 LSAs describe routes to networks within the local area and are sent to the backbone area. Type 4 describes reachability to ASBRs. These link entries are not flooded through totally stubby areas. |
| 5 | Autonomous system external link entry (E1—OSPF external type 1) (E2—OSPF external type 2) (AS external link states) | Originated by the ASBR. Describes routes to destinations external to the autonomous system. Flooded throughout an OSPF autonomous system except for stub, totally stubby, and not-so-stubby areas. |

**6**  Describe the path a packet must take to get from one area to another.

**The packet must go through the source area, through the ABR, through the backbone area, through the next ABR, and then through the internal routers to its final destination.**

**7**  When is a default route injected into an area?

**When the area is configured as a form of a stub area**

**8**  What are the four types of OSPF routers?

**The four types of OSPF routers are internal, backbone, ABR, and ASBR.**

**9**  Which router generates a type 2 LSA?

**A DR generates a type 2 LSA.**

**10** What are the advantages of configuring a totally stubby area?

**The routing tables in the routers in a totally stubby area will be smaller because external and summary routes are not injected into this type of area. This will result in less routing information being sent, and increased stability and scalability of the OSPF network.**

**11** What command is used on an ABR to summarize routes for a specific area?

**The area *area-id* range *address mask* command is used on an ABR to summarize routes for a specific area.**

# Chapter 5

**1** How are IGRP and EIGRP different in their metric calculation?

**IGRP and EIGRP use the same metric calculation, but EIGRP's metric value is multiplied by 256 to give it more granularity in its decision making.**

**2** Why are EIGRP routing updates described as reliable?

**EIGRP update packets are generated by the Reliable Transport Protocol (RTP) within EIGRP and must be acknowledged by the receiving device.**

**3** What does it mean when a route is marked as a feasible successor?

**A route is marked as a feasible successor when the next-hop router's advertised distance is less than the feasible distance for the current successor route to the destination network. A feasible successor route is an alternate or backup route to the primary route specified by the successor route in the routing table.**

**4** What is the recommended practice for configuring bandwidth on a Frame Relay point-to-point subinterface?

**Configure the bandwidth on a Frame Relay point-to-point subinterface based upon the number of virtual circuits divided into the bandwidth of the physical interface. For example, if the physical interface was a T1 and there were 12 VCs, each subinterface would have a configured bandwidth of 1.544 Mb ÷ 12 = 128 kbps.**

**5** In this exercise, you can test your understanding of EIGRP by matching terms with statements. Place the letter of the description in front of the term that the statement describes. A statement may describe more than one term.

Statements:

— A. A network protocol that EIGRP supports

— B. A table that contains feasible successor information

— C. Administrative distance to determine routing information that is included in this table

— D. A neighbor router that has the best path to a table destination

— E. A neighbor router that has the best alternative path to a destination

— F. An algorithm used by EIGRP that assures fast convergence

— G. A multicast packet used to discover neighbors

— H. A packet sent by EIGRP routers when a new neighbor is discovered and when a change occurs

| Answer | Term |
|--------|------|
| D | Successor |
| E | Feasible successor |
| G | Hello |
| B | Topology table |
| A | IP |
| H | Update |
| A | AppleTalk |
| C | Routing table |
| F | DUAL |
| A | IPX |

**6** Answer true or false for the following statements:

— EIGRP performs autosummarization. **True**

— Autosummarization can't be turned off. **False**

— EIGRP supports VLSM. **True**

— EIGRP could maintain three independent routing tables. **True**

— The hello interval is an unchangeable fixed value. **False**

# Chapter 6

**1** When would it be appropriate to use static routes to interconnect autonomous systems?

**It would be appropriate to use static routes if you have one of the following conditions:**

— **A single connection to the Internet or another AS**

— **No concern for routing policy and route selection for your AS**

— **Lack of memory or processor power on routers to handle BGP constant updates**

— **Limited understanding of route filtering and BGP path selection process**

— **Low bandwidth between autonomous systems**

**2** What protocol does BGP us as its transport protocol? What port number does BGP use?

**BGP uses TCP as its transport protocol; port 179 has been assigned to BGP.**

**3** Any two routers that have formed a BGP connection can be referred to as what two terms?

**Any two routers that have formed a BGP connection are called BGP peers or BGP neighbors.**

**4** Write a brief description of the following:

Internal BGP—**When BGP is running between routers within one AS, it is termed internal BGP (IBGP).**

External BGP—**When BGP is running between routers in different autonomous systems, it is termed external BGP (EBGP).**

Well-known attributes—**A well-known attribute is one that all BGP implementations must recognize. Well-known attributes are propagated to BGP neighbors.**

Transitive attributes—**A transitive attribute that is not implemented in a router can be passed to other BGP routers untouched.**

BGP synchronization—**The BGP synchronization rule states that a BGP router should not use or advertise to an external neighbor a route learned by IBGP until a matching route has been learned from an IGP.**

**5** For an external update advertised by IBGP, where does the value for the next-hop attribute of an update come from?

**For an external update advertised by IBGP, the value of the next-hop attribute is carried from the EBGP update.**

**6** Describe the complication that an NBMA network can cause for the next-hop attribute of an update.

**When running BGP over a multiaccess network, a BGP router will use the appropriate address as the next-hop address to avoid inserting additional hops into the network. The address used is of the router on the multiaccess network that advertised the network. On Ethernet networks, that router will be accessible to all other routers on the Ethernet. On NBMA media, however, all routers on the network may not be accessible to each other, so the next-hop address used may be unreachable.**

**7** Complete the table to answer the following questions about these BGP attributes:

— In which order are the attributes preferred (1, 2, or 3)?

— For the attribute, is the highest or lowest value preferred?

— Which other routers, if any, is the attribute sent to?

| Attribute | Order Preferred In | Highest or Lowest Value Preferred? | Sent to Which Other Routers? |
|---|---|---|---|
| Local Preference | 2 | **Highest** | **Sent to internal BGP neighbors only** |
| MED | 3 | **Lowest** | **Sent to external BGP neighbors only** |
| Weight | 1 | **Highest** | **Not sent to any BGP neighbors; local to router only** |

**8** How is the BGP router ID chosen?

**The BGP router ID is an IP address assigned to a router and is determined on startup. The BGP router ID is chosen the same way that the OSPF router ID is chosen—it is the highest active IP address on the router, unless a loopback interface with an IP address exists, in which case it is the highest such loopback IP address.**

**9**  What command disables BGP synchronization?

**Use the no synchronization router configuration command to disable BGP synchronization.**

**10**  What are the four BGP message types?

**The four BGP message types are: open, keepalive, update, and notification.**

**11**  How does BGP-4 support CIDR?

**BGP-4 support for CIDR includes the following:**

— **The BGP update message includes both the prefix and the prefix length. Previous versions included only the prefix; the length was assumed from the address class.**

— **Addresses can be aggregated when advertised by a BGP router.**

— **The AS-path attribute can include a combined unordered list of all autonomous systems that all the aggregated routes have passed through. This combined list should be considered to ensure that the route is loop-free.**

**12**  Which command is used to activate a BGP session with another router?

**The neighbor {*ip-address* | *peer-group-name*} remote-as *autonomous-system* router configuration command is used to activate a BGP session with another router.**

**13**  Which command is used to display information about the BGP connections to neighbors?

**The show ip bgp neighbors command is used to display information about the BGP connections to neighbors.**

# Chapter 7

**1**  Describe the BGP split horizon rule.

**The BGP split horizon rule specifies that routes learned via IBGP are never propagated to other IBGP peers.**

**2**  What effect do route reflectors have on the BGP split horizon rule?

**Route reflectors modify the BGP split horizon rule by allowing the router configured as the route reflector to propagate routes learned by IBGP to other IBGP peers.**

**3**  Write a brief description of the following:

Route reflector—**A route reflector is a router that is configured to be allowed to advertise (or reflect) routes that it learned via IBGP to other IBGP peers.**

Route reflector client—**A route reflector client is a router that is connected via IBGP only to a route reflector.**

Route reflector cluster—**The combination of the route reflector and its clients is called a cluster.**

4 Routers configured as route reflectors do not have to be fully meshed with IBGP. True or false?

**False**

5 When a route reflector receives an update from a client, it sends it to where?

**When a route reflector receives an update from a client, it sends it to all nonclient peers and all client peers (except the originator of the route).**

6 What is the command used to configure a router as a BGP route reflector?

**The neighbor *ip-address* route-reflector-client router configuration command is used to configure the router as a BGP route reflector and to configure the specified neighbor as its client.**

7 Describe the advantages of using prefix lists rather than access lists for BGP route filtering.

**The advantages of using prefix lists include these:**

— **A significant performance improvement over access lists in loading and route lookup of large lists.**

— **Support for incremental modifications. Compared to the normal access list in which one no command will erase the whole access list, prefix list entries can be modified incrementally.**

— **More user-friendly command-line interface. The command-line interface for using extended access lists to filter BGP updates is difficult to understand and use.**

— **Greater flexibility.**

8 In a prefix list, what is the sequence number used for?

**The sequence number of the prefix-list statement is used to determine the order in which the statements are processed when filtering.**

9 What command is used to clear the hit count of the prefix list entries?

**The clear ip prefix-list *name* [*network/len*] command resets the hit count shown on prefix list entries.**

**10**  What is BGP multihoming?

**Multihoming is the term used to describe when an AS is connected to more than one ISP. This is usually done for two reasons:**

— **To increase the reliability of the connection to the Internet so that if one connection fails, another will still be available**

— **To increase the performance so that better paths can be used to certain destinations**

**11**  What command is used to assign a weight to a BGP neighbor connection?

**The neighbor *ip-address* weight *weight* router configuration command is used to assign a weight to a neighbor connection.**

**12**  What is the preferred method to use to advertise an aggregated route from an AS into BGP?

**The preferred method to advertise an aggregated route from an AS into BGP is to use the aggregate-address command. With this command, as long as a more specific route exists in the BGP table, then the aggregate gets sent. If the aggregating router loses all of its specific connections to the networks being aggregated, then the aggregate route will disappear from the BGP table and the BGP aggregate will not get sent.**

# Chapter 8

**1**  List three reasons you might use multiple routing protocols in a network.

**Some reasons you may need multiple protocols are as follows:**

— **When you are migrating from an older IGP to a new IGP, multiple redistribution boundaries may exist until the new protocol has displaced the old protocol completely.**

— **You want to use another protocol but need to keep the old protocol due to the needs of host systems.**

— **Different departments might not want to upgrade their routers, or they might not implement a sufficiently strict filtering policy. In these cases, you can protect yourself by terminating the other routing protocol on one of your routers.**

— **If you have a mixed-router vendor environment, you can use a Cisco-specific protocol in the Cisco portion of the network and then use a common protocol to communicate with non-Cisco devices.**

**2** What two parameters are used by routers to select the best path when they learn two or more routes to the same destination from different routing protocols?

**For routers to select the best path when they learn two or more routes to the same destination from different routing protocols, Cisco uses two parameters:**

— **Administrative distance—Administrative distance is used to rate the believability of a routing protocol. Each routing protocol is prioritized in order of most to least believable (reliable) using a value called administrative distance. This criterion is the first that a router uses to determine which routing protocol to believe if more than one protocol provides route information for the same destination.**

— **Routing metric—The metric is a value representing the path between the local router and the destination network. The metric is usually a hop or cost value, depending on the protocol being used.**

**3** What are the components of the EIGRP routing metric?

**The components of the EIGRP routing metric are as follows:**

— **Bandwidth—Minimum bandwidth of the route in kilobits per second**

— **Delay—Route delay in tens of microseconds**

— **Reliability—Likelihood of successful packet transmission expressed in a number from 0 to 255, where 255 means that the route is 100 percent reliable**

— **Loading—Effective loading of the route expressed in a number from 1 to 255, where 255 means that the route is 100 percent loaded**

— **MTU—Maximum transmission unit, the maximum packet size along the route in bytes, an integer greater than or equal to 1**

**4** Consider that you have a dialup WAN connection between site A and site B. What can you do to prevent excess routing update traffic from crossing the link, but still have the boundary routers know the networks that are at the remote sites?

**Use static routes, possibly in combination with passive interfaces.**

**5** What command is used to cause RIP to source a default route?

**When running RIP, you can create the default route by using the ip default-network command. If the router has a directly connected interface onto the network specified in the ip default-network command, RIP will generate (or source) a default route to its RIP neighbor routers.**

**6** If no filter is associated with an interface, what happens to packets destined for that interface?

**If a filter is not associated with the interface, the packets are processed normally.**

**7** What command can be used to discover the path that a packet takes through a network?

**To discover the routes that a packet follows when traveling to its destination from a router, use the traceroute privileged EXEC command.**

**8** How can a routing loop result in a network that has redundant paths between two routing processes?

**Depending on how you employ redistribution, routers can send routing information received from one autonomous system back into that same autonomous system. The feedback is similar to the routing loop problem that occurs in distance vector protocols.**

**9** What is redistribution?

**Cisco routers allow internetworks using different routing protocols (referred to as autonomous systems) to exchange routing information through a feature called route redistribution. Redistribution is defined as the capability of boundary routers connecting different autonomous systems to exchange and advertise routing information received from one autonomous system to the other autonomous system.**

**10** What is the default administrative distance for IGRP? For RIP? For OSPF?

**The default administrative distance for IGRP is 100.**

**The default administrative distance for RIP is 120.**

**The default administrative distance for OSPF is 110.**

**11** When configuring a default metric for redistributed routes, should the metric be set to a value *larger* or *smaller* than the largest metric within the AS?

**Larger**

**12** What command is used for policy-based routing to establish criteria based on the packet length?

**The match length *min max* route map configuration command can be used to establish criteria based on the packet length between specified minimum and maximum values.**

**13** What command is used to configure filtering of the routing update traffic from an interface? What command mode is this command entered in?

**To assign an access list to filter outgoing routing updates, use the distribute-list {*access-list-number* | *name*} out *interface-name* command. This command is entered in Router(config-router)# command mode.**

**14** What does the following command do?

```
distance 150 0.0.0.0 255.255.255.255 3
```

The distance **150 0.0.0.0 255.255.255.255 3** command is used to change the default administrative distance of routes, from specific source addresses, that are permitted by an access-list. The parameters mean the following:

| Parameter | Meaning |
| --- | --- |
| 150 | Defines the administrative distance that specified routes will be assigned. |
| 0.0.0.0 255.255.255.255 | Defines the source address of the router supplying the routing information—in this case, any router. |
| 3 | Defines the access list to be used to filter incoming routing updates to determine which will have their administrative distance changed. |

Routes matching access list 3, from any router, will be assigned an administrative distance of 150.

15 What are the benefits of policy-based routing?

**The benefits that can be achieved by implementing policy-based routing in networks include these:**

— **Source-based transit provider selection**

— **Quality of service (QoS)**

— **Cost savings**

— **Load sharing**

16 Policy-based routing is applied to *what* packets?

**Incoming**

# Chapter 9

1 Name the two major functions performed by routers.

**Routers perform both a routing and a switching function.**

2 What are the benefits of VLSMs?

**The benefits of VLSMs include these:**

— **Even more efficient use of IP addresses**

— **Greater capability to use route summarization**

**3** If the subnet 172.17.2.32/28 was further subnetted with a /30 prefix, how many more subnets would be created? How many hosts would be available on each of these new subnets?

**The additional 2 subnet bits would create $2^2 = 4$ more subnets. There would be $2^2 - 2 = 2$ hosts available on each of these subnets.**

**4** Define the following terms:

**IGP—Interior gateway protocol—A routing protocol used to exchange routing information *within* an autonomous system. RIP, IGRP, OSPF, and EIGRP are examples of IGPs.**

**EGP—Exterior gateway protocol—A routing protocol used to connect *between* autonomous systems. BGP is an example of an EGP.**

Autonomous system:

— **BGP autonomous system—A set of routers under a single technical administration, using an Interior Gateway Protocol and common metrics to route packets within the AS, and using an Exterior Gateway Protocol to route packets to other autonomous systems.**

— **Another definition of autonomous system—Internetworks using different routing protocols.**

Redistribution—**The capability of boundary routers connecting different autonomous systems to exchange and advertise routing information received from one autonomous system to the other autonomous system.**

**5** Describe some of the characteristics of BGP.

**BGP is a distance vector protocol, but it has many differences from the likes of RIP:**

— **BGP uses TCP as its transport protocol, which provides connection-oriented reliable delivery. In this way, BGP assumes that its communication is reliable; therefore, it doesn't have to implement any retransmission or error-recovery mechanisms. BGP uses TCP port 179. Two routers speaking BGP form a TCP connection with one another and exchange messages to open and confirm the connection parameters. These two routers are called peer routers or neighbors.**

— **When the connection is made, full routing tables are exchanged. However, because the connection is reliable, BGP routers need send only changes (incremental updates) after that. Periodic routing updates are also not required on a reliable link, so triggered updates are used. BGP sends keepalive messages, similar to the hello messages sent by OSPF and EIGRP.**

— BGP routers exchange network reachability information, called path vectors, made up of path attributes, including a list of the full path (of BGP AS numbers) that a route should take to reach a destination network. This path information is used in constructing a graph of autonomous systems that is loop-free. The path is loop-free because a router running BGP will not accept a routing update that already includes its AS number in the path list; this would mean that the update has already passed through its AS, and accepting it again would result in a routing loop. Routing policies can also be applied to the path of BGP AS numbers to enforce some restrictions on the routing behavior.

**6** Policy-based routing is applied to packets going in which direction on an interface?

**Policy-based routing is applied to incoming packets on an interface.**

**7** What distinguishes classful routing protocols from classless routing protocols?

**The characteristics of classful routing protocols include these:**

— **Subnet masks are not advertised.**

— **Routes are exchanged to all subnetworks within the same major classful network.**

— **The receiving device must know the mask associated with any advertised subnets; therefore, all the subnetworks in the major network should have the same routing mask.**

— **The subnetwork information from foreign networks (different major networks) must be summarized to a classful boundary using a default routing mask before inclusion in the routing update.**

— **The creation of a classful summary route at major network boundaries is handled automatically by classful routing protocols. Summarization at other bit positions within the major network address is not allowed by classful routing protocols.**

**The characteristics of classless routing protocols include these:**

— **Subnet masks are advertised for each route.**

— **The summarization process is manually controlled and can usually be invoked at any bit position within the network. Because subnet routes are propagated throughout the routing domain, summarization is often required to keep the size of the routing tables at a manageable size.**

**8** A router has networks 192.168.160.0/24 through 192.168.175.0/24 in its routing table. How could it summarize these networks into one route?

**The addresses in binary are:**

| Decimal | Binary |
|---|---|
| 192.168.160.0/24 | **11000000 10101000 10100**000 00000000 |
| 192.168.161.0/24 | **11000000 10101000 10100**001 00000000 |
| 192.168.162.0/24 | **11000000 10101000 10100**010 00000000 |
| 192.168.163.0/24 | **11000000 10101000 10100**011 00000000 |
| 192.168.164.0/24 | **11000000 10101000 10100**100 00000000 |
| 192.168.165.0/24 | **11000000 10101000 10100**101 00000000 |
| 192.168.166.0/24 | **11000000 10101000 10100**110 00000000 |
| 192.168.167.0/24 | **11000000 10101000 10100**111 00000000 |
| 192.168.168.0/24 | **11000000 10101000 10101**000 00000000 |
| 192.168.169.0/24 | **11000000 10101000 10101**001 00000000 |
| 192.168.170.0/24 | **11000000 10101000 10101**010 00000000 |
| 192.168.171.0/24 | **11000000 10101000 10101**011 00000000 |
| 192.168.172.0/24 | **11000000 10101000 10101**100 00000000 |
| 192.168.173.0/24 | **11000000 10101000 10101**101 00000000 |
| 192.168.174.0/24 | **11000000 10101000 10101**110 00000000 |
| 192.168.175.0/24 | **11000000 10101000 10101**111 00000000 |

**To determine the summary route, the router determines the number of highest-order (left-most) bits that match in all the addresses. Referring to the list of IP addresses here, 20 bits match in all the addresses. Therefore, the best summary route is 192.168.160.0/20.**

**9** In the BGP selection process, which attribute is checked first: AS path, weight, or local preference?

**In the BGP selection process, the weight is the first attribute checked of the three listed.**

# Appendix A

## Supplement 1 Review Questions

**1** You need to design an IP network for your organization. Your organization's IP address is 172.16.0.0. Your assessment indicates that the organization needs at least 130 networks of no more than 100 nodes in each network.

As a result, you have decided to use a classful subnetting scheme based on the 172.16.0.0/24 scheme. In the space that follows, write any four IP addresses that are part of the range of subnetwork numbers. Also, write the subnet address and subnet mask for these addresses. One address is provided as an example.

| IP Address | Subnet Address and Mask |
|---|---|
| 172.16.1.0/24 | 172.16.1.0 255.255.255.0 |
| **172.16.2.9/24** | **172.16.2.0 255.255.255.0** |
| **172.16.3.11/24** | **172.16.3.0 255.255.255.0** |
| **172.16.4.12/24** | **172.16.4.0 255.255.255.0** |
| **172.16.255.2/24** | **172.16.255.0 255.255.255.0** |

**2** Your network has the address 172.16.168.0/21. Write eight IP addresses in this network.

**172.16.168.1**

**172.16.168.255**

**172.16.169.1**

**172.16.175.253**

**172.16.168.2**

**172.16.169.0**

**172.16.169.2**

**172.16.175.254**

**3** Write the four IP addresses in the range described by the 192.168.99.16/30 address.

**192.168.99.16**

**192.168.99.17**

**192.168.99.18**

**192.168.99.19**

**4** Of the four addresses in question 3, which two could you use as host addresses in a point-to-point connection?

**192.168.99.17 and 192.168.99.18**

# Supplement 2 Review Questions

**1** The following figure shows the network for this question.

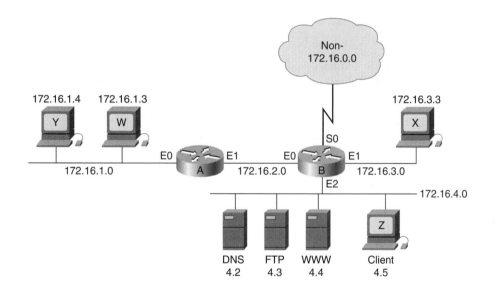

Create an access list and place it in the proper location to satisfy the following requirements:

— Prevent all hosts on subnet 172.16.1.0/24 except host 172.16.1.3 from accessing the web server on subnet 172.16.4.0. Allow all other hosts, including from the outside world, to access the web server.

— Prevent the outside world from pinging subnet 172.16.4.0.

— Allow all hosts on all subnets of network 172.16.0.0 (using subnet mask 255.255.255.0) to send queries to the DNS server on subnet 172.16.4.0. The outside world is not allowed to access the DNS server.

— Prevent host 172.16.3.3 from accessing subnet 172.16.4.0 for any reason.

— Prevent all other access to the 172.16.4.0 subnet.

Write your configuration in the spaces that follow. Be sure to include the router name (A or B), interface name (E0, E1, or E2), and access list direction (in or out).

**Global commands: Configuration for Router B**

```
access-list 104 deny ip host 172.16.3.3 172.16.4.0 0.0.0.255
access-list 104 permit tcp host 172.16.1.3 172.16.4.0 0.0.0.255 eq 80
access-list 104 deny tcp 172.16.1.0 0.0.0.255 172.16.4.0 0.0.0.255 eq 80
access-list 104 permit tcp any any eq 80
access-list 104 permit udp 172.16.0.0 0.0.255.255 172.16.4.0 0.0.0.255 eq dns
```

**Interface commands:**

```
interface e2
ip access-group 104 out
```

**2**   What do bits set to 1 in a wildcard mask indicate when matching an address?

**Bits set to 1 in a wildcard mask indicate that the corresponding bits in the address are ignored when matching an address in a packet to the address in the access list.**

**3**   By default, what happens to all traffic in an access list?

**By default, all traffic is denied by an access list.**

**4**   Where should an extended access list be placed to save network resources?

**An extended access list should be placed close to the source to save network resources.**

**5**   Using the keyword **host** in an access list is a substitute for using what value of a wildcard mask?

**The keyword host is a substitute for a wildcard mask of 0.0.0.0.**

This appendix contains information on the equipment requirements for the Configuration Exercises in this book, along with the configuration commands for the backbone routers.

This appendix is organized in the following sections:

- Configuration Exercise Equipment Requirements
- Configuration Exercise Setup Diagram
- Configuration Exercise Equipment Wiring
- Backbone Router Configuration

# Configuration Exercise Equipment Requirements and Backbone Configurations

## Configuration Exercise Equipment Requirements

In the Configuration Exercises in this book, you are in control of a pod of three routers; there are assumed to be 12 pods in the network. The pods are interconnected to a backbone. In most of the exercises, there is only one router in the backbone; in some cases, another router is added to the backbone. Each of the Configuration Exercises in this book assumes that you have completed the previous chapters' Configuration Exercises on your pod.

The equipment listed in Table H-1 is for 12 pods (each with 3 routers) and the backbone (with 2 routers).

**Table H-1** *Configuration Exercise Equipment Requirements for 12 Pods and the Backbone*

| Quantity | Required Product Description | Recommended Product Number |
|---|---|---|
| 12 | Personal computer, running Win95 and Hyperterminal, with one COM port. (A dumb terminal would be sufficient.) (One per pod.) | — |
| 1 | PC running Win95 (or WinNT) and Hyperterminal, with one COM port. | — |
| 13 | A/B/C switch to connect pod and backbone PC to routers. | — |
| 12 | Router with four serial ports (One per pod). | Cisco 2520 (or Cisco 2522) |
| 24 | Router with two serial ports and one Ethernet port (two per pod). | Cisco 2501 (or Cisco 2503, Cisco 2514, Cisco 2520, Cisco 2522, or others) |
| 36 | Version 12.0(3) (or later) Cisco IP-only IOS software for 25*XX* routers (requires 8 MB Flash memory and 4 MB RAM). | c2500-i-l_120-3.bin |
| 36 | Optional 8 MB Flash SIMM. | MEM-1X8F |
| 36 | Optional 8 MB DRAM memory. | MEM-1X8D |
| 2 | Router for backbone. | Cisco 3640 |

*continues*

**Table H-1** *Configuration Exercise Equipment Requirements for 12 Pods and the Backbone (Continued)*

| Quantity | Required Product Description | Recommended Product Number |
|---|---|---|
| 4 | 8-port asynchronous/synchronous serial network module (for 3640 routers, with 12 serial ports required per router). | NM-8A/S |
| 2 | Version 12.0(3c) Cisco 3640 series IOS Enterprise Plus (requires 8 MB Flash memory and 48 MB DRAM). | c3640-js-mz_120-3c.bin |
| 2 | 8 MB to 16 MB Flash Factory Upgrade for the Cisco 3600 (not required for 12.0[3c], but may be for future releases). | MEM3600-8U16FS |
| 2 | 32 MB to 64 MB DRAM Factory Upgrade for the Cisco 3640. | MEM3640-32U64D |
| 38 | Power cord, 110V. | CAB-AC |
| 60 | V.35 cable, DCE, female 10 feet. | CAB-V35FC |
| 60 | V.35 cable, DTE, male 10 feet. | CAB-V35MT |
| 12 | Ethernet crossover cable. | — |

The lab diagrams and configurations provided for the 3640 routers assume that the 3640 router has the serial port network modules installed as follows:

- Slot 1 (bottom left): NM-8A/S
- Slot 2 (top right): NM-8A/S

The information and configurations provided in the rest of this appendix assume that you have 12 pods. However, if you are configuring only one pod, you will need only the equipment specified in Table H-2. You will need to modify the wiring information provided in the "Configuration Exercise Equipment Wiring" section and the backbone router configurations provided in the "Backbone Router Configuration" section.

**Table H-2** *Configuration Exercise Equipment Requirements for One Pod and the Backbone*

| Quantity | Required Product Description | Recommended Product Number |
|---|---|---|
| 1 | Personal computer, running Win95 and Hyperterminal, with one COM port. (A dumb terminal would be sufficient.) | — |
| 2 | A/B/C switch to connect pod and backbone PC to routers. | — |

**Table H-2**    *Configuration Exercise Equipment Requirements for One Pod and the Backbone (Continued)*

| Quantity | Required Product Description | Recommended Product Number |
|---|---|---|
| 1 | Router with four serial ports for pod. | Cisco 2520 (or Cisco 2522) |
| 2 | Router with two serial ports and one Ethernet port for pod. | Cisco 2501 (or Cisco 2503, Cisco 2514, Cisco 2520, Cisco 2522, or others) |
| 2 | Router for backbone with one serial port. | Cisco 2501 (any router with 1 serial port will be sufficient) |
| 5 | Version 12.0(3) (or later) Cisco IP-only IOS software for 25XX routers (requires 8 MB Flash memory and 4 MB RAM). | c2500-i-l_120-3.bin |
| 5 | Optional 8 MB Flash SIMM. | MEM-1X8F |
| 5 | Optional 8 MB DRAM memory. | MEM-1X8D |
| 5 | Power cord, 110V. | CAB-AC |
| 5 | V.35 cable, DCE, female 10 feet. | CAB-V35FC |
| 5 | V.35 cable, DTE, male 10 feet. | CAB-V35MT |
| 1 | Ethernet crossover cable. | — |

# Configuration Exercise Setup Diagram

There are 12 pods, each with three routers named p$x$r1, p$x$r2, and p$x$r3, where $x$ = the pod number. There are two backbone routers, named backbone_r1 and backbone_r2.

The Configuration Exercise setup diagram is shown in Figure H-1. Only 1 of the 12 pods is shown in this diagram.

The backbone router addresses, shown in Figure H-1, are in the configurations provided (see the "Backbone Router Configuration" section, later in this chapter). The addresses shown for the pod routers will be configured in the Configuration Exercises.

**Figure H-1**   *Configuration Exercise Setup Diagram*

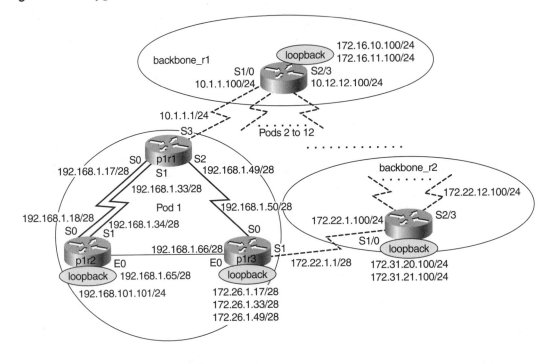

# Configuration Exercise Equipment Wiring

Each of the backbone 3640 routers requires 12 serial ports, one to each of the pods. All interfaces on the 3640 routers are DCE. The Serial 0, Serial 1, and Serial 2 interfaces on the p*x*r1 routers are DCE. All other serial interfaces are DTE.

The backbone_r1 router interfaces should be cabled as shown in Table H-3.

**Table H-3**   *backbone_r1 Cabling*

| backbone_r1 Interface (All DCE) | Pod Router and Interface (All DTE) |
|---|---|
| S1/0 | p1r1 S3 |
| S1/1 | p2r1 S3 |
| S1/2 | p3r1 S3 |
| S1/3 | p4r1 S3 |
| S1/4 | p5r1 S3 |
| S1/5 | p6r1 S3 |

**Table H-3**    *backbone_r1 Cabling (Continued)*

| backbone_r1 Interface (All DCE) | Pod Router and Interface (All DTE) |
| --- | --- |
| S1/6 | p7r1 S3 |
| S1/7 | p8r1 S3 |
| S2/0 | p9r1 S3 |
| S2/1 | p10r1 S3 |
| S2/2 | p11r1 S3 |
| S2/3 | p12r1 S3 |

The backbone_r2 router interfaces should be cabled as shown in Table H-4.

**Table H-4**    *backbone_r2 Cabling*

| backbone_r2 Interface (All DCE) | Pod Router and Interface (All DTE) |
| --- | --- |
| S1/0 | p1r3 S1 |
| S1/1 | p2r3 S1 |
| S1/2 | p3r3 S1 |
| S1/3 | p4r3 S1 |
| S1/4 | p5r3 S1 |
| S1/5 | p6r3 S1 |
| S1/6 | p7r3 S1 |
| S1/7 | p8r3 S1 |
| S2/0 | p9r3 S1 |
| S2/1 | p10r3 S1 |
| S2/2 | p11r3 S1 |
| S2/3 | p12r3 S1 |

The remaining pod router interfaces should be cabled as shown in Table H-5.

**Table H-5**    *Other Pod Interface Cabling*

| This Interface | Goes to This Interface |
| --- | --- |
| p*x*r1 S0 (DCE) | p*x*r2 S0 (DTE) |
| p*x*r1 S1 (DCE) | p*x*r2 S1 (DTE) |
| p*x*r1 S2 (DCE) | p*x*r3 S0 (DTE) |
| p*x*r2 E0 | p*x*r3 E0 |

# Backbone Router Configuration

The configuration for the backbone 3640 routers changes for the different Configuration Exercises. Configurations have been created for each of the backbone_r1 and backbone_r2 routers.

The text of the configurations is provided in the following sections. To use the configurations, create text files from the information provided. These configurations were written to be sent from the Transfer, Send Text File menu from Hyperterminal into the console port of the devices. The configurations are additive—in other words, the first configuration is assumed to be in the device before the second one is loaded, and so on. The first configuration assumes that the router has no configuration—in other words, it assumes that the startup configuration has been erased and that the router has been reloaded.

Before sending a configuration file, go into privileged EXEC mode on the router. The configurations have **config t** commands at the beginning, followed by the necessary configuration commands and then commands to save the configuration into NVRAM.

---

**NOTE**   The last command in each configuration is **copy run start**. When creating the text files, enter a carriage return after this command and then another carriage return. This will ensure that the configuration is saved and that the router will return to the privileged EXEC prompt.

---

When testing similar configurations, I ran into a problem on the 3640 routers. Loading the files from Hyperterminal was too fast for the 3640—it would lose some of the commands, and then the rest of the file would get mixed up. To fix this problem in Hyperterminal, do the following:

- From the File menu, select Properties.
- Click the Settings tab.
- Click the ASCII Settings button.
- Set the Line Delay to 200 milliseconds. (You may have to increase the line delay further if you get errors.)

Table H-6 identifies when the various configurations should be loaded on each 3640 router.

**Table H-6**   *When Configurations Should Be Used on the Backbone Routers*

| Configuration Exercise | Use This Configuration in This Device (Load the Configuration at the Beginning of the Configuration Exercise) | |
|---|---|---|
| | **backbone_r1** | **backbone_r2** |
| Discovering the Network (Chapter 1) | bbr1 discovery.txt | — |
| Configuring OSPF for a Single Area (Chapter 3) | bbr1 ospf single.txt | — |
| Configuring OSPF for a Single Area in an NBMA Environment (Chapter 3) | Continue to use bbr1 ospf single.txt | — |
| Configuring a Multiarea OSPF Network (Chapter 4) | Continue to use bbr1 ospf single.txt | — |
| Configuring EIGRP (Chapter 5) | bbr1 eigrp.txt | — |
| Configuring EIGRP in an NBMA Environment (Chapter 5) | Continue to use bbr1 eigrp.txt | — |
| Configuring BGP (Chapter 6) | bbr1 bgp.txt | — |
| Configuring BGP Route Reflectors and Prefix-List Filtering (Chapter 7) | Continue to use bbr1 bgp.txt | — |
| Configuring Multihome BGP (Chapter 7) | Continue to use bbr1 bgp.txt | bbr2 bgp multihome.txt |
| Configuring Policy-Based Routing (Chapter 8) | Continue to use bbr1 bgp.txt | Continue to use bbr2 bgp multihome.txt |
| Configuring Route Redistribution Between OSPF and EIGRP (Chapter 8) | Continue to use bbr1 bgp.txt | Continue to use bbr2 bgp multihome.txt |
| Super Lab, Part I and Part II (Chapter 9) | bbr1 super.txt | Continue to use bbr2 bgp multihome.txt |

# Backbone_r1 Configurations

This section provides the text of the configuration files for the backbone_r1 router. Use Configuration H-1 through Configuration H-5, as specified in Table H-6.

**Configuration H-1**   *bbr1 discovery.txt*

```
!
!backbone_r1 discovery configuration exercise configuration
!
! This file is designed to be copied and pasted into an erased router, at
! the # prompt.
!
! This configuration was tested with the c3640-js-mz_120-3c.bin
! IOS image and with the c3640-js-mz_120-5_T1.bin image.
!
conf t
!
!
no service config
hostname backbone_r1
!
enable password cisco
!
ip subnet-zero
no ip domain-lookup
!
interface Loopback100
 ip address 172.16.10.100 255.255.255.0
 no ip directed-broadcast
!
interface Loopback101
 ip address 172.16.11.100 255.255.255.0
 no ip directed-broadcast
!
interface Serial1/0
 ip address 10.1.1.100 255.255.255.0
 clockrate 64000
 bandwidth 64
 no shutdown
!
interface Serial1/1
 ip address 10.2.2.100 255.255.255.0
 clockrate 64000
 bandwidth 64
 no shutdown
!
interface Serial1/2
 ip address 10.3.3.100 255.255.255.0
 clockrate 64000
 bandwidth 64
 no shutdown
!
interface Serial1/3
```

**Configuration H-1**    *bbr1 discovery.txt (Continued)*

```
  ip address 10.4.4.100 255.255.255.0
  clockrate 64000
  bandwidth 64
  no shutdown
!
interface Serial1/4
  ip address 10.5.5.100 255.255.255.0
  clockrate 64000
  bandwidth 64
  no shutdown
!
interface Serial1/5
  ip address 10.6.6.100 255.255.255.0
  clockrate 64000
  bandwidth 64
  no shutdown
!
interface Serial1/6
  ip address 10.7.7.100 255.255.255.0
  bandwidth 64
  clockrate 64000
  no shutdown
!
interface Serial1/7
  ip address 10.8.8.100 255.255.255.0
  clockrate 64000
  bandwidth 64
  no shutdown
!
interface Serial2/0
  ip address 10.9.9.100 255.255.255.0
  clockrate 64000
  bandwidth 64
  no shutdown
!
interface Serial2/1
  ip address 10.10.10.100 255.255.255.0
  clockrate 64000
  bandwidth 64
  no shutdown
!
interface Serial2/2
  ip address 10.11.11.100 255.255.255.0
  clockrate 64000
  bandwidth 64
  no shutdown
!
interface Serial2/3
  ip address 10.12.12.100 255.255.255.0
  clockrate 64000
  bandwidth 64
  no shutdown
```

*continues*

**Configuration H-1**   *bbr1 discovery.txt (Continued)*

```
!
interface Serial2/4
 shutdown
!
interface Serial2/5
 shutdown
 !
interface Serial2/6
 shutdown
!
interface Serial2/7
 shutdown
!
router igrp 200
 network 10.0.0.0
 network 172.16.0.0
!
ip classless
!
!
ip host p1r1 192.168.1.17 192.168.1.33 192.168.1.49 10.1.1.1
ip host p1r2 192.168.1.65 192.168.1.18 192.168.1.34
ip host p1r3 192.168.1.66 192.168.1.50
ip host p2r1 192.168.2.17 192.168.2.33 192.168.2.49 10.2.2.2
ip host p2r2 192.168.2.65 192.168.2.18 192.168.2.34
ip host p2r3 192.168.2.66 192.168.2.50
ip host p3r1 192.168.3.17 192.168.3.33 192.168.3.49 10.3.3.3
ip host p3r2 192.168.3.65 192.168.3.18 192.168.3.34
ip host p3r3 192.168.3.66 192.168.3.50
ip host p4r1 192.168.4.17 192.168.4.33 192.168.4.49 10.4.4.4
ip host p4r2 192.168.4.65 192.168.4.18 192.168.4.34
ip host p4r3 192.168.4.66 192.168.4.50
ip host p5r1 192.168.5.17 192.168.5.33 192.168.5.49 10.5.5.5
ip host p5r2 192.168.5.65 192.168.5.18 192.168.5.34
ip host p5r3 192.168.5.66 192.168.5.50
ip host p6r1 192.168.6.17 192.168.6.33 192.168.6.49 10.6.6.6
ip host p6r2 192.168.6.65 192.168.6.18 192.168.6.34
ip host p6r3 192.168.6.66 192.168.6.50
ip host p7r1 192.168.7.17 192.168.7.33 192.168.7.49 10.7.7.7
ip host p7r2 192.168.7.65 192.168.7.18 192.168.7.34
ip host p7r3 192.168.7.66 192.168.7.50
ip host p8r1 192.168.8.17 192.168.8.33 192.168.8.49 10.8.8.8
ip host p8r2 192.168.8.65 192.168.8.18 192.168.8.34
ip host p8r3 192.168.8.66 192.168.8.50
ip host p9r1 192.168.9.17 192.168.9.33 192.168.9.49 10.9.9.9
ip host p9r2 192.168.9.65 192.168.9.18 192.168.9.34
ip host p9r3 192.168.9.66 192.168.9.50
ip host p10r1 192.168.10.17 192.168.10.33 192.168.10.49 10.10.10.10
ip host p10r2 192.168.10.65 192.168.10.18 192.168.10.34
ip host p10r3 192.168.10.66 192.168.10.50
ip host p11r1 192.168.11.17 192.168.11.33 192.168.11.49 10.11.11.11
ip host p11r2 192.168.11.65 192.168.11.18 192.168.11.34
```

**Configuration H-1**  *bbr1 discovery.txt (Continued)*

```
ip host p11r3 192.168.11.66 192.168.11.50
ip host p12r1 192.168.12.17 192.168.12.33 192.168.12.49 10.12.12.12
ip host p12r2 192.168.12.65 192.168.12.18 192.168.12.34
ip host p12r3 192.168.12.66 192.168.12.50
!
!
line con 0
 transport input none
 exec-timeout 0 0
 logging synchronous
line aux 0
line vty 0 100
 password cisco
 login
!
exit
exit
copy run start
```

**Configuration H-2**  *bbr1 ospf single.txt*

```
!
!backbone_r1 OSPF single area configuration exercise configuration
!
! This file is designed to be copied and pasted into a router that already
! has the previous BSCN configuration files loaded, at the # prompt
!
conf t
!
no router igrp 200
!
router ospf 200
 redistribute connected subnets route-map passext
 network 10.0.0.0 0.255.255.255 area 0
!
!
access-list 1 permit 172.16.10.0
access-list 1 permit 172.16.11.0
route-map passext permit 10
 match ip address 1
!
!
exit
exit
copy run start
```

**Configuration H-3**  *bbr1 eigrp.txt*

```
!
!backbone_r1 EIGRP configuration exercise configuration
!
! This file is designed to be copied and pasted into a router that already
! has the previous BSCN configuration files loaded, at the # prompt
!
conf t
!
!
no router ospf 200
!
router eigrp 200
  redistribute connected metric 10000 100 255 1 1500 route-map passext
  network 10.0.0.0
!
!
exit
exit
copy run start
```

**Configuration H-4**  *bbr1 bgp.txt*

```
!backbone_r1 BGP configuration exercise configuration
!
! This file is designed to be copied and pasted into a router that already
! has the previous BSCN configuration files loaded, at the # prompt
!
conf t
!
!
no router eigrp 200
!
router bgp 65200
 no synchronization
 neighbor 10.1.1.1 remote-as 65101
 neighbor 10.2.2.2 remote-as 65102
 neighbor 10.3.3.3 remote-as 65103
 neighbor 10.4.4.4 remote-as 65104
 neighbor 10.5.5.5 remote-as 65105
 neighbor 10.6.6.6 remote-as 65106
 neighbor 10.7.7.7 remote-as 65107
 neighbor 10.8.8.8 remote-as 65108
 neighbor 10.9.9.9 remote-as 65109
 neighbor 10.10.10.10 remote-as 65110
 neighbor 10.11.11.11 remote-as 65111
 neighbor 10.12.12.12 remote-as 65112
 network 10.0.0.0
 network 172.16.10.0 mask 255.255.255.0
```

**Configuration H-4**  *bbr1 bgp.txt (Continued)*

```
 network 172.16.11.0 mask 255.255.255.0
 !
exit
exit
copy run start
```

**Configuration H-5**  *bbr1 super.txt*

```
!
! backbone_r1 Super lab configuration exercise configuration
!
! This file is designed to be copied and pasted into a router that already
! has the previous BSCN configuration files loaded, at the # prompt
!
conf t
!
no router bgp 65200
!
router ospf 200
 redistribute connected subnets route-map passext
 network 10.0.0.0 0.255.255.255 area 0
!
no access-list 1
access-list 1 permit 172.16.10.0
access-list 1 permit 172.16.11.0
route-map passext permit 10
 match ip address 1
!
exit
exit
copy run start
```

# Backbone_r2 Configurations

This section provides the text of the configuration file for the backbone_r2 router. Use the configuration in Configuration H-6, as specified in Table H-6.

**Configuration H-6**  *bbr2 bgp multihome.txt*

```
!
!backbone_r2 BGP multihome configuration exercise configuration
!
! This file is designed to be copied and pasted into an erased router, at
! the # prompt.
!
! This configuration was tested with the c3640-js-mz_120-3c.bin
! IOS image and with the c3640-js-mz_120-5_T1.bin image.
!
conf t
```

*continues*

**Configuration H-6** *bbr2 bgp multihome.txt (Continued)*

```
!
!
no service config
hostname backbone_r2
!
!
enable password cisco
!
ip subnet-zero
no ip domain-lookup
!
interface Loopback100
 ip address 172.31.20.100 255.255.255.0
 no ip directed-broadcast
!
interface Loopback101
 ip address 172.31.21.100 255.255.255.0
 no ip directed-broadcast
!
interface Serial1/0
 ip address 172.22.1.100 255.255.255.0
 clockrate 64000
 bandwidth 64
 no shutdown
!
interface Serial1/1
 ip address 172.22.2.100 255.255.255.0
 clockrate 64000
 bandwidth 64
 no shutdown
!
interface Serial1/2
 ip address 172.22.3.100 255.255.255.0
 clockrate 64000
 bandwidth 64
 no shutdown
!
interface Serial1/3
 ip address 172.22.4.100 255.255.255.0
 clockrate 64000
 bandwidth 64
 no shutdown
!
interface Serial1/4
 ip address 172.22.5.100 255.255.255.0
 clockrate 64000
 bandwidth 64
 no shutdown
!
interface Serial1/5
 ip address 172.22.6.100 255.255.255.0
 clockrate 64000
```

**Configuration H-6**    *bbr2 bgp multihome.txt (Continued)*

```
 bandwidth 64
 no shutdown
!
interface Serial1/6
 ip address 172.22.7.100 255.255.255.0
 clockrate 64000
 bandwidth 64
 no shutdown
!
interface Serial1/7
 ip address 172.22.8.100 255.255.255.0
 clockrate 64000
 bandwidth 64
 no shutdown
!
interface Serial2/0
 ip address 172.22.9.100 255.255.255.0
 clockrate 64000
 bandwidth 64
 no shutdown
!
interface Serial2/1
 ip address 172.22.10.100 255.255.255.0
 clockrate 64000
 bandwidth 64
 no shutdown
!
interface Serial2/2
 ip address 172.22.11.100 255.255.255.0
 clockrate 64000
 bandwidth 64
 no shutdown
!
interface Serial2/3
 ip address 172.22.12.100 255.255.255.0
 clockrate 64000
 bandwidth 64
 no shutdown
!
interface Serial2/4
 shutdown
!
interface Serial2/5
 shutdown
!
interface Serial2/6
 shutdown
!
interface Serial2/7
 shutdown
!
router bgp 65201
```

*continues*

**Configuration H-6**    *bbr2 bgp multihome.txt (Continued)*

```
 no synchronization
 neighbor 172.22.1.1 remote-as 65101
 neighbor 172.22.2.2 remote-as 65102
 neighbor 172.22.3.3 remote-as 65103
 neighbor 172.22.4.4 remote-as 65104
 neighbor 172.22.5.5 remote-as 65105
 neighbor 172.22.6.6 remote-as 65106
 neighbor 172.22.7.7 remote-as 65107
 neighbor 172.22.8.8 remote-as 65108
 neighbor 172.22.9.9 remote-as 65109
 neighbor 172.22.10.10 remote-as 65110
 neighbor 172.22.11.11 remote-as 65111
 neighbor 172.22.12.12 remote-as 65112
 network 172.31.20.0 mask 255.255.255.0
 network 172.31.21.0 mask 255.255.255.0
!
ip classless
!
!
ip host p1r1 192.168.1.17 192.168.1.33 192.168.1.49 10.1.1.1
ip host p1r2 192.168.1.65 192.168.1.18 192.168.1.34
ip host p1r3 192.168.1.66 192.168.1.50
ip host p2r1 192.168.2.17 192.168.2.33 192.168.2.49 10.2.2.2
ip host p2r2 192.168.2.65 192.168.2.18 192.168.2.34
ip host p2r3 192.168.2.66 192.168.2.50
ip host p3r1 192.168.3.17 192.168.3.33 192.168.3.49 10.3.3.3
ip host p3r2 192.168.3.65 192.168.3.18 192.168.3.34
ip host p3r3 192.168.3.66 192.168.3.50
ip host p4r1 192.168.4.17 192.168.4.33 192.168.4.49 10.4.4.4
ip host p4r2 192.168.4.65 192.168.4.18 192.168.4.34
ip host p4r3 192.168.4.66 192.168.4.50
ip host p5r1 192.168.5.17 192.168.5.33 192.168.5.49 10.5.5.5
ip host p5r2 192.168.5.65 192.168.5.18 192.168.5.34
ip host p5r3 192.168.5.66 192.168.5.50
ip host p6r1 192.168.6.17 192.168.6.33 192.168.6.49 10.6.6.6
ip host p6r2 192.168.6.65 192.168.6.18 192.168.6.34
ip host p6r3 192.168.6.66 192.168.6.50
ip host p7r1 192.168.7.17 192.168.7.33 192.168.7.49 10.7.7.7
ip host p7r2 192.168.7.65 192.168.7.18 192.168.7.34
ip host p7r3 192.168.7.66 192.168.7.50
ip host p8r1 192.168.8.17 192.168.8.33 192.168.8.49 10.8.8.8
ip host p8r2 192.168.8.65 192.168.8.18 192.168.8.34
ip host p8r3 192.168.8.66 192.168.8.50
ip host p9r1 192.168.9.17 192.168.9.33 192.168.9.49 10.9.9.9
ip host p9r2 192.168.9.65 192.168.9.18 192.168.9.34
ip host p9r3 192.168.9.66 192.168.9.50
ip host p10r1 192.168.10.17 192.168.10.33 192.168.10.49 10.10.10.10
ip host p10r2 192.168.10.65 192.168.10.18 192.168.10.34
ip host p10r3 192.168.10.66 192.168.10.50
ip host p11r1 192.168.11.17 192.168.11.33 192.168.11.49 10.11.11.11
ip host p11r2 192.168.11.65 192.168.11.18 192.168.11.34
```

**Configuration H-6**    *bbr2 bgp multihome.txt (Continued)*

```
ip host p11r3 192.168.11.66 192.168.11.50
ip host p12r1 192.168.12.17 192.168.12.33 192.168.12.49 10.12.12.12
ip host p12r2 192.168.12.65 192.168.12.18 192.168.12.34
ip host p12r3 192.168.12.66 192.168.12.50
!
line con 0
 transport input none
 exec-timeout 0 0
 logging synchronous
line aux 0
line vty 0 100
 password cisco
 login
!
exit
exit
copy run start
```

# Glossary

This glossary assembles and defines terms and acronyms used in the *Building Scalable Cisco Networks* coursebook and in the internetworking industry. Many of the definitions have yet to be standardized, and many terms have several meanings. Multiple definitions and acronym expressions are included where they apply. These definitions can be found on CCO at www.cisco.com under the title, "Internetworking Terms and Acronyms."

**10BaseT**—10-Mbps baseband Ethernet specification using two pairs of twisted-pair cabling (Category 3, 4, or 5): one pair for transmitting data and the other for receiving data. 10BaseT, which is part of the IEEE 802.3 specification, has a distance limit of approximately 328 feet (100 meters) per segment.

**802.x**—Set of IEEE standards for the definition of LAN protocols.

**AAA**—Authentication, authorization, and accounting (pronounced "triple a").

**ABR**—Area Border Router. A router located on the border of one or more OSPF areas that connects those areas to the backbone network. ABRs are considered members of both the OSPF backbone and the attached areas. Therefore, they maintain routing tables describing both the backbone topology and the topology of the other areas.

**access layer**—Layer in a hierarchical network that provides workgroup/user access to the network.

**access list**—List kept by routers to control access to or from the router for a number of services (for example, to prevent packets with a certain IP address from leaving a particular interface on the router).

**access method**—Generally, the way in which network devices access the network medium.

**access server**—Communications processor that connects asynchronous devices to a LAN or WAN through network and terminal emulation software. Performs both synchronous and asynchronous routing of supported protocols. Sometimes called a *network access server (NAS)*.

**accounting management**—One of five categories of network management defined by ISO for management of OSI networks. Accounting management subsystems are responsible for collecting network data relating to resource usage.

**accuracy**—The percentage of useful traffic that is correctly transmitted on the system, relative to total traffic, including transmission errors.

**ACK**—1. Acknowledgment bit in a TCP segment. 2. See *acknowledgment*.

**acknowledgment**—Notification sent from one network device to another to acknowledge that some event (for example, receipt of a message) occurred. Sometimes abbreviated *ACK*. Compare with *NAK*.

**ACL**—See *access list*.

**AD**—Administrative Distance. Rating of the trustworthiness of a routing information source. Administrative distance is often expressed as a numeric value between 0 and 255. The higher the value, the lower the trustworthiness rating.

**address**—A data structure or logical convention used to identify a unique entity, such as a particular process or network device.

**address mapping**—A technique that allows different protocols to interoperate by translating addresses from one format to another. For example, when routing IP over X.25, the IP addresses must be mapped to the X.25 addresses so that the IP packets can be transmitted by the X.25 network. See also *address resolution*.

**address resolution**—Generally, a method for resolving differences between computer addressing schemes. Address resolution usually specifies a method for mapping network layer (Layer 3) addresses to data link layer (Layer 2) addresses.

**adjacency**—A relationship formed between selected neighboring routers and end nodes for the purpose of exchanging routing information. Adjacency is based on the use of a common media segment.

**administrative distance**—A rating of the trustworthiness of a routing information source. The higher the value, the lower the trustworthiness rating.

**Advertised distance**—The cost between the next-hop router and the destination.

**Advertising**—Router process in which routing or service updates are sent at specified intervals so that other routers on the network can maintain lists of usable routes.

**agent**—1. Generally, software that processes queries and returns replies on behalf of an application. 2. In NMSs, a process that resides in all managed devices and reports the values of specified variables to management stations.

**aggregation**—See *route summarization*.

**alarm**—A message notifying an operator or administrator of a network problem.

**algorithm**—Well-defined rule or process for arriving at a solution to a problem. In networking, algorithms are commonly used to determine the best route for traffic from a particular source to a particular destination.

**analog**—An electrical circuit that is represented by means of continuous, variable physical quantities (such as voltages and frequencies), as opposed to discrete representations (such as the 0/1, off/on representation of digital circuits).

**analog transmission**—Signal transmission over wires or through the air in which information is conveyed through variation of some combination of signal amplitude, frequency, and phase.

**ANSI**—American National Standards Institute. Voluntary organization composed of corporate, government, and other members that coordinates standards-related activities, approves U.S. national standards, and develops positions for the United States in international standards organizations. ANSI helps develop international and U.S. standards relating to, among other things, communications and networking. ANSI is a member of the IEC and the ISO.

**API**—Application programming interface. A specification of function-call conventions that defines an interface to a service.

**AppleTalk**—A series of communications protocols designed by Apple Computer. Two phases currently exist. Phase 1, the earlier version, supports a single physical network that can have only one network number and be in one zone. Phase 2, the more recent version, supports multiple logical networks on a single physical network and allows networks to be in more than one zone. See also *zone*.

**application layer**—Layer 7 of the OSI reference model. This layer provides services to application processes (such as electronic mail, file transfer, and terminal emulation) that are outside the OSI model. The application layer identifies and establishes the availability of intended communication partners (and the resources required to connect with them), synchronizes cooperating applications, and establishes agreement on procedures for error recovery and control of data integrity. It corresponds roughly with the transaction services layer in the SNA model.

**area**—A logical set of network segments and their attached devices. Areas are usually connected to other areas via routers, making up a single autonomous system. See also *AS*.

**ARIN**—American Registry for Internet Numbers. Nonprofit organization established for the purpose of administrating and registering IP numbers to the geographical areas currently managed by Network Solutions (InterNIC). Those areas include, but are not limited to, North America, South America, South Africa, and the Caribbean.

**ARP**—Address Resolution Protocol. An Internet protocol used to map an IP address to a MAC address. It is defined in RFC 826.

**ARPA**—Advanced Research Projects Agency. Research and development organization that is part of DoD. ARPA is responsible for numerous technological advances in communications and networking. ARPA evolved into DARPA and then back into ARPA (in 1994).

**ARPANET**—Advanced Research Projects Agency Network. Landmark packet-switching network established in 1969. ARPANET was developed in the 1970s by BBN and was funded by ARPA (and later DARPA). It eventually evolved into the Internet. The term ARPANET was officially retired in 1990.

**AS**—Autonomous system. A collection of networks under a common administration sharing a common routing strategy. Autonomous systems may be subdivided into areas.

**ASBR**—Autonomous System Boundary Router. An ABR located between an OSPF autonomous system and a non-OSPF network. ASBRs run both OSPF and another routing protocol, such as RIP. ASBRs must reside in a non-stub OSPF area.

**ASCII**—American Standard Code for Information Interchange. An 8-bit code for character representation (7 bits plus parity).

**assigned numbers**—RFC [STD2] documents the currently assigned values from several series of numbers used in network protocol implementations. This RFC is updated periodically, and current information can be obtained from the IANA. If you are developing a protocol or application that will require the use of a link, socket, port, protocol, and so forth, contact the IANA to receive a number assignment.

**asynchronous transmission**—Term describing digital signals that are transmitted without precise clocking. Such signals generally have different frequencies and phase relationships. Asynchronous transmissions usually encapsulate individual characters in control bits (called start and stop bits) that designate the beginning and end of each character.

**ATM**—Asynchronous Transfer Mode. An international standard for cell relay in which multiple service types (such as voice, video, or data) are conveyed in fixed-length (53-byte) cells. Fixed-length cells allow cell processing to occur in hardware, thereby reducing transit delays. ATM is designed to take advantage of high-speed transmission media, such as E3, SONET, and T3.

**AUI**—Attachment unit interface. IEEE 802.3 interface between an MAU and an NIC. The term AUI can also refer to the rear panel port to which an AUI cable might attach.

**authentication**—In security, the verification of the identity of a person or process.

**AUX**—Auxiliary port on Cisco Routers.

**average rate**—Average rate, in kilobits per second (kbps), at which a given virtual circuit will transmit,

**backbone**—Part of a network that acts as the primary path for traffic that is most often sourced from and destined for other networks.

**backward explicit congestion notification**—See *BECN*.

**bandwidth**—Difference between the highest and lowest frequencies available for network signals. The term is also used to describe the rated throughput capacity of a given network medium or protocol.

**bandwidth reservation**—Process of assigning bandwidth to users and applications served by a network. It involves assigning priority to different flows of traffic based on how critical and delay-sensitive they are. This makes the best use of available bandwidth; if the network becomes congested, lower-priority traffic can be dropped. This sometimes is called bandwidth allocation.

**Basic Rate Interface**—See *BRI*.

**baud**—Unit of signaling speed equal to the number of discrete signal elements transmitted per second. Baud is synonymous with bits per second (bps) if each signal element represents exactly 1 bit.

**Bc**—Committed Burst. Negotiated tariff metric in Frame Relay internetworks. The maximum amount of data (in bits) that a Frame Relay internetwork is committed to accept and transmit at the CIR.

**BCRAN**—Building Cisco Remote Access Networks.

**BDR**—Backup Designated Router. The BDR does not perform any DR functions when the DR is operating. Instead, it receives all information, but allows the DR to perform the forwarding and synchronization tasks. The BDR performs DR tasks only if the DR fails.

**Be**—Excess burst. Negotiated tariff metric in Frame Relay internetworks. This is the number of bits that a Frame Relay internetwork will attempt to transmit after Bc is accommodated. Be data is, in general, delivered with a lower probability than Bc data because Be data can be marked as DE by the network. See also *Bc* and *DE*.

**BECN**—Backward explicit congestion notification. A bit set by a Frame Relay network in frames traveling in the opposite direction of frames encountering a congested path. DTE receiving frames with the BECN bit set can request that higher-level protocols take flow control action as appropriate. Compare with *FECN*.

**Bellman-Ford routing algorithm**—See *distance vector routing algorithm.*

**best-effort delivery**—Delivery in a network system that does not use a sophisticated acknowledgment system to guarantee reliable delivery of information.

**BGP**—Border Gateway Protocol. An interdomain routing protocol that replaces EGP. BGP exchanges reachability information with other BGP systems. It is defined in RFC 1163. See also *BGP-4* and *EGP*.

**BGP-4**—BGP version 4. This is version 4 of the predominant interdomain routing protocol used on the Internet. BGP-4 supports CIDR and uses route aggregation mechanisms to reduce the size of routing tables. See also *BGP*.

**BIA**—Burned-in address, another name for a MAC address.

**binary**—Numbering system characterized by 1s and 0s (1 = on, 0 = off).

**bit**—Binary digit used in the binary numbering system. This can be 0 or 1.

**BOD**—Bandwidth on demand.

**BOOTP**—Bootstrap Protocol. Protocol used by a network node to determine the IP address of its Ethernet interfaces in order to affect network booting.

**BRI**—Basic Rate Interface. The most common kind of ISDN interface available in the United States. BRI contains two B channels, each with a capacity of 64 kbps, and a single D channel (with a capacity of 16 kbps) that is used for signaling and call progress messages. Compare with *PRI*.

**broadcast**—Data packet that will be sent to all nodes on a network. Broadcasts are identified by a broadcast address. Compare with *multicast* and *unicast*.

**BSCN**—Building Scalable Cisco Networks.

**buffer**—Storage area used for handling data in transit. Buffers are used in internetworking to compensate for differences in processing speed between network devices. Bursts of data can be stored in buffers until they can be handled by slower processing devices. This sometimes is referred to as a packet buffer.

**byte**—Term used to refer to a series of consecutive binary digits that are operated upon as a unit (for example, an 8-bit byte).

**cable**—Transmission medium of copper wire or optical fiber wrapped in a protective cover.

**CCITT**—Consultative Committee for International Telegraph and Telephone. International organization responsible for the development of communications standards. It is now called the ITU-T. See *ITU-T*.

**CCDA**—Cisco Certified Design Associate.

**CCDP**—Cisco Certified Design Professional.

**CCNA**—Cisco Certified Network Associate.

**CCNP**—Cisco Certified Network Professional.

**CCO**—Cisco Connection Online. Cisco's web site.

**CDP**—Cisco Discovery Protocol. Media- and protocol-independent device-discovery protocol that runs on all Cisco-manufactured equipment including routers, access servers, bridges, and switches. Using CDP, a device can advertise its existence to other devices and receive information about other devices on the same LAN or on the remote side of a WAN. Runs on all media that supports SNAP including LANs, Frame Relay, and ATM media.

**channel**—Communication path. Multiple channels can be multiplexed over a single cable in certain environments.

**Channelized E1**—Access link operating at 2.048 Mbps that is subdivided into 30 B channels and 1 D channel. It supports DDR, Frame Relay, and X.25.

**Channelized T1**—Access link operating at 1.544 Mbps that is subdivided into 24 channels (23 B channels and 1 D channel) of 64 kbps each. The individual channels or groups of channels connect to different destinations. It supports DDR, Frame Relay, and X.25. It is also referred to as fractional T1.

**checksum**—Method for checking the integrity of transmitted data. A checksum is an integer value computed from a sequence of octets taken through a series of arithmetic operations. The value is recomputed at the receiving end and is compared for verification.

**CIDR**—Classless interdomain routing. Developed for Internet service providers (ISPs). This strategy suggests that the remaining IP addresses be allocated to ISPs in contiguous blocks, using geography as one consideration.

**CIR**—Committed information rate. Rate at which a Frame Relay network agrees to transfer information under normal conditions, averaged over a minimum increment of time. CIR, measured in bits per second, is one of the key negotiated tariff metrics. See also *Bc*.

**circuit**—Communications path between two or more points.

**CiscoSecure**—A complete line of access-control software products that complement any dial network solution, enabling the centralization of security policies.

**classful routing protocols**—Routing protocols that do not transmit any information about the prefix length. Examples are RIP and IGRP.

**classless routing protocols**—Routing protocols that include the prefix length with routing updates; routers running classless routing protocols do not have to determine the prefix themselves. Classless routing protocols support VLSM.

**CLI**—Command-line interface. An interface that enables the user to interact with the operating system by entering commands and optional arguments.

**client**—A node or software program that requests services from a server. See also *server*.

**client/server computing**—Computing (processing) network systems in which transaction responsibilities are divided into two parts: client (front end) and server (back end). Both terms (*client* and *server*) can be applied to software programs or actual computing devices. This is also called distributed computing (processing).

**collapsed backbone**—A nondistributed backbone in which all network segments are interconnected by way of an internetworking device. A collapsed backbone might be a virtual network segment existing in a device such as a hub, a router, or a switch.

**collision**—In Ethernet, the result of two nodes transmitting simultaneously. The frames from each device impact and are damaged when they meet on the physical media.

**Committed burst**—See *Bc*.

**Committed information rate**—See *CIR*.

**cost**—An arbitrary value, typically based on hop count, media bandwidth, or other measures, that is assigned by a network administrator and used to compare various paths through an internetwork environment. Cost values are used by routing protocols to determine the most favorable path to a particular destination: The lower the cost, the better the path. In OSPF, this is the value assigned to a link. This metric is based on the speed of the media. It is sometimes called path cost.

**CPE**—Customer premises equipment. Terminating equipment, such as terminals, telephones, and modems, supplied by the telephone company, installed at customer sites, and connected to the telephone company network.

**CR**—Carriage return.

**CRC**—Cyclic redundancy check. Error-checking technique in which the frame recipient calculates a remainder by dividing frame contents by a prime binary divisor and then compares the calculated remainder to a value stored in the frame by the sending node.

**CSU**—Channel service unit. Digital interface device that connects end-user equipment to the local digital telephone loop. It is often referred to, together with DSU, as CSU/DSU. See also *DSU*.

**customer premises equipment**—See *CPE*.

**cyclic redundancy check**—See *CRC*.

**DARPA**—Defense Advanced Research Projects Agency. U.S. government agency that funded research for and does experimentation with the Internet. It evolved from ARPA and then, in 1994, back to ARPA.

**Data Encryption Standard**—See *DES*.

**Data Network Identification Code**—See *DNIC*.

**data terminal equipment**—See *DTE*.

**datagram**—Logical grouping of information sent as a network layer unit over a transmission medium without prior establishment of a virtual circuit. IP datagrams are the primary information units in the Internet. The terms *cell*, *frame*, *message*, *packet*, and *segment* are also used to describe logical information groupings at various layers of the OSI reference model and in various technology circles.

**data-link connection identifier**—See *DLCI*.

**DB**—Data bus connector. Type of connector used to connect serial and parallel cables to a data bus. DB connector names are in the format DB-*x*, where *x* represents the number of wires within the connector. Each line is connected to a pin on the connector, but in many cases, not all pins are assigned a function. DB connectors are defined by various EIA/TIA standards.

**DBD**—Database description packets. Describes the contents of the topological database. These messages are exchanged when an adjacency is initialized.

**DCE**—Data circuit-terminating equipment (ITU-T expansion). Devices and connections of a communications network that comprise the network end of the user-to-network interface. The DCE provides a physical connection to the network, forwards traffic, and provides a clocking signal used to synchronize data transmission between DCE and DTE devices. Modems and interface cards are examples of DCE. Compare with *DTE*.

**DDR**—Dial-on-demand routing. Technique whereby a router can automatically initiate and close a circuit-switched session as transmitting stations demand. The router spoofs keepalives so that end stations treat the session as active. DDR permits routing over ISDN or telephone lines using an external ISDN terminal adapter or modem.

**DE**—Discard eligible indicator. When the router detects network congestion, the FR switch will drop packets with the DE bit set first. The DE bit is set on the oversubscribed traffic— that is, the traffic that was received after the CIR was sent.

**decryption**—Reverse application of an encryption algorithm to encrypted data, thereby restoring that data to its original, unencrypted state. See also *encryption*.

**dedicated line**—Communications line that is indefinitely reserved for transmissions rather than switched as transmission is required. See also *leased line*.

**default route**—A routing table entry that is used to direct frames for which a next hop is not explicitly listed in the routing table.

**default router**—The router to which frames are directed when a next hop is not explicitly listed in the routing table. Also called a default gateway.

**delay**—Time between the initiation of a transaction by a sender and the first response received by the sender. Also, the time required to move a packet from source to destination over a given path.

**demarc**—Demarcation point between carrier equipment and CPE.

**DES**—Data Encryption Standard. Standard cryptographic algorithm developed by the U.S. National Bureau of Standards.

**destination address**—Address of a network device that is receiving data. See also *source address*.

**DHCP**—Dynamic Host Configuration Protocol. Provides a mechanism for allocating IP addresses dynamically so that addresses can be reused when hosts no longer need them.

**dial backup**—Feature that provides protection against WAN downtime by allowing the network administrator to configure a backup serial line through a circuit-switched connection.

**dial-on-demand routing**—See *DDR*.

**dialup line**—Communications circuit that is established by a switched-circuit connection using the telephone company network.

**Diffusing Update Algorithm**—DUAL. A convergence algorithm used in Enhanced IGRP that provides loop-free operation at every instant throughout a route computation. This allows routers involved in a topology change to synchronize at the same time, while not involving routers that are unaffected by the change.

**digital**—The use of a binary code to represent information, such as 0/1 or on/off.

**distance vector routing algorithm**—A class of routing algorithms that call for each router to send all or some portion of its routing table, but only to its neighbors. This is also called the Bellman-Ford routing algorithm and DBF.

**DLCI**—Data-link connection identifier. Value that specifies a PVC or an SVC in a Frame Relay network. In the basic Frame Relay specification, DLCIs are locally significant (connected devices might use different values to specify the same connection). In the LMI extended specification, DLCIs are globally significant (DLCIs specify individual end devices). See also *LMI*.

**DNIC**—Data Network Identification Code. Part of an X.121 address. DNICs are divided into two parts: the first specifying the country in which the addressed PSN is located, and the second specifying the PSN itself.

**DNS**—Domain Name System. System used in the Internet for translating names of network nodes into addresses.

**DoD**—Department of Defense. U.S. government organization that is responsible for national defense. The DoD has frequently funded communication protocol development.

**domain**—In the Internet, a portion of the naming hierarchy tree that refers to general groupings of networks based on organization type or geography.

**Domain Name System**—See *DNS*.

**dot address**—Refers to the common notation for IP addresses in the form *n.n.n.n*, where each number *n* represents, in decimal, 1 byte of the 4-byte IP address. This is also called dotted notation or four-part dotted notation.

**dotted decimal notation**—Syntactic representation for a 32-bit integer that consists of four 8-bit numbers written in base 10 with periods (dots) separating them. It is used to represent IP addresses in the Internet, as in 192.67.67.20. This is also called dotted quad notation.

**DR**—Designated router. OSPF router that generates LSAs for a multiaccess network and has other special responsibilities in running OSPF. Each multiaccess OSPF network that has at least two attached routers has a designated router that is elected by the OSPF Hello protocol. The designated router enables a reduction in the number of adjacencies required on a multiaccess network, which in turn reduces the amount of routing protocol traffic and the size of the topological database.

**DS**—Digital signal.

**DSL**—Digital subscriber line. Public network technology that delivers high bandwidth over conventional copper wiring at limited distances. There are four types of DSL: ADSL, HDSL, SDSL, and VDSL. All are provisioned via modem pairs, with one modem located at a central office and the other at the customer site. Because most DSL technologies do not use the whole bandwidth of the twisted pair, there is room remaining for a voice channel. See also *ADSL* and *HDSL*.

**DSU**—Data service unit. Device used in digital transmission that adapts the physical interface on a DTE device to a transmission facility such as T1 or E1. The DSU is also responsible for such functions as signal timing. It is often referred to, together with CSU, as CSU/DSU. See also *CSU*.

**DTE**—Data terminal equipment. Device at the user end of a user-network interface that serves as a data source, a destination, or both. DTE connects to a data network through a DCE device (for example, a modem) and typically uses clocking signals generated by the DCE. DTE includes such devices as computers, protocol translators, and multiplexers. Compare with *DCE*.

**DUAL**—See *Diffusing Update Algorithm*.

**DVMRP**—Distance Vector Multicast Routing Protocol. Internetwork gateway protocol, largely based on RIP, that implements a typical dense mode IP multicast scheme. DVMRP uses IGMP to exchange routing datagrams with its neighbors.

**dynamic address resolution**—Use of an address resolution protocol to determine and store address information on demand.

**E1**—External Type 1. Autonomous system external link entry. Originating from the ASBR, they describe routes to destinations external to the autonomous system. They are flooded throughout an OSPF autonomous system except for stub, totally stubby, and not-so-stubby areas. If a packet is an E1, then the metric is calculated by adding the external cost to the internal cost of each link the packet crosses.

**E2**—External Type 2. Autonomous system external link entry. Originating from the ASBR, they describe routes to destinations external to the autonomous system. They are flooded throughout an OSPF autonomous system except for stub, totally stubby, and not-so-stubby areas. If a packet is an E2, then it will always have only the external cost assigned, no matter where in the area it crosses. Use this packet type if only one router is advertising a route to the autonomous system. Type 2 routes are preferred over type 1 routes unless two same-cost routes exist to the destination.

**EBGP**—External BGP. When BGP is running between routers in different autonomous systems it is called EBGP. Routers running EBGP are usually directly connected to each other.

**EGP**—Exterior Gateway Protocol. An Internet protocol for exchanging routing information between autonomous systems. It is documented in RFC 904. This is not to be confused with the general term exterior gateway protocol; EGP is an obsolete protocol that has been replaced by BGP.

**EIA/TIA**—Electronic Industries Association/Telecommunications Industry Association.

**EIGRP**—Enhanced Interior Gateway Routing Protocol. An advanced version of IGRP developed by Cisco. It provides superior convergence properties and operating efficiency, and combines the advantages of link-state protocols with those of distance vector protocols.

**e-mail**—Electronic mail. Widely used network application in which text messages are transmitted electronically between end users over various types of networks using various network protocols.

**encapsulation**—Wrapping of data in a particular protocol header. For example, Ethernet data is wrapped in a specific Ethernet header before network transit. Also, when bridging dissimilar networks, the entire frame from one network is simply placed in the header used by the data link layer protocol of the other network.

**encryption**—Application of a specific algorithm to data to alter the appearance of the data, making it incomprehensible to those who are not authorized to see the information. See also *decryption*.

**Enhanced IGRP**—See *EIGRP*.

**Excess burst**—See *Be*.

**Extended Super Frame**—ESF. Framing type used on T1 circuits that consists of 24 frames of 192 bits each, with the 193rd bit providing timing and other functions. ESF is an enhanced version of SF.

**exterior gateway protocol**—Any internetwork protocol used to exchange routing information between autonomous systems. This is not to be confused with Exterior Gateway Protocol (EGP), which is a particular instance of an exterior gateway protocol. See also *BGP*.

**exterior routing protocols**—See *exterior gateway protocol*.

**FCC**—Federal Communications Commission. U.S. government agency that supervises, licenses, and controls electronic and electromagnetic transmission standards.

**FCS**—Frame check sequence. Extra characters added to a frame for error control purposes. This is used in HDLC, Frame Relay, and other data link layer protocols.

**FD**—Feasible Distance. In EIGRP, the FD is the lowest cost route to a destination.

**Feasible Distance**— See *FD*.

**Feasible Successor**— See *FS*.

**FECN**—Forward explicit congestion notification. Bit set by a Frame Relay network to inform the DTE receiving the frame that congestion was experienced in the path from the source to the destination. The DTE receiving frames with the FECN bit set can request that higher-level protocols take flow-control action as appropriate. Compare with *BECN*.

**FIFO**—First in, first out. With FIFO, transmission occurs in the same order as messages are received.

**filter**—Generally, a process or device that screens network traffic for certain characteristics, such as source address, destination address, or protocol, and determines whether to forward or discard that traffic based on the established criteria.

**firewall**—Router or access server, or several routers or access servers, designated as a buffer between any connected public networks and a private network. A firewall router uses access lists and other methods to ensure the security of the private network.

**flapping**—Intermittent interface failures.

**flash update**—A routing update sent asynchronously in response to a change in the network topology. Compare with *routing update*.

**floating static route**—A static route that has a higher administrative distance than a dynamically learned route so that it can be overridden by dynamically learned routing information.

**flooding**—A traffic-passing technique used by switches and bridges in which traffic received on an interface is sent out all the interfaces of that device, except the interface on which the information was originally received.

**flow**—Stream of data traveling between two endpoints across a network (for example, from one LAN station to another). Multiple flows can be transmitted on a single circuit.

**flow control**—Technique for ensuring that a transmitting entity, such as a modem, does not overwhelm a receiving entity with data. When the buffers on the receiving device are full, a message is sent to the sending device to suspend the transmission until the data in the buffers has been processed.

**FR**—See *Frame Relay.*

**fragmentation**—Process of breaking a packet into smaller units when transmitting over a network medium that cannot support the original size of the packet.

**frame**—Logical grouping of information sent as a data link layer unit over a transmission medium. This often refers to the header and trailer, used for synchronization and error control, that surround the user data contained in the unit. The terms *cell*, *datagram*, *message*, *packet*, and *segment* are also used to describe logical information groupings at various layers of the OSI reference model and in various technology circles.

**Frame Relay**—Industry-standard, switched data link layer protocol that handles multiple virtual circuits using HDLC encapsulation between connected devices. Frame Relay is more efficient than X.25, the protocol for which it is generally considered a replacement. See also *X.25*.

**frequency**—Number of cycles, measured in hertz, of an alternating current signal per unit time.

**FS**—Feasible Successor. EIGRP neighbor that is downstream with respect to the destination, but is not the least cost path and therefore is not used for forwarding data.

**FTP**—File Transfer Protocol. Application protocol, part of the TCP/IP protocol stack, used for transferring files between network nodes. FTP is defined in RFC 959.

**full duplex**—Capability for simultaneous data transmission between a sending station and a receiving station.

**full mesh**—Term describing a network in which devices are organized in a mesh topology, with each network node having either a physical circuit or a virtual circuit connecting it to every other network node. A full mesh provides a great deal of redundancy, but because it can be prohibitively expensive to implement, it is usually reserved for network backbones. See also *mesh* and *partial mesh*.

**gateway**—In the IP community, an older term referring to a routing device. Today, the term *router* is used to describe nodes that perform this function, and *gateway* refers to a special-purpose device that performs an application layer conversion of information from one protocol stack to another.

**GRE**—Generic routing encapsulation. Tunneling protocol developed by Cisco that can encapsulate a wide variety of protocol packet types inside IP tunnels, creating a virtual point-to-point link to Cisco routers at remote points over an IP internetwork. By connecting multiprotocol subnetworks in a single-protocol backbone environment, IP tunneling using GRE allows network expansion across a single-protocol backbone environment.

**half duplex**—Capability for data transmission in only one direction at a time between a sending station and a receiving station.

**HDLC**—High-Level Data Link Control. Bit-oriented synchronous data link layer protocol developed by ISO. Derived from SDLC, HDLC specifies a data encapsulation method on synchronous serial links using frame characters and checksums.

**header**—Control information placed before data when encapsulating that data for network transmission.

**hello packet**—A multicast packet that is used by routers for neighbor discovery and recovery. Hello packets also indicate that a client is still operating and network-ready.

**Hello protocol**—A protocol used by OSPF systems for establishing and maintaining neighbor relationships.

**High-Speed Serial Interface**—See *HSSI*.

**holddown**—A state into which a route is placed so that routers will neither advertise the route nor accept advertisements about the route for a specific length of time (the holddown period); in this way, the entire network has a chance to learn about the change. Holddown is used to flush bad information about a route from all routers in the network. A route is typically placed in holddown when a link in that route fails.

**hop**—The passage of a data packet between two network nodes (for example, between two routers). See also *hop count*.

**hop count**—A routing metric used to measure the distance between a source and a destination. IP RIP uses hop count as its sole metric.

**HSRP**—Hot Standby Router Protocol. Provides a way for IP workstations to keep communicating on the internetwork even if their default router becomes unavailable, thereby providing high network availability and transparent network topology changes.

**HSSI**—High-Speed Serial Interface. Network standard for high-speed (up to 52-Mbps) serial connections over WAN links.

**hub**—Hardware or software device that contains multiple independent but connected modules of network and internetwork equipment. Hubs can be active (when they repeat signals sent through them) or passive (when they do not repeat, but merely split, signals sent through them).

**IANA**—Internet Assigned Numbers Authority. Organization operated under the auspices of the ISOC as a part of the IAB. IANA delegates authority for IP address-space allocation and domain-name assignment to the InterNIC and other organizations. IANA also maintains a database of assigned protocol identifiers used in the TCP/IP stack, including autonomous system numbers.

**IBGP**—Internal Border Gateway Protocol. When BGP is running between routers within one AS it is called Internal BGP.

**ICMP**—Internet Control Message Protocol. Network layer Internet protocol that reports errors and provides other information relevant to IP packet processing. It is documented in RFC 792.

**ICND**—Interconnection Cisco Network Devices

**IEEE**—Institute of Electrical and Electronic Engineers. Professional organization whose activities include the development of communications and network standards. IEEE LAN standards are the predominant LAN standards today.

**IETF**—Internet Engineering Task Force. Task force consisting of more than 80 working groups responsible for developing Internet standards. The IETF operates under the auspices of ISOC.

**IGMP**—Internet Group Management Protocol. Used by IP hosts to report their multicast group memberships to an adjacent multicast router.

**IGP**—Interior Gateway Protocol. An Internet protocol used to exchange routing information within an autonomous system. Examples of common Internet IGPs include IGRP, OSPF, and RIP.

**IGRP**—Interior Gateway Routing Protocol. An IGP developed by Cisco to address the problems associated with routing in large, heterogeneous networks. Compare with *Enhanced IGRP*.

**Integrated Services Digital Network**—See *ISDN*.

**interior routing protocols**—Routing protocols used by routers within the same autonomous system, such as RIP, IGRP, and Enhanced IGRP.

**Internet**—A term that refers to the largest global internetwork, connecting tens of thousands of networks worldwide and having a "culture" that focuses on research and standardization based on real-life use. Many leading-edge network technologies come from the Internet community. The Internet evolved in part from ARPANET. At one time, it was called the DARPA Internet. This is not to be confused with the general term *internet*.

**internet**—Short for internetwork. Not to be confused with the Internet. See also *internetwork*.

**internetwork**—A collection of networks interconnected by routers and other devices that functions (generally) as a single network. It is sometimes called an internet, which is not to be confused with the Internet.

**internetworking**—The industry that has arisen around the problem of connecting networks. The term can refer to products, procedures, and technologies.

**intranet**—A network, internal to an organization, based on Internet and World Wide Web technology, that delivers immediate, up-to-date information and services to networked employees.

**I/O**—Input/output. Typically used when discussing ports on a device where data comes in or goes out.

**IOS**—Internetwork Operating System. Cisco system software that provides common functionality, scalability, and security for all products under the CiscoFusion architecture. Cisco IOS allows centralized, integrated, and automated installation and management of internetworks, while ensuring support for a wide variety of protocols, media, services, and platforms.

**IP**—Internet Protocol. A network layer protocol in the TCP/IP stack offering a connectionless internetwork service. IP provides features for addressing, type-of-service specification, fragmentation and reassembly, and security. It is documented in RFC 791.

**IP address**—A 32-bit address assigned to hosts using TCP/IP. An IP address belongs to one of five classes (A, B, C, D, or E) and is written as four octets separated with periods (dotted decimal format). Each address consists of a network number, an optional subnetwork number, and a host number. The network and subnetwork numbers together are used for routing, and the host number is used to address an individual host within the network or subnetwork. A subnet mask is used to extract network and subnetwork information from the IP address. It is also called an Internet address.

**IP multicast**—A routing technique that allows IP traffic to be propagated from one source to a number of destinations or from many sources to many destinations. Rather than send one packet to each destination, one packet is sent to a multicast group identified by a single IP destination group address.

**IPSec**—Standards-based method of providing privacy, integrity, and authenticity to information transferred across IP networks. It provides IP network layer encryption.

**IPv6**—IP version 6. Replacement for the current version of IP (version 4). IPv6 includes support for flow ID in the packet header, which can be used to identify flows. It formerly was called IPng (IP next generation).

**IPX**—Internetwork Packet Exchange. A NetWare network layer (Layer 3) protocol used for transferring data from servers to workstations.

**IS**—Information systems. A broad term used to describe the use of information technology in organizations. This includes the movement, storage, and use of information.

**ISDN**—Integrated Services Digital Network. Communication protocol offered by telephone companies that permits telephone networks to carry data, voice, and other source traffic.

**IS-IS**—Intermediate System-to-Intermediate System. An OSI link-state hierarchical routing protocol based on DECnet Phase V routing whereby ISs (routers) exchange routing information based on a single metric to determine network topology.

**ISO**—International Organization for Standardization. International organization that is responsible for a wide range of standards, including those relevant to networking. ISO developed the OSI reference model, a popular networking reference model.

**ISOC**—Internet Society. International nonprofit organization, founded in 1992, that coordinates the evolution and use of the Internet. In addition, ISOC delegates authority to other groups related to the Internet, such as the IAB. ISOC is headquartered in Reston, Virginia (United States).

**ISP**—Internet service provider. Company that provides Internet access to other companies and individuals.

**ITU-T**—International Telecommunication Union Telecommunication Standardization Sector. International body that develops worldwide standards for telecommunications technologies. The ITU-T carries out the functions of the former CCITT.

**Kb**—Kilobit. Approximately 1,000 bits.

**kbps**—Kilobits per second.

**keepalive message**—A message sent by one network device to inform another network device that the circuit between the two is still active.

**Kerberos**—Developing standard for authenticating network users. Kerberos offers two key benefits: It functions in a multivendor network, and it does not transmit passwords over the network.

**LAN**—Local-area network. High-speed, low-error data network covering a relatively small geographic area (up to a few thousand meters). LANs connect workstations, peripherals, terminals, and other devices in a single building or other geographically limited area. LAN standards specify cabling and signaling at the physical and data link layers of the OSI model. Ethernet, FDDI, and Token Ring are widely used LAN technologies. Also see *MAN* and *WAN*.

**LAPB**—Link Access Procedure, Balanced. Data link layer protocol in the X.25 protocol stack. LAPB is a bit-oriented protocol derived from HDLC.

**leased line**—Transmission line reserved by a communications carrier for the private use of a customer. A leased line is a type of dedicated line. See also *dedicated line*.

**LED**—Light emitting diode. Semiconductor device that emits light produced by converting electrical energy. Status lights on hardware devices are typically LEDs.

**link**—Network communications channel consisting of a circuit or transmission path and all related equipment between a sender and a receiver. It is most often used to refer to a WAN connection and sometimes is referred to as a line or a transmission link.

**link-state routing algorithm**—A routing algorithm in which each router broadcasts or multicasts information regarding the cost of reaching each of its neighbors to all nodes in the internetwork. Compare with *distance vector routing algorithm*.

**LMI**—Local Management Interface. Set of enhancements to the basic Frame Relay specification. LMI includes support for a keepalive mechanism, which verifies that data is flowing; a multicast mechanism, which provides the network server with its local DLCI and the multicast DLCI; global addressing, which gives DLCIs global rather than local significance in Frame Relay networks; and a status mechanism, which provides an ongoing status report on the DLCIs known to the switch. It is known as LMT in ANSI terminology.

**load balancing**—In routing, the capability of a router to distribute traffic over all its network ports that are the same distance from the destination address. Good load-balancing algorithms use both line speed and reliability information. Load balancing increases the use of network segments, thus increasing effective network bandwidth.

**local loop**—Also known as "the last mile." Line from the premises of a telephone subscriber to the telephone company CO.

**LSA**—Link-state advertisement. In OSPF, broadcast packet used by link-state protocols that contains information about neighbors and path costs. LSAs are used by the receiving routers to maintain their routing tables.

**LSAck**—Link-state acknowledgment. In OSPF, a packet in which the router acknowledges the receipt of the DBD.

**LSP**—Link-state request. In OSPF, packet sent to the master router if the DBD has a more up-to-date link-state entry.

**LSU**—Link-state update. In OSPF, the master router responds with the complete information about the requested entry in a LSU packet.

**MAC**—Media Access Control. Lower of the two sublayers of the data link layer defined by the IEEE. The MAC sublayer handles access to shared media, such as whether token passing or contention will be used.

**MAC address**—Standardized data link layer address that is required for every port or device that connects to a LAN. Other devices in the network use these addresses to locate specific ports in the network and to create and update routing tables and data structures. MAC addresses are 6 bytes long and are controlled by the IEEE. Also known as a hardware address, MAC-layer address, and physical address.

**MAN**—Metropolitan-area network. Network that spans a metropolitan area. Generally, a MAN spans a larger geographic area than a LAN, but a smaller geographic area than a WAN. Compare with *LAN* and *WAN*.

**maximum transmission unit**—See *MTU*.

**MD5**—Message digest algorithm 5. Algorithm used for message authentication. MD5 verifies the integrity of the communication, authenticates the origin, and checks for timeliness.

**MED**—Multi-Exit-Discriminator. In BGP, the MED attribute is an optional nontransitive attribute.

**mesh**—A network topology in which devices are organized in a manageable, segmented manner with many, often redundant, interconnections strategically placed between network nodes. See also *full mesh* and *partial mesh*.

**message**—An application layer (Layer 7) logical grouping of information, often composed of a number of lower-layer logical groupings such as packets.

**metric**—A standard of measurement, such as performance, that is used for measuring whether network management goals have been met.

**modem**—Modulator-demodulator. Device that converts digital and analog signals. At the source, a modem converts digital signals to a form suitable for transmission over analog communication facilities. At the destination, the analog signals are returned to their digital form. Modems allow data to be transmitted over voice-grade telephone lines.

**modulation**—Process by which the characteristics of electrical signals are transformed to represent information. Types of modulation include AM, FM, and PAM.

**MP**—Multilink PPP.

**MTU**—Maximum transmission unit. Maximum packet size, in bytes, that a particular interface can handle.

**multiaccess network**—Network that allows multiple devices to connect and communicate simultaneously.

**multicast**—Single packets copied by the network and sent to a specific subset of network addresses. These addresses are specified in the Destination Address Field. Compare with *broadcast* and *unicast*.

**multiplexing**—Scheme that allows multiple logical signals to be transmitted simultaneously across a single physical channel.

**NAK**—negative acknowledgment. Response sent from a receiving device to a sending device indicating that the information received contained errors. Compare to *acknowledgment*.

**NAS**—See *access server*.

**NAT**—Network Address Translation. Mechanism for reducing the need for globally unique IP addresses. NAT allows an organization with addresses that are not globally unique to connect to the Internet by translating those addresses into globally routable address space. Also known as Network Address Translator.

**NBMA**—Nonbroadcast multiaccess. Term describing a multiaccess network that does not support broadcasting (such as X.25) or in which broadcasting is not feasible (for example, an SMDS broadcast group or an extended Ethernet that is too large).

**neighboring router**—In OSPF, two routers that have interfaces to a common network.

**NetBEUI**—NetBIOS Extended User Interface. Enhanced version of the NetBIOS protocol used by network operating systems such as LAN Manager, LAN Server, Windows for Workgroups, and Windows NT. NetBEUI formalizes the transport frame and adds additional functions. NetBEUI implements the OSI LLC2 protocol.

**network**—Collection of computers, printers, routers, switches, and other devices that are capable of communicating with each other over some transmission medium.

**NLSP**—NetWare Link Services Protocol. Link-state routing protocol based on IS-IS.

**NNI**—The standard interface between two Frame Relay switches meeting the same criteria.

**non-stub area**—A resource-intensive OSPF area that carries a default route, static routes, intra-area routes, interarea routes, and external routes. Compare with *stub area*. See also *ASBR*.

**NSSA**—Not-so-stubby area. In OSPF, a not-so-stubby area imports a limited number of external routes. The number of routes is limited to only those required to provide connectivity between backbone areas.

**NVRAM**—Nonvolatile random access memory.

**OC**—Optical carrier. Series of physical protocols (OC-1, OC-2, OC-3, and so forth) defined for SONET optical signal transmissions. OC signal levels put STS frames onto multimode fiber-optic lines at a variety of speeds. The base rate is 51.84 Mbps (OC-1); each signal level thereafter operates at a speed divisible by that number (thus, OC-3 runs at 155.52 Mbps).

**octet**—Eight bits. In networking, the term *octet* is often used (rather than *byte*) because some machine architectures employ bytes that are not 8 bits long.

**ODBC**—Open database connectivity.

**OLE**—Object linking and embedding. Compound document standard developed by Microsoft Corporation. It enables creating objects with one application and then linking or embedding them in a second application. These objects keep their original format and links to the application that created them.

**OSI**—Open System Interconnection. International standardization program created by ISO and ITU-T to develop standards for data networking that facilitate multivendor equipment interoperability.

**OSI reference model**—Open System Interconnection reference model. Network architectural model developed by ISO and ITU-T. The model consists of seven layers, each of which specifies particular network functions such as addressing, flow control, error control, encapsulation, and reliable message transfer. The lowest layer (the physical layer) is closest to the media technology. The lower two layers are implemented in hardware and software, while the upper five layers are implemented only in software. The highest layer (the application layer) is closest to the user. The OSI reference model is used universally as a method for teaching and understanding network functionality.

**OSPF**—Open Shortest Path First. A link-state, hierarchical IGP routing algorithm proposed as a successor to RIP in the Internet community. OSPF features include least-cost routing, multipath routing, and load balancing. OSPF was derived from an early version of the IS-IS protocol. See also *EIGRP, IGP, IGRP, IS-IS,* and *RIP.*

**OUI**—Organizationally unique identifier. Three octets assigned by the IEEE, used in the 48-bit MAC addresses.

**packet**—Logical grouping of information that includes a header containing control information and (usually) user data. Packets are most often used to refer to network layer units of data. The terms *datagram, frame, message,* and *segment* are also used to describe logical information groupings at various layers of the OSI reference model and in various technology circles. See also *PDU.*

**packet switching**—Networking method in which nodes share bandwidth with each other by sending packets.

**partial mesh**—Network in which devices are organized in a mesh topology, with some network nodes organized in a full mesh, but with others that are connected to only one or two other nodes in the network. A partial mesh does not provide the level of redundancy of a full-mesh topology, but it is less expensive to implement. Partial-mesh topologies are generally used in the peripheral networks that connect to a fully meshed backbone. See also *full mesh* and *mesh*.

**payload**—Portion of a cell, frame, or packet that contains upper-layer information (data).

**PDM**—Protocol-dependent modules. In EIGRP, PDMs are responsible for network layer, protocol-specific requirements for IP, IPX, and AppleTalk.

**PDN**—Public Data Network. Network operated either by a government (as in Europe) or by a private concern to provide computer communications to the public, usually for a fee. PDNs enable small organizations to create a WAN without all the equipment costs of long-distance circuits.

**PDU**—Protocol data unit. OSI term for *packet*.

**peak rate**—Maximum rate, in kilobits per second, at which a virtual circuit can transmit.

**permanent virtual circuit**—Virtual circuit that is permanently established. PVCs save bandwidth associated with circuit establishment and teardown in situations in which certain virtual circuits must exist all the time. In ATM terminology, this is called a permanent virtual connection.

**ping**—Packet internet groper. ICMP echo message and its reply. This is often used in IP networks to test the reachability of a network device.

**PIX**—Cisco's Private Internet Exchange firewall. See also *firewall*.

**playback**—Reuse of a packet captured from a line by a sniffer.

**point of demarcation**—The physical point at which the phone company ends its responsibility with the wiring of the phone line.

**POP**—Point of presence. A long-distance carrier's office in your local community. A POP is the place where your long-distance carrier, or IXC, terminates your long-distance lines just before those lines are connected to your local phone company's lines or to your own direct hookup. Each IXC can have multiple POPs within one LATA. All long-distance phone connections go through the POPs.

**PPP**—Point-to-Point Protocol. Successor to SLIP that provides router-to-router and host-to-network connections over synchronous and asynchronous circuits. Whereas SLIP was designed to work with IP, PPP was designed to work with several network layer protocols, such as IP, IPX, and ARA. PPP also has built-in security mechanisms, such as CHAP and PAP. PPP relies on two protocols: LCP and NCP. See also *CHAP* and *PAP*.

**PRI**—Primary Rate Interface. ISDN interface to primary rate access. Primary rate access consists of a single 64-Kbps D channel plus 23 (T1) or 30 (E1) B channels for voice or data. Compare with *BRI*.

**PVC**—Permanent virtual circuit. Virtual circuit that is permanently established. PVCs save bandwidth associated with circuit establishment and teardown in situations in which certain virtual circuits must exist all the time. In ATM terminology, this is called a permanent virtual connection. See *SVC*.

**QoS**—Quality of service. A measure of performance for a transmission system that reflects its transmission quality and service availability.

**query**—Message used to inquire about the value of some variable or set of variables.

**queue**—1. Generally, an ordered list of elements waiting to be processed. 2. In routing, a backlog of packets waiting to be forwarded over a router interface.

**RADIUS**—Database for authenticating modem and ISDN connections and for tracking connection time.

**rate enforcement**—See *traffic policing*.

**redistribution**—Allowing routing information discovered through one routing protocol to be distributed in the update messages of another routing protocol. This is sometimes called route redistribution.

**RFC**—Request For Comments. Document series used as the primary means for communicating information about the Internet. Some RFCs are designated by the IAB as Internet standards. Most RFCs document protocol specifications such as Telnet and FTP, but some are humorous or historical. RFCs are available online from numerous sources.

**RIP**—1. Routing Information Protocol. A distance vector IGP, RIP uses hop count as a routing metric. See also *Enhanced IGRP*, *hop count*, *IGP*, *IGRP*, and *OSPF*. 2. IPX Routing Information Protocol. A distance vector routing protocol for IPX.

**RJ-45**—Registered jack connector. Standard connectors used for 10BaseT and other types of network connections.

**route summarization**—The consolidation of advertised addresses in a routing table. Summarizing routes reduces the number of routes in the routing table, the routing update traffic, and overall router overhead. Also called route aggregation.

**router**—A network layer device that uses one or more metrics to determine the optimal path along which network traffic should be forwarded. Routers forward packets from one network to another based on network layer information. It is occasionally called a gateway (although this definition of gateway is becoming increasingly outdated).

**routing**—The process of finding a path to a destination host. Routing is complex in large networks because of the many potential intermediate destinations that a packet might traverse before reaching its destination host. Routing occurs at Layer 3, the network layer.

**routing domain**—A group of end systems and intermediate systems operating under the same set of administrative rules.

**routing metric**—A standard of measurement, such as path length, that is used by routing algorithms to determine the optimal path to a destination. This information is stored in routing tables. Metrics include bandwidth, communication cost, delay, hop count, load, MTU, path cost, and reliability. It is sometimes referred to simply as a metric.

**routing protocol**—A routing protocol supports a routed protocol by providing mechanisms for sharing routing information. Routing protocol messages move between the routers. A routing protocol allows the routers to communicate with other routers to update and maintain routing tables. Routing protocol messages do not carry end-user traffic from network to network. A routing protocol uses the routed protocol to pass information between routers. Examples of routing protocols are IGRP, OSPF, and RIP.

**routing table**—A table stored in a router or some other internetworking device that keeps track of routes to particular network destinations and metrics associated with those routes.

**routing update**—A message sent from a router to indicate network reachability and associated cost information. Routing updates are typically sent at regular intervals and after a change in network topology. Compare with *flash update*.

**RTO**—Retransmission timeout. This is the amount of time the EIGRP waits before retransmitting a packet from the retransmission queue to a neighbor.

**RTP**—Reliable Transport Protocol. RTP is responsible for guaranteed, ordered delivery of Enhanced IGRP packets to all neighbors.

**SA**—Source address.

**SAP**—Service access point; also Service Advertising Protocol (Novell).

**SDLC**—Synchronous Data Link Control. SNA data link layer communications protocol. SDLC is a bit-oriented, full-duplex serial protocol that has spawned numerous similar protocols, including HDLC and LAPB.

**server**—Node or software program that provides services to clients. See also *client*.

**SIA**—Stuck in active. In some circumstances, it takes a very long time for an EIGRP query to be answered. So long, in fact, that the router that issued the query gives up and clears its connection to the router that isn't answering, effectively restarting the neighbor session. This is known as a SIA route.

**SIN**—Ships-in-the-night. Ships-in-the-night routing advocates the use of a completely separate and distinct routing protocol for each network protocol so that the multiple routing protocols essentially exist independently.

**SMTP**—Simple Mail Transfer Protocol. Internet protocol providing e-mail services.

**SNA**—Systems Network Architecture.

**SNAP**—SubNetwork Access Protocol.

**SNMP**—Simple Network Management Protocol.

**SOF**—Start of frame.

**SONET**—Synchronous Optical Network. High-speed (up to 2.5 Gbps) synchronous network specification developed by Bellcore and designed to run on optical fiber. STS-1 is the basic building block of SONET. It was approved as an international standard in 1988.

**source address**—Address of a network device that is sending data. See also *destination address*.

**SPF**—Shortest path first algorithm. Routing algorithm that iterates on length of path to determine a shortest-path spanning tree. Commonly used in link-state routing algorithms. Sometimes called Dijkstra's algorithm.

**split-horizon**—Routing technique in which information about routes is prevented from exiting the router interface through which that information was received. Split-horizon updates are useful in preventing routing loops.

**spoofing**—Scheme used by routers to cause a host to treat an interface as if it were up and supporting a session. The router spoofs replies to keepalive messages from the host to convince that host that the session still exists. Spoofing is useful in routing environments such as DDR, in which a circuit-switched link is taken down when there is no traffic to be sent across it to save toll charges.

**SQL**—Structured Query Language.

**SRAM**—Static RAM.

**SRTT**—Smooth round-trip time. This is the number of milliseconds it takes for an EIGRP packet to be sent to a neighbor and for the local router to receive an acknowledgment of that packet.

**SSAP**—Source service access point (LLC).

**SSE**—Silicon switching engine.

**SSP**—Silicon switch processor.

**static route**—A route that is explicitly configured and entered into the routing table.

**STP**—Shielded twisted-pair; also Spanning-Tree Protocol.

**stub area**—An OSPF area that carries a default route, intra-area routes, and interarea routes, but that does not carry external routes. Compare with *non-stub area*.

**stub network**—Part of an internetwork that can be reached by only one path; a network that has only a single connection to a router.

**subinterface**—One of a number of virtual interfaces on a single physical interface.

**subnet**—See *subnetwork*.

**subnet mask**—A 32-bit number that is associated with an IP address; each bit in the subnet mask indicates how to interpret the corresponding bit in the IP address. In binary, a subnet mask bit of 1 indicates that the corresponding bit in the IP address is a network or subnet bit; a subnet mask bit of 0 indicates that the corresponding bit in the IP address is a host bit. The subnet mask then indicates how many bits have been borrowed from the host field for the subnet field. It sometimes is referred to simply as mask.

**subnetwork**—In IP networks, a network sharing a particular subnet address. Subnetworks are networks arbitrarily segmented by a network administrator to provide a multilevel, hierarchical routing structure while shielding the subnetwork from the addressing complexity of attached networks. It is sometimes called a subnet.

**Successor**—A successor is a neighboring router used for packet forwarding that has a least cost path to a destination that is guaranteed not to be part of a routing loop.

**SVC**—switched virtual circuit. Virtual circuit that is dynamically established on demand and is torn down when transmission is complete. SVCs are used in situations in which data transmission is sporadic. It is called a switched virtual connection in ATM terminology. Compare with *PVC*.

**switch**—1. A network device that filters, forwards, and floods frames based on the destination address of each frame. The switch operates at the data link layer of the OSI model. 2. An electronic or mechanical device that allows a connection to be established as necessary and terminated when there is no longer a session to support.

**SYN**—Synchronize (TCP segment).

**synchronization**—Establishment of common timing between sender and receiver.

**T1**—Digital WAN carrier facility. T1 transmits DS-1-formatted data at 1.544 Mbps through the telephone-switching network using AMI or B8ZS coding.

**TAC**—Technical Assistance Center (Cisco).

**TACACS**—Terminal Access Controller Access Control System.

**TCP**—Transmission Control Protocol. Connection-oriented transport layer protocol that provides reliable full-duplex data transmission. TCP is part of the TCP/IP protocol stack. See also *TCP/IP*.

**TCP/IP**—Transmission Control Protocol/Internet Protocol. Common name for the suite of protocols developed by the U.S. DoD in the 1970s to support the construction of worldwide internetworks. TCP and IP are the two best-known protocols in the suite. See also *IP*, *TCP*, and *UDP*.

**TDM**—Time-division multiplexing.

**Telco**—Telephone company.

**TFTP**—Trivial File Transfer Protocol.

**TIA**—Telecommunications Industry Association.

**Topology table**—In EIGRP, the topology table contains all destinations advertised by neighboring routers.

**ToS**—Type of service.

**traffic policing**—Process used to measure the actual traffic flow across a given connection and compare it to the total admissible traffic flow for that connection. Traffic outside of the agreed-upon flow can be tagged (where the CLP bit is set to 1) and can be discarded en route if congestion develops. Traffic policing is used in ATM, Frame Relay, and other types of networks.

**traffic shaping**—The use of queues to limit surges that can congest a network. Data is buffered and then sent into the network in regulated amounts to ensure that the traffic will fit within the promised traffic envelope for the particular connection. Traffic shaping is used in ATM, Frame Relay, and other types of networks. It is also known as metering, shaping, and smoothing.

**Transmission Control Protocol**—See *TCP*.

**TTL**—Time To Live. A field in an IP header that indicates how long a packet is considered valid.

**tunneling**—An architecture that provides a virtual data link connection between two like networks through a foreign network. The virtual data link is created by encapsulating the network data inside the packets of the foreign network.

**twisted pair**—Two insulated wires, usually copper, twisted together and often bound into a common sheath to form multipair cables. In ISDN, the cables are the basic path between a subscriber's terminal or telephone and the PBX or the central office.

**UDP**—User Datagram Protocol. Connectionless transport layer protocol in the TCP/IP protocol stack. UDP is a simple protocol that exchanges datagrams without acknowledgments or guaranteed delivery, requiring that error processing and retransmission be handled by other protocols.

**UNC**—Universal Naming Convention or Uniform Naming Convention. A PC format for specifying the location of resources on a local-area network (LAN). UNC uses the following format: \\server-name\shared-resource-pathname.

**unicast**—Message sent to a single network destination. Compare with *broadcast* and *multicast*.

**URL**—Uniform Resource Locator.

**UTC**—Coordinated Universal Time (same as Greenwich Mean Time).

**UTL**—Utilization.

**UTP**—Unshielded twisted-pair wire.

**V.35**—ITU-T standard describing a synchronous, physical layer protocol used for communications between a network access device and a packet network. V.35 is most commonly used in North America and in Europe, and is recommended for speeds up to 48 Kbps.

**VC**—See *virtual circuit*.

**VIP**—Versatile Interface Processor.

**virtual circuit**—Logical circuit created to ensure reliable communication between two network devices. A virtual circuit is defined by a VPI/VCI pair and can be either permanent (PVC) or switched (SVC). Virtual circuits are used in Frame Relay and X.25. In ATM, a virtual circuit is called a virtual channel. It is sometimes abbreviated VC.

**VLSM**—Variable-length subnet mask. The capability to specify a different subnet mask for the same network number on different subnets. VLSM can help optimize available address space. Some protocols do not allow the use of VLSM. See also *classless routing protocols*.

**vty**—Virtual terminal.

**WAN**—Wide-area network. Data communications network that serves users across a broad geographic area and often uses transmission devices provided by common carriers. Frame Relay, SMDS, and X.25 are examples of WANs.

**weighted fair queuing**—Abbreviated as WFQ. Congestion-management algorithm that identifies conversations (in the form of traffic streams), separates packets that belong to each conversation, and ensures that capacity is shared fairly between these individual conversations. WFQ is an automatic way of stabilizing network behavior during congestion and results in increased performance and reduced retransmission.

**wildcard mask**—A 32-bit quantity used in conjunction with an IP address to determine which bits in an IP address should be ignored when comparing that address with another IP address. A wildcard mask is specified when setting up access lists.

**window**—The number of data segments that the sender is allowed to have outstanding without yet receiving an acknowledgment.

**windowing**—A method to control the amount of information transferred end to end, using different window sizes.

**workgroup**—A collection of workstations and servers on a LAN that are designed to communicate and exchange data with one another.

**World Wide Web**—See *WWW*.

**WWW**—World Wide Web. A large network of Internet servers providing hypertext and other services to terminals running client applications such as a WWW browser.

**WWW browser**—A GUI-based hypertext client application, such as Mosaic, used to access hypertext documents and other services located on innumerable remote servers throughout the WWW and Internet. See also *Internet* and *WWW*.

**X.25**—ITU-T standard that defines how connections between DTE and DCE are maintained for remote terminal access and computer communications in PDNs. X.25 specifies LAPB, a data link layer protocol, and PLP, a network layer protocol. To some degree, Frame Relay has superseded X.25.

**xDSL**—Group term used to refer to ADSL, HDSL, SDSL, and VDSL. All are emerging digital technologies using the existing copper infrastructure provided by the telephone companies. xDSL is a high-speed alternative to ISDN.

**XNS**—Xerox Network Systems.

**ZIP**—Zone Information Protocol. AppleTalk session layer protocol that maps network numbers to zone names. ZIP is used by NBP to determine which networks contain nodes that belong to a zone.

# INDEX

# Numerics

# F

# G

# H

# M

# P

# Q-R

# S

# T